THE SORCERER's APPRENTICE

The Life of Franz von Papen

Richard W. Rolfs, S.J.

University Press of America, Inc.
Lanham • New York • London

Copyright © 1996 by
University Press of America,® Inc.
4720 Boston Way
Lanham, Maryland 20706

3 Henrietta Street
London, WC2E 8LU England

Library of Congress Cataloging-in-Publication Data

Rolfs, Richard W.
The sorcerer's apprentice : the life of Franz von Papen / Richard W.
Rolfs.
p.   cm.
Includes bibliographical references and index.
1. Papen, Franz von, 1879-1969. 2. Diplomats--Germany--
Biography. 3. Germany--Foreign relations--20th century. 4.
Conservatism--Germany--History. 5. Germany--Politics and
government--1918-1933. 6. Germany--Politics and government-
1933-1945. I. Title.
DD247.P3R65   1995   327.2'092 --dc20   95-43733 CIP

ISBN 0-7618-0162-6 (cloth: alk: ppr.)
ISBN 0-7618-0163-4 (pbk: alk: ppr.)

⊖™ The paper used in this publication meets the minimum
requirements of American National Standard for information
Sciences—Permanence of Paper for Printed Library Materials,
ANSI Z39.48—1984

Contents

Franz von Papen

LIST OF PICTURES

PREFACE

Because of his association with Adolf Hitler and the role he played in the Third Reich, Franz von Papen has been variously described as a clever intriguer, an urbane but devious and unreliable diplomat, or as an ambitious but incompetent lackey who served as a front man, first for General von Schleicher, and then for Hitler. According to many historians, Papen's only claim to fame was that he "held the stirrup for Hitler in his rise to power." Even his contemporaries had little positive to add. The French ambassador to Berlin, François Poncet, once remarked that "there is something about Papen that prevents either his friends or his enemies from taking him entirely seriously."

When I mentioned to one German historian my interest in writing about Papen's life and activities in the Third Reich, he asked me why I would bother writing about such a "*belangloser mensch*" (irrelevant person)? This remark merely whetted my curiosity. How could a man who played such a significant role in Hitler's rise to power be considered "irrelevant?" Did he deserve the reputation he had acquired? If so, why? More to the point, what was there about his personality that prompted him to continue to serve under Hitler and a government that proved to be the most heinous in modern, if not of all, time?

In order to find the answer to these and many other questions, I launched on what became an eight year study of a very complex personality. I discovered a person who, in many ways, deserved the criticisms leveled against him. On the other hand, as a conservative Catholic aristocrat, Papen considered himself as the voice of those dedicated to the restoration of the pre-World War I sociopolitical order, based on what he perceived to be Christian principles. This quixotic conviction became the basis of his appeal for a coalition of all national forces in Germany to establish a "New State." In the process of attempting to see the fulfillment of this idea, he - like many others - underestimated Hitler, and over-estimated his own abilities. Instead of becoming the architect of this "New State," Papen became an apprentice to the Sorcerer who created a "New Order." And while Papen never considered himself a part of this barbarous system, he was never able to fully remove the stigma of his association with it.

Although there have been many persons who made this study possible, I wish to single out those in particular to whom I am especially grateful for their support and assistance. Dr. Jürgen Real of the *Bundesarchiv* in Koblenz was particularly helpful with his wise advice and generous assistance. I would also like to thank the efficient Staff at the *Bundesarchiv* who were most helpful and always ready to assist me. My research took me to many archives in Germany and Austria, and I am especially thankful to the archivists in all of them for their assistance: Former Director, Dr. Klaus Weinandy, and the Assistant Director, Frau Dr. Maria Keipert, of the *Polkitisches Archiv, Auswärtiges Amt*, Bonn; Dr. Schumann, Director, *Staatsarchiv*, Nuremberg; Dr. Neugebauer, Director of the *Bundesarchiv, Abteilung Militärarchiv*, Freiburg/B; Dr. Martin Broszat, Director, *Institut für Zeitgeschichte*, Munich; Frau Dr. Anna Benna, Director, *Oesterreichisches Haus-Hof-und Staatsarchiv*, Vienna; Frau Bahr, *Sachbearbeiterin, Spruchkammerakten, Amstgericht*, Munich.

Although I received little information from the Papen family archives, I deeply appreciate the time given to me by Isabella and Margaret von Papen. Not only did I spend some time with them as a guest in their home at Obersasbach, but they continued to correspond with me on my return to America. Their conversations and correspondence helped me to understand more fully their father's deep love for his family, his Church, and his country. I would also like to thank the following for their support and encouragement: Mik and Sigi Real who permitted me to share their hearth and home on so many occasions; Reverend John Cantwell and the generous people of Corpus Christi Parish; Sister Mary Milligan, RSHM, Dean of the College of Liberal Arts at Loyola Marymount University, in Los Angeles; the German Jesuits of the South German Province, and the Sisters of the Holy Family in Munich, who made my year-long stay a most pleasant one, and offered a welcome relief from the long hours spent pouring over hundreds of documents and letters in the archives. I also wish to express my thanks to Howard B. Fitzpatrick, Edward F. Slattery, and

Henry K. Workman, Directors of the University Hill Foundation who provided me with a grant, which enabled me to finish this study.

Although there are many more whose names do not appear here, I wish to express my gratitude to them for their support and encouragement. I owe a very special thanks to Alexis Dolan for her careful proof-reading , and retyping of the text. It goes without further comment that any errors in this account can only be attributed to me.

Richard W. Rolfs, S.J.

CHAPTER 1:
THE EARLY YEARS

A. The Salters From Werl[1]

On January 18, 1781, in the Hall of Mirrors at the Palace of Versailles, Wilhelm II was proclaimed Kaiser of the Second German Empire. This final act of German unification not only represented the inauguration of a new Emperor, but it also introduced an entirely new set of factors into the European balance of power equation, which would determine the course of events that led to the outbreak of World War I.

The hero of this significant event, however, was not the Kaiser, Wilhelm II, but the Chancellor, Otto von Bismarck. As the architect of German unification, Bismarck accomplished what no other German was able to achieve since the collapse of the Holy Roman Empire of the German Nations in 1804, when Napoleon Bonaparte crowned himself Emperor. It was Bismarck who had successfully waged three limited wars to gain advantages for Prussia within the German-speaking world. As Minister President in Prussia - the largest in population, territory, and wealth - the "Iron Chancellor" established a constitutional monarchy that protected the Junker class and thwarted the efforts of the "liberals" to achieve anything resembling popular rule.

While Bismarck piloted the German ship of state through the stormy waters of European diplomacy, there was another event of much smaller dimensions taking place in a quiet and peaceful corner of the western province of predominantly Catholic Westphalia. Just eight years after Bismarck's triumphant declaration of the Second Reich, on October 29, 1879, in the small town of Werl, located about three hours from Soest, the one-time capital of Westphalia, the third child - a boy - was born to Friedrich Franz Michael, and Anna Laura v. Steffens von Papen. A few days later, in the baptistery of the ancient Franciscan monastery church, Franz Joseph Hermann Michael Maria received the waters of baptism.

The von Papen family belonged to a small group of hereditary salters who held the rights to the salt mines in the district of Soest as early as the ninth century. However, it was not until the end of the thirteenth century (1298) that the family name was first mentioned in a decree identifying a certain Albert Pape as holding long-standing rights to the brine wells in Werl.[2] From the fifteenth century onwards, the family became something more than country squires. In December, 1485, Wilhelm Pape was given the knightly estate of Köningen by Count Claudius von Tecklenburg. On April 15, 1708, the Papen ambition was fulfilled when a decree promulgated in Vienna by the Habsburg Emperor ennobled the Papen family for all time, permitting them to use the prefix "von," which carried with it all the rights and privileges of the noble class.[3]

According to the family records, the von Papens had for centuries contributed scientists, economists, and clerics to Germany. An especially devoted loyalty to the Archbishop of Cologne, and allegiance to the Catholic Hapsburgs of Austria, had been a long-standing tradition in the Papen family. When Franz's father, Friedrich Franz, entered the 5th Westphalian Uhlan regiment, and became a Prussian army officer, military service became another badge of honor on the von Papen coat of arms. He served with distinction in Bismarck's wars of 1864, 1866, and the Franco-Prussian war of 1870-71.[4]

Both in his childhood, as well as during his adolescence, Franz was heavily influenced by these family traditions: pride in his aristocratic heritage as the salters of Werl; his intense commitment to his Catholic faith, which stemmed from his deeply religious parents; his passionate loyalty to the Prussian military system and to the

German Kaiser. Because of this background and education, the values, and attitudes towards God and nation were deeply etched into his character, and throughout his long life his actions were guided by them.

After attending elementary school in Werl, young Franz expressed a desire to attend a military school. No doubt the impressionable boy was not only influenced by his father, but also by the events taking place in Europe and Germany at that time. The 1880s and 1890s were years during which the Kaiser, Wilhelm II, proclaimed to the world Germany's right to a place in the sun. These were years in which pan-Germanism was popular, and the glories of the Prussian armies were extolled both in the classroom and from the pulpit. Franz was deeply impressed by these signs of patriotism, and like many other young boys, saw himself as a hero in the service of the Fatherland. Although his mother resisted, Franz's father took him at age eleven to Bensberg where he was accepted as a cadet in the academy.[5]

For the next four years, between 1891 and 1895, Franz attended the Cadet Academy. Like most of the German upper class, Franz received very little education in the liberal arts. The stress was placed on the traditional virtues of a Prussian soldier, with special emphasis on loyalty to the Kaiser, perseverance under stress, physical exercise, and duty to one's country. At Easter in 1895, when only fifteen years old, Franz became a non-commissioned officer, and was transferred to the main corps of cadets at Gross-Lichtenfelder near Berlin.

For the next two years he became acquainted with the cultural and scientific riches of Berlin. Visiting museums, institutes, the theater, and opera, Papen developed an appreciation for the arts and German culture which had been ignored in his training. In his last year at Lichtenfelder, at the age of seventeen, Papen was selected, along with ninety other cadets, to remain another year. As a member of the senior group (the *Selekta*), Papen was given the opportunity to develop his leadership abilities. At the end of that year he was commissioned as a second lieutenant - six months earlier than the other cadets. He was also invited to enter the Imperial Corps of Pages.[6] During this year he enjoyed the court life, and especially the chance to mingle with prominent people.

When it came time for him to select the branch of military service in which he intended to enlist, Franz's passion for horses, which dated from his earliest years, naturally dictated his desire to join the cavalry. On March 15, 1898, he was commissioned in the 5th Westphalian

Uhlan regiment (his father's old regiment), and stationed in Düsseldorf. As a Lancer, Papen's training consisted mainly of horseback riding in military formation. While becoming an excellent military rider, he also became interested in the steeplechase, which had become extremely popular in Germany. Thus began his career as a *Herrenreiter*, which lasted through 1906, and brought him many victories. In his later years he claimed that this form of competition not only required "considerable self-discipline, endurance and powers of decision," but also "a fine contempt for broken bones - by no means a bad training for a politician."[7] After completing his training in Düsseldorf, the young lieutenant was stationed in Hanover to attend the cavalry riding school. While in Hanover, Franz was given the opportunity to go to England where he spent several months riding superb thoroughbreds, engaging in fox hunts, and especially enjoying a very active social life. Endowed with the cultivated manners of an aristocrat, Papen was naturally charming, possessed a quick wit, and was a good conversationalist. Throughout his political and diplomatic career these qualities were to play an important role, not only for the advancement of his career, but also rescued him from serious set-backs.

When he returned to Germany from England to complete his cavalry training, Franz was a frequent visitor at the home of the wealthy industrialist, René von Boch-Galhau.[8] It was there that he met von Boch-Galhau's youngest daughter, Martha, with whom he soon fell in love. Martha von Boch-Galhau was a typical wealthy socialite. She was not interested in politics, or any form of intellectual discipline. She was quite conscious of her aristocratic background, and proud of her French ancestry. Although she was a bit of a snob, Martha did not hesitate to help the less fortunate, and engaged in numerous charities. Like her future husband, she was a devout, conservative Catholic.[9] Throughout Franz's political and diplomatic career, especially in the most trying times, Martha remained both loyal and supportive.

On May 3, 1905, after six months of courtship, Franz and Martha exchanged their wedding vows in Mettlach, Martha's home. After a three week honeymoon in Italy, the couple returned to Düsseldorf where Franz resumed his military training, while Martha took up housekeeping and other domestic duties.[10] It was during this period that Martha gave birth to Antoinette, the first of five children, on April 16, 1906.

In the meantime, Franz continued to prepare for his fondest dream, which was to become a General Staff officer. Finally at twenty-eight years of age, he passed the rigorous qualifying examinations, and, leaving his family in Düsseldorf for the time being, went to Berlin to begin his new career.

For the next three years Franz was engaged in a rigorous program including lectures, discussions, and a comprehensive in-depth study of military science. This was interspersed with summer assignments in Strasbourg and Trier, while his third and final summer he spent in France where he also improved his knowledge of French. Finally, he was chosen, along with 150 officers, to serve on the General Staff for a trial period, which lasted until April 1911. He was then informed that he would continue for another two years during which time he was instructed in intelligence operations.

It was during this period of his training that Papen enthusiastically adopted the *Weltanschauung* (world view) of Friedrich von Bernhardi, who wrote that war is "not only an integral part of humanity, but the great civilizing influence of the world," therefore it is the duty of every citizen to be prepared for war.[11] Bernhardi also declared that Germany was the coming power, and, in fact, she was civilization's greatest asset. It was the duty of Germany therefore, to utilize every means to protect her legitimate interests, and if might is not right, it is so alike as to be hardly distinguishable from it. Papen translated this crude interpretation of social Darwinism into a passionate loyalty to the Fatherland, which called for him to faithfully and completely follow the wishes of his Emperor to whom he had taken a solemn oath. As a sincerely religious man, Papen viewed the connection between Throne and Altar as real, consequently service to the Kaiser became a religious duty, and that duty took precedence over right. Of what account were the rights of other nations compared with the allegiance he owed his emperor, and through him, to God? This basic philosophy - which he stated quite simply as "my conscience is my guide" - served to justify all of his activities later on, both as a politician and as a diplomat.

By 1913 he had completed his training and was promoted to the rank of Captain. Later in autumn he was asked whether he would accept a dual assignment as military attaché to the German Embassy in the United States, and the German Legation in Mexico. After discussing the offer with his wife, Papen accepted the post and was briefed on his new assignment by the War Office to whom he was to report. Finally, after a short farewell visit with his wife and his family, Franz left Bremerhaven on January 6, 1914, for the United States.[12]

B. Mission USA - Mexico

The young officer arrived in New York on January 14, 1914, after a very stormy sea voyage. The weather was about zero. He then traveled to Washington DC, where he reported to the German Ambassador, Count Johann Bernstorff.[13] Franz was well-suited for his post as military attaché, both by training as well as by temperament. His duties included gathering information about the military movements of the host country and then advising his government through the German Ambassador and the War Office in Berlin. He was also the official representative of the German Army, and therefore served as the liaison between the military forces of both countries.

During times of peace a military attaché's duties were not very difficult nor complicated. During those first months in Washington, Papen's calendar was filled with social events including numerous invitations to dinner parties, the theater, and opera. On those occasions, he met a number of important personalities including Franklin Delano Roosevelt, the future president of the United States, with whom he would have some indirect dealings much later in his career. He also met President Wilson to whom he extended the Kaiser's greetings. However, while interested in meeting these important people, Franz was eager for more action. Both by temperament and training he was anxious, one could add ambitious, to prove his worth as a representative of the Kaiser and the Fatherland.

He did not have long to wait for his first assignment. The United States was involved in a tense international situation with Mexico. In February 1913, General Victoriano Huerta had overthrown the Mexican government and declared himself president. While this *coup* was regarded as a favorable one in some quarters, not everyone supported the new government. Not only did the United States refuse to recognize Huerta's regime, but in Mexico the opposition came from a revolutionary coalition headed by Venustiano Carranza and Francisco "Pancho" Villa. There was also opposition from the Zapatista irregulars south of Mexico City. Eventually these forces coalesced around Villa who within a year gained control of all Chihuahua.

Besides the United States, other governments, including Great Britain and Japan, were carefully monitoring the events in Mexico. Both the German Foreign Office and the War Office were interested in observing how the political situation in Mexico was developing. Moreover, the German armaments industry wanted to take advantage of the revolutionary conditions in Mexico, and requested permission to engage in the sale of armaments to the Huerta regime. It was at this juncture that Bernstorff commissioned Papen to go to Mexico.

Papen, who had been cooling his heels back in Washington, D. C., was eager to become involved in a more challenging situation than existed in the American capital. Therefore he accepted his assignment with enthusiasm. Although he said his plans "were vague enough," it does not seem likely that he went to Mexico just to see the country.[14] A sightseeing trip to Mexico hardly fits the image or intentions of a Government that was pursuing an aggressive foreign policy.[15] What little evidence exists seems to indicate that he was sent to Mexico to try and influence the political development in such a way as to favor German interests. Apparently the German Foreign Office favored the Huerta regime, and was therefore eager to buy him off with rifles and money which he desperately needed.[16]

One obstacle standing in the way of this policy was the attitude of the German Minister to Mexico, Admiral Hintze. Since the United States refused to recognize the Huerta regime, Hintze advised the German nationals not to criticize U.S. policy. Papen was directed to try and persuade Hintze to change his attitude and back Huerta, while at the same time he was to keep the War Office informed about the growing revolutionary activities in Mexico. Moreover, there were rumors that the United States might intervene militarily in the revolutionary situation in Mexico. Such an invasion would not only affect German commercial interests in Mexico, but could also pose a threat to German nationalists residing in Mexico. Since Papen was accredited to both countries, he was assigned to keep the Washington Embassy and the War Office informed of the military, as well as the diplomatic, developments going on in Mexico and the United States.

Meanwhile, what had started out as an internal affair between several Mexican factions, soon took on an international flavor. The United States practiced "gunboat diplomacy" when it landed troops in Vera Cruz on April 21, 1914. President Wilson's government considered this military intervention a "reprisal" for the Huerta government's refusal to salute the American flag. The Mexican government viewed it as an invasion of a sovereign nation. Huerta was now being attacked not only by the Mexican revolutionaries, Zapata and Carranza, but also by the American troops.

While Papen was eager to observe the conflict from both sides and submit his observations to Berlin, his first duty was to prepare the German colony in Mexico City to defend themselves against attack from the revolutionaries. Mexico City was becoming an armed camp. Stores were barricaded to prevent looting. The American Embassy was heavily guarded by Mexican police. Under Papen's supervision, security measures were undertaken at the German legation.[17] Once this was accomplished, the restless attaché requested that he be allowed to observe the American military operations in Vera Cruz. However, he was informed by his superiors in Berlin that he was to remain where he was, and Major Ritter would accompany the American troops, and take over part of Papen's duties.

However, before Papen received this information, he had already gone to Vera Cruz where he met Admiral Badger of the USS *Arkansas*, and General Funston. In his conversation with both men he was unable to find out if American troops were going to attack Mexico City. However, he did submit a report to Hintze in which he indicated military data including troop units, war material, and total American troop strength. He also reported on American industrial capacity, and suggested that for this reason alone, America could become a major factor if war broke out in Europe.

Aside from these exploits, Papen's mission to Mexico was uneventful, and contributed very little to German diplomacy in Mexico. However, from a personal standpoint the experiences gained from this assignment proved to be invaluable. Not only did he become more familiar with the diplomatic policies and procedures of the Foreign Office, but more importantly, he was initiated into the world of espionage and subterfuge associated with the activities of the German Foreign Office. These experiences would serve him in good stead when he served as Hitler's ambassador to Austria in 1938, and Turkey during World War II.

C. Apprenticeship in Intrigue

Papen learned of the German declaration of war against Russia on August 1, 1914 from the American General Frederick Funston.[18] The next day, he boarded an American ship and after a rather unpleasant passage arrived in Galveston, Texas, on August 4. From there he continued on to Washington D. C. For the next two years Papen's activities in the United States were clouded by intrigue, charges of espionage and even sabotage. Finally, in December, 1916, he was expelled from the United States because of his schemes to circumvent American neutrality laws.[19]

By the time Papen arrived in Washington, Europe had turned into a battlefield. The German declaration of war against Russia was followed by French and English mobilization, the German declaration of war against France, the invasion of Belgium by the Kaiser's army, and Britain's entrance into the war. Like his German colleagues in the Foreign Office and the War Ministry, Papen fully supported the violation of Belgian neutrality by German troops. He agreed with the German Chancellor, Bethmann-Hollweg's public announcement, that "necessity knows no law," which in this case was defined by Germany as a move in self-defense! Moreover, Papen believed that the time had come for Germany to be recognized as a great world power. This belief provided him with the justification to carry on what later proved to be violations of America's declaration of neutrality.

In the early stages of the war, the question of supplies was not too clearly visualized. German military successes held out the false promise of a short war followed by an armistice, and a settlement in favor of the Kaiser's empire. The more immediate task was to convince America that Germany was winning the war, and therefore deserved American neutrality if not support. One way to accomplish this was through highly colored press reports about the success of German arms, and the weakness of the Allied defenses. One of Papen's lesser responsibilities was to serve as a press officer, passing on to the *New York Sun* articles written by German officers like von Bernhardi, in which German military successes were emphasized at the expense of the true picture of events on both the eastern and western fronts. By 1915, "vituperous editorials against the President, Mr. Bryan, and Mr. Lansing" appeared in a newspaper called *The Fatherland*, whose editor, Mr. Viereck, was receiving money from Mr. Heinrich Albert, the financial advisor to the German Embassy in Washington, DC[20] Papen not only knew Viereck, but he was also familiar with Albert's financial dealings with this pro-German editor.[21] One of the charges against Papen, that he had publicly criticized the Government, grew out of these highly inflammatory articles that appeared in a newspaper financed by German money.

Papen's chief responsibility as military attaché was to gather intelligence information about the movement of troops, the shipment of weapons, and all other military matters that affected the course of the war. This was the function of the attachés of all the belligerents. In order to carry out this function, Papen set up a connection with G. Amsinick & Company on Wall Street in New York. The Director was Adolph Pavenstedt, a German citizen who knew Papen through the German Club where Papen lived. He also employed the former military attaché, Captain Boy-Ed, to "arrange business for me," which meant the establishment of the cover operation.[22] In addition, Papen had at his disposal a network of agents spread from Ottawa to New Orleans, and from Seattle to New York. These agents kept him informed of the nature and amount of the cargoes, shipping schedules, destinations, etc.[23] The Amsinick Company served as a blind through which Papen was able to contact these agents undetected by the British or the U.S. officials. This company also served as a front through which Papen furnished the funds with which these agents financed their covert operations.[24]

Of course, the Germans were not the only nation to establish this system of intelligence in the United States. The British also organized an intelligence system in America together with a network of agents. As a cover for their operations the British set up Wisdom Films, Inc. As long as neither side violated American laws or its position as a neutral nation, the United States Government did not interfere.

Meanwhile, after the collapse of the supposedly infallible Schlieffen Plan, both sides turned to trench warfare. What had once been regarded as a short war now became a long war of attrition. This resulted in an increased demand for more armaments and other war materials. As a neutral nation far from the battle grounds, and in possession of enormous natural resources, the United States became the most important source of these materials.

From the very beginning of the war, the English, French and Russian agents started placing large munitions and armament orders with American factories. These countries were especially interested in the purchase of American shells, which were particularly desirable because their steel casings made them infinitely more effective than the old iron ones. The German Government tried, through the agency of their military attaché in Washington, to purchase these shells as well as other armaments. Although smaller purchases were successful, the transport of larger quantities was practically impossible because the British and French navies controlled the sea lanes, and seized nearly every vessel carrying war materials destined for Germany or her allies.

Initially, Papen proposed to the Foreign Office that Germany should buy up as much war materials as possible from American firms, in order to prevent the British and her allies from obtaining them. However, the German War Department rejected this proposal.[25] For one thing, so many American companies converted to war production, that this method of preventing or even delaying the dispatch of war materials to the British and her allies was not feasible. At this juncture, Papen proposed that Germany build its own ammunition factory in the United States, give it an American name and an American manager. Under this cover, Germany could buy for herself everything in the nature of war materials purchasable on the American market, and store them in their own facility until they could be shipped to Germany. An added advantage was that by acquiring all the obtainable supplies the British and her allies would find none available.[26]

However, Papen did not stop with this project. In March 1915, he was able to set up a covert operation with the help of an American friend, Mr. George Hoadley. A large factory called the Bridgeport Projectile Company was built, which had all the appearances of an American firm, and from whom the Allies could (theoretically) purchase war materials.[27]

One of the most essential pieces of equipment required in the manufacture of artillery ammunition is the hydraulic press. In order to prevent the growing American armament manufacturers from acquiring these presses, Papen proceeded to purchase every hydraulic press that the U.S. companies could produce over the next two years.[28] In this way, he hoped to curtail the American output of artillery ammunition, which would in turn reduce the Allied purchases.

Papen did the same thing with regard to gunpowder. He bought up all the powder that the United States was able to produce over the next two years.[29] He was also able to conclude long-term contracts with industries that produced the acid-proof containers required in the production of gun-powder. This tied up their deliveries for about eighteen months, and again, curtailed Allied orders for gun-powder. In another effort to restrict trade with the Allies, Papen induced the German engineers and firms that built coke ovens used in the production of gun-powder, to slow down and even sever relations with American armament companies who wanted to install these ovens.[30] Papen insisted that all of these operations were not illegal. However, the United States Department of Justice viewed them as violations of the laws in restraint of trade.[31]

Papen was also engaged in the business of forging passports, which was clearly against U.S. laws. He justified this activity on the grounds that the Allied blockade forced Germany to issue fraudulent passports. There were many German reservists in the United States, Mexico, and probably other Latin American countries, who stormed the consulates and the Embassy anxious to get back to Germany to join their units.[32] In America, the task of providing these reservists with false passports was assigned to a reserve officer, Captain Hans Adam von Wedell.[33]

Without realizing it, Wedell was forging passports under the eyes of American and British agents. In early December Papen apparently became aware that U.S. agents were prepared to arrest Wedell. He therefore advised the forger to leave the country, and provided him and his wife with funds to go to Havana.[34]

With von Wedell's departure, the passport operation continued under the direction of Karl Ruroede. A naturalized citizen, Ruroede worked for Papen as a shipping agent arranging passenger tickets for these reservists. He was also associated with Wedell's passport operation. On January 2, 1915, undercover agents trapped and arrested Ruroede.[35] His testimony revealed Papen's connection with this fraudulent operation. Papen would give one of his personal cards or a letter of recommendation to any reservist seeking help, who was then told to contact Ruroede. He also testified that Papen insisted on nothing in writing, and there was to be no connection between them. If either of them were arrested they would swear that they had never met each other. The accumulation of this evidence, which was supported by the captured Falmouth Papers, resulted in charges by the Justice

Department accusing Papen of becoming an accessory after the fact to von Wedell's crime:

> It would seem that Captain von Papen is guilty also of violation of Section 146 of the penal code in that he had actual knowledge of the commission of a felony...It might be difficult in the absence of admissions from von Papen or von Wedell's testimony to clearly prove knowledge on von Papen's part...but there seems to be no room for doubt...[36]

Violation of federal laws governing the issuance of passports paled in comparison with Papen's other efforts to obstruct Allied war efforts. Among the more notorious incidents was Papen's indirect involvement in a plot to blow up the locks of the Welland Canal in Canada. Shortly after the outbreak of the war, in August, 1914, a Mr. Bridgeman-Taylor came to Papen with a plan to delay the arrival of Canadian troops to France.[37] Papen thought the idea of blowing up the locks of the Welland canal was a good idea, and gave the man $500.00 to purchase the explosives. The attempt, however, was unsuccessful, and the saboteur was arrested along with his accomplice, Werner Horn.[38]

The Welland Canal project was not Papen's last attempt at sabotage. Sometime in January, 1915, Werner Horn proposed to blow up the Vanceboro bridge, the most important railway line between Canada and the United States. Just as in the case of the Welland affair, Horn was caught and arrested on February 2, 1915, while attempting to carry out the plot. Under intense cross-examination Horn confessed that he had carried out the attempt on Papen's orders. It was hoped that this would cut off an important artery for sending war material from America to Britain's ally, Canada. Horn's confession caused an enormous sensation in the American and Canadian press. An official denial by the German Embassy stated that Papen had never met the man, nor had any connection with him. However, it was later proven that Papen had paid Horn the sum of $700 to carry out this act of sabotage.[39]

After the Vanceboro fiasco, Papen claimed that he opposed further illegal activities.[40] However, it is more probable that Berlin no longer wanted Papen to become involved in these acts of sabotage because of the careless manner with which he had handled them. However, Berlin was still prepared to carry out a policy of espionage and sabotage.

Consequently, a Captain von Rintelen, who was attached to the Naval Intelligence Staff, was sent to America to continue this policy.

From the outset Papen did not get along with von Rintelen. For one thing, he resented the purpose of his mission. Rintelen's plan called for German and Irish dock workers to stow incendiary objects in various places on munitions ships chartered by the Allies. After a few days, when the ships were on the high seas, these incendiary devices would cause fires forcing the captains to return to port. Rintelen also developed an explosive device which could be attached to the steering wheel of a vessel. The constant turning of the wheel would cause these devices to explode and thus render the ship rudderless. Finally, he wanted to stage strikes on the docks and prevent the loading of vessels. Through these means, Rintelen hoped to either curtail the shipment of munitions to the Entente or at least delay them.[41]

Papen and the Naval Attaché, Captain Boy-Ed, were afraid that Rintelen's illegal activities would endanger their covert operations. Consequently they agreed to send a coded cable to the War Office requesting the immediate recall of Captain Rintelen. After a few weeks Rintelen was recalled, but on his way back to Germany he was taken off the Dutch boat, and arrested by British authorities.[42]

Papen's connection with Rintelen's sabotage activities was traced through a check made out to a German chemist, Dr. Scheele. According to Papen, he had employed Scheele to try and find a method of pulverizing oil, a scarce fuel in Germany, and essential for the war.[43] Papen argued that the money Scheele received from him was for this purpose. He further asserted that the whole process of bomb-making was unknown to him, and he had kept himself as far away as possible from Rintelen's schemes.[44] Rintelen, on the other hand, maintained that Scheele presented himself through a letter from Papen, and showed him the incendiary device he had invented. The German naval officer purchased and successfully used the device on a number of occasions. While he does not directly indicate where the money came from, Rintelen implies that he received it from Papen.[45]

While Papen continued his efforts to obstruct aid of any sort to the Entente Powers, the U.S. Justice Department was keeping a close watch on the activities of the German Embassy. One of the most closely watched besides Papen was Heinrich Albert, financial advisor to the Embassy, who was also instructed to subsidize writers and speakers whose job it was to influence public opinion against the Allies.

On a very hot summer day in 1915, Albert and the pro-German editor of *The Fatherland*, George Viereck were traveling in one of the Sixth Avenue elevated trains to Albert's lodgings in the German Club. Albert carried with him a large dispatch case full of documents relating to his bureau. The July heat made the train stifling hot. After Viereck got off, Albert settled back and, due to a long day's work plus the heat, he dozed off. Waking up just as he arrived at his destination Albert jumped up, rushed for the door, and once on the platform realized that he had forgotten his briefcase. Leaping back into the train just before it departed, he saw that the case was gone. Dejectedly he returned to the German Club where he recounted the sad tale to Papen. The Chargé immediately telephoned the police, and every effort was made to recover the case, but without success. It had been the work of an American secret service operative, Frank Burke, who took the briefcase to his chief, Treasury Secretary, William McAdoo.[46]

The portfolio contained documents dealing with German economic and propaganda activity, as well as important political papers. However, since the United States and Germany were not on a collision course at this time, the only documents that President Wilson and Colonel House permitted to be published dealt with economic and propaganda information. Although there was nothing criminal in these documents, they did pave the way for another anti-German press campaign.

While the published contents of the purloined Albert briefcase certainly did not help Papen's public image, his carelessness about his correspondence was even more damaging to his reputation in America. In a personal letter to his wife, who was then living in Germany, Papen recounted the case of the stolen briefcase, and then made a very dangerous comment: "Well! One must after all expect things like this to happen. How splendid on the Eastern Front. I always say to these idiotic Yankees they should shut their mouths, or better still, express their admiration for all that heroism."[47] This comment proved to be the last bit of evidence the State Department used to have him declared a *persona non grata*, which meant expulsion from America.

The way in which this damaging comment made its way into the press was one of those unlucky episodes that seem to have pursued Papen throughout his life. An American journalist James F. Archibald and a friend of Papen's, also served as a courier for the German government. In August 1915, Archibald was going to Germany taking with him some important political documents from the German Embassy in Washington, DC to the Foreign Office in Berlin. Papen gave him this letter for his wife. On August 30, the neutral vessel *Rotterdam* arrived at Falmouth for the usual British customs inspection. In searching Archibald's luggage, the English discovered the portfolio, and as luck would have it, Papen's letter to his wife along with several other incriminating documents.[48]

When the contents of the Archibald portfolio were published in the press, a new wave of anti-German feelings developed. This was intensified when the political documents were also revealed. This consisted of a letter from the Hungarian Ambassador, Constantin Dumba, to his Foreign Minister in Prague. Dumba questioned America's neutral status, and proposed that it might be possible to arrange for strikes in U.S. munitions factories. This would hold up the production of armaments for the Entente Powers, and aid the cause of the Central Powers. Since this was similar to Papen's project to get German workers out of war industries, the press immediately sought to question him.

On September 5, he was interviewed about the mention of his name in the Dumba letter. In what was to become characteristic of his responses to questions from the press, Papen admitted his connection with Dumba, claimed that he knew nothing about the proposed strikes, and went on to accuse the British officials of fostering anti-German propaganda. Topping the interview, however, was his blunt comment that he had nothing to say about the letter to his wife. Naturally, the anti-German press charged Papen with anti-Americanism, and connected this with the allegations of espionage and sabotage which had already made the headlines.[49]

While the press began to call for Papen's expulsion, the Secretary of State, Lansing, issued a sharply-worded dispatch to Vienna demanding Dumba's recall. Lansing charged Dumba with conspiracy against American industry, and violating diplomatic privileges.[50] It was only a question of time before Papen would receive the same treatment.

In the meantime, Papen's "idiotic Yankee" remark would not go away. In an effort to get away from the constant questions by reporters, and the pressures of the job, Papen decided to travel to San Francisco where the World Exposition was being held. Accompanied by a friend,

Prince Hatzfeldt, Papen was able for the most part to avoid publicity. However, in San Francisco he was cornered by reporters who raised the derogatory "Yankee" remark. Once again, he committed a bad mistake. Perhaps out of sheer weariness, or unmindful of the way comments can be interpreted by a hostile press, Papen declared that the remark was not directed against the American public, but against a certain New York newspaper. The hostile press now accused him of lying. Adding this latest charge to all the other allegations, which were supported by the documents recovered in the Albert and Archibald portfolios, Papen's days in America were numbered.

At the end of November the storm broke over Papen's head. The *Providence Journal*, a strongly pro-British newspaper, published a series of articles against Papen. Although the "idiotic Yankee" remark precipitated Papen's recall, it was bolstered by a number of other accusations including, passport frauds, charges of espionage and attempted sabotage such as the Welland Canal and Vanceboro bridge miscarriages, and association with men like Dumba who had allegedly conspired against American industry.

Perhaps many of the accusations made against Papen were hardly serious enough to have him expelled from the country. However, there were instances in which he did violate U.S. laws, and therefore constituted valid grounds for his recall. Papen tended to dismiss these by claiming that he was either inexperienced or that his illegal activities did no harm to the American people. Perhaps the greatest damage came from Papen's own indiscretions such as the "Yankee" comment and his feeble explanation to justify it.

While Papen's indiscreet remarks and implausible justifications did a great deal to injure his reputation, the anti-German press and highly influential British propaganda certainly fueled the demands for Papen's recall. To this one must add that the American Secretary of State, Lansing, was inordinately anti-German, and sought every means to have the German Embassy shut down. In order to accomplish this, he enlisted the support of the Justice Department and the Secretary of the Treasury, Mr. McAdoo, who was also pro-British.

There were other extraneous circumstances that also contributed to Papen's recall. Among the more significant was the sinking of the *Lusitania*, which caused the anti-German press to heap abuse on the German government, the Embassy, and everyone connected with it, including Papen. Nor can one overlook Ambassador von Bernstorff's lame defense of German nationals, Papen's activities, and Germany's desire to remain on friendly terms with America despite all the anti-American activities reported in the jingoist press. Finally, while Papen probably had nothing to do with many of the foolish acts of espionage and sabotage, his reputation identified him with every rumor and crackpot activity.[51]

On December 1, 1915, Ambassador Bernstorff was called to the State Department where he was informed that his attachés were no longer acceptable, and he was requested to withdraw them from the country.[52] On Wednesday, December 22, 1915, having been relieved of his duty as military attaché to the United States and Mexico, Papen set sail from New York aboard a neutral vessel, the SS *Noordam* of the Holland-American Line. He took with him some personal correspondence, private letters, and records of canceled checks and checkbook stubs. On January 22, the *Noordam* arrived at Falmouth for customs clearance. Papen, bearing a legitimate passport, assumed that he was traveling under diplomatic immunity. In spite of the fact that the guarantee of safe conduct excluded carrying official documents, and he had been warned not to carry with him any potentially incriminating papers, Papen gave it little thought.[53] The British officials not only searched his person, but also his belongings, and confiscated incriminating written and printed materials. Once again Papen's carelessness endangered not only himself and his government, but also private people who had trusted him unconditionally in their service to Germany. On the other hand, it furnished the United States with additional evidence with which to charge Papen, and further tarnish his reputation.[54] Despite protestations of innocence, Papen was never able to completely remove that stain.

Papen arrived in Germany on January 8, 1916. After spending a few days with his wife and family in Düsseldorf, he went to Berlin where he reported to his superior, General Erich von Falkenhayn. In the two hour meeting with the General, Papen not only briefed him on his activities in America, but he also wanted to make certain that his superiors regarded his mission as honorable and worthy of a Prussian officer. Later on, in February, when the Falmouth incident was reported in the press, Papen wrote his version in a memo to the Foreign Office. He insisted that several of the published letters were never in his possession at Falmouth. He also listed the documents that were confiscated along with a summary of their contents and explanation of their importance.[55]

Once Papen had given his report, he awaited further orders. As a military man, he was anxious to go to the Front where he felt his training would be best put to the test. In many ways, this proved to be true. His record as a soldier proved to be far better than his activities as a diplomat.

NOTES

[1] The only account of Papen's early life is found in his *Memoirs*, (New York: E.P. Dutton & Company, Inc., 1953), a translation by Brian O'Connell of *Die Wahrheit eine Gasse* (Munich: Paul List Verlag, 1952). Other biographies are either incomplete or are biased, and poorly researched narratives, e.g., Oswald Dutch *The Errant Diplomat* (London: Edward Arnold & Co., 1940); H.W. Blood-Ryan *Franz von Papen His Life and Times* (London: Rich & Cowan, Ltd., 1940). There is only one recent, complete account by Henry M. and Robin K. Adams, *Rebel Patriot* (Santa Barbara: McNally & Loftin Publishers, 1987). Unfortunately, this long, tedious account relies too much on Papen's untrustworthy *Memoirs*, ignores previous scholarship, and selectively chooses what serves the authors' purposes. Moreover, the disproportionate number of pages dedicated to irrelevant material further characterizes this flawed chronicle.

[2] *Albertus dictus Papa et Hermanus filius ejus, Sälzer zu Werl* ("Albert by name Papa, and his son Hermann, the Salters of Werl"), "Papen Stammtafel," published in *Gothaischen Genealogischen Taschenbuch* (Marburg: Deutsches Adelsarchiv, 1933), pp. 396-397.

[3] Ibid.

[4] *Memoirs, pp. 4-5*

[5] Ibid.

[6] Blood-Ryan, ibid., p. 20

[7] *Memoirs, p. 8*

[8] René von Boch-Galhau was the Privy Councilor at Mettlach in the Saar. He was a partner in the very profitable pottery industry, Villeroy & Boch, and held directorships in many large manufacturing firms in the Rhineland, France, Belgium and Luxembourg. He died in 1908, and left the bulk of his fortune to his daughter, Martha and son-in-law. This enabled Franz to remain financially independent in his pursuit of a political career.

[9] For this reason more than any other, Martha hated the Nazi regime and what it did to the Catholic church in both Germany and Austria. She despised Hitler and the entire Nazi hierarchy, and never gave the Nazi salute to anyone, or on any occasion. Her favorite nick-name for Hitler was "Dodo!"

[10] *Memoirs*, p. 9.

[11] Friedrich von Bernhardi, *Germany and the Next War* (Berlin: 1911). Bernhardi was both a diplomat and a General in the German Army before and during World War I. His book ran through numerous editions, and was regarded by many military men as the bible of Prussian diplomacy.

[12] During his time at the War Academy, Martha gave birth to a second daughter, Margaret, on April 14, 1908. Then on October 10, 1911, they were blessed with their third child, Franz Friedrich.

[13] Count Johann Heinrich von Bernstorff's principle objective in the first few months of the war was to make relations between his Government and Washington as friendly as possible.

[14] Ibid., p. 16

[15] With the exception of the Kaiser himself, the persons who did most to give German foreign policy a European reputation for dangerous irrationality were Foreign Secretary Bernhard von Bülow and Admiral Alfred von Tirpitz. Both were committed to a policy of world domination by Germany. It was Tirpitz' strategy of unrestricted submarine warfare that eventually brought America into the war on the side of the Allies.

[16] The United States refused to recognize the Huerta government and imposed an embargo on arms shipped to Mexico. However, all along the border arms were being smuggled in to Villa and Carranza under the advertent eyes of the U.S. customs officials.

[17] *Memoirs*, p. 17.

[18] Ibid., p. 20

[19] Papen's account of his activities in America is perhaps the most self-serving and erroneous section of his *Memoirs*, which are notoriously regarded as unreliable. In *Rebel Patriot*, pp. 5-103, Henry and Robin Adams attempt to justify Papen's illegal activities. Their account is not only full of irrelevant material, but often includes misleading information.

[20] Memorandum of the Secretary of State, Lansing, concerning Heinrich Albert, November 21, 1915. On June 29, 1915, Mr. Viereck sent a letter to Mr. Albert enclosing a statement requesting payment of $1,500.00. Albert's reply, dated July 1, acknowledged the amount due, and promised to remit it within a week. *Dept. of Justice Report*, Microfilm #701.6211/321, National Archives, Washington, DC (hereafter cited *Lansing Rept.*)

[21] Although Papen was not directly involved in these transactions, he was well aware of Albert's financial support of Viereck's pro-German newspaper. A copy of a letter from George Sylvester Viereck to Captain von Papen dated December 4, 1915, was among the papers confiscated by British authorities at Falmouth. "Selection from Papers of Captain von Papen," Falmouth, January 2 & 3, 1916 (London: HMSO, 1916), No. 23, p. 12, National Archives, No. 701.6211/358, (hereafter cited *Falmouth Papers*).

[22] Translation of rough draft cable from Captain von Papen to Captain Boy-Ed, Military Attaché, Mexico, July 29, 1914, *Falmouth Papers*, No. 6, p. 3.

[23] Papen's reports to the Foreign Office in Berlin not only included copies of press reports from the major U.S. newspapers, but also a complete breakdown of all shipping departing from U.S. ports. The schedules included the name of

the vessel, date of departure, and destination, along with the contents and its value. Cf. *Akten, vom 1 Jannuar 1914 bis Februar 1914*, Bd. 16, 1335/3 *Auswärtiges Amt, Abteilung A: Politisches Archiv. d. Auswärt. Amts*, Bonn (hereafter cited *Akten, A. Amt/Abt. A*).

[24] Analysis of certain of Captain von Papen's checks between September 1, 1914, and December 21, 1915, *Falmouth Papers*, Annex 2, pp. 19-24. Photostats of these checks are included, (Annex 3), which indicate the name of the Amsinick Company as the recipient, and also on the record of the transaction the purpose for which the check was written. This made it very easy for anyone to know to whom the money was to be paid through the Amsinick "Laundromat."

[25] Statement of Major v. Papen to the Investigating Committee of the German National Assembly, Friday, April 16, 1920. Trans. in *Official German Documents Relating to the World War*, 2 vols., Carnegie Endowment for International Peace (New York: Oxford University Press, 1923), vol. 2, pp. 1307-16 (hereafter cited *Invest. Com./CNA*).

[26] *Invest. Com./CNA*, p. 1311. Although Papen refused to consider this as illegal, the U.S. Justice Department would label this "in restraint of trade," and therefore against American laws. This was one of the major reasons why Papen was designated a "persona non grata," and "invited" to leave in December, 1916.

[27] Memorandum on Captain von Papen, Military Attaché, *Lansing Rept.*, pp. 11-12, mentions Papen's efforts to convince the German Ambassador to have the Bridgeport Company buy up all the phenol used in the production of armaments, and also the rights of the Wright Aeroplane patent.

[28] *Invest. Com./CNA*, p. 1311.

[29] The Bridgeport Company was able to tie up the Aetna Powder Company's entire production of gun-powder until the end of 1915, and stored it in the Bridgeport facility, *Invest. Com./CNA,* pp. 1311-1312; cf. also Papen's report to the Imperial German Ambassador, April 16, 1915, in which he lists the amount of powder purchased from Aetna together with the dates and the cost: 3,250,000 pounds of smokeless powder to be delivered between August, 1915 and February, 1916, at a cost of $8,250,000, *Akten, Aus. Amt/Ab, 2A.*

[30] *Invest. Com./CNA*, pp. 1311-12. Papen also initiated a program designed to get German, Austrian and Hungarian workers in munitions and war production plants to quit their jobs and take up work in non-war production industries. The number of German nationals and others who might have participated in this program is uncertain, nor is it known how successful this operation was.

[31] Memorandum concerning Captain von Papen, *Lansing Rept.*, p. 10 ff.

[32] *Memoirs*, p. 35.

[33] Hans Adam von Wedell was an American citizen and New York lawyer. In 1914, he went to Germany to join the German army, carrying with him

dispatches, reports and a recommendation from the German Embassy in Washington, DC As an American notary, he was in an excellent position to provide these reservists with forged passports. He arrived in New York in November, 1914, with instructions for Papen. From November 21, 1914, until he left the United States for Havana in December, Wedell received funds from Papen through the Amsinick company. After Wedell departed, Ruroede carried on the passport operation until he was arrested.

[34] Among the documents confiscated by the British at Falmouth was a checkbook with no fewer than seven checks totaling $3,000 made out to von Wedell and his wife. One of them was for $300 with the note "journey money for Wedel." These checks were written out to the Amsinick Company, and signed by Papen. *Falmouth Papers*, Check No. 52, Annex 3, p. 28.

[35] Lansing memorandum concerning Captain von Papen, *Lansing Report*, pp. 12-14a, national Archives, Washington, DC The Justice Department planted an agent in Heinrich Albert's office, posing as Ruroede. The agent discovered the passport operation and its connection to Papen one day when the German Naval Attaché from Tokyo, on his way to Europe, presented a letter of recommendation from Papen thinking the agent was Ruroede. When the letter was compared with lists of names, addresses, rank, etc. who had applied for passports found in Ruroede's desk, it was discovered that both were written with the same typewriter.

[36] Memorandum concerning Captain von Papen, *Lansing Rept.*, p. 14.

[37] Bridgeman-Taylor's real name was Horst von der Golst, alias Wachendorf. Apparently, this devious character had a long history of intrigue. In 1910, he had been extradited from Belgium to Germany because of attempted swindles. In Mexico, where he had met Papen, he was an arms merchant on behalf of Pancho Villa. He was also involved in other nefarious schemes. Papen claims that after the Welland Canal incident, he had nothing to do with Golst. However, Golst presented a letter of recommendation from Papen to the German Consul in Baltimore in order to obtain an American passport, which he received under the name Bridgeman-Taylor.

[38] Bridgeman-Taylor was later tried for espionage. Horn was released for lack of evidence.

[39] *Falmouth Papers*, check #87, $700.00, January 18, 1915, "for Horn."

[40] *Memoirs*, p. 36

[41] Captain Franz von Rintelen, *The Dark Invader, War-time Reminiscences of a German Naval Intelligence Officer*, (London: Lovat Dickson, 1933).

[42] Eventually Rintelen was returned to the United States, and stood trial in may, 1917. His testimony further implicated Papen in numerous sabotage activities.

[43] *Memoirs*, p. 48

[44] Ibid.

[45] Rintelen, ibid. Since the veracity of Rintelen's testimony is no more reliable than Papen's protestations of innocence, the entire episode remains unresolved. The only thing that can be said is that given the unreliability of Papen's recollections in so many other instances, one might also question his explanation in this case.

[46] *Memoirs*, pp. 44-45. Papen's account of the "theft" is fairly close to the event. A more detailed version is found in W.F. Houghton, "The Albert Portfolio," *Saturday Evening Post*, August 17, 1929.

[47] Memorandum concerning Captain von Papen, *Lansing Rept.*, p. 12, National Archives, Washington, DC

[48] Page to Lansing, August 31, 1915, *FRUS, Suppl.*, Vol. I, 1915, p. 932

[49] *New York World*, September 6, 1915, p. 2, col. 5-6

[50] Lansing to Penfield, September 8, 1915, *FRUS, Suppl.*, 1915, pp. 933-934.

[51] For example, in his trip to San Francisco, the press gave out the speculation that Papen was on his way to war-torn Mexico. Cf. *San Francisco Chronicle*, Saturday, September 25, 1915, p. 2, col. 1; Sunday, September 26, p. 2, col. 3; Tuesday, September 28, p. 1, col. 2. He was also accused of organizing the famous "Black Tom" explosions in July, 1916 and January, 1917, after he had already returned to Germany.

[52] Lansing memorandum of interview with Bernstorff, December 1, 1915, *FRUS, Lansing Report*, pp. 86-87. The Naval Attaché, Boy-Ed, was also requested to leave America because he also engaged in acts of espionage.

[53] Boy-Ed had been much more cautious, and had either hidden or destroyed all of his records. One can only speculate that Papen ignored the advice and took these incriminating documents with him because he wanted to defend his activities in America against possible criticisms. It is also instructive to note that among the documents confiscated were a number of letters praising him for his efficient and loyal service to the Fatherland. *Falmouth Papers*.

[54] The U.S. Justice Department charged that Papen's efforts to prevent the sale of war materials to Britain and her allies was in violation of the restraint of trade laws. He was, therefore, subject to penalties for these violations. Lansing memorandum concerning Captain von Papen, pp. 10-15.

[55] This *apologia* does not excuse his carelessness. The fact is that the British confiscated them and it did not matter how or when. Moreover, if these reports were of such a sensitive nature, why didn't Papen send them in code? This would have prevented their contents from being used by the British to generate more anti-German feelings in America.

CHAPTER 2:
THE KAISER'S FAITHFUL SERVANT

A. On the Western Front

When the war broke out in August, 1914, the German armies enjoyed initial success. On the eastern front, under the leadership of Generals Hindenburg and Ludendorff, the army was particularly successful against the Russians. By mid-September, East Prussia was free of Russian troops, and the German public had found in Hindenburg and Ludendorff the military heroes it so ardently sought.

However, the gratifying results in the east tended to blot out the terrible failure of the German armies in the west. In spite of the collapse of the supposedly infallible Schlieffen Plan, public opinion was still confident that the German offensive would resume in the near future. Even as late as the last months of 1914, no one even dimly discerned the true shape the war was to assume in the west - the long bloody halt in the mud that was to destroy a whole generation of young men.

In the middle of February, 1916, Captain von Papen received his orders to proceed to the front. After bidding his wife and family good-bye, he departed on February 20 for Flanders where he took command of the 2nd Battalion Reserve Regiment No. 93, 4th Guards Infantry Division.[1]

On August 22 Papen's division was thrown across the Somme and moved into position opposite Schwaben near Thiepval. Under extremely heavy artillery fire, Papen's battalion stood its ground, but suffered severe losses. By November, the Guards Division had been driven back to a line a few miles south of Bapaume, and Papen's division attempted to stand its ground near Warlencourt, where the battle raged until the beginning of 1917. On February 23, Papen's division moved into the Siegfried line.[2] All told, Papen's division engaged in battle three times during the spring and summer of 1917. On Easter Sunday, April 11, 1917, he was once again in action at Vimy Ridge and Arras. For four weeks his division managed to keep the Canadian forces at bay. However, once again the final losses were staggering. As a consequence, Papen introduced certain modifications in the army's defensive tactics along the Artois front. Papen's new tactics proved to be highly successful , and he was requested to visit General Headquarters and report his success to Hindenburg and Ludendorff.[3]

During all of this fighting, Papen never lacked courage. In spite of the constant danger of death, and the dreadful losses he witnessed, Papen never seemed to fear anything. From his steeplechasing days to his escapades in Mexico and the United States, he always seemed to possess a certain reckless form of courage that has often been interpreted as a careless disregard for consequences. While this characteristic served him well on the battlefield, it often proved to be a serious obstacle when he embarked on a political career after the war.

Papen continued to serve in the 4th Guards Division, experiencing action in the Lens sector. However, he was growing restless with the defensive battles and longed for more action. Finally, after several more months on the Western Front, Papen received orders to go to Mesopotamia as head of the Operations Department of Army Group Falkenhayn. Along with these orders, Papen was promoted to the rank of Major.[4] Papen joined Falkenhayn, and together with a small staff, went on to Constantinople where they arrived at the end of June, 1917.

In Constantinople, Falkenhayn, Papen, and a small force of picked men, formed what became known as the Asia Corps. The Corps, which included a newly organized Turkish Army Group F, was composed of only three infantry battalions equipped with artillery, mortars, aircraft, wireless and mechanical transport.[5]

Although Papen had anticipated active engagement in battles, he spent several tedious weeks at a desk working in the debilitating mid-August heat of Constantinople. It was just about this time that the British General, Allenby, took command of the British forces in Palestine, and was threatening to breakthrough the Palestine front which extended from Gaza on the Mediterranean southeastward to Beersheba. Realizing that a British break-through on the Palestine front would endanger the German operation against Baghdad, Falkenhayn, accompanied by Papen, set out for that theater of operations. For two days, September 9 and 10, they inspected the waterless, shadowless, and unmercifully hot desert region. After assessing the strengths and weaknesses, Falkenhayn decided to postpone the Baghdad offensive and commit all available forces to the Palestine front. Papen was sent back to Palestine to reorganize the defenses around Jerusalem, and make arrangements for the arrival of the 7th Turkish army and the German Asia Corps.[6]

Between October and December, 1917, Papen engaged in several major bloody battles against General Allenby. Towards the close of 1917, the British occupied Beth-Horon only twelve miles from Jerusalem. On the night of December 7, the British began their second attack on Jerusalem in a driving rain. The Turkish army appeared to give up hope, and they retreated that night and all the next day. On December 11, Allenby entered Jerusalem and claimed the city for the Allies. One version recorded that Papen was forced to flee Jerusalem in his pajamas leaving his clothing and all his papers behind.[7] However, Papen claimed that he was in Germany visiting his family at the time. He also insisted that the papers were nothing more than some private letters "with comments on the general situation and the likely outcome of the war."[8]

In the meantime, the British had captured El Salt and on September 20, 1918, had reached Nazareth, and headed for the headquarters of Liman von Sanders, the new commander who had replaced Falkenhayn. Papen, accompanied by his adjutant Franz von Spee, reached Constantinople in October, but was unable to return to the Palestine front. Instead, after the Turkish High Command decided to surrender in October, Papen was assigned to facilitate the return of what was left of the German Asian Corps to the mountains in Karapunar. It was in those mountains that Papen and his troops learned of the end of the war. An armistice had been declared, the Kaiser had abdicated and fled to Holland. Proud Imperial Germany was no more. Major Franz von Papen could only see dark days ahead for himself and for the Fatherland.

B. The Agony of Defeat

Von Papen's reaction to the announcement of Germany's surrender was one of shock: "...it was the collapse of every value we had ever known, made even more painful by exile." Even more depressing was the news that the Kaiser had been forced to abdicate because President Wilson refused to deal with the existing regime. "It was the end of everything we had believed in for generations, the disappearance of all that we had loved and fought for."[9]

Sometime after November 9, 1918, Papen was instructed to proceed with his troops to Moda near Constantinople. But it was not until late in November that they arrived at Moda where they were interned until transport back to Germany could be arranged. General Von Sanders, who had lost his post as Commander-in-Chief after the Armistice, was allowed to take up residence on the island of Prinkipo and, according to Papen, visited the internment camp every morning. It was on one such visit that Papen and von Sanders engaged in a stormy argument that almost resulted in a court martial for the outspoken Major. According to Papen, the argument developed over von Sanders' desire to organize soldier's councils similar to those which, according to reports, were being organized by revolutionaries in Germany. Papen strongly opposed such a move, maintaining that if this happened, the authority of the officers would disappear, and the Allies would impose stricter internment regulations. Papen boldly suggested that von Sanders give up his command of the troops and return to Germany, and then insisted on appealing directly to Field-Marshal von Hindenburg in Germany. In one of those rare instances in which prudence overruled boldness, Papen decided against such a precipitous action because all of the telegraph lines were in the hands of the Allies.

Meanwhile, angered by what he considered to be insubordination, von Sanders decided to have Papen arrested and court-martialed.[10] Realizing that he would probably not receive a fair trial at Moda, Papen decided to return to Germany as quickly as possible and present his case to Field Marshal von Hindenburg. Dressed in civilian clothes purchased at a local bazaar, Papen and his adjutant, Count Spee, smuggled themselves aboard the German hospital ship *Jerusalem*, and remain undetected until the ship arrived at Spezia, Italy. From there they made their way to the Swiss border, and finally arrived at the main train station in Munich on January 6, 1919.[11]

The scene that Papen witnessed on his arrival in Munich was one he never forgot. The Wittlesbach monarchy had been deposed in the November revolution, and the left-wing Socialist, Kurt Eisner, had proclaimed a Socialist Republic in conservative Catholic Bavaria. Opposing Eisner were the Majority Socialists and the more radical Communists who had established soldiers' councils composed of war veterans and unemployed workers. Disillusioned and angry, they roamed the streets of Munich creating an atmosphere of violence. Members of the soldiers' council who were on duty in the train station tried to tear off Papen's epaulets. With the help of the leader of one of the bands of embittered ex-soldiers and disillusioned youth known as Free Corps units, he was able to fight his way out of Munich.[12]

Papen eventually reached Hindenburg's headquarters at Kolberg on the Baltic Sea, where he reported the collapse of the Turkish Empire, the last battles, and the internment of the German troops. He also recounted his dispute with von Sanders, and justified his actions on the grounds that some steps had to be taken to maintain the honor of German army in Turkey. Accepting full responsibility for his actions, Papen requested an investigation into the entire affair, and told Hindenburg he was prepared to stand trial. Hindenburg smiled and replied "I know General Liman von Sanders' vanity pretty well. I don't need any further information about his attitude...there is no need for either investigation or court-martial. You may consider the matter closed."[13] This was the last time that Papen met Hindenburg as an active soldier, but he left the Field-Marshal's presence with a strong impression that "here was one personality to whom the nation could turn in time of stress."[14]

Meanwhile, on January 9, while Papen was reporting to von Hindenburg, an insurrection led by the Communists Karl Liebknecht and "Red Rosa" Luxemburg, erupted in Berlin. Friedrich Ebert, the Socialist president of the Provisional Government, was determined to prevent the revolution from turning further left. He therefore called on Defense Minister Gustav Noske to crush the rebellion. On the cold, rainy morning of January 11, at the head of some 3,000 men including the Free Corps unit known as Maercker's Volunteer Rifles, Noske, the self-styled "bloodhound of the revolution," entered Berlin by way of *Potsdamer Strasse*, and systematically occupied the city. By January 15, the capital was completely in the hands of the government. Liebknecht and Luxemburg were brutally murdered by members of the Free Corps unit who had been ordered to deliver them to the Spandau prison.[15]

Viewing this scene of revolution and violence, Papen grew even more depressed: "The world I had known and understood had disappeared. The whole system of values into which I had integrated myself and for which my generation had fought and died had become meaningless...Germany was defeated, ruined, her people and institutions a prey to chaos and disillusionment."[16] For the first time in his life, Papen's sense of self-confidence and buoyant optimism faded, and he began to wonder what the future held, not only for Germany, but also for himself and his family.

During the war, Martha and the four children had lived on the family estate at Wallerfangen in the Saar. When Papen returned to Germany he was finally able to notify his wife, and they made arrangements to meet at his mother's home in Düsseldorf. According to Papen, the Allies refused to allow him to return to Wallerfangen, but it is more probable that he was afraid that he would be arrested by the French.

Unable to return to the Saar, and unwilling to continue to serve in an army that was now called upon to defend the Republic for which he had little regard or loyalty, Papen decided to relocate his family and return to civilian life. The decision to resign from the army was not an easy one, but he was aided in making it when the Allies demanded that Germany reduce the Army to one hundred thousand men and officers. "With a heavy heart, I sent off my resignation from the Army, requesting permission, which was later granted, to wear the uniform of the General Staff on formal occasions, in memory of the work to which I had devoted most of my life."[17] Thus, after almost twenty-nine years in the service of the Empire and the Hohenzollern dynasty, Papen laid aside his officers epaulets, and prepared to embark on a new and completely different career.

C. *Haus Merfeld*

While waiting for the Army to acknowledge his request to resign, Papen decided to go back to the country life in which he had grown up. He had always admired the people who worked the land, which he believed was the "well-spring" of Germany's strength, and where he felt that he would be in good company "...to combat the materialist spirit of the twentieth century and ward off the threat of decay, hopelessness and moral degeneration," which, in his opinion, characterized post-war Germany.[18] With this in mind, he leased an estate in his native Westphalia near Dülmen not far from the Ruhr.

Haus Merfeld consisted of an old country house with adjoining stables partially hidden by giant oak trees. A narrow path wound its way through a lush green meadow dotted with wild flowers, and circled around several ponds lined with willow trees. Idyllic as it seemed, Martha found living there primitive in comparison with the family home in the Saarland. There was no electricity, sewage or water mains, and the estate was miles from the main road and the railway.[19] In spite of these drawbacks, however, the von Papens quickly adjusted to their new surroundings.

The neighbors were simple farmers with "...both feet planted firmly on the ground, strong in their religious beliefs and upright in their behavior."[20] Although normally wary of new-comers, they soon came to realize that the "Baron" not only shared their conservative, Catholic outlook, but also was willing to come to their aid whenever approached. It was not long before Papen gained the confidence and respect of his neighbors, and the friendships he developed in Merfeld remained strong throughout his controversial career.

During the first two years in *Haus Merfeld*, Papen lived the life of a gentleman farmer. Unlike many ex-officers, who had no income except their Army retirement pay, Papen was financially secure as a result of a patrimony he inherited, and the dowry he received from his father-in-law. This not only provided him with the means to develop his estate and agricultural interests, but also allowed him to pursue his favorite hobbies-riding and hunting.

Papen had grown up around horses, and the many trophies won in numerous competitions were proof of his expert horsemanship. At Merfeld he had several fine horses, and every morning his neighbors would see the "gentleman rider" astride his favorite chestnut stallion trotting down a country road or through the wooded areas that crisscrossed the rolling hills of the Westphalian countryside. Next to riding, Papen's favorite hobby was hunting. On brisk fall mornings, accompanied by young Franz, who flushed the game out of the brush, Papen would go in search of game. An expert marksman, he would more often than not return home with several fat partridges which Martha would roast over an open spit.

Although he was not unfamiliar with farming, Papen preferred to lease his acreage to tenant farmers. As a landlord, he treated his tenants fairly, and it was not too long before he became looked upon as the champion of agricultural interests around Dülmen. Over the course of time, Papen's reputation as a defender of agricultural interests caught the attention of local political leaders who began to see the former army officer as a possible representative in the Prussian *Landtag*.

When he was not overseeing his agricultural or business interests, Papen found his greatest pleasure in the company of his children. Isabella recalled those happy years in Dülmen, when her father would sit her on his horse, or take her brother, Franz, and her sisters, Margaret and Marie Antoinette swimming in a nearby lake. In winter he would yoke one of the horses to a sleigh, and bundling the children in warm blankets, skillfully pilot them over the frozen turf. Then they would return home where Martha had prepared steaming cups of hot chocolate, and listen to the excited chatter of the children as they recounted every detail of the sleigh ride. Margaret recalls her childhood in Dülmen as years filled with many wonderful days in which her father "... quietly and lovingly taught them by example to have respect for all persons, live a life close to God, and always place duty above pleasure."[21] It was in this peaceful setting on June 14, 1919, that Martha gave birth to her fifth and last child, Stephanie Marie Antoinette. She, along with her brother, Franz, and her three sisters were to spend many happy days in *Haus Merfeld* - perhaps the most peaceful of their lives.

Although Papen enjoyed the life of a country gentleman, he was disturbed by the events which were taking place in Germany. The Weimar coalition government under the presidency of the Socialist, Friedrich Ebert, had been forced to accept the humiliating terms of the Versailles Treaty. For Papen, as well as millions of Germans who had hoped for a peace of reconciliation based on Wilson's Fourteen Points, the Treaty turned out to be a document based on hate and vengeance.

Bitterly disappointed with the peace terms, Papen wrote that "...for the first time in history the victors applied the principle of totality...totality in the imposition of war guilt and its punishment, in the unilateral solution of territorial and ethnic problems, and all questions of reparations and finance: totality in the sequestration of all enemy private property, even in neutral countries, and totality in the formation of a League of Nations, from which only the vanquished were excluded."[22]

There is no question that the Versailles Treaty was not a wise peace. But its wisdom or folly is less important than how the French interpreted it, and what the Germans chose to make of it. From its inception, the Weimar Republic suffered under the burden of the Treaty. Instead of using their power as victors to help democracy in Germany, the allies made the Republic's position infinitely more difficult. In treating the Weimar government with the same contempt that they had for the Junker-dominated Germany of 1914, they strengthened the hands of the reactionaries who effectively exploited the unbridled hatred of those who had democratized Germany and accepted the peace terms. The myth that the Army was "stabbed-in-the-back" by the liberals, coupled with the fear of communism and the disillusionment of the de-mobilized veterans, produced a strong resurgence of extreme conservatism and nationalism. Right-wing politicians and journalists portrayed the leaders of the new government as cowards and traitors who cared nothing for Germany, and by their betrayal had abandoned all of the old ideals and traditions that had made Germany great in the past.

While he was never openly as hostile to democracy as the right wing extremists, Papen never really reconciled himself to the advent of the Republic. His family background, and early military training, predisposed him to favor the return of the prewar social and political order. To Papen's way of thinking, the democratic ideals embodied in the Weimar Constitution not only destroyed the proper balance between the nation's citizens and the authority of its rulers, but the thesis that "all power derives from the people" prepared the way for the conversion of the masses into a Marxist weapon in the struggle to overturn both Christianity and capitalism. The example of the Russian Revolution and its consequences was still fresh in his mind, and he never believed for one minute that the secular, liberal Weimar Republic ever could or would protect Germany against the threat of

Communism.   Papen was confirmed in this belief when a
communist-led revolt in the Ruhr broke out in the Spring of 1920. For
months, the Ruhr Communists had made plans to seize power if the
opportunity presented itself. The occasion arose on March 13, 1920,
when an anti-republican force under the leadership of Wolfgang Kapp
and General Walter von Lüttwitz seized Berlin with the intention of
overthrowing the Republic.[23] When Chief of the *Truppenamt*, General
von Seeckt, informed the government that the Army would not fire on
the Volunteers, President Ebert called for a general strike to paralyze
the nation and force Kapp to capitulate. The general strike was
extremely successful. Life in the capital came to a halt, "all public
service ceased throughout Berlin; no streetcar ran, no light went on, no
news was printed."[24] Kapp proved incapable of imposing his dictatorship on the passive Berliners. After five days the *putsch* collapsed and
Kapp fled to Sweden.[25]

Meanwhile, when Ebert called for the general strike he not only
supplied the Communists in the Ruhr with their long-awaited
opportunity, but he also furnished them with weapons to carry out their
revolution. More interested in fomenting unrest than supporting the
government, the Ruhr Communists, widely supported by non-
Communist workers, launched their attack against the Ruhr industrial
centers.

Alarmed by this turn of events, Ebert called off the strike on
March 16, but the Communists in the Ruhr simply ignored the order,
and continued to create unrest and disorder. While the Ebert
government attempted to negotiate a peace between the Communists
and the Free Corps units, both sides used the armistice period to
increase and consolidate their forces. The failure of the government to
achieve a compromise between the opposing forces finally led to
further violence and bloodshed. When the echoes of the Ruhr
insurrection reached Dülmen, Papen hastily organized a volunteer
company of local farmers in order to protect their property and
valuables from the approaching "Red marauders." The ex-Major soon
realized his small unit was no match for the invading Communist
forces, and he appealed to the Free Corps leaders in Münster for
soldiers to stiffen his defenses.[26] By April 8, the entire area was cleared
of the Red Army, and a certain measure of order was restored in the
Ruhr.[27] Thoroughly disgusted with what he termed "...the moral
degeneration of civil war," Papen wanted to rally all the conservative

forces under the banner of Christianity, in order to sustain in the new Republic the basic conceptions of continuing tradition.[28]

As an Army officer, Papen had spent most of his life in the service of his country. Now that Germany appeared to be on the verge of total collapse, the ex-major felt an even stronger obligation to offer his services. In the course of considering several possibilities, Papen's thoughts turned more and more to a political career. By the fall of 1920, after a great deal of soul-searching, he decided to enter the world of partisan politics.

NOTES

[1] Blood-Ryan, ibid., pp. 70

[2] Ibid., pp. 70-71; Papen, *Memoirs*, pp. 66-67.

[3] *Memoirs*, p. 67.

[4]Blood-Ryan, ibid., p. 75; *Memoirs*, p.68. After the terrible defeat at Verdun, Falkenhayn was relieved of his post as Chief of the German General Staff. After a successful invasion of Rumania in June 1917, he was sent to take over the Turkish forces from Field Marshal von der Goltz.

[5] Blood-Ryan, ibid., pp. 9-80

[6] *Memoirs*, p. 72.

[7] Blood-Ryan, ibid., p. 83, This account described the papers as important documents that revealed Papen's plot to blow up the Suez Canal, foment revolutionary and secessionist activities in nearly all the British colonies, and correspondence with the Irish revolutionary Sir Roger Casement.

[8]*Memoirs*, pp. 81-82. Papen claimed that the British played up the importance of the papers as part of a propaganda campaign against him. According to Blood-Ryan, the documents turned over to the U.S. authorities were incriminating evidence used by the Justice Department in successfully prosecuting a number of German espionage agents (p. 78). However, it seems highly unlikely that Papen would have carried such documents with him into battle. It is more likely that the confiscated papers were military plans or strategies along with some letters from his wife.

[9]*Memoirs*, p. 82.

[10] Ibid., pp. 84-85

[11] Ibid., p. 85

[12]Throughout Germany these Freikorps bands roamed the streets cutting down any and all factions they felt threatened their ideas about what the Germany nation should be. Usually the Government called upon these volunteer units to suppress strikes and other forms of turmoil. But very often they indulged in all forms of violence simply for the sake of violence, thus relieving pressing psychological needs that had arisen with the sudden collapse in 1918. For a full account of the Free Corps movement see Robert G. L. Waite, *Vanguard of Nazism: The Free Corps Movement in Post-War Germany, 1918-1923* (Cambridge, Mass., 1952).

[13] *Memoirs*, p. 85

[14] *Memoirs*, p. 85

[15] Gorden Craig, *Politics of the Prussian Army 1640-1945*, (New York: Oxford Press, 1964), p. 359-360.

[16] *Memoirs*, p. 85

[17] Ibid., p. 86

[18] Ibid., p. 91

[19] Ibid., p. 96

[20] Ibid.

[21] Correspondence to author from Isabella v. Papen, November 14, 1984.

[22] Ibid., p. 94

[23] General Walther von Lüttwitz was the commander of the *Reichswehr's* Berlin district. Wolfgang Kaap was an East Prussian politician who had helped found the right wing, rabidly nationalistic *Vaterland Partei* during World War I. They were supported by the German Nationalist and the People's party politicians, and relied on one of the most politicized Free Corps units, the Erhardt Brigade, to carry out the actual "putsch."

[24] Erich Eyck, *The History of the Weimar Republic*, Vol. 1 (Atheneum: New York, 1970), p. 152.

[25] When it came time to prosecute the *putschists*, only three were indicted for treason and stood trial before the Supreme Court. Only one of these was sentenced to five years in prison. Kapp returned to Germany in the spring of 1922, but before he could be tried, death "took him to a higher court." (Eyck, ibid., p. 160).

[26] *Memoirs*, p. 97. In his account, Papen gives the impression that he played an important role in restoring order in Dülmen. However, the military records make no mention of his name.

[27] Robert Waite, *Vanguard*, pp. 169-182

[28] *Memoirs*, p. 91

CHAPTER 3:
FROM EPAULETS TO TOP HAT

A. The Prussian *Landtag*

Several months after the Ruhr insurrection, the president of the Westphalian Farmers' Association, Freiherr Engelbert von Kerkerinck zur Borg, together with some friends, approached Papen with the request that he stand for election to the Prussian *Landtag* as a Center party candidate. Papen recalls that it was some time before he could make up his mind to accept this invitation, because he was not certain about which political party to join.[1]

Among the parties on the right, the one that appealed to Papen's conservative background and training was the German National People's Party (DNVP).[2] Formed in 1918, the DNVP presented an image of "progressive" conservatism. It stood for the traditional bourgeois values of free enterprise, protection of private property, and Christian ethics. It rejected all experiments in "Marxist collectivism." However, the Party's openness to the new times did not last long. Within a year, it was denouncing the Republic, democracy, parliamentarianism and the Jews, while demanding a return of the Hohenzollern monarchy. Papen agreed with most of these conservative ideas, but he was opposed to what he believed were many prejudices and "...too many obsolete ideas."[3]

The other conservative party that Papen considered joining was Gustav Stresemann's German People's Party (DVP). It represented big business and industry, and embraced the bulk of the conservative wing of the former National Liberal Party. Although monarchist at heart, the party supported the Republic once it was clear that it was more or less firmly established. Papen seems to have had a great deal of respect for Stresemann, and he certainly supported the party's "laissez faire" policies. However, the party's poor showing in the election for the National Assembly in January 1919, convinced the ambitious Papen that the party offered little chance for him to be elected. He therefore decided to join his conservative friends in the Catholic Center party.

Founded in 1870 as a counter-force to widespread anti-Catholic sentiments in Bismarck's Germany, the Center party became one of the mainstays of the Weimar Republic. Except in those instances where the autonomy of the Catholic Church, freedom of religious education, or the defense of states' rights was at stake, the Center had always reflected a greater freedom of action than the other parties. It unequivocally rejected the idea of a socialist state, and after the armistice in November 1918, it discarded its pro-monarchist attitude and insisted that the regime must be a democratic republic. As a party of the middle, it was prepared to share with other moderate groups the task of consolidating the republican regime. The Center also had a long history in matters of social reform, and had pledged themselves to implement the programs laid down by Pope Leo XIII. In his encyclical *Rerum Novarum*, Pope Leo called for workers' cooperatives, Christian trade unions, and other measures designed to help the poor raise their standard of living. Papen agreed with the party's commitment to defend the rights of the Catholic Church, and its pledges to carry out social reforms based on the social doctrines of Pope Leo XIII. But, he was opposed to the liberal wing of the party.

Headed by Matthias Erzberger and Josef Wirth, the liberals had co-operated with the Social Democrats and the Democrats after the Armistice in calling for the abdication of the Kaiser and the establishment of a Republic. As one of the coalition parties after the national elections in January 1919, the Center also shared in the responsibility for signing the Versailles Treaty, and, as a consequence, were accused by the Nationalists, the Army General Staff, and other Right-wing groups, of stabbing Germany in the back.

As a member of the nobility, and a former officer under the Kaiser, Papen shared these views. However, as the son-in-law of a wealthy industrialist, and a staunch Catholic opposed to all forms of Marxism, he disapproved of the Center's participation in the Weimar Coalition which included the Social Democrats (SPD).[4] Papen saw little difference between the Communists and the Socialists, both of whom, in his opinion, advocated the idea of class struggle and extolled the atheistic doctrines of Karl Marx.[5] Papen wanted the Center to break its ties with the Socialists, and to cooperate with the right-wing parties because he believed they were dedicated to the restoration of the values and traditions that had made Germany the bulwark of Christianity in the heart of Europe.[6]

Although he was strongly opposed to the liberal wing of the party, his close association with men like von Kerkerinck and the encouragement he received from his Catholic neighbors influenced him to accept the invitation to be a candidate for the Center party in the Prussian *Landtag* elections scheduled for February, 1921.[7] Naturally, the party liberals opposed Papen's nomination. However, they were unable to prevent it because of the strong support he received from his conservative friends. Moreover, there were other important, practical political reasons why Papen's nomination was successful.

Ever since the foundation of the party, the Westphalian faction had been dominated by the nobility and the large land owners. For many years they delivered the votes that gave the Center political leverage in both the *Reichstag* and the *Landtag*. Many of the local leaders, who also shared Papen's conservative views, were among his closest friends. Carl Herold, a wealthy, conservative landowner, and one of the leading party members in Westphalia, was one of Papen's sponsors. Freiherr von Kerkerinck, in addition to being the President of the Westphalian Agrarian Association, and chairman of the powerful Federation of German Agrarian Associations, was also a member of the National Executive Council of the Center party. Papen's circle of friends included Count Clemens von Galen and Friedrich von Landsburg, both of whom had held important party posts for many years. With such influential friends, Papen knew that his chances of being accepted on the Center ticket were almost guaranteed.

On December 18, 1920, von Kerkerinck and several other members of the Agrarian Association met with the leaders of the Center party to settle the question of candidates for the February elections. Although the liberals must have realized that conservatives like Papen would be more of a hindrance than a help when it came to supporting the party platform, they had little choice. It was a well known fact that the Agricultural Association, the Nationalists, and the People's Party closely cooperated with the Center in agricultural legislation in the *Landtag*. Consequently, the liberals feared that if they rejected von Kerkerinck's nominee, the Association would either form an independent party, or cast its votes in favor of the German Nationalists who, after the Ruhr insurrection, had attracted many former Center voters to its ranks. In either case, the Center would suffer a major defeat at the polls, and as a consequence be effectively out of power in Prussia. With these considerations in mind, therefore, the liberals were obliged to assume a conciliatory attitude, and Papen was accepted as a candidate from North Westphalia.[8]

Just as the national elections held on June 6, 1920, proved to be a critical turning point in Weimar politics, so too did the Prussian elections of February 20. In both elections there was a swing to the right. The conservative People's Party and the German Nationalists increased their representation in the *Landtag* by more than 10%, while the Democratic Party dropped more than 10%. The Center suffered a slight setback, but still remained the second largest party next to the Majority Socialists who also lost several seats. The farmer's of North Westphalia gave overwhelming support to their candidate, Franz von Papen. With this mandate, the neophyte politician embarked on his first political voyage resolved to faithfully represent his neighbors interests, and to promote his own peculiar brand of conservatism.

Papen admits that it was "...a bad time to embark on a political career. The country's position was at its nadir. We had been beaten in war, we were embroiled in a civil war that threatened the very foundations of the State, and labored under a dictated peace which, in its reparations demands, seemed to threaten the very basis of our economic existence. Nevertheless, I threw myself into my career with the greatest enthusiasm."[9] Although his critics maintain that he was a "cipher" in the *Landtag*, the minutes of the *Landtag* sessions indicate that during his first term (1921-24), as the Secretary of the Central Committee, Papen was one of the chief spokesman for the agrarian interests.[10] The Central Committee was one of the most important committees in the *Landtag* because its main function was to advise the government on budget questions. As a member of this Committee, Papen demonstrated considerable expertise not only with regard to technical financial questions, but also in dealing with complex agricultural issues.[11]

However, just as the liberals had anticipated, Papen proved to be a difficult colleague. He readily admits that he "...was impatient with party dogma and the narrow egocentric outlook which determined much of the current thinking on internal and external problems."[12] It was his opinion that a member of parliament should not be bound by a party platform, but had the responsibility of representing the interests of his constituency, even when those interests were not in accord with those of the party.[13] This disregard for the role of political parties was characteristic of Papen and his aristocratic colleagues. When the time came for him to assume the role of chancellor, Papen along with his conservative cabinet members did everything possible to diminish the importance of the party system, and as a consequence, significantly contributed to the demise of parliamentary democracy in Germany.

Meanwhile, in his first speech before the Prussian *Landtag* on June 6, 1921, Papen began his campaign to move the Center to the Right. The issue before the *Landtag* was the annual budget. The government proposed a budget that would leave Prussia with a 2.3 million mark deficit. In order to balance the budget, Papen recommended severe cuts in administrative areas by calling on the private sector and local governments to take the lead. He argued that a reduction in certain administrative services would diminish the number of state employees, and result in a lowering of the deficit. Papen also opposed raising taxes, and suggested that government incentives to industry and agriculture would automatically increase government revenues under the existing tax structure.[14]

Consciously aware that his conservative economic proposals were diametrically opposed to the ideas and programs of the liberals and the socialists, Papen hoped to persuade the conservatives of all parties to join forces against what he considered to be a coalition of forces that threatened the very Christian foundations of the German nation. He laid particular emphasis on this idea in the same talk when he sharply rebuked the Socialists' call for separation of Church and State, and the support of secular education as the fundamental basis on which to reconstruct the German nation. Countering the Socialist's argument, Papen responded that "an inner regeneration of the German *Volk* could come to pass only on the solid principles of Christian ethics."[15]

Almost one month after his first speech, Papen stood before the *Landtag* again. This time he rose to protest the Social Democratic charges that the large landlords were ruthlessly exploiting their tenant farmers. Sharply criticizing the SPD, Papen accused them of trying to subvert the traditional, friendly relations between landlord and tenant in order to "socialize" agriculture. "The farmers will not permit themselves to be socialized...Any arrangement between the landlord and tenant will not be achieved by government interference as the Socialists are demanding. The tenants are not workers, they are farmers, and therefore as a worker's party the SPD has wandered into foreign territory."

For the next two years, Papen vigorously defended the interests of the land-owners, accusing the Socialists and the liberal wing of his own party of attempting to "socialize" agriculture. Papen's defense of the patriarchal relationship between landowner and renter was reminiscent of the socioeconomic order that had existed in Europe during the middle ages. While these medieval notions angered his own liberal party colleagues, he further irritated them by his demand that all government controls on agriculture be abolished. In calling for this policy, Papen hoped to organize a united front of independent farmers who would extend their allegiance from the Center to the German Nationalists.[16] In this way he expected that eventually the Center party would also abandon its association with the Socialists in other areas. Although these rather feeble efforts were unsuccessful, they do point to Papen's determination to try and align the Center party with the conservatives.

In the meantime, the burden of reparations demanded under the Versailles Treaty intensified the economic distress in Germany. Finally, in January, 1923, the Government abandoned the policy of fulfillment which resulted in the occupation of the Ruhr by the French and Belgian troops. President Ebert reacted with a call for passive resistance. This policy contributed to the galloping inflation that reached its height in November, 1923. Not only did the German currency completely collapse wiping out the savings of many citizens, but this crisis was accompanied by separatist movements in the Rhineland, and Communist insurrections in Hamburg and Saxony. On November 9, 1923, Adolph Hitler's Nazi party attempted to overthrow the Bavarian government, and was defeated by Government troops.[17]

Chancellor Gustav Stresemann's efforts to stabilize the economy were coupled with the need to readjust the reparations claims. Due to the efforts of the British and American governments, a new reparations agreement was finally reached in April, 1924, known as the Dawes

Plan.[18] Thanks to the stabilization programs, the Dawes Plan, and foreign investments, the German economy became relatively stable until 1929. But it was a hollow recovery fraught with political and economic dangers. The German Nationalists resented foreign supervision of the nation's finances, and consequently refused to cooperate with any government that would not assume a more aggressive foreign policy. Moreover, the Dawes Plan assumed a favorable balance of trade in order that Germany could earn foreign credits. But Germany's balance of trade was unfavorable during most of this period requiring her to live on borrowed funds, which resulted in even deeper indebtedness.

On the eve of the *Reichstag* vote on the Dawes plan, Papen addressed the Westphalian Farmer's Association, in which he declared his support for the Dawes Plan. He pointed out that it was an unavoidable but necessary step in stabilizing the German economy, even though it might threaten the economic sovereignty of the nation. He was convinced that a rejection of the Plan would lead to the complete collapse of the *Rentenbank*, and increase the instability of the currency, which would then "lead to the ruin of the German Reich." Then, turning to the "gentlemen on the Right," Papen pointed out that a certain measure of economic independence would have to be surrendered as the price for the preservation of State sovereignty.[19]

Aside from the economic arguments, Papen had another reason for his overtures to the Nationalists. The *Reichstag* elections in May 1924 resulted in almost doubling the representation of the conservative parties - The German Nationalists and Hitler's National Socialists - from 62 to a combined total of 127 seats. The Communist Party jumped from 16 to 62, while the Socialists fell from 171 to 100, and the People's Party from 62 to 44 seats. The Democrats sank to a new low giving them only 28 places in the new *Reichstag*. Only the Center held steady, dropping from 69 to 65 seats not because of the popular vote, which increased, but because of the loss of Upper Silesia, now a part of Poland.[20] Papen believed that these elections were a sign that the voters were continuing to desert the pillars of the Republic, and that the time was ripe to push for a coalition government composed of the Center and the Nationalist parties. In order to accomplish this, he had to convince the Nationalists to vote for the Dawes Plan, which was supported by all factions in the Center. If the Nationalists refused to vote for the Dawes Plan, Papen knew that he would be unable to convince his conservative colleagues, much less the liberals, that the DNVP was capable of co-operating with the Center party.[21]

On August 29, the *Reichstag* voted on the Dawes legislation. While the Marx government could count on the Center, the Democrats, the Social Democrats and the People's party, the growing strength of the Nationalists posed a problem. In the course of the debates it became clear that the Nationalist die-hards lead by Tirpitz, Westarp, and Hugenburg were unwilling to listen to any arguments. Finally, after certain promises were made to the Nationalists by Marx's government, the delegates were instructed to vote as they saw fit. As a result of the combined vote of the industrial and agricultural interests in the DNVP, the necessary two-thirds majority needed to pass the legislation was reached.[22] Despite the close vote, Papen viewed the Nationalist support as a sign that cooperation between the Center and the Nationalists was possible. [23] But, he would have to wait until after the December elections to find out if his optimism was justified.

The elections for both the *Reichstag* and the Prussian *Landtag* were set for December 7, 1924. Once again, Papen was selected as a candidate from Westphalia-North, and since he was sixth on the *Landeslist* his reelection was practically assured. In his campaign, Papen promised to work for a protective tariff on farm products, a call for lower taxes, and the removal of all price controls on agricultural products, or farm subsidies if price controls were not removed. His other campaign theme was a promise to work for the formation of a government that he believed represented the interests of the majority, and that operated on the basis of Christian principles. He was convinced that the May elections proved that Germany was becoming more conservative, and that the December elections would justify this view. A conservative victory would mean that the Nationalists would be invited to participate in the new government along with the Center party. Using all of his persuasive powers, Papen boldly declared that the time for temporizing and accommodation was past, and that he was prepared to wage an all out battle to unite the Center with the Nationalists in a conservative coalition.[24]

While the December election was, for the most part, a vote of confidence for the supporters of the Dawes legislation, it spelled the end of the Marx government. The Social Democrats captured 131 seats, while the Centrists, Democrats and People's Party registered far smaller gains. The big surprise was the showing of the Nationalists, who added seven *Reichstag* seats for a total of 103. As soon as the elections results were confirmed, Marx resigned, and finally on January 9, 1925, at Stresemann's suggestion, Hans Luther was appointed Chancellor.[25]

In the Prussian *Landtag* elections the Social Democrats also suffered losses, while the Nationalists captured an additional 6 seats for a total of 109, thus making it the second largest party in the Prussian parliament.[26] The losses sustained by the Social Democrats meant that the days of Braun's "Great Coalition" were numbered. In order for the Braun cabinet to remain in office it would need the continued support of the People's party. But, that party refused to participate in a new government unless the Nationalists were also given cabinet posts. In order to put pressure on Braun to accept the DNVP in a new cabinet, the Peoples' representatives withdrew from the government. Although Braun could no longer count on an absolute majority in the *Landtag* as a result of this action, he hesitated to resign. Consequently, on January 20, 1925, the Nationalists, the People's party and the Communists submitted motions of no-confidence in the Braun government.

On January 23, 1925, these motions were presented in the *Landtag*. Even though Papen wanted to see the Braun government resign, he could not bring himself to vote for the Communist motion, which was defeated in the end. Then, when the Nationalists presented their three motions, Papen and three of his colleagues left the chambers, and by this action gave the conservatives a narrow victory.[27] Although Braun could have remained in office because the vote to unseat him fell short of an absolute majority, he submitted his resignation explaining that the position taken by the parties as a result of the vote would leave him in no position to work for the welfare of the State.[28]

Papen's action was sharply criticized in the liberal press. Even the Center newspaper *Germania*, in which he had become the principal stock-holder, declared that "the Center voters would not understand how certain delegates in the Parliament could thwart (*durchkreuzen*) the politics of the entire party." The editorial went on to state that in spite of this defeat, "the formation of a bourgeoisie coalition is out of the question."[29] The most critical comments about Papen's action were published in the left-liberal *Berliner Tageblatt*. The paper printed an anonymous letter supposedly written by "a well-known member of the Berlin Center party," who charged that Papen's action was the result of "a variety of intimacies among the secessionists who betrayed [Center] Party discipline."[30] Not only was this an attack against Papen, but it was also a denunciation of the industrial and agricultural interests who stood behind Papen, and had "spun a web of intrigue with the political Right against the Center."[31]

With Braun's resignation, the way was open for the election of a new Minister President, which took place on January 30, 1925. Once again Otto Braun was chosen over the Nationalist candidate, Wolfgang Kries by 221 to 175 votes.[32] The next morning, the liberal press attributed Braun's victory to the close cooperation of the coalition partners, and stressed the fact that even the "three dissidents who had opposed Braun a week earlier" now supported him.[33] A few days later, the *Kölnische Zeitung*, reported that Braun's election was made possible because a compromise had been reached between the liberal and conservative factions, i.e., that the Center Party would not participate in the coalition unless the DVP was included.[34] In a letter to Felix Porsche, the Vice President of the *Landtag*, Papen explained why he voted in favor of Braun this time.[35] Papen said he was prepared to cooperate with the Center fraction if Braun would agree to form a government in which the DVP was represented and not one composed exclusively of parties of the Weimar Coalition.[36]

While the liberals commended Papen's support of Braun, his action was sharply criticized by the monarchists whose opinion he greatly respected. Crown Prince Wilhelm and his aristocratic circle of friends, including some of the Catholic nobility who still supported the Center party, were shocked that people like Papen would remain members of a party that had abandoned its earlier support of the Hohenzollerns, and fraternized with republicans.[37]

These objections induced Papen to address a letter to the Crown Prince explaining the reasons for his actions. While the contents of this letter are not known, the reaction of the Crown Prince was passed on to Papen by Count Praschma, who wrote that Wilhelm told him (Praschma) that Papen's reasons for cooperating with the Center "eluded him." In an even sharper criticism, the Crown Prince told another aristocratic friend of Papen that he found Papen's support of Braun "incomprehensible," and his (Papen's) explanation had not convinced him otherwise.[38]

These criticisms, and the reproaches he received from his aristocratic fraternity, strengthened Papen's resolve to coerce the

Center into a coalition with the right wing parties. If successful, he would not only prove his loyalty to the Hohenzollerns, but he would also convince the aristocratic skeptics that he was still a monarchist at heart. Probably this also explains why Papen was prepared to commit political suicide when he refused to go along with the Center in the election of Wilhelm Marx as the Minister President of Prussia, and his decision to support Hindenburg over Marx in the Reich presidential elections in 1925.

In the meantime, unable to persuade the DVP to join in a new cabinet, Braun informed the *Landtag* president, Friedrich Bartels, that he would not accept the post of minister president.[39] Braun's resignation meant that once again the *Landtag* would have to elect a new minister president. On February 10, 1925, former Reich Chancellor, Wilhelm Marx, was elected on the second ballot. The *Landtag* records show that Papen voted for the moderate Centrist with the proviso that the new government would include representatives from the right, or at least that the cabinet would include "experts," regardless of party affiliation. Papen also warned Marx that a cabinet composed of the parties in previous coalitions was not acceptable to him.[40]

On February 18, Marx presented his cabinet to the *Landtag*. Along with representatives from the Democratic and Center parties, Marx announced that he intended to retain the Social Democrat, Carl Severing, as Interior Minister. For the next two days there was a heated debate over the Severing appointment. The Nationalists and the People's party, joined by Papen and twenty of his colleagues, objected to Severing, and called for a vote of confidence. When the *Landtag* convened to vote on February 20, Papen and Friedrich Loenartz deliberately stayed away, while two of Papen's associates, Roeingh and Baumann, excused themselves on the grounds of "illness." Since these men were close associates of Papen, it would seem that this "sickness" was an excuse to avoid responsibility.[41] Because of these obstructionist tactics, Marx lacked the necessary support to defeat the no-confidence vote, and he submitted his resignation.

Immediately following Marx's defeat, an angry group of Center delegates met and issued a sharply-worded memo to the Center Executive Council demanding that the Party call for the immediate resignation of Papen and Loenartz because the *Landtag* fraction could no longer work with them.[42] In an effort to justify his action, Papen addressed a letter to the fraction Chairman, Felix Porsche, stating that his action was not directed against the person of Marx, but that Marx had "formed a Weimar Coalition cabinet in spite of his [Papen's] warning."[43] For this reason, Papen continued, he saw no reason why he should resign. Then, revealing his disregard for party discipline, Papen insisted that his mandate did not come from the Center fraction, but "from the agrarian voters in the election district of North Westphalia," with whom the decision to resign was lodged.[44] With this tactic, Papen cleverly shifted the judgment of his case to the provincial committee of the Westphalian Center party who was in complete accord with his views. It was also generally known that some of the provincial party leaders favored leaving the Center party and joining the Bavarian People's Party.[45] Therefore, if the Party leaders forced Papen to resign, party unity in Westphalia would be in jeopardy. The fact that Party Chairman, Marx, decided to attend a provincial meeting of the Westphalia Center is indicative of the concern that he felt about a possible schism. While the Papen issue was brought up at the provincial meeting, no decision was reached. Two days later, on February 25, the Agricultural Advisory Board, which was known to be in sympathy with Papen's views, was scheduled to discuss the entire issue. If the Provincial Committee had issued any criticism it might have prevented any possible compromise with the Advisory Board. In fact, it might even have provoked a split in the party ranks.[46]

When the Agricultural Advisory Board met, Papen explained the reasons for his action, while Roeingh explained his "sick leave" and declared his support of Papen's position. At the end of a long and lively session in which there was little disagreement, the Board (1) approved the actions of the two delegates and gave them a vote of confidence; (2) rejected the recommendation to expel them from the *Landtag*; (3) directed the Center fraction in the *Landtag* to "revise" its original decision.[47]

Preoccupied with maintaining party unity, the Executive Council agreed not to call for Papen's resignation, but as a disciplinary measure, he was banned from all committee assignments.[48] Although a serious division in the Center party had been avoided, the "Papen question" continued to be a problem. Acclaimed a hero by his conservative associates, Papen was declared a "black sheep" in the party. Seemingly unaffected by this label, this "uncomfortable *frondeur*," as he proudly boasted in his *Memoirs*, continued to engage in activities that proved he was more loyal to the traditions of the *ancien régime* than to the ideals of the Weimar Constitution.

B. From Ebert to Hindenburg

Three days after the Agricultural Advisory Board proclaimed its support of Papen's actions in the Marx affair, President Ebert died. For the first time in their history, the German people were about to discharge the duty of electing a chief executive. For the next several weeks, the parties busied themselves with the task of selecting suitable presidential candidates. The parties on the Right formed a committee under the leadership of the former Prussian Minister of the Interior, Wilhelm Loebell. The Social Democrats chose the Prussian Minister President, Otto Braun as their candidate. Since Braun was selected without consulting the Center leaders, the Catholic party turned to the Loebell group. But, when Loebell's committee recommended the Democrat, Dr. Karl Jarres, both the Center and the Bavarian People's Party, rejected him and withdrew from the discussions.[49] After a brief but unsuccessful attempt by the two Catholic parties to agree on a candidate, the Center chose Wilhelm Marx, while the Bavarians selected Heinrich Held as their candidate.[50]

From the very outset, Papen favored the nomination of a candidate who would unite all parties opposed to socialism. His choice was Otto Gessler, the Minister of Defense. Although Gessler was a Democrat, his defense of the military against attacks in the press and the *Reichstag*, and his conservative, Catholic background were qualities, which, in Papen's view, would make him acceptable to all parties except the Socialists and Communists. However, Papen's plan to nominate a candidate that would unite all parties against the Left failed to materialize.[51] Gustav Stresemann opposed the Gessler nomination on the grounds that foreign governments would react unfavorably to Gessler's election. They might jump to the conclusion that the Army was in the saddle once again, and Germany was gearing up for another war.

The election took place on March 25, 1925, and since none of the seven candidates obtained the absolute majority required by law, a second election was scheduled for April 26. This time the Center, joined the Social Democrats, and Democrats in the "People's Bloc," thus abandoning their resolution to refrain from entering into another coalition with the Left. After a series of maneuvers the Center agreed to back Braun's bid to head the Prussian government in return for Social Democratic support in Marx's campaign for the Reich presidency. Papen was opposed to this arrangement because he was afraid that if Marx became Reich president as a result of Social Democratic support, the Center would become so dependent on the them that he would be unable to fulfill his cherished dream of a coalition with the right wing parties.

While the People's Bloc was preparing for the forthcoming presidential election, the conservative parties made efforts to agree on a suitable candidate. The Loebell committee (recently renamed the Reich Bloc) were determined to keep the Reich presidency out of republican hands, and so they turned to the hero of Tannenberg, Field Marshall Paul von Hindenburg[52]

In his *Memoirs*, Papen records his reaction when he heard that his former superior officer intended to accept the nomination: "Here, it seemed to me, was an opportunity to reawaken some of those traditions that had been lost with the collapse of the monarchy. I was never for a moment in doubt as to where my allegiance lay."[53] His decision to support the old Field Marshall was in direct conflict with his party's mandate to support Marx. But Papen's loyalty was not to the republic and its "rationalistic and atheistic premises," which was, in his opinion, destroying the Center party traditions and with it Catholicism in Germany.[54]

In order to insure Hindenburg's election, Papen set out to win support from the voters in his electoral district of North Westphalia. He was supported in his efforts by his long-time associates, von Kerkerinck and von Loe. In mid-April Papen and his friends issued a statement declaring that "important sections of the population had lost faith in the type of society sought by the Weimar Coalition, based as it was, to too great an extent, on rationalistic and atheistic premises." The declaration went on to argue that "it was not possible to elect a member of the Zentrum Party with the help of millions of socialist votes and then proceed with an anti-socialist policy." Appealing to the Reich's nationalistic traditions, the statement called for "a return to the old Christian conception of government, [and]...proclaimed anew Germany's historical duty to act as watchman and bulwark of the western tradition in the heart of Europe." It was, therefore, imperative that Hindenburg, "such a God-fearing and devout personality," be elected as "the best guarantee for a return to this fundamental policy."[55] Naturally, the Center party reaction to this statement was one of outrage. Not only did Papen deliberately come out in support of the opposition, but his statement implied that he was the true defender of Center founder, Windthorst's, political principles. On April 26, Hindenburg was elected by the narrow margin of 7% over the Center candidate, Wilhelm Marx.

In his *Memoirs* Papen gives the impression that his efforts on behalf of the old Field Marshall "in the slender balance of forces, had probably been decisive."[56] Although it is not possible to assess the impact of Papen's support on the outcome of the election, the results of the North Westphalian electoral district were not as significant for Hindenburg's victory as the Bavarian People's party, which controlled about one million votes.[57]

Needless to say, Papen and his conservative colleagues were elated at the results of the election. Moreover, if there were any doubts about Papen's loyalty to the Hohenzollerns and the "other Germany," his congratulatory telegram to the new president put them to rest. Published in the *Frankfurter Zeitung*, the telegram read:

> On this historic day when the Nation spoke out, may this most obedient undersigned not fail to be among those to give thanks to their great leader from even greater times for his willingness to sacrifice, and once again to take in his skillful hands the fate of the Nation. Even as a delegate in the Center party I never grew weary of fighting under the slogan of our unforgettable leader: "The Fatherland above the Party!" This solemn vow is the best wish that I can offer to our General Field Marshall today.[58]

This pledge of allegiance to his Commander in Chief and to the German nation was not only an affront to the Republic and parliamentary democracy, but it was also a signal to his own political party that he placed loyalty to the *ancien régime* above party politics and parliamentary democracy. A few days after the election Papen confirmed his fidelity to this "solemn vow" when he refused to go along with the Center's decision to enter into a coalition with the Socialists.

On May 5, the *Landtag* convened to approve the formation of a new government under the leadership of Socialist Otto Braun. With stubborn consistency, Papen refused to support a government that included the Social Democrats. But this time Papen and a conservative colleague, Carl Baumann, pleaded "illness" as the reason for their absence. While the ex-Major's strategy did not prevent a victory for the Braun government, it did draw criticisms from the press and his own party.[59] The liberal *Frankfurter Zeitung* raised the question, "Why did he [Papen] continue to place any value on his membership in the Center party?"[60] According to Papen, the Center had betrayed its Christian heritage when it proclaimed its loyalty to a secular Republic. As a Catholic nobleman he felt that it was his duty to revive the Center party's pre-war spirit of dedication and loyalty to the Fatherland, and the only way to accomplish this was from within.[61]

Although this might explain Papen's reasons for remaining in the Center party, it does not answer the question, why the Center party tolerated Papen, especially after he publicly supported von Hindenburg, who represented everything that the liberals opposed. The answer to this question sheds light on the dilemma in which the Center found itself in 1925.

The drastic socio-political changes in Germany after 1918 found the postwar Center lacking the integrating forces which had bound the old party together in spite of its heterogeneous composition. While the prewar party was just as diverse, it possessed a much more clearly defined platform and a stronger sense of mission. All of this gradually changed so that by the end of the war, very little of that platform remained, and along with it the strong sense of unity among the diverse factions. This resulted in a crisis over the role of political Catholicism in postwar Germany. While the left wing of the party accommodated itself to the liberal principles embodied in the Weimar Constitution, the conservative wing representing the old aristocracy and the rural sections of the country insisted that the party return to the Christian principles upon which it had been founded. Concern for the image of party unity, the Center leaders wanted to avoid all signs of internal disagreements. They were afraid that if Papen were to be dismissed, it would only call attention to the acute differences within the party, and this could jeopardize its standing with the voters.

A more important reason for the reluctance of the party leaders to oust Papen was his financial control of *Germania*, the semi-official

Center newspaper. As the major stockholder, Papen could exercise enormous influence on the editorial policies of *Germania*, and this caused the party leaders to handle this *frondeur* with discretion. Moreover, because of his association with the Westphalian Farmer's Association, Papen was in close contact with the agricultural movement throughout Germany. Backed by this important block of votes, Papen did not hesitate to remind the party leaders that it would be advisable to tolerate his "independent stand."

It should come as no surprise, therefore, when the Center Party Chairman in the *Reichstag* issued a weak statement reprimanding Papen and his sympathizers for their failure to support Marx in the presidential elections. The statement called for a closing of the ranks and an appeal for understanding and trust among all party members.[62] But this plea for unity had little effect on Papen, who was determined to exert every effort to move the party to the right.

While the national leaders lacked the courage to discipline Papen, the Center faction in the Prussian *Landtag* took steps to weaken his influence in Prussian political circles. Papen was removed from his position on the Agriculture Committee to which he had been appointed on January 23, 1925.[63] As a consequence of this action, Papen became more and more isolated. Regarded as an "outsider," his strategy to exploit the parliamentary system to move the Center to the right had failed. During his last two years in office, Papen was rarely seen with the Center faction. On the two occasions when he did speak in the *Landtag*, he tried to regain some credibility with his colleagues. However, he was unsuccessful on both occasions.

In spite of this, Papen's attitude remained astonishingly one of confidence, "I was not entirely dependent on the party for my activity and had plenty of opportunity for expressing my convictions.[64] The opportunity he referred to was the influence he expected to exercise over the editorial policies of *Germania*, the semi-official Center party newspaper. As the major stockholder and Chairman of the Board of Directors, Papen intended to use the newspaper as a forum for his political views.[65]

Papen also compensated for his loss of political influence through his association with numerous clubs and leagues, which included the "*Herrenklub*," the "League for Restoring the Reich," the "League for the Preservation of Western Culture," and the "Mayrisch Committee" established to improve Franco-German relations. Moreover, as an honorary member of the Board of Directors in the Westphalian Farmers' Association, he was able to keep his contacts with influential politicians on the local level, as well as a large measure of support from the voters in his district. Therefore, when President Hindenburg dissolved the *Reichstag* and called for new elections on May 20, Papen's name appeared on the election list.

Even though the Center leaders had all but excommunicated Papen from the party, they were well aware of his influence in the Westphalian electoral district. However, as a result of some clever maneuvering by the left-wing of the party, this time Papen was in the tenth spot on the *Landesliste*, which meant that he had very little chance of re-election.[66] The results of the election showed a strong shift to the left both in Prussia and in the Reich. In Westphalia, as expected, the Center was able to win only nine seats, and therefore Papen's bid for re-election was unsuccessful.

Although Papen lost his seat in the *Landtag*, his career as a politician was not over yet. He returned to the *Landtag* in February 1930, when his conservative colleague, Theodor Roeingh, resigned for reasons that are still unknown.[67] But during the next two years, until the elections in April 1932, Papen never once addressed the assembly, and after he moved his family back to Wallerfangen in the Saar in 1931, he seldom went to Berlin - much less to the *Landtag* sessions. As far as he was concerned, "party politics had lost much of its *raison d'etre* when it came to calling on the nation as a whole to make a great combined effort."[68] He believed that Germany should be run by "experts" regardless of party affiliation, "who would use the last remnants of State authority to impose solutions designed to meet the emergency of the times."[69]

By 1932, the deteriorating economic conditions resulting from the Great Depression, and the alarming rise of the Nazis, convinced Papen that, "the formation of a trustworthy, conservative national opposition...is the only road to recovery, and to conquer the chaos of partisan politics that the mechanistic Weimar democracy had introduced *ad absurdum*."[70] Less than two months after he had penned these words, Papen was appointed Chancellor by President von Hindenburg. Papen saw this as a golden opportunity to achieve in a short time what he had been unable to accomplish during his eleven years in the *Landtag*. But instead of negotiating with Nationalists who were no longer a force in German politics, Papen was confronted with the specter of Nazism, and his limited political talents proved to be no match in his futile efforts to "tame" Hitler.

On May 12, 1925, President-elect von Hindenburg entered the hall of the nation's parliament to swear allegiance to the Weimar Constitution. Seated with his conservative colleagues in the crowded auditorium, Franz von Papen proudly viewed this moment of "glorious history." At last, Germany had elected a true leader who would re-awaken some of those traditions that had been lost with the collapse of the monarchy.

Count Harry Kessler described the scene: "By eleven o'clock the galleries inside the *Reichstag* were full to overflowing...The hall was skimpily decorated. Just the black-red-gold presidential standard affixed to a wall-covering behind the *Reichstag* President's chair and a black-red-gold banner, flanked by blue hydrangeas, draped over the presidential table..."

"Hindenburg, standing on the spot where Rathenau's coffin had stood, swore the oath of office...and read a declaration from a piece of paper inscribed with such huge letters that it would have been possible, with the aid of an opera-glass, to read them from the gallery. The old gentleman nevertheless had some trouble deciphering them...The impression was of a somewhat self-conscious old general enunciating unaccustomed and incomprehensible material."[71] The emphasis laid in the declaration on the constitution's "republican" and "democratic" character...was however, stronger than expected:

> *Reichstag* and Reich President belong together, for they both are elected directly by the German people...Together only they are the embodiment of popular sovereignty which today is the basis of our national life...the Reich President must work for the cooperation, above all parties, of all those forces of our nation which are ready and willing to make a contribution...[72]

This appeal neither allayed the fears of the Left nor raised the hopes of the Right. But to the surprise of all, in the five years that followed, Hindenburg's actions were governed by the spirit as well as the letter of the Constitution. He not only used his authority judiciously, but he also worked with parties to find ways out of the dilemmas created by inter-party strife.

Shortly before Hindenburg took office, Germany was beginning to recover from the economic crisis that had plagued it since the end of the war. The Dawes Plan, Hjalmar Schacht's financial wizardry, and American and British loans and investments, rejuvenated industry, supported public works and social services, increased unemployment benefits and subsidized agriculture.[73] Huge sums were spent on all sorts of enterprises, while the mounting deficits were covered by foreign credits, mostly of the short-term variety. Caught up in this new-found prosperity, many Germans regarded the next few years as a period of affluence and stability. Despite warnings from Parker Gilbert, the American banker and Agent General of the reparation payments, that the Reich was borrowing and spending too much, the Government contested the validity of his assertions, and refused to acknowledge the dangerous path on which they had set out.[74] "It was too easy, after so many years of uninterrupted hardship, to cling to pleasurable delusions."[75]

The return to prosperity was accompanied by the relaxation of tensions between Germany and the Allies. Gustav Stresemann, the architect of German foreign policy from June 1924 until his untimely death in October 1929, devoted all his efforts to achieving a *modus vivendi* with the Allies. Despite persistent opposition from the conservatives in Germany, Stresemann's diplomacy brought about the removal of almost all of the restrictions imposed on German sovereignty by the peace treaty.

Among his more notable accomplishments were the Locarno Treaties of October, 1925, which marked the beginning of a period of reconciliation between Germany and the Allies. The following year, Germany was admitted to the League of Nations and given a seat on the Permanent Council. In Stresemann's words, "the attempt to create a new and better Europe by methods of compulsion, dictation and violence has been a failure. Let us try to achieve this objective on the basis of peace and of equal rights and liberty for Germany."[76] However, the "spirit of Locarno," hailed by many as the beginning of a period of international good will, did very little to stem the growing disillusionment with parliamentary democracy in Weimar Germany.

In spite of economic recovery and diplomatic gains, the middle years of the Weimar Republic were marked by a steady erosion of parliamentary democracy. A major contributing factor was the inability of parties to work together. Representation in the *Reichstag* was shared by so many parties that majorities could be obtained only by coalition governments. But, since many of the parties were more concerned with promoting their own interests over those of the nation at large, the mortality rate of coalition governments was high. Between 1919 and 1928 there were fifteen separate cabinets, none performing longer than eighteen months and several less than three.[77] There is no doubt that Hindenburg's election reflected the frustration of many voters who had grown weary of these internal conflicts and longed for the return of the old virtues of order and discipline which, in their minds, the Field Marshall personified.

C. The *Germania* Episode

Hindenburg's victory not only raised the hopes of many, but it also renewed Franz von Papen's determination to break up the Prussian democratic coalition. Although his efforts in the *Landtag* had failed, the ex-cavalry officer refused to surrender. He decided to wage his campaign against the left in the pages of *Germania*, the semi-official Center newspaper.

Although *Germania* had a limited circulation (about 10,000), it exercised considerable influence for several reasons. In the first place, many of the articles were written by the Center's leading personalities, and therefore reflected official party views. Moreover, since its offices were located in Berlin, the paper was able to give first-hand reports about the political issues debated in both the *Reichstag* and the Prussian *Landtag*. Consequently, the other parties and newspapers followed *Germania's* editorials with great attention. Finally, because of the special political circumstance in the Weimar Republic, no government could command a parliamentary majority without the participation of the Center. Consequently, *Germania* enjoyed a special influence over the governments in which the Center either headed the coalition or held cabinet positions under one of the other parties. Thus in 1917, when Erzberger and the left wing of the Center gained control of the party's *Reichstag* faction, *Germania* began to reflect Erzberger's democratic views.

In spite of Erzberger's influence over the newspaper, the stock in the corporation was almost completely in the hands of conservative, Catholic noblemen from the Rhineland, Westphalia and Silesia. Therefore, it was just a matter of time before these aristocratic stockholders would attempt to seize complete control of the corporation.

An opportunity presented itself in May 1920, when two aristocrats were elected to the Board of Directors.[78] The next step was to call for a recapitalization of the corporation. The new stock would be sold to members of the aristocracy, and then with the additional voting rights they could take control of the corporation and the newspaper. However, the plan failed because of the lack of wealthy buyers.[79] Eventually the corporation sold a large number of shares to several wealthy businessmen, among them were the Berlin banker, Franz Semer, and the wealthy industrialist, Dr. Florian Klöckner, who was also acquainted with Franz von Papen.[80]

In 1924, during the days of wild inflation, Papen had the opportunity to purchase Semer's stock in *Germania*. But, since the by-laws of the corporation required a majority of the Board to approve any sale of stock, Papen appealed for help to Klöckner and Praschma. The only way Papen could get an approval to purchase the Semer stock was if a member of the Board could be authorized to vote in Semer's name. Therefore, Papen asked Praschma to obtain Semer's voting rights. In the meantime Semer's wife obtained a court order preventing the sale of her stock on the grounds that her husband did not have her authorization to do so.[81]

To make matters worse for Papen, Frau Semer's action also prevented him from exercising any voting rights connected with these stocks. Meanwhile, after a series of charges and counter-charges between Semer and his wife concerning the sale, the court decided that Semer was entitled to sell the stock, but a Board approval of the transfer was required before Papen could exercise the voting rights connected with the stock.[82]

When the Board met on May 18, 1925, the first order of business was to approve the transfer of Frau Semer's 600 shares to Papen. Although Papen had 1,685 votes at his disposal, he did not have an absolute majority, and therefore he appealed to Florian Klöckner and other aristocratic friends to vote approval of the stock transfer.[83] After a heated debate in which Spiecker and his supporters argued against the transfer, the vote was cast in favor of Papen.[84] With the 600 additional shares Papen came close to having an absolute majority of votes at his disposal. His next step was to make certain that any new members elected to the Board were in agreement with his plans to convert the newspaper into an organ of the Right.

Changes in the Board membership due to retirement called for the election of eight new members. Prior to the Board meeting, Klöckner presented the party's Executive Committee with a list of candidates. Since the list contained the names of two liberals, the Executive Committee had no objections.[85] Papen was satisfied because, regardless of who was elected, the Board would clearly favor the conservative wing of the party. However, when the list was presented to the Board, there was a considerable difference of opinion, especially over the question of a representative from the Berlin Center faction. The liberals suggested the former Board member, Dr. Wilhelm Koch, but he was completely unacceptable to Papen. Eventually a compromise was reached in which the proposed list was to be accepted without any changes, and at a later date another Board meeting would take up the Berlin faction's nomination.[86] The last action taken by the Board was to elect Papen as its Chairman. The stage was now set for the Westphalian aristocrat to launch his attack against the left-wing of the party through the pages of *Germania*.

Papen's claims that he "had no intention of altering the paper's character" are unfounded. Nor does the evidence support his contention that when he forced one of the editors to resign in 1925, "this was not due to any attempt on my part to impose a political line on them."[87] For one thing, he readily admits that he purchased Semer's shares for the purpose of serving his "political interests," and not for financial gain.[88] In a letter to Count Praschma, Papen criticized the "Wirth clique," who, under the managing editor Karl Spiecker, were "in complete control of *Germania*," and who "tried by every means to prevent the realization of a coalition with the German Nationalists."[89] Papen added that every effort must be made to prevent Spiecker from delaying the approval of the stock transfer from Semer to himself, "...if we are to express our political line of thought."[90] With Semer's stock, Papen would have forty-seven percent of the voting capital in his hands. This would enable him to pack the Board of Directors with conservatives, and then alter the orientation of the newspaper in order to influence party policies.

If Papen's intentions before he joined the Board of Directors were a signal that he wanted to control the newspaper's policies, his actions after his appointment were even more obvious. After his election as

Chairman of the Board, Papen found himself in continual conflict with the publisher, Dr. Hermann Katzenberger, and the managing editors, Karl Spiecker and Heinrich Teipel, because "...they refused to allow me any expression at all of my political convictions." One of his first actions as chairman was to force Teipel to resign his post in August 1925. However, since Teipel had aggravated the Center party leaders because of his sharp disagreement with party policy to remain the "party in the middle," Papen's action did not arouse any objections from the party leaders.[91]

Encouraged by this success, Papen took even bolder steps. He wanted to remove the editor-in-chief who was blocking his efforts to change the paper's orientation.[92] However, this time he was unsuccessful, because his friend Klöckner refused to support him, and without Klöckner's vote, Papen lacked the necessary majority to carry out his plan.

But, an even more significant reason why he was not able to control the paper's editorial policies was due to the opposition of Joseph Hess. The newspaper was in financial difficulties, and was able to survive only because of the support it received from the Center publishing house in Berlin. In his position in the Prussian Center Party, Hess was able to threaten Papen with the withdrawal of this aid if he tried to turn the newspaper into a right-wing organ. Without the financial support from Berlin, Papen's control would have disappeared along with the paper.[93]

In spite of Papen's dictatorial methods in his dealings with the newspaper staff, the party Executive Committee refused to sever its connections with *Germania* fearing that it might shatter the illusion that the Center represented all German Catholics. Moreover, as long as the editors remained independent of Papen's influence, there was no point in creating a crisis that might endanger party unity. This fainthearted attitude only served to encourage Papen and his conservative associates on the Board to attempt even more radical changes.

Teipel's removal was followed the next year by the replacement of the publisher, Hermann Katzenberger who was an outspoken critic of Papen's actions. Heinrich Bungartz, who was employed in the business office of the newspaper, was promoted to Katzenberger's position.[94] But, despite these changes, Papen was still unable to alter the editorial policies of *Germania*.[95]

Although Papen would have preferred to force the resignation of the "senior members" of the editorial staff, his failure to do so the previous year prompted him to pursue a different strategy. Instead of trying to remove an editor, Papen decided to appoint a journalist to the editorial staff who sympathized with his political views. His plan was to have an informant on the inside who could carefully monitor the editor's strategies, and report them to him. He also wanted someone on the editorial staff who might be able to propose alternatives that would weaken the liberal influence over the newspaper. For these reasons, Papen contacted the former Catholic military chaplain, Dr. Friedrich Esser with an offer to become the "theological editor" on the *Germania* staff. Esser had been a member of the *Germania* staff until he was "encouraged" by Speicker to become a Center party correspondent for Hugenberg's right-wing newspaper, the *Telegraph-Union*.[96]

In what came to characterize many of his later undertakings, Papen arranged for Esser to join the *Germania* staff without consulting the Board of Directors, Hermann Orth, editor-in-chief of the newspaper, or even his closest ally, Florian Klöckner.[97] The irate editor immediately informed the Center party headquarters, *Germania's* Board of Directors, and other newspapers of Papen's action, and called for their support to block the appointment.[98] While Papen expected opposition from the *Germania's* editorial staff and the other liberal newspapers, he was not prepared for the Board's reaction. Board members Theodor Guérard, Johann Giesberts, and Joseph Ersing opposed the appointment. Guérard informed Papen that he would object to Esser's appointment at the next Board meeting, and if Papen insisted, Guérard would submit his resignation.[99] Guérard represented Klöckner's viewpoint, while the other two Board members acted on behalf of the Center Executive Council. Therefore, if Papen insisted on Esser's appointment he would not only clash with the majority fraction of the Center party, but also with Klöckner. With this realization in mind Papen decided to withdraw Esser's name.

This unsuccessful attempt to infiltrate *Germania's* editorial staff had important consequences for both the newspaper's editors and for Papen. The editors were successful in their efforts to prevent Papen from taking control of the newspaper, while the Executive Council of the party became more wary of Papen's intrigues. As a result, Papen was no longer able to appoint personnel without the party's approval.[100]

Papen's failure to challenge the newspaper's editorial staff was not only a moral but also a political defeat for which he had only himself to blame. Acting on the assumption that Klöckner would agree to Esser's appointment, Papen failed to take into consideration the fact that he needed Klöckner's vote to have an absolute majority. But even if Klöckner would have been willing to work out a compromise, Papen's impulsive action made this impossible once the party leaders publicly denounced the appointment. Klöckner might have been willing to confront the newspaper's editors, but he was not prepared to defend Papen against the majority faction in the party. In the final analysis, the plan was ill-conceived, based as it was more on the element of surprise than on careful planning. This was not the first, nor would it be the last time, in which the ex-cavalry officer over-estimated his own abilities and acted in a precipitous manner with negative results.[101]

While Papen failed to gain control over the editorial policies of *Germania*, he did manage to improve the efficiency of the newspaper, and put it on a sounder financial footing. Outmoded equipment and lack of space, coupled with growing competition, endangered the economic existence of the corporation. Since neither credit nor loans sufficient to cover the costs of modernization were available, the only other solution was through recapitalization. This meant that the corporation would have to issue more stock. Papen saw the need to sell more stock, but he wanted to make sure that whoever purchased the shares would not upset the conservative composition of the Board. He therefore approached Count Nikolaus Ballestrem with the hope that he and his conservative friends would purchase the new shares.[102]

After Papen had explained the financial situation of the corporation to Ballestrem, he came to the real point of his letter. Since he was not in a position to purchase any of the new stock, Papen stated that he was prepared to sell his shares to someone who, together with the new stock would possess a majority in the corporation. He then added that Ballestrem could "...take it for granted that he [Papen]...was willing to assume the political trusteeship of the stock portfolio."[103] In other words, Papen wanted to withdraw his investment in *Germania* stock without losing his influence over the corporation. Then, in an effort to put pressure on the Silesian aristocrat, Papen informed him that he would be forced to sell the stock to his political enemies if Ballestrem declined.[104] When, in spite of this appeal, Ballestrem turned him down, Papen approached Count Friedrich von Schaffgotsch through Hans Praschma with the same arguments. But the wealthy Silesian landowner politely refused the offer.[105]

Bitterly disappointed but undefeated, Papen turned to Praschma with a plea that the Silesian nobleman find purchasers among his friends. Praschma responded that there was little chance that he [Papen] could find any buyers among the landholders at this time.[106] Praschma then recommended that Papen should turn to his industrial friends in the Rhineland, "actually people like Klöckner, Hagen, and Thyssen could raise the money in preparation for the next election."[107] Papen knew that this advice was practical, but he also was afraid that as a result of his strained relationship with Klöckner, the industrialist would set limits on his influence over the Board as well as the newspaper, and Papen was not prepared to accept this.

Thus, for the second time in a year Papen's plans were frustrated. This time, however, it was not the left-wing that defeated him, but members of his own aristocratic class, who were willing to offer him moral support but nothing more. Unable to sell his stock, and unwilling to surrender his position, Papen decided to retain his stock rather than take a chance that his shares would come into the hands of someone opposed to his schemes to control *Germania*. In the meantime, he found a way to secure the financial resources it would take to make the newspaper more competitive, while at the same time allowing him to maintain control over the corporation.

In April, 1924, Hugo Stinnes, the wealthy industrial magnate died and one of his newspapers, the *Deutsche Algemeine Zeitung (DAZ)*, was put up for sale. Through a series of complex financial transactions, the newspaper eventually ended up in the hands of the Prussian government. It was at this point that Werner von Alvensleben, a member of the *Herrenklub*, to which Papen also belonged, offered to purchase the newspaper on behalf of a group of interested persons. Alvensleben made his offer to the Foreign Minister, Stresemann, on September 17, 1926, promising that the newspaper would support Stresemann's foreign policy objectives. While General Kurt von Schleicher was one of this group, it is not certain whether Papen was also involved. However, given the fact that Alvensleben, Schleicher and Papen were all members of the *Herrenklub*, it is not unreasonable to speculate that Papen at least knew of the proposed purchase.[108] This is supported by the fact that two months later, Papen approached

Stresemann with an offer that *Germania* was interested in purchasing the *DAZ* printing presses.

Two months later, Papen offered to purchase the *DAZ* printing presses, and divide the stock between the Prussian government and *Germania*.[109] Papen's offer proves that he was well-informed of the Alvensleben-Schleicher scheme to purchase the *DAZ*. Stresemann, however, was not interested in surrendering such a large number of shares (51% to *Germania* and 49% retained by the State). He probably also suspected that Alvensleben's reasons for purchasing the newspaper went beyond supporting his foreign policy objectives. Although nothing came of this offer, Papen was able to negotiate with the consortium that purchased the presses from the State.[110]

Papen's efforts to obtain new equipment were the result of his close contacts, his ability to carefully follow the course of events, and his talent for taking advantage of every opportunity to gain his objectives. In the end, he managed to modernize *Germania's* facilities at a minimal cost to the stock-holders, while at the same time *Germania* was able to operate more efficiently and meet the competition more successfully.

However, the co-operative arrangement between the *DAZ* and *Germania* was not without its problems. Difficulties between Papen and the party over political issues would continue to surface, especially since Papen's friend, Hans Humann, the publisher of the *DAZ*, was a right-wing conservative.

The personnel changes in *Germania* went hand in hand with the beginning of close cooperation with the *Kölnische Zeitung (KVZ)*. In November, 1927, an *Interessengemeinschaft* was formed between the publishing concern of the *KVZ* and the *Germania* press for the "express purpose of obtaining a unified representation of the Center program and the interests of the Catholic population."[111] Members of both boards of directors were exchanged, and Papen was chosen to represent *Germania* on the *Volkszeitung* board. A few months later, a number of local Catholic papers from towns throughout Westphalia and the Rhineland were incorporated in the *Germania* publishing house. While this cartelization naturally expanded the influence of *Germania*, it reduced Papen's role in the press. Papen himself admitted that the consolidation of these Catholic papers would not necessarily serve his political goals.[112] At the same time, however, this cooperative movement helped to solve *Germania's* financial situation since the

KVZ was financed through west German industry, especially by Florian Klöckner.[113]

Because of the arrangement between the *KVZ* and *Germania*, Papen was able to obtain the necessary financial means to modernize the newspaper. A large percentage of the new stock was purchased by the *KVZ* with Klockner's help. Even Papen purchased some of the new stock, but there are no records to indicate how many shares he purchased or how much he paid.

With the resources to improve the press, *Germania* moved into new quarters on *Puttkamerstrasse*, and set up new printing presses, which increased both the efficiency as well as the capacity of the newspaper to meet the competition. A few weeks after the new offices were blessed by Bishop Schreiber of Berlin, the stock market crash on Wall Street ushered in the era of the Great Depression.

In retrospect, Papen's efforts to take over control of the Center Party organ, and convert it into a right-wing newspaper, are another example of the manner and methods he used to accomplish his goals. Not only was he a bold, unscrupulous, and energetic entrepreneur; but he also reflected the interests of the wealthy land-owners and big business. Both of these groups would prove to be very useful when the invitation to assume the post of chancellor was presented to him. Once appointed, he hoped to introduce a *Reichsreform* that would replace the "bankrupt parliamentarian system" with a "New State." This authoritarian regime would rest on the *potestas* of the army and the *auctoritas* of the president.[114]

With a successful political reform accomplished, Papen expected that he would be able to reconcile the economic interests of those groups that helped bring him to power. Unfortunately the role he ended up playing did not result in a "New State," but a "New Order." And the architect was not the aristocratic Westphalian Catholic Franz von Papen, but the Austrian corporal, Adolf Hitler.

NOTES

[1] Papen, *Memoirs*, p. 97.

[2] In November, 1918, the three wings of the prewar German Conservatives, Free Conservatives, and what was left of the Christian Socialists, formed the DNVP. While it continued to be led by the old conservative aristocrats, the DNVP attempted to broaden its voting appeal to include white-collar workers, professionals, and businessmen.

[3] *Memoirs*, p. 97. There was a strong anti-Catholic bias among the pre-war conservatives which carried over into the Weimar period. For example, when negotiations for a concordat between the Vatican and Prussia were going on in the mid-1920's, the DNVP strongly opposed any state-support of private Catholic schools.

[4] The Socialists split into two separate parties during World War I. The Social Democrats were referred to as the Majority Socialists to distinguish them from the Independent Socialists (USPD). The USPD represented various socialist views from revolution to revisionism. A third group, organized by Rosa Luxemburg and Karl Liebknecht known as the Sparticus League, later became the Communist Party (KPD).

[5] Papen, *Memoirs*, p. 104

[6] In *The Face of the Third Reich*, Joachim Fest offers a less gracious, but perhaps more correct, description of the future chancellor. Fest portrays Papen as a social reactionary "disguised behind a pseudo-Christian vocabulary; [a] sprinkling of monarchistic ideas...[and] nationalistic jargon...[with] a tendency to think in long-outdated categories. ...a perfect model of that type of the ruling class...[who]...with an almost unparalleled blindness imagined itself to be once more called upon by history to assume leadership." (Ace Books: New York, 1970), pp. 224-25.

[7] *Memoirs*, p. 97

[8] Jürgen A. Bach, *Franz von Papen in der Weimarer Republik*, (Düsseldorf: Droste Verlag, 1977), pp. 27-30.

[9] *Memoirs*, p. 100

[10] Bach, p. 32

[11] F.F. von Papen, *29.10.79 zum 100 Geburtstag meines Vaters*, (Wallerfangen: 1979), p. 15

[12] *Memoirs*, p. 100

[13] Ibid., p. 106

[14] Bach, pp. 37-38

[15] Ibid., p. 39

[16] Bach, ibid., pp. 41-46

[17] For a complete account of Hitler's "beer hall *putsch*" see Alan Bullock, *Hitler, A Study in Tyranny*, (New York: Bantam Books, 1961), pp. 73-85; Harold Gordon, *Hitler and the Beer Hall Putsch*, (New Jersey: Princeton University Press, 1957).

[18] Among other things, the Dawes Plan recommended that reparations should be based on Germany's capacity to pay. Funds were to be raised in Germany by new taxes and by income from the railroads, which were placed under international supervision. The transfer of marks into foreign currency was to be carefully regulated. Finally, payments were to begin on a low level assisted by foreign loans, and by 1928-29 would reach the full payments amounting to two billion marks a year. However, the Dawes Commission refused to set any total figure.

[19] Bach, p. 54

[20] Karl Dietrich Bracher, *The German Dictatorship* (New York: Praeger Publishers, 1970), pp. 122-23.

[21] Bach, pp. 55-56

[22] Bullock, ibid., pp. 102-103; Gordon Craig, *Germany 1866-1945*, (New York: Oxford University Press, 1978), pp. 514-516. The Nationalist vote was split between the anti-republicans and those who were more moderate in their views. Out of a total of 95 votes, those who favored the legislation won by the narrow margin of 48-47!

[23] Bach, ibid., p. 57.

[24] Ibid., p. 56.

[25] Luther served as Finance Minister in the Cuno Cabinet. Prior to that he was Minister of Food and Nutrition in the Wirth Cabinet.

[26] Herbert Höemig, *Das Preussische Zentrum in der Weimarer Republik*, (Mainz: Matthias-Grünewald-Verlag, 1979), pp. 121-22

[27] Besides Papen, the conservative agricultural block included Friedrich Loenartz, Carl Baumann, Andreas Hermes, and Theodor Roeingh. It was Papen, Loenartz, and Roeingh who walked out of the chambers. Cf. Hoemig, ibid., pp. 125-26.

[28] Bach, ibid., p. 69.

[29] Ibid., p. 70.

[30] Ibid.

[31] Ibid.

[32] Bach, ibid., p. 74.

[33] *Frankfurter Zeitung*, January 31, 1925.

[34] *Kölnische Zeitung*, February 2, 1925.

[35] *Kölnische Zeitung*, February 22, 1925.

---

[36] "*Eine Erklärung des Abgeordneten v. Papen*," *Kölnische Zeitung*, February 22, 1925.

[37] Bach, ibid., pp. 75-76.

[38] Letter of Graf Schaffgotsch-Warmbrunn to Praschma, February 11, 1925. Quoted in Bach, pp. 77-78.

[39] Bach, ibid., p. 78.

[40] *Kölnische Zeitung*, February 22, 1925.

[41] Homig, ibid., p. 125; Bach, p. 81. According to Papen, only six delegates ended up in opposition because "the rest had submitted to party pressure." *Memoirs*, p. 106.

[42] *Frankfurter Zeitung*, February 21, 1925.

[43] Papen's letter to Felix Porsche, February 21, 1925. Quoted in Bach, pp. 83-84

[44] Ibid.

[45] The Bavarian People's Party, which was formed in November, 1918, has been described as separatist and monarchist. This was true insofar as its leaders disliked the Republic, and gave only grudging recognition to the Weimar Constitution. In January, 1920, the party severed its ties with the Center Party.

[46] Bach, p. 85.

[47] Reported in the *Frankfurter Zeitung*, February 26, 1925.

[48] It was through the efforts of the leading spokesman for the left-wing of the Center, Joseph Hess, that Papen was removed from the Agricultural Committee, and the Principle (Steering) Committee. Cf., Eric D. Kohler, "The Successful Center-Left: Joseph Hess & the Prussian Center Party 1908-1932." *Central European History*, 23 #4 (December, 1990) 313-348.

[49] Karl Jarres, Reich Minister of the Interior (1923-25), and lord mayor of Duisburg, belonged to the right wing of the People's party. As a Protestant, he had risen to importance in Catholic Rhineland, and expected to attract the conservative Catholic vote. But the Bavarian People's party refused to support Jarres because of his objections to the Bavarian Concordat with the Vatican.

[50] The Center proposed Marx, but the BVP felt he was too leftist and co-operated too readily with the Social Democrats. The BVP would have accepted Stegerwald, but he was out of the picture as far as the left wing of the Center was concerned.

[51] Papen's involvement in the nomination of Gessler is based on a letter from Major Mueldner von Muelnheim, personal adjutant to the Crown Prince, to Graf Praschma dated March 16, 1925. Cf. Bach, p. 89.

[52] For a full account of the negotiations between the conservatives from all parties, and von Hindenburg, cf. Andreas Dorpalen, *Hindenburg and the Weimar Republic* (New York: Princeton University Press, 1964), pp. 68-75.

---

[53] *Memoirs*, p. 107.

[54] Ibid., p. 108.

[55] Ibid., p. 108. The Nationalist press gave full coverage to this statement. Cf. Bach, pp. 92-93.

[56] Ibid., p. 108.

[57] For a complete analysis of the election returns and the significance of the Bavarian People's Party vote in this election, see John K. Zeender's article, "The Presidential Election of 1925," *Journal of Modern History*, 35 (1963), 366-381.

[58] Papen's telegram was printed in the *Frankfurter Zeitung* on April 30, 1925.

[59] The *Kölnische Zeitung*, May 9, 1925, commented that it "was a remarkable coincidence that Papen and Baumann - both outspoken critics of the Weimar Coalition - were ill when the vote was taken."

[60] *Frankfurter Zeitung*, April 30, 1925.

[61] When questioned at the Nuremberg Trials about why he continued to serve Hitler during the Third Reich, Papen justified his actions on the same grounds.

[62] "*Eine Kundgebung des Zentrums*," *Kölnische Zeitung*, May 15, 1925, p. 1.

[63] Because of their strong showing in the December elections, the conservatives were able to have Papen re-instated to this committee over the objections of the left-wing.

[64] Papen, *Memoirs*, p. 108.

[65] Papen had purchased a controlling block of stock in *Germania*, "during the wild inflation days of 1924." Bach, ibid., pp. 255-315.

[66] By placing Papen tenth on the election list, the Center leaders hoped to capture all of the votes that Papen's candidacy might attract. At the same time, they did not expect that he would be re-elected to the *Landtag* because of anticipated losses on the national level. As it turned out, the Center did suffer losses in both the Prussian *Landtag* and the *Reichstag* elections.

[67] The speculation that Roeingh disagreed with Papen's appointment to his seat has never been proven. Cf. Bach, p. 181.

[68] Papen, *Memoirs*, p. 109.

[69] Ibid., pp. 105-106.

[70] *Der Ring*, 16 (April 15, 1932), p. 58.

[71] Harry Kessler, *Tagebücher 1918-1937*, (Frankfurt am/M: Wolfgang Pfeiffer-Belli, 1961)

[72] Dorpalen, *Hindenburg and the Weimar Republic*, p. 88.

[73] It has been estimated that between 1924 and 1929, Germany received 8 billion dollars in foreign loans - most of which were of the short-term variety.

[74] Both Gilbert and Stresemann were alarmed at the large scale of public spending on non-productive enterprises. Stresemann remarked prophetically in

1928, "If ever a crisis hits us and the Americans recall their short-term loans, we face bankruptcy." Cf. S. William Halperin, *Germany Tried Democracy* (New York: W.W. Norton & Company, Inc., 1964), pp. 347-349; Erich Eyck, *A History of the Weimar Republic* (New York: Athenaeum, 1970), II, pp. 137-38.

[75] Halperin, pp. 349-350.

[76] Halperin, ibid., p. 333.

[77] Craig, *Germany*, p. 509.

[78] Bach, ibid., pp. 199-201. Schönburg-Glauchau was a member of the agrarian wing of the Center party. He also had stock in the *Germania* Corporation. The two new board members were Count Hans Praschma, a Catholic nobleman from Silesia, and Count Clemens August von Galen, a Roman Catholic priest, and a monarchist at heart. Later, as the bishop of Münster, he was known as the "lion of Münster" because of his public protestations against Hitler's euthanasia program. He was made a cardinal in 1946 and died shortly thereafter.

[79] Bach, ibid., pp. 204-210. Schönburg and Galen sent letters to their aristocratic friends urging them to purchase stock in *Germania* in order to gain control of the newspaper's editorial policies. However, many of those who were approached had no confidence in the ability of the stockholders to alter the newspaper's liberal policies.

[80] Florian Klöckner was a wealthy Westphalian industrialist who had served in the *Reichstag* from 1920 to 1933. He initially purchased 100,000 Marks worth of *Germania* stock, and became a member of the Board of Directors. He also supported Papen's bid to purchase Semer's stock. Franz Semer was the Director of the Berlin Commercial-Discount Bank. He purchased 700,000 Marks in stock, and assigned 200,000 to his wife.

[81] It was the liberal Center party member, Karl Spiecker, who encouraged Frau Semer to challenge her husband's action. Spiecker wanted to prevent Papen from taking over control of the newspaper because he knew that Papen intended to use the paper as a propaganda tool for his conservative ideology.

[82] Bach, pp. 261-262.

[83] Bach, pp. 266-267.

[84] Bach records that the stockholders voted 3332 to 1236 with 363 abstentions in favor of Papen (p. 268). It is estimated that Papen purchased the stock for about 200,000 Gold marks. In his *Memoirs* (p. 111), Papen states that the purchase consumed a considerable portion of his personal wealth. While it is not certain, it was probably Praschma who suggested to Papen that he purchase Semer's shares. The next day, Papen was elected to the Board and after

Johannes Bell was re-elected Chairman, Papen was appointed to act as chairman when Bell was absent.

[85] Recommended were Theodor von Guérard as Klöckner's delegate, Senate President Karl Zimmerle representing Erzberger's shares held by his widow, Msgr. Ludwig Kaas, future chairman of the party, Pastor count von Galen, Franz von Papen. Frh. Heeremann was Papen's candidate on the Board, while Giesberts belonged to the liberal wing of the party. Bach, pp. 265-66.

[86] Bach, pp. 268-269. There is no record of another meeting; probably because the opposition realized that with his large majority of votes Papen would reject any candidate they might suggest.

[87] *Memoirs*, pp. 111-112.

[88] *Memoirs*, p. 111: "The war and inflation had seriously reduced our personal wealth and it was no means easy to decide to invest a considerable proportion of the remainder in a way which might serve one's political interests but which would produce a very uncertain income."

[89] Bach, p. 221, n. 2. Papen to Praschma, May 4, 1924. Quoted in Bach, p. 256. Dr. Karl Spiecker belonged to the Wirth faction and was a staunch defender of the Republic and the Weimar Constitution. Because of his association with the left-wing of the Center, and his many friends on *Germania's* editorial staff, Spiecker became Papen's principal adversary, and the one man that Papen wanted to remove from the newspaper.

[90] Bach, p. 256.

[91] Teipel had published a book in which he called for the Center party to abandon its "middle course" strategy, and line up with the more radical parties. This caused a great debate within the Executive Council, with the result that Teipel became a "persona non grata" in party circles.

[92] Papen's *Report* to Count Praschma, May 18, 1925, quoted in Bach, p. 271.

[93] Eric D. Kohler, "The Successful German Center-Left: Joseph Hess & the Prussian Center Party 1908-1932," *Central European History* 23, #4 (December, 1990) p. 336.

[94] Papen informed Praschma of this change in a letter dated May 17, 1926. Bach, p. 275.

[95] An unsigned article appeared in *Germania* on May 23, 1924, in which the author sharply criticized the Board of Director's interference with the "inner freedom of the German press." The article made it clear that the transfer of stock to Papen might alter the political position on the Board, but any attempt to do so was out of the question. Cf. Bach, pp. 263-64.

[96] Papen's letter to Praschma on October 27, 1927. According to Bach, p. 277.

[97] Orth was informed of Esser's appointment only two days before he was to join the newspaper staff. Klöckner only found out about the appointment when

he was informed that a special meeting of the Board was called to approve Papen's action.

[98] Bach, p. 277. The *Frankfurter Zeitung,* among other newspapers, published a detailed account of Papen's action on October 20, 1927. Heinrich Teipel's close connections with the *Frankfurter Zeitung*, enabled him to provide that newspaper with all of the details.

[99] Ibid.

[100] For example, a short time after the Esser affair, Papen appointed Dr. Ernst Buhla in place of Orth as editor-in-chief, but this was done with Center party approval.

[101] Kohler's comment that Papen's "...boldness [was] exceeded only by his stupidity" accurately reflects the attitude that Hess and the other members of the Center-Left had for Papen's reckless policies and actions. Kohler, ibid., p. 336.

[102] Count Nikolaus Ballestrem was a wealthy Silesian landowner and a close friend of Hans Praschma and Bishop von Galen.

[103] Papen's letter to Count Nikolaus Ballestrem, July 25, 1927, quoted in Bach, pp. 283-84.

[104] Ibid.

[105] The Schaffgotsch family not only possessed enormous land-holdings in Silesia, but they were also one of the largest mining corporations in the Reich. Praschma appealed to Gerhard Werner, the Director of the Schaffgotsch corporation, who acted on behalf of the family's interests. Bach, pp. 287-88.

[106] Bach, pp. 289-90, "Papen's letter to Praschma, October 27, 1927." The main reason for the refusal to supply the funds was due to the decline in farm prices, and not because of any antipathy towards Papen.

[107] Ibid. Praschma assumed that the conservatives would like to have control of the newspaper in order to promote their own candidates for election to the *Reichstag.*

[108] Cf. Bach, pp. 292-96 for a full account of the transactions.

[109] Cf. Bach, ibid.

[110] Bach, pp. 295-96. Actually, Papen and the Danat Bank agreed to share the expenses involved in financing the installation of the presses in *Germania's* new location.

[111] Cf. Bach, pp. 292-98, for a full account of the cartelization of the Catholic press in the Rhineland.

[112] Bach, p. 298

[113] Florian Klöckner was a major investor in the *Klöckner Zeitung* and therefore was interested in supporting *Germania*.

[114] Papen resigned from the Board of Directors after he was appointed Chancellor in 1932. Florian Klöckner replaced him as chairman of the board, and Rudolf von Twickel assumed the chairmanship from Klöckner until Himmler suppressed the newspaper in 1938. Bach, p. 304, note #5.

CHAPTER 4:
THE CABINET OF BARONS

A. The "Cardinal"

By March of 1930, the future of democracy in Germany was very much in doubt. Hermann Müller, the Social Democratic Chancellor and head of the "Great Coalition," was forced to resign because of the economic crisis brought on by the depression.[1] Although Hindenburg never concealed his preference for the monarchy, during his first five years in office he faithfully adhered to the democratic principles embodied in the constitution. However, by the Spring of 1930, faced with deteriorating economic conditions, growing political unrest, and a hopelessly divided *Reichstag*, the aging president's patience with parliamentary politics ran out. Consequently, in choosing Müller's successor, Hindenburg was influenced by those who thought there were better ways of using presidential authority to cope with the national emergency. The master-mind behind these plans was General Kurt von Schleicher, General Wilhelm Gröner's "Cardinal in politics."[2]

Kurt von Schleicher came from an old Brandenburg family, and like many from his background, entered the army where he formed a close friendship with Hindenburg's son, Oskar. He became a frequent visitor in the Hindenburg household, where the Field Marshall took a great liking to this sociable, urbane young officer whose quick wit amused him. Schleicher's unusual talent for organization, his penchant for intrigue, and his ability to make acquaintance with important individuals, assisted him in rising rapidly in the military hierarchy. Hand-picked by General Gröner to serve on the General Staff in 1913, von Schleicher became the General's aide-de-camp when the latter succeeded Ludendorff as Quartermaster General in October, 1918. After the war, Gröner was instrumental in getting his protégé transferred to the war ministry where Schleicher began his politico-military career. From his small office in the *Bendlerstrasse* overlooking the Landwehr Canal, the ambitious and calculating young officer set out to make himself the invisible commander-in-chief of the *Reichswehr*. What he wanted was power without responsibility, influence rather than position.[3]

From 1920 to 1926 Schleicher remained in the War Ministry, and under the commander-in-chief of the *Reichswehr*, Hans von Seeckt, continued to demonstrate his abilities. He soon became Seeckt's right-hand man, and although the commander-in-chief never liked Schleicher personally, he appreciated the ambitious officer's political talents and entrusted him with the delicate task of maintaining the political contacts of the Defense Ministry.[4] But as long as Seeckt remained the commander-in-chief, Schleicher's schemes to become the invisible power in the *Reichswehr* were frustrated.[5] Therefore, when Seeckt, largely through his own fault was forced to resign, the unscrupulous Brandenburger became the controlling influence in the *Bendlerstrasse*.[6]

The advent of Hindenburg as *Reichspresident* proved to be another step in Schleicher's bid to become the power behind the throne. Taking advantage of his friendship with Hindenburg's son, Schleicher was able to gain admittance to the presidential palace at will. He became an intimate with all of Hindenburg's staff, especially Otto Meissner, Hindenburg's secretary.[7] When he realized how much influence Meissner exercised over the president, Schleicher decided more could be gained through collaboration than through competition for Hindenburg's favor. The result was the formation of a "palace *camarilla*" consisting of Schleicher, Meissner and Hindenburg's son, Oskar. But it was Schleicher, with the support of his patron, General Gröner, who came to exercise the greatest influence over the aging president.

In 1928 Schleicher's good fortunes continued. Otto Gessler, the War Minister was forced to resign as a result of his involvement in illicit financial transactions.[8] Because of his close association with the

President, Schleicher was able to persuade Hindenburg to appoint Gröner as Defense Minister. With his former patron in charge of the *Reichswehr*, Schleicher was rewarded for his loyalty by becoming the head of the newly created *Ministeramt*, a political liaison office between the armed forces and the cabinet and the political parties. In this post Schleicher was able to expand his activities beyond the war ministry and into the national political arena.[9]

In the meantime, the national scene in 1929 was one of growing political and economic chaos in which all of the ills that had plagued Germany in 1923 revived with a vengeance. Unemployment continued to rise while the voices of the anti-republicans grew more strident. Political extremism accompanied economic decline, and the Republic rapidly became polarized. On the Left, the Communist party showed signs of revival, while on the Right, Hitler's National Socialists were becoming a force of political significance.[10] Meanwhile, the other parties showed no ability to cooperate, with the result that parliamentary bankruptcy, and the increase in anti-republican sentiment among the masses, furnished Schleicher with the opportunity to become the secret arbiter of German destinies. Not only did he exercise a controlling influence in the *Reichswehr*, but Hindenburg came to rely almost completely on his advice. In a position to dominate the inner political life of the nation, Schleicher wanted to liberate Germany from the inefficiency of parliamentary democracy, and restore the sense of discipline and order that had existed under the monarchy.

Convinced that further efforts to form a coalition government would be fruitless, Schleicher, with Gröner's blessings, went to Hindenburg with a plan to meet the national emergency. The plan called for a cabinet composed of men unhampered by narrow party loyalties, willing to govern from the standpoint of national interests, and relying for its authority upon the support of the *Reichspresident*.[11] Schleicher convinced Hindenburg that the formation of a government independent of parties, and equipped with the emergency powers provided by Article 48 of the Constitution, could deal more effectively with the extremists of both right and left, and bring stability to the nation.[12] But the crafty General's political instincts told him that the *Reichstag* could not be completely ignored, and so he recommended the Centrist, Heinrich Brüning, be appointed chancellor.[13] Brüning would presumably have the cooperation of his own party, while his conservative fiscal views would provide him with support from the industrialists in the People's party. Moreover, the idea of a strong "presidential cabinet" would appeal to the moderate wing of the Nationalist party and free it from the reactionary leadership of Alfred Hugenberg.[14] Schleicher's plan was successful, and after assuring Brüning that he could rely on the President's support, the Center leader agreed to accept the post.[15]

Brüning's appointment gave Schleicher his first experience as a king-maker, but it was not to be his last. When the experiment with the Brüning government proved to be unworkable, Schleicher managed to dispose of him and replace him with another "agent" whom he intended to manipulate in order to protect the glory of the German Army, save the nation from the growing Nazi menace, and eliminate the last vestiges of parliamentary democracy in the Reich. The man he selected as Brüning's successor, the person he was confident would do his bidding, was the dashing ex-cavalry officer, Franz von Papen.[16]

B. The Westphalian Candidate

Franz von Papen became acquainted with Schleicher prior to the war when they both served on the General Staff. After the war when he was a delegate in the Prussian *Landtag*, he saw Schleicher "whenever former members of the Headquarters or General Staff got together."[17] Even after he lost his bid for reelection to the Prussian *Landtag* in 1928, Papen kept up his contacts with Schleicher. In 1930, Schleicher invited Papen to observe military maneuvers, which Papen accepted with gratitude.[18] As members of the *Herrenklub*, they saw each other on numerous occasions, and undoubtedly shared their views about the economic and political issues at the moment.[19]

Although they were both monarchists at heart, Schleicher probably would have tolerated any government that permitted the Army to go its own way, and who would also allow him to rule from behind the scenes. Papen, on the other hand, objected to the *Reichswehr* mixing in politics, and clung to the centuries-old tradition that the Army's function was the defense and maintenance of the unity of the Reich. They both agreed that the Social Democrats should be eliminated as a political force, and were prepared to take any steps to achieve this. Insofar as he expressed any opinion of Schleicher, Papen described the General as a "man of great clarity and vision, with a caustic wit and a cheerful extrovert manner."[20] Schleicher's opinion of Papen, on the other hand, was less than flattering. Prior to Papen's appointment as chancellor, when someone remarked to Schleicher that the Westphalian aristocrat was not known to have a strong head, the General replied, "He doesn't have to have. He's a hat!" From this statement, as well as the manner with which he treated Papen in November of 1932, it is clear that Schleicher intended to control the Westphalian aristocrat just as he had manipulated Brüning. What in fact happened, was that "Fränzchen," turned out to be more ambitious, and possessed a greater capacity for intrigue than the General had bargained for. In the end, both men were the victims of their own intrigues. But it was Schleicher who paid the greater price.

When Brüning was appointed Chancellor, Papen was still serving as a member of the Prussian *Landtag*. He also wrote articles in *Germania*, and delivered occasional lectures to various conservative groups, in which he called harped on his favorite theme, viz., a call for the Center party to break its ties with the Socialists and join ranks with the Right. When he was not engaged in these activities, Papen, as the honorary mayor of Dülmen from 1928 to 1930, managed to reduce the community deficit and through the imposition of rigorous economic measures created a surplus in a little more than six months.[21]

In the spring of 1929, when it became clear that the Müller cabinet was about to fall, Papen came out in favor of Brüning's appointment, describing him as "a man of upright and impartial character [who] seemed ideally suited to the task of solving the social problems involved in the maintenance of the country's economy."[22]

Although Papen supported the Chancellor's conservative economic policies, he criticized him for his tolerance of the Social Democrats. Papen argued that if Brüning had turned to the right wing parties for support instead of relying on the Social Democrats, he could have carried out his reforms without resorting to presidential authority.[23] By placing all the blame for the collapse of parliamentary democracy on the Social Democrats, Papen hoped to escape the left wing charges that he was "the grave-digger" of democracy.

While it would be a misrepresentation of the facts to place all of the blame on Papen for the collapse of Weimar, it would be equally erroneous to accept Papen's explanation. Papen contended that Brüning "chose to form a Government which did not enjoy a parliamentary majority."[24] However, when Brüning formed his cabinet, the parties that were represented in the coalition accounted for 249 *Reichstag* seats

- a clear majority. Therefore, Brüning was hopeful that his coalition would work together, but if that failed, he intended to rely on the president's powers to accomplish his goals. From the very outset of his chancellorship, it was not only the Social Democrats who failed in their responsibilities, but also Nationalists who were just as unwilling to accept a responsible role in government. Even though Hindenburg urged on more than one occasion, no Nationalist leader would assume the duty of forming a government. The obstructionist tactics of Hugenberg and the Nationalists, whose ultimate objective was the destruction of the Republic, were as much to blame for the crippling of parliamentary democracy as the Socialists.[25]

Finally, Papen failed to acknowledge that members of his own aristocratic class and the landed gentry were also culpable. Not only did most of them refuse to participate in civic life, but those like Papen who did, wanted a more authoritarian government, and by supporting anti-republican causes contributed to the collapse of Weimar.

Meanwhile, the rapid decline of the nation's economy aggravated already existing tensions and led to an ominous increase in the number of clashes between rival extremist groups. Nazi Storm Troopers under their chief, Ernst Röhm, fought pitched battles against red-shirted Communists. While the streets of the cities were turning into battle grounds, Brüning was locked in a duel with the *Reichstag*. On July 16, 1930, the *Reichstag* rejected an essential part of the Chancellor's fiscal program, and he retaliated by threatening to resort to an emergency decree. The Social Democrats denounced Brüning's threat as contrary to the constitution, and with the support of Hugenburg's Nationalists, the Nazis and Communists voted 236 to 221 in favor of revocation of the emergency decrees. Instead of resigning in the wake of the adverse vote, Brüning carried out his threat. For the first time since the founding of the Republic, the principle of ministerial responsibility was violated. Brüning retaliated by dissolving the *Reichstag* and calling for new elections to be held on September 30, 1930.[26]

The Republic's fifth national election produced ominous results. The extremists on both sides showed huge gains, while the moderate parties dropped in strength.[27] The Nazis, who in 1928 had secured only 12 seats in the *Reichstag* with 810,00 votes, were now supported by over 6 million voters and became the second largest party with 107 seats.[28] The Social Democrats survived rather well, and with their 143 seats remained the strongest party in the *Reichstag*.

For Brüning, the election results were a heavy blow. Not only did they crush his hopes for a majority on the Right, independent of Hitler and Hugenberg, but they also eliminated any possibility of a majority that would support his economic reforms. Nevertheless, he decided to remain in office hoping that with Hindenburg's support he could weather the coming parliamentary storm.

Between 1931 and his resignation in May, 1932, Brüning tried desperately to stem the economic and financial crisis by measures designed to balance the budget - lower salaries for government employees, lower pensions and welfare payments, less government housing, etc. In order to put this unpopular, and unsuccessful, policy into effect, he was forced to rely completely on Article 48. The opposition forces in the *Reichstag* - the Communists, the Nazis and the Nationalists - repeatedly rejected his programs. Not only did the Chancellor's emergency decrees fail to resolve the economic crisis, but he was unable to cope with the advancing Brown Tide. In one state after another, the number of Nazis in local governments increased, and their voices became more strident, accusing the "Hunger Chancellor" of being the embodiment of all the evils of the "System" that had governed Germany since 1918. Moreover, with every Nazi victory the level of violence increased. Clashes between Nazis and Communists on the one hand, and the police and the rioters on the other, threatened to erupt in civil war. By the spring of 1932 the only thing that stood between Brüning and the collapse of his government was the aging President who became increasingly exasperated with the Chancellor's inability to resolve the crises.[29]

After the presidential elections in April, 1932, Schleicher was convinced that Brüning was not the man to tame the Nazis.[30] As the sentiment against Brüning mounted, Schleicher was preparing his *coup de grace*. Through his influence with Hindenburg, supported by the president's son, Oskar, and private secretary, Meissner, Schleicher plotted the Chancellor's downfall.

The complicated web of intrigue spun by the unscrupulous General involved plans to eliminate the Social Democrats as a political force, and to prorogue the *Reichstag* indefinitely pending a new Constitution. In the meantime, the President, the *Reichswehr*, and a Cabinet of the President's "friends" would govern the nation. To accomplish this risky plan, Schleicher was prepared to gamble on the support of the Nazis and the Nationalists. Once they had served his purpose, the crafty

General intended to restrain Hitler by taking the more moderate elements of the party into the government, and persuading the SA to abandon its allegiance to the Führer and join the Army.

Both before and after the presidential elections, Schleicher met with Hitler and Röhm on several occasions in an effort to persuade the Nazi leaders to join a coalition government, but none of these meetings proved to be successful. On May 8, after Hindenburg's reelection, Hitler and Schleicher met in the latter's apartment where the General laid out his plan for the Führer. The Brüning government was to fall piecemeal; first Gröner, then the Chancellor. A Presidential cabinet was to replace Brüning's, the *Reichstag* would be dissolved, and the decrees against the SA and SS would be rescinded. In return for these solid advantages, Schleicher requested Hitler to "tolerate" a presidential cabinet.

While Schleicher was weaving his web of intrigue, the beleaguered Chancellor sought the advice of Otto Meissner. The State Secretary told him that the President wanted a new government that would be exclusively rightist and would be tolerated by Hugenberg and Hitler. Meissner also told Brüning that the President would refuse to sign any new emergency decrees and, in the strictest confidence, added that Schleicher had influenced the President to take this hard line. On hearing this, Brüning said that he was fed up and wanted to call it quits; he was prepared to tender his resignation to Hindenburg in their next meeting scheduled for the next day.[31]

The end came with dramatic suddenness. On the morning of May 30, 1932, two months after Hindenburg's reelection, the Chancellor was dismissed without so much as a hearing. As Brüning departed from the President for the last time, Hindenburg turned to Meissner and muttered, "Now I can have a Cabinet of my friends." Schleicher, who was at the height of his power and influence with Hindenburg, intended to make sure that the President's "friends" were also his.

Two days later, Schleicher presented Hindenburg with the Chancellor of his choice, the man who, under his guidance and with the support of the *Reichswehr*, he, von Schleicher, would control as Defense Minister. This combination, Schleicher assured the President, would "tame" the Nazis, eliminate the Social Democrats as a political force, and establish an authoritarian regime. The man Schleicher proposed to accomplish this was none other than the ex-cavalry officer military attaché to America,   famous gentleman-rider, and arch-conservative monarchist, Franz von Papen.

Papen's life style, personality and background appealed to Schleicher. As a friend of many years, a fellow-member of the *Herrenklub*, and a former military officer, Schleicher believed he could work well with Papen. As the first German Chancellor to come to power without holding a major government or diplomatic position, Papen lacked experience, thus assuring Schleicher of a submissive spokesman who would follow the General's advice. Schleicher also counted on Westphalian aristocrat's wit, charm, and *savoir faire* to relieve the aging Field Marshal's depression and thus insure his control of government policies. What Schleicher failed to realize was that Papen's ambition and tenacity, no less than his capacity for intrigue, were equal to, and in some ways surpassed, his own.

While Papen probably played no role in his selection, it is highly unlikely that he did not hear the rumors that were circulating in Berlin. As early as the end of April, the well-informed French Ambassador to Germany, Andre François-Poncet, was telling people that Papen would be the next chancellor.[32] Reports in the daily press mentioned Papen's name as a possible candidate for the post. Papen also learned from other sources that Schleicher was proposing him for Chancellor.[33]

Whether or not Papen's claim that he knew nothing of his candidacy was true, he did in fact meet with Schleicher on May 28. Schleicher gave him "a general survey of the political situation, described the crisis within the Cabinet, and told me that it was the President's wish to form a Cabinet of experts, independent of the political parties."[34] The General also told Papen that "in the present parliamentary crisis, the instrument of law and order (the Army) could only be spared from intervention in the civil war that threatened, if an authoritarian Cabinet were to replace the tottering party system."[35] This was a theme that Papen had been preaching for many years, and he was overjoyed to think that he now would have the support of the Army in his plans to create a "New State."

Although Papen was in complete agreement with Schleicher's plans for an authoritarian government, he was cautious about the General's solution for all of Germany's ills. Papen told Schleicher that the real root of Germany's problems was the system of proportional representation with its thirty parties. He proposed to amend the Constitution and introduce a system of individual constituencies.[36]

The conversation then turned to the question of whom ought to lead the government: "Looking at me with his humorous and somewhat sarcastic smile, he seemed to me to appreciate my astonishment. 'This offer takes me completely by surprise...I very much doubt if I am the right man. I know I seem to be agreed on the measures that have been taken, and I shall be glad to help in any way that I can - but the Reich Chancellor! That is a very different matter.' " [37] Schleicher replied that he had already submitted Papen's name to Hindenburg who wished "very much" to appoint him to the office. When Papen told the General that he was taking things too much for granted, and that he could not "undertake such an immense responsibility on the spot," Schleicher took his arm and in his most congenial and confidential manner said, "You have simply got to do Hindenburg and myself this service. Everything depends on it, and I cannot think of anyone who would do it better. You are a man of moderate convictions, whom no one will accuse of dictatorial tendencies, and there is no other right wing man of whom the same could be said. I have even drawn up a provisional Cabinet list which I am sure you will approve."[38]

Although flattered by this appeal to his vanity, Papen was concerned about how the Nazis could be persuaded to collaborate in a Presidential Cabinet. Schleicher responded that in a recent conversation with Hitler, he had promised the Führer to repeal the ban on the SA and dissolve the *Reichstag* in return for Nazi toleration of a new government. On hearing this, Papen told the General that he would think the whole matter over during the weekend and give him his answer on Monday.

Uncertain about accepting Schleicher's offer, Papen went to Neubabelsberg, on the outskirts of Berlin, to seek the advice of his old friend Hans Humann, a frequenter of the *Herrenklub*. In the idyllic calm and expanse of the Wannsee the two men spent most of the weekend discussing the pros and cons of Schleicher's offer. Humann was quick to warn Papen that if he accepted the General's offer his greatest difficulties would come from the Center party. Not only was Brüning their "idol," but they would never forgive Papen for wishing to usurp his position. Humann went on to say that he understood why Schleicher and the President wanted Papen, "They are looking for someone who understands people, knows the situation here and abroad, and has the courage of his convictions. On the other hand," Humann continued, "I don't think that the parties have yet realized that the whole apparatus of government under the present Constitution will break down completely if it is not reformed in some way. If we only had a competent right wing opposition, who could combine an enlightened outlook with their conservatism." Since this was not the case, Humann counseled Papen to reject the offer.[39]

Returning to the *Bendlerstrasse* on Monday morning, Papen was determined to reject Schleicher's offer. "Well, my dear Papen," the General asked, "what is the verdict?" Then, without waiting for a reply, he added that "someone as active as you are is not going to decline such an opportunity of serving his country." Papen responded, "I have been trying to answer your question all the weekend, but I am sorry to have to tell you that it can't be done. We can only resolve this situation by combining every constructive force in the country, both inside and outside the parties, and I am simply not the right man."[40] Papen explained that not only the Center but also the Socialists and Trade Unions would oppose him. Under these conditions, it would be senseless to inaugurate a new government with a constitutional crisis.

Schleicher was not to be put off by Papen's remarks. Applying all of his charm, the General smiled and told Papen, "We have taken all this into consideration, and I think you will find you are exaggerating the difficulties." Schleicher then said that the best way to overcome opposition is to work out a comprehensive program for reducing unemployment. Once this was accomplished, he continued, "the people who support the Nazis will soon quiet down."[41] He then added, "Hitler has already promised tacit cooperation with a Papen cabinet, and you will see what a difference it will make if we can get away from this civil war atmosphere." Although Schleicher's arguments impressed Papen, he remained an elusive quarry. He told Schleicher that he wanted to confer with Kaas about the offer, and promised him a "definite decision" on the following day.[42]

At three o'clock the next afternoon, Papen visited the Center leader. Kaas made it clear that his party would not support Papen if he replaced Brüning who was the party's choice. When Papen explained that Schleicher had convinced him of the wide breach between Hindenburg and Brüning, Kaas refused to change his position. Leaving Kaas, Papen thought that any man who did not enjoy the support of the moderate parties "would be to all intents and purposes powerless." With this thought in mind he was ushered into Hindenburg's office fifteen minutes later.

The President greeted Papen with a certain air of "paternal kindness." "Well, my dear Papen, I hope you are going to help me out of this difficult situation." Papen replied that he was unable to do so even though he "fully agreed with the necessity for a change of course." When he suggested that Brüning might be able to take the necessary steps, Hindenburg replied that there was little chance of that. He then added that he wanted a cabinet composed of men whom he knew personally; a cabinet that would govern "without being dependent on parliamentary negotiations for even the most insignificant action." Expressing his agreement with this objective, Papen still tried to convince the President that without the support of the Center, his government would incur the hate and enmity of his own party, and therefore "he might just as well call upon the German Nationalists for the task."[43] Papen vividly describes the scene that followed: "Rising heavily from his chair, the old Field Marshal put both hands on my shoulders: 'You cannot possibly leave an old man like me in the lurch. In spite of my age I have had to accept the responsibilities of the nation for another period. I am asking you now to take over the task on which the future of our country depends, and I am relying on your sense of duty and patriotism to do what I ask you. ...You have been a soldier and did your duty in the war. When the Fatherland calls, Prussia knows only one response - obedience.'"[44] Moved by this appeal, Papen struck his colors. Shaking Hindenburg's hand, he accepted the post. Schleicher, who had been waiting in the next room, came in to offer his congratulations. In view of the burden Papen had assumed, and the course on which he was about to embark, the General should have offered his condolences.

C. The *Herrenklub* Takes Over

As the new Cabinet ministers filed into the President's spacious office, Papen could not help but reflect that not since the days of the Kaiser had any government been formed so quickly. The bickering and bargaining between political parties, which had often kept the nation in suspense for weeks, had been avoided.[45] This was mainly due to the efforts of Schleicher and Hindenburg who, in fact, had most of the selections in mind before Papen's appointment.

The new government under Papen's leadership represented no particular political party, and was not supported by the labor unions, or even a majority of businessmen. Seven of the ten ministers were members of the *Herrenklub*, while eight of them had also served as officers in the Kaiser's army. Their loyalty to Hindenburg was based more on his rank as Field Marshall than on his role as President of the Republic. Recalling the oath-taking ceremony, Magnus von Braun, Minister for Food and Agriculture, observed, "...we all sensed that the *Reichspresident* felt comfortable and contented with his new Cabinet members...Papen, Gayl, Elitz and I had belonged to the Potsdam Guard Regiment, Schleicher had been in the same regiment as the Hindenburgs (father and son), Gürtner was a Bavarian artillery man, Neurath had been with the Olga Dragoons at Württemberg, Krosigk had been a Pomeranian Uhlan."[46]

On June 2, Papen announced the existence of his government of "national concentration" to the German public and to an astonished world. The news of Papen's appointment met with criticisms from all sides. The Socialist newspaper, *Vorwärts*, denounced the new regime as "...a conspiracy of the great land-owners and captains of industry...who want inflation and are behind those who have unleashed the crisis."[47] The liberal *Kölnische Volkzeitung*, recalling Papen's unsavory activities as a military attaché in Washington during World War I, labeled his appointment a "national embarrassment."[48] *Germania*, the semi-official Center newspaper, expressed its attitude towards the new Cabinet: "Regardless of how it may appear, the Center Party does not support the new regime. [The Party] will adopt an objective attitude towards the practical work of the new Cabinet, and in each instance will make its decisions on this basis."[49]

Even the Right-wing press received the news of the new Cabinet with cautious restraint. The lead article in *Junge Nation*, a newspaper sympathetic to the ideals of the *Stahlhelm*, made the tentative comment that it would not extend its confidence to Papen on credit, "...but we will also not distrust him from the very outset."[50] The *Lokalanzeiger*, closely allied with Alfred Hugenburg, observed that "... the DNVP and the National Socialists had nothing officially to do with the formation of this Cabinet."[51] Hans Zehrer, a friend of von Schleicher, writing in the *Tägliche Rundschau*, a newspaper linked with the conservative "Tat" circle, warned that Papen's only achievement would be "...to smooth the path to power for the NSDAP."[52]

If most of the press were opposed to the new government, there were others who also expressed their dismay or amazement at the announcement. Bavarian nobleman, Erwin von Aretin, who was also an acquaintance of Papen, commented that the Chancellor "...no longer represented a political solution for the problem of government, but was adventurism pure and simple."[53] Perhaps the cruelest remark of all came from the pen of Harry Kessler, who wrote that Papen "...looked like a billy-goat attempting to maintain his poise in top-hat and frock coat-a character out of Alice in Wonderland!"[54]

Even the ambassadors from France and England were less than kind in their comments about the new chancellor. The French Ambassador, Andre François-Poncet, recorded his reaction to the news of Papen's appointment in his diary:

> Papen's appointment was at first greeted with incredulous amazement; when the news was confirmed, everyone smiled. There is something about Papen that prevents either his friends or his enemies from taking him entirely seriously...He is one of those people who are considered capable of plunging into a dangerous adventure; they pick up every gauntlet, accept every wager. If he succeeds in an undertaking he is very pleased; if he fails it doesn't bother him.[55]

The British Minister, Sir Horace Rumbold, perhaps more closely reflecting the truth of the matter, observed that Papen was probably chosen because "...no candidate of any standing was willing to take the office."[56]

These criticisms should have served as a warning to Papen that he would have difficulties in finding support for his solutions to Germany's problems. However, even more disastrous for the future of his government, was Papen's betrayal of Msgr. Ludwig Kaas and the Center Party .

On May 31, 1932, while Papen discussed his appointment as chancellor with Hindenburg, Kaas was closeted with the members of the Center Party *Reichstag* delegation just a few doors down the street. At that meeting Kaas informed his colleagues that Papen had assured him that he would not seek the chancellorship, and promised he would urge Hindenburg to seek an alternative candidate.[57] When informed of what actually had happened, Kaas jumped up and "...literally clapped his hands above his head, repeatedly screaming impossible, impossible and left the room cursing."[58] Later that day, after he had calmed down, Kaas tried to reach Papen by telephone to no avail. The Chancellor had gone to Schleicher's house for dinner to discuss the cabinet appointments and plan their course of action.

Papen's failure to contact Kaas immediately is difficult to explain. He claimed that "someone...telephoned the information to the outside world...the news spread like wildfire...had I any idea that the information would leak out so soon, I would have telephoned to Dr. Kaas myself and told him why I had changed my mind."[59] Even if one accepts this dubious explanation, it does not change the course of events which led to an irreparable breach between the new regime and the Center Party.

On June 1, 1932, Papen received a sharply worded statement from the Center Party delegation in the *Reichstag* accusing the Chancellor of "capricious intrigues" in cooperation with irresponsible persons not bound by the constitution - a reference, no doubt, to General Schleicher who had managed the entire affair. The resolution included an avowal that the Party would refuse to accept responsibility for any difficulties that might result from the actions of the new government.[60]

The appearance of the Center Party charges in the press prompted the Chancellor to publicly state his reasons for accepting the post. In a letter addressed to Kaas dated June 2, 1932, Papen explained that he had accepted the position in "...one of the most fateful hours of German history...not as a member of a party but as a German, and certainly not with a light heart." Pointing to the present crisis as an ideological one, Papen declared that the new Germany must be built on a foundation that ruthlessly espouses the eternal principles of a Christian outlook.[61]

Once again, Papen misjudged the effects of his actions. When the Center Party received the letter, they determined that Papen's action was not only a betrayal of the Party, but also an insult to Brüning. In a sharply worded reply, Kaas reprimanded Papen for going back on his word, and challenged his assertion that he was motivated to accept the position in hopes that he could bring about a unification of all truly national forces. If this was his true purpose, Kaas went on, then the new regime should have included prominent political figures of the Left; since Papen had neglected to form such a government, he had abandoned the idea of the *Volksgemeinschaft*, -- a notion sacred to the

Center party. Since the Chancellor chose to ignore this Kaas warned, he was entering on a path that would lead him astray.[62]

Fearing that his public image could be seriously damaged as a result of Kaas' reprimand, Papen committed an even more serious blunder. He issued an official communiqué in which he offered an explanation that was completely unsatisfactory. The communiqué stated that the President had first requested him to undertake the formation of a new cabinet as a member of the Center party. However, Papen said he had refused because of his promise to Kaas. Then later on the president asked Papen to accept the offer as a "private person." Papen concluded that he was unable to refuse the aging Field Marshals' appeal, and accepted the post not as a member of the Center party but as a German patriot.

When the Center party Executive Committee learned of this latest vindication, they called for Papen's expulsion from the party. In order to avoid the stigma attached to expulsion, Papen announced his resignation from the Center on June 2, 1932.[63]

Having severed his ties with the Center, Papen was acutely aware that his government would now have to secure Hitler's promise of toleration, which could be as ephemeral as the wind. If he could bring the Nazis into his cabinet, he was convinced that once saddled with responsibilities, Hitler would abandon his radical schemes. This presumption was based on Schleicher's assurances to Papen, prior to his appointment, that Hitler had agreed not to oppose the new regime if it would lift the ban on the Storm Troopers and the SS, dissolve the *Reichstag* and call for new elections.[64]

On June 3, two days after Hindenburg announced the new government, Schleicher and Hitler met at the Fürstenberg estate in Mecklenberg. In return for the agreement to remove the ban on the SA and SS and dissolve the *Reichstag*, Hitler promised to tolerate the Papen government until after the elections, and this implied that he would also join the cabinet thereafter.[65] The next day, at Papen's request, Hindenburg issued an emergency decree dissolving the *Reichstag*. The Chancellor defended this action on the grounds that the recent elections in the *Länder* indicated that the *Reichstag* no longer reflected the political will of the people. However, this explanation hardly squared with the conditions required to declare a state of emergency as defined in Article 48. To the insiders, it was obvious that the dissolution of the *Reichstag* was the result of the "political deal" between Schleicher and Hitler.[66]

If Papen had anticipated that the Nazis would be satisfied with this action, he must have been very disappointed. In the immediate aftermath of the dissolution, the Nazis became increasingly critical of the government. Speaking at Dömitz on June 4, Gregor Strasser declared that his party had no "common bond" with Papen's cabinet, and they would vigorously oppose any efforts to win them over. Besides, Strasser continued, they were determined to "take the tiller of the state" into their own hands after the *Reichstag* elections.[67] Goebbels also attacked the Papen regime in a series of articles in his propaganda sheet, *Der Angriff*. The future Propaganda Minister charged the Papen government with failure to ensure law and order in these "wild times." Of course, Goebbels failed to mention the fact that much of the violence and disruption was caused by Hitler's Storm Troopers! Under the impact of these indictments and the growing level of violence, Papen arranged a meeting with Hitler to determine for himself what arrangements Schleicher had made with the Nazi leader.

They met on June 9, in the apartment of Papen's *Herrenklub* colleague, Werner von Alvensleben. The Chancellor vividly recalled his first impressions of the Nazi leader: "He was wearing a dark blue suit and seemed the complete petit-bourgeois. He had an unhealthy complexion, and with his little moustache and curious hair style had an indefinable bohemian quality. His demeanor was modest and polite..."[68]

After an exchange of polite formalities, Papen asked Hitler whether or not the National Socialists would tolerate his government. Hitler replied with his usual complaints about the decision of previous governments to exclude a political party with such wide-spread support from sharing in the affairs of state, especially at a time when all-out efforts should be taken to correct the errors of Versailles and restore full German sovereignty. Hitler also made it clear that he regarded the Papen government as a temporary solution, and that the neither he nor his Party would be satisfied with a subordinate role. He concluded the one-hour conversation with a promise that he would continue to make his party the strongest in the country, and then the chancellorship would be his.[69]

Papen came away from the meeting with the belief that the fate of his government would depend to a large extent on Hitler's willingness to back him up, both at the forthcoming international reparations conference in Lausanne, and in his program to combat the massive unemployment at home. He also knew that this would not be easily accomplished, especially since Hitler demanded that the government lift the ban against the SA and the SS. Despite Schleicher's agreement with Hitler, Papen was reluctant to remove the ban. For one thing, he feared that if the SA and SS were permitted to freely roam the streets, there would be a resurgence of violence and disorder that could lead to a civil war. But, a more compelling reason was the opposition of Bavaria, Württemberg, and Baden to such a move.

Spearheading the southern opposition was the Prime Minister of Bavaria, Heinrich Held, a member of the Bavarian People's Party and a staunch defender of south German interests in the Reich. Held's opposition to the removal of the ban was only one of his quarrels with the central government. A more serious problem involved rumors that Papen intended to remove the Braun-Severing "care-taker" government in Prussia and replace it with a Reich Commissioner. The Bavarian statesman was convinced that once Prussia was swallowed up, the other *Länder* would soon fall victim to the same fate.

Faced with this situation, Papen tried to convince Held and the other southern leaders that he had no intention of experimenting with a Reich Commissioner because such an appointment would be justifiable only as an *ultima ratio* to be used only if the vital interests of the Fatherland were at stake. As for the ban, Papen explained, it had been imposed on the formation of the Nazi Party, but not on the formations of the other parties, and the removal of the ban was simply a matter of restoring equality before the law; if there were any danger of civil war, Papen added, all paramilitary organizations would be outlawed at once.[70]

Under the pretext of wishing to discuss the financial crisis in Prussia, Papen invited Held, Joseph Schmitt, the Minister President of Baden, and Eugen Bolz of Württemburg to a meeting in Berlin in June.[71] Suspecting that the real reason for the meeting had little to do with the financial situation in Prussia, the three southern statesmen met on June 9, at Karlsruhe, to plan their strategy. They also sent a telegram to President Hindenburg calling for a meeting with him and Papen on June 12, and then took the train to Berlin.

The meeting between Papen and the southern officials turned out to be a stormy one. Papen started out by sketching the state of affairs in

Prussia, and the need for certain reforms. He argued that he was trying to bring together those factions in the Reich who would cooperate to resolve the economic problems facing the government. Moreover, the Chancellor insisted that without cooperation between the more important political parties and the government, there was little prospect of success at the forthcoming Lausanne conference. If Germany obtained no relief in the reparations issue at Lausanne, Papen went on, there would be little hope of solving the financial crisis at home. The Chancellor then noted that the role of Hitler and the Nazis could not be ignored, but that there was little chance of getting their support unless the ban on the SA and SS were lifted.[72]

In a sharp rebuttal, Held accused Papen of harboring reactionary ideas aimed at eliminating federalism. He told the Chancellor that the southern *Länder* mistrusted the government because of the support it had received from the large landowners and big business, while there was no representation in the cabinet for the bulk of the Bavarian population. He also criticized Papen for wanting to lift the ban, calling it a "license for murder." Echoing the same sentiments, Schmitt and Bolz accused the Papen government of duplicity and insincerity in its dealings with the other *Länder*. By the time the meeting had adjourned, the chasm separating them was as wide, if not wider, than before.[73] The results of the meeting with President Hindenburg the next morning were equally unproductive. Held charged the government with attempts to alter the federal structure, and expressed the fear that "what happens in Prussia today might well be repeated in other states tomorrow." He then demanded to know if the rumors about a commissional government were true. Finally, he argued that if the ban on the SA and SS were to be lifted, the result would lead to civil war. Held concluded by calling for a decree to ban all para-military organizations. In their remarks to Hindenburg, the other two southern statesmen supported Held's observations, and Schmitt added that Baden "would decline all responsibility for the preservation of public order within its borders if the ban were lifted."[74]

Applying all his charm in an effort to persuade these heads of state that the government wanted to preserve the *Rechtsstaat*, Papen claimed that he had "no intention" of experimenting with a Reich Commissioner, and added that such a move was possible only as a last ditch stand to save the nation. With regard to the ban, the Chancellor argued that he was simply trying to see that all parties were treated fairly, and he noted that other formations like the *Stahlhelm* and the *Reichsbanner* currently enjoyed freedom of action. He also reminded the southern leaders that the government had to take into account the fact that thirteen million votes were cast for the Nazis in the recent presidential elections. After another heated exchange by Held, the President cut off the discussion by stating that he intended to lift the ban, and added that he would immediately cancel the decree should he be deceived by the outcome. Hindenburg concluded with the remark that the rumors concerning a possible change in the relationship between the states and the government were false. On this cool note, the conference came to an end.[75]

In the minds of Held, Schmitt, and Bolz, the President's remarks confirmed their suspicions that Papen was nothing more than a puppet commissioned to carry out the President's orders with little regard for his position as a representative of the people. Whatever confidence they might have had in Papen no longer existed after this meeting. The Chancellor's failure to win support from these heads of state would come back to haunt him when it came time to account for his stewardship.

Papen's unsuccessful meeting with the southern leaders made him more skeptical about lifting the ban against the Nazis. However, at the suggestion of Schleicher, the Chancellor met again with Hitler on June 13, to discuss the situation. The Nazi leader refused to compromise, and insisted that Papen take action. Later that same day, Papen reported his conversation with Hitler to the Cabinet, and sought their advice. There followed an exchange of views with von Gayl, Minister of the Interior, arguing in favor of lifting the ban. Opposition to this recommendation resulted in the Cabinet adjourning without reaching any decision.[76]

Meanwhile, the Nazis continued to put pressure on the government. Goebbels complained to Schleicher that the government was vacillating, while Göring told von Gayl that he was convinced that the hesitation to lift the ban stemmed from a fear of adverse public opinion should the government capitulate to Nazi demands. On that same afternoon the Cabinet reconvened and voted to lift the ban.[77] Two days later on June 16, Hindenburg promulgated the decree lifting the ban on the SA and SS.

The reaction of the states to the government's action was extremely negative. In the north, Prussia and Hamburg announced that they would continue to enforce the prohibitions on demonstrations. In the south, Württemberg forbade open-air demonstrations while Baden and Bavaria banned all outdoor meetings as well as the wearing of uniforms.[78]

This opposition was embarrassing for Papen at a time when he sorely needed all the support he could muster. The Chancellor was about to leave for Lausanne where he hoped to get the other nations to settle the reparations question in favor of Germany. Leaving behind him a government that lacked the support of the southern states would place him in a difficult position. The French and the British would wonder whether or not the Papen government would be around long enough to implement any decisions made at Lausanne. Moreover, Papen's political standing at home was insecure. In his first few weeks as Chancellor, he had acted on behalf of the Right, and, consequently, alienated the Center and the Left. With the *Reichstag* elections set for July 31, Papen realized that unless he was able to bring back from Lausanne what the Right demanded of him, he would risk losing their support in the elections.

If Papen was worried about his performance at Lausanne, he did not reveal it as he smilingly waved good-bye to his wife, Martha, from the window of the train in the Anhalt Station.

NOTES

[1] Hermann Müller, the veteran Social Democrat, replaced Wilhelm Marx after the May, 1928 elections. He governed as the head of the "Great Coalition," a parliamentary majority composed of five parties ranging from right to left. As long as the major issues centered around foreign policy and the survival of the Republic, Müller's cabinet managed to stay in power. But when the issue of unemployment benefits came up, the cabinet was divided and Müller was forced to resign on March 27, 1930.

[2] Gröner retired from active military service at the end of 1919. Between 1920 and 1923 he served as Minister of Transportation, but returned to private life after the resignation of the Cuno cabinet in the Fall of 1923. President Hindenburg appointed him *Reichswehr* Minister in 1928 where he remained until 1932.

[3] John W. Wheeler-Bennett, *The Nemesis of Power* (New York: St. Martin's Press, Inc., 1954) p. 182.

[4] Hans von Seeckt was appointed commander-in-chief of the *Reichswehr* in June 1920. During the French occupation of the Ruhr, Seeckt formed the "Black *Reichswehr*" composed of former Free Corps soldiers, the *Stahlhelm*, and the Socialist *Reichsbanner*. Seeckt was also responsible for suppressing the Hitler *putsch* in Bavaria, and the Communist uprisings in Saxony and Thuringia in 1923.

[5] Following the centuries-old tradition of the officer corps, Seeckt insisted that his officers be strictly non-political. In this respect Schleicher differed markedly from the commander-in-chief with the result that there was constant friction between them.

[6] Seeckt was dismissed from his post in October 1926. Although Schleicher's name has been connected with Seeckt's dismissal, there is no solid evidence to support this. Seeckt himself believes that jealousy on the part of Hindenburg caused his downfall. Cf. Gordon Craig, *The Politics of the Prussian Army*, pp. 421-422.

[7] Otto Meissner was a Prussian civil servant who became State Secretary to President Ebert in March 1920. He continued to serve as a secretary to Ebert, Hindenburg and Hitler. Although he exercised great influence on Ebert and Hindenburg, his authority diminished under Hitler. He was placed on trial as a War Criminal at Nuremberg in November, 1947, and was acquitted of all charges in April, 1949.

[8] In February 1928 Gessler was associated with attempts by the *Reichswehr* to increase their funds through heavy speculation in the shares of a film company called "Phoebus," which then collapsed. This disclosure caused the Socialists in the *Reichstag* to demand a complete investigation and a call for reforms. These

demands were almost immediately forgotten after Gessler's dismissal. Gordon Craig, ibid., p. 425.

[9] The new post carried with it numerous duties and enormous powers. Gröner gave him a free hand, and Schleicher quickly consolidated his position through his contacts with politicians, journalists, and foreign observers who happened to visit Berlin. Schleicher had agents in every Ministry and Government bureau including the chancellor's office. "Not since Holstein had there been so pertinacious a prier into the secrets of the official world," Wheeler-Bennett, *Nemesis*, p. 184.

[10] After his release from the Landsberg prison in December, 1924, Hitler announced his intention to pursue the path of legality to political power. This meant a drive to expand the party membership and participate in the electoral process. The first signs that this new strategy was working occurred in the May, 1928, elections, in which the Nazis did surprisingly well in Schleswig-Holstein, Lower Saxony, Thuringia, and Upper Bavaria. Cf. Thomas Childers, *The Nazi Voter* (Chapel Hill: The University of North Carolina Press, 1983), pp. 125-28; Richard F. Hamilton, *Who Voted for Hitler?* (Princeton New Jersey: Princeton University Press, 1982), pp. 235-37.

[11] Schleicher's goal was to identify the President with the Army, both as its Supreme Commander and as Chief of State. Schleicher was convinced that only the President could save Germany, but he also held the position that the *Reichswehr* was the sole source of Hindenburg's power.

[12] Article 48 of the Weimar Constitution stated that, "Should public order and safety be seriously disturbed or threatened, the President may take the necessary measures to restore public order and safety; in case of need, he may use armed force...and he may, for the time being, declare the fundamental rights of the citizen to be wholly or partly in abeyance."

[13] Heinrich Brüning's political career began in 1924 as a protégé of Stegerwald. By 1929 he had established himself as an expert on finance, and in 1930 he was elected chairman of the Center fraction in the *Reichstag*. As an officer in the war, Brüning had acquired a deep respect for the German officer corps, and after his retirement from the military kept up his connections with the *Reichswehr*. Through these connections he met General Kurt von Schleicher. Brüning's war record made him more acceptable to Hindenburg, who at first was not interested in appointing the Centrist as Chancellor.

[14] Hugenberg had managed to oust Otto Kirdorff from the leadership of the DNVP in October 1928. Schleicher saw no possibility of dealing with this arch-enemy of democracy who had turned against Hindenburg when the president approved the new reparations schedule outlined in the Young Plan. If the moderates in the DNVP could be persuaded to successfully challenge Hugen-

berg's leadership, Schleicher hoped that a government composed of the DNVP, Center, DVP and Democrats under Brüning's leadership could be formed.

[15] At first not only Brüning, but also Hindenburg was opposed to Schleicher's plan. But mounting pressures and Schleicher's persuasive manner, caused Hindenburg to yield. Brüning also changed his mind because he said that he "could not reject the President's appeal to my soldierly sense of duty." Cf. Dorpalen, *Hindenburg*, p. 177.

[16] It is uncertain on what date Schleicher had actually decided to recommend Papen to Hindenburg. In his *Memoirs* (pp. 150-51), Papen claims that he only learned of Schleicher's interest in him on May 26, 1932.

[17] *Memoirs*, p. 124.

[18] Papen to Schleicher, September 24, 1930, *Schleicher Papers*, N 42/80/6-6a, *Bundesarchiv-Militärarchiv*, Freiburg/i.B   (Hereafter cited: *Schleicher*, BA, Freiburg).

[19] It will be recalled that when Papen was raising money to modernize *Germania* he became involved in Werner von Alvensleben's plans to purchase the *Deutsche Allgemeine Zeitung*, and that Schleicher was also involved in that effort.

[20] *Memoirs*, p. 124.

[21] "*Von Papen-Ausgabe*," *Dülmener Heimatblaetter*, Vol. 3, May 1933, p. 40. Quoted in Bach, *Franz von Papen*, pp. 144-45.

[22] *Memoirs*, p. 133.

[23] *Memoirs*, p. 133. It is ironic that Papen should make this observation about Brüning. As chancellor, he tried without success to gain the support of the Right, and ended up depending on the presidential powers just as Brüning did.

[24] Ibid., p. 132. It is true that since the Center party did not have a majority in the *Reichstag*, Papen could make this claim. But since Brüning's cabinet represented a majority, he did have the necessary votes to carry out his reforms.

[25] Between 1919 and 1932, the Nationalists participated in only two of nineteen parliamentary cabinets, and the total period of their participation over thirteen years was twenty-seven months.

[26] On July 26, Hindenburg issued a number of emergency decrees submitted to him by the Chancellor. Meanwhile, Hugenberg's decision to go along with the Social Democrats' motion against Brüning caused a split in the Nationalist party under the leadership of Count Cuno von Westarp. Stung by this turn of events, Hugenberg began to seek an accommodation with Hitler and the Nazis.

[27] The Communist delegation increased from 54 to 77 representatives in the *Reichstag*, while the moderate parties dropped in strength with the SPD, the DVP and the DDP losing the most votes. Cf. Hamilton, *Who Voted for Hitler?*, pp. 236 ff.

[28] Hamilton, ibid., pp. 236-38. The growth of the party began before the 1930 elections. In May, 1928, before the depression, the Nazis were already increasing

their strength in the state elections in Baden, Lübeck, Thuringia, and Saxony. However, the September election was the first time the Nazis exploded on the national scene.

[29] Hindenburg was also annoyed with Brüning because he failed to gain the support of the Right to have the president's term of office prolonged rather than a call for national elections.

[30] Hindenburg was reelected president on April 10, 1932. He decisively defeated Hitler and the Communist, Ernst Thälmann, on a second ballot. It was a bitter contest in which many of those who had supported Hindenburg in 1925 now voted for Hitler, while many voters on the left voted for the President.

[31] "Memorandum of June 10, 1932, by Otto Meissner," *Nachlass Hindenburg*, vol. X, No. 12, reprinted in Walther Hubatsch, *Hindenburg und der Staat: Aus den Papieren des Generalfeldmarschalls und Reichspräsidenten von 1878 bis 1934* (Göttingen: Musterschmidt Verlag, 1966), p. 328. (Hereafter cited: *Hubatsch*).

[32] Otto Schmidt-Hannover, *Umdenken oder Anarchie: Männer, Schicksale, Lehren* (Göttingen: Göttinger Verlaganstalt, 1959), p. 366.

[33] Franz von Papen, *Vom Scheitern einer Demokratie 1930 - 1933* (Mainz: V. Hase & Köhler Verlag, 1968), p. 191.

[34] Ibid.

[35] Papen, *Memoirs*, p. 151.

[36] Ibid. Papen criticized the list system of voting, which he maintained "corrupted the very basis of a healthy democracy." He believed that an individual party member was more responsible to the party committee than to the constituency that elected him. Papen is correct in pointing out that this system gave rise to far too many political parties. But the constant bickering that characterized German politics in the 1920's stemmed from other causes that were only indirectly related the question of proportional representation.

[37] Ibid., p 152.

[38] Ibid.

[39] Ibid., p. 154.

[40] Ibid.

[41] Ibid., p. 155.

[42] Ibid.

[43] Ibid.

[44] Ibid.

[45] Ibid., p. 160.

[46] Magnus von Braun, *Durch vier Zeitepochen: Vom ostprüssischen Gutslebender Väter bis zur Weltraumforschung des Sohnes*, 3rd. ed. revised (Limburg/a.d.Lahm: C. A. Starke Verlag, 1965), p. 226.

[47] *Vorwärts*, June 3, 1932

[48] *Kölnische Volkzeitung*, June 1, 1932.

[49] *Germania*, June 1, 1932.

[50] *Junge Nation*, June 9, 1932.

[51] *Die Lokalanzeiger*, June 1, 1932.

[52] *Tägliche Rundschau*, June 2, 1932.

[53] Erwein von Aretin, *Krone und Ketten: Errinnerungen eines bayrischen Edelmannes*, eds. Karl Bucheim u. Karl Otmar v. Aretin (München: Süddeutscher Verlag, 1955), p. 1109.

[54] Harry Klemens Ulrich Graf Kessler, *Tagebücher 1918-1937*, ed. Wolfgang Pfeiffer-Belli (Frankfurt am Main: Insel Verlag, 1961), p. 671. Count Harry Kessler was the son of a Hamburg banker who had been ennobled by Kaiser Wilhelm I. He was a member of the Uhlan Guards and fought in Belgium and on the eastern front in World War I. A skilled diplomat and something of an intriguer, but also a collector and patron of art, Kessler's diary is a remarkable portrait of personalities, issues, and events in Berlin in the 1920's. He left Germany in 1933, and died in France on December 4, 1837, at the age of 69.

[55] Andre François-Poncet, *Souvenirs d'une ambassade a Berlin Septembre 1931 - Octobre 1938* (Paris: Flammarion, 1946), p. 42.

[56] "Report of 9 June 1932, by Sir Horace Rumbold to Sir John Simon," No.129. E. L. Woodward & Rohan Butler, eds. *Documents on British Foreign Policy, 1919-1929*. Second Series, Vol. III, p. 166 (Hereafter cited: *DBFP*).

[57] *Memoirs*, p. 156.

[58] Joseph Joos, *So Sah ich sie* (Augsburg: Verlag Winfried-Werk, 1958), p. 96. Rudolf Morsey, "*Deutsche Zentrumspartei*," in *Das Ende der Parteien 1933*, ed. Erich Matthias/Rudolf Morsey (Düsseldorf: Droste Verlag, 1979), p. 307, note 6.

[59] *Memoirs*, p. 158.

[60] Resolution of June 1, 1932, by the *Parteivorstand* of the Center Party. Cited in Morsey, "*Die Deutsche Zentrumspartei*," p. 308.

[61] Letter of Papen to Kaas. Reprinted in *Berliner Tageblatt*, June 2, 1932.

[62] "*Kaas antwortet Papen*," *Berliner Tageblatt*, June 3, 1932.

[63] Morsey, "*Die Deutsche Zentrumspartei*," p. 308, n. 12.

[64] Hitler was confident that in a new election he would increase his *Reichstag* representation beyond its existing 107 seats, and the president would be forced to call on him to form a government.

[65] Joseph Goebbels, *Vom Kaiserhof zur Reichskanzlei: Eine historische Darstellung in Tagebuchblättern vom 1. Januar 1932 bis zum 1. Mai 1933* (Munich: Zentralverlag der NSDAP, Franz Eber Nachf., 1934), p. 106.

[66] If nothing else, this explanation reveals how easy it had become for the palace *camarilla* to pull the wool over the aging Hindenburg's eyes!

[67] "*Will Hitler ohne Papen regieren? Strasser über die Wahlziele der Nationalsozialisten*," *Vossische Zeitung*, June 5, 1932.

[68] *Memoirs*, p. 162.

[69] Ibid.

[70] Memorandum of June 12, by Otto Meissner, reprinted in Hubatsch, *Nachlass Hindenburg*, pp. 332-335.

[71] Friedrich Fischbein, "Diary," *Kleine Erwerbungen*, 295/194, Bundesarchiv, Koblenz.

[72] Fischbein, ibid.

[73] Memorandum of June 12, 1932, by Otto Meissner. Reprinted in Hubatsch, ibid., pp. 332-335.

[74] Hubatsch, p. 334.

[75] "*Niederschrift Dr. Meissner*", June 12, 1932, MA-87, *Institut für Zeitgeschichte* (Hereafter cited: *IfZg*).

[76] Cabinet Session June 13, 1932, 4:30 P.M., *RKz*, 43 I/154, BA, Koblenz.

[77] Cabinet Session June 14, 1932, *RKz*, R 43 I/1546, BA, Koblenz.

[78] *Augsburger Postzeitung*, June 18, 1932. In Bavaria the prohibition caused a tumultuous scene in the *Landtag* on June 17. When the Nazi delegation attended the session in full uniform, Georg Stang, the presiding president, asked them to leave. When they refused, he adjourned the session. Upon its resumption, the Nazi delegation, now dressed in civilian clothes, returned to the chamber and started to heap abuse on Stang. Their leaders, Julius Streicher and Hermann Esser were ejected by the police.

CHAPTER 5:
PINSTRIPE DIPLOMACY

A. Off to Lausanne

As Papen settled back in the seat of his private compartment, he reflected on the importance of his mission in Lausanne.[1] If there was any one issue on which the German population was united, it was their dislike for the harsh terms of the Versailles Treaty, especially its punitive reparations and war guilt clauses. Spurred on by the inflammatory rhetoric of Hitler and pressures from the German Nationalists, Papen recalled how public outrage over the Versailles "*Diktat*" mounted as the economic conditions deteriorated, and how the Nazis had exploited the crisis so that by 1930, they became the second largest delegation in the *Reichstag*. The Chancellor remembered his first meeting with the Nazi leader and how this "Bohemian corporal" told him that he regarded his (Papen's) cabinet as a "temporary solution." With the *Reichstag* elections set for July 31, Papen was well aware that if he failed in Lausanne, the Nazis would charge his government - as they had every regime in the past - with failing to restore German honor by repudiating the Versailles Treaty. He also realized that Lausanne offered him the opportunity for increasing his popularity at home. With this increased support, he was confident that his government could "take the wind out of Hitler's sails."[2]

As the train sped towards the Swiss border, Papen reviewed the notes he jotted down at the cabinet meetings prior to leaving Berlin. Like his predecessor Brüning, Papen was anxious to obtain complete cancellation of Germany's obligation to pay reparations to the victorious nations.[3] More importantly, he wanted to "reach agreements with the outside world which would permit what could best be called the moral rearmament of Germany."[4] He dreamed of the day when the causes of Germany's "inferiority complex" would be removed, and his country could "play its true part in the peaceful development of Europe." The only way this could be accomplished was to convince the Allied Powers of Germany's genuine desire to cooperate, and devise some peaceful way of removing the discriminatory clauses of the Versailles Treaty. Papen's list of grievances included what he considered to be "the deprivation of many attributes of sovereignty," [viz.] "...the limitations placed on defensive armaments, the defenselessness of the Rhineland, the corridor that cut off East Prussia from the Reich, the international control of the Saarland, and above all paragraph 231 of the Versailles Treaty, the 'war guilt' clause." As far as Papen was concerned "the reparations problem was largely incidental."[5]

In order to prepare himself more thoroughly for the conference, Papen had with him a rather bulky document entitled "Comments and Plans of Foreign Nations in the Reparations Question."[6] This report contained excerpts from newspaper interviews, speeches in the House of Commons, and public pronouncements by prominent British statesmen and economists. Of particular interest to Papen were the statements of economist John Maynard Keynes and former British prime minister Lloyd George. Both men strongly advocated cancellation of the reparations, and the abrogation of the war guilt clause in return for certain political concessions by Germany.[7]

The documents also included statements by the current Prime Minister, J. Ramsay MacDonald, who headed the British delegation in Lausanne. MacDonald also favored the ideas of Lloyd George and Keynes. Among his reasons was his desire to lessen the tensions between Germany and France, which he feared might escalate into another war. In order to accomplish this, MacDonald intended to propose the abrogation of the "war guilt" clause, which would reduce German antagonisms against France. However, in order to achieve this, MacDonald realized that the Conference would have to address the question of French security. Therefore he intended to propose a fifteen-year political truce, in which no political questions touching the interests of the signatories could be reopened without that nation's consent.[8]

Armed with this information, Papen regarded the British position as a favorable sign that could work to his advantage. Papen also felt that the recent elections in France, in which the Left, who had returned to power, favored a revision of the Versailles Treaty. The new premier, Edouard Herriot, seemed eager to set European affairs off on a new footing, and his previous record on that score was impressive.[9] However, Papen failed to understand Herriot's precarious political position. For one thing, the French Premier's coalition government could be easily defeated by his vocal right wing opponents. Moreover, previous governments had included reparation payments in their budgets. Should Herriot agree to cancellation, he would have to find new sources of revenue through new taxes or loans. He knew that this would never be acceptable to the conservatives, much less to the taxpayers.[10] Therefore, like every other French political figure, Herriot was forced to insist on reparations for France.

Another problem that Papen failed to understand was the position of the United States. The United States refused to "wipe the slate clean" or even scale down the payments owed by the Allies.[11] No American politician was willing to saddle the American public with financing a European war. Clearly, any settlement would have to take the American position into account.

In spite of these difficulties, which would tax the abilities of even the most accomplished diplomat, Papen felt confident that he could meet the challenges. After all, did he not represent the German national forces of concentration, and therefore speak for the Right? He also believed that his French family ties, and his long-standing association with a French-German Study Group were additional assets.[12] Finally, if these advantages were insufficient, he was convinced that the compelling needs stemming from the international financial crisis would dictate no other choice but cancellation.

Although Papen was a man of charm, a gifted speaker, and clever negotiator, his personal style of diplomacy at Lausanne is open to question. In part, this was due to his impulsive nature. Unlike the cautious Brüning, Papen lacked the patience required of a diplomat. Instead of moving around an obstacle, the ex-cavalry officer's tendency was to try and hurdle it, often without regard to consequences. Characteristically, Papen appeared to be unaffected in the face of these obstacles.

Another shortcoming was Papen's conviction that diplomacy could be carried on through the press. While some of his capricious remarks to the press made good copy, they also served to place him in awkward negotiating positions. In an effort to extricate himself, he would often resort to abrupt reversals of policy, even ignoring the advice of his own delegation. Not only did these sudden shifts irritate the British and increase French doubts about German sincerity, but they also weakened his credibility at home.

The German delegation arrived in Lausanne on June 15, 1932.[13] Located on the northern shore of Lake Geneva, this favorite retreat of exiled royalty, and the haunt of famous European men of letters (Voltaire, Victor Hugo, Rousseau and Dickens), rivaled Geneva as the intellectual and cultural center of French Switzerland. Lausanne was also the site of several international conferences, the last one occurring in 1922-23 between the Turkish Republic and the World War I Allies.

In what was to become one of a number of political "gaffs," Papen left his delegation to register at the Beau Rivage Hotel, and drove directly to the press headquarters. He did not even bother to contact other foreign dignitaries first. Anxious to gain public support for his position, Papen told the correspondents that Germany pinned its hopes on the conference, and he "asked for the objective support of the world's organs of public opinion."[14] While this unorthodox tactic made for good headlines, it did little to ingratiate him with the British and French delegations. However, this was not the only time that Papen's impulsive actions would irritate the French and British delegation. Later encounters with the press made this action pale in comparison.

The formal inauguration of the conference took place in the banquet hall of Hotel Beau Rivage on the morning of June 16. Prime Minister J. Ramsay MacDonald gave an eloquent speech calling for cooperation among all nations. He emphasized the urgency of finding a solution to the economic crisis: "The whole world looks to us, as it has never looked to an international conference before, to find agreements which will help to put an end to its existing distress." While speedy action was essential, MacDonald requested that the delegates acknowledge the principle that "engagements solemnly entered into cannot be set aside by unilateral repudiation." The British Prime Minister then added that this principle carried with it an important corollary, viz. "if default is to be avoided, engagements which have been proved incapable of fulfillment should be revised by agreement."[15] This was a clear indictment of the current reparations policy, and indicated that the British favored cancellation.

Shortly after the first session adjourned, Papen paid a visit to the French Premier. The German Chancellor expressed his hopes for the conference and suggested that the moment had arrived for complete cancellation of reparations. Herriot voiced his disagreement with this abrupt proposal, but indicated his "readiness" to find a reasonable solution to the problem.[16] Papen interpreted Herriot's remarks to mean that rapprochement with the French was feasible. Determined to press for a radical revision of the Versailles Treaty - abrogation of the reparations and removal of the "war guilt" clause - Papen felt justified in continuing his efforts to bring about a reconciliation.[17] What the Chancellor either failed to recognize, or refused to acknowledge, was that even if Herriot was willing to negotiate a compromise, his political constituency would never permit him to agree to a complete cancellation of reparations.[18]

In the second plenary session, a favorable impression was created when it was decided to postpone all payments until the conclusion of the conference in July. In his opening speech, which he delivered in French instead of German, Papen applauded this decision, "as the first visible proof of the firm determination of the Powers concerned to facilitate the work of the Conference and to take those comprehensive and final decisions which the present situation demands." He then stated that Germany would not argue its case "on purely legal grounds, or question the validity of earlier international agreements."[19] It was his intention, he declared, to consider the realities which confronted Europe and the world and to derive from them certain incontrovertible lessons. Papen followed this with a brief but impressive description of the deleterious effects of the depression on the German economy, and the depressing psychological effects on the German population who, he warned, were losing confidence in the capitalistic system. Arguing that the crisis was in large measure due to the reparations payments, Papen called for immediate steps to be taken , "to rescue the world from total catastrophe." He concluded his remarks with the observation that "the time for palliative, respites and postponements is finally past. We want to serve as an equal partner in the reconstruction of a unified and peaceful Europe."[20]

Delivered with moderation and clarity, Papen's speech left a favorable impression on the assembled delegates. One French newspaper commented that, "if Papen understands the French as well as he speaks French, the prospects for agreement are excellent."[21] But as things turned out, Papen's talent for diplomacy did not match his oratorical skills.

The optimism generated by Papen's speech was quickly dispelled by the French premier's rebuttal. Herriot took issue with Papen's claim that cancellation would not place Germany in a favorable competitive position. Supporting his arguments with statistics, Herriot pointed out that the elimination of reparations would reduce the capital charges of the German railways in comparison to the French and British railways, and this would result in considerable reductions in the rates of transported goods. The German coal industry would also benefit since the weight was high in proportion to the value, therefore making it possible to reduce coal prices by as much as 15 to 25% as compared with the present prices.[22] Furthermore, this proposal would place undue burdens on the French budget by canceling the receipts without doing the same for debts. Citing the "Basel Report," the French premier rejected the argument that Germany's present incapacity to pay precluded her future ability to do so.[23] Herriot concluded his remarks with the declaration that France, "without passion or prejudice, but with the most sincere desire for European fraternity, derives...the opinion that the cancellation of reparations would constitute no effective or fair solution...In our view it is a mistake to imagine that the cancellation, even outright, of reparations would bring about a return to the desired equilibrium."[24]

While the opening speeches revealed the differences between the negotiating parties, their tone was moderate. No provocative declarations of unalterable policy were made even though the tacit positions were understood. Nevertheless, MacDonald realized that little progress would be accomplished in general sessions, therefore, it was agreed that after a short adjournment, private meetings between the British, French and German delegations would be more beneficial in resolving the Franco-German impasse. If and when the differences could be ironed out, there would be a final plenary conference to ratify what had been previously decided in these private sessions.

B. The Bargaining Table

The first series of meetings between the British and French began in the second week of the conference. MacDonald reiterated his position that the simplest resolution of the impasse was to cancel reparations. He also told Herriot that any "political difficulties" resulting from cancellation could be resolved by reaching "understandings" on other issues, viz., good trade and armaments agreements. Herriot replied that, "there was no French Government, not one, which would support before the chambers the thesis of cancellation."[25]

Later on that same day, MacDonald met with Papen and Neurath and informed them that the other delegations expected Germany to give something. Papen rejected the notion of any form of payment, declaring that this would be tantamount to asking his people to work in order that the surplus of their labor should be given to other people: "If we are to pay from normal balances, there is no inducement to work." Papen also told MacDonald that his government "was probably the last bourgeois Government likely to hold power in Germany," and then he warned, "If we returned home without achieving any success, we would be succeeded by the extremists, either of the left or of the right."[26] MacDonald replied that he appreciated Papen's predicament, and assured the Chancellor that he would press for cancellation. However, he added that if the French position called for a compromise, he would have to accede.[27]

The next day, June 21, Papen sent a memo to MacDonald summarizing the German opposition to any final payment to her creditors. Papen added that, in his opinion, the world crisis was mainly due to the lack of trust occasioned by the many "unsuccessful" attempts in the past to "realize obligations which were not the result of economic events." Papen promised that his government would be willing to contribute to the "rapid realization of satisfactory solutions in related areas" (i.e., the issues of trade, disarmament, etc.) if the Allied Powers would agree to abandon the notion of reparations. He concluded by outlining several areas in which Germany would cooperate: (1) German participation in all financial and economic measures for the reconstruction of Europe; (2) maintaining armaments within the framework of a five-year disarmament convention; and (3) contribute to the lessening of tensions in Europe by entering into a consultative pact between France, Germany, Italy and Great Britain for the purpose of ensuring French security.[28]

The idea of Franco-German friendship had always been one of Papen's obsessions, and now he thought "the time seemed ripe" to take some practical steps.[29] The German Chancellor believed that a consultative pact would relieve French fears that Germany might threaten her security. In return, the German Chancellor hoped to obtain cancellation of reparations, equality in armaments, and the removal of Article 231 - the "war guilt" clause - in the Versailles Treaty. Papen also hoped that such a pact would be the forerunner of an alliance between France and Germany, but he realized that "public opinion in both countries was not ready for this."[30]

While Papen's insistence that the only way to resolve the impasse was through a political solution and not by an economic settlement, the French delegation rejected this proposal. In spite of these differences, MacDonald continued to hold out hopes that some resolution was possible. MacDonald met again with the French premier who told him that as far as he was concerned, the conference had failed. Unwilling to give up, MacDonald urged the French premier to make one more effort to break the deadlock. If this failed, the matter would be turned over to the Bureau of Invited States (Japan, Italy, and Belgium). Unwilling to submit the question to this body, Herriot suggested that a fixed sum or ("*forfait*") would be acceptable to him. Once agreement was reached between them on the principle of a fixed sum, the German, French and British ministers of finance could decide on the method of payment. MacDonald replied that if "fixed sum" meant the continuation of the present methods of payment, his government could not agree with it; but if it meant a lasting settlement for the future, there was hope of an agreement.[31] The meeting concluded on this note.

Two days later, on June 23, the two delegations re-convened, and the French Finance Minister, Louis Germain-Martin, sought to clarify what the French meant by a fixed sum. Without stating any amount, he defined it in theoretical terms as a payment in money that should not endanger the collapse of Germany on the one hand, nor should it threaten France because of her payments to the United States.[32] As an example, Germain-Martin suggested that Germany's railways were almost completely debt-free, and therefore were ideally suited for the creation of bonds up to the total or partial values of the railways' assets. He concluded with a warning that if the British were unwilling to go along with the idea of a fixed sum, Europe would see a general collapse of credit because the French refused to go along with cancellation. With these harsh words ringing in their ears, the delegates adjourned for a brief recess.[33] When the meeting reconvened, MacDonald stated that if the French could get the Germans to agree to the fixed sum "in a private understanding," his government would "be quite willing to accept it."[34] MacDonald then urged Herriot to arrange a meeting with the German delegation as soon as possible.

The importance of the British willingness to consider the idea of a fixed sum was not lost on Papen. For one thing, it would mean that if MacDonald went along with the French proposal, Germany's demands for cancellation of all reparations would go up in smoke, and this could spell political defeat for Papen's government in the forthcoming *Reichstag* elections. It would also mean that his efforts to create a more friendly atmosphere between Germany and France would be shattered, and therefore any hope of achieving equality of arms or a repudiation of Article 231 in the Versailles Treaty would be ended. Faced with possible defeat, the German Chancellor resorted to his own personal style of diplomacy. Over the objections of Under Secretary of State von Bülow, Papen met the French Premier on Friday morning on June 24, about an hour before the two delegations were scheduled to resume discussions. It was their first private meeting since Papen's arrival in Lausanne.[35]

Papen opened the discussion with the offer to grant France economic and political compensations, including support for a joint Franco-German program of economic revitalization of southern Europe, if the French abandoned all claims to reparations. Then, to Herriot's complete amazement, the German Chancellor proposed a military alliance which would include continuous contact between the general staffs of both armies. Next, Papen suggested that "on the basis of reciprocity, French General Staff officers should be allowed access to all the departments of our General Staff. France would then be informed of all German military matters."[36] He also submitted a memorandum calling for a "consultative pact," in which Germany promised not to take any action regarding revision of its eastern borders or an *Anschluss* with Austria, without consulting France: it could function as a "kind of Locarno."[37] In return for this pact, Papen wanted all the powers represented at Lausanne to pass a resolution canceling paragraph 231 of the Versailles Treaty, specifying Germany's war guilt.[38]

The German offer of a bilateral military alliance between two nations who had quarreled for centuries, and were a constant threat to European peace, was in itself a generous - almost magnanimous - offer. But was Papen's proposal all that sincere?[39] Like most Frenchmen, Herriot did not have complete confidence in the alleged German desire for reconciliation, especially while arrogant German nationalists, some of whom supported Papen's government, were singing another song. Moreover, Herriot was quite aware that Papen's domestic position was precarious. Enjoying practically no public support, Papen kept himself in office only through dissolution of the *Reichstag*, the backing he received from an aging president, and the uncertain tactics of a few generals. Under these circumstances, how could Papen's generous proposal guarantee French security? Was it not one of those maneuvers that made Bismarck wonder: "Who is fooling whom here?"[40] Therefore, when the delegations met later that morning, the French declared that they were unable to agree to cancellation, and requested the German delegates to present an offer which might serve as the basis for a discussion of a fixed sum. Since the German delegation was unwilling to consider this request, the meeting broke up on a negative note.

Even if Papen's private offer to Herriot was motivated by the well-intentioned desire to reach some agreement with the French on a broader basis than reparations, his next diplomatic *faux pas* destroyed any hopes of accomplishing that goal. As the delegations filed out of the conference room, Herriot and Papen met separately with the press. Herriot contended himself with the cryptic remark from the Lorelei song that "the air is cool but not dark." Papen's interview, on the other hand, proved to be as startling as his private offer to the French premier. Speaking with the French newspaperman Stephen Lauzanne, the German chancellor remarked that, while the time was not yet ripe for a military alliance between France and Germany, it was the goal of his foreign policy and therefore, the Lausanne conference could serve as a successful beginning.[41] Caught up in the vortex of his own rhetoric, the Chancellor indiscreetly added that he was the first person "to acknowledge France's right to compensation for the renunciation of reparations." He then boasted, "France need have no fear about

Germany's good faith because unlike Brüning, I represent all of the national forces of Germany."[42]

While Papen hoped that his statements to the French journalist would "rally French public opinion," he failed to reckon with the storm of protest they raised in Berlin. News of his interview was published in the German press, and when Papen arrived in Berlin, he was greeted with headlines in the right wing press flatly denying that Papen spoke for them. The *Deutsche Allgemeine Zeitung* charged Papen with laying the onus of making proposals on Germany and therefore, had placed his nation in an unfavorable bargaining position: "The Chancellor is wrong in saying that all Germany would endorse his signature. Germany would not follow him on this path."[43] The *Deutsche Tageszeitung* acidly commented that Papen's references to reparations "are not what national Germany expects from a national chancellor." Realizing his blunder, Papen issued a denial in the German press questioning the truthfulness of Lauzanne's account. If he thought that this would end the matter, Papen was sadly mistaken. Lauzanne replied to Papen's charges with a public claim that he could defend every word of the interview. Disregarding the possible negative repercussions his statements to the press might have provoked, the Chancellor stubbornly refused to admit he was wrong. He issued a second denial, but Lauzanne now challenged Papen to publish his version of what had been discussed. This time Papen declined to respond, leaving it to the public relations office to defuse the issue through an evasive reply.

Meanwhile in Paris, Herriot met with "severe opposition" from the right who charged him with betraying French interests. However, when the French premier put the alternative of reparations payments or compensations to his cabinet with the appeal that Franco-German reconciliation was better than a "mere money payment," his cabinet accepted this interpretation. Even the influential and normally anti-German *Temps* stated that the principle of reparations should be upheld, but if compensation meant "certain common agreements or an agreement as the starting point of genuine economic cooperation," continued negotiations might be worth the effort.[44]

On Monday, June 27, Herriot and Papen were back in Lausanne. However, the German chancellor's diplomatic "gaffe" had altered the entire atmosphere of the conference. Still smarting from the attacks of the Right resulting from the Lauzanne interview, Papen shifted his stand. Conferring with Herriot that same afternoon, the French premier found the German chancellor "in quite a different mood." Herriot told MacDonald later that Papen "said nothing except that Germany could not pay any further reparations." With regard to compensations, which they had discussed the previous Friday, Papen spoke vaguely of certain kinds of aid for Central Europe and some minor advantages for Hungarian and Rumanian wheat.[45] Herriot, who had returned with his cabinet's support to seek reconciliation, was completely bewildered at Papen's change of heart, and confessed that their negotiations had broken down. Reluctantly both men agreed to meet one last time on the following day.

Following this meeting, MacDonald met separately with the two leaders. Soon after Herriot departed, Papen met with the British leader and recounted his earlier discussion with Herriot. The German chancellor told MacDonald that he had spoken "plainly" of complete cancellation because the German delegation would not consider any alternative. Papen also told the Prime Minister that he "had done all he could to clear away the obstacles between France and Germany, even in the face of domestic criticism."[46] MacDonald then asked whether it was true that the Chancellor had proposed a Franco-German military alliance as "security?" Papen responded that he had, and then quickly added, "but the idea was, of course, preposterous whether in France or Germany...he had been misrepresented."[47] Then the German chancellor blamed the French journalist for publishing the interview in which, Papen told MacDonald, "he had attributed to me [Papen] all sorts of statements as to what had been promised in compensation to France..."[48] By trying to place all of the blame on Lauzanne, Papen hoped to avoid risking the loss of British support for Germany's demands. In point of fact, however, Papen had proposed a military understanding, which Herriot was asked not to repeat to MacDonald. Therefore, by telling MacDonald the alliance suggested by the press was "preposterous," Papen was either deceiving the French or MacDonald. Regardless of how one wishes to interpret his statements, Papen's indiscreet interview had placed him in an awkward situation, out of which he tried to extricate himself by a bold denial that he had ever made such an offer.[49]

Meanwhile, exasperated with Papen's attitude, the British Prime Minister reproached him for the offer of an alliance as well as his habit of giving press interviews which, he warned, increased the obstacles to finding reasonable solutions. When both men had cooled down,

MacDonald broached the subject of final payment in return for the elimination of all reparations. As an example, he suggested that Germany issue a certain number of bonds which would not be redeemable until German securities on the open market were quoted at par. Then Germany could redeem the bonds either by a single payment or by the operation of a sinking fund. Furthermore, the payments could go directly into a European pool, and this would be Germany's "contribution" to the economic revival of Europe.

The German chancellor was interested in MacDonald's proposal, but he countered with his own version of a compromise, viz., that some parts of the Treaty of Versailles must be "wiped out" and matters must be "cleared up" with regard to certain questions of disarmament. "If these conditions could be met, why should they not reach an agreement?" MacDonald replied that as far as he was concerned, Papen was "pushing at an open door."[50]

Papen's bid to improve Franco-German relations by cutting "through the maze of diplomatic niceties" were probably motivated by good intentions. However, his characteristic tendency to act precipitously with little preparation resulted in damaging his own cause. From this point on, the discussions revealed Herriot's increasing mistrust of the German chancellor, while MacDonald's attitude was reflected in his attempts to cement Franco-British ties at Germany's expense. Therefore, if it had been Papen's intention to drive a wedge between Britain and France, he had unwittingly produced the opposite result. Papen also discovered that the French premier's initial interest in a consultative pact faded, and that he would not accept any "political" clauses in the final agreement.

Despite Papen's change of heart and Herriot's aroused suspicions, MacDonald still held out hopes for a compromise. After speaking separately with both delegations, the Prime Minister requested a three-way meeting on the following day, June 28.

This meeting not only revealed Papen's changed position, but also Herriot's distrust for political agreements with Germany, stating that confidence, not documents, was necessary for political peace. Herriot also rejected Papen's proposals for a common fund for assistance to financially depressed countries, equality of armament rights, and a consultative pact in which no questions interesting other cosigners could be discussed without prior consultation with all of them. Declaring that France was only interested in the payment question, the

French premier said that there were only two solutions to the reparations problem: either a fixed sum, or by an arrangement between France and Germany based on economic and political compensations. He concluded by announcing that he was ready to accept either one or the other, but to discuss anything else was a waste of time.[51]

Later that same day, the delegations reconvened. MacDonald requested the German delegation to state under what conditions they would accept a fixed sum. Foreign Minister von Neurath repeated the conditions discussed in the morning session: (1) complete cancellation of reparations; (2) an international monetary settlement as part of a constructive plan for world reorganization, which implied the establishment of a common fund; and (3) a settlement of Disarmament on the basis of equality of rights.[52]

MacDonald then introduced the question of the relationship between reparations and war debts. Papen and Neurath argued that Germany never recognized this relationship, and emphasized that German confidence could never be restored if the settlement was contingent upon American assent. The British and French delegations rejected this argument out of hand. Unable to resolve their differences on this point, the discussions moved to the more difficult question of final payment. It was over this question that disagreement was most acute.

Herriot bluntly charged the Germans with a contradictory attitude towards payment. On the one hand Germany argued that she was unable to pay either at the present or in the future. Now she was prepared to contribute to a common fund if her political and disarmament terms were met at Lausanne. In effect, Herriot concluded, the Germans were contradicting their previous thesis concerning her inability to pay.[53] Papen weakly responded that Germany was willing to help reconstruct Europe, but he would pay no more tribute. In either case, Germany could pay nothing at the present. He then added that disarmament was included only "as a means of clearing up the whole situation," since admittedly Germany "had little to offer."[54]

Exasperated over this argument, Herriot said he understood how Papen could "take account of German feelings." But to argue that Germany's demand for disarmament in return for final payment was what a French deputy or peasant wanted, was absurd. The French premier was irritated with the German Chancellor's disingenuous arguments and his underestimation of Herriot's ability to see through such fallacious arguments.

At this point in the meeting, the delegations agreed with Neville Chamberlain, the British Chancellor of the Exchequer, who suggested that progress was more probable if they concentrated their attention on three matters: the fixed sum, economic compensations and security. While the discussions were more amiable, the results were equally unsatisfactory. By the end of this session, the positions lined up as follows: Herriot believed that disarmament was not on the Lausanne agenda and that Germany's compensations were inadequate; MacDonald and Chamberlain also thought that the disarmament issue did not belong in the Lausanne deliberations; Papen thought that the "essential object of Lausanne was to wipe out the various discriminations against Germany under the Versailles Treaty." He argued that if a final payment were made, "that would help clear up the situation but...why could not Disarmament be settled in Lausanne under a friendly agreement with France?"[55] Shortly after this meeting, Papen met with Herriot in a private conversation and agreed to the idea of a fixed sum as a means of resolving the impasse over reparations.

Following his meeting with Herriot, Papen returned to his quarters with a heavy heart. He realized that his efforts to include political agreements in the final settlement had suffered a serious blow. Papen blamed MacDonald for Herriot's refusal to consider his proposals.[56] However, the records of the conference indicate that it was the German Chancellor's diplomatic "blunders" and his sudden, unprepared shifts of position that had caused the French premier to become disenchanted with the idea of any political conditions. Moreover, in spite of MacDonald's efforts to bring about an accord between the French and German delegations, it was Papen's stubborn insistence that political guarantees be attached to any final payment that continued to plague the discussions and even threatened to undermine the conference.

Meanwhile, believing that Papen was resigned to the idea of a final payment, MacDonald decided that the determination of the amount to be paid and the method of payment could best be accomplished if the other invited powers - Belgium, Italy and Japan - were requested to join the discussions. Therefore, with the approval of the German and French delegations, a committee was established with one representative from each country, and the meetings began the following afternoon, June 29.

The Bureau of Inviting Powers focused on the amount and method of payment. Differences immediately surfaced over the question of "contingencies" resulting from subsequent unsatisfactory agreements with the United States over war debts. MacDonald informed German finance minister Krosigk, that the solution to German debts without agreement with the United States would place the British and French at the unfair disadvantage of renouncing their credits, while remaining in debt to their creditors. Fearing that domestic public opinion would not accept this explanation, the German delegation informed MacDonald that it was withdrawing from further meetings of the Bureau. However, Papen yielded on this point after MacDonald assured him that the probable economic situation would prevent any increase in Germany's contribution should ratification not be secured.[57]

The problem of the amount was not so easily settled. During the weekend of July 2, after a series of meetings with the British delegation, the French hesitantly agreed to the sum of four billion *Reichsmarks*.[58] Later that day, when the Bureau of the Inviting Powers met, Georges Bonnet officially announced France's acceptance of this amount.[59]

Meanwhile, Papen realized that, since cancellation was out of the question, the German delegation faced an important decision. Should they maintain a firm attitude, break off the conference, and return home empty-handed; or would it be better to return with some modest achievements? Papen knew that any sum granted would provoke a storm of protest from his opponents at home. The left wing parties would claim that Brüning would have achieved a big success in the circumstances, and that the failure at Lausanne was due to the incompetence of the Papen government. The Chancellor was afraid that "...All this would have had its effect on the elections due to take place at the end of July."[60] If he was to gain any popular support for the Lausanne agreements, Papen knew that the final amount granted must be small, and that political concessions must also be included. After a lengthy discussion it was decided to stay and negotiate for the best possible agreement, and hope that future developments would provide Papen's government with fresh opportunities to achieve a more satisfactory settlement.

Domestic politics was not the only issue that influenced Papen's decision to bargain for a lower payment and political guarantees. Throughout the course of the negotiations, Papen kept the cabinet informed of the issues and proposals. When Berlin received word of the proposed four billion-mark payment, several cabinet ministers opposed Papen's rejection of the offer claiming that Germany could pay that amount.[61] This split became even sharper as negotiations proceeded, and played an important part in Papen's determination to include political guarantees in the final agreement.

On Sunday morning, July 3, 1932, MacDonald met with the German delegation, and told them that he had been authorized by the Bureau to propose the figure of four billion *Reichsmarks*, "nearly half what could have been offered a fortnight ago." Papen replied that he was "very grateful for the way in which the question had been handled," but wondered how the German people would react to such a settlement. The chancellor said there was a limit to what he could or could not do, and added that "if some way could be found to make it definite, he could sign an agreement to pay two billion *Reichsmarks*."[62] Finally, when the negotiations resumed after a long recess, Papen informed MacDonald that he could not accept the figure of four billion. Once again, political pressures had influenced Papen's decision. He begged MacDonald to imagine his position, stating that he had come to Lausanne with the conviction that they could not pay a penny, and now he was willing to pay a share. Papen recalled that Brüning had always maintained that Germany could not pay. If the German people now discovered that his Government had done no better, "it would be knocked out, both by the Left and by the Right. The scheme," Papen concluded, "could never get through the *Reichstag*."[63]

After discussing Papen's rejection of the four billion mark payment with the Bureau, MacDonald met privately with the French on the morning of July 5. The British prime minister informed Herriot, who had just returned from Paris where he was busy drawing up the new French budget, that the German delegation had rejected the four billion sum for "political reasons," but were willing to consider the sum of two billion *Reichsmarks*. Herriot testily replied that he too had "political considerations." He informed the British minister that his Government was in danger of falling because he had been obliged to introduce a finance bill requiring the French taxpayers to cover the Hoover annuity which the Germans were refusing to cover.[64] And then he skeptically remarked that the Germans would not pay in any circumstances, and therefore the conference was going through a great deal of trouble to secure a signature that was worthless. However,

MacDonald eventually persuaded Herriot to meet with Papen and explain why he could not go below four billion.[65]

Before the French and German delegations reconvened, MacDonald hastened to see Papen with a statement upon which he wanted the Lausanne conference to agree. This statement was the same one he had proposed to Herriot, and contained six points: (1) a resolution that reparations were at an end and consequently Article 231 was dead; (2) a desire to reach a disarmament agreement at Geneva equitable towards all; (3) a general agreement on currency was desired in the future; (4) the birth of a new spirit of co-operation among the European powers; (5) an agreement of the Six Inviting Powers that no political question affecting the interests and arising out of treaties to which they were a party should be raised involving two or more of them without prior consultation; (6) the post war period was finally declared closed.[66]

The German chancellor was impressed with this offer and declared his willingness to agree to a figure "rather above" two billion if Germany received suitable concessions on disarmament. Papen then telegraphed the contents of this offer to Berlin. Although he had insisted up to this point that Germany could not pay more than two billion *Reichsmarks*, Papen apparently had a change of heart after his meeting with MacDonald. He now recommended an offer of 2.6 billion R.M. as suggested by Sir Walter Layton, editor of the British journal, "The Economist." Papen also wired that the "political terms" were generally acceptable, although he had argued for a tightening of the ambiguous wording regarding the war guilt clause.[67] After virtually no discussion, the cabinet forwarded its reaction to Papen's telegram.

That same afternoon Papen met with MacDonald and submitted his cabinet's proposals. They called for a 2.6 billion R.M. payment under the following conditions: (1) all mention of war guilt and the origin of reparations, not limited exclusively to Article 231, must be renounced; (2) the principle of equality is to govern future disarmament conferences; (3) German sovereignty must prevail over the *Reichsbank* and the German Railway Company. The proposal also contained several stipulations concerning the sale of the bonds.[68] MacDonald did not think that 2.6 billion would "bridge the gap," and asked Papen to accept three billion since "it would put matters in a much smoother position." In reply to Papen's reference of the terrible German economic distress, MacDonald pointed out that Germany would not pay anything until their economic situation had changed. "Surely the moment had come," MacDonald pleaded, "when the two sides should agree to split the difference." Papen replied, "it was always Germany which was asked to undertake everything."[69]

When MacDonald met with the French delegation later that afternoon, Herriot angrily stated that he would accept no political conditions: "Disarmament was one thing; responsibility for the war another; reparations was a third matter." In any event, "he would not sell the rights of his country." And maliciously he added that Germany was trying to settle reparations, disarmament and the responsibility for the war through a payment of 2.6 billion R.M. Although he was interested in reconciliation, "he would not accept the German conditions, which reeked of bad faith." MacDonald replied that he thought they had agreed "to wipe out the past and begin afresh." Aware that the French premier was excited and angry, MacDonald broke off the discussion.

Fearing that the negotiations would break down completely, MacDonald met with the leaders of the various delegations and begged them to "use their good offices to find some way out of the impasse." Later that evening, Papen and Herriot joined this meeting and, after a drawn-out discussion, agreed to meet the next day.[70] However, the conference between Papen and Herriot the next morning ended badly. Herriot refused to make any concessions either on war guilt or disarmament. Papen stubbornly insisted that Germany could not pay one *pfennig* more than two billion *Reichsmarks*.

Once again, MacDonald intervened by conferring privately with Papen. He warned the Chancellor that if the conference failed, a financial crisis would occur and many people would blame Germany. Papen would be doing the "right thing," if he told Herriot he was prepared to accept a figure of three billion.[71] Disturbed by MacDonald's warning, Papen decided to accept the three billion figure, but still tried to include some sort of a political declaration, "which would justify Germany in accepting the settlement."[72] The next morning, MacDonald informed Papen that the French were willing to make a general declaration. Papen then telephoned his cabinet, and informed them of the proposed amount and the French declaration.[73] Realizing that the fate of the conference hung in the balance, Papen urged the divided cabinet members not to undermine the conference over political questions and the insistence on a lower amount. He added that the favorable terms of payment necessitated the acceptance of a higher sum.[74] Shortly after noon on Friday, July 8, Papen told the prime minister that his colleagues in Berlin had agreed to this amount, and to a vague political formula that granted none of his requests. "It was a terrible decision to take," he confessed.[75]

With the negotiations drawing to a close, the delegations met Friday evening at 10 p.m. to review and approve the final declarations, which constituted the "Lausanne Agreements." The most important ones provided that reparations should be abolished subject to Germany's depositing with the Bank of International Settlements 5% redeemable annuities with a 1% sinking fund in the amount of three billion *Reichsmarks*; and that the Bank had the authority to negotiate any of these annuities by public issue at a price not lower than 90% three years after the date of the agreement.

The next morning at 10 a.m., the delegates met for the final plenary session. In his closing speech, MacDonald pointed out how difficult it had been to reach an agreement: "There are too many old memories, and there is nothing harder to uproot than an old memory." In spite of this, he continued, "we have done much...Not a continuation of the old...the writing we have put on the pages of history is not the end of an old chapter, it is the beginning of a new. We have closed the book, we have put the book on the shelf, we have opened a new book. No more Reparations!"[76] The British statesman concluded his remarks with a warning that "there can be no peace and security until there is a will to peace and the will to give security all round. We all hope that Geneva will register a great success...but unless the world and the big nations in the world have arrived at a stage when they trust each other and cooperate with each other...disarmament alone is not going to relieve us of our burden."[77] On this note, the Lausanne Conference came to an end.

With the conclusion of the conference, all the delegations returned home, but to varied reactions. MacDonald and Herriot received standing ovations from their parliaments, while the British and French press praised their efforts as "the beginning of greater things." Even Papen was complimented by the foreign press. Writing for the *Observer*, J. L. Garvin expressed the reaction of a large section of British and French public opinion when he wrote that "whatever we may think about the present German regime as regards domestic politics in the troubled Reich, we are bound to recognize that Herr von

Papen showed much more of the spirit of effectual statesmanship than had been expected."[78]

C. Reaction at Home

If Papen and the German delegation had hoped to be welcomed as returning heroes, they were sadly disillusioned. Arriving in Berlin, the German delegation was pelted with a shower of bad eggs and rotten apples.[79] The German press was almost unanimous in its merciless condemnation of the Agreement. The British Ambassador to Germany, Sir Horace Rumbold remarked that "the Lausanne settlement is not being judged on its merits by the press...Its hostile reception by practically all parties is mainly due to political and tactical considerations connected with the elections on July 31..."[80]

As in the past, whenever issues of foreign policy were introduced into political campaigns, the most extreme views prevailed. *Germania*, Papen's former newspaper, indicted him for departing from Brüning's foreign policy, while Hugenberg's *Lokalanzeiger* criticized Papen for making political demands and then not insisting on them at all cost. The *Deutsche Algemeine Zeitung*, previously supportive of Papen's government, published a headline that screamed "Ransom!"[81]

The sharpest criticism, however, came from the Nazi press. The *Volkischer Beobachter* accused Papen of following the same policy of fulfillment as his predecessors because his nerves were not equal to the task. Goebbels propaganda sheet, *Der Angriff*, dismissed the whole agreement as "catastrophic," and promised that the Nazis would oppose its ratification in the *Reichstag*. The *Tägliche Rundschau* called the Lausanne Agreement a disaster, and wondered why Hindenburg did not dismiss Papen immediately.[82]

Strangely enough, the only favorable support Papen received was from the democratic press. The *Berliner Tageblatt*, the *Vossische Zeitung*, and the *Börsen-Courier*, expressed a qualified commendation by stating that the removal of the discriminatory clauses in the Versailles Treaty was a precondition for the world's economic recovery.[83]

While Papen might have expected a negative reaction from the German press, he hardly anticipated criticisms from his own cabinet. Yet, on July 11, when he reported to the cabinet about the negotiations, he was surprised at the disappointment registered by von Gayl who acknowledged some dissatisfaction with the results. However, the most scathing criticism came from von Schleicher who castigated the delegation for what he called embarrassing reversals of position. First, he complained, the delegation announced that Germany was unable to pay; then they declared that Germany was able to pay if political concessions were included; finally they agreed to pay without these concessions. In the light of such a "severe defeat," Schleicher said the only course of action was for the cabinet to resign. While others in the cabinet might have agreed with the General's criticisms of the delegation's tactics, none expressed themselves in that way. Nor were they willing to support his proposal that the cabinet should resign. Instead, they issued a public statement expressing gratitude for the results obtained.[84]

Meanwhile, Papen held a press conference, at which he began by denying what every reporter knew to be true; that the negotiations in Lausanne were influenced by domestic politics. In an effort to present the bright side of the negotiations, he stressed Germany's renewed sovereignty over the *Reichsbank* and the German Railway Company. He also stated that the terms of the settlement did not endanger Germany's economic recovery, but rather it was a prerequisite for payment. Not content with these moderate remarks, Papen then attempted to respond to the charges that he had launched into a series of political questions without adequate prior preparation. Alluding to a recent scholarly investigation that questioned the findings of war guilt, Papen boldly declared that cancellation of further reparation obligations constituted a formal abrogation of Part VII of the Versailles Treaty along with its hated war-guilt clause (Art. 231).[85] Not only did this old unilateral renunciation remain unconfirmed in London and Paris, but it also failed to silence Papen's critics; nor would it help his cause in the forthcoming elections.

Nevertheless, in spite of what one may think of Papen or his methods, it must be admitted that he did achieve a significant victory at the Conference. The terms of the payment not only granted Germany a three year moratorium, but enabled her to pay only when she was able to do so. As it turned out, the Lausanne Agreements were never ratified and Germany never paid a single *pfennig* of the three billion *Reichsmarks*.

Admittedly, Papen did not obtain the desired political concessions concerning the war guilt clause and Germany's right to some measure of rearmament. However, these issues were not irrevocably ended and, in fact, the question of Germany's rights in the matter of armaments was taken up again in December after Papen's resignation.[86] Unfortunately the Papen government had become the victim of right-wing rhetoric. The Nationalists, and other conservative groups, had fostered the attitude that reparations was a dead issue, and that anything less than complete renunciation of payments would be unacceptable to the German people. Moreover, the scheduling of a national election shortly after the conference was a guarantee that a highly politicized atmosphere would surround the negotiations. It is indeed ironic that the Papen government became the victim of severe criticisms over an action they had hoped to exploit. In an effort to recover from this unexpected turn of events, Papen decided to embark on another scheme to strengthen the credentials of his government with the right, and hopefully improve his chances in the forthcoming elections - the replacement of the Prussian Government.

NOTES

[1] It was in Bessinge near Geneva, Switzerland early in 1932 that Brüning had laid the foundations for German participation in an international conference to discuss the implications of the reparations schedule of the Young Plan and the economic crisis attending those issues

[2] Hindenburg, at Papen's request, had dissolved the *Reichstag* on June 4, and elections were set for July 31, 1932. Banking on successful negotiations at Lausanne, Papen hoped to increase his popularity in order to make political gains in the forthcoming elections.

[3] *Niederschrift über die Ministerbesprechung*, June 13, 1932, 11:30 a.m., *Vorbereitung der Lausanne Konferenz, RKz,* R 43 I/338, BA, Koblenz.

[4] Papen, *Memoirs*, p. 172.

[5] Ibid., p. 172.

[6] *Stimmen und Pläne des Auslandes zur Reparationsfrage*, May 31,1932, pp. 14-49a. *RKz.*, R 43 I/337, BA, Koblenz.

[7] Ibid., p. 22-44; pp. 44-46.

[8] *DBFP*, No. 135, pp. 177-82

[9] Edouard Herriot served both as the prime minister and foreign minister in a "left alliance" in 1924. Unlike the passionate nationalist Poincare, Herriot was interested in a reconciliation with Germany, but wanted some measure of security in return.

[10] Telegram of L. von Hösch to the Foreign Office, June 10, 1932, *RKz.*, R 43 I/338, BA, Koblenz. Hösch, who was the German Ambassador in Paris, informed the Foreign Office of Herriot's pessimistic outlook for the Lausanne conference.

[11] Ibid.

[12] The Franco-German Study Group was formed in May 1926, by Emil Mayrisch, a highly respected Luxembourg industrialist. Mayrisch believed that economic cooperation between Germany and France was essential for the preservation of peace between the two nations. Although Papen attended a number of the meetings, he did not play a significant role in the Group's activities. Cf. Jürgen Bach, *Franz von Papen in der Weimarer Republik*, pp. 149-51.

[13] The Chancellor was accompanied by Foreign Minister von Neurath, Undersecretary of Foreign Affairs von Bülow, Finance Minister Schwerin-Krosigk and Economics Minister Warmbold.

[14] *Memoirs*, p. 172.

[15] Stenographic Notes of the First Plenary Session of the Conference, Thursday, June 16, 1932, at 10 a.m., *DBFP*, No. 137, pp. 191-193.

[16] Edouard Herriot, *Jadis: D'une guerre a l'autre 1914-1936* (Paris: Flammarion, 1952), II, p. 322.

[17] *Memoirs*, pp. 172-73.

[18] *DBFP*, No. 135, pp. 177-82,. Herriot had expressed this view to MacDonald in their preliminary meeting on June 11, 1932.

[19] Papen was referring to the Hague Agreements concluded in August 1929. The Germans accepted the Young Plan and were rewarded with the French evacuation of the Rhineland.

[20] Stenographic Notes of the Second Plenary Session of the Conference, Friday, June 17, 1932, at 10 a.m., *DBFP*, No. 138, pp. 196-202; *Memoirs*, pp. 173-74.

[21] Paul Schmidt, *Statist auf diplomatischer Bühne, 1923-1945. Erlebnisse des Chefdolmentschers im Auswärtigen Amt mit den Staatesmännern Europas* (Bonn: Athenaeum Verlag, 1950), p. 243.

[22] Stenographic Notes, of the Second Plenary Session of the Conference, Friday, June 17, 1932, at 10 a. m., *DBFP*, No. 138, pp. 202, 204-205, 206.

[23] Ibid. The "Basel Report," issued by a Committee of Experts in December 1931. This Report declared that Germany would be unable to resume payments at the expiration of the Hoover Moratorium in June 1932. However, it did not rule out such payments at a future date.

[24] *DBFP*, ibid.

[25] Notes of a conversation between Great Britain and France, Monday, June 20, 1932, at 10 a.m., *DBFP*, No. 140, pp. 220-2.

[26] *Memoirs*, p. 175.

[27] *DBFP*, No. 141, p. 231; Report of Neurath to Acting State Secretary, June 20, 1932, *RKz* R 43 I/338, BA, Koblenz.

[28] *DBFP*, No. 141, pp. 251-52; Papen to MacDonald, June 21, 1932, *RKz.*, R 43/I338, BA, Koblenz; Papen, *Memoirs*, p. 176.

[29] *Memoirs*, p. 175.

[30] Ibid., p. 176.

[31] Notes on a conversation between Herriot and MacDonald held on Tuesday, June 21, 1932, at 4 p.m., *DBFP*, No. 143, pp. 244-45.

[32] Notes of a conversation between Great Britain and France held on Thursday, June 23, 1932, at 10 a.m., *DBFP*, No. 145, pp. 254-57. In plain language, the French tied the reparations payments to her war loans from the United States.

[33] Ibid.

[34] Notes of a conversation held on Thursday, June 23, 1932, at 4 p.m., *DBFP*, No. 146, pp. 267-68. The British change of heart occurred shortly after

President Hoover issued the announcement on June 22, calling for a reduction of world armaments. Germany and Italy supported Hoover's appeal while the British exhibited little enthusiasm, and the French flatly opposed it.

[35] Although Papen thought that Herriot had received him quite cordially in their first meeting, this was not the case thereafter. Not only did Herriot disagree with Papen on many important issues, but as an anticlerical, antimilitary liberal, he also disliked the German Chancellor's conservative politics, military background, and staunch Catholicism. The British Foreign Secretary, Sir John Simon, recalled one occasion in which Herriot expressed his low esteem of Papen: "...as he [Herriot] looked across the conference table at von Papen, he whispered in my ear, 'the more I study the face of a German cavalry officer, the more I admire -- his horse!'" John Simon, *Retrospect The Memoirs of the Rt. Hon. Viscount Simon* (London: Hutchinson, 1952), p. 188.

[36] *Memoirs*, p. 176.

[37] Herriot, *Jadis*, II, pp. 338-39; Schwerin-Krosigk, *Observations on Schäffer's Tagebuch*, ZS A/30, *IfZg*). *DBFP*, No. 148, p.271.

[38] *Memoirs*, pp. 175-76.

[39] *Memoirs*, pp. 176-77. Papen claims that Herriot was attracted to his proposal for improving Franco-German relations, and even asked one of his secretaries to prepare a draft of it as a basis of an accord between the two countries. What Papen fails to mention, however, is that Herriot's interest in this proposal came before the recess on Friday. When the two met on the following Monday, Papen's accommodating attitude had disappeared. Herriot reacted by showing little interest in discussing political questions.

[40] Eric Eyck, *A History of the Weimar Republic*, II, p. 403.

[41] Quoted in Walter Schotte, *Das Kabinett Papen, Schleicher, Gayl* (Leipzig: R. Kittler Verlag, 1932), p. 34; Notes of a conversation between Britain and France held on Monday, June 27, 1932, at 10 a.m., *DBFP*, No. 148, pp. 271, 274.

[42] *Memoirs*, p. 179. For some undisclosed reason, the translator of the English edition, Brian Connell, omitted Papen's disclosure of his plan for a military alliance with France. This is not the first time that the English translation significantly departs from the German original.

[43] Quoted in John Wheeler-Bennett, *The Pipedream of Peace: The Story of the Collapse of Disarmament* (New York: William Morrow and Company, 1935), p. 46.

[44] Notes of a conversation between Britain and France held on Monday, June 27, 1932, at 10 a.m., *DBFP*, No. 148., p. 271.

[45] Notes of a conversation between Britain and France held on Monday, June, 27, 1932, at 10 p.m., *DBFP*, No. 148, p. 271. Herriot told MacDonald that he

thought Papen's change of heart was due to the criticisms in the Berlin press and Italy's new support for Germany's position.

[46] *Memoirs*, p. 179.

[47] Great Britain and Germany: Notes of a conversation held on Monday, June 27, 1932, at 10:30 p.m., *DBFP*, No. 148, p. 272-75.

[48] *DBFP*, No. 148, pp. 272-75.

[49] In a later meeting between the British and French delegations (July 5), Herriot is quoted as telling MacDonald that "Herr von Papen had offered him a military understanding...which he [Herriot] had been asked not to repeat to Mr. MacDonald." This explains why the British prime minister knew so little about the proposed alliance, and why he probably thought Papen was trying to undermine Franco-British relations. *DBFP*, III, No. 175, p. 387.

[50] Notes on a conversation between Great Britain and Germany held on Monday, June 27, 1932, at 10:30 p.m., *DBFP*, No. 149, pp. 272-75.

[51] Notes of a conversation between Great Britain, France, and Germany, Tuesday, June 28, 1932, at 12 noon, *DBFP*, No. 150, pp. 276-77.

[52] Great Britain, France and Germany: Notes of a conversation held on Tuesday, June 28, 1932, at 4 p.m., *DBFP*, No. 151, p. 281.

[53] *DBFP*, No. 151, p. 281.

[54] Ibid.

[55] Great Britain, France and Germany: Notes of a conversation held on Tuesday, June 28, 1932, at 4 p.m., *DBFP*, No. 151, pp. 286-287.

[56] *Memoirs*, p. 181.

[57] Legally, however, MacDonald could make no guarantee, since the *de jure* status reverted to the Hague Agreements, which meant a return to the Young Plan of 1929.

[58] Initially, the French finance minister, Germain-Martin, had indicated that the lowest figure that the French government could accept was four billion *Reichsmarks*, excluding the Hoover Year Annuities worth an additional two billion. Neville Chamberlain knew that the Germans would never accept a figure of five billion, and finally persuaded the French to accept the four billion sum. Great Britain and France: Notes of a conversation held on Saturday, July 2, 1932 at 9 a.m., *DBFP*, No. 163, p.323; No. l64, p. 334.

[59] *DBFP*, No. 165, pp. 336-337.

[60] *Memoirs*, p. 182.

[61] Von Gayl and von Braun supported Papen in opposing the sum of four billion R.M., while Krosigk, Schäffer, and Warmbold believed Germany could manage to pay that amount. "*Verhandlungen* in Lausanne," *RKz* R 43 I/338, BA, Koblenz.

---

[62] Great Britain and Germany: Notes of a conversation held on Sunday, July 3, 1932, at 9 a.m., *DBFP*, No. 166, pp. 343-344. Papen added that the sum of four billion R.M. was the same indemnity paid by France after the Franco-Prussian war in 1870: "After twelve years of peace such a figure was impossible."

[63] Great Britain and Germany: Notes of a conversation held on Sunday, July 3, 1932, at 5 p.m., *DBFP*, No. 168, p. 354.

[64] The four billion agreed upon by the French consisted of two billion as the final payment and two billion to cover the French war debts to the United States and Great Britain.

[65] Great Britain and France: Notes of a conversation held on Tuesday, July 5, 1932, at 9 a.m., *DBFP*, No. 172, pp. 354-55.

[66] The fifth point was inserted as a guarantee to the French that Germany would not seek to unilaterally negotiate with any of the signatories and thus undermine the financial agreement concluded with France at Lausanne. Great Britain and France: Notes of a conversation held on Tuesday, July 5, 1932, at 9 a.m., *DBFP*, No. 172, pp. 368-373.

[67] "Telegram: Deutsche Delegation Lausanne," July 5, 1932, *RKz* R 43 I/1457, BA, Koblenz.

[68] Great Britain and Germany: Notes of a conversation held on Tuesday, July 5, 1932, at 3:45 p.m., *DBFP*, No. 174, pp. 380-81.

[69] *DBFP*, No. 174, pp. 378, 380-81.

[70] Notes of a private meeting of delegates of the Six Inviting Powers, held on Wednesday, July 6, 1932, *DBFP*, No. 180, p. 399; No. 181, p. 403.

[71] MacDonald had collapsed from exhaustion and Neville Chamberlain spent the night of July 7 trying to convince Herriot to accept the three billion amount. The French premier finally agreed, but only if there were no political guarantees included in the conditions for payment.

[72] Great Britain and Germany: Notes of a conversation held on Thursday, July 7, 1932, at 4:45 p.m., *DBFP*, No. 182, pp. 406, 410.

[73] The French declaration consisted of a communiqué specifically excluding any political agreements and only vaguely mentioned a new restoration of confidence and mutual respect in Europe. Great Britain and France: Notes of a Conversation held on Friday, July 8, 1932, at 10:15 a.m., *DBFP*, Appendix to No. 184, "French Draft of a Political clause (first prepared July 7, 10 p.m.)," pp. 419-420.

[74] "*Bericht über die Verhandlungen in Lausanne,*" *RKz* R 43 I/338, BA, Koblenz.

[75] Great Britain and Germany: Notes of a conversation held on Friday, July 8, 1932, at 12:25 p.m., *DBFP*, No. 185, p. 422.

[76] Stenographic notes of the Fifth Plenary Session of the Conference, Saturday, July 9, 1932, 10 a.m., *DBFP*, No. 188, p. 434.

[77] *DBFP*, No. 188, p. 434.

[78] J. L. Garvin, "Clearing up and Cutting down: The Lessons of Lausanne...," *The Observer*, Sunday, July 10, 1932.

[79] *Memoirs*, p. 186.

[80] Rumbold to Simon, July 13, 1932, *DBFP*, No. 192, pp. 441-442.

[81] *DBFP*, No. 192, pp. 441-442.

[82] *DBFP*, No. 192, pp. 441-442.

[83] *DBFP*, No. 192, pp. 441-442.

[84] Cabinet Session, July 11, 1932, *RKz* R 43 I/1457, BA, Koblenz.

[85] *Memoirs*, pp. 184-85.

[86] Von Neurath and Schleicher unsuccessfully tried to reach an agreement with the French by direct negotiation. However, on December 11, 1932, the Allied Powers and Germany agreed on the formula of "equality of rights within a system of security for all nations."

CHAPTER 6:
TOWARDS THE "NEW STATE"

A. The Prussian "Triumph"

One of the most troublesome problems facing every chancellor during the Weimar period was the relationship of Prussia to the central government. The origins of this problem go back to the days of Frederick the Great, when the Hohenzollern monarch managed to transform some fragments of north German territory into a great power on which the peace of Europe depended. Although Prussia ceased to exist as a separate state when the new German Reich was proclaimed in the Hall of Mirrors at Versailles on January 1, 1871, it continued to exercise extraordinary influence over the Reich's foreign and domestic policies. This was due in large measure to the efforts of Otto von Bismarck, who created a political system that enabled him, as the Minister President of Prussia and Reich Chancellor, to manipulate the authority of both offices in such a manner as to prevent the federal government from succumbing to the forces of liberalism or democracy, and to leave Prussia with sufficient power to protect the aristocratic-monarchical system.[1] With the backing of the powerful Prussian state, Bismarck also saw to it that the federal government had enough leverage to keep the particularism of the southern states from curbing Prussian influence in national affairs. When Bismarck retired to his estate in 1890, Prussia still dominated the Reich. But the Iron

Chancellor left a legacy of ambiguities and contradictions that aggravated the already existing tensions between Prussia and the other German states.

When the delegates to the National Assembly met at Weimar in February, 1919, the old debate of centralization versus state's rights was reopened. It was clear that any solution to this complex problem would make little sense unless Prussia's position in the Reich were reduced. However, the framers of the new Constitution rejected a proposal to divide Prussia into various smaller provinces.[2] Consequently, Prussia remained the largest state, while Berlin continued to be the capital of both governments, with bureaucracies that often duplicated each other's work. Even under the best of circumstances, when political harmony existed between the two governments, administrative conflicts occurred; when their political ideologies were in opposition, the situation became noticeably strained.[3]

Although the National Assembly had failed to resolve the problem of dualism between the Reich and Prussia, the issue of constitutional reforms continued to be discussed among various political groups throughout the history of the Republic.[4] One of the last attempts to introduce reforms that would bring Prussia more under the control of the central government was a proposal by Papen's predecessor, Heinrich Brüning. The presidential elections in the Spring of 1932 had alerted Brüning to the growing popularity of the National Socialists. With the Prussian *Landtag* elections scheduled for April 24, Brüning was afraid that a National Socialist victory in Prussia would result in a demand to participate in a new coalition government there. He also shuddered at the thought that Hitler might demand the Prussian Ministry of Justice or Police as part of a compromise for not receiving the minister president's office. If the Nazis held either of these important ministries, they would be in a position to significantly increase their influence not only in Prussia, but also in the Reich.[5] To prevent this, Brüning proposed to merge these two ministries under the leaders of the corresponding ministries of the Reich. He even considered extending this arrangement to other states, and establishing Reich Commissioners to increase administrative efficiency and effect savings in government.[6] But before he could bring this plan to fruition, Brüning was forced out of office - the victim of General Schleicher's intrigues.

Brüning was not the only one to foresee the dangers of a Nazi victory in the forthcoming *Landtag* elections. On April 12, the ruling Weimar Coalition in Prussia (Social Democrats, the Democrats reconstituted as the State Party, and the Center), voted to change the electoral procedures so that a new minister president could be elected only by a two-thirds majority vote instead of by a relative majority. This change would prevent the Nazis from assuming control of the Prussian government. Papen, who was still a member of the *Landtag* at that time, argued against this proposal claiming that it "was an affront both to the letter and spirit of parliamentary procedure." As a final act of defiance against his party's policies, he voted with the Right against the proposal.[7]

The results of the Prussian elections on April 24, demonstrated how farsighted the Coalition cabinet had been. The National Socialists scored heavily in Bavaria, Württemberg, Anhalt, and Hamburg. But their most impressive victory was in Prussia where they increased their representation from 9 to 162 seats, making them the largest party in the *Landtag*. The Social Democrats, who had shared power with the Center and Democratic parties in every Prussian regime since 1919, sank from 137 to 94 seats.[8] Despite this dramatic victory, the National Socialists could not muster enough votes to satisfy the new requirements.[9] As a consequence, the Cabinet of Socialist Otto Braun, remained in office as a "caretaker" government. Since prospects for a speedy solution to this situation seemed unlikely, it appeared that this interim government would continue for some time. Meanwhile, the *Landtag* reconvened on May 25, and the Nazi Hans Kerrl, was elected *Landtag* President. On the same occasion, the Communists and Nazis joined together and voted "no confidence" in the Braun government. Not long afterwards, on June 6, an exhausted and depressed Otto Braun took a leave of absence "for reasons of health."[10] Replacing Braun as the acting minister president was the moderate Center party Minister of Welfare, Heinrich Hirtsiefer.

In the meantime, Schleicher, who was at the height of his power and influence over the aging Hindenburg, had concluded that the Brüning experiment was a failure. He had hoped that the Brüning government would free Germany "from the anarchy of party politics and parliamentary instability." In order to accomplish this, Schleicher had unsuccessfully urged Brüning to pursue a policy that would eliminate the Social Democrats as a political force, prorogue the

Reichstag until a *Reichsreform* could be carried out, and govern the nation by presidential decree supported by the *Reichswehr*, with a Chancellor and a Cabinet of "the President's friends."[11] To attain this risky goal, Schleicher was prepared to gamble on the support of the Nazis and the Nationalists. Once accomplished, the crafty Schleicher planned to dispose of the Nazis by splitting Hitler's party and taking the more conservative elements into the government.[12]

With Brüning out of the way, Schleicher was able to convince the aging Hindenburg to appoint Franz von Papen to head a non-party government. The new Chancellor and the General had known each other in the Army, and had renewed their friendship after the war as members of the conservative *Herrenklub*. Schleicher and Papen shared certain common concerns about the future of the Republic, and saw eye to eye in finding a solution to the political and economic crisis. They were both avowed enemies of the Social Democrats, and wanted to eliminate them as a political force. Both men favored a *Reichsreform* that would replace the "bankrupt, mechanical parliamentarianism" with the "New State," whose authority "would rest on the *potestas* of the army and the *auctoritas* of the president."[13] As members of the conservative *Herrenklub*, Papen and Schleicher had often discussed the need for constitutional reforms that would reestablish the prestige of the conservative military caste, restore Germany's image as a strong, united nation, and return political power and social prestige to their own class. Schleicher knew that Hindenburg would be attracted by these qualities, while he (Schleicher) planned to use Papen as a pawn in his own schemes to enhance the power of the Army, and to engage in the risky game of "cut-throat" which he was playing with the Nazis.

Meanwhile, the tensions between the Reich and Prussia continued to mount after Papen assumed the chancellorship. Rumors spread that the new government intended to appoint a Reich Commissioner in Prussia.[14] There were also reports that this was a condition Hitler demanded from Schleicher in return for Nazi toleration of the Papen cabinet. Although evidence to support this conjecture is incomplete, there are strong indications that both Papen and Schleicher had discussed this with Hitler. If we are to believe Joseph Goebbels, when Schleicher met with Hitler on June 4, 1932, it was agreed that the Papen government would lift the SS and SA ban, dissolve the *Reichstag*, and either establish a Commissioner in Prussia or allow the Nazis to have the office of minister president.[15] Other evidence seems to support Goebbels' remarks that an agreement had been reached. A memo dated June 6, written by Heinrich von Gleichen, the managing director of the *Herrenklub*, reveals that certain "agreements" were reached between the Papen Government and the Nazis that called for the establishment of "a trustworthy man as Minister President or a Reich Commissioner." In return, the Nazis promised to tolerate the new Reich government at least until the *Reichstag* elections.[16] Further evidence links Papen with these agreements. On June 7, two days before Papen met with Hitler to discuss the conditions under which the Nazis would tolerate the new regime, Count Bodo von Alvensleben, President of the *Herrenklub*, wrote to Finance Minister Schwerin-Krosigk, "Since we will hardly come to a government of the Right in Prussia, then we ought to steer a course for a Reich Commissioner."[17] In light of this evidence, it is highly improbable that Papen was unaware of these rumors. It is even more unlikely that he did not discuss them with Schleicher before he met with Hitler at Alvensleben's home! Moreover, given the purpose of Papen's decision to meet with the Nazi leader, it is hard to imagine that the subject of a Commissioner was not one of the issues they discussed.[18]

Although Papen was not opposed to resolving the Prussian question by establishing a Reich Commissioner, he initially preferred to see a coalition government composed of the National Socialists, Nationalists, and Center parties. While still a member of the *Landtag*, Papen wrote an article in the conservative weekly, *Der Ring*, in which he called for the inclusion of the National Socialists in the Prussian government. He maintained that if the Nazis shared responsibilities, they would be less revolutionary in their activities. He also wanted to take advantage of Hitler's popularity to gain support for his proposed *Reichsreform*.[19]

However, Papen's efforts to bring about a coalition between the Nazis, the Center and the Nationalists held little promise of success from the very beginning. For one thing, the Center party would have nothing to do with the Chancellor whom they regarded as a traitor. Moreover, the National Socialists and the Center continued to bitterly attack each other in the *Landtag*, and all indications in that forum pointed to the impossibility of reconciling their differences. Goebbels comments illustrate how fruitless these efforts were: "One wants to bind us into responsibility in Prussia. Papen and Schleicher have invited the German Nationalists and Center to the Reich chancellery...[We] prefer to remain in the opposition, until we get complete power."[20] A few days later he described how his party intended to sabotage any negotiations: "In the Prussian question we are placing conditions that the Center cannot fulfill."[21]

Having failed in his efforts to bring the Center, the Nazis, and the German Nationalists together in a right wing coalition government in Prussia, Papen decided to try another course of action that was as controversial as it was novel. At the first Cabinet meeting on June 2, the Chancellor informed the Prussian representative that he was not to attend any future cabinet meetings unless matters directly concerning Prussia were on the agenda.[22] A few days later, the Papen government withheld a payment of 100 million marks promised to Prussia by the Brüning government. Using this action as a pretext for interfering in Prussia's internal affairs, the Chancellor side-stepped Acting Minister President Hirtsiefer, and sent a letter to the *Landtag* president Kerrl, requesting him to reconvene the *Landtag* as soon as possible in order to form a permanent government. Papen explained that the Reich would be unable to assist Prussia in resolving her financial problems as long as an interim government was in power.[23] This action only served to increase the tensions between the two governments because this step was perceived to have been a pretext to intervene in Prussia's internal affairs.[24]

Meanwhile, the implications of this irregular procedure for forming a state government was not lost on Hirtsiefer. In a carefully worded statement, he accused the Chancellor of by-passing the present government as if it did not exist, and requested him to refrain from engaging in such procedures in the future.[25] In his response, Papen acknowledged that he had ignored the normal channels, but he pointedly stated that if an emergency should arise in the future, he would not hesitate to act in a similar manner.[26]

While Papen engaged in this bizarre behavior vis-à-vis the Prussian government, the rumors about a Reich Commissioner aroused the fears of the South German *Länder*, who were afraid that if the Reich swallowed up Prussia, the same thing might happen to them. Consequently, the leaders of the southern *Länder* met with President Hindenburg, the Chancellor, and Secretary Meissner on June 12, and expressed their concerns in no uncertain terms.[27] Papen denied the charge that he intended to establish a Reich Commissioner in Prussia, but he qualified this by adding that "...the establishment of a Reich

Commissioner was the *ultima ratio* if the really vital interests of the entire Fatherland were at stake."[28] While this statement indicates that Papen still preferred to resolve the Prussian issue through negotiations leading to a coalition government, it was also a signal that if this was not possible, he would support more drastic measures.

One of the reasons for Papen's reluctance to take more forceful action in Prussia was his fear of adverse reaction from abroad. The Allies were scheduled to meet with a German delegation at Lausanne in the middle of June to discuss the difficult reparations question. Papen wanted to get the Allies to cancel all war reparations in order to relieve Germany of one of the reasons for her financial crisis. He was also thinking about the forthcoming *Reichstag* elections, and hoped that a successful agreement at Lausanne would improve his sagging popularity with the German voters. Thus, in their last minute preparations for the Lausanne conference, the cabinet agreed to suspend any further decisions with regard to the Prussian question until after the conference.

When Papen decided to head the delegation to Lausanne, he appointed Wilhelm von Gayl as the Acting Chancellor. However, during the Chancellors' absence, domestic tensions continued to plague the Reich. The emergency decree of June 16, which had lifted the ban on the SA and SS, was ignored by Bavaria, Baden, Württemberg, and Hesse who countered with bans of their own.[29]

From the Right and Left, pressures on the Government to resolve the crisis mounted. On June 20, Hitler met with Gayl and complained that the Nazis were not being allowed to defend themselves against the Communists. The Nazi leader charged that the Communists, with Russian members of the "*Cheka*" at their head, were launching a reign of terror. He also said that the Prussian police were no longer in control of the situation, and demanded that his Storm Troopers be given permission to "clear the streets."[30]

A few days later, on June 24, five Nazi *Landtag* deputies protested the efforts of the Communists and Socialists to form a popular front in Prussia against Hitler, and accused the Prussian police of showing favoritism to the Left.[31] The Nazis also complained to Kurt von Bredow of the *Ministeramt*, an office of the *Reichswehr* primarily concerned with maintaining close liaison with the political parties. They demanded official recognition of their right to defend themselves against the Left in what they described as a state of emergency.[32]

Although neither Gayl nor von Bredow gave the Nazis any direct encouragement, Gayl did observe that if the Prussian government was unable to restore order, the Reich would abandon its "customary procedures" in order to do so.[33]

The Nazis were not the only party to bring pressure on the Papen Government. On June 8, State Secretary Erwin Planck met with two leaders of the German Nationalist *Landtag* delegation, Friedrich von Winterfeld and Eldor Borck. They urged the Reich to intervene in Prussia because of her weak financial position, and the failure of the *Landtag* to take appropriate steps to check the mounting disorders. They also accused the Prussian government of undertaking personnel changes favorable to the Left.[34] On that same day, Winterfeld wrote a letter to von Papen in which he repeated what he had told Planck earlier. He also accused the Social Democrats of having close connections with the Communists and concluded with a plea that the Papen government must intervene in Prussia or else "the decision about Germany's fate would be settled in the streets in civil war."[35]

Pressure on the Government also came from Count Rüdiger von der Goltz, President of the United Associations. In a letter to Papen dated July 11, von der Goltz appealed to the Chancellor not to repeat the weakness his government had shown during the controversy with the South German *Länder* over the lifting of the ban on the SA and SS. He urged Papen to intervene in Prussia immediately after the *Reichstag* elections.[36] Joining these cries for action was Crown Prince Wilhelm von Hohenzollern who insisted that it was justifiable for the Reich to force a recalcitrant state to obey the Reich laws by imposing a commissional government upon it.[37]

Meanwhile Gayl, whose sympathies were aligned with those of the Nationalists, refrained from proposing the appointment of a Reich Commissioner because of the delicate negotiations in which the Chancellor was engaged at Lausanne. Any forceful action taken in Prussia might scuttle the conference and with it any hopes of improving Germany's financial situation. Moreover, a failure in Lausanne could seriously damage the already shaky position of the Papen regime in the forthcoming elections.

However, by the end of June, the situation in Prussia had become so unstable, and the pressures on the Government so intense, that Gayl decided the time had come to take forceful action in Prussia. On July 9, Gayl met with the *Reichswehr* Minister at the latter's apartment.

Although Schleicher had agreed to postpone the Prussian question until after the Lausanne Conference, he now concurred with the Interior Minister's suggestion that the time had come to take action. Both men agreed that a speedy overthrow of the caretaker cabinet of Centrists and Socialists would serve a number of useful purposes: it would please Hindenburg, who found the conflict between the Reich and Prussia intolerable; it would placate the Nazis who could scarcely oppose any assault against the Social Democrats; it would place the control of the Prussian police forces at the disposal of the Reich, and thus strengthen its bargaining position with the Nazis after the election; and the removal of a liberal socialist regime in Prussia would help to gain more support from the Right in the forthcoming election.[38] The next day Gayl hurried to the railway station to meet Papen on his return from Lausanne to inform him of the proposed action.

Upon his return from Lausanne, the Chancellor found Germany in a state of near-collapse. Unemployment had risen to more than six million, about one-third of the work force, and street fights between uniformed gangs of Nazis and Communists broke out almost every day in every quarter of the Reich. In The Berlin Stories Christopher Isherwood describes the chaotic situation in Berlin: "Hate exploded suddenly, without warning out of nowhere....at street corners, in restaurants, cinemas, dance halls, swimming-baths; at midnight, after breakfast, in the middle of the afternoon. Knives were whipped out, blows were dealt with spiked rings, beer mugs, chair legs or leaded clubs; bullets slashed the advertisements on the poster-columns."[39] According to Albert Grzesinski, the Police President of Berlin, there were 461 political riots in Prussia alone between June 1 and July 20, 1932, in which eighty-two people were killed and four hundred seriously wounded.[40]

Although Papen had little time to rest from either his journey or the exhausting negotiations at Lausanne, it took Gayl little time to convince the Chancellor that the Prussian crisis required the Government's immediate attention. At the Cabinet meeting the next afternoon, July 11, Papen introduced the subject, stating that the incidence of terrorism had created a serious challenge for the Reich. He urged the ministers to find a quick and effective solution to this crisis, and then turned the meeting over to Gayl. The Interior Minister reported that the Communist party had stepped up its activities in Prussia, while the measures taken by the caretaker government to curb them were "inadequate."[41] Gayl warned that the increase of Communist power posed a real threat for the Prussian government. He also noted that the Nazis were increasing in size and influence, while Carl Severing's actions against this growing movement were ineffective.[42]

Gayl's list of criticisms of the caretaker government also included the failure of the *Landtag* to reconvene until August 24, and the uncertain state of the Prussian budget, which had been temporarily alleviated by a credit from the *Reichsbank*. After criticizing Severing's protest against the Reich's 5-day ban of the Socialist newspaper, *Vorwärts*, Gayl concluded that the Braun government no longer had the capacity for the kind of concerted action required in this situation.[43] Therefore, since the "psychological moment" for intervention had arrived, he proposed that the Chancellor should arrogate to himself the powers of Reich Commissioner, and appoint someone to assist him.

The Interior Minister went on to state that it was essential to maintain a Commissioner in Prussia until the administrative and constitutional reforms putting an end to the dualism between the Reich and Prussia had been completed. Anticipating the objection that the caretaker government would challenge this action in the courts, Gayl said he was convinced that its chances of success were slim. Schleicher applauded this proposal and added that since the authority of the caretaker government was "shattered" it was crucial to resolve the problem of dualism once and for all.[44] Among the remainder of the Cabinet members, only the Minister of Labor, Hugo Schäffer, felt that this action was premature. Hindenburg's secretary, Meissner, suggested that if the Cabinet expected to obtain Hindenburg's blessings on this project, it was absolutely essential to find a valid reason for intervention.[45] At the end of this session Papen, who had contributed very little to the discussion, summarized the results with the statement that the cabinet was united on the proposal to establish a Reich Commissioner in Prussia.[46]

The next afternoon July 12, when the Cabinet reconvened, Gayl read the draft of an emergency decree, which contained the proviso that the Reich chancellor would be named Reich commissioner in Prussia.[47] In the discussion that followed, Magnus von Braun, Minister of Food and Agriculture, raised the question about what would happen if the Prussian Acting Minister President, Hirtsiefer, should refuse to accept the order to resign? Schleicher replied that the military commander of the district could be granted executive power. To the question what measures could be taken if the workers should call a general strike in support of the caretaker government, Gayl replied that the Reich could always resort to emergency military action.[48] Meissner suggested that Prussia should be issued an ultimatum before any action was taken. He pointed out that in previous situations when commissioners had been appointed, opposition from the state government involved had resulted in bad publicity for the central government. He concluded with a warning that in case of litigation, failure to issue an ultimatum could result in the a ruling against the Government. Gayl and Schleicher thought that there was some merit in this suggestion, and proposed a number of questions to be submitted to the Prussian government. If they failed to respond to them, the Reich would have legitimate grounds to appoint a commissioner. Gürtner as Minister of Justice was concerned that if the Reich could not put a stop to the disorders, which had resulted in hundreds of deaths, then any intervention in Prussia would be worthless. Agreeing with this observation, Papen and the other ministers approved Gayl's proposal that the Government should issue a decree suspending all outdoor assemblies and demonstrations for the next few days.[49]

Although the ministers were virtually unanimous in their decision to intervene in Prussia, it was necessary to discover legal grounds that were so irrefutable that the southern *Länder* would accept them, and that Hindenburg's scruples about authorizing such action would be removed. The issue that seemed to offer the best prospects of success turned on Prussia's alleged inability to cope with the Communist threat.[50] Unsettling reports kept coming into Gayl's office that the Communists were forming "socialist action groups" in Prussia.[51]

A justification, given later by the Papen Government for its action in Prussia was Schleicher's report about a meeting between William Abegg, and two Communist Party politicians, Wilhelm Kaspar and Ernst Torgler.[52] Schleicher learned of this meeting through a minor official, Rudolf Diels, who was one of Abegg's trusted assistants.[53] Diels told Schleicher that he was present at a meeting on June 4, between Abegg and two Communist deputies, Wilhelm Kaspar, a member of the Prussian *Landtag*, and Ernst Torgler, a member of the *Reichstag*. According to Diels, Abegg invited the Communists to join the Social Democrats in a coalition government in Prussia for the purpose of forming a common front against Papen's Government. Abegg vigorously denied this charge, and claimed that all he wanted was to win the support of the Communist Party in a common struggle against the Nazis. He also requested that they give up their terrorist activities which were not only "illegal," but also "senseless."[54]

Although the validity of Diels' allegations may never be known, Abegg's version of the meeting is probably closest to the truth.[55] In support of Abegg's account, is the fact that neither the Socialists nor the Communists had any desire to form an alliance.[56] Moreover, from the day of the reported meeting between Abegg and the Communist deputies until Papen's trip on July 14, nothing happened to indicate that the relationship between the two parties had changed. This alone should have been enough to assure Papen that regardless of the topic, Abegg's conversation with the Communist delegates was totally unsuccessful.[57]

Regardless of how one wishes to judge the truth or error of either version, the evidence that the Papen Government was not stating its case correctly to the public is much clearer. In his explanation to the German public on the evening of the intervention, Papen justified the Government's action on the grounds that Abegg's negotiations would lead to a Marxist coalition government in Prussia. This would give the Communists control of the highly trained Prussian police force, which would present a threat to the very existence of the Reich.[58] However, this explanation is not reflected in the minutes of the Cabinet meeting at which Schleicher gave his report. The ministers were virtually unanimous in their belief that intervention was not only proper, but also necessary. The Abegg affair was not even discussed in connection with the plans to intervene.[59] Papen would have been more correct if he had admitted that he used Abegg's meeting with the two Communists to remove Hindenburg's scruples about signing the emergency decree authorizing the Government to intervene in Prussia.[60]

In the meantime, after approving Gayl's draft of the emergency decree, the cabinet discussed the question of personnel changes in the police. It was also decided that Papen should meet with three members of the Prussian cabinet, Hirtsiefer, Severing, and Klepper (Finance Minister) in the Reich chancellery on July 20, to inform them about the cabinet's decisions with regard to Prussia. At the end of the meeting the ministers agreed that the *Sprung* into Prussia should take place at 10 o'clock on the morning of July 20.[61]

The next evening, July 13, Papen and Gayl went to report the domestic and foreign affairs to the President, and to obtain his endorsement for the government's impending intervention in Prussia.[62] However, Hindenburg had not forgotten the warnings from the southern German ministers, and he was worried that he might be impeached before the Supreme Court. He therefore insisted on a thorough briefing of the facts before he would give his approval. The two men promptly presented their arguments, and recited a litany of doleful statistics of death and injury as a result of the political conflicts in Prussia. They also informed him the Abegg affair. When Hindenburg realized that Prussia could be in the hands of a Marxist coalition, he reacted by granting the government a virtual blank check, since he signed the decree without dating it. He also agreed to another measure which provided for the imposition of martial law in Berlin and Brandenburg should the government's action provoke any resistance.[63]

In the meantime, Prussia was on the verge of a civil war. Brown-shirted Nazis clashed with Communists in street battles that resulted in many deaths and serious injuries. The Prussian government tried desperately to cope with the growing violence. On July 13, the President of the SPD, Otto Wels and the leader of the *Reichstag* delegation Rudolf Breitscheid had a conference with Gayl, to whom they supplied evidence of the gravity of the situation, and pleaded for the reinstitution of the ban on uniforms. But Gayl refused the request with the biting comment that the maintenance of law and order was the responsibility of the local governments.[64]

These weeks of terror culminated in a street battle in Altona near Hamburg on Sunday, July 17. Count Harry Kessler describes the bloody scene: "The Nazis, several thousand strong and doubtless meaning to provoke an incident, marched in their spick-and-span uniforms through the poorest quarters of Altona. The predictable result occurred. The unemployed and the loafers, probably criminal elements too, attacked them. But the guilt rests upon those who provided the provocation."[65] The toll in this riot was 19 dead and 285 wounded. The next day Gayl reluctantly issued a national prohibition of political parades. When a Socialist member of the Prussian *Staatsrat* demanded the renewal of the ban on uniforms, the Interior Minister left the chamber.[66]

Altona provided Papen with the pretext he needed to intervene in Prussia. He invited Hirtsiefer, Severing and Otto Klepper the Prussian Finance Minister, to meet with him on the morning of July 20. When Severing inquired about the subject matter of the meeting, the

Chancellor informed him that the agenda consisted of financial and agricultural matters. However, this bit of deception on Papen's part was uncovered by Klepper while visiting in Herne, Westphalia with the director of the Prussian mining association "*Hibernia*." Klepper's host told him that Franz Bracht, the mayor of Essen, would be installed to head a commissional regime in Prussia.[67] The next day July 19, Berlin was crawling with rumors about the possible appointment of a commissioner in Prussia. That evening at a dinner party for the cabinet members and their wives, Papen informed Bracht of the plans to appoint a commissioner in Prussia the next day.[68]

Meanwhile, unknown to Papen or the other ministers, Severing had met with the Executive Committee of the Social Democratic Party to inform them of the rumors about a commissorial government in Prussia.[69] He asked them if they thought it permissible for the police, supported by the Iron Front, "to resist such unlawful action," even though the imposition might be backed by the Army. The members advised him that resistance was imprudent and unconstitutional. As the editor of Vorwärts, Friedrich Stampfer, remarked, "Severing had no right to be brave with the lives of the Prussian police."[70]

The next morning July 20, at 10 o'clock, Severing, Hirtsiefer and Klepper arrived at the chancellery where they met with Papen, Gayl and Planck. As usual, Papen was charming and friendly, although Klepper thought he was nervous. The Chancellor wasted little time on preliminaries, declaring that as a result of the disturbances over the past several weeks it had become quite clear that the caretaker government could no longer maintain law and order within its borders. As a consequence, he said he had obtained an emergency decree from President Hindenburg. Then, with trembling hands Papen unfolded the decree and read it aloud to the Prussian ministers.[71] It provided for the immediate establishment of a commissional government in Prussia. Papen was to be appointed as the Commissioner with the authority to dismiss the caretaker government. Accordingly, Braun and Severing would be the first to feel the impact of the Chancellor's new powers, for naturally he would assume the functions of Premier and Bracht would replace Severing as Interior Minister.[72]

Severing was incensed by Papen's accusation that law and order had broken down in Prussia, and he challenged the Chancellor to produce evidence of a single case in which his government had failed to carry out its responsibilities. When Severing also charged that the

Reich's action was unconstitutional, Papen replied that he could not prevent the Prussian ministers from appealing to the Supreme Court (*Staatsgerichthof*). Anxious to know if Severing would offer any resistance, the Chancellor then diplomatically inquired about the circumstances under which he would surrender his office. The Interior Minister replied that because of the unconstitutionality of the Reich's action, he would yield only to force.[73]

Severing was not the only one to criticize the Reich's action. Acting Minister President Hirtsiefer protested this unwarranted interference into a State's rights, characterizing the government's action as so bizarre that "in the whole of history" he could think of no precedent. He complained that "Without having been informed about what was wrong in Prussia, without having been given any opportunity to resolve possible complaints...we have been commanded to appear here." Even a prisoner has a final chance to be heard prior to sentencing.[74] According to Severing, Papen unabashedly declared that the government's action was "ultimately one of *raison d'etat*."[75] The Prussian Minister replied that there was nothing in the first two paragraphs of Article 48 to support such claims. At that point, Papen got up from his chair to signify that the meeting was at an end.[76] It had lasted just twenty minutes.

Severing's declaration that he would yield only to force prompted Papen to confer with Gayl, Planck and Bracht. They decided to proclaim a state of emergency in Berlin and Brandenburg if Severing carried out his threat.[77] Accordingly, General-Lieutenant Gerd von Rundstedt, the ranking military commander of the area, was appointed to execute the decree. Soldiers were dispatched to guard all public buildings, and other positions considered militarily important.[78]

Meanwhile, at about 11 o'clock that morning, von Rundstedt telephoned the Berlin Police-President, Albert Grzesinski, and informed him that he, together with the Vice-president of the police, Dr. Bernhard Weiss, and the commander of the police forces, Manfried Heimannsberg, were to be dismissed according to the decree of martial law issued for Berlin and the province of Brandenburg.[79] Grzesinski immediately got in touch with Severing, and after informing him of von Rundstedt's action, pleaded with him to take immediate counteraction. However, Severing refused to go along with the plan. Not only did he refuse to condone any bloodshed, but he also believed the proclamation of marshal law was a legal procedure under which a military commander was within his rights to dismiss the police president and his staff.[80] Severing, who had refused to abandon his office, was given the opportunity to yield to a show of force, which was all that it was, since only the new police president and two soldiers were required to remove him from his office.[81]

Although Otto Braun had withdrawn from his post as Minister President in Prussia early in June, he received word of his dismissal by messenger at his residence in Zehlendorff. At first he intended to try and regain his office, but in a telephone conversation he was informed that several *Reichswehr* officers had occupied his quarters and would not permit him to enter or use his official automobile. After several unsuccessful attempts to contact Severing and other members of the State Ministry, Braun settled for a written protest to Papen.[82]

Meanwhile, in order to prevent any opposition from developing, Papen addressed the nation that evening on the radio. His theme was essentially the same one which had convinced Hindenburg to sign the emergency decrees. The threat of Communist subversion of law and order in Prussia had persuaded him to take this action. He also explained that the recently elected *Landtag* was unable to form a majority for the election of a minister president because of the change in the manner of electing someone to that post. The result was a predicament, Papen continued, in which the parties on the right with 47% of the seats were unable to take power from the present caretaker government. Placing a great deal of the blame for this situation on the Center leaders for refusing to form a coalition with the Right, the Chancellor warned that the Communists, with 16% of the seats, "were [now] in a key position to overthrow the State and the Constitution." He then recited a litany of reasons why the Communists were the sworn enemies of the State: "...their method [was] the destruction of the religious, moral, cultural values of our people. Their terrorist groups had introduced violence and murder as political weapons." He capped off these charges by accusing the Social Democrats of negotiating with the Communists, thus implying that they were part of the same conspiracy.[83] He concluded his address with assurances that his government did not wish to destroy Prussian autonomy.[84] Always conscious of his Government's image abroad, Papen also issued a statement to America via NBC, in which he explained that his governmnet had been forced to intervene in order to prevent a civil war. Then, with an eye to winning the sympathy of conservatives and other anti-Communists, Papen pointed out that since the Communists were prepared to take over Prussia and then the Reich, his regime had no other course of action.[85] The following day, in spite of his assurances the night before, the Papen government proceeded to purge not only the Prussian State Ministry, but also local officials on the pretext that this was part of the administrative reforms being undertaken by the Reich.[86]

Papen's victory in Prussia marked his first effort to restore what he often called "the other Germany." But, this was an illusion - the Germany he desired no longer existed. And his allegiance to an illusion, led him to serve as an apprentice to a Sorcerer who had his own vision of a new Germany.

B. Elections of July 31, 1932

The German nation was preparing to go to the polls once again on July 31. Not only would the voters pass judgment on Papen's negotiations at Lausanne, but more importantly his actions against the Prussian government. The atmosphere was tense as all parties campaigned intently. The level of violence steadily increased as the election day approached. There were even rumors of a plot to overthrow the government by the Hitler's SS Charges and counter-charges by all the parties increased the already hostile mood, with the most extreme charges coming from the Nazis and the Communists.

Naturally, the major issue was the performance of the Papen government. However, unlike previous elections, in this one the voters found it difficult to voice their opinions because the cabinet was not represented by any one specific party. In fact Papen had renounced any such claim, maintaining that it was a government above political parties. In spite of this declaration, Papen did attempt to form a moderate conservative grouping of parties around President Hindenburg. However, those efforts foundered not only on the petty rivalries among the parties, but also on Hindenburg's apparent coolness to the idea.[87] Therefore, the only alternative that remained for voters who did not favor either the Communists or Nazis, was to vote for either the DNVP or the DVP. However, since the death of Gustav Stresemann, the DVP had been steadily declining. This was also true of the DNVP, headed by the mass-media tycoon, Alfred Hugenburg.[88] Consequently, those who might have favored Papen's policies, but were put off by Hugenburg's leadership had no recourse but to vote for another party or abstain.

Although this situation helps to explain the weakness of Papen's position with the voters, it masks the fundamental problem, which was the lack of a broadly based support among the voters. The constant refrain of "cabinet of barons," echoed relentlessly in the speeches by the Social Democrats, the Communists, and especially the Nazis. Even the Nationalists tried to put some distance between themselves and Papen's government. On July 23, Hugenburg wrote the Chancellor requesting that he prevail on the cabinet to lift both the Prussian emergency decree of June 8, and the Reich emergency decree of June 14. Although Papen politely rejected this appeal, the exchange of these memos demonstrated that even the Nationalists did not want to be too closely identified with the Papen government.[89]

Finally, in a last minute bid to increase the Government's support among the voters, Papen and Schleicher took to the air to deliver radio addresses. Schleicher stressed two points: Germany was prepared to a) pursue whatever armament course was necessary if France refused Germany parity, and b) renounce any government supported only by bayonets.[90] On the eve of the election day, Papen gave a spirited defense of the Lausanne Agreements, calling them the end of a system of tribute and the basis for economic recovery. Papen also stressed that Germany must liberate itself from the fruitless arguments over the merits of capitalism and socialism. The welfare of the community, he declared, must take precedence over the welfare of the individual.[91]

C. Aftermath

On July 31, the German public went to the polls and chose a *Reichstag* vastly different from its predecessor. The DNVP and the DVP, most closely connected with the Papen regime, were only able to marshal 44 seats between them. The Nazis emerged as the largest party in the *Reichstag*, their representation increasing from 107 to 230! The SPD held second place but, having failed to resist the Prussian coup, fell from 143 to 133. On the other hand, the Center party and the BVP rose from 87 to 97, while the Communists showed a modest increase from 77 to 89 seats. The remaining splinter parties were virtually wiped out. But the most striking result was that the Nazis and the Communists, two sworn enemies of the Republic, now possessed

*Vice Chancellor von Papen with his wife and daughter
leaving the polling place in the Jaegerstrasse, Berlin,
July 1932*

52.5% of the *Reichstag* seats.[92] Moreover, aside from the fact that the results proved that the German voters had disavowed the cabinet of barons, the returns produced "no conclusive" decision.[93]

Despite these results, Papen appeared to be unconcerned. In an interview on August 1 with Louis P. Lochner, head of the Associated Press in Berlin, Papen had the audacity to claim that the election results marked an endorsement of his efforts to free Germany from the domination of political parties. In a tone bordering on the blasé, Papen boasted that he would not bother with coalitions, and would make no attempt to find a majority in the *Reichstag*.[94] "My colleagues and I," he continued, "want to go before the *Reichstag* with our constructive program and force its members to decide whether or not they want to dislodge us from the saddle despite the pressing need for objective non-partisan work."[95] In this connection he also mentioned the need for a *Reichsreform*, which included the elimination of proportional representation. If such reforms had been in place before the elections Papen boasted, he would have been elected as a candidate of the Center in his native Westphalia. Shortly after the interview Papen slipped away to his estate in Wallerfangen for a rest from the hectic pace of the past sixty days.

NOTES

[1] The constitution of 1871 was a curious mixture of federalism and centralism. The Constitution called for the administration of federal legislation by the state bureaucracies. Since Prussia occupied two-thirds of German territory and possessed three-fifths of her population, it was responsible for the implementation of most of the Reich laws. Moreover, the Prussian king and the chancellor dominated the *Bundesrat* and the *Reichstag*.

[2] While the Social Democrats favored centralization in principle, they were not prepared to support a division of Prussia into smaller states at the cost of their own political dominance in Prussia. Consequently many Socialists were at one with the soldiers and bureaucrats in opposing any changes. Bavaria would also have been happy to see Prussia's position reduced, but the idea of a more centralized system was unacceptable because of a certain measure of autonomy it enjoyed, even under Bismarck. Cf. Arnold Brecht, *Federalism and Regionalism: The Division of Prussia* (London: Oxford University Press, 1945), p. 72 ff.

[3] Frequent political clashes between the Reich and the Prussian governments resulted from the fact that the Prussian government was controlled by the liberal Weimar Coalition, while the Reich cabinets, with few exceptions, were composed mainly of conservative, anti-democratic parties. Cf. Arnold Brecht, *Prelude to Silence* (New York: Oxford University Press, 1944), pp. 51-55.

[4] In 1928 a committee for constitutional reform was established. After more than two years of debate, the committee drafted several proposals which would have significantly changed the state of Prussia. However, the proposals came to naught because of the objections of the Bavarian Minister President Held, and public apathy. Arnold Brecht, *Federalism and Regionalism; The Division of Prussia* (London: Oxford University Press, 1945), pp. 174-75.

[5] Prussia was strategically important for all the political parties because of its size and voter population. It also had a 60,000 man police force, which represented the most powerful official armed force outside of the *Reichswehr*. Control of this body would place the Nazis in a position to dictate their own terms to the Reich, since it depended on the Prussia police for protection.

[6] This was the second attempt by Brüning to initiate a constitutional reform. In 1931 he asked Otto Braun to merge the Reich and Prussian ministries of finance under the Reich Minister. Braun turned the offer down when he realized that he would be politically responsible for fiscal policies over which he had only limited control. Cf. Heinrich Brüning, *Memorien* 1918-1934 (Stuttgart: Deutsche Verlagsanstalt, 1970), pp. 569-70; Thomas Trumpp, *Franz von Papen, der*

preussische-deutsche Dualismus und die NSDAP in Preussen. Ein Beitrag zur Vorgeschichte des 20 Juli 1932, Diss. Tübingen 1963, p. 99.

[7] Papen, *Memoirs*, p. 110. In his account of this incident, Henry Adams labels the *Landtag* proposal "a slick maneuver," designed to preserve the SPD's "power position" in Prussia (*Rebel Patriot*, p. 152). There is no question that the Braun-Severing government wanted to remain in power in Prussia, but a more fundamental motive for the proposal was to block the Nazis from seizing control of the Prussian police. While Adams condemns the Social Democrats for this action, he approves Papen's decision to intervene in Prussia for the same reason!

[8] The approximately 420 *Landtag* seats were divided as follows: Nazis, 162; Nationalists, 31; Social Democrats, 94; Center, 67; Communists, 57; German People's Party, 7; State Party, 2. Cf. Halperin, *Germany Tried Democracy*, p. 481.

[9] With the possible exception of the DNVP, there was little enthusiasm for a coalition government composed of the National Socialists, Nationalists, and Center parties. Although several Centrists continued to be interested in a sharing power with the Nazis, Goebbels recorded the Nazi attitude: "In the Prussian question we are placing conditions that the Center cannot fulfill." Goebbels, *Kaiserhof,* entry for June 9, 1932, p. 109.

[10] Otto Braun later wrote that he was "a finished man," with no desire "to expose myself to gutter cries of parliamentary rowdies, in a legislative chamber that has become no better than a den of thieves." He never again returned to his position in the Prussian government. Otto Braun, 2nd. ed., *Von Weimar zu Hitler* (New York: Europe Verlag, 1940), p. 396.

[11] Wheeler-Bennett, *The Nemisis of Power*, p. 245; Gordon Craig, *Politics of the Prussian Army*, p. 454.

[12] Wheeler-Bennett, ibid. What Schleicher intended after he had disposed of the Nazis is not clear. He was probably interested in the return of the monarchy since he was in close personal contact with the crown prince throughout this period.

[13] Werner E. Braatz, "Franz von Papen and the *Prüssenschlag*, July 20, 1932; a move by the 'New State' toward *Reichsreform,*" *European Studies Review*, Vol. 3 No. 2 (April, 1973), p. 157; Franz von Papen, "*Konservative Staatsführung,*" *RKz.*, R 43 I/1934, BA, Koblenz.

[14] "*Wie Papen konzentriert,*" *Berliner Tageblatt,* June 1, 1932; "*Die Pläne um Preussen,*" *Vossische Zeitung,* June 8, 1932.

[15] Goebbels, *Kaiserhof,* entry for June 4, 1932, p. 107.

[16] *Preussen contra Reich vor dem Staatsgerichtshof; Stennogrammbericht der Verhandlungen vor dem Staatsgerichtshof in Leipzig von 10. bis 12. und von Oktober 1932.* (Berlin: J.H.W. Dietz., 1933), p. 38.

[17] Alvensleben to Schwerin-Krosigk June 7, 1932, *Preussen contra Reich*, p. 37.

[18] There are different opinions about what the Nazis wanted in return for tolerating the Papen regime. Thomas Trumpp, *Papen, NSDAP, und Reich-Prüssen Dualismus*, p. 73, 104, argues that the Nazis were more interested in rescinding the April 12 decision in the Prussian *Landtag*, which stated that an absolute majority was required to elect the minister president. Jürgen Bay, *Der Prüssen Konflikt*, p. 102, n. 548, argues that Trumpp underestimates the Nazi's desire to have a Reich Commissioner.

[19] Michael Carl Sterling, "The *Herrenreiter* in Politics: The Government of Franz von Papen, May 31, 1932 - December 2, 1932," (Ph.D. dissertation, Indiana University 1975), pp. 171-172.

[20] Goebbels, *Kaiserhof*, entry for June 6, 1932, p. 108.

[21] Ibid., entry for June 9, 1932, p. 109.

[22] Cabinet Meeting, June 2, 1932, 1600 hrs, *RKz.*, R 43 I/1456, BA, Koblenz.

[23] Papen to Kerrl, June 6, 1932 *RKz.*, R 43 I/2280, BA, Koblenz.

[24] The Prussian regime blocked this attempt by introducing the *Schlachtsteuer* (slaughtering tax), and reducing government salaries by 2.5% to 5%. State Ministry Meeting, June 7, 1932, *Preussisches Geheimesstaatsarchiv-Berlin-Dahlem*, Rep. 90/1932/ Bd. 39/ 44-46.

[25] Hirtsiefer to Papen, June 7, 1932, *RKz.*, R 43 I/2280, BA, Koblenz.

[26] Papen to Hirtsiefer, June 9, 1932, *RKz.*, R 43 I/2280, BA, Koblenz.

[27] Cf. Chapter 7 for more details. As in Prussia, the April elections in the southern *Länder* resulted in caretaker governments. The three minister presidents were afraid that if a commissioner was established in Prussia, they would be the next victims.

[28] "*Niederschrift über eine Besprechung des Reichspräsidenten mit den Süddeutschen Minister*," June 12, 1932, *MA* 87, *IfZg.*

[29] Trumpp, ibid., pp. 76-77.

[30] Gayl's report to the Cabinet, June 25, 1932. R 43 I/1456, BA, Koblenz.

[31] Joachim Petzold, "*Der Staatsstreich vom 20 Juli 1932 in Preussen*," *Zeitschrift für Geschichtswissenschaft*, IV (1956), p. 1160; "*Kurzorientierung für Herrn General von Bredow*," F 41, *IfZg*; Cabinet Meeting, June 25, 1932, *RKz.*, R 43 I/1456, BA, Koblenz.

[32] Short Notation of June 25, 1932 by *Ministeramt, Sammlung Photokopien und Einzeldokumente*, F 41, *IfZg.*

[33] Notes of a conversation between the Prussian *Fraktion* of the NSDAP and Wilhelm von Gayl, June 24, 1932, *Reichsministerium des Innern: Akten betreffend Zusammenstösse, Gewalttätigkeiten*, No. 25706, Deutsches Zentralarchiv, Potsdam. (Hereafter cited as *RMI*, DZA, Potsdam)

[34] Minutes of a meeting between State Secretary Planck and *Landtag* deputies Winterfeld and Borck, July 8, 1932, *RKz.*, R 43 I/2280/19-20, BA, Koblenz.

---

[35] Winterfeld to Papen, July 8, 1932, *RKz.*, R 43 I/2280/23-24, BA, Koblenz.

[36] Von der Goltz to Papen, July 11, 1932, *RKz.*, R 43 I/678, BA, Koblenz.

[37] *Privatschreiben des Prinzen Wilhelm v. Preussen an Frhr. v. Gayl vom 9. Juni 1932, Nachlass Gayl* 24, BA, Koblenz. (Hereafter cited as *NG*) Karl D. Bracher, *Die Auflösung der Weimarer Republik: Eine Studie zum Problem des Machtverfalls in der Demokratie.* 3rd.rev.ed., Villigen, Schwarzwald, 1960), p.577, n.97.

[38] Cabinet Session, July 11, 1932, *Rkz.*, R 43 I/1457, BA, Koblenz; Andreas Dorpalen, *Hindenburg*, pp. 401-402.

[39] Christopher Isherwood, *The Berlin Stories* (New York: New Directions Publishing Corporation, 1963) p. 86.

[40] Alan Bullock, *Hitler*, p. 177.

[41] Cabinet Session, July 11, 1932, *RKz.*, R 43 I/1457, BA, Koblenz.

[42] Gayl agreed with Schleicher that a more cooperative approach towards Hitler's movement would produce better results.

[43] *Vorwärts* was banned for five days because of an article critical of lifting the ban on the SA. The *Kölnische Volkszeitung* had also been banned because of criticism of Papen's handling of foreign policy. Cf. Horkenbach, *Das Deutsche Reich* (1932), pp. 218-19. For Gayl's remarks to the Cabinet see Cabinet Session, July 11, 1932, *RKz.*, R 43 I/1457, BA, Koblenz.

[44] Cabinet Session, July 11, 1932, *RKz.*, R 43 I/1457, BA, Koblenz.

[45] Ibid.

[46] Cabinet Session, July 11, 1932, *Rkz.*, R 43 I/1457, BA, Koblenz. Gayl and the Justice Minister Gürtner, were commissioned to draft an appropriate emergency decree.

[47] Cabinet Session, July 12, 1932, *Rkz.*, R 43 I/1457/108-109, BA, Koblenz.

[48] Ibid.

[49] Cabinet Session, July 12, 1932, *Rkz.*, R 43 I/1457, BA, Koblenz.

[50] Affidavit of testimony by General-Major Eugen Ott, *Sammlung Zeugenschrifttum*, No. 279, *IfZg*, Munich; Dorpalen, *Hindenburg*, p. 342; Cabinet Session, July 11, 1932, *Rkz.*, R 43 I/1457, BA, Koblenz.

[51] Gayl informed the Cabinet that the Communist party was trying to organize a popular front against fascism. In Berlin the shop workers at the Sieman's plant and the union members of the AEG plant at Henningsdorf responded positively to these appeals. The Government also received reports of Communist agitation in Breslau, Düsseldorf, Wuppertal and Elberfeld. Situation Report of July 16, 1932, *RMI Akten*, No. 26177, DAZ, Potsdam.

[52] Cabinet Session, July 11, 1932, *RKz.*, R 43 I/1457, BA, Koblenz.

[53] It is not certain whether Diels served as an informer to Schleicher on his own initiative or was persuaded to do so by persons who were in the direct pay of the

General. Diels later became a prominent member of the Gestapo. In 1934 he was replaced by Heinrich Himmler.

[54] Letter of May 21, 1947 by Wilhelm Abegg to Carl Severing, *Sammlung Zeugenschrifttum*, No. 536, *IfZg*; Communication of August 4, 1932 by Wilhelm Abegg to Carl Severing, *Sammlung Photokopien und Einzeldokumente*, Fa 4, *IfZg*.

[55] Diels' report to Schleicher is open to question because of his reputation as being very ambitious. He might have presented an exaggerated picture of this meeting in order to ingratiate himself with Schleicher for personal gain. There is also the unanswered question posed by Arnold Brecht during the proceedings in Leipzig before the Supreme Court. Why did Diels wait over a month before presenting his information to Schleicher? Was it perhaps because he waited for a better opportunity to enhance his position? Quoted in Carl Severing, *Mein Lebensweg* II (Köln: Greven Verlag, 1950), p. 342.

[56] Ever since the formation of the Republic there was bad blood between the two Marxist parties. The Communists considered the Social Democrats as traitors to Marxism because they abandoned their revolutionary posture. The Social Democrats, on the other hand, regarded violence as something evil, and for this reason insisted on parliamentary democracy as the only road to bring about socialism.

[57] Erich Eyck, *Weimar Republic*, II, p. 413.

[58] Cabinet Session of July 11, 1932, *RKz.*, R 43 I/1457, BA, Koblenz. Papen defended his actions with the same argument in his *Memoirs*, and at the Nuremberg Trials.

[59] Cabinet Session on July 12, 1932, *RKz.*, R 43 I/1457, BA, Koblenz; Severing, ibid., p. 342.

[60] Otto Meissner, was present when Gayl and Papen met with Hindenburg. At Nuremberg, Meissner testified that Hindenburg was very reluctant to approve the emergency decree. But when Papen informed him of Abegg's talk with the two Communists, his misgivings quickly vanished. Meissner Document Book, I, 63, *International Military Tribunal*, War Crimes Case No. 11. (Hereafter cited as *I.M.T.*)

[61] Cabinet Session, July 12, 1932, *RKz.*, R 43 I/1457/100, BA, Koblenz

[62] Hindenburg received Papen and Gayl with warm cordiality. When the Chancellor offered to resign because of the poor domestic reception of the Lausanne settlement, the president would not hear of it. Cf. Dorpalen, *Hindenburg*, p. 344.

[63] Information given by Otto Meissner to Hans Otto Meissner, in Hans Otto Meissner & Harry Wilde, *Die Machtergreifung: Ein Bericht über die Technik des*

nationalsozialistischen Staatsstreichs (Stuttgart: J. G. Cottische Buchhandlung, 1958), p.91.

[64] Quoted in Eyck, ibid., p. 409. Gayl voided the local government prohibitions on party uniforms with the cutting remark that "the misgivings which are frequently expressed about the renewed exercise of this right [i.e., wearing of uniforms] are exaggerated."

[65] Kessler, *Diary*, p. 423.

[66] Eyck, ibid., p. 409.

[67] Otto Klepper, "*Das Ende der Republik*," *Die Gegenwart*, Vol. II, No. 42/43 (September 30, 1947), p. 21. Bracht belonged to the conservative wing of the Center party with a reputation of being a solid administrator. Since he agreed with Papen that a *Reichsreform* was necessary, this made him an excellent candidate for the position of Interior Minister in Prussia.

[68] Gayl, *NG*, 36/8, BA-Militärarchiv, Freiburg.

[69] In his *Memoirs* (p. 190), Papen states that his information about this meeting came from an article by Klepper published in the German magazine *Die Gegenwart*, in September 1947.

[70] Severing, ibid., p. 347; Papen, *Memoirs*, pp. 190-91. In his account of this meeting, Papen fails to include the fact that Severing and the others had decided not to offer any resistance out of fear that it would provoke a civil war.

[71] Otto Klepper, "*Das Ende der Republik*," *Die Gegenwart*, Vol II, No. 42/43 (September 30, 1947), p. 21.

[72] Memorandum of August 1, 1932 by the Reichs Chancellery about the course of action against the Prussian State Government on July 20, 1932, *RKz.*, R 43 I/2280, BA, Koblenz; Memorandum of August 5, 1932 concerning the meeting on July 20, 1932 between the Reichs Chancellor and the representatives of the Prussian State Government, Ibid.

[73] Severing, ibid., p. 349; Memorandum of August 5, 1932, *RKz.*, R 43 I/2280, BA, Koblenz.

[74] Memorandum of State Minister Hirtsiefer, *Anlageheft zu der Erklärung des preussischen Staatsministeriums*, August 10, 1932, Anlage I; quoted in Bracher, *Auflösung*, p. 584.

[75] Severing, ibid., II, p. 350.

[76] Papen, *Memoirs*, p. 190.

[77] Notes about the events of July 20, 1932, entitled "*Mittwoch 20. Juli 1932*," *RKz.*, R 43 I/2280/221, BA, Koblenz.

[78] Memorandum of August 1, 1932 by Reichs Chancellery concerning the course of action against Prussia on July 20, 1932, *RKz.*, R 43 I/2280, BA, Koblenz.

[79] Albert Grzesinski, *Inside Germany*, trans. Alexander S. Lipschitz (New York: E. P. Dutton & Co., Inc., 1939), pp. 157-160. The police chief of Essen, Kurt

Melcher, was appointed in Grzesinski's place, and the conservative police Colonel Poten replaced Weiss. The latter was especially hated in right wing circles because of his liberalism, and Jewish origin.

[80] Albert Grzesinski, ibid., pp. 157-159. He disagreed with Severing over the question of resistance, and was arrested along with his associates later that day after waiting in vain for opposition to the *coup* to surface.

[81] Severing, ibid., p. 352. In his *Diaries*, Count Kessler characterized Severing's statement about bowing to force alone as "simply a case of playing to the gallery." According to Klepper, Severing's conduct was "only explicable in terms of being a little man who...believes that...nothing should be done to infringe the ruling class' conventions." (*Diaries*, p. 432.)

[82] Letter from Braun to Papen July 20, 1932, *RKz.*, R 43 I/2280/231, BA, Koblenz. Papen's response to Braun, ibid., 179.

[83] Papen, *Memoirs*, pp. 191-192.

[84] Ibid.

[85] Ibid., p. 192.

[86] For example, the presidents of Lower Silesia, Saxony, Schleswig-Holstein, Hesse-Nassau - all provinces lying within Prussia's boundaries - were immediately replaced. The same held true for the *Regierungspräsidenten* of Frankfurt on the Main.

[87] Dorpalen, *Hindenburg*, p. 347. Differences concerning attitudes towards the Papen government can be found in the *Berliner Tageblatt*, June 13, 1932. Papen's attitude towards the formation of a presidential party can be found in *Wahrheit*, p. 238, where he places most of the blame on the failure to form a presidential party on Hugenberg. The weakness of Papen's non-party position is affirmed by Nickolaus Graf von Ballestram in his letter to Papen, January 16, 1933, *RKz*, R 53 I/71/70-71, BA, Koblenz.

[88] Hugenberg failed to gain many supporters because of his complete lack of rapport with the voters, as well as his excessively strident nationalism, and extremely intolerant attitude towards parliamentarianism.

[89] Papen to Hugenberg, July 23, 1932. Schleicher Papers, N-42/22/76-81, M.A., *IfzG*, Munich; also Papen to Hugenberg, July 26, 1932, R 43 *RKz I/339/138-140*, BA, Koblenz.

[90] Horkenbach, *Das Deutsche Reich* (1932), p. 260 for a detailed summary of Schleicher's speech.

[91] Horkenbach, ibid., p. 263. This was a substantial departure from his earlier views enunciated on June 4, when he criticized previous governments for perpetuating the welfare state. One expects that this was simply campaign rhetoric since he followed those remarks with the declaration that the common good demanded the strong protection of private-property rights.

[92] *Reichstag* Elections 1919-1933, Appendix B in Koppel S. Pinson, *Modern Germany: Its History & Civilization* (2nd ed.; New York, 1966), p. 604.

[93] Dorpalen, *Hindenburg,* p. 348.

[94] Interview of August 1, 1932 by Franz von Papen with Louis P. Lochner, quoted in *Vossische Zeitung*, August 2, 1932. The prospect of a no confidence vote in the *Reichstag* seemed "not in the slightest to disturb him" (ibid.).

[95] Interview, ibid.

CHAPTER 7:
THE "NEW STATE" IN ACTION

A. The Nazis & the "New State"

On Monday morning after the election, the nation awoke to the news that Nazis had gone on a rampage in Königsberg, killing two Communist leaders in their beds at night, and wounding several Social Democrats. Although Reich commissioner Bracht issued a warning that he would not hesitate to take strong action to end the current violence, his exhortation had little effect. For the next ten days acts of violence were reported in East Prussia, Silesia, Schleswig-Holstein, the Ruhr, Saxony and Bavaria.[1] The British Ambassador in Berlin, Sir Horace Rumbold, reported that on August 2, SA thugs planted bombs in ten towns in Holstein, fired pistol shots in Marienburg and hand grenades were thrown at a land-title office in the county of Labiau. For the next eight days the police reported bombings in Breslau, Gleiwitz, Ratibor. The Mayor of Norgau was gunned down in the streets on August 3. On August 7, Storm Troopers murdered two leaders of the *Reichsbanner*. In Britz, a working-class suburb of Berlin, the SA threw an incendiary bomb at the Town Hall.[2]

While the public were deeply distressed over the current wave of violence, the press of the Left and Center charged the Government with dragging its heels. *Germania* accused Papen of being no more successful in restoring order in Prussia than the Socialist government, which he had ousted from power. Even the right wing press called for punishment of the perpetrators regardless of party affiliation. The Nazi press, on the other hand, made no effort to disavow the wave of terror unleashed by the Storm Troopers, and even threatened future acts of violence.[3] Meanwhile the *Volkische Beobachter* defended Nazi outrages, claiming that they were acts of desperation prompted by the necessity for self-defense against the communists.[4]

Despite this growing crisis, Papen decided to spend a few days with his family while Hindenburg retreated to his estate in East Prussia. However, under the chairmanship of Gayl, the Cabinet met on August 4, to discuss ways to restore peace to the country. Gayl proposed the establishment of special courts in areas where particularly heavy violence had been reported, and suggested that a ban on the carrying of weapons should be imposed along with the death penalty for killing or wounding other citizens. Franz Bracht, the newly appointed Reich Commissioner in Prussia, expressed concern about the growing Communist threat, and complained that the Government was too ready to exaggerate out of all proportion the actions of the Right. This was not too surprising, he continued, "if one considers the fact that for more than ten years the police served the Weimar Coalition by harassing the Right almost exclusively."[5] This criticism was directed against the Social Democrat, Carl Severing, who had been the Prussian Minister of Interior, and in charge of the police. But it was also an attempt to minimize the obvious complicity of the Nazis in most of the violence. After further discussion, the ministers agreed that some emergency legislation was necessary, but they were still uncertain about the form it should take.[6]

When Papen returned to Berlin on August 8, Gayl informed him of the Cabinet's deliberations. Upon hearing that nothing had been decided, the Chancellor announced that the government would use all of its power, including brute force if necessary, to halt the violence.[7] When the ministers met the next day, the Cabinet proposed emergency legislation calling for an end to terrorism. The most significant part of this legislation was a decree that called for the death penalty for any person who killed a political opponent, a police officer, or a member of the army.[8] The decree also established special courts to try the political cases that might arise as a result.

The Government did not have to wait long to test these new measures. That same night, nine uniformed Storm Troopers, who had been drinking excessively, roamed the streets of the Silesian town, Potempa, looking for trouble. Forcing their way into the home of a known communist, Konrad Pietzruch, they pulled him out of bed, and beat him to death before his mother's eyes.[9] When news of this brutal act reached the ministers, they voted to charge the perpetrators with murder in a special court that had been established at Beuthen. On August 22, five of the men were condemned to death for their part in the crime. The National Socialists who were present throughout the trial loudly protested the verdict, proclaiming that "the German people will reach another verdict in the future; the verdict of Beuthen will be a beacon to German freedom."[10] Hitler immediately rushed to the defense of the convicted men, assuring them that "in the face of this most monstrous and bloody sentence," he remained joined to them "in boundless loyalty." He concluded with a pledge to fight for their immediate release, and attacked Papen for deliberately undertaking a persecution against the "nationally minded elements" in Germany.[11] A few days later this bold challenge to the Papen government was answered by a commutation to life imprisonment. In announcing the decision, the Government rationalized that the new decrees had gone into effect only hours before the crime was committed. "It was therefore possible to claim that the culprits had not been aware of the legal consequences of their actions; in which case it might be proper to commute the sentence to one of life imprisonment."[12] Thus Papen, who just one month before had justified his intervention in Prussia on the grounds that the Braun-Severing regime had failed to secure law and order, now failed to live up to the same objective.[13]

In his *Memoirs*, Papen offers a different version concerning the Cabinet's actions. He maintains that the decision to commute the sentences was based on his unwillingness to "provide the more radical National Socialists with unnecessary propaganda material" in the forthcoming *Reichstag* elections. He also claims that this decision was intended to be a "display of mercy," which would have a "calming effect" on the nation![14] However, this rather weak attempt to minimize the significance of this action does not stand up to the facts. How could the decision to commute the sentences be based on the forthcoming elections when the decision to hold elections was not decided until the *Reichstag* session of September 12? Perhaps an even more acceptable explanation is that Papen's own over-estimation of his personal ability to control the situation, along with the support he anticipated from the President and the Army, led him to simply ignore the consequences. This was not the first time - nor would it be the last - that this happened. In any case, neither Papen nor his ministerial colleagues were ready to admit that they were giving in to Nazi pressure. Further evidence that this was the case can be seen from the fact that over the next several weeks both Papen and Schleicher tried to bring Hitler to accept some form of partnership with the presidial government.

B. Hitler Rebuffed

Since the elections settled nothing, Papen was confident that he could remain in office. He was not impressed by Hitler's gains in the elections since the Nazis had failed to win a majority. He also knew that he enjoyed Hindenburg's favor more than any previous chancellor. Papen expressed confidence that he could wrest a majority from the *Reichstag*, after which an Enabling Act would be passed authorizing him to govern by decree for a specified period of time. If the *Reichstag* refused to pass this law he would dissolve it.[15]

A course of action favored by Gayl was to dissolve the *Reichstag* for an indefinite period, during which time the Government would undertake a series of constitutional reforms that would lead to the restoration of the pre-1918 political order.[16] However, since this clearly unconstitutional approach would probably lead to violent opposition, there was only one remaining option, namely the dissolution of the *Reichstag* and the announcement of new elections within the constitutionally defined limit of sixty days. Probably the most distasteful option for Papen's government would have been to resign in favor of a Nazi-Center coalition government. Although some members in the Center advocated such an arrangement, many National Socialists were opposed to it. While Schleicher thought this could happen, Gayl, whose political thinking was considerably different from the General's saw little likelihood that these two parties could reach an agreement in the long run.[17] In any event, Papen intended to maintain an independent government that stood above all parties. With this in mind he left Berlin in early August to spend a few days with his family in the Saarland, and prepare for what proved to be a series of unsuccessful meetings with Hitler and other political groups.

In the meantime, flushed with electoral success, Hitler had no intention of being fobbed off with second place. He wanted the chancellorship for himself, and several important ministerial posts for his Nazi colleagues. In his view, the German public expected him to take power at once; if he failed to do so, many would see no purpose in voting for the party in the future. An analysis of the July election results indicated that the vote totals were approximately the same as those in the presidential runoff in April. There were some among the Nazi hierarchy who thought this was a sign that the popularity of the Nazi movement had apparently peaked. On August 9, Strasser and Frick joined Hitler at Berchtesgaden with some disquieting news. The violent behavior of the SA along with some wilder election and post-election statements were causing people to wonder if the Nazis were fit to have power. Schacht reported, for example, that business and industrial circles were becoming worried lest a Hitler government should lead to radical economic experiments along the lines Gottfried Feder and Gregor Strasser had often proposed.[18] Consequently, Hitler was compelled to consider the prospects of negotiating not only with Papen but also with the Center Party.

An opportunity arose just a few days after the elections. At a post-election meeting in Cologne, the Center leaders decided to explore the possibilities of forming a coalition government with the National Socialists.[19] When the news of this rapprochement between the Center and the National Socialists reached Schleicher's ears, he called together some of his closest advisors. Not a little disturbed, the General told them that a government under Hitler's leadership was impossible because Hindenburg would never agree to it. Therefore, it was his intention to try and talk Hitler out of this plan.[20]

When the two met on August 5, at the Fürstenberg Barracks north of Berlin, Hitler defended his claim to the chancellorship, and also demanded the post of minister president in Prussia along with other ministerial posts.[21] The Führer also expressed confidence that he could wrest a majority from the *Reichstag*, after which an Enabling Act would be passed authorizing the chancellor to govern by decree for a specified period of time. If the *Reichstag* refused to pass this law he would dissolve it.[22] Schleicher responded that with a majority in the *Reichstag* nobody could question Hitler's right to govern. In spite of the ambiguity of this reply, the Führer took it to mean that Schleicher had promised him the chancellorship.[23]

Having failed in his efforts to talk Hitler out of demanding the chancellorship, Schleicher now had to try to persuade the President to go along with the Führer's demands. On August 9, "either on a hurried visit to Neudeck or through phone calls to Oskar," Schleicher spoke with Hindenburg.[24] The General insisted "most emphatically" on the appointment of Hitler as chancellor. But Hindenburg rejected the suggestion, and sharply rebuked him: "I am told that you want to hand me over to the Nazis." He then added that he would resign rather than appoint Hitler if "by some compact with the Center" he were able to obtain a majority in the *Reichstag*.[25]

When Hindenburg returned to Berlin the next day, he met with Papen and discussed Schleicher's reported meeting with Hitler. The Chancellor informed Hindenburg of the Center party's interest in joining the Nazis to form a majority in the *Reichstag*, and then entrust the leadership of the government to Hitler. Papen said that he was sympathetic to such a prospect, and that he was even willing to resign as chancellor, and accept the post of foreign minister in a Hitler cabinet.[26] In spite of this offer, Hindenburg remained strongly opposed to a Hitler-led government. He reminded the Chancellor that the Nazi leader had recently promised to support the Papen government after the election, but was now prepared to break this promise. As far as he was concerned, Hindenburg concluded, there was no guarantee that as chancellor Hitler would "preserve the character of a presidial government." However, Hindenburg added that he did not exclude the possibility of eventually inviting into the government one or two "reliable and hard-working National Socialists." Then the President requested Papen to discuss this possibility with both the Nazis and the Center party.[27]

Later that same day, Papen reported his conversation with Hindenburg to the cabinet. Summarizing this conversation, Papen told the ministers he wanted to obtain Hindenburg's permission to try and get Hitler to join his government. The real task, he continued, was to "find a middle way between the retention of a presidial cabinet and the desire of the Nazis to assume the leadership of the government."[28] Then switching to his favorite subject, Papen concluded his report with what he considered to be the most essential tasks facing the Cabinet in the immediate future: (a) the settlement of the constitutional relationship between the Reich and Prussia; (b) a reform of the voting system and the creation of an Upper House; (c) administrative reforms in both the Reich and Prussia.[29]

Enlarging on Papen's report, Schleicher informed the ministers that in his recent meeting with Hitler he became convinced of how impossible it was to satisfy the Nazis with two or three cabinet posts.

Although one could never be certain just what the cagey General was plotting from one moment to the next, he suggested that this left the Government with two possibilities: the Cabinet could decide to resist any change in its composition and hope to ultimately swing the majority behind it through "successful practical achievements;" or attract the National Socialists into a ruling coalition of some sort. Schleicher pointed out that he did not see much chance of success for the first alternative because all parties (except the DNVP) would probably declare themselves against the Papen regime. Consequently, the government would then be forced to admit that there was no possibility of forming a majority government. He then pointed out that there existed in the Center party a strong inclination to bypass the present government and negotiate directly with the National Socialist. Should this effort be successful, this could lead to a presidential crisis because Hindenburg refused to appoint a cabinet composed of political parties, especially with Hitler as chancellor.[30]

While Schleicher thought the idea of taking the Nazis into the present government was the simplest solution, he expressed doubts that the cabinet would be willing to pay the price that Hitler would demand, namely, the top cabinet posts. He concluded his remarks by suggesting that before the cabinet could make any final decision it would have to await the outcome of further negotiations.[31]

The discussion that followed revealed differing views. Gayl and Braun were opposed to any participation of the National Socialists in the government. The Interior Minister predicted bitter opposition from the Left, which would result in increased acts of terror, worsening of the economy, and the prevention of implementing the necessary constitutional and administrative reforms indicated by the Chancellor. Like Gayl, Braun dreaded the public outcry that would undoubtedly arise from the southern *Länder* who were opposed to the idea of a Hitler chancellorship. Neurath and Schäffer also opposed any political changes at this time lest they provoke further unrest. On the other hand Warmbold, Krosighk and Gürtner were not against some participation of the Nazis in the government. Summarizing the discussion, the Chancellor agreed to try and find a way to preserve the government's power as much as possible in his forthcoming talks with the party leaders. But he emphasized that the crucial issue was the degree of participation in the government which must be conceded to the Nazis in order to get them to cease their opposition.[32]

Against this backdrop of the impending political negotiations, the official anniversary celebration of the Weimar Republic took place on August 11. The *Reichstag* and all public buildings in Berlin were decorated with the Black-Red-Gold of the Republic. The President, dressed in frock-coat and top hat, sat with Siegfried von Kardorff, one of the vice presidents of the *Reichstag*. On Hindenburg's left sat Schleicher as the representative of the government.[33] After several stirring Prussian marches by a military band, Interior Minister Gayl stepped up to the podium and gave the major address. Unlike previous anniversaries in which speeches heaped great praise on the Constitution, Gayl announced the urgent need to amend it. While the constitution remained the only firm ground on which all alike must stand who wished to maintain the German state, a constitution that was not the source of union but of dissension required revision. The present turmoil was evidence of this fact. Gayl then outlined those changes which reflected Papen's notions about the "New State:" (a) amend Article 22 which called for election by lists, and establish the principle of one man one vote; and (b) turn the relationship between the Reich and Prussia into a working union without reducing the independence or separate identity of the German states. But the Reich must be given those powers which were essential to maintain itself.[34] The Chancellor then concluded the ceremony with a short speech in which he stated that only the march of time could confirm the value of great legislative work; what proved to be temporary disappeared quickly, but even what remained vital for a number of years lost its relevance when circumstances were completely changed. Germany in 1932, he stressed, was not the same Germany as in 1919; consequently, the form of government that was suitable thirteen years ago no longer satisfied the requirements of the present day in which powerful national forces were at work. Although he did not spell them out, Papen suggested that the constitution included certain fundamental ideas and procedures which could be of help in setting the German house in order. He then concluded with an invitation to the crowd to join him in a cheer, not, as was customary, for the German Republic, but for the German Reich. Then, as only the Germans can sing it, the ceremonies concluded with a rousing version of "*Deutschland, Deutschland über Alles.*"[35] The most perceptive assessment of the entire affair appeared in the *Bayerische Staatszeitung*, where the editorial observed that the whole event was essentially a leave-taking from the Weimar Constitution.[36]

A few hours after the ceremonies, Papen, at Hindenburg's request, met with the party leaders of the Right in order get their opinions about participating in a coalition government with the Nazis. His first discussions were with Hugenberg and the German Nationalists. This stubborn old man expressed no interest in joining what he referred to as a "Harzburg cabinet," and he stated that he preferred to see Papen remain in office.[37] Later that same day, the Chancellor met with Center party delegate, Josef Joos, and Eugene Bolz of the Bavarian People's Party. With a certain boldness that also hinted of contempt for these two representatives of parliamentary democracy, Papen requested the two politicians to refrain from forming a coalition government with the National Socialists since it would impede his efforts to win their support for his government. The response of the two men was indication that the Center had neither forgotten nor forgiven Papen for breaking his promise to Kaas in May when he accepted the chancellorship. They responded by demanding that he resign, and added that their party would give its positive consideration to any solution which corresponded to "a clear conception of political responsibility and constitutional legality." In other words, this meant that they were in the process of negotiating with the Nazis, and would support a cabinet under Hitler's leadership.[38]

Meanwhile, for reasons that are not clear even today, there was a growing feeling among the Storm Troopers that a Hitler chancellorship was imminent. Goebbels noted in his diary that "The entire party is already preparing itself for power. Not only did the SA leave their places of work in order to make themselves ready...If all goes well everything is in order, but if things go badly there will be a terrible setback."[39] On August 10, while Papen was in session with the cabinet, the SA in Berlin were placed on alert and reinforcements from nearby provinces camped in the suburbs of the capital. Refusing to be intimidated, the Government stood firm, and Count Wolf von Helldorf, the commander of the Berlin SA, issued a proclamation enjoining his troops to avoid illegal actions and demonstrate their loyal obedience to the Führer's orders.[40]

Neither the SA's attempts to put pressure on the Government, nor Hindenburg's rumored opposition to a Hitler chancellorship, halted the negotiations. Probably because he had sworn never again to attempt a *putsch*, Hitler decided to arrange for another meeting with the president. The Nazi leader arrived in Berlin on August 12, with the intention of meeting Hindenburg the next day. However, when his personal adjutant, Wilhelm Bruckner, went to the *Wilhelmstrasse* to arrange for the meeting, Otto Meissner suggested that Hitler should confer with Papen before meeting with the President. Annoyed at this suggestion, Hitler resorted to a typical Nazi ploy. He sent the leaders of the SA, Röhm and Helldorf, with a message that the Nazis and the SA would accept no solution short of their leader's appointment as chancellor. Papen refused to be intimidated by Röhm, whom he described in his *Memoirs* as, "...a powerfully-built man, with a big red face scarred with dueling marks, and a disfigured nose, part of which had been shot away."[41] The interview, according to Papen, was inconclusive, since he told the two Nazis that he had no desire to discuss the subject with a third party, but preferred to deal directly with Hitler. As he turned to leave, Röhm responded that Hitler should be appointed chancellor, and then added, "the Party will accept no other solution."[42]

If the SA leader had intended this remark to be a threat, it had little effect on Papen. The next day, August 13, after a brief meeting with Schleicher, Hitler accompanied by Röhm and Frick, called on Papen. Mustering all of his charm, the Chancellor told Hitler that the President was unwilling to entrust the chancellorship to him because "he did not know him well enough." Papen also indicated that Hindenburg expected the Nazi leader to exercise his patriotic duty by refraining from further opposition, and by placing his "politically dynamic movement" at the service of the country during these trying times. Then, in an effort to placate Hitler, Papen assured him that he personally was not wedded to the chancellorship, and that he would have no compunction about resigning in Hitler's favor at some point in the near future. However, he suggested that if the Nazi leader joined the government as vice chancellor, the president would have the opportunity to become better acquainted with him, and undoubtedly become more receptive to the idea of appointing him as chancellor.[43]

Having listened in silence to Papen's assurances, Hitler finally gave vent to his anger. He severely criticized the policies of Papen's government; its leniency in dealing with the political parties was a terrible mistake because it permitted the Marxists to win an additional three million votes in the last election. The only way to deal with these parties on the Left was to exterminate them with fire and sword regardless of how much blood might run in the streets. As for the vice chancellorship, Hitler said it was out of the question since the party regarded him as their leader and not one of its flunkies.[44] Since further discussion was futile, Hitler demanded to know whether he was to regard their conversation as finished, in which case he wanted to know whether this meant his party was free to oppose the government. That answer, the Chancellor replied, could only be settled by a discussion between Hindenburg and the Nazi leader. Papen added that he would inform the President that this conversation had produced no positive results.[45] When Hitler replied that a conference with the president would be pointless, Papen countered that the nation would not understand a refusal on the part of the Nazi leader to see the president in this hour of crisis. On this icy note the meeting came to an end with Hitler reluctantly agreeing to meet with Hindenburg that afternoon.[46]

Leaving the chancellery an angry and frustrated man, Hitler drove to Goebbels' apartment in one of Berlin's western suburbs.[47] At 3 o'clock that afternoon, a call came from Papen's secretary, Planck. When Hitler asked whether the President had made up his mind not to appoint him Chancellor, Planck's reply was evasive: the President wished to talk to him first. Bolstered by this vague reply, Hitler along with Röhm and Frick set out for the Presidential Palace.

In the presence of Papen and Meissner, Hindenburg received Hitler with great courtesy. The meeting lasted just over twenty minutes. The President opened the discussion by telling his visitors that he would welcome Nazi participation in the government. Then he asked Hitler point-blank whether he was prepared to join Papen's government. Hitler replied that he could not become a member of such a government, and reiterated his demand for a new cabinet with himself as chancellor and with freedom to fully exercise the powers of state.[48] Hindenburg then explained his reasons for not appointing Hitler as chancellor: "Before God, his conscience and the Fatherland," he declared, "he could not justify turning over the complete power of the state to one party, especially a party that was negatively disposed towards all who were at variance with it."[49] When Hitler insisted that there was no other alternative, the President wanted to know if he intended to go into opposition. The Führer replied that he had no other choice. In his response to this answer, Hindenburg reprimanded Hitler for the acts of violence and terror that the SA had visited upon the nation. He then warned Hitler that he would not hesitate to use the full powers of his office against any future outbreaks.[50]

In this strained atmosphere the meeting ended. In the ante-chamber of the presidential suite, Papen and Meissner met briefly with Hitler and his two lieutenants. There followed a heated discussion in which Hitler sharply rebuked the Chancellor for permitting the discussion with the President to take place, knowing all along that there was no possibility that Hindenburg would appoint him to the post. Opinions differ about whether Hitler made any threats to overthrow the President, or that he had merely inquired about the likelihood that Papen would pursue a course of military dictatorship.[51] Whatever the case may have been, Hitler left the meeting bitter at Papen for having subjected him to what he thought was a superfluous and humiliating experience.

The bitterness that resulted from this meeting was intensified when the Government released the official version of the meeting. In an official communiqué composed by Schleicher with Papen's approval, Hitler was portrayed as having refused the president's request to join Papen's government because he wanted the complete control of the state handed over to him. The communiqué went on to state that Hindenburg declined to do this because of the one-sided manner in which the Nazis would apply their power. The meeting concluded with the president urging the Nazi leader to challenge his opposition in a civil manner, while warning him that he would not shrink from using the *Reichswehr* to curb SA excesses.[52]

This communiqué was one of the few times that Goebbels propaganda-machine was caught napping. Hitler was furious. After an embarrassing delay the Nazis published their own version of the meeting denying that Hitler had demanded the complete control of the state, but only requested "unambiguous leadership of the government."[53]

Aside from this *faux pas*, Hitler had to deal with another equally difficult task. Ever since the aborted beer hall *putsch* in November 1923, Hitler was determined to avoid open conflict with the Army and to come to power "legally."[54] Now, in light of the dressing down he had received from Hindenburg, this policy appeared to have been discredited and bankrupt. As a consequence, there was strong pressure from the more radical element in the Party to give the SA their head, and "let the smug bourgeois politicians see whether he was just a revolutionary with a big mouth." If ever Hitler needed confidence in his own judgment it was now. Calling together the SA leaders at the

Hotel Kaiserhof, the Führer had to confess that the victory had once again eluded them, and there was nothing they could do but wait for a better time to seize power. Assisted by SA leader Röhm, Hitler was able to convince these men that armed action was futile.

The collapse of the negotiations between the Papen Government and the National Socialists left both parties with a problem about their future course of action. Papen was faced with the difficulty of continuing to govern without the likelihood of much support in the *Reichstag*. Hitler, on the other hand, faced the prospect of further opposition while the possibility of seizing power remaining as elusive as ever.

Two days after Hitler's meeting with Hindenburg, Papen met with his cabinet. Reporting on what had taken place during the negotiations, Papen told his colleagues that in spite of the Nazi leader's attitude, it was still necessary to try to win the support and participation of the Nazi movement. However, since Hitler would not be satisfied unless he was given full control over the state, every effort would have to be made to anchor the government more securely in the people. In order to accomplish this, the Chancellor proposed a massive publicity campaign to capture the support of the youth, by expanding the newly instituted plan of voluntary work service. He also suggested that a popular basis of support for the government could come from the *Stahlhelm*. The Chancellor emphasized the need to reorganize the government's press department in order to defend and promote the government's program. He concluded with the declaration that the time had come for "action, action, action."[55]

Schleicher agreed with Papen, stating that the most important tactic was to make the Nazis appear to be in the wrong. The General also suggested two possibilities for the future. One was for the government to allow the *Reichstag* to reconvene in order to prove that it could not form a majority favorable to the government. The other possibility was for the government to declare beforehand that the convening of the *Reichstag* was pointless.[56] Gayl agreed with Schleicher's analysis. Now that parliamentarianism had reached the end of the line, the government must fulfill all justifiable wishes of the Nazis in order to steal their thunder in subsequent confrontations. Gayl proposed, for example, that the high interest rates should be lowered, and agricultural interests should receive greater protection.[57] After further comments by Warmbold, Gürtner, Braun and Papen, the

Cabinet devoted the rest of the meeting to the question of how to deal with the economic crisis.

Although in their meetings the ministers appeared to have little concern about the likelihood of an agreement between the Center and the National Socialists, Papen and Schleicher were concerned about such a possibility. They had every reason to be concerned since Hitler, not surprisingly, turned to the Center shortly after his humiliating meeting with the president on August 13. The initiative came from the Prussian leader of the Center party, Fritz Grass. While the Center might have appeared to be pursuing a vendetta against Papen, there was a sincere desire to develop "clear lines of responsibility" between the *Reichstag* and the government.[58] Grass met with Hans Richter, the deputy-leader of the Nazis in the *Landtag*. When Grass stressed the need, in light of present political uncertainties, for renewing negotiations between the two parties, Richter's reaction was one of caution. He stated that the decision to open negotiations would have to come from the Führer himself.[59] However, several days later, Hans Kerrl contacted Grass and informed him that Hitler was prepared to enter into negotiations. A short time later, the two men met for preliminary talks. Kerrl said his party demanded the minister presidency and control of the ministers of interior, culture and finance. Grass replied that his party could not condone a cabinet in which the Center was a minority; a coalition government was possible only if the Center shared an equal number of portfolios with the National Socialists. In addition, Grass added, his party would reserve for itself the right to appoint state secretaries in those ministries headed by Nazis. If the minister presidency fell to the Nazis, he continued, his party would also want to appoint the state secretary in the State Ministry. Kerrl replied in a reassuring tone that the Nazis intended to govern legally; they were quite aware of the fact that a coalition government implied "mutual cooperation between its members." The meeting ended with the Nazi's promise to leave that evening for Obersalzburg to consult with the Fuhrer.[60]

On August 20, Grass met with Kerrl who had just returned to Berlin from Obersalzburg. The Nazi told Grass that Hitler was ready to concede parity to the Center in the Prussian government in return for the minister presidency. However, when Grass informed the party leaders about this proposal they were disappointed, and told him to temporarily break off the negotiations, while they considered what action to take. When Kerrl met with Grass the next day, the Nazi agreed to delay further negotiations until August 24.[61]

After receiving Grass' report, the leaders of the Center fraction in the *Reichstag*, Joos, Bolz and Stegerwald, met in Stuttgart with their counterparts in the Bavarian People's Party, Schäffer and Pfeiffer. In the course of this meeting it was agreed that the Prussian negotiations were just a prelude to the real issue, which was to try and get to co-operative arrangement in the national government as well.[62] On August 21, Brüning met with Gregor Strasser in Constance to arrange for a Black-Brown coalition in the *Reichstag*, and set the date of August 29, for negotiations to begin.[63]

When the Center leaders received this news, the *Reichstag* delegation met with the Bavarian People's Party leaders to draw up a basic proposal that they would present to the Nazis. They resolved to cooperate in the establishment of a government that would be supported by a majority of the *Reichstag*, and would be willing to work with the *Reichstag*. In effect this would mean the end of Papen's presidial government and a return to what they said was the "clear intent" of the Constitution.[64] Later, when the Center leaders met with Hitler, they were impressed with the Führer's explanations; but there was no agreement about the formation of a coalition government.[65]

In the meantime, Papen gave the impression that he cared very little about the rumored negotiations between the Center and the Nazis.[66] He was confident that by a process of "wearing-down" the Nazis, by keeping them waiting in the vestibule of power, he could force Hitler to accept his terms. He was also convinced that armed with the threat to dissolve the *Reichstag* and call for new elections, he held the ace of trumps, and, if necessary, he resolved to play it.[67] Undoubtedly, the Chancellor hoped that this tactic would discourage any further negotiations between the Nazis and the Center, and afford him more time to implement administrative and constitutional reforms that would bolster his authoritarian government.

But Schleicher, who was not as confident as the Chancellor, wanted to try once again to win over the Führer by offering him the vice chancellorship, several cabinet posts and control of Prussia.[68] With this plan in mind, Schleicher managed to persuade Papen to meet with Hitler on August 29, one day before the *Reichstag* was to begin its new session. Although Papen intended to go to Neudeck in order to get a decree of dissolution from the President, he agreed to meet with Hitler one more time. But when they met with Hitler, the Nazi leader flatly rejected the offer and demanded "full power" to form a government.[69]

Left with no other alternative, Papen, along with Schleicher and Gayl, journeyed to Neudeck the next morning to submit their plans to the President.[70] The Chancellor expressed doubts that a working majority would result from the series of negotiations between the Nazis and the Center party. But, if such a coalition were to be formed, Papen reminded Hindenburg that the constitution did not compel the president to confer power upon its leaders. It was his belief, Papen continued, that the Center leaders were engaged in this maneuver in order to avoid a dissolution of the *Reichstag*, while at the same time they wanted to see the Nazis destroy themselves by assuming governmental responsibility. The Chancellor went on to suggest that as far as the Nazis were concerned, they wanted to establish a "pseudo-majority" in the *Reichstag* and then put the blame on Hindenburg for refusing to entrust the government to this "majority." Once it became clear that there was no possibility of obtaining a working majority that would cooperate with the government, Papen suggested that the President was justified to dissolve the *Reichstag*. Hindenburg agreed with Papen's analysis since he too thought a working majority could not be found in the *Reichstag*. If this disregard for the spirit of the constitution was not sufficient proof that neither Papen nor his colleagues had any use for parliamentary democracy, the next topic of discussion was proof positive of their contempt for it.

With the fate of parliamentarianism sealed, the question of what to do after dissolution still remained to be answered. The Constitution prescribed another election was to be held within sixty days of dissolution. Papen agreed that any delay beyond this limit was technically a violation of the Constitution. But, with the subtlety of a medieval philosopher, he told Hindenburg that since the government was faced with a state of emergency, a postponement of elections was justified. Aware of Hindenburg's scruples about faithfully adhering to his presidential oath, the Chancellor cleverly argued that, after all, in his oath of office the President had sworn to protect the German Volk from harm; new elections in times of political turmoil such as was witnessed in July, would cause great harm. Seeing the old man beginning to waver, Gayl agreed that people would understand why the elections were postponed, therefore it was simply a matter of whether "we would allow the wording of the constitution to prevent us from doing it." The Interior Minister concluded that as long as an emergency situation continued to exist, the reelection of a *Reichstag* within the prescribed time limits could be ignored. Papen summed up the arguments with the pious reflection, "If the General Field Marshal and Reichs President von Hindenburg, who had upheld the constitution so conscientiously, decides in the case of a special emergency to depart just once [sic!] from the constitution the German people will fully accept it."[71]

Papen's persuasive manner won the day. The President replied that in good conscience he could interpret Article 25 of the constitution in such a way as to permit him to postpone new elections until a later time because of the "unusual situation" in the country. He then signed a decree dissolving the *Reichstag* with the date and the reasons to be filled in later. At Papen's request, he also signed another decree placing the Prussian police under the jurisdiction of the Reich Interior Minister in the event that the Center and the Nazis formed a coalition government in Prussia.[72] Armed with these documents, the three men returned to Berlin post-haste, confident that the president would back them to the limits of his authority.

In the meantime, the newly elected *Reichstag* met for the first time on the same afternoon that Papen was meeting with Hindenburg. However, unlike previous sessions, this one was quite orderly. Clara Zetkin, the veteran Communist deputy gave the opening address. "Red Clara" called on the deputies to impeach the president and the cabinet for violations of the constitution. While her Communist colleagues gave her only perfunctory applause, the Nazi delegation maintained an exemplary discipline. It appeared as if the one thing all these parties had in common was their opposition to the Papen government. This outlook was reinforced by the last-minute arrangements between the Center and the National Socialists, which resulted in the election of Hermann Göring as president of the *Reichstag*. The election of a representative from the Center, the German Nationalists, and the Bavarian People's Party to the three vice-presidential posts appeared to give further evidence that collaboration between the parties was possible.[73] Göring closed the first session with the declaration that the election of the presidium was proof that the *Reichstag* could work effectively. He asked the *Reichstag* for the authority to request the president "to receive the newly elected officers of that body not, as the regulations prescribed when the opportunity offered, but without delay."[74]

C. The Münster Program

As important as it was for the Papen government to seek greater political maneuverability, the most urgent problem facing it was the staggering unemployment. By early 1932 there were 6 million unemployed and that figure continued to mount throughout the summer. Papen realized that if he expected to restore confidence in his government it was imperative to establish a program that would alleviate at least some of the depression's effects. Moreover, he knew that without a successful economic program his dreams of a *Reichsreform* would vanish along with his personal ambition to go down in history as Bismarck's successor. While the government had been wrestling with this crisis since early June, the growing strength of the Nazi movement, the sharp increase in electoral strength of the Communist party in the July elections, and the public disaffection with Papen's government prompted the Cabinet to agree with the Chancellor that the economic crisis had to receive top priority.[75]

On Friday, August 26, at 11 o'clock, Economics Minister Warmbold presented the draft of a proposal for the government's economic program. And although several days were still required before a final draft could be published, the Cabinet agreed that the salient features of the plan should be announced prior to the first session of the new *Reichstag*.[76]

The Chancellor wasted little time in fulfilling the cabinet's wishes. On August 28, he delivered a speech in Münster to the Westphalian Farmer's and Peasants Association. What came to be known as the "Münster Program" was implemented by means of emergency decrees one week later on September 4 and 5. The plan approached the problem of unemployment from two directions. The first section of the plan sought to resolve the problem of unemployment by provided credit for business expansion. Under this arrangement, the government would introduce a 1.5 billion R.M. tax abatement plan for taxes paid in any year from 1932 to 1938. Firms would be granted a 40% rebate on the *Umsatzsteuer* (turnover tax), the *Gewerbesteuer* (trade tax), and a complete remission on the *Beförderungssteuer* (transportation tax). The rebates would be given in the form of tax certificates that could be sold on security markets or used as collateral for loans. If held to maturity by the owner, they would yield annual premiums of 4%. It was hoped that the funds obtained either through sale of the certificates or used to secure loans would be used to expand business.[77] As businesses expanded, more workers would be employed.

In another section of the plan, firms were encouraged to employ more workers in one of two ways. One inducement was by a direct payment of 400 R.M. for each new worker employed by a firm beyond the number at work from June to August 1932. The money for these payments would come from a fund of 700 million R.M. set aside by the government. The second and more controversial section allowed employers to lower wages if they employed additional workers. Employers could reduce wages in the last ten hours of the week up to 50% if the labor force was increased by 25%, provided that the total payroll did not decline.[78]

The reaction to Papen's economic program was immediate and mixed. The executive board of the Free Trade Unions sent a telegram to Hindenburg complaining that Papen's proposal was nothing more than "a one-sided enrichment of the employer at the expense of the worker."[79] Labor leaders also argued that this program would further erode the purchasing power of the worker and consequently prolong the current economic crisis. Even more critical was the charge made by *Vorwärts*, the Social Democratic organ, that the government's cancellation of wage agreement was another step toward dictatorship.[80] The National Socialists joined with the Center in condemning the government's new economic measures as unfair to Germany's workers. On the same day of the no confidence vote, the Nazis launched an abrasive attack against the Papen regime. Branding the Chancellor as a reactionary, they charged that his entire economic policy was "nothing more than a throwback to *manchestertum*" (a derisive term for laissez-faire economics).[81]

While these criticisms must have upset the Chancellor, he could console himself with the thought that they came from quarters that were consistently at odds with his government. Moreover, the enthusiastic response of the business community to the Münster Program suggested to Papen that perhaps he was gaining much needed support from that quarter. This was confirmed by the sharp rise of the stock market and the congratulatory letter the Chancellor received from the *Reichsverband der Deutsche Industrie*, an extremely influential business organization.[82]

While these positive reactions from the business community were encouraging, Papen was stung by the sharp rebukes his program received from the agricultural community. In a letter to the Chancellor, Alfred Hugenburg demanded that the government should introduce measures to alleviate the plight of the farmers, such as an immediate introduction of quotas on agricultural imports and a lower interest rate on foreign debts.[83] Similar criticism came from the influential president of the Reich Agrarian League (*Reichslandbund*), Count Kalkreuth, who accused some members of the cabinet of failing to support agriculture minister, von Braun's call for import quotas and protective tariffs.[84]

Papen had every reason to be concerned about these criticisms because his government depended heavily on political support from Hugenburg and the agricultural associations. Nevertheless, the close ties that his wife's family had with industrial interests in France made him aware of the harmful effects a strong protectionist policy could have on the German economy. Caught in this dilemma, Papen tried to steer a middle course. Although during the first two months in office he seemed to favor industry, by September he had shifted his position and now gave his complete support to Braun's quota policies and other measures designed to aid agriculture.[85] This about face can be explained by two reasons. First, the dissolution of the *Reichstag* on September 12, and the cabinet's decision to schedule new elections in November necessitated the support of agriculture. Second, the powerful agrarian interests in East Prussia had stepped up their campaign to force the government to award them further concessions.[86]

To Papen's credit, he had some understanding of the need for salvaging the German economy, and his Münster Program contained measures that could have worked had the political situation been more stable, and, even more importantly, if his government had been willing to cooperate with the *Reichstag*. As it was the Münster program never lived up to its expectations. For one thing, the section that permitted the employer to lower wages if he hired extra workers was bitterly opposed by the unions who threatened to strike if firms introduced this measure. As a consequence many employers, fearing labor unrest, refused to initiate this plan.[87] By mid-November Labor Minister Schäffer urged that the decree be revoked by January 1, because the estimated 70,000 employed under it provisions were the maximum to be expected.[88]

While not as controversial as the wage cut measure, the bonus payment plan also failed to achieve its original purpose. One fundamental weakness was that this program did not strengthen worker purchasing power because low-paid workers were generally hired. Another factor was the uneven effect that this measure had among competing firms. When the decree was promulgated, businesses that expanded seasonally were now being paid to grow when they would have normally done so anyway. Moreover, firms that might have reduced their payrolls recently had the advantage while those that had recently added workers did not.[89]

While the wage cuts and bonus provisions of the plan were important, the key to the success of the program was the tax-certificate section. The basic goal of this section was to encourage expansion by making capital available for investment that would have normally been used to pay taxes. Despite Papen's high hopes for this plan, it failed to stimulate business sufficiently to start an upswing in the economy.

Although the Münster plan never lived up to its expectations, this was not the principle reason for the collapse of Papen's chancellorship in December. Ironically, it was Papen's close associate, General von Schleicher, who undermined his position in the Cabinet, and used his influence as the head of the Army to pressure Hindenburg into reluctantly calling for Papen's resignation. It was indeed a tragedy for the Republic that at this fateful point in her history, the cunning and devious activities of a General Staff officer in competition with a crafty, impetuous ex-cavalry officer greedy for prestige and power, should result in the pursuit of policies that would result in defeat for democracy and victory for dictatorship.

NOTES

[1] "Bredow Aktennotiz, July 26, 1932," F 41,Bd. I/65, *IfZg*, Munich.

[2] "Report of August 10, 1932, by Sir Horace Rumbold to Sir John Simon," *DVFP*, IV, No. 10, pp. 23-24.

[3] In *Der Angriff*, Goebbels warned the editor of the *Vossische Zeitung*, George Bernard, that some night a small bomb would fall on his bed cover! Cf. "Report," Sir Horace Rumbold, *DBFP*, No. 10, p. 24.

[4] "*Das Reichsbanner bewaffnet sich*," *Der Volkische Beobachter*, Bayernausgabe, August 4, 1932.

[5] Cabinet Session August 4, 1932, *RKz*, R 43 I/1457, BA, Koblenz; Schultess, ibid., LXXIII, pp. 136-137.

[6] Ibid.

[7] Ibid.

[8] Ibid. In effect the death sentence was so expanded as to include cases which did not constitute murder under the regular criminal code.

[9] Pietzruch's brother was forced to face the wall in the room where the murder took pace, and he too was savagely beaten. Cf. Paul Kluke, "*Der Fall Potempa*," *VjHfZg*, Vol. V, No. 3 (July, 1957), pp. 279, 282.

[10] Horkenbach, *Das Deutsche Reich*, p. 279.

[11] Dorpalen, *Hindenburg*, p. 365.

[12] Horkenbach, ibid. p. 307.

[13] In a speech to the Farmer's Association in Münster on August 28, Papen made a glowing defense of the principles of German justice. He also emphasized that his Government intended to continue to be the defender of order and stability. Schultess', ibid., p 44.

[14] *Memoirs*, p. 201. Papen attempts to cover up this pusillanimous action by humbly admitting that, "in light of later developments...mercy in this case was a grave political error."

[15] Ibid., p. 199.

[16] Constitutional reforms advocated later on by Gayl and Papen included a first chamber composed of delegates from the *Länder*, representatives from occupational groups, and presidential appointments. The voting age would be raised, and proportional representation would give way to single-member voting districts. The problem of relations between Prussia and the Reich would be resolved by uniting the offices of chancellor and minister president. Bracher, *Auflösung*, pp. 536-545.

[17] Thilo Vogelsang, "*Zur Politik Schleichers genenüber der NSDAP 1932*," *VjHfZg*, VI (January, 1958), pp. 95-96.

[18] Bullock, *Hitler*, p. 182.

[19] "Neither we nor the BVP have any doubt that the Nazis must participate in the government." Joos to Graf von Galen, August 5, 1932. In Morsey, "*Die Deutsche Zentrumspartei*," in *Das Ende der Parteien 1933*, eds. Erich Matthias and Rudolf Morsey (Düsseldorf, 1960) p. 424-425.

[20] Affidavit of testimony by Hans Henning von Holtzendorff, *Sammlung Zeugenschrifttum*, No. 248, *IfZg*.

[21] Hitler demanded the Reich and Prussian ministries of the Interior, Justice, Agriculture, Aviation and a new ministry of Popular Enlightenment and Propaganda. He also agreed that Schleicher was to remain at the head of Defense.

[22] Wheeler-Bennet, *Nemesis*, p. 258; Goebbels, *Kaiserhof*, entry of August 6, 1932, p. 139.

[23] Wheeler-Bennett, ibid., p. 258; Bracher, *Auflösung*, p. 613. Goebbels, who distrusted Schleicher, suspected that Hitler had been duped. He expressed his skepticism, and added "once we have the power we will never give it up." *Kaiserhof*, August 6, 1932.

[24] Kurt von Schleicher to Sate Secretary Paul Korner, August 5, 1932, *Buro des Reichsprasidenten*, VIII, No. 47, *DZA* Potsdam. Papen claimed that he had informed Hindenburg of Schleicher's meeting with Hitler on August 10. Memorandum of November 12, 1957 by Franz von Papen, *Sammlung*, No. 354, *IfZg*. Paul Löbe, supporting Schleicher, said he told him: "...the wave has become so large we cannot stop it...we must...take the fellow and place him in the middle with two weights suspended on each side. On the one side me and the *Reichswehr*...on the other side the old gentleman and his authority." Paul Lobe, *Erinnerungen eines Reichstags präsidenten* (Berlin: Arani Verlag, 1949), p. 142.

[25] Holtzendorff, Affidavit, *Sammlung*, No. 248; Lobe, *Erinnerungen*, p. 142.; Thilo Vogelsand, *Reichswehr, Staat und NSDAP, Beiträge zur deutschen Geschichte 1930-1932* (Stuttgart: Deutsche Verlags-Anstalt, 1962), pp. 259-260.

[26] Edgar von Schmidt-Pauli, 2nd ed. rev. *Hitler's Kampf um die Macht: Der Nationalsozialismus und die Ereignisse des Jahres 1932* (Berlin: Verlag von George Stilke, 1933), p. 87; Walter Görlitz, *Hindenburg: Ein Lebensbild* (Bonn: Athenaum Verlag, 1953), p. 381. Papen vigorously denied that he ever supported Hitler's bid for the chancellorship at that time: "...if I had supported Hitler's demand for the chancellorship...my agreement to resign would have been necessary. Such an act would never have slipped my memory." "Memorandum of November 12, 1957 by Franz von Papen," *Sammlung*, No. 354, Archives, *IfZg*, Munich. However, Papen's "memory" proved to be

unreliable in so many other instances, that one hesitates to accept his explanation in this case, and rely on the testimony of Görlitz and Schmidt-Pauli.

[27] Memorandum of August 11, 1932 by Otto Meissner, *Nachlass Hindenburg*, Vol. X, No. 13; Hubatsch, *Hindenburg*, pp. 335-336.

[28] Cabinet Session August 10, 1932, at 5:30 p.m., *Rkz*, R 43 I/1457/273-275, BA, Koblenz.

[29] Ibid.

[30] Ibid.

[31] Ibid. Although for tactical reasons, Schleicher refrained from proposing that Hitler should be appointed chancellor, outside of the cabinet meetings he continued to believe that the Nazi leader "must be appointed as chancellor." Quoted by Hans Schäffer, *Tagebuch*, August 12, 1932, p. 740, Archives, *IfZg* Munich.

[32] Cabinet Session August 10, 1932 at 5:30 p.m., *RKz*, R 43 I/1457, BA, Koblenz.

[33] Dorpalen, *Hindenburg*, P. 357.

[34] Schultess, ibid., Vol. LXXIII (1932), 139. What is so perfidious about Gayl's presentation is the hypocrisy with which these proposals were presented. None of the cabinet ministers were interested in preserving the parliamentary system.

[35] Report of August 12, 1932 by Sir Horace Rumbold to Sir John Simon, No 11, *DBFP*, Second Series, Vol. IV, p. 28.

[36] *Bayerische Staatszeitung*, August 12, 1932. Quoted in Dorpalen, *Hindenburg*, p. 357.

[37] Vogelsand, *Reichswehr, Staat und NSDAP*, p. 261.

[38] Morsey, *Zentrumspartei*, pp. 316-317.

[39] Goebbels, *Kaiserhof*, entry for August 8, 1932, p. 140.

[40] Goebbels, ibid., entry for August 10, 1932, pp. 141-142. An important reason for Helldorf's proclamation was the fact that the *Reichswehr* took immediate countermeasures in response to the Nazi troop deployments.

[41] Papen, *Memoirs*, p. 195.

[42] Ibid.

[43] Dorpalen, ibid., pp. 352-353; Papen, ibid., pp. 196-197; Testimony of Franz von Papen, *IMT*, Vol. XVI, p. 253. Papen was not authorized to offer Hitler a vice chancellorship since the post had not yet been sanctioned by Hindenburg However, he was confident that the President would agree to such an arrangement.

[44] Papen's report to the Cabinet on 15 August 1932, *Rkz*, R 43 I/1457, BA Koblenz.

[45] Papen, *Memoirs*, p. 197.

[46] Cabinet Session, August 15, 1932, *Rkz*, R 43 I/1457, BA, Koblenz.

[47] Goebbels, *Kaiserhof*, entry of August 13, 1932, p. 144.

[48] Memorandum by Otto Meissner concerning a conversation between Paul von Hindenburg and Adolph Hitler on August 13, 1932, at 4:15 p.m., *Nachlass Hindenburg*, Vol. X, No. 14. Reprinted in Hubatsch, *Hindenburg und der Staat*, p. 338; Cabinet Session 15 August 1932, *RKz*, R 43 I/1457, BA, Koblenz.

[49] Memorandum by Otto Meissner, *Nachlass Hindenburg*, ibid.

[50] "*Aufzeichnung des Staatssekretars Dr. Meissner über eine Besprechung Hindenburg/Hitle*," *Rkz*, R 43 I/1309/215-219, BA, Koblenz.

[51] The Meissner version, which was only one paragraph in length is surprisingly less truthful than the considerably longer and more complete Nazi version. *RKz*, R 43 I/1309/219; 229-232, BA, Koblenz.

[52] Wolf Telegraph Bureau, August 13, 1932, Nr. 1732, "*Nachtausgabe*." Papen and Schleicher were responsible for this tersely worded statement. Alluding to Bismarck's "doctored" telegram of Kaiser Wilhelm to the French government in 1871, Planck labeled this statement as an "*Ems Dispatch*." Brüning, *Memorien*, p. 622.

[53] *Der Angriff*, Nr. 165, August 16, 1932.

[54] To Hitler's way of thinking, "legality" was a relative term meaning that the movement would not try to seize power forcefully. This did not exclude street brawls, frequent disruptions in the *Reichstag* debates, or even brutal beatings that often resulted in death to the victim - such as the Potempa case.

[55] Cabinet Session, August 15, 1932 at 4:30 p.m., *RKz*, R 43 I/1457/290-294, BA, Koblenz.

[56] Ibid. Schleicher was clearly stretching the meaning of the Constitution with this interpretation, probably in an effort to spare the Papen regime another election campaign.

[57] Ibid., 296-297.

[58] Resolution of August 29, 1932 by the *Reichstagsfraktion* of the Center Party, quoted in Morsey, *Zentrumspartei*, p. 320.

[59] Ibid., p. 319, n. 16.

[60] Memorandum of August 16, 1932 by Fritz Grass, *Nachlass Lauscher*, reprinted in Morsey, Ibid., p. 425.

[61] Memorandum of August 25, 1932 by Fritz Grass, ibid., p. 318, n. 18.

[62] Ibid.

[63] Brüning, *Memorien*, pp. 623-624. The two men discussed a cabinet consisting of Strasser as Chancellor, Brüning as Foreign Minister, and

Goerdeler as Prussian Minister President. However, Brüning said he removed himself from participating in any future cabinet.

[64] Morsey, *Zentrumspartei*, p. 320.

[65] Letter of August 31, 1932 by Eugen Bolz to his wife, quoted in Max Miller, *Eugen Bolz: Staatsmann und Bekenner* (Stuttgart: Schwabenverlag, 1951), II, p. 425.

[66] Papen told Sir Horace Rumbold on August 22nd, that even if Hitler could convince the President that he could form a coalition government with a working majority in the *Reichstag*, it was still the President's prerogative to appoint a Chancellor. In other words, Hindenburg would never appoint Hitler to the chancellorship. Report of August 22, 1932 by Sir Horace Rumbold to Sir John Simon, No. 18, *DBFP*, Second Series, Vol. IV, p. 41.

[67] On August 26, Papen announced that he intended to request Hindenburg to approve a decree calling for the dissolution of the *Reichstag*.

[68] In a conversation with Schleicher on August 26, Goebbels got the distinct impression that the General was afraid of a possible rapprochement between the Nazis and the Center party. Goebbels, *Kaiserhof*, entry of August 29, 1932, p.152.

[69] Ibid., entry of August 26, 1932, p. 150.

[70] The only written record of this meeting at Neudeck is from the pen of Otto Meissner. He sent the report to Schleicher later on. "Memorandum of August 30, 1932 by Otto Meissner concerning a conversation at Neudeck on Tuesday, August 30 between Paul von Hindenburg, Franz von Papen, Wilhelm von Gayl, Kurt von Schleicher and Otto Meissner," *Nachlass Hindenburg*, Vol. X, No. 15, reprinted in Hubatsch, *Hindenburg*, pp. 340-341.

[71] Minutes of the Neudeck Conference, August 30, 1932, *RKz*, R 43 I/678/247-256, BA, Koblenz. This appalling display of contempt for the constitutional structure was one of the identifying characteristics of the Papen regime. The tragedy was that Hitler and the Nazis shared this resentment and made it the basis for an enormously popular movement which not only brought about the destruction of Papen's dream to restore the pre-1918 order, but engulfed Germany and eventually the world in a terrible catastrophe.

[72] Memorandum of August 30, 1932 by Otto Meissner, *Nachlass*. Reprinted in Hubatsch, *Hindenburg*, pp. 340-341.

[73] Schultess, ibid., p. 150. Although the SPD was entitled to the first vice-presidency as the second largest party, its claim was ignored.

[74] Schultess, ibid.

[75] Cabinet Session of August 15, 1932, *RKz*, R 43 I/1457, BA, Koblenz.

[76] Papen was gambling that the announcement of economic reforms would gain public support, and therefore when he presented his program to the new *Reichstag* they would be hard pressed to reject it.

[77] Schultess, ibid., pp. 152-156.

[78] Ibid.

[79] Horkenbach, *Das Deutsche Reich*, p. 299.

[80] Ibid.

[81] Henry Ashby Turner, Jr., *German Big Business & the Rise of Hitler* (New York: Oxford University Press, 1985), p. 279.

[82] The *Reichsverband* argued that, "the entire German economy has reason to look favorably upon the Government's attempt to bring about a stimulation of the economy by emphasizing personal initiative." Horkenbach, ibid., (1932), p.333.

[83] Ibid., p. 307.

[84] Ibid., p. 319. There was a great deal of truth in Kalkreuth's charges. Von Braun and Gayl had close ties to East Prussian agricultural interests. Warmbold was a former director of the giant chemical and dye trust, I.G. Farben. and he was supported in his defense of industrial interests by Neurath and Krosigk.

[85] For example, Papen tried to compensate industry for any losses as a result of import duties by agreeing with Warmbold's proposal for wage reductions. Later this became part of the government's economic program. Cabinet Session of 21 July 1932, R 43 *RKz*, R 43 I/1457, BA, Koblenz. On September 23, Papen informed the cabinet that he favored the autonomous establishment of quotas should the negotiations over commercial agreements be unsuccessful.

[86] Hundreds of letters poured into the chancellery from wealthy eastern landowners pressuring Papen to lower interest rates, impose higher tariffs on butter, and establish support payments on rye and corn. *RKz*, R 43 I/1859, BA, Koblenz.

[87] Letter to Papen from representatives of industry and the Chamber of Commerce of Lower Saxony-Kassel, October 3, 1932, *RKz*, R 43 I/2046/38-42, BA, Koblenz. By the end of October, the Labor Ministry told Papen that no further increases in employment could be expected.

[88] Cabinet Session of November 7, 1932, *RKz*, R 43 I/1457, BA, Koblenz

[89] Gerhard Colm, "Why the Papen Plan for Economic Recovery Failed," *Social Research*, I (1934), pp. 83-96.

CHAPTER 8:
THE "NEW STATE" IS CHALLENGED

A. *Reichsreform*

While Papen's cabinet was preoccupied with efforts to alleviate the economic crisis, Göring, who had just been elected president of the *Reichstag*, accompanied by Frick and Strasser, resumed negotiations on September 1, for the purpose of forming a parliamentary coalition with the Center Party. In the course of the discussions, both parties rejected Papen's economic program.[1] They also agreed that the restoration of public confidence in the government could only be achieved through the establishment of a working majority in the *Reichstag*. Bolz and Esser, representing the Center Party, stated that their party was prepared to accept a Nazi as chancellor if he could gain the confidence of the president.[2]

Hopes to accomplish this goal were dampened when Hindenburg met with the newly-elected members of the *Reichstag* presidium on September 9.[3] Göring claimed that a large majority of the *Reichstag* were of the opinion that the *Reichstag* was able to function and therefore should not be dissolved. The two vice presidents, Esser and Rauch agreed with Göring, but the German Nationalist, Graef, objected that the *Reichstag* president had no right to make political statements on behalf of the *Reichstag*. He added that his colleagues welcomed the president's efforts to create a government devoid of party intrigues, and assured him they would not interfere.[4]

Noticing that the presidium members were in disagreement, Hindenburg replied that he saw no reason to dismiss the Papen regime simply because this was the wish of a few parties. Then, revealing his true disdain for parliamentarianism, Hindenburg added that even if there was a vote of no confidence, he would still support Papen.[5] The meeting was over in twenty minutes, and so was any possibility of forestalling the dissolution of the *Reichstag* or forming a coalition government. The stage was now set for the turbulent *Reichstag* session of September 12, 1932.

It was Papen's intention to present a report on the nation's economic situation and explain how his program would alleviate the crisis.[6] What actually occurred, however, caught the Chancellor completely by surprise. No sooner had Göring called the session to order when, as previously arranged, the Communist Ernst Torgler, stood up and proposed two changes in the agenda: first, to repeal the emergency decree of September 4, containing the government's economic program; secondly, to record a vote of no confidence in Papen's government. Torgler also requested that both motions should be voted on before the Chancellor read his declaration of policy. When Göring put the question to the chamber, and asked if there was any objection to Torgler's motions, none was forthcoming. Consequently, both items were placed on the agenda.[7]

In the meantime, Papen, who had entered the *Reichstag* shortly before with the look of a man in complete control of the situation, now turned pale. Not anticipating a vote of no-confidence at this session, he had left the decree of dissolution in his office. He had assumed that a debate on his proposals would last several days.[8] Further disaster was averted when Wilhelm Frick moved for a thirty minute recess in order to discuss Torgler's motions with the other Nazi deputies. This tactical blunder gave the chancellor time to dispatch a courier to bring back the decree of dissolution.

When the *Reichstag* reconvened, Göring called for an immediate vote on Torgler's motions. Just at that moment Papen reentered the chamber holding high over his head the red leather portfolio easily recognized by all as the one that contained the decree of dissolution. Making his way to the government bench Papen raised his hand to indicate his wish to address the chamber, but Göring pretended not to

Celebration of the anniversary of the Weimar Constitution,
August 11, 1932
On Papen's right - Secy. Meissner; rear left - Agricultural Minister von
Braun; rear right - Interior Minister von Gayl

notice him. The battle for political power in Germany now became a contest between Papen and Göring. Papen wanted to dissolve the *Reichstag* before the vote of censure could be taken, while the Nazi official wanted to force the resignation of the government, and thus keep the *Reichstag* from being dissolved. In this clash of wills, the Nazi proved to be far more unscrupulous if not more skillful than the debonair Chancellor.

At this point the session became a scene of complete disorder. From the government bench, Erwin Planck stood up and explicitly called Göring's attention to the Chancellor's request for recognition, but the Nazi waved him aside. Papen then jumped up and demanded the floor, which both by custom and the Constitution was accorded him. Göring refused to recognize him and shouted instead that the voting had already begun, and no one was allowed to speak until it was completed. White with anger Papen strode up to the rostrum in order to hand the portfolio over to Göring, but the Nazi refused to acknowledge it. When Planck approached the rostrum and tried to shove the decree plainly into view, the Nazi demonstratively pushed it to one side amidst the cheers of his brown-shirted colleagues and Communists. Infuriated by this cavalier treatment, the Chancellor and his colleagues marched out of the chamber to the accompaniment of catcalls and derisive laughter.[9] Meanwhile, the final tally proved to be a complete defeat for Papen's government with the vote against him 512 to 42. After announcing the results, Göring took formal notice of the dissolution order only to immediately declare that it was invalid, since it had been countersigned by a Chancellor and a cabinet who were no longer in office![10]

This entire episode is a tragic example of how parliamentary democracy was rapidly deteriorating in Weimar Germany. Not only was Göring's role as loyal defender of the Weimar constitution ludicrous, but his refusal to accord the Chancellor his right to address the chamber was a flagrant violation of Article 33, Paragraph 3 of the Constitution. Nor can the defenders of parliamentary democracy, the Centrists, be absolved from blame. Their willingness to go along with the no-confidence vote, based more on their intense dislike for the "cabinet of barons" than on a respect for parliamentary procedures, made them equally responsible. Finally, Hugenberg and the German Nationalists pursuing their own private war against the Republic, were prepared to engage in any plot to overthrow it.[11]

Perhaps the most distressing feature of this entire episode was the Government's callous disregard for the opinions of the *Reichstag*. Papen and his colleagues operated on the principle that as long as they had the President's support, the opinions of the *Reichstag* were irrelevant. This attitude was apparent in the very wording of the dissolution order, which stated that the dissolution was necessary "because of the danger that the *Reichstag* will demand the repeal of the Emergency Decree of September 4." It should be recalled that the framers of the Constitution had originally anticipated that emergency decrees would be used only in cases of extreme necessity such as a threat of civil war or revolution, where immediate action was absolutely necessary. Moreover, according to the Constitution (Art. 48), the *Reichstag* had the right to rescind these orders. Hindenburg's intention to dissolve that body before it could exercise its constitutional rights was an obvious effort to use his own authority to make temporary measures permanent. In effect this meant changing the role of the president from that of a limited legislator to one of unrestricted power.[12]

Returning from the turbulent *Reichstag* session, the cabinet met in the chancellery at 4:40 that same afternoon to discuss the day's events and decide what actions to take. Papen informed his colleagues that he intended to appeal to the German nation in a radio address. Meissner reported that Hindenburg was deeply disturbed, and added that the president was prepared to endorse any measures by the government, even the declaration of martial law. The Prussian Minister of Interior, Franz Bracht, offered to arrest all the Communist members of the *Reichstag* in order to prevent the *Reichstag* from effectively convening.[13] The cabinet also decided to have the Chancellor send Göring a letter in which he accused the Nazi of acting contrary to Article 33 of the constitution by refusing to allow him to address the chamber. The latter went on to argue that from that moment the *Reichstag* was dissolved, the continuation of the session, along with the vote, were a breach of the constitution.[14]

That same evening, in a radio address to the nation, Papen gave his version of what had happened in the *Reichstag*. The Chancellor criticized the deputies for failing to grant the head of the national government the same courtesy they had awarded the Communist Clara Zetkin several days earlier.[15] But he saved his sharpest attack for

Göring and the Nazis whom he castigated for their inability to think beyond the interests of their party.

He also gave a shorter version of the speech he was denied at the *Reichstag* session. This included an assessment of the economic crisis and a justification for his enactment of his economic program by emergency decree. Papen's final remarks touched on the question of reorganization of political life in Germany. Trotting out his neo-conservative ideology, Papen called for an end to parliamentary democracy and the restoration of a non-party national political leadership based on the power and authority of the president. He then listed his proposed political reforms which included everything from eliminating popular sovereignty to regulating relations between the Reich and Prussia. Summing up his address, Papen argued that the government would be neglecting its duty if it were to resign in favor of any coalition with all its attendant uncertainties. Then, in a burst of patriotic rhetoric, he called upon the German public to join with Hindenburg and the government in fulfilling his program for the welfare of the nation.[16]

Although Papen's radio speech did nothing to increase public support for his programs, it did provoke a sharp debate about the constitutionality of Göring's actions. Responding to the Chancellor's radio address, Göring defended his actions at a press conference stating that no one could have the floor while a vote was in progress. He argued that since the vote was against the government, the decree of dissolution was invalid because the government was no longer in power to exercise it.[17] There followed an exchange of letters with Hindenburg and Papen in which Göring maintained that the *Reichstag's* action had been completely legal. Meissner, responding on behalf of the President, declared that Hindenburg regarded the vote of no confidence as "contrary to the constitution," and therefore would "draw no conclusions from these (the *Reichstag's*) decisions."[18]

Meanwhile, in an attempt to further discredit the government, Göring, supported by the Communists, demanded that the Chancellor appear before a special *Reichstag* investigative committee.[19] Initially, Papen refused on the grounds that since the *Reichstag* had been dissolved, any agreement to attend a meeting of a *Reichstag* committee would be interpreted as a denial of the dissolution decree. Finally, realizing the matter would not go away, and seeing that the Nazis would try and use this as an issue in the forthcoming election campaign, the government agreed to appear before the committee on condition that the agenda would be limited to questions about the parliamentary debate of September 12. However, when the Chancellor, accompanied by Gayl and Planck, appeared before the committee on September 27, neither side was willing to alter its version of events. Finally the Social Democrat, Paul Loebe, introduced a motion defending the legality of the dissolution.[20] Although this motion was defeated by the Nazi-Communist majority, a compromise motion, stating that the dissolution decree was contrary to the *spirit* of the constitution, was approved. Then, in order to avoid the impression that the *Reichstag* had capitulated to the Papen government, the motion added that its acceptance by the committee was without prejudice to the majority view of the *Reichstag* that the dissolution had been illegal.[21] Thus after more than two weeks of bitter arguments, the Nazis had to yield to the inevitable. On the other hand, while Papen seemed to have gained from this encounter, the entire incident did embarrass his government and demonstrated how limited its support was among the public at large. Nevertheless, Papen continued to govern, secure in the knowledge that as long as the president backed him, he would continue in office.

The other important activity that continued to preoccupy the Chancellor during the fall election campaign was his determination to eliminate Reich-Prussian dualism through a series of administrative reforms, which he had initiated on July 20. As a result of that action, and the failure to reach any agreement with either Prussia or the other states, the case was scheduled to be heard by the Supreme Court.

B. The Leipzig Verdict

On October 25, the Supreme Court rendered its verdict in the case of Prussia vs. the Reich.[22] Defending Hindenburg's action of July 20, the Court ruled that the President had the right to intervene in a state's affairs if there was a major threat to law and order. Moreover, he was not limited to police actions, but if he was convinced that the state of emergency required the removal of the entire state government, he was entitled to do so. On the other hand, the actions of the Reich were invalid if they implied a permanent dismissal of Prussian officials. The Court also ruled that the Prussian State Ministry could not be removed, even temporarily; specifically it retained the right to represent Prussia in the *Reichsrat*, in the Prussian *Landtag*, and in its relations with the other states. In effect, the Court upheld the constitutional guarantees of the states against infractions by the Reich.[23]

Pleasantly surprised by the court's verdict, Braun and his caretaker government publicly claimed that their honor had been vindicated.[24] On the other hand, at a meeting of the Prussian commissional government on October 27, Papen demonstrated how little regard he had for the ruling. Referring to the court's decision to divide the two powers in Prussia as "a very inconvenient one," the Chancellor declared that his government was determined not to permit the caretaker government (i.e., Braun, etc.) to "...talk itself into any exercise of executive powers."[25] For Papen, the cornerstone of his *Reichsreform* rested on the elimination of dualism between the Reich and Prussia.

Papen's attitude towards the Court's decision became even more evident at a cabinet meeting the next day. Deploring the court for its lack of "creative thinking," he announced his determination to bring about constitutional reforms in Prussia "today or tomorrow (October 28 or 29)." Launching into specifics, the Chancellor notified the ministers that he would start with the "coordination" (a euphemism for "control") of the portfolios of several Prussian ministries with those of the Reich. He then announced that the Reich Minister of Agriculture, Magnus von Braun would, "...be entrusted with the portfolio of the Prussian Agriculture Minister." Commissioner Bracht and former secretary of state in the Reich Finance Ministry, Johannes Popitz, were to be designated ministers without portfolios.[26] The Chancellor also informed his colleagues that in an emergency decree to be announced in a day or two, the Ministry of Welfare in Prussia would be eliminated and its functions transferred to the Ministries of Agriculture, Economics, Finance, Education, and the Interior.[27] This decision to charge full steam ahead was another example of Papen's impatience to fulfill his dream of restoring the *ancien régime* regardless of the consequences for the welfare of the nation.

Meanwhile, although he was fighting a losing cause, Braun hoped to recover some of his lost powers as a result of the Supreme Court's decision. Thus he met with Hindenburg in the presence of Papen and Meissner at Neudeck on October 29.[28] In his opening remarks, Hindenburg informed Braun that the Court's verdict had finally laid to rest the entire controversy between the Reich and Prussia. Swallowing the bitterness he felt about the way he was removed from office after serving almost fourteen years as Minister President, Braun replied that he would deal with the issues in an objective manner. Referring to the Court's ruling, he maintained that the removal of the Prussian minister was unconstitutional and should not have been allowed. He reminded Hindenburg that the Court had also rejected the view that the Prussian government had not fulfilled its duty. Since he did not believe the alleged reason for intervention in Prussia continued to exist, Braun concluded that "...the State Ministry...should be restored to power."[29]

It should come as no surprise that Papen did not share these views. He rejected out of hand Braun's opinion that the situation in Prussia no longer required intervention by the Reich. He also insisted that the State Ministry's powers were limited to representing Prussia in the *Landtag* and the *Reichsrat*. The Chancellor even refused Braun's more modest request that the State Ministry officials be given office space and access to all information. When the Prussian minister warned Papen that this reform from above could have serious consequences, Hindenburg interjected with the ominous remark that control of the Reich and Prussia must be concentrated in the hands of a single authority.[30] The sixty-five minute meeting with the President and the Chancellor left no doubt that the Government was not going to allow the Leipzig decision stand in the way of its plans for Prussia. This was confirmed when several hours later, Papen issued an emergency decree that brought to a close the process of political coordination in Prussia.[31]

The announcement of these changes, however, did not settle the bitter controversy between the Prussian caretaker government and the Reich. Braun wrote to Hindenburg on November 3, in which he supported the complaints of the Prussian officials against Reich Commissioner Bracht. Then, on November 7, he sent a second letter accusing the Government of planning to dismiss a number of Prussian officials because of their political convictions.[32]

When the cabinet met to discuss their strategy in dealing with Braun and his colleagues, Papen impatiently called for the president to simply issue an executive order to carry out the Supreme Court's verdict. But fearing another Prussian appeal to the Supreme Court, Minister of Justice, Gürtner and Popitz opposed this tactic and agreed to seek an alternative solution. It was Popitz who came up with a plot to prevent the Supreme Court from interfering any further in the Reich vs. Prussia conflict. He suggested to Papen that Hindenburg should issue an emergency decree, based on Paragraph Two of Article 48, which would serve to regulate the various issues raised by the caretaker government.[33]

This was a deliberate attempt to unilaterally settle questions that in the original Court ruling were to be agreed upon through negotiation. Then, in order to conceal the true nature of this settlement, Popitz suggested that Papen should invite Braun to another meeting, which like the previous one, would undoubtedly prove to be unsuccessful. When it became obvious that the two sides were unable to reach any agreement, Hindenburg's emergency decree would appear justified. More importantly, the Supreme Court would have no basis for reviewing or overturning the decree. The meeting was held on November 10, and as predicted, it was as unfruitful as the first one.

With this deception successfully concluded, Papen now undertook to convert the *de facto* control over Prussia into a *de jure* status. He persuaded Hindenburg to issue an emergency decree that enlarged the executive powers of the Reich commissioner and the many, recently appointed "deputies" who, in fact, had replaced the caretaker officials.[34]

Faced with this *fait accompli*, a very weary President Braun protested this latest violation of the spirit, if not the letter, of the Supreme Court's verdict. Before a meeting of the old Prussian State Ministry - the one Papen had ousted from power after July 20 - Braun denounced this travesty of justice. The State Ministry followed up with a rather futile appeal to its personnel to defend its sovereign prerogatives before any parliamentary body that would listen.[35] Upon hearing this, the Papen government immediately responded that the State Ministry had exceeded its powers through unwarranted interference with the Commissioner's executive rights. In a final attempt to justify its position, the State Ministry argued that it was perfectly within its authority as recognized by the Supreme Court's October verdict.[36]

This was the last confrontation between Papen and the Prussian State Ministry. However, even though Papen gave way to a cabinet headed by Schleicher at the beginning of December, the significance of his intervention for the future of Prussia did not diminish with his departure from office. Schleicher continued to refuse to allow the old system of Reich-Prussian dualism to return. In February, after his appointment as chancellor, Hitler dissolved the Prussian *Landtag*, and two months later the *Reichstatthalter* law eliminated virtually all the remaining vestiges of federalism within the Reich. Chancellor Hitler now exercised direct control over the appointment of the Prussian Minister President as well as power over all functions of the Prussian administration.

Although it was Hitler's government that hammered the final nails into the Prussian coffin, the Papen government's responsibility for its ruin cannot be easily dismissed. These old guard conservatives, who longed for a return to the pre-war socio-political order, took great pleasure in crushing the Social Democratic party's control in Prussia. They were also delighted to see the end of the old problem of Reich-Prussian dualism, which Gayl considered as one of the two principal accomplishments of the Papen cabinet.[37] While one may quarrel with Gayl about the value of this achievement, there is little doubt that this action against Prussia was of critical importance for the continued existence of the Republic. By removing the last citadel of republicanism, the *Herrenkabinet* won a notable victory in their battle to transform the Weimar parliamentary system into the "New State." By disregarding the Supreme Court's verdict, Papen's government struck a decisive blow against the idea of "a state of laws, and not of men," one of the crowning achievements of the Republic's founding Fathers.

C. Southern Reaction

Meanwhile, the relative ease with which Papen's regime was able to depose the Prussian government alarmed the southern states who were afraid that the Reich might take similar action against them. From almost the beginning of his chancellorship, Papen had clashed with the southern states over the question of lifting the SA ban. Thus the anxiety in the South, especially in Bavaria, was revealed almost immediately following the Reich's intervention in Prussia. It will be recalled that in order to remove these fears, Papen had entered into a series of discussions with the southern political leaders. Throughout the month of August and into September, an exchange of letters, followed by a series of meetings between the Reich and the southern states, took place.[38]

By September, relations between the Reich and the southern states had improved to the point that Papen decided to pay a visit to

Bavaria.[39] Not only did he hope to further improve his relations with the Bavarian government, but he also intended to deliver a campaign speech to a Bavarian businessmen's association in order to gain their support for his programs.

Accompanied by State Secretary Planck, Papen arrived in Munich on the morning of October 11. Greeted warmly by Held, the two men seemed in public to be on good terms. Nevertheless, within twenty-four hours Papen's tactless demeanor during his conversations with Held and his associates caused them to revert to their former mistrust of the Chancellor. Although there was ample opportunity to discuss the whole issue of *Reichsreform* with the Bavarian officials, Papen referred to it only in passing. Even more puzzling was the fact that he failed to inform Held that he intended to address this issue in detail when he spoke to the members of the Bavarian Industrial Association the next day. If one of his primary reasons for his visit to Munich was to improve relations between his government and the South, why did he fail to discuss the one issue that had caused the greatest friction between them? The main reason was his continued reliance on the authority of Hindenburg to carry out his plans for a *Reichsreform*, regardless of any opposition that he might encounter. He also believed that he would be able to persuade the southern businessmen to support his programs and thus put pressure on the southern politicians to follow suit.

The address itself was vintage Papen. Always an impressive speaker, the Chancellor rose to the occasion once again. He presented the major issues of his earlier speeches which embraced both domestic and foreign policy statements and programs of his government. Not only did he present statistics reflecting the early success of his economic program, but, mindful that the Bavarian economy was largely agricultural, Papen assured his listeners that his government was prepared to do everything in its power to preserve agricultural production from complete collapse. Turning to his pet theme, *Reichsreform*, he announced that it was his government's intention to remodel the constitution along authoritarian lines so that it would lead to the creation of a federal government that would withstand the test of time and parliamentary parties. Moreover, he continued, the relationship between the government and the representatives of the people must be so regulated that the full power of the state would be exercised by the government in close cooperation with the states, but not by the *Reichstag*. He sanctimoniously added that this was precisely why he had rejected all measures that might contribute to the destruction of Prussia! Warming to his subject, the Chancellor called for an end to the dualism between the Reich and Prussia by "merging the most important organs of the Reich and Prussia." Aware of Bavaria's concern for the protection of its own self-interests, Papen assured his audience that his government's action in Prussia was intended solely for the purpose of restoring the "organic unity" between the Reich and Prussia. He also proposed other ideas for strengthening the position of the federal states. Then expounding his interpretation of the Constitution, Papen proclaimed that the founding fathers had not assigned popular representation to the *Reichstag* alone, but "...in the office of the president...created an organ at once authoritarian and democratic."[40] Charging political parties with almost destroying the Reich as exemplified by the *Reichstag* fiasco of September 12, Papen proclaimed his determination to unite all the national forces and successfully fulfill President Hindenburg's charge to reconstruct the political and economic life of the nation. He concluded his address with an emotional appeal to his audience: "With Hindenburg for a new Germany!"[41]

Although this speech brought Papen's audience to their feet cheering as no chancellor before had ever been cheered in Bavaria, Held and his colleagues reacted quite differently. They felt that Papen had deceived him. Later, when the Bavarian President told the chancellor this, Papen cavalierly dismissed the address as unimportant! Held was appalled. If Papen could be that indifferent about a public policy speech, how serious would he be about his negotiations with the southern states? Held, Fritz Schäffer and Anton Pfeiffer of the BVP were so upset with what they thought was a case of double-dealing that they refused Papen's request to speak to a group of party leaders.[42]

In truth, Papen's dealings with the southern political leaders were about as honest as his dealings with Braun and the caretaker government. Almost two weeks before his trip to Munich, the Chancellor met in his office with Gayl and Bracht to discuss a memorandum that was strongly supported by Gayl.[43] Entitled, *The Coordination of the Reich & Prussia*, the memorandum called for a much closer relationship between the two governments, including measures that would merge certain Prussian ministries with those of the Reich. Among the more important changes would be the appointment of the Reich chancellor as the Prime Minister of Prussia, and the Reich president would become the Prussian State President. Then, in order to solicit support from the states, the memorandum called for the participation of the non-Prussian states in any discussion. The date for implementation was set for December 1. Although he had ample opportunity to discuss this proposal with Held, Papen failed to do so. This could only mean that he intended to carry out his program of constitutional reform regardless of what the southern states might say.[44]

Although Held and the other southern leaders were unaware of this memorandum, a series of measures undertaken by the Papen regime shortly after the Supreme Court's ruling quickly dispelled their ignorance. Believing that the Reich was now taking steps to control Prussia without consulting the other states, or granting them any concessions, Held sent a message to Hindenburg protesting against what he believed were illegal actions.[45] For the next several weeks the southern states carried on a correspondence with Reich officials with little success. In order to put more pressure on Papen's government to grant them concessions in return for their approval of the *Reichsreform*, Held sought to rally the other state governments into a united front against the Reich. On October 30, before a gathering of Center party members, Held accused Papen not only of breaking the law in his dealings with the states, but he was also a man who did not keep his word. Expressing his disappointment at Papen's failure to respect the promises he made to him, Held told his audience that he was "constrained to oppose him (Papen) publicly and...take up battle against his measures."[46] Since the Center party had never trusted Papen, Held's opinions merely confirmed their judgment of the Chancellor. More importantly, if Papen had expected the Bavarian politician to "use his influence" with the Center party, this latest blunder put an end to those hopes.[47]

In the meantime, sensing the growing tide of opposition against his actions in Prussia, and fearing another round in the Supreme Court that might result in a set-back for his *Reichsreform*, Papen decided to try another tactic - the one previously proposed by Popitz. Acting as if he wished to reach some accord over his latest actions against Prussia, Papen invited Braun and Held to meet with him in Berlin on November 10. But, almost immediately, the extent of the differences separating both sides became evident. It was, of course, Papen's intention to prove that further negotiations were futile, and therefore to stress that he had been justified in taking *de facto* control over the Prussian government. Therefore, there would be no legal reason for the Supreme Court to intervene as it had done previously.

While there is little doubt about Papen's motives, one should not overlook the fact that the southern leaders' intentions were almost as selfish, although more justifiable in light of the fact that their very existence was at stake. Their opposition was based less out of respect for Prussia's integrity, than out of fear that the federalist nature of the constitution would endanger their own interests. Consequently, with both sides approaching the negotiations with such different aims and even less mutual confidence, the failure of reaching an agreement should hardly come as a surprise. Nevertheless, the failure to reach an agreement proved not only to be detrimental for Papen's government and the interests of the states south of the Main, but also more inauspicious for the future of parliamentary democracy in Germany.

Meanwhile, the dissolution of the *Reichstag* meant that the Government would have to call for new elections which, according to the Constitution, had to be held within sixty days. Therefore, when the cabinet met on September 14, two days after the turbulent *Reichstag* session, Papen called for a discussion about the advisability of holding new elections.[48] Speaking first, Gayl proposed that the elections should be postponed indefinitely. However, if the cabinet decided otherwise the elections should be held at the last possible moment. In that case, Gayl warned, there were certain disadvantages. Two months was not enough time to introduce basic government reforms, nor would this be sufficient time to organize those voters who stood between the Nazis and the Center. Furthermore, new elections would not produce a clear majority in the *Reichstag*. Gayl warned that new elections would introduce a new wave of violence. Therefore, the cabinet would have to decide which course was the least dangerous for the Reich, an indefinite postponement or the other disadvantages mentioned. He did admit that an indefinite postponement would be in violation of the Constitution, but he justified this on the grounds that the welfare of all the people stood higher than a formal observance of the constitution.[49] Showing some support for the Interior Minister's position, Schleicher argued that, barring any cooperation with the existing party constellation, it would be impractical to call for new elections because the voters were weary of elections.[50] Other members of the cabinet expressed reservations about an indefinite postponement because they were afraid that the Nazis and Communists would try to force the president out of office for violating the constitution. After a lengthy discussion, Papen summed up the discussion with the observation that even though the economic crisis called for a departure from the constitution, the time was not yet ripe for such action. Therefore, he reluctantly agreed to go ahead with the elections, but proposed that the date should be moved as far forward as possible within the sixty-day limit. Three days later the Cabinet set November 6 as election day.[51]

Papen hoped that the elections would result in stemming the growth of the Nazi party. But regardless of the outcome, he expected that no party would be able to obtain a majority, and therefore he would continue to govern under the protection of the aging President. With this support he intended to keep calling for new elections until the opposition either acknowledged his presidential government or they were completely exhausted. In either case Papen intended to take advantage of the delays that this strategy would cause, in order to complete his program of constitutional reform. Once the "New State" was in place, his anxieties about Germany's future would be replaced by the realization that he had helped to turn the clock back to the "good old days" of Bismarck and the rule of the aristocracy.

NOTES

[1] Morsey, "*Die Deutsche Zentrumspartei,*" p. 322.

[2] Ibid., p. 321.

[3] "Minutes of the conference of Hindenburg and the *Reichstag* Presidium, September 9, 1932," *Schleicher Papers*, *N 26/2*, MA, Freiburg. Göring was elected president of the *Reichstag* on August 30. Cf. Schultess' ibid., Vol. LXXIII (1932), p. 150.

[4] Ibid.

[5] Ibid., Morsey, *Zentrumspartei*, p. 323

[6] Papen, *Memoirs*, p. 207.

[7] Eyck, *Weimar Republic*, II, pp. 429-430.

[8] Papen, *Memoirs*, p. 208.

[9] Ibid., p. 208; Report of September 13, 1932, by Sir Horace Rumbold to Sir John Simon, No. 24, *DBFP*, Second Series, Vol. IV, pp. 49-50.

[10] Eyck, *The Weimar Republic*, II, pp. 429-431.

[11] Alfred Hugenberg knew that Papen was empowered to dissolve the *Reichstag*. In order to block what he thought might be a last-minute agreement between the Nazis and the Center, Hugenberg decided to force Papen to use the dissolution order. Unfortunately, Hugenberg failed to inform Papen of his change of plans, so that the chancellor, certain that a no-confidence vote would not be taken that day, came without the decree.

[12] Eyck, ibid., pp. 432-433. According to the Weimar Constitution the emergency powers granted to the president were intended to be *temporary* interventions into the legislative domain. According to the same Article (Art. 48), the *Reichstag* had the right to repeal such emergency measures as they saw fit.

[13] 13. Cabinet Session of September 12, 1932 at 4:30 p.m., *RKz*, R 43 I/1457, BA, Koblenz. The cabinet took no action on Bracht's proposal.

[14] Cabinet Session of September 12, 1932 at 4:40 p.m., *RKz.*, R 43 I/1457, BA, Koblenz; Schultess, ibid., p. 159.

[15] According to the *Reichstag* rules of procedure, the oldest member, regardless of party affiliation, presided over the meeting during which the new *Reichstag* elected its officers. The seventy-five year old Zetkin was accorded this honor on this occasion. Papen's complaint, therefore, was irrelevant.

[16] Schultess, ibid., Vol. LXXIII (1932), p. 161.

[17] Ibid., p. 160.

[18] Cabinet Session, September 14, 1932, 11:00 A.M., *RKz*, R 43 I/1457, BA, Koblenz. Cf. Horkenbach, *Das Deutsche Reich* (1932), pp. 326-327.

[19] Goebbels, *Kaiserhof*, p. 164, entry for September 14, 1932.

[20] Horkenbach, ibid., p. 337.

[21] Ibid.

[22] At the heart of the controversy was the extent of presidential power in a state of emergency as stipulated in Article 48. "The Decision of the Supreme Court concerning the Reich President's Decree of July 20, 1932," *Rkz*, R 43 I/1901, BA, Koblenz.

[23] Schultess, p. 184.

[24] Ibid., p. 188.

[25] "Memorandum of a Meeting of the Commissional Prussian State Government," October 27, 1932, *Rkz*, R 43 I/2281, BA, Koblenz.

[26] Cabinet Session, October 28, 1932, *Rkz*, R 43 I/ 2281, BA, Koblenz. Papen revealed his complete disregard for the southern states' religious sensitivities when he shrugged off Gürtner's warning that Popitz, as a strict Unitarian, would evoke serious objections from Catholic Bavaria.

[27] "Decree for the Simplification and Reduction in Cost of Administration." Ibid.

[28] "Memorandum concerning a discussion of the Reich President with Reich Chancellor von Papen and Minister President Braun, October 29, 1932, at 12:15 noon," *Rkz.*, R 43 I/2281, Ba, Koblenz. Although Papen's planned decree had not yet been published, Braun knew from rumors about the proposed changes.

[29] Ibid.

[30] "Memorandum Concerning the Discussion of the Reichs President with Reichs Chancellor von Papen and Minister President Braun," October 29, 1932, *Rkz.*, R 43 I/2281/175-187, BA, Koblenz.

[31] Schultess, ibid., p. 192. Popitz became the Chancellors' special representative in the Prussian ministry of finance. Von Braun was appointed Papen's special representative in the Prussian ministry of agriculture. Wilhelm Kaehler became the Papen's special representative in the Prussian ministry of education, art, and culture.

[32] "Memorandum, October 29," ibid., 227-233; 271-283.

[33] The Court had ruled in favor of the President's intervention in Prussia on the basis of Paragraph II which granted the President the right to intervene in a state's affairs if there was a major threat to law and order.

[34] Wolf Telegram Bureau, November 18, 1932, Nr. 2417.

[35] "Directives for the Continuance of Business," Horkenbach, ibid., p. 383.

[36] Ibid., pp. 394-395.

[37] "Nachlass Gayl," *Kl. Erw.*, 4/63, BA, Koblenz. The other accomplishment was the ushering in of a new order of things.

[38] *"Stellungnahme und Förderungen Bayern zur Verfassungs und Reichsreform,"* August 20, 1932, *RKz,* R 43 I/1883/59-89, BA, Koblenz. Dr. Held listed a number of conditions under which Bavaria would accept reforms in the Reich: (a) reforms would not be implemented under Article 48, and any changes that effected the federal character of Germany could be undertaken only with the consent of all the states; (b) Bavaria would accept the union between Prussia and the Reich if the other states were guaranteed their rights; (c) the Upper House would be involved in any changes.

[39] *Memoirs,* pp. 213-14. Papen claimed that the purpose for the visit to Bavaria was to persuade Dr. Held, "to use his influence on the Zentrum and German Nationalists."

[40] Schultess, ibid., pp. 178-179; *"Papen's Münchener Rede-Wortlaut der Kanzlerede," Vossische Zeitung,* October 12, 1932. This explanation can hardly be understood as anything but a clear reference to his plans for the establishment of an authoritarian regime that would ensure a government by the "elite" instead of a democratic parliamentary government by "inferiors."

[41] Ibid.

[42] Papen claimed that when he spoke to the Bavarian Cabinet they "...expressed full agreement with my plans" (*Memoirs,* pp. 213-214). Papen's memory is either weak on this point or he preferred to ignore the fact that Held, Schäffer and Pfeiffer expressed their disappointment with his views quite openly. He also overlooked the fact that in the no-confidence vote of September 12, the BVP *Reichstag* delegation voted with the majority! Cf. Fritz Schaeffer, *"Die Bayerische Volkspartei (BVP)," Politische Studien,* Vol. XIV, No. 147, (Jan-Feb 1963), pp. 58-61.

[43] *"Memorandum, Die Zusammenfuehrung von Reich und Preussen," RKz.,* R 43 I/1883, BA, Koblenz.

[44] *"Vermerk über die Niederschrift ueber die Besprechung in der Reichskanzlei, September 28, 1932,"* Ibid., /44-45. Koblenz.

[45] "Bavarian State Minister's Meeting of 29 October, 1932," *MA* 99/524, *Bayerisches Hauptarchiv,* Munich (Hereafter cited: *BHA*).

[46] *Deutsches Volksblatt,* November 2, 1932, quoted in Waldemar Besson, *Württemberg und die deutschen Staatskrise 1928-1933.* (Stuttgart, Deutsche Verlagsanstalt, 1959), pp. 315-316.

[47] After the elections, Papen sought to improve his relationships with the southern states. He called for a meeting in Berlin on November 11. Despite his efforts to persuade the southern politicians that he did not intend to disturb the equilibrium between the Reich and the states, his professions of good faith fell on deaf ears. "Memorandum of a meeting in the Reichs Chancellery on November 11, 1932 at 6 p.m.," *RKz.,* R 43 I/ 2281, BA, Koblenz.

---

[48] Cabinet Session, September 14, 11:00 A.M., *RKz*, R 43 I/1457, BA, Koblenz.

[49] Ibid.

[50] Ibid. It should be recalled that Prussia and the southern states (Bavaria, Baden, Hesse) were challenging the legality of Papen's actions of July 20.

[51] Cabinet Session of September 14, 1932, *RKz.*, R 43 I/1457, BA, Koblenz.

CHAPTER 9:
THE CARDINAL vs. THE BARON

A. The November Elections

The announcement of new elections did not cause a great outburst of enthusiasm among the voters. In fact, the German electorate was exhausted from going to the polls four times that year. Nevertheless, the Nazi campaign, spearheaded by Goebbels' campaign rhetoric, directed its attack against the "clique of the nobles," the "bourgeois young bravos," and the "corrupt Junker regime." While Nazi speakers denounced the business-oriented economic policies of Papen's government, brown-shirted rowdies broke up communist meetings and organized attacks against *Stahlhelm* leaders. In spite of this stepped-up campaign, Hitler's movement began to ebb as demonstrated by the decline of attendance at party rallies. Among the first to abandon the Nazi movement were conservative businessmen who had welcomed Hitler as an avowed enemy of communism. Now, shocked by the Nazi's cooperation with the communists in the Prussian *Landtag*, and in the Berlin transit strike a few days before the elections, many decided to vote for the DNVP and other conservative parties.[1] Other conservatives, who had voted for the Nazis in July, abandoned the party in November because of Hitler's inflexible opposition to joining Papen's government. Finally, many voters were appalled at Hitler's public expressions of support for the five storm troopers who had brutally murdered a Polish miner in the Upper Silesian village of Potempa in August.

While the popularity of the National Socialists appeared to be declining, representatives from big business as well as the wealthy, conservative East Elbian landowners began to show more support for the Papen government.[2] Alarmed by Hitler's radical campaign and concerned about the precarious position of Papen's government, politically active industrialists Carl Friedrich von Siemans and steel magnate Fritz Springorum invited other businessmen to a special meeting in Berlin on October 19. Joining them at the Berlin Club was the state secretary of the Reich Chancellery, Erwin Plank. He told his audience that Papen had no intention of returning to parliamentary rule, and added that in order to prevent this, the Chancellor was prepared to introduce certain constitutional reforms. The only obstacle to this plan would be a Nazi-Center coalition in the *Reichstag*. In order to prevent this, Papen wanted to offer financial support in the forthcoming election to those political parties and organizations that he knew would not cooperate with the Nazis or the Center. In response to Planck's appeal, this group of businessmen agreed to raise two million marks. They also pledged further financial support on behalf of the government's planned constitutional reforms.[3]

While Papen's efforts to obtain patronage from big business met with success, his appeal for support from the working class went largely unheard. The trade unions criticized his economic policies, which they regarded as favoring the rich. Naturally, the Communists opposed the bourgeois politics of the Papen cabinet, and in order to discredit the government, engaged in crippling strikes throughout the country. Papen was also in danger of losing the support of his agrarian constituency who had been one of his principal backers throughout his political career.[4] Finally, the Chancellor found himself in the position that even those who wanted to support his government were unable to do so directly since it was not directly associated with any political party.[5] The only way one could vote for Papen was to vote for the German Nationalist party. But this proved to be a liability because Hugenberg's popularity was at its lowest point.[6]

As the November elections drew near, parties stepped up their campaign activities. As usual, Hitler managed to out-shout everyone else, denouncing Hugenberg's party as "bourgeois reactionaries." Papen was also the recipient of bitter personal attacks by the Nazis concerning his actions during the war in the United States and his wife's alleged close French ties.[7] The voters were also bombarded with Communist propaganda. Borrowing Nazi propaganda techniques in hopes of attracting the more radical elements in the Nazi party, the Communists condemned the Versailles Treaty and called attention to Polish atrocities against Germans in Silesia. However, the Social Democrats waged one of the weakest campaigns in its Weimar existence. Papen's move against the Prussian government in July deprived the Party of all positions of power in Prussia and left the party leaders struggling to hold together the pieces of a rapidly disintegrating organization.[8]

Meanwhile Papen and his associates were also busy on the campaign trail. On October 28, Gayl spoke to the Berlin Press Club on the government's domestic programs including the government's economic reforms, and plans for further administrative reforms in Prussia. In his campaign speeches, Papen called for equality of treatment by the other nations, and a repeal of the disarmament provisions in the Versailles Treaty. The Chancellor addressed numerous business groups pointing out the advantages of supporting candidates who backed his government in the *Reichstag*. Defending his economic program against his critics, the Chancellor presented statistics that supported his claims that unemployment had declined since the previous year. Appealing to the farmers, Papen promised that his government, unlike previous ones, would not favor industrial production at the expense of agriculture. To Nazi charges that he had prevented them from accepting a position in the government, Papen responded that Hitler had bluntly refused his offer. He usually ended his campaign speeches with a promise to unite the truly national forces and carry through to success the commission of President Hindenburg to reconstruct the political and economic life of the nation.

On November 6, the German public went to the polls for the fifth time that year. For the first time since 1930, the Nazis lost two million of the 13,745,000 votes they had registered in the July 1932, cutting their percentage from 37.3 to 33.1, and reducing their representation in the *Reichstag* from 230 to 196 seats.[9] The Nazi defeat was thrown into sharper relief by the success of the Nationalists and the Communists. Hugenbergs' party, benefiting from the Nazi cooperation with the Communists in the Berlin Transit strike and the radical nature of Hitler's campaign, raised its number from 37 to 52 seats. The

Communists who polled close to six million votes secured 100 *Reichstag* seats[10] Many of those who voted for the Communists had supported the Nazis or the Social Democrats in the July election. But, disillusioned with these parties, they now gave their support to what they thought was a genuinely revolutionary party.[11]

Papen and those sympathetic with his government were delighted with the results. They viewed these modest gains as a moral victory for the Government. He saw the results as a revelation of the emptiness of Hitler's claims, and had reduced the Führer "to the proportions of any other politician scrambling for power."[12] The Chancellor was now convinced that Hitler's fall would be as meteoric as his rise. If Hitler wanted power he had better seek to negotiate or suffer further electoral defeats. The odds did appear to be against Hitler, but a combination of Schleicher's intrigues and Papen over-playing his hand led to some unexpected results.

When the cabinet met on November 9, to discuss the political situation in the wake of the election, differences of opinion about the government's attitude towards the Nazis surfaced. Schwerin-Krosigk, Gürtner and Braun-Neucken favored their inclusion in the government. However, Gayl asserted that under no circumstances should Papen give way to a different government. If the parties would not agree to tolerate the present government, the *Reichstag* should be dissolved and the Cabinet should continue to govern by emergency decree. Of course, he concluded, this would mean that, "for a certain period a dictatorship could not be avoided."[13] Under these circumstances, Schleicher interjected, the question of the right kind of tactics was extremely important because, at least in the eyes of the public, the government should appear to be completely in the right. In order to accomplish this, the crafty Defense Minister suggested that Hindenburg should entrust the Chancellor with a commission to undertake negotiations with the party leaders. Above all, he declared, the favorable outcome of these talks depended on Hitler's reaction since the position of the government could only be strengthened with the support of the Nazis. (Schleicher was almost certain that none of the parties would cooperate with Papen's government, and he felt certain that Hitler would not accept a position in the cabinet other than the chancellorship, which Hindenburg would reject out of hand.) When it became clear that none of the parties would cooperate with the government, Schleicher continued, the Chancellor could inform Hindenburg who would then be free to dissolve the *Reichstag* and allow Papen's cabinet to continue ruling by emergency decree.[14]

Papen, at least up until this point, continued to be a pawn in Schleicher's game, agreed whole-heartedly with the general's analysis of the situation. He promised that he would do everything in his power to establish a government of national concentration. The cabinet also accepted Braun's recommendation that, Schleicher should deal with the Nazis because of his previous negotiations with Hitler and Röhm. Meanwhile, Papen would see if there was any basis for cooperation with the other parties.[15]

Following the strategy meeting, Papen received from Hindenburg instructions to negotiate with party leaders. In the course of the next few days invitations went out to the party leaders for consultations. No one expected anything to come of these discussions, and the results bore out this cynical prediction. The first effort ended in failure when the Social Democrats flatly refused to meet with Papen or even discuss the possibility of cooperating with his government.[16] Papen's attempt to reach some agreement with the Center party was equally unsuccessful. In rejecting the Chancellor's offer, the Party leaders, Joos and Kaas, warned that the nation was drifting into a revolutionary situation not unlike that of 1918. Kaas added that, "The only solution to the present untenable situation is to form a Government which - in protecting the rights of the President, and with full authority - restores contact with the people's representatives and ensures the parliamentary majority the situation demands."[17]

Unlike the Center, the Bavarian People's Party favored the formation of a government of national concentration, but since the Chancellor could not find adequate backing, it too thought he should resign. Only Hugenberg's German Nationalists and the declining German People's Party were prepared to fully endorse Papen's government.[18] But this favorable reaction meant very little since, as Schleicher observed later, only through Nazi support or toleration could the political position of the Cabinet be materially strengthened.

In the meantime, negotiations with the Nazis proceeded along two separate lines. On November 13, Papen wrote to Hitler, requesting him to put aside their past personal and political differences and enter into negotiations with the hope of coming to some mutual agreement about the Government's economic and political programs.[19] Still smarting from the humiliation he had suffered on August 13, Hitler refused to enter into direct negotiations with the Chancellor. In his reply, the Nazi leader stated that he did not want to see the hopes of his followers, raised by renewed talks, dashed to the ground when his demand to become the chancellor was turned down again. Furthermore, he was unwilling to accept a subordinate role in a Papen-led cabinet since he was afraid that as a second man in the government he would soon disappear in the background. Asserting that he would not be outmaneuvered as he had in August, Hitler added certain conditions under which he was willing to continue these discussions.[20] He concluded with a stinging rebuke in which he charged the policies of the Papen cabinet with being "in part inadequate, in part as poorly thought out, in part as completely useless and even dangerous."[21]

Papen's efforts to persuade Hitler to join him were countered by Krosigk's attempts to meet with Gregor Strasser about a possible future role for him in the cabinet. Although Krosigk had previously kept aloof from the political controversies surrounding Papen's government, he began to play an increasingly important role in the weeks ahead.[22] However, Krosigk's meeting with Strasser never took place because Hitler threatened all National Socialist leaders with expulsion from the party if they accepted any offer other than a Hitler chancellorship.[23]

Meanwhile, although he gave the impression that he favored continuing with the presidial cabinet under Papen's leadership, Schleicher was beginning to question the Chancellor's ability to continue to lead the Government. Not only was he becoming more irritated with Papen's increasingly independent attitude, and his close relationship with the President, but he was also beginning to see the Chancellor's personal quarrel with Hitler as an obstacle to his plans to concentrate all the "national forces." Up until this point it was the policy of this modern Richelieu to play the role of the power behind the throne. Now it began to dawn on him that he might have to emerge from the shadows and take over the chancellorship himself. Therefore, in order to find a formula for success before it was too late, the crafty General laid plans to get rid of Papen, just as he had eliminated Brüning six months earlier.[24] With Papen out of the picture, Schleicher hoped to persuade the Nazi leader Gregor Strasser and his supporters who favored a truce with the government, to enter the government under his (Schleicher's) chancellorship.

Meanwhile, Papen was determined to remain in office so that he could complete the formation of the "New State." In order to accomplish this, he continued to rely on Hindenburg's backing as well as the support of the *Reichswehr*. Therefore, even if he began to suspect that Schleicher was plotting against him, Papen continued to rely on the General to complete his ambitious project. Schleicher, on the other hand, needed Papen's influence with Hindenburg in order to pursue his own intricate schemes. In spite of the growing mistrust between the two, they continued to cooperate in one scheme after another.

When the latest effort to find a solution to the political crisis failed, Schleicher and Papen entered into one of the most cynical plots ever devised against the continued existence of parliamentary democracy in Germany. On November 17, shortly before the cabinet met to discuss the current political crisis, Schleicher suggested to Papen that, in view of his failure to form a government of national concentration, it would be best for him to submit his resignation to Hindenburg in order to give the latter a free hand to undertake negotiations with the party leaders to form a new government. Papen agreed to go along with this scheme since, like Schleicher, he was confident that Hindenburg would return him to power once it became clear that a parliamentary majority could not be fashioned by any of the parties, and Hitler's reawakened hopes would be shattered once again.[25] They both knew therefore, that this was not going to be a *real* resignation, but only a sham one. This would signal a victory for Papen, who could then go ahead with his *Reichsreform* unhampered by parliamentary politics. For Schleicher, it meant more time and opportunity to bring a chastised Hitler to the bargaining table where he could dictate the terms of a coalition.

When the cabinet met on November 17, Papen informed his colleagues of his limited success in finding parliamentary support, and therefore decided to submit his resignation in order to allow the President the opportunity to rally the nationalistic forces of the Reich. It came as no surprise that Schleicher swiftly concurred with the Chancellor's assessment of the situation. He pointed out that it would be wise for the entire government to resign before and not after the President conferred with the party leaders. Meissner, who was not privy to the plot at that time, objected to this proposal and pointed out that Hindenburg wanted to retain the present government. Gayl interjected that if this was the case, the cabinet should not resign until it was absolutely certain that a new government could be formed. In spite of these objections, however, the ministers finally agreed to submit to the President the government's petition for permission to resign.[26] That same afternoon, Papen met with Hindenburg in order to present him with the cabinet's petition.

That Papen had no intention of resigning became clear in the course of his conversation with the old man. Pointing out that neither the President nor he wanted a return to parliamentary government, Papen stated that negotiations with the party leaders were essential in order to prove to the German public that a working majority was impossible. Once this was established, he continued, a new presidial government could act with much greater authority. He also reminded Hindenburg that members of his cabinet were prepared to accept any future summons that might be forthcoming. With these assurances, Hindenburg reluctantly accepted Papen's resignation, and in accordance with customary practice asked him to remain in office until a new government took over.[27]

It was now the "*Herrenkabinet's*" turn to become a "caretaker government."[28] During this interregnum, Hindenburg engaged in a number of conferences with the leaders of the more important political parties for the purpose of trying to form a new government.[29] Already irritated by the whole affair, the President approached these conferences with little intention of finding a solution. Determined to make this unpleasant matter as brief as possible, Hindenburg began each meeting by reading a prepared statement, undoubtedly drafted by Meissner with Papen's approval.[30] Each party leader was asked to give his political assessment of the situation and the conditions under which his party would cooperate in forming a government of national concentration. The President also asked each leader what kind of a program should such a government pursue, and who ought to serve as chancellor. He concluded the meeting with two conditions: he would not permit a return to party government, and he refused to accept a return of the former Reich-Prussian dualism.[31]

Even if Hindenburg had been interested in solving the impasse, he received precious little advice during the first round of meetings with he bourgeois parties. The leaders were generally in favor of a concentration of all "national forces." They all agreed that the Nazis should be taken into the government, but stated that the choice of a chancellor was the prerogative of the president. With the exception of Center leader Kaas, they all had reservations about appointing Hitler as chancellor.[32]

After meeting with these party leaders Hindenburg was prepared to meet with Hitler who had arrived in Berlin on November 18. Unlike the August 13 meeting, this one was more cordial. A second, but much shorter, conference followed the next day. The heart of Hindenburg's offer was contained in three sentences from the official minutes recorded on November 21:

> You have declared that you will only place your movement at the disposal of the government of which you, the leader of the Party, are the head. If I consider your proposal, I must demand that such a cabinet should have a majority in the *Reichstag*. Accordingly, I ask you, as the leader of the largest party, to ascertain if, and on what conditions, you could obtain a secure workable majority in the *Reichstag* on a definite program.[33]

Neither Hindenburg nor the "palace *camarilla*" thought that Hitler could find a "workable majority" in the *Reichstag*. They also knew that the Nazi leader did not want to be a parliamentary chancellor, shackled by a coalition. He declared that he wanted to be a presidial chancellor, with the same sweeping powers Hindenburg had granted to Papen. This, of course, was refused outright by the President. What was the point of replacing Papen, Hindenburg argued, if Germany was to continue to be governed by emergency decree? The only reason for inviting Hitler to become chancellor would be to provide something Papen was unable to secure, namely, popular support for the Chancellor's reforms. Two days later, November 26, the two met again, with the same results. Neither party had anything new to add to what had already been said. At the conclusion of this meeting, Hitler said he would respond to Hindenburg's proposal in writing that same afternoon.[34]

Over the course of the next three days, Hitler and Meissner exchanged a series of letters that enlarged on the points discussed in the meetings.[35] Schleicher worked closely with Meissner throughout these days. Not only did he receive the minutes of Hindenburg's talks with Hitler, but the crafty General read and revised the letters Meissner was writing to the Nazi leader in Hindenburg's name.[36]

Schleicher, who had always insisted on exhausting every avenue, no matter how hopeless, persuaded Hindenburg to meet again with

Kaas in a last ditch effort to find a solution after the talks with Hitler failed.[37] Late in the afternoon of November 24, Hindenburg met with Kaas and requested him to undertake negotiations with other party leaders for the purpose of finding a working majority in the *Reichstag*. Although he thought Brüning more suited to undertake this commission, the prelate promised to reflect on the matter and communicate his decision to the President the next day.[38] Then, in a series of conversations with Hitler and the other party leaders, Kaas asked each one whether he would join in a coalition government with the Center. Hitler and Hugenberg opposed the idea of a parliamentary government, while the other leaders said they were prepared to help. Discouraged by this limited success, Kaas reported to Hindenburg on November 25, that he could not accept the commission. When asked by Hindenburg what to do, Kaas replied that the reappointment of Papen would be a tragic mistake that would lead to civil insurrection. When Hindenburg wanted to know why the Center objected so strongly to Papen, Kaas replied rather tactlessly that Papen was not only inexperienced, but also a poor leader. Cut to the quick by this observation, and Kaas' feeble attempts to mollify him, Hindenburg concluded his conversation with the trenchant remark that, "they show me a carrot on the one hand, and a stick on the other."[39] The meeting ended on this negative note.

Meanwhile, Schleicher, who had been regularly and completely informed of these negotiations through the good graces of Meissner, became increasingly concerned about the political impasse. He realized that if the Papen Government was unable to secure a substantial popular backing, it would be forced to rely on the *Reichswehr* to compensate for the sagging balance of power. Alarmed at the increase of the Communist vote in the recent elections, the growing radicalism of the National Socialists and their cooperation with the Communists in the Berlin Transit strike, Schleicher became convinced that the prospects for a civil war were looming, and he envisioned the army at the barricades facing the Nazis and the Communists.

On November 25, the day after Hitler's final correspondence with Meissner, the cabinet met to discuss the political crisis. Disenchantment with Papen was beginning to set in among certain members of the cabinet as a result of Schleicher's subtle lobbying. Finance Minister Krosigk, openly opposed another Papen-led cabinet. He was joined by von Braun who was afraid that the retention of Papen would not only drive twenty to thirty thousand Storm Troopers into the streets of Berlin, but also provoke a general strike. Backing Papen was Transport Minister Eltz-Rübenbach, who declared that Papen should remain at the head of the cabinet because of his "idealism and energy." Gürtner's support was more modest. The Justice Minister argued that there was no advantage to changing the chancellorship at this time because Hitler would not be satisfied unless the Nazis were able to take over other cabinet posts as well. Gayl, who up until this point, was a consistent supporter of Papen agreed with Gürtner. He added that the Nazis would also purge the bureaucracy in order to provide positions for their supporters.[40]

When it became his turn to speak, Schleicher reported his lack of success in his meeting with Hitler. Then in a rather surprising move, he suggested that since Hindenburg had refused to appoint Hitler, Papen ought to remain in the post. When the cabinet expressed great concern about the possibilities of a general strike or an armed Nazi uprising, Schleicher assured them that: "In the *Reichswehr* there is no longer enthusiasm for Hitler." As for the technical preparations, the Defense Minister said that all questions of a state of military emergency were being worked out at the *Reichswehr* ministry.[41]

Schleicher's skill at covering up his real intentions is no better exemplified than in this instance. While seemingly eager to support a Papen-led cabinet, the crafty General had become convinced by this time that Papen's usefulness had come to an end. If the nation was to be preserved from a total collapse, it was imperative that the present government had to resign and a presidial cabinet composed of "national forces" be appointed in its place. Through his network of carefully planted "spies," the General heard that the long-time follower of Hitler, Gregor Strasser, was dissatisfied with the Nazi chieftain's policy of "all or nothing." As the head of the Party Organization, Strasser was not only more in touch with the local branches than anyone else, but he was also more disturbed than any of the other leaders by the election results that had culminated in the loss of two million votes in November, many of whom defected to the Communist party. He was convinced that the only way to keep the Party from falling to pieces would be to get into power at once, even if this meant joining in a coalition government. However, before Schleicher could approach Strasser with a proposal to enter a cabinet under his own leadership, Hitler issued an order that forbade anyone but himself to engage in any further negotiations.[42]

Meanwhile, Schleicher had gained an ally in Otto Meissner who, at the General's prompting, was putting pressure on the aging President to appoint a new chancellor. Meissner suggested that the mayor of Leipzig, Carl Goerdler, might be a good choice to lead a coalition cabinet composed of Brüning, Hugenberg, and other trusted conservatives.[43] Although Hindenburg was extremely reluctant to part with his dear "Fränzchen," as he had come to affectionately call the Chancellor, he did dispatch Meissner to seek Brüning's advice. Convinced that Papen was clinging to office mainly because he enjoyed the sudden prestige and power, Brüning recommended that Schleicher should be appointed chancellor, and appoint Papen to an important cabinet post as a palliative for his bruised ego.[44] Still unwilling to dismiss his favorite chancellor, Hindenburg chose to ignore Meissner's report.

While Papen continued to enjoy Hindenburg's protection and support, he found himself increasingly isolated, except for some backing from the Nationalists and the Stahlhelm. In the meantime, Schleicher had managed to persuade Krosigk that the continuation of a Papen-led government would lead to civil war. Gayl, who until now had been one of the Chancellor's closest allies in the cabinet, indicated to Krosigk that he would welcome a Schleicher chancellorship if it would help to eliminate the conflicting policies that were emanating from the Chancellery and the office of the Defense Minister. Schleicher had also undermined the confidence of Gürtner and Neurath, and implied that a cabinet under his leadership offered more promise than continuing with Papen.[45]

In spite of the growing dissatisfaction with his leadership, Papen stubbornly refused to accept defeat.[46] Impatient with what he considered "useless negotiations" with Hitler, and anxious to get on with his constitutional reforms, Papen realized that if he was to remain in office he would have to form a *Kampfkabinet*. This would consist of a group of ministers who would be willing to dispense with the constitution and employ every means available to maintain order, while steps would be taken to bring about a systematic return to an authoritarian system. With this in mind, Papen devised a plot to eliminate Schleicher and his allies from the government. Up until this point, neither had openly confronted the other. However, the moment had arrived when Hindenburg summoned them to a meeting in his chambers on December 1, 1932.

B. "*Ich hatt' einen Kameraden!*"

Papen, and Schleicher met with the president at 6 o'clock in the evening of December 1, 1932.[47] At Hindenburg's request Papen spoke first, summarizing the present state of affairs. Hitler had refused to enter into discussion with the other parties, and insisted on being appointed chancellor, which Hindenburg had refused on two occasions. In his opinion, the unruly actions of the Nazis over the past several months gave the Chancellor no reason to recommend a change in Hindenburg's opposition. Meanwhile, a state of emergency existed requiring extraordinary measures not provided for by the Constitution. Papen proposed that he remain in office in order to continue reorganizing the economy and complete the reform of the constitution. Since he expected the newly elected *Reichstag* to behave exactly the same way as the previous one, it should be prorogued for a period of three to six months. A new Constitution could then be ratified through a popular referendum or a National Assembly. Of course, Papen pointed out, this would be a violation of the Weimar Constitution, but he assured Hindenburg that the gravity of the situation demanded such an infraction. He added that he was deeply aware of the President's desire not to violate the sacredness of his oath to preserve the constitution. Then, appealing to Hindenburg's partiality for the prewar German institutions, Papen compared his actions with those of Bismarck, who had advised King William I of Prussia to ignore the constitution for the sake of the nation.[48] Once the constitutional reforms were in place, Papen concluded, the *Reichstag* could then regain its legislative function. Understood, but not mentioned, was the fact that the *Reichstag*, under the revised constitution, would be considerably different in composition and authority from the present one.[49]

When the Chancellor finished, Hindenburg turned to listen to Schleicher's proposed solution. Aware of Hindenburg's desire to remain faithful to his oath, the wily General charged that Papen's plan was a flagrant breach of the Constitution, and it would plunge the nation into a bloody civil war. He also reminded the President that the vast majority of the nation had declared themselves emphatically opposed to Papen in two national elections. He then proposed a plan which made any violation of the constitution unnecessary. There were factions in the Nazi party that were ripe for revolt, and this faction, headed by Gregor Strasser, along with the Social Democrats and the Center could be the basis for a coalition government[50] Fearing that the president might be swayed by these arguments, Papen interrupted the Defense Minister countering that it would not be easy to split the Nazis who were bound to Hitler by an oath of allegiance. Furthermore, Schleicher's proposal would defeat the President's original reason for appointing a cabinet independent of the *Reichstag*. Was it not appointed precisely for the purpose of bringing about constitutional changes that would result in a more satisfactory relationship between the administration and the *Reichstag*? Schleicher's plan would definitely scrap this objectives. Then he added sarcastically that "Herr von Schleicher has much more intimate connections with the party, and probably sees things more clearly than I do!"[51] After a brief discussion of the two proposals, an exhausted Hindenburg rose from his chair indicating that he had made up his mind. Turning to Papen, Hindenburg ordered him to undertake negotiations for the formation of a new government that would enable him to carry out his plan.[52] Taken back by this directive, Schleicher remained silent; but silence did not mean submission.

Leaving the President's office, Papen, Schleicher and Meissner met briefly in the antechamber to discuss Hindenburg's decision. Papen records the tense conversation that followed: "As we both left, I made one last appeal to him...I can well understand that you should wish to take over the reins of Government after directing its activities behind the scenes for so long. But I have severe doubts about the advisability of your present plan. Would it not be better to solve the problem once and for all by a reform of the Constitution, rather than resort to yet another temporary expedient?"[53] Papen then offered to hand over the post of chancellor to Schleicher if he agreed to carry out his (Papen's) solution to the crisis. Then, perhaps out of fear that Schleicher might accept this offer, the Chancellor quickly added that he thought it would be more advantageous if the Defense Minister would wait until the reforms had been completed. Once this had been accomplished, Schleicher could become Chancellor without receiving the blame for the changes and the attendant unpopularity they would arouse. Papen was now offering the very opposite of what Schleicher had proposed at the November 25 cabinet meeting!

The Defense Minister listened incredulously to Papen's proposal. As they parted he warned the Chancellor, "*Mönchlein, Mönchlein, du gehst einen schweren Gang.*" (Little Monk, you have chosen a difficult path.)[54] After Papen left, the General turned to Meissner and said, "Papen enjoys no popularity. Besides, he is always unlucky. People who are unlucky have no right to be in politics."[55]

Meanwhile, Papen returned to the Reich Chancellery where he discussed Hindenburg's decision with two of his most loyal supporters, Justice Minister Gürtner and Transport Minister Elz-Rübenach. He also invited them to join in a reconstructed cabinet. Although both men declared their willingness to support him, they warned Papen that over the past two weeks Schleicher had suggested to several cabinet members that the Chancellor's reappointment would mean civil war, in which the army's resources were inadequate to protect the state. Papen was stunned by these revelations. He assured the two ministers that neither in private conversations nor in the presence of Hindenburg did Schleicher express doubts about the *Reichswehr's* ability to maintain order in a state of emergency. Thereupon they suggested that the Chancellor should convene the cabinet immediately to clarify this issue. Although it was very late, the Chancellor contacted the other ministers and informed them of a meeting scheduled for the next morning.[56]

It was a group of somber men who met on December 2, at 9 o'clock in the Gartensaal of the Reichs Chancellery.[57] Papen reported on the previous days' conference with the President and the announcement of his commission to form a new presidial government. He then called on the Defense Minister to explain his case. Schleicher now launched one of his famous torpedoes, declaring that the Army no longer had confidence in Papen and was convinced that Papen's plan entailed the enormous danger that the Nazis and Communists would resort to violence. This, he warned, could lead to a civil war, and the Army supported by the Prussian police were not equal to quelling a large scale revolt, even if supported by voluntary civilian formation. Schleicher assured the ministers that he did not speak unadvisedly or without careful reflection. He explained that he had ordered his ministry to organize so-called "war games" under theoretical conditions, in order to ascertain the ability of the Army to deal with an invasion or, as in this instance, the possibility of both an invasion and a civil war. The crafty Defense Minister then called on Lt. Colonel

Eugen Ott, the officer who had been in charge of the operation, to corroborate in detail the findings of these war games. Ott, a close confidant of Schleicher's, reported that in the judgment of all the military authorities participating in this game there was no hope; the *Reichswehr* could not be expected to cope with such a situation.[58] Upon hearing this report, the majority of the cabinet agreed with Schleicher that Papen's plan to violate the Constitution should be abandoned. Once again the Army had shown itself to be the supreme arbiter in German politics. Papen realized that Schleicher had won the day, and so he terminated the meeting without further discussion and hurried to report these latest developments to the President.[59]

Although he had lost the support of some of his closest collaborators, and the *Reichswehr* was unwilling to follow his lead, Papen refused to acknowledge defeat. Instead of submitting his resignation, he asked Hindenburg whether the Field Marshal still wanted him to carry out his plan. Of course, this would mean that another Defense Minister would have to be appointed. He assured the President that if the German people could be convinced of his sincerity to give them bread and work and to restore a functional democracy, there would be no recourse to civil disorder. However, he continued, if the President thought his analysis was incorrect, he could appoint Schleicher to the chancellorship. With bowed head the old gentleman listened in silence. Then he rose slowly from his chair and with a saddened voice said: "My dear Papen, you will not think much of me if I change my mind. But I am too old and have been through too much to accept the responsibility for a civil war. Our only hope is to let Schleicher try his luck."[60] As he turned to leave, Papen noticed two large tears rolling down Hindenburg's cheeks. That same day he received a photograph of the President on which he had written the words of an old soldier's song: "*Ich hatt' einen Kameraden.*"[61]

Shortly after Papen left the President's office, Schleicher was called and Hindenburg asked him to form a new cabinet and carry out his proposed program. Still reluctant to assume the chancellorship, he would have preferred to use his influence behind the scenes, Schleicher replied, "I am the last horse in your stable, and ought to be kept in reserve." But the old man, still bitter about the manner in which Schleicher forced him to part with his favorite, von Papen, now insisted on his appointment. Let the General succeed if he could; but if he failed, and turned to Hindenburg for support, he could expect no more loyalty or mercy than he had shown to the other victims of his intrigues - Müller, Gröner, Brüning, and now Papen. Therefore, on December 2, Schleicher became the last chancellor of pre-Hitler Germany.

Schleicher was the first general since Caprivi to occupy the position of *Reichschancellor*.[62] He now had to make good his claims to succeed where Papen had failed. His desire was to find a way out of the predicament in which Germany had been governed for years without a parliament and even against parliament. He hoped to find a parliamentary majority in the *Reichstag*, ranging from the moderate Nazis on the Right to the moderate Social Democrats on the Left.

At first it appeared that the new Chancellor might find more support in parliament than Papen. The Center were willing to work with him, and the German Nationalists, though cooler to him than Papen, also accepted him. As expected, he received no support from either the Communists or the Social Democrats who still regarded him as Papen's accomplice in the coup against Prussia. However, he did, at first, have the support of the Trade Unions under the leadership of Theodor Leipert. But ultimately Schleicher's political future depended on the attitude of the Nazis. Aware of this, the chancellor resorted to his customary tactics of "divide and conquer." If he could split the Nazi party by appealing to the moderate wing led by Gregor Strasser, he could force Hitler to come to terms or become a political cipher.

Schleicher's first act, therefore, was to send for Strasser to offer him the cabinet post of Vice Chancellor and Minister President in Prussia. This was a clever move since Strasser could take over Schleicher's plans for dealing with unemployment and help establish cooperation with the Trade Unions.[63] Even more importantly, the offer would not only split the Nazi party leadership, but it would also strengthen Schleicher's position since Strasser would bring with him a substantial segment of the Party. However, this plan failed when, in a heated confrontation with Hitler, who accused him of trying to go behind his back and oust him from the leadership of the Party, Strasser quit the Party.[64] With Strasser's resignation Schleicher's hopes to divide the Nazis had collapsed, and with it all hope of forming a coalition with the National Socialists.

While Strasser's resignation gave Hitler time to recover his confidence and restore the threatened unity of his Party, Schleicher tried to persuade the other parties to join his government. On December 15, Schleicher delivered a radio address to the nation in which he announced his program. Calling on his listeners to accept him, not as a soldier, but as an "impartial trustee of the interests of all in an emergency," he declared that he supported neither capitalism nor socialism. He also announced the appointment of a Reich Commissioner to draw up plans for reducing unemployment. He announced the end of agricultural quotas which Papen had introduced to the benefit of the large landowners in the eastern provinces; he came out strongly in favor of a huge land settlement for the peasants to be taken out of the bankrupt estates in eastern areas of the Reich.[65] Not only did his radio address fail to win him support from the moderate Socialists, the Trade Unions, or the Center party, but he also stirred up violent opposition from the powerful industrial and agricultural interests.[66]

In spite of his inability to bring the Nazis into his government, and his failure to find a parliamentary majority in the *Reichstag*, Schleicher remained suavely and resolutely optimistic.[67] But by January 20, 1933 his imperturbable mien was shaken to some degree when the Nationalist Party withdrew its support from the government. Schleicher had now successfully alienated the respect and confidence of every party in the *Reichstag* from the extreme Right to the extreme Left. There was little hope left for even a remote chance of fulfilling the mandate with which he had been entrusted by Hindenburg just six weeks earlier. The Chancellor, who had promised that he would either reach an agreement with Hitler or split the party, had failed to accomplish either objective. He had made enemies of every party in the *Reichstag*, and his statement on January 20, that he no longer attached any importance to a parliamentary majority was simply an admission of a situation that had existed for some time.

C. The Baron's Revenge

While Schleicher's futile efforts to reestablish some form of parliamentarianism threatened to bury him, it was his former colleague and fellow conspirator, Franz von Papen, who brought about his fall from power. In his *Memoirs* Papen denies that he felt any personal animosity towards Schleicher, and claims that their differences were on matters of policy and that he "had no wish to reduce it to a personal issue."[68] Yet it is difficult to accept this in light of his activities from the day of his resignation until the appointment of Hitler as Chancellor on January 30, 1933.

Schleicher, who probably recognized the danger of seeing the former chancellor remain close to the president, proposed that Papen be appointed ambassador to France. Papen said that he was attracted to the idea because it would offer him the opportunity to improve Franco-German relations. But after discussing it with the President he declined the post, stating that Hindenburg wanted him to be available for advice from time to time.[69]

While Hindenburg's decision to retain Papen as his personal advisor came as a shock to Schleicher, Papen was overjoyed. He was firmly convinced that the political fortunes of the NSDAP were beyond recovery, and that he could now call the tune to which the Nazi leader would be forced to dance.[70] He considered it only a matter of time before Schleicher would be a victim of Lassalle's dictum, "It might cost a man his head to be too clever in great affairs." Surrounded by his son Otto, his private secretary, Meissner, and Papen, there was little chance for Schleicher to influence the President or call upon him for support. At the appropriate moment, therefore, Papen intended to answer Hindenburg's call to form a new government.

One of the first - Papen would probably say providential - pieces of good fortune was the fact that repairs in the President's palace caused Papen to offer his apartments in the Reichs chancellery to Hindenburg and his son, Otto, on a temporary basis. Papen moved a few houses down to the vacant lodgings of the Prussian Minister of Interior. Schleicher, on the other hand, lived in the official residence of the Defense Minister in the *Bendlerstrasse* where he was separated from Hindenburg by about half a mile. Papen could walk through the gardens of the *Wilhelmstrasse* in a matter of minutes. Both the Field Marshal and his son enjoyed the witty conversation of the dapper ex-chancellor who took full advantage of this situation to mix in items of political importance along with his clever and always amusing stories.[71]

While Schleicher was desperately attempting to woo the parties into some type of cooperation with his government, Papen was busy laying the foundations for his return to power. The day after Chancellor Schleicher's first radio speech to the nation, on December 16, Papen delivered a speech in the *Herrenklub*, at a banquet in his honor. Although he spoke as a private citizen, in the eyes of his audience he was more than just that. These politicians, important businessmen, and high officials were well informed of what was going on in the *Wilhelmstrasse*. They also knew that Papen was a special confident of the President and anything he said was taken, rightly or wrongly, as reflecting the views of the old gentleman himself. In the course of his speech, the former Chancellor appealed to the Nazis to see him as a friend who was anxious to see them participate in the government. Later Papen claimed that his appeal to Hitler was an effort to assist Schleicher's attempts to gain Nazi support. However, both in substance and manner, the speech conveyed a different impression, which was not lost on his audience. Many, in fact, interpreted his remarks as an effort to undermine Schleicher's efforts to split the Nazis.[72] The historian, Theodor Eschenberg, who was present at the banquet, regarded this as "a stab in Schleicher's back," and warned that "this offer to the Nazis to enter the government is bound to provide them with new momentum. They know that Papen is Hindenburg's confidant."[73]

This reaction was not far from the truth. Among the three hundred guests who had gathered to hear Papen was the wealthy Cologne banker, Kurt von Schröder.[74] Like many others at the banquet, Schröder believed that Papen represented the President's thinking, and he was impressed with Papen's appeal to the Nazis. At the end of the banquet, Schröder approached the former Chancellor, and in the course of the discussion both agreed that there was a need for coming to terms with the Nazis.[75] Although Papen claimed that beyond this nothing specific was said, this contradicts Schröder's testimony at Nuremberg.[76]

After the banquet Papen left for his estate in the Saar to spend the Christmas holidays with his family. On December 28, he claims he received a telephone call from Schröder inviting him to come to Cologne to meet with Hitler. Papen told the banker that he intended to return to Berlin via Düsseldorf on January 4, and he could stop at Cologne on the way if he wished.[77] It was this meeting that has given rise to a lively controversy about what Papen and Hitler might have discussed and upon which they came to some agreement.[78]

According to Schröder's testimony at the Nuremberg Trials in 1945, Hitler arrived his house on January 4, 1933, accompanied by Himmler and Keppler. After a brief informal reception, Hitler and Papen went into the den where they were closeted alone for about two hours. Although he was not present at that private meeting, Schröder testified that Hitler and Papen began with a discussion about the government's action against the Potempa case. Then changing the subject, Papen told Hitler he had urged the President to appoint the Nazi leader as Chancellor after the July 31 elections. When Hindenburg refused to do so, Papen said he was shocked, and said that he suspected Schleicher was behind the President's rejection. Papen then suggested the concentration of all national forces of the Right - the Nazis, German Nationalists, and the *Stahlhelm* - to form a government headed co-equally by Hitler and himself. Papen also insisted that his friends should become ministers in the cabinet provided they accept his (Hitler's) policy, and agreed to the necessary changes that the Nazi leader intended to make. Among the changes, he included the elimination of all Social Democrats, Jews and Communists from leading public positions, and the restoration of law and order. According to Schröder, Hitler and Papen, "...had reached an agreement in principle so that many points which had brought them into conflict could be eliminated and they could find a way to get together."[79]

Papen vehemently denied this testimony, stating that he met with Hitler because the Schleicher government was "proving itself unworkable." He also said that the rumors concerning the weakness of the Nazi party were exaggerated, and Hitler was regaining momentum. For these reasons, therefore, he decided to meet with the Führer in hopes that he could persuade him to accept the post of vice chancellor in Schleicher's cabinet. He also says that he "even went so far as to suggest that Schleicher might be agreeable to some sort of *duumvirat*," and that he would be happy to suggest this.[80]

However, this account is open to question. Would there have been any point in asking Hitler to become vice chancellor after he had refused it on numerous other occasions? Moreover, would either Schröder or Keppler have been in favor of a meeting if all Papen intended to offer Hitler was a slightly different version of what the Führer had already refused in August? Finally, a vice chancellorship, with the assurance that the powers would be equally shared, would scarcely have interested Hitler either. After all, Papen had offered him a similar proposal earlier, when he agreed to step down after a period of collaboration had proven that Hitler was willing to work in a coalition.

That Papen was set on getting rid of Schleicher is further supported by a letter from Keppler to Hitler on December 19, 1932.

According to Keppler, who was present at the banquet on December 16 when Papen met Schröder, Papen had complained about Schleicher's intrigues which had led to his (Papen's) resignation. Keppler quoted Papen as stating that he expected a speedy change in the political situation as both possible and necessary, and that he [Papen] "...espouses you [i.e., Hitler] for the Chancellorship." Keppler also reported that Papen wanted to have a confidential discussion with the Führer "...in order to clear up earlier events, and discuss future political arrangements."[81]

In response to this allegation, Papen insisted that Keppler's letter was written to overcome Hitler's aversion to him, and that he had never spoken to Keppler before February 1933.[82] However, Keppler would scarcely have told Hitler categorically that Papen would back his candidacy for the chancellorship if he intended to offer him only the vice chancellorship, or a shared chancellorship. One has to conclude, therefore, that the meeting was held in January because Papen, as he admitted to Schröder on December 16, realized that Hitler and the Nazis had to come to power. What Papen wanted, was to be in a position to not only keep Hitler in check, but even to prepare for his own return to the chancellorship after Hitler's attempts had failed.

Support of this version is to be found in Goebbels' diaries. While it is certainly true that Goebbels is hardly a reliable source, one must ask what interest he could possibly have had in falsifying his record of these events? According to Goebbels, Hitler told him that "things were looking up. If nothing extraordinary occurs, we shall probably succeed this time."[83] What else could Hitler mean, if not that he expected to come to power through Papen's efforts? This becomes even clearer from his "Table Talk," in which he is reported as having said the following:

> In the face of the increasingly tense political situation, the Old Gentleman [Hindenburg] had made contact with him [Hitler] through Papen, letting the former Chancellor explore the terrain, so to speak, in their well-known conversation at Cologne. *At this meeting he, Hitler, had gained the impression that his prospects were excellent* (italics added). He had therefore made it absolutely clear that under no circumstances would he be a party to any compromise solutions.[84]

Finally, Otto Meissner, Hindenburg's private secretary, and a man in whom the aging president often confided, recorded that, after Papen's talks with Hitler (in August & November), the President told him (Meissner) that Hitler was no longer demanding the Chancellorship, and that he was prepared to participate in a coalition government. Meissner also reported that Hindenburg gave his permission for Papen to remain in personal and strictly confidential contact with Hitler *on this basis*, (i.e., on the basis of participating in a coalition government).[85] In his testimony at Nuremberg, Meissner added that Hindenburg had requested him to make no mention of Papen's commission - *even to Schleicher*! From this statement, it appears quite clearly that Hindenburg and Papen had agreed that Schleicher must go.[86]

From all of this evidence, it appears that Papen went to Cologne with the precise intention of inviting Hitler to join him in a coalition government with conservatives and nationalists. But in order to accomplish this, Schleicher had to be dismissed. Papen knew from previous talks with the Führer, that he would not join any coalition unless he was the chancellor. Consequently, Papen was forced into offering him at least an equal share of power along with himself.

Papen devotes several pages in his *Memoirs* in an unsuccessful attempt to deny this. The only response he makes to all the evidence against him is that he "had not the slightest intention of causing Schleicher difficulties."[87] If that was his intention, why did he not approach Schleicher and offer to cooperate with the General in his efforts to split the Nazi party and therefore weaken Hitler's position? Papen never intended this to happen because he hoped to use Hitler as a means to return to power, either as chancellor, or as vice chancellor.

In the meantime, events continued to develop that were more and more unfavorable for Schleicher. On January 15, 1933, a *Landtag* election in the tiny state of Lippe-Detmold secured the Nazis 36.6% of the votes, a rise of 17 per cent. Although this state, half the size of Rhode Island, revealed very little in terms of claiming a resurgence of Nazi strength throughout the Reich, Goebbels and his propaganda machine blared forth the election results as if they constituted a major triumph. On January 22, with a full escort of armed Prussian police, ten thousand SA men paraded on the *Bülowplatz* and listened to a ranting speech by Hitler. They also staged a mass demonstration in front of the

Communist headquarters in Berlin. "We shall stake everything on one throw to win back the streets of Berlin," Goebbels wrote in his diary.[88]

Schleicher now realized that his hopes to split the Nazis had all but disappeared. At the same time he had not helped his cause when he gave a Christmas eve address to the nation in which, among other things, he said that he planned to resettle thousands of unemployed on 750,000 acres of "our thinly populated East." There arose an enormous outcry from the Nationalists and the powerful Agrarian Association, who represented their protest to Hindenburg, and clamored for the Chancellor's dismissal. This was followed by the Nationalist's withdrawal of their support for the government.[89]

Meanwhile, Papen still hoped to persuade Hitler to join him in forming a new government. In order to accomplish this, he accepted an invitation to meet with the Nazi leader at von Ribbentrop's home on January 10.[90] Hitler insisted on being appointed Chancellor, while Papen said that Hindenburg would never agree to this. The meeting ended with Hitler refusing to meet for any more discussions until after the Lippe elections scheduled for January 15, 1933.[91]

Three days after the Lippe elections, on January 18, Papen met with Hitler at Ribbentrop's house again. Heartened by the results of the Lippe elections, Hitler was unyielding on the question of the chancellorship.[92] As a compromise, he said he was willing to have only two Nazis in the government: a new department of aviation, and the post of Reich Commissioner in Prussia for himself.[93] Realizing that Hitler would not settle for anything less, and anxious to find a solution to the impasse, Papen accepted Hitler's new terms as a basis for further discussions. He was now determined to try and work out some way to convince Hindenburg to accept Hitler as the chancellor. Before the meeting broke up, Ribbentrop suggested that a talk between Oskar von Hindenburg and the Führer would be helpful.[94]

Following this meeting, Papen went to Hindenburg and informed him of Hitler's new offer. Still reluctant to appoint the Nazi leader, Hindenburg called in both Meissner and his son, Oskar to listen to Papen's latest report. Repeating Hitler's terms, Papen said that as the leader of the largest party, Hitler could insist on the chancellorship, and that, after all, he was asking for only two cabinet posts. Papen added that he would be satisfied with the vice chancellorship. Meissner, who up until this point, had opposed Hitler's demands, now supported Papen's suggestion. But, he added that certain safeguards would have to be taken to avoid any possible abuses of power. Papen assured him that there were a number of safeguards: the constitutional rights of the president; his position as commander-in-chief of the *Reichswehr*; the rights of the parliament. Papen was convinced that by getting the Nazis to participate in the government, he could maneuver them away from their revolutionary ideas and put a stop to their incendiary tactics.

In spite of Papen's persuasive arguments, Hindenburg was not convinced. No doubt his misgivings were based more on his instinctive aversion to Hitler than on the weaknesses of Papen's so-called "safeguards." He therefore said he wanted time to think this over. Oskar's position remained unchanged, and he continued to warn his father against Papen's plan.[95]

Papen now realized that before Hindenburg could be converted to his proposal, the younger von Hindenburg would have to be won over. Therefore he decided to accept Ribbentrop's offer for another meeting with Hitler on January 22. Papen requested Oskar and Meissner to accompany him "in order to make sure of my position." Hitler was accompanied by Frick, Röhm and Himmler, and was joined later by Göring. After some rather awkward small talk, Hitler invited the President's son to join him in an adjoining room. There is no record of their conversation which lasted for more than an hour.[96] According to Oskar, Hitler did most of the talking, and used all the familiar arguments to change his mind: only he could save Germany from Communism; only he would be an effective chancellor; no government could survive without his support, etc. Although no proof exists, it has been suggested that Hitler used threats and bribes to influence the President's son to support his demand.[97] But whatever the reason, on their way home Oskar told Meissner: "It cannot be helped, the Nazis must be taken into the government."[98] The next morning when Papen reported to Hindenburg, he tried to convince the President of the advantages of Hitler's offer. However, the President was still adamantly opposed to appointing the "Austrian Corporal" to the chancellorship.[99]

Meanwhile, all of Schleicher's efforts to gain political support from the other parties had collapsed. Alone and isolated, especially after the German Nationalists abandoned him on January 20, he realized that it was only a question of time before the President would call for his resignation. He was also aware of Papen's efforts to return to power, either in a Hitler-Hugenburg coalition, or with the Führer alone. He was convinced that a Hitler-Hugenburg government would result in a civil war, and the Army would not support the Papen government. The crafty General also knew about the meetings at Ribbentrop's home.[100] Now that Oskar was involved he knew he had to act swiftly if he was to remain in control of the situation.

On January 23, Schleicher went to the president and told him that his efforts to split the Nazi party had failed, and the only solution was to dissolve the *Reichstag* and postpone new elections until conditions became stable once again. In order to suppress any possible Nazi resistance, he asked for emergency powers. Ironically, Schleicher had now come to the exact position Papen had been in at the beginning of December. As expected, Hindenburg balked at this plan invoking the horrors of a civil war. The General tried to assure the president that the Communists would not rise, and there would be no general strike because the labor unions supported him. Moreover, he stated that the *Reichswehr* could be reinforced with volunteers, and therefore easily deal with the Nazis.[101]

Hindenburg was not impressed by Schleicher's arguments, and told him that, for the time being, he would not postpone new elections beyond the appointed time. He also said he would think about dissolving the *Reichstag*. Moreover, in spite of all the pressure being brought to bear, he told Schleicher that he was still opposed to a Hitler chancellorship. Hindenburg's objections to a Hitler appointment did not prevent Papen from pursuing his plans to return to power in some capacity. He was certain that Schleicher was finished, and he now saw that the moment had arrived for which he had been waiting. Since the president was still reluctant to appoint Hitler, he thought, perhaps there was a better chance to ally himself with Hugenburg and the Nationalists. Not only would this be more acceptable to Hindenburg, who wanted Papen to resume the chancellorship, but to Oskar who had consistently urged his father to appoint Papen.

Since Hindenburg seemed quite set on reappointing Papen, the ex-chancellor decided to pursue this possibility knowing that there was only a slim chance that he could succeed. In any event, he realized that success would only come if he could convince Hugenburg and the Nationalists to join him along with the Nazis in a coalition cabinet. Up until very late in the negotiations he probably was uncertain as to what positions would be held by which individuals, but it was clear that

Hitler would have to play an important role - possibly even the chancellorship.

On January 23, the same day that Schleicher visited the President, Papen met with Frick, and Göring and they agreed to "form a national front to support Papen's position with Hindenburg." The next day Oskar had tea with Ribbentrop, who told him that it looked as if "...a Hitler chancellorship under the auspices of a new national front is not entirely hopeless." Oskar promised to have another talk with Ribbentrop before his father made up his mind.[102]

While Ribbentrop hoped that, Oskar could convince his father to appoint Hitler, Papen had reached the decision to support Hitler's candidacy for the chancellorship. On January 25, Ewald Kleist accused Papen with attempting to cajole Hindenburg into appointing Hitler chancellor. Papen candidly replied that "there is no other course left but to get the old gentleman to do so."[103]

The last weeks before Hitler's appointment were so filled with plots and manipulations that it is almost impossible to unravel the tangled web. Not only is much of the documentation confused and often fragmentary, but statements spoken or written long after the event are frequently hazy and even self-contradictory. But while they are not wholly accurate, all the sources reveal a conspiratorial atmosphere on the part of the main participants. Caught up in their own schemes, they were all attracted to Hitler like moths to a candle, and in which all would ultimately perish.[104]

Schleicher and his colleague General von Hammerstein had come to the conclusion that Hitler would be better than Papen. They decided to present their views to the President. On January 26, Hindenburg received Hammerstein, but he was furious with the general for meddling in politics. After a withering dressing-down, he told Hammerstein that he would, under no conditions, appoint that "Austrian Corporal."[105] Upon hearing this news, Schleicher knew his time was up unless he could appeal personally to Hindenburg to accept Hitler rather than Papen. When Hindenburg heard this he angrily requested Schleicher to submit his resignation.[106]

Word of Schleicher's meeting with the president spread like wildfire. Rumors poured into the *Bendlerstrasse* that a Papen-Hugenburg cabinet was all but reality.[107] On the morning of January 29, the situation was still unresolved. Hindenburg stubbornly clung to his desire to see a Papen-Hugenburg cabinet. Meanwhile, Papen learned from Oskar that Schleicher wished to remain as Defense Minister, and in order to insure this, he had mobilized the Potsdam garrison, which was on its way to the capital to prevent Hitler from becoming chancellor. Papen hurried over to see the President to inform him of this latest development. Although the old man found it hard to believe that one of his generals would betray him, he accepted Papen's suggestion that Schleicher had to be replaced immediately. The President decided to appoint General von Blomberg, the chief military delegate at the Disarmament Conference. Blomberg received word that he was to report immediately to the President, and left Geneva for Berlin, arriving at the Anhalter Railroad Station the next morning, January 30.[108]

Although this report of a possible coup by Schleicher was wholly unfounded, it is difficult to discover from which quarter it originated. Papen could have circulated it in order get rid of Schleicher once and for all, and to put final pressure on Hindenburg to accept Hitler as chancellor. On the other hand, the rumor could have started in the Hitler camp.

Werner von Alvensleben, a leading member of the *Herrenklub*, and formerly one of Schleicher's chief liaison men with the Nazis agreed to go to Hitler at Goebbels' home and find out what was going on. He discovered a qualified celebration in progress. Hitler was still demanding the chancellorship, but it was not certain that the President had yielded. Without thinking, Alvensleben allowed his zeal to outrun discretion, turning to Hitler he warned: "If the Palace crowd are only playing with you, the *Reichswehr* Minister and the Chief of the *Heeresleitung* will have to turn out the Potsdam garrison and clean out the whole pig-sty from the *Wilhelmstrasse*."[109] Upon hearing this, a wild panic spread through government quarters in Berlin. Called from his bed at two o'clock in the morning, Meissner was informed that von Hammerstein was preparing to transport the President and his son to Neudeck, and that he (Meissner) and Papen were to be arrested.[110] Whether or not the rumors of a *coup* were true, this episode reveals the polluted atmosphere of intrigue and conspiracy that hung over Berlin those final January days.

Meanwhile, Blomberg arrived at the railroad station where he was met by Oskar von Hindenburg and also by von Hammerstein's adjutant, Major von Kuntzen. He was greeted with conflicting demands; one ordering him to report to Schleicher, and the other to go at once to the President's office. Blomberg went to Hindenburg, and at nine o'clock in the morning he was appointed Defense Minister in a still-to-be-appointed cabinet.[111]

The final arrangements between Hitler and Papen centered around the cabinet appointments. It was finally agreed that Hitler would have two of his lieutenants in the cabinet, Herman Göring as Prussian Minister of the Interior, and Wilhelm Frick, who was the Reich interior minister, appointed as a minister without portfolio. Papen was to be appointed Vice Chancellor and Reich Commissioner in Prussia. The remainder of the cabinet was composed of conservatives, some of whom were hold-overs from Papen's cabinet. However, Hugenberg was the only one whom the Nationalists could expect to stand up against Hitler. During the last-minute negotiations, Hitler insisted on new *Reichstag* elections. When Hugenburg strongly objected to the idea, Hitler promised that he would make no changes in the cabinet regardless of the outcome of the elections. Papen, who was afraid that his carefully orchestrated scheme was about to collapse, turned to Hugenburg and sarcastically remarked, "But Herr *Geheimrat* do you wish to endanger the alliance that took so much work to form? Certainly you cannot question a German gentleman's solemn word of honor." About two hours later Hitler was sworn in as Chancellor, and the Third Reich was about to be born.

NOTES

[1] In cooperating with the Communists in a *Landtag* resolution, Hitler hoped to force Hindenburg into appointing him chancellor. Cf. Dorpalen, ibid., p. 364. The transit workers walked out on strike after the city-owned Berlin Transit Corporation announced it would have to cut wages. Not only did the strike fail, but Hitler suffered his first major election set-back since 1930. E. Eyck, ibid., p.435.

[2] Henry Ashby Turner Jr. *German Big Business & The Rise of Hitler*, pp. 294-300. Turner gives a good account of the financial support Papen's government received from big business in the fall election campaign. According to Turner, money was raised that was ticketed for parties who supported the Papen government.

[3] The business community came out in support of a return of the Papen government in an appeal issued on the eve of the election. Among the 339 signatures were several prominent figures from the business world. The most notable was Albert Vögler, general director of United Steel. Turner, pp. 293-296.

[4] Agrarian interests put pressure on Papen's government to increase the duties and quotas on agricultural imports. Since he was expecting their support in the November elections, the Chancellor was forced to yield to their requests. This did not meet with the approval of the Ruhr industrialists who saw tariffs as an obstacle to foreign trade.

[5] Papen turned down an invitation from Paul Reusch and other members of the influential *Ruhrlade*, to take over the leadership of the DNVP from Hugenberg. Turner, ibid., p. 322.

[6] Several notable industrialists, including Krupp von Bohlen and Paul Reusch had a long-standing opposition to Hugenberg, and refused to sign an election appeal calling for support of the DNVP candidates. H. A. Turner, ibid., p. 296.

[7] The attacks against Papen's wife came from the Crown Prince August Wilhelm who was an avid supporter of the Nazi party.

[8] Richard F. Hamilton, *Who Voted For Hitler?* (Princeton, New Jersey: Princeton University Press, 1982), p. 281. The party leaders "refused all active intervention" after the Papen government assumed control over Prussia in July.

[9] "Report of November 8, 1932 by Basil Newton to Sir John Simon," No. 32, *DBFP*, ibid., Second Series, Vol. IV, p. 71. Cf. Thomas Childers, *The Nazi Voter* (Chapel Hill: University of North Carolina Press, 1983), pp. 210-211.

[10] The Center lost five seats in polling 15% of the national vote, leaving it with 70 seats in the new *Reichstag*. In the South, the Center's Catholic counterpart,

the BVP, also suffered a decrease from 22 to 20 seats. Cf. Dorpalen, pp. 372-373; Eyck, ibid., pp. 434-43; Childers, ibid.

[11] Bullock, ibid., p. 193.

[12] Ibid., p. 194.

[13] Cabinet Session, November 9, 1932, *RKz.*, 43 I/1458, BA, Koblenz.

[14] Ibid.

[15] Ibid. From the summer of 1931 until his dismissal from office as Chancellor eighteen months later, Schleicher's activities became increasingly devious and difficult to follow. Although it is almost certain that he never wanted to see the Nazis in a position of supreme power, he wanted to use every means to bring Hitler and his movement under his influence since he believed that he, and he alone could guide the German ship of State through the troubled political waters.(Wheeler-Bennett, *Nemesis*, p. 226).

[16] The Social Democrats were understandably still angry over the Prussian "coup," and especially the wholesale removal of Prussian officials (many of them members of the SPD). They were also incensed over the Chancellor's refusal to reach a compromise with Braun and his "caretaker government," after the Leipzig verdict.

[17] Papen, *Memoirs*, p. 212; "Memorandum of a Conversation between Franz von Papen, Ludwig Kaas, and Joseph Joos, November 16, 1932," quoted in Morsey, *"Zentrumspartei,"* pp. 329-330; *"Beratungsgegenstände,"* November 17, 1932, R43 I/1458, Ba, Koblenz.

[18] Karl Schwend, *"Die Bayerische Volkspartei,"* in Matthias and Morsey, *Ende der Parteien*, p. 475.

[19] Letter of November 13, 1932, by Franz von Papen to Adolf Hitler, *IMT*, Document 633-D, Vol. 35, pp. 223-224.

[20] "Letter by Adolf Hitler to Franz von Papen, November 16, 1932," Document 634-D, *IMT*, pp. 225-230. Hitler insisted on the following conditions: (1) negotiations must be conducted in writing; (2) the Chancellor must agree to take full responsibility for his actions, and not try to hide behind the coat-tails of the President as he had in August; (3) Hitler would be informed in advance of what policy he was being asked to support; (4) the Chancellor would assure him that the DNVP leader, Hugenberg, would be prepared to enter a national bloc.

[21] Ibid., 371-383.

[22] Krosigk was coming more and more under Schleicher's influence, and eventually abandoned the idea of retaining Papen as Chancellor.

[23] Schwerin-Krosigk, *Diaries*, entry for November 20, 1932, No. 145, Archive, *IfZg*, Munich.

[24] In 1957 Papen said he was convinced that Schleicher had systematically struggled (*planmässig angestrebt*) to become the chancellor after the *Reichstag* fiasco of September 12, 1932. "*Niederschrift des Reichskanzlers a. D. Franz von Papen, 1957 November 12, Obersasbach,*" *Zeugenschriftum*, Nr. 354, fol. 6, Archiv *IfZg*, Munich.

[25] Schwerin-Krosigk, *Diaries*, entry for November 18, 1932, ibid., Archives, *IfZg*, Munich.

[26] Cabinet Session, November 17, 1932, *RKz*, R 43 I/1458, BA, Koblenz.

[27] Cabinet Session, November 18, 1932, *Rkz*., R 43 I/1458, BA, Koblenz.

[28] Gürtner's comment that "the constitution recognizes no limitation on the powers of a caretaker government," is a pathetic commentary on the ethics of the same men who had used such a status as justification for removing the Braun-Severing cabinet in July!

[29] Neither the Social Democrats nor the Communists participated in these discussions, leaving the President to meet with the leaders of the DNVP (Hugenberg), Center (Kaas), DVP (Dingeldey), BVP (Schäffer), and Hitler.

[30] Meissner was only one of the players in this game. The other members of the "palace *camarillo*" who were using the President's authority to obtain their own selfish ends included Oscar Hindenburg, Schleicher, and Papen. It is not certain whether the other cabinet members were privy to the plot.

[31] Dorpalen, ibid., p. 376. The statement also requested each party leader to suggest the conditions they regarded as necessary for cooperating in the formation of a government. He also asked them what program such a government should adopt, and who ought to be the chancellor. Cf. "Notes for the Conversations of the Reich President with the Leaders of the German National People's Party, the German People's Party, the Center, and the Bavarian People's Party," MA-106, Archiv, *IfZg*, Munich.

[32] Kaas' willingness to accept Hitler as chancellor stemmed from his fear that another Papen-led cabinet without any popular support would plunge the nation into a civil war. The Catholic prelate was also afraid that the decline of the Nazis would benefit the Communists as indicated by the results of the November 6 elections. Cf. Dorpalen, ibid., p. 377.

[33] Quoted in Bullock, ibid., p. 196; Cf. "*Aufzeichnung über die Becprechung des Herrn Reichspräsidenten mit Herrn Adolf Hitler am November 19, 1932,*" reprinted in Hubatsch, *Hindenburg und der Staat*, pp. 350-352.

[34] "*Aufzeichnung über die Besprechung des Herrn Reichspräsidenten mit Herrn Adolf Hitler am November 21,1932,*" *Rkz*, R 43 I/ 1309, BA, Koblenz.

[35] The correspondence between Meissner and Hitler can be found in *Schultess'*, ibid., pp. 209-213; Hubatsch, ibid., pp. 356-362; Hans Otto Meissner and Harry Wilde, *Die Macht-ergreifung: Ein Bericht über die Technik des*

national-sozialistische Staatsstreichs (Stuttgart: J. G. Cotta, 1958), pp. 115-118.

[36] Dr. Otto Meissner was a conscientious - but also ambitious - bureaucrat, who had risen rapidly in the ranks of the civil service. He became a technical and legal advisor to President-elect Ebert in 1919. Suave and affable in his personal relations, Meissner's contacts with cabinet ministers, *Reichstag* delegates, and other official agencies provided him with important political connections. Under Hindenburg his influence grew steadily as the old man came to depend more and more on his advice. Schleicher was quick to see how valuable Meissner could be and was able to persuade the secretary to support his intrigues.

[37] "Memorandum by Otto Meissner of a meeting between Paul von Hindenburg and Ludwig Kaas, November 22 & 25, 1932, 5 p.m.." Reprinted in Hubatsch, ibid., pp. 362-363; 374-345. Schleicher was also certain that Kaas would warn the President once again about the danger of reappointing Papen.

[38] Memorandum by Otto Meissner of a meeting between Hindenburg and Kaas, November 24, 1932, at 5 p.m., *Nachlass Hindenburg*, Vol. X, No. 27, reprinted in Hubatsch, ibid., pp. 364-365.

[39] Memorandum by Otto Meissner of a meeting between Hindenburg and Kaas on November 25, 1932 at 5 p.m., ibid., No. 28, reprinted in Hubatsch, ibid., pp. 364-365.

[40] It is ironic that Gayl should accuse the Nazis of doing precisely what the Papen government did after the July "*coup.*"

[41] Cabinet Session, November 25, 1932, *Rkz.*, R 43 I/1458, BA, Koblenz. Schleicher had commissioned one of his staff, Lt. Col. Ott, to arrange for war games at the Ministry on November 25-26 to test the army's ability to cope with a general strike and/or armed rising. Some authors have accused Schleicher of deliberately withholding the negative results of this exercise in order to have an alternative plan in case his other schemes to oust Papen were unsuccessful. However, if the war games were still going on November 25, Schleicher could not have had the results in time for the cabinet meeting.

[42] This did not prevent Schleicher from sending Colonel Ott to offer the Nazi chieftain the vice chancellorship in a Schleicher-led government, with the possibility of naming several other Nazis to cabinet posts. But the only response he received was a report that Hitler spent two hours ranting and raving at Ott about why he could not accept Schleicher's proposal.

[43] This was not the first time that Gördler's name came up as a possible choice for the chancellorship. In May, Brüning suggested that the former *Oberbürgermeister* of Leipzig would be a good choice to succeed him. Schleicher also confided to his closest associates in the *Bendlerstrasse* that

Goerdler would make a good chancellor. Schwerin-Krosigk *Diaries*, No. 145, Archives, *IfZg*, Munich.

[44] Dorpalen, ibid., p. 388. When Schleicher was appointed chancellor in December, he offered Papen the post of Foreign Minister, which the ex-chancellor rejected.

[45] Papen denied that among the cabinet members there were strong reservations about his remaining as chancellor. But in an hour long conversation with the Chancellor on November 26, Krosigk explained to Papen why he should not remain in office. Three days later, Krosgik repeated his remarks, and predicted that strikes and possible armed resistance might occur if he remained in office. Schwerin-Krosgik, *Diaries*, November 29, 1932, ZS A/20, Archives, *IfZg*, Munich.

[46] According to Gordon Craig ibid., pp. 458-59, despite all disclaimers which he makes, Papen "had developed a love for office."

[47] There are two versions of this meeting. One as recorded by Meissner, "Memorandum of December 2, 1932 by Otto Meissner," reprinted in Thilo Vogelsang, "*Zur Politik Schleichers gegenüber der NSDAP 1932*," *VhfZg*, Vol. VI, No. 1 (January 1958),p.106. The other version is recorded by Papen in his *Memoirs*, pp. 215-218. Vogelsang also published Papen's criticism of Meissner's account in which he (Papen) claimed that Meissner's memorandum did not correspond to the facts. Papen suggested that Schleicher had dictated the memo to Meissner sometime in the afternoon or evening of December 2, *after* he had accepted the chancellorship: "*Niederschrift des Reichskanzlers a.D. Franz von Papen, 1957 November 12, Obersasbach*," Doc. Nr. 7, pp. 112-113. Archives, *IfZg*, Munich. However, Papen is unable to provide any proof of this. Given the unreliability of his *Memoirs* on so many other occasions, one tends to discount his explanation in this case.

[48] "Memorandum of December 2, 1932 by Otto Meissner concerning conversations by Paul von Hindenburg on December 1 and 2," reprinted in Thilo Vogelsang, ibid., p. 106.

[49] Delegates to the *Reichstag* would be indirectly elected by a franchise weighted in favor of wealth and age. This plan was a direct descendant of Bismarck's constitution system established in 1871!

[50] Papen's account of this meeting differs from his testimony made under interrogation at Nuremberg in September, 1945. In his *Memoirs* (p. 217) he claimed that Schleicher offered to "take over the Government" At Nuremberg, under interrogation, he failed to repeat this assertion. "Testimony of Franz von Papen," *IMT*, Vol. XVI, p. 259; According to Meissner, "Memorandum of December 2, 1932," reprinted in Vogelsang, ibid., p. 106, Schleicher told the

President he could achieve a parliamentary majority, which is not the same thing as offering to head a new government.

[51] Meissner, ibid.

[52] Ibid.

[53] *Memoirs*, p. 218.

[54] Ibid. This was the famous warning Martin Luther received as he left the Diet of Worms in 1521.

[55] Quoted in Otto Meissner and Harry Wilde, *Die Machtergreifung: Ein Bericht über die Technik des nationalsozialistischen Staatsstreichs* (Stuttgart: J.G. Gotta'sche Buchandlung, Nachf., 1958), p. 122. Considering his own fate, Schleicher should have taken his own advice.

[56] *Memoirs*, p. 219; Testimony of v. Papen, *IMT*, Vol. XVI, p. 259.

[57] There are several brief accounts, which when combined, provide a fairly accurate picture of what occurred at this meeting. Memo of December 2, 1932, by Meissner, reprinted in Hubatsch, ibid., p. 367; Memo of Franz v. Papen, *Sammlung*, No. 354, Archives, *IfZg*, Munich; Bracher, ibid., p. 674.

[58] "Memorandum of December 2, 1932 concerning a report by Eugen Ott," *Sammlung Photokopien und Einzeldokumente*, F 41, Archives, *IfZg*, Munich. This meeting took the form of a colloquy among the leaders of the major divisions of the *Reichswehr*, navy commanders, representatives of the Prussian government, the Prussian state police and of the "Technical Emergency Service" (TNH), a special unit designed to provide essential functions interrupted by a general strike.

[59] Schleicher's tactics recall his actions of the previous May when he seduced his fellow generals into withdrawing their confidence from their civilian chief, Gröner. As in that case, so too in the case of Papen, the crafty General's objective was to obtain the withdrawal of the confidence of the Army from the person whom at the moment he wished to eliminate from Cabinet.

[60] Papen, *Memoirs*, p. 223.

[61] Meissner & Wilde, ibid., p. 129; Papen, ibid., pp. 222-23; Dorpalen, ibid., pp. 394-95. The affection Hindenburg had for Papen was reflected in a personal note the former Chancellor received the next day: "My trust in you and my respect for your person and for your work remains undiminished." Always cool and detached, Hindenburg had never found words of such warmth for any other departing chancellor.

[62] General Count Georg Leo von Caprivi (1831-1899) was appointed Imperial Chancellor by Wilhelm II on Bismarck's dismissal in 1890. He continued in office, with little significant achievements, until 1894, when he was replaced by Prince Hohenlohe-Schillingsfurst.

[63] Gregor Strasser espoused nationalization of heavy industry and the big estates together with the decentralization of political power, and the break-up of Prussia. Hitler had little sympathy for these ideas. Schleicher was aware of this and his invitation was intended to use them to draw Strasser and his Nazi followers into support for his government.

[64] A fuller account of this affair can be found in Bullock, ibid., pp. 199-202. If Strasser had stayed to fight out his quarrel with Hitler, he could have carried a majority of the Party with him. But lacking the toughness to challenge the Führer was characteristic of Strasser as earlier capitulation's had revealed.

[65] Bullock, ibid., p.202; Wheeler-Bennett, ibid., pp. 274-75.

[66] Because of his role in the rape of Prussia neither the Trade Unions nor the Social Democrat trusted him. Recalling his role in the overthrow of Brüning, the Center party refused to come to his support. He also stirred up violent opposition from the powerful industrial interests because of his conciliatory policies towards labor. Farmers were furious at his reduction of agricultural protection. The East Elbian landowners denounced his land settlement program as "agrarian Bolshevism."

[67] When Kurt Schuschnigg, the future Austrian chancellor, paid a call on Schleicher, the Chancellor said Herr Hitler was no longer a problem and that "his movement had ceased to be a political danger." Quoted in Bullock, ibid., p.203.

[68] *Memoirs*, p. 225.

[69] *Memoirs*, pp. 223-24. No doubt Papen was already contemplating ways and means of returning to power. As long as Hindenburg was President, the wily ex-chancellor intended to remain close enough to plot Schleicher's downfall, and reclaim the chancellorship for himself. Paris was too far away from Berlin.

[70] There was no doubt that Hitler's party had reached the low-point of its existence. The most immediate problem was a shortage of funds. Even more serious was the sense of defeatism in the Party. The Strasser crisis had caused deep divisions within the Party, so that Hitler, Goebbels, and Göring traveled from one *Gau* to another in an effort to restore confidence in the local party leaders. Goebbels records in his diary that "the past was sad, and the future looks dark and gloomy; all chances and hopes have quite disappeared." *Kaiserhof*, p. 215.

[71] Meissner's affidavit at Nuremberg, *IMT*, ibid. This was denied by Papen in his testimony at Nuremberg, *IMT*, ibid.

[72] According to Fritz Thyssen, "Herr von Papen had developed an intense hatred of General von Schleicher, whom he planned to eliminate as Chancellor of the Reich." Quoted in Wheeler-Bennett, *Nemesis*, p. 271, n. 1.

[73] Theodor Eschenberg, "Franz von Papen," *VjHfZg*, I (1953), p. 163. Eschenberg was of the opinion that the real purpose of Papen's address was not "to see Schleicher's government off to a good start...On the contrary, von Papen again demanded that the National Socialists be taken into a coalition cabinet."

[74] Baron Kurt von Schröder was a wealthy Cologne banker who had been one of the initiators of a petition sent to Hindenburg in November requesting the president to appoint Hitler to the chancellorship.

[75] Through the efforts of his friend von Lersner, Papen came into contact with Schröder. During the fall election campaign, Lersner received a letter from the Cologne banker, in which he urged Papen to persuade Hindenburg to appoint Hitler as Chancellor. Papen replied that he was in favor of this idea, but that Hindenburg would not hear of it. Papen added that if there was a chance that this situation could change he would certainly not stand in the way! Papen mentions none of this in his *Memoirs*. Cf. Heinrich Muth, "*Das Kölner Gespräch" am 4. Januar 1933*, Karl Dietrich Erdmann u. Joachim Rohlfes (eds.) "*Geschichte in Wissenschaft und Unterricht*", Vol. 37, No. 8, Part I.

[76] Schröder affidavit, Nuremberg *NCA*, Vol. II, pp. 922-924.

[77] According to his testimony at Nuremberg, Schröder claimed that Papen approached him first. Cf., Schröder affidavit, ibid. Under cross-examination at Nuremberg on 10/9/1946, Papen denied that he had made the first advances for the meeting with Hitler, claiming that it was Hitler himself who had requested the conference. Copy of the testimony of Franz v. Papen, Archives, *IfZg*, NG/1948.

[78] Cf. Theodor Eschenberg, "Franz von Papen," *VjhfZg*, I (1953), pp. 163-64; Keppler's deposition at the Nuremberg Trials, *IMT*; Schröder's Affidavit, December 5, 1945, Case No. 5, Prosecution Document-Book, No. XIV-A, *IMT*; Axel Kuhn, "*Die Unterredung zwischen Hitler und Papen im Hause des Barons von Schröder*," *Geschichte in Wissenschaft und Unterricht*, Vol. 24, No. 12 (January, 1973), pp. 709-722. Heinrich Muth's study has been already noted. There are other accounts, which tend to corroborate these studies, e.g., Meissner and Wilde, ibid., 148-174, plus notes pp. 287-292.

[79] Affidavit of Kurt Freiherr von Schröder, ibid.

[80] *Memoirs*, p. 228.

[81] Keppler's letter to Hitler, December 19, 1932, cited in Kuhn, ibid., p. 716; also cited in Vogelsang, *Reichswehr*, Doc. 39, pp. 485-486.

[82] Copy of the testimony of Franz v. Papen, 10/9/1946, Nuremberg, NG 1948, Archives, *IfZg*, Munich.

[83] Entry, January 9, 1933. *Kaiserhof*, p. 235; Quoted in Eyck, ibid., p.467.

[84] Entry for May 21, 1942, Henry Pickard & Gerhard Ritter (eds.), *Tischgespräche im Führerhauptquartier, 1941-1942* (Bonn, 1951), p. 428.

[85] Otto Meissner, *Staatssekretär unter Ebert-Hindenburg-Hitler. Der Schicksalsweg des deutschen Volkes von 1918-1945, wie ich ihn erlebte*, 3rd. ed. (Hamburg: Hoffman und Campe, 1959), p.263.

[86] Eyck, ibid., p. 469. One can conclude that if Meissner's report is true, Papen had severely exaggerated Hitler's readiness to compromise. More importantly, he failed to inform Hindenburg that Hitler was still demanding the chancellorship, which was the single important objection the president had.

[87] *Memoirs*, p. 227.

[88] Goebbels, *Kaiserhof*, p. 231.

[89] Hugenburg had already discussed a possible agreement with Hitler on January 17, and they would meet again at Ribbentrop's home on January 22 at which meeting Papen was also present. Wheeler-Bennett, ibid., pp. 274-76.

[90] Joachim von Ribbentrop, *Zwischen London und Moskau, Erinnerungen und letzte Aufzeichnungen*, ed. by Annelies von Ribbentrop (Starnberger See: Leoni Verlag, 1953), pp. 38-39.   Michael Bloch. *Ribbentrop, A Biography* (New York: Crown Publishers, Inc., 1992) pp. 29. At the denazification trial in 1949, Papen denied that he met with Hitler at Ribbentrop's house. The only meeting he claims to have attended was the one on January 22, *Proceedings and Decisions of the German Denazification Court of Appeal, 1949*, p. 31. Since Papen's memory has been unreliable in many other instances, and Ribbentrop had no reason to fabricate the meeting, the latter's version appears to be more reliable.

[91] Dorpalen, ibid., pp. 419-20

[92] Although he makes no mention in his *Memoirs*, at the denazification trial in 1949, Papen denied that he met Hitler on the 18, *De-Nazification Trial*. Bloch, ibid., p. 30 quotes Ribbentrop's *Memoirs*, which indicated that Papen was present.

[93] Dorpalen, ibid., p. 421. These proposals were not all that generous. As Reich Commissioner in Prussia Hitler would have control of the Prussian police, while a Nazi commissioner of aviation would be able to build up a military air force.

[94] Oskar was known to be one of the most strongly opposed to Hitler's appointment, therefore if his resistance could be overcome, the president might change his mind. Cf. Dorpalen, ibid., p. 420; Eyck, ibid., pp. 471-72; Ribbentrop's diary, ibid.

[95] Dorpalen, ibid., p. 422-23. Meissner "Affidavit," *IMT*, Trial IX, pp. 248-249.

[96] There are several versions of this meeting. Ribbentrop's account, which Papen claims is inaccurate, records that after Meissner and Oskar left, Papen

promised to recommend the appointment of Hitler as chancellor to Hindenburg. Papen denies that he said this. The reconstruction of this meeting is offered by several historians. Cf. Bracher, *Auflösung*, pp. 708-709; Vogelsang, *Reichswehr*, pp. 371-372; Dorpalen, *Hindenburg*, pp. 423-424; Meissner and Wilde, *Machtergreifung*, pp. 161-163; Bloch, *Ribbentrop*, p. 30. In his account Henry Adams accepts Papen's version, ibid., p. 204.

[97] Dorpalen *Hindenburg*, p. 424. Bullock, ibid., pp. 208-09, speculates that Hitler may also have revived the threat of impeachment proceedings against the President, and threatened to disclose Oskar's part in the *Osthilfe* scandals and tax evasion on the presidential estate in Neudeck. Although it may be a coincidence, in August 1933, five thousand tax free acres were added to the Hindenburg estate, and one year later Oskar was promoted from colonel to the rank of major-general.

[98] Meissner, "Affidavit," *IMT*, ibid., p. 4494; Meissner and Wilde, ibid., pp. 161-164. While Hitler was closeted with Oskar von Hindenburg, Göring spoke with Meissner, and confirmed Papen's report of Hitler's proposals. There was even a hint that Hitler might be able to fulfill the President's ardent desire to see the monarchy restored. Meissner and Wilde, ibid.; Meissner "Affidavit," ibid.

[99] Dorpalen, ibid., p. 424.

[100] When Meissner arrived at his office the day after the meeting he received a telephone call from Schleicher who wanted to know how the food tasted at Ribbentrop's house! Obviously his network of spies was still active.

[101] Dorpalen, ibid. p. 425.

[102] Quoted in Dorpalen, ibid., p.427.

[103] Ewald Kleist-Schmenzin, *"Die letzte Möglichkeit. Zur Ernennung Hitler's zum Reichskanzler am 30. Januar 1933,"* *Politische Studien,* Vol. X, No. 106 (February 1959), 89-90.

[104] Dorpalen, ibid., p. 428.

[105] Quoted in Dorpalen, ibid., p. 280.

[106] Dorpalen, ibid., p. 280.

[107] By this time, however, Papen had abandoned the idea of a Papen-Hugenburg cabinet, and was negotiating with Göring for the formation of a Hitler-Papen-Hugenburg-Seldte government.

[108] Papen, *Memoirs*, p. 242; Wheeler-Bennett, *Nemesis*, p. 282; Dorpalen, ibid., p. 439.

[109] *Hammerstein Memorandum* Archives, *IfZg* Munich.

[110] Schwerin-Krosigk, *Diaries*, entry for February 5, 1933, ibid., Archives, *IfZg*, Munich.

[111] Wheeler-Bennett, ibid., p. 284.

CHAPTER 10:
UNDER THE SWASTIKA

A. The Veil of Illusions

The announcement of Hitler's appointment as Chancellor was greeted with a vast torchlight parade. Assembling at 7 o'clock in the evening, thousands of jubilant uniformed men, Storm Troopers, *Stahlhelm*, and Himmler's SS marched in military fashion, with bands playing "*Deutschland Über Alles*," and the Nazi party song, "*Die Fahne Hoch*" (Raise the Flag High). They wound their way onto the *Charlottenburger Chaussee* and eastward to the Brandenburg Gate where the goddess of victory in her chariot whipped the stone horses forward. Just beyond the Brandenburg Gate at the *Pariser Platz*, the columns swung to the right and trooped down the *Wihelmstrasse*. With thousands of onlookers lining both sides of the broad avenue, the troops marched in review before President von Hindenburg standing behind the window of the *Reichschancellor's* palace. About one hundred yards away, Hitler stood on a small balcony of the new chancellery. Goebbels captured the excitement of that evening:

> Endlessly, endlessly the crowds march by the Chancellery. Storm troopers, Hitler-youths, civilians, men, women, fathers with their children held up high to see the Führer. Indescribable enthusiasm fills the streets. A few yards from the Chancellery, the President of the Reich stands at his window, a towering, dignified, heroic figure, invested with

> a touch of old-time charm. Now and then with his cane he
> beats time to the military marches. Hundreds and hundreds
> of thousands march past our window in never-ending
> uniform rhythm. The rising of a nation![1]

In the room behind the balcony Papen and his wife heard the jubilant shouts and "frantic applause" of the crowds. Even Papen was stirred by the endless triumphal cries of "*Heil, Heil, Sieg Heil*," which "rang in my ears like a *tocsin*." As he watched the parade, Papen was struck by the way the crowd marched "with restrained joy," as they passed by the window at which Hindenburg - "a symbol of the past" - appeared; and how they broke out in frenzied applause as they marched by the balcony on which the Führer - the Messiah of their hopes - stood. "I had the feeling of listening to a fanfare announcing a period of radical changes."[2] The parade lasted until long after midnight. Goebbels describes the final scene: "At length the square is empty. We close the windows and are surrounded by absolute silence. The Führer lays his hands on my shoulders in silence...The German Revolution has begun!"[3]

While Goebbels rejoiced at the thought that the revolution had begun, Papen celebrated what he naively thought was to be a complete victory for his "new state." Not only had he evened the score with Schleicher, but he had pulled off what neither the crafty General nor anyone else was able to accomplish - he thought he had employed Hitler to work for him and his conservative allies on their own terms. "In two months we'll have pushed Hitler into a corner so hard he'll be squeaking," he boasted to his friend Kleist-Schmenzin.[4] Hitler might be the Chancellor, but the real power, Papen assured his friends, rested with the Vice Chancellor. After all, was it not the Vice Chancellor, and not the Chancellor, who enjoyed the special confidence of the President? And was it not also agreed that the Vice Chancellor had the right to be present on all occasions when the Chancellor reported to the President? Moreover, it was the Vice Chancellor who held the key post of Minister-President of Prussia, and therefore controlled the Prussian administration and the police.

Papen had further reason to think that Hitler was a prisoner tied hand and foot by the conditions he had accepted. Only three of the eleven cabinet posts were held by Nazis, and apart from the Chancellorship, both were of secondary importance. Frick received the

Opening of the Reichstag in the Garrison Church in Potsdam. Hitler's cabinet marching between the ranks of the Reichswehr.

Reich Ministry of the Interior (which did not control the State police forces), and Göring as a minister without Portfolio. And while Göring was also appointed Prussian Interior Minister, he would have to report to Papen who headed the Prussian government.[5]

Papen was so confident this was to be his cabinet, that during the preliminary process of selecting the ministers he was more interested in posts and power than policies or programs.[6] Once the government was in place, he intended to control the agenda of the cabinet. Papen regarded the new Chancellor in his old role of "Drummer." He would be like the barker of a circus in which he had his name as a partner at the top of the bill, but the real decisions would be made by those who out-numbered him eight to three. How badly Papen and his conservative colleagues had judged both Hitler and his movement became patently clear within six months; at the end of which they were to discover, like the young lady of Riga, the dangers of going for a ride on a tiger.[7]

Twenty years later, reflecting on Hitler's appointment as Chancellor, Papen claimed that "he had been brought to power by the normal interplay of democratic processes."[8] However, this veiled criticism of the democratic system does not stand up against the evidence. The plain fact is that Hitler came to power, not through a popular victory at the polls, nor any national movement sweeping him into power, but as a part of a shoddy political deal with the "old gang" against whom he had campaigned for months past. "Hitler did not seize power; he was jobbed into office by a backstairs intrigue."[9] With this explanation, did Papen hope to receive a kinder judgment of history? Or did he sincerely believe that Germany would have been spared this demagogue if an authoritarian system had been in place? Whatever his motives, his rambling attempts to explain the rise of Hitler and the success of the Nazi movement not only add nothing to what is already known, but even tend to be misleading.[10]

Although Papen had assured his associates that he would be able to control Hitler, the course of events over the next six months proved this to be a large dose of wishful thinking. With astonishing speed, Hitler began to consolidate his political position through what the Nazis, who were masters at creating bureaucratic euphemisms, termed the first step in the process of "synchronization" or *Gleichschaltung*. In essence, *Gleichschaltung* constituted a series of measures that prohibited all organized political activity other than that of the Nazi party, established an increasingly efficient system of state-sponsored terror, converted the country's vestigial parliamentary democracy into Hitler's personal dictatorship, and attempted to infuse all traditionally non-political activities with the Nazis' ideology.

Ironically, the Nazis' *Gleichschaltung* was implemented largely by Papen and the New Conservatives, who envisioned that Hitler and his movement would be junior partners in fulfilling the idea of a New State.[11] While Hitler's more radical moves were still unknown and untried - at least in the early stages of the *Gleichschaltung* - the New Conservative goals matched those of Hitler: to destroy democracy; to rebuild the military power of Germany; to reverse the decision of 1918, and to restore Germany to a dominant position in Europe. Blinded by interest and prejudice, these New Conservatives forsook the role of true conservatism, abandoned its own traditions and made the terrible mistake of supposing that in Hitler they had found a man who would enable them to achieve their goals.

Initially, the two most important goals of the self-styled "government of national awakening" were the attainment of a monopoly of political power for the "nationalist parties," and getting people back to work. Between that first cabinet meeting held the day after the triumphal torchlight parade, and the *Reichstag* fire on the evening of February 27, Hitler was well on the way to accomplishing these goals, thanks to Papen's naive belief that he had Hitler cornered, and was assured of the cooperation of the New Conservatives.

The first indication that Hitler and Papen were in agreement about the future of parliamentary democracy in Germany can be traced to the cabinet meeting on January 31. Papen proposed that the forthcoming *Reichstag* elections should be the last, and that there should be no return to the parliamentary system.[12] Papen wanted to bring about the end of parliaments and political parties that could interfere with his *Reichsreform*. But for Hitler, it meant that he could use all of the resources of the State in the forthcoming campaign in order to capture 51% of the vote.[13] This would give him the necessary *Reichstag* majority to pass an Enabling Act, which would grant him complete power for a period of four years. After assuring the cabinet that the results of the election would not alter the composition of the cabinet, the last elections in the Reich were scheduled for March 5, 1933.[14]

At that same meeting, it was agreed - despite the State Supreme Court's ruling in October, 1932 - to transfer all remaining functions of the Braun-Severing caretaker government to Papen. From the very beginning of his Chancellorship, Papen had wanted to oust the Social Democrats from power in Prussia; now he realized this dream. And while his non-Nazi colleagues supported this move thinking they were strengthening Papen's hand, it was Hitler and the National Socialists who were the actual beneficiaries.[15]

Further steps to consolidate political power were introduced on February 2. Using the rumored threat that the Communists and the trade unions were preparing to strike against the State, Frick presented the cabinet with the draft of a decree "for the protection of the German people." It provided for far-reaching controls over political meetings and demonstrations, as well as censorship of the press and other publications. Thus for all practical purposes the Nazis were empowered to neutralize rival parties and leaders, and manage public opinion.[16] Papen was so eager to cooperate in the elimination of the Left, that he and his non-Nazi colleagues supported this decree. What they failed to realize was that the Nazis could, and did use it not only against the Communists, but also against any and all opponents to their movement.

In the meantime, Göring was conducting a wholesale purge of the Prussian police. As the Prussian Interior Minister, he was hard at work replacing "unreliable" police officers with trusted SA leaders. Papen went along with this because he considered this a continuation of his policy to rid the Prussian administration of all Left wing politicians.[17] However, Göring had other ideas. Without consulting Papen, he published an order on February 22, establishing an auxiliary police force on the grounds that the resources of the regular police were stretched to the limits. Fifty thousand men were called up, among them twenty-five thousand from the SA and fifteen thousand from the SS. All they had to do was to put on a white arm-band over their brown or black shirts.[18] The enforcement of the law was now in the hands of criminals. Consequently, it became more dangerous for a citizen to appeal to the police for protection than to suffer assault or robbery in silence.

Meanwhile, Papen mistakenly thought that Hitler would become more responsible as Chancellor, and for this reason continued to co-operate with him during those first weeks. "We believed Hitler," Papen wrote, "when he assured us that once he was in a position of power and responsibility he would steer his movement into more ordered channels."[19] However, events began to unfold that should have made the Vice Chancellor more uneasy about Germany's future. Reflecting on this twenty years later he wrote: "Looking back, I see that there were many times when I should have invoked the President's authority."[20] At the same time, he wrote that Hindenburg was neither willing nor able, due to his age, to use his authority. This was Papen's justification for not appealing to the president for help.[21]

Not only was the aging President becoming less receptive to complaints, but under the "protection" of his son, Oskar, and Meissner, who was always looking out for his own good, he grew out of touch with events outside of his estate. Moreover, Hitler had learned to ingratiate himself with the President. Employing his immense powers of persuasion, he gained the trust of the Field Marshal. Within a few weeks the arrangement was dropped by which Papen was to be present whenever Hitler called upon the President.[22]

B. The Last Election

In the meantime, the process of *Gleichschaltung* was rapidly reducing any possible challenge to Hitler's government. The only remaining barriers, were the *Reichstag* and the Army. The events between the burning of the *Reichstag* and the Enabling Act in March would eliminate the parliamentary threat, while Hitler would settle his differences with the Army in the summer of 1934. For the German voters, the announcement that the *Reichstag* elections would take place on March 5, meant that it would be the last time they would have the opportunity to elect their representatives. For Hitler, it meant the removal of one more barrier to total power. This time, Goebbels wrote in his diary, there would be no mistake.[23] True to his word, Goebbels mapped out a campaign that took Hitler and other leading party speakers to every corner of Germany.

On February 10, Hitler launched his campaign from the *Sport-Palast* in Berlin, which was broadcast throughout the nation. Then, in order to leave no doubt that they intended to be victorious, the Führer met with a group of prominent businessmen at which Dr. Schacht served as the host.[24] Hitler spoke quite frankly about his determination to stay in power regardless of the outcome of the elections: "Now we stand before the last election. Whatever the outcome, there will be no retreat. One way or another, if the election does not decide, the decision must be brought about by other means."[25] After a short thank you speech by Krupp, Schacht urged those present to raise an election fund of three million *Reichsmarks*. The fund was to be divided between the partners in the coalition government, but the Nazis claimed, and got, the lion's share.

Throughout the campaign, Hitler refused to outline any program for his government. At Munich he said, "If today we are asked for the program of this movement, we can summarize it in a few quite general sentences: programs are of no avail, it is the human purpose which is decisive...Therefore, the first point in our program is: Away with all illusions!"[26]

But Hitler's campaign was not waged with words alone. As Prussian minister of interior, Göring used his Brown-Shirted auxiliary police to break up meetings of the opposition, assault their speakers, and tear down their posters. When the former Chancellor, Brüning, attempted to give a speech in favor of the Center Party, he was prevented from doing so by Göring's forces. Adam Stegerwald, a Center leader, was actually beaten up by Nazi thugs on another occasion. Violence and terror were two weapons commonly employed by the Nazis in every election, and this one was no exception.

In the meantime, Papen had his own ideas about the forthcoming elections. He saw this last election as an opportunity to rally the conservative elements in the Reich and thereby strengthen his position in the cabinet and the *Reichstag*. To this end, he proposed to Hugenberg, and some of the leaders of the smaller right wing parties, that the time had come when the older members of the *Reichstag* should make way for the youth who were drifting into the Nazi camp.[27] When Hugenberg insisted on retaining his candidates on the election list, Papen's plan was rejected. In its place, he formed what he called a "Combat Front Black-White-Red," which consisted of Papen, Hugenberg, and the *Stahlhelm's* Franz Seldte. It was hoped that this combination would see the conservatives in the government emerge from the elections greatly strengthened.[28]

Although Papen campaigned vigorously on behalf of the Combat Front, it turned out to be what Papen later admitted was "a half-hearted initiative."[29] "The weakness of our position was that we were not able to criticize our new coalition partner openly. I could only attempt to convince the electorate of the positive aspects of our program, in the hope that they would be compared with the negative side of the Nazi doctrine. But either through lack of intelligence or because of mental laziness, this hope was never fulfilled."[30] While this arbitrary opinion of the German voters may have eased Papen's conscience, it does not alter the fact that he had never been a popular choice with the German public.

On the other hand, it was also true that the voters failed to see the difference between the two camps. An analysis of the speeches by both Papen and Hitler reveals a similarity in points of view which led the greater part of the population to vote for Hitler instead of the conservative program. For example, both condemned the Communists, the injustices of the Versailles Treaty, and called for the restoration of the spiritual and political unity of the German people. Both called for the restoration of national discipline, and the reorganization of the economy. Both condemned the Weimar Republic, claiming that fourteen years of Marxism had ruined Germany. Both set forth the tasks of the new National government to be accomplished under the leadership of the venerable *Reichspresident* with the loyal cooperation of the German *Volk*.[31]

His denunciation of the middle class for their failure to distinguish between his program and that of the Nazis is further weakened by the fact that Papen himself saw the difference between conservatism and National Socialism merely as a matter of tactics.[32] Even the staunchly conservative and influential member of the German Nationalists, Oldenburg-Januschau made the following declaration in a public meeting: "If I were not a German Nationalist, I should like to be a Nazi."[33] A remark of this kind tells us more than any analysis could about the degeneration of conservatism in Germany. Hermann Rauschnigg summed up the convergence of the conservative Nationalist's ideology with that of the NASDP as follows:

> In judging violence there is no contradiction between reaction and revolution. Hence the German Nationalist viewpoint was in essence merely a politically more moderate, but fundamentally, equally as nihilistic a doctrine of force as that of the National Socialists. This is the basic reason for the combination of bourgeois nationalism, of reactionary pseudo-conservative forces with revolutionary dynamism. It is also the essential reason for the later capitulation of those bourgeois forces before National Socialism, because the more consistent expression of any viewpoint always triumphs over the more irresolute.

> There had, for a long time, been no conservatism left in
> Germany, but only a bourgeois form of the doctrine of
> force coexisting with the consistent revolutionary form.[34]

While Papen might have protested that his program was essentially
different from the Nazis, many conservative interests were simply
seized and swept away by clever manipulation of the current "national
awakening," as Hitler labeled his program. Consequently, all the
nervous attempts by Papen and his associates to assert their own image
beside that of the Nazi mass movement were simply not taken seriously
by the general public.

The election campaign was interrupted by the burning of the
Reichstag late in February. Papen was giving a dinner in honor of
Hindenburg at the Guard Cavalry Club, when about 9 p.m., the diners
noticed a red glow in the distance. Throwing open the window they
saw, with shocked amazement, the dome of the *Reichstag* in flames
and smoke. Papen drove the President home and then went straight to
the burning building where he joined Göring, who was issuing orders
to the firefighters. The Nazi minister turned to Papen and shouted in an
angry voice: "This is a Communist crime against the new
Government." By the time the fire was extinguished and he was
leaving for home, Papen said he was "firmly convinced that the cause
had not been accidental."[35]

The next day, when the cabinet met, Hitler declared that the time
had come for an all-out fight against the Communists. Referring to the
fire as an obvious manifestation of a threat against the government,
Hitler proposed a series of measures, among them the promulgation of
a decree for the protection of society against the Communist danger.
Göring offered his analysis of Communist involvement in the fire, and
described certain acts of terrorism being planned by the Communists
including the destruction of public buildings, poisoning food in public
kitchens, and kidnapping the wives and children of high officials in the
government. Göring also proposed certain safety measures in the light
of these threats. Among these, he suggested the temporary closing of
museums, banning the SPD press, closing the KPD offices and
arresting all Communist deputies and functionaries. Frick then rose and
read a draft of a decree for the protection of the state and nation. These
decrees canceled the constitutional protection of many basic personal
freedoms, e.g., freedom of speech, the press, assembly, the mail and

telephone, protection against unlawful search and seizure.[36] Papen's only objection to these decrees was to warn that any attempt to take over the full powers of the states would cause further conflicts between the states south of the Main and the Reich. Finally, after the acceptance of a minor modification of the enabling section, the decree was passed unanimously.[37] In the hands of the Nazis these decrees meant that Hitler would be able to "legally" realize his plan to establish a totalitarian state.[38]

Meanwhile, when the results of the March 5, election were tallied, the Nazis had increased their vote from 11.7 million to 17.2 million, and had increased their seats in the *Reichstag* from 195 to 288. Despite the methods of repression, harassment, and outright terror against all anti-Nazi forces during the campaign, the Nazis gained only 5.5 million votes. This did not give Hitler the majority he had expected. For Papen and the *Kampffront*, the setback was even more serious. Although the coalition gained 200,000 votes over the November elections, its relative share dropped from 8.3 to 8 per cent. In Hindenburg's home province of East Prussia the *Kampffront* suffered its worst set-back, dropping from 14.4 to 11.3 per cent, while Hugenberg's party dropped from 1.9 to 1.1 per cent. This combined vote resulted in 52 deputies representing the conservatives in the *Reichstag*. On the other hand, despite the hammering by the Nazis during the campaign, the SPD returned 119 delegates, only a loss of two seats, while the Communists returned 81, a loss of eight seats; the Center and the BVP had only moderate losses (from 11.9 to 11.7, & from 3.1 to 2.7 per cent).[39]

Disappointing though the results were, the Nazis still managed to hold on to a bare majority in the new *Reichstag* (288 plus 52 seats in a house of 647 deputies). But even though Hitler had received only 43.9 per cent of the vote, he was strong enough to remain in power. Moreover, it did not escape the attention of the Nazi leaders that with the Communists banned by the decrees of February 28, they would have a parliamentary majority without the Nationalist votes. Given the experiences over the past few weeks, the chances of Papen, Hugenberg and the Nationalists acting as an effective brake on the Nazis now appeared slight.

Although Papen's position was considerably weakened after the elections, he was still convinced that he could tame Hitler, and in the process complete his plans for the restoration of the monarchy in a "New State." For this reason, he continued to lend his support to

Hitler's proposals. Among these was the Führer's decision to have the opening ceremonies of the new *Reichstag* in the Potsdam Garrison Church on March 21. Papen had no objection to this decision, although he thought it probably arose from Hitler's "own distorted romanticism combined with the propaganda value of old traditions."[40] However, Hitler was more clever than Papen had ever imagined. What the Nazi leader aimed at was arbitrary power. And while it took time to achieve this, he had no intention from the very outset of having his hands tied by any constitution. His plan was to secure the passage of a "Law for Removing the Distress of People and Reich." This Enabling Law would transfer the law-making powers for a period of four years to the Reich government. Since this represented an alteration of the Constitution, a two-thirds majority in the *Reichstag* was required for passage. The 81 Communist deputies could be left out since either they had already been arrested, or would be if they showed up. Some of the Socialists would be jailed for conspiring with the Communists, and others could be expelled on some pretext during the deliberations. The Center party seemed ready to go along with the law under certain conditions. In the meantime Hitler showed himself most conciliatory towards Papen and the Nationalists. It was probably for this reason that Hitler chose the Garrison Church for the opening ceremonies of the *Reichstag*. It was more than a propaganda value - it was a stroke of absolute genius!

Hitler wanted to give the impression of total dedication to German traditions and at the same time conciliate Hindenburg, the Nationalists, and the Army. Potsdam was the royal town of the Hohenzollerns, and the Garrison Church, which had been founded by Frederick William I and contained the grave of Frederick the Great, stood in complete contrast to Weimar, which was the city of Goethe and Schiller, and where the National Assembly and the "November criminals" established the Weimar Republic - traitors to everything German. March 21, was selected for two reasons. On another March 21, Bismarck had opened the first *Reichstag* of the Second German Reich, and it would be on March 21, 1933 that Hitler would open the *Reichstag* of the Third Reich. Moreover, two days later, March 23, the Enabling Act was to be presented to the *Reichstag* for approval.

The Potsdam affair was a brilliant success for Hitler and the Nazi movement.[41] On the houses, huge swastika banners hung side by side with the black-white-red flags of the old empire. In the Garrison church, one whole gallery was filled with generals, admirals, and marshals, all attired in their pre-war uniforms. Out of respect for the Imperial family, some seats had been set aside, and one chair was left vacant as a special tribute to the ex-Emperor. On the floor of the church were ranged the brown-shirted Nazi delegates, flanked by the Center and Nationalist deputies. There was not one Social Democrat present.

As the door was thrown open, the audience rose to greet the members of the government. Hitler dressed in formal morning-dress with a cut-away coat stood a bit self-consciously next to the massive figure of the old Field Marshal, Hindenburg. Leaning on his cane, the president came down the aisle and, as he reached the center, turned and solemnly saluted the empty throne with his Field-Marshal's baton.[42]

Following a brief speech by Hindenburg, Hitler addressed the assembly with an eye to the representatives of the old regime who sat before him. After closing with a special tribute to the Field Marshal, Hitler crossed over to the President's chair, and bending low, grasped his hand. Outside the guns roared in salute and, to the crash of cymbals and drums, with trumpets blaring, the German army followed by the SA and the Stahlhelm, paraded before the President, the Chancellor and the Crown Prince. The parade wound its way back to Berlin, through the Brandenburg Gate, where the cheers of thousands greeted the marchers.[43]

C. The Enabling Act

Two days later the *Reichstag* assembled in the temporary quarters of the Kroll opera house. The main order of business was the enactment of the Enabling Act. Discussions about this bill had been going on in the cabinet since March 7. Since the Communists were outlawed, and the Socialists could not muster sufficient strength to oppose the bill, there was only the possibility that the Center might vote against it. Always anxious to observe constitutional niceties, Hitler needed a qualified majority in order to obtain passage of the bill. If the Center could be persuaded to go along with Hitler, the Enabling Act was assured of passage. Hitler and Frick met with Center leaders, Kaas, Stegerwald, and Hackelsberger, to discuss under what conditions they would support the passage of the bill.[44] The rights of the President and the *Reichstag*, they falsely promised, would not be infringed. But according to the text of the bill, which was published that evening, the rights of the President would actually be greatly reduced since he could not examine the laws passed by the cabinet.[45]

The Center leaders knew that the effectiveness of any governmental concessions would depend on the future status of the Reich president. Therefore, in a second meeting with Hitler they asked for the inclusion of a provision that would grant the President the right to sign and promulgate laws, or give him the right of veto. While Hitler refused to include this request, he assured them that he would enact laws of far-reaching importance only after consultation with the President. However, he did agree to a number of other requests including a pledge to protect the confessional schools, and to respect the concordats between the Vatican and Bavaria, Prussia, and Baden. He also promised that he would mention these commitments in his speech before the *Reichstag*. With these assurances, the Center agreed to vote for the Enabling Act.[46]

The Enabling Law was passed 441 to 94, with all parties except the SPD voting in favor, each for its own reasons. The importance of this vote was that the *Reichstag* had voted itself out of existence as a viable legislative body. Furthermore, with the passage of this Act, Hitler secured his independence not only from the *Reichstag* but also from the President. Three previous chancellors, Brüning, Papen, and Schleicher, had all been dependent on the President's emergency powers granted to him in Article 48 of the Constitution; now Hitler had that right for himself. "The gutter had come to power."[47]

At the Nuremberg trials, Papen defended his reasons for supporting the passage of this law. For one thing, the parliamentary system was clearly finished. The only political parties defending parliamentary democracy, the SPD and the Center, were unable to command a majority, while the anti-parliamentary bloc composed of the National Socialists, the German Nationalists, and Papen's Black-White-Red Front had a majority. Furthermore, Papen maintained that the Enabling Act was a grant of powers to the cabinet, not to Hitler, and the cabinet was a coalition in which only the Chancellor and Frick could vote. Thus, Papen felt the majority could always vote against Hitler, and the President would sustain them since he had the right of veto. Finally, Papen said he believed Hitler's promise not to misuse the authority, and that he would respect the integrity of the *Länder*. But despite these justifications, neither Papen and his non-Nazi colleagues, nor the Center party delegates and the German Nationalists can escape the charge that they had betrayed parliamentary democracy and opened the door to dictatorship.[48]

With the passage of the Enabling Act, Papen found himself more and more in isolation - ironically an isolation of his own making. At Hindenburg's request, he had accepted the post of vice chancellor "in order to counter the influence of the Nazi ministers." Papen had expected that his special relationship with Hindenburg would provide him with the necessary power not only to influence cabinet decisions but also to control Hitler. As it turned out, he failed to accomplish either objective. Hitler was considerably more clever than Papen had imagined. By mid-April, Papen's special relationship with Hindenburg was becoming more and more restricted, while Hitler's influence increased significantly.[49]

Papen's plan to curb the new Chancellor's influence in the cabinet were as unsuccessful as his intentions to control Hitler through Hindenburg. This, too, was the result of his own doing. The office of vice chancellor had no constitutional basis, and therefore he held no ministerial post. Papen says that he had accepted the post "for the purpose of countering the influence of the Nazi ministers in the cabinet." But having no ministerial position, he was unable to have any influence over the execution of the laws passed by the government. This relegated him to the role of an observer, which limited him to listening to the debates, and offering his opinions. Papen's influence was further curtailed by the fact that Hitler would never permit him to act as his deputy since he never allowed himself to be represented.

While Papen's position as vice chancellor proved to be an anomaly, the attitudes of his non-Nazi colleagues in the cabinet were even more disappointing. One of the safeguards that Papen hoped would curb Hitler's radical ideas was to appoint ministers who would support Papen's strategies. However, the vice chancellor discovered that the main concern of his conservative colleagues was to establish friendly relations with the new Chancellor in the interests of good working relationships. For this reason, they concerned themselves exclusively with the purely administrative work of their respective departments, and usually refrained from engaging in any general debates, or criticizing Hitler's ideas. According to one of his staff, Papen was the only member of the cabinet who attempted to influence Hitler both privately as well as in cabinet meetings.[50] But while he spoke out quite openly in opposition to a number of Hitler's proposals, he was not supported by his non-Nazi colleagues. For example, when Hitler informed the cabinet that he wanted the swastika flag to replace the Republic's black, red, and gold, Papen presented his reasons for opposing the move and tried to rouse the cabinet against it. But when Blomberg supported the proposal, the other ministers voiced no objections.[51] There were also several cabinet members who were more than sympathetic to the ideas of National Socialism.[52] Papen seems to have been surprised at this, but he should not have been since he had selected ministers whose anti-democratic ideas were in sympathy with his own, and who, therefore, were susceptible to Hitler's skillful manipulations. For all of these reasons, plus Papen's own mistaken idea that Hitler would soon come around to his way of thinking, the cabinet became a meaningless body in the Third Reich. Finally, in 1937, it ceased to exist except on paper in the Weimar Constitution, which Hitler never bothered to abrogate.[53]

The failure of Papen's conservative colleagues to stand up to Hitler was matched by the skillful manner with which the Chancellor imposed his will on them. Papen attributes this to the force of his personality: "He had immense powers of persuasion and an extraordinary and indefinable capacity for bending individuals, and above all, the masses to his will." Papen confessed that he was as much a victim as everyone else, and he admitted that he believed in Hitler's "protestations" until the Röhm *putsch* in 1934, when Hitler "showed the full measure of his duplicity."[54] The force of the Chancellor's personality was enhanced by the tactics he employed at cabinet meetings. Instead of proceeding on the basis of majority decisions, Hitler based his actions on Article 56 of the Constitution, which stated that the Chancellor was responsible for policy and for the adherence of individual ministers to it. Therefore, decisions were a matter between the Chancellor and the responsible minister alone, and this way he could avoid any joint opposition. Whenever rare differences of opinion became apparent he would cut short the discussion and in private impose his will on the minister involved.[55]

Hitler was supported by Göring and Goebbels, against whom the non-Nazi ministers were no match. Goebbels, who was invited into the cabinet by Hitler with no objections from the ministers, was one of the few real powers in the movement's leadership, and one of the most astonishingly gifted propagandists of modern times.[56] Even if the non-

Nazi ministers had been prepared to oppose Hitler, they stood little chance of success because of the illusive dialectics of these two Nazi leaders.

Further evidence that Hitler was not going to be squeezed into a corner was his attack against the state governments. With little regard for the opinions of his vice chancellor, Hitler proceeded with the process of *Gleichschaltung* against the state governments. The extent to which Papen had been pushed into a corner was clearly seen in the case of Bavaria.

Ever since the July *coup* in Prussia, Papen had promised the Bavarian government that the Reich government would never do the same in Bavaria. Even as late as February 1933, the vice chancellor assured Dr. Schäffer, the Bavarian Finance Minister, that there was absolutely no truth in the rumor that Reich Commissioners were to be installed in the states.[57] In spite of these assurances, on March 9, Franz Ritter von Epp carried out a *coup d'etat* in Munich. So much for Papen's efforts to control Hitler.

The overthrow of the Bavarian government was followed by similar action in other states. By virtue of the decree of February 28, Reich Police Commissioners were appointed in Baden, Württemberg and Saxony. Papen supported these actions because Göring had informed the cabinet of rumored communist revolt in those states. By the end of March, all local parliaments were turned out. By the end of the first week in April, Hitler had nominated Reich governors in every state, and given them the power to dissolve the legislatures, to prepare and publish state laws, and appoint and dismiss state officials.[58] These actions reveal how bankrupt the conservative bloc was, since neither Papen nor his conservative colleagues raised any objections.

Papen was still Reich Commissioner in Prussia, but Göring paid little attention to his complaints over the removal of senior posts in the Prussian administration and the assignment of Nazis.[59] Further decrees called for the replacement of the Reich Commissioners of each state with Reich governors, who had the authority to appoint and remove state governments, to dissolve state *Diets* (legislative bodies), to prepare and publish laws, and to appoint and dismiss state officials.[60] Hitler appointed himself Reich Governor of Prussia and immediately delegated his powers to Göring as Prussian Minister-President. Seeing the writing on the wall, Papen "asked to be relieved of his post," and the office of Reich Commissioner for Prussia was abolished.

Papen's resignation as Reich Commissioner in Prussia did not mean that he was prepared to give up on his efforts to steer Hitler into a more moderate path. But, realizing that the conservative bloc in the cabinet was rapidly losing its influence over the Nazis, he decided to try and exert influence in other areas of both internal and international affairs. For this reason he decided to develop a staff that would serve these purposes. He carefully selected several young Catholic noblemen, a number of experienced civil servants, ten clerks and a private secretary. His personal adjutants were Fritz-Gunther von Tschirschky, an expert in matters of protocol, and Count Hans Kageneck who was particularly well-informed about domestic political affairs. Herbert von Bose took over the task of the press, publicity and propaganda, while at the same time he continued to serve as director of the press office in the Prussian state ministry to which Papen had appointed him in February 1933. Baron William von Kettler, a passionate anti-Nazi who developed a close relationship with one of Papen's daughters, also served as an aide along with Dr. Oscar Wingen, a specialist on the Saar question in the foreign ministry. Papen's legal advisor as well as his consultant on religious and social affairs was the conservative Friedrich Carl von Savigny. Conrad Josten, who was the youngest member of the staff, served as a courier. Papen's personal secretary Fräulein Rose, remained with him until the end of his mission in Turkey in 1944.[61] The one person with whom Papen was not in complete agreement, was the brilliant young Munich lawyer, Edgar Jung.[62] It was Jung who wrote Papen's famous Marburg speech, for which the young speech writer would suffer the consequences on the "Night of the Long Knives" in June, 1934.

Papen's intention was to use this staff as a means of keeping informed about what was going on in the various ministries, and make representations either to Hitler directly or to the heads of the governmental ministries. No doubt he had learned from Schleicher the importance of developing an efficient and loyal underground network designed to infiltrate the various ministries and use the information to influence the government. However, unlike Schleicher, Papen faced an adversary far more unscrupulous than either he or the General had ever envisioned. And for this reason, the record of his successes was far from impressive. With rare exception, the advice he did offer to Hitler was either ignored or the Führer managed to utilize it for his own ends. Moreover, Papen's continued public support of the Nazi-led cabinet tended to identify him with Hitler's policies and programs. So that even if he wanted to show the German public a different face, he failed to do so. He justified this on the grounds that he could not bring himself to publicly criticize the regime to which he also belonged as a member of the cabinet.

Although most of the documentary evidence contained in the files of the Vice Chancellery were destroyed in June 1934, the surviving files reveal that the bureau received numerous petitions of all kinds, many requests for personal interviews, appointments, copies of Papen's numerous speeches, and many telegrams and letters of congratulations as well as expressions of concern and understanding for the work of the Vice Chancellor and his staff. There were also complaints from disgruntled opponents who criticized his office for failing to bring about any important changes in the repressive measures employed by Göring's Gestapo, the SA and the SS.

Meanwhile, Hitler did not stop the process of *Gleichschaltung*. In order to destroy Marxism in Germany, he had to break the power of the trade unions, which were the foundation of the Social Democratic party. The SA and the SS were instrumental in accomplishing this goal. They occupied trade union offices all over the country, arrested many union officials, beat them, and threw them into concentration camps.[63] Like the Trade Unions, the political parties were also victims of the *Gleichschaltung*. In May, Göring ordered the occupation of the Social Democratic Party headquarters and newspaper offices. On June 22, Frick banned the SPD as an enemy of the people under the decree of February 28, and like the Communists, Social Democrats were no longer able to hold any elected public office.[64]

The other parties represented a more difficult problem, but they too disappeared in the summer of 1933. The Center Party dissolved itself on July 5, while the Democrats and the People's Party, reduced to mere shadows, had already ceased to exist. Even the German Nationalists fell victim to Hitler's "purge." National leaders were arrested, others dismissed from public office, and party meetings terrorized or broken up by the SA. Hugenberg resigned, and on that same day, the German National leaders decided to dissolve their party.[65] Thus by the middle of the summer in 1933 all the political parties except the National Socialists had ceased to exist.

NOTES

[1] Goebbels, *Vom Kaiserhof*, entry of January 30, 1933, pp. 253-54.

[2] *Memoirs*, p. 264.

[3] Goebbels, Ibid.

[4] Kleist-Schmenzin, "*Letzte Möglichkeit*," p. 92.

[5] The composition was as follows: Hitler as Chancellor; Papen as Vice Chancellor; Foreign Minister, von Neurath; Finance, Schwerin-Krosigk; Trade and Agriculture, Hugenberg; Defense, Blomberg; Chief of Office of Defense Ministry, Reichenau; Labor, Seldte (Stahlhelm Leader); Interior, Frick; Justice, Gürtner; Transport, Elz-Rubenach; without Portfolio, Göring; Secy. for Unemployment, Gereke.

[6] For example, when the Finance Minister, Schwerin-Krosigk, met Hitler for the first time at the swearing-in ceremony on January 30, he inquired of the Führer whether he should continue to pursue an orderly financial policy. Hitler simply replied that it was fine with him. Schwerin-Krosigk, *Es geschah*, p. 147.

[7] Bullock, *Hitler*, pp. 216-217:

> There was a young lady of Riga,
> Who smiled as she rode on a tiger.
> They returned from the ride
> With the lady inside,
> And a smile on the face of the tiger.

[8] *Memoirs*, p. 250.

[9] Bullock, ibid., p. 213. Later Hitler admitted that the Party was on its last legs when the unexpected intervention of Papen offered them a chance they could scarcely have foreseen.

[10] Papen devotes an entire chapter to the reasons why Hitler became Chancellor, and why the Nazi movement was so successful. While he admits to mistakes, the greater portion of the chapter suggests that the delusions, misunderstandings, blunders, failures and mistakes of others were more responsible for Hitler's rise to power than his own. *Memoirs*, pp. 250-263.

[11] The New Conservative movement is treated by Klemens von Klemperer, *Germany's New Conservatism* (Princeton, New Jersey: Princeton University Press, 1968). Papen was a member of the *Herrenklub*, which was the most active center of neo-conservatism in Berlin. Primarily a meeting place for the Junkers, and the leaders in heavy industry and finance, the *Herrenklub* also exercised significant influence on the German Right. Many of Papen's ideas for a *Reichsreform* originated from his contacts with this organization.

[12] Cabinet Meeting of January 31, 1933, *RKz*, R/332, BA, Koblenz. Although the question of new elections had come up during the course of negotiations between Papen and Hitler on January 30, there is no record that they had agreed that this was to be the last *Reichstag* election. Papen completely omits this in his *Memoirs*.

[13] Cabinet meeting of January 31, 1933, *RKz*, R/332, BA, Koblenz. Goebbels recorded that for the last time the Germans would go to the polls: "This time," he wrote, "there would be no mistake. The struggle is a light one now, since we are able to employ all the means of the State...we shall achieve a masterpiece of propaganda. Even money is not lacking this time." Goebbels, ibid., entry for February 3, 1933, p. 240.

[14] *Memoirs*, p.265. Papen claims that Hitler proposed the idea of an Enabling Act for the first time at this cabinet meeting. However, the minutes of the first cabinet meeting held on January 30 at 4 p.m., indicate that it was Papen who suggested that Hitler go to the President and request an Enabling Act! Cf. the minutes of Hitler's cabinet meeting for January 30, 1933, Karl-Heinz Minuth, *Die Regierung Hitler* (Bundesarchiv, Koblenz), Vol. 1, Doc. # 1, p. 3.

[15] Cabinet Meeting of January 31, 1933 at 4 p.m. *RKz.*, R 43 I/332, BA, Koblenz; Dorpalen, ibid., p. 449. Hugenberg proposed that the Braun-Severing government be eliminated immediately or those members of the civil service who had been appointed by Papen after the Prussian coup, would be in danger of being replaced by those loyal to the Socialist Braun. Meissner proposed that the application of Art. 48 would be in line with the State Supreme Court's action of October, 1932. Cabinet Meeting of February 3, 1933, *RKz.*, R 43 I/1459.

[16] Cabinet Meeting of January 31, 1933, at 4 p.m., *RKz.*, R/332, BA, Koblenz; Dorpalen, ibid., p. 448. Complaints registered against the enforcement of this decree had to be lodged with the police and with Frick himself, before an appeal to the courts. This meant that any immediate recourse remained, in Prussia at least, in the hands of the Nazi police commissioners.

[17] The position of Prussian Interior Minister was more important than its Reich counterpart because the Prussian police were the largest and most efficient in Germany. This made Göring, next to Hitler, the most important Nazi during 1933-34.

[18] Bullock, ibid., p. 221. About a week earlier, Göring had issued an order to the Prussian police ordering them to "avoid anything suggestive of hostility to the SA, or SS, and *Stahlhelm*." He also exhorted the police to show no mercy to the activities of "organizations hostile to the State," i.e., the Communists and Marxists in general.

[19] *Memoirs*, p. 257.

[20] Ibid., p. 258.

[21] This bit of hindsight reveals how Papen failed to realize that Hindenburg's influence could not have prevented the growing radicalism.

[22] By April Hitler had so skillfully managed to gain the confidence of Hindenburg that the President told Papen it was no longer necessary to continue the practice of being present whenever Hitler met with him. Dorpalen, ibid., pp. 453-454.

[23] Goebbels, ibid., entry for February 3, 1933, p. 240.

[24] Bullock, ibid., p. 218. Among those present were Krupp von Bohlen, Vögler of United Steel, Schnitzler and Basch of I.G.Farben, and Walter Funk.

[25] Bullock, ibid., pp. 218-219.

[26] Bullock, ibid., p. 219.

[27] Memo from Vice Chancellor von Papen to Hugenberg, 12. 2. 1933, Matthias & Morsey (ed.) *Das Ende der Parteien*, p. 635.

[28] Larry E. Jones. "Edgar Julius Jung: The Conservative Revolution in Theory and Practice." *Central European History*, 21 #2 (June 1988) 160-61.

[29] Edgar Jung had been engaged as Papen's speech writer in early February, 1933. His first speech that bore the imprint of Jung's conservative philosophy was Papen's address to the students at the University of Berlin on February 21. Papen called for the fusion of all the "forces of the conservative revolution" so that "...the Nazis, the Stahlhelm and the Christian-conservative forces" could restore the state and bring about a better future. Jones, ibid., p. 161.

[30] *Memoirs*, p. 266.

[31] Adolf Hitler, "Proclamation to the German people," February 1, 1933. Quoted in Bracher, Sauer, Schulz, *Machtergreifung*, pp. 51-52. This radio address was partly composed by Papen and partly by Hitler; "Campaign speech to Berlin University Students, February 21, 1933," Papen, *Memoirs*, pp. 266-268.

[32] In a speech in Breslau on March 17, 1933, he declared that "it was no accident that not only the sensibilities and aims of National Socialism headed in the same direction, but that the conservative trains of thought also played a decisive part in National Socialist circles. The difference between the conservative revolutionary and the Nationalist Socialist movement was clearly one of tactics." Papen, *Appell an das deutsche Gewissen. Reden zur nationalen Revolution*, Oldenburg. Archives, *IfZg.*, Munich.

[33] Elard von Oldenburg-Januschau was a veteran leader of the Agrarian reactionaries. He was an uncompromising opponent of the Weimar Republic, and played an important role in sustaining Hindenburg's hostility against republican elements. He also was a firm backer of Papen's "New State."

[34] Hermann Rauschnigg, *The Revolution of Nihilism: Warning to the West* (New York: Alliance Book Corporation, Longmans Green & Co., 1939).

[35] *Memoirs*, pp. 268-269. The question of who set the fire need not be explored here. What is important, however, is that the Nazis used this as means of winning

more support in the forthcoming elections. Hitler told the cabinet that he was confident that the government would capture 51% of the vote because of the fire.

[36] Minutes of the cabinet meeting, February 28, 1933, at 11:30 a.m., & 4:15 p.m. *RKz.*, 43 I/1459, BA Koblenz; Bracher, Sauer, Schulz, *Machtergreifung*, pp. 82-88

[37] The amended version of the article authorized intervention *insofar as* a state was doing nothing. Minutes of the Cabinet Meeting at 4:15 p.m., *RKz.*, 43 I/1459, BA Koblenz.

[38] Bracher (ibid., p. 351) maintains that the passage of these two decrees was all the "legal" excuse Hitler needed to establish his dictatorship. Even the Enabling Act, according to Bracher, was not necessary. If Papen was so opposed to Hitler's dictatorship, as he often maintained at Nuremberg, why did he vote for this piece of legislation?

[39] Election returns in the *Frankfurter Zeitung*, Reich ed., March 7, 1933; Matthias & Morsey, *Das Ende der Parteien*, pp. 792-793. In Prussia, the *Landtag* gave the NSDAP the majority, due in part to the exclusion of the Communists. Had not Papen dismissed the Braun-Severing caretaker government and dissolved the *Landtag*, a Left or even moderate government there might have retained power and possibly served to check Nazi ambitions.

[40] *Memoirs*, p. 272.

[41] Bullock, ibid., pp. 226-229.

[42] Ibid.

[43] Ibid.

[44] Rudolf Morsey, *"Zentrumspartei,"* in *Ende der Parteien*, pp. 353-367.

[45] Morsey, ibid., pp. 258-59.

[46] Rudolf Morsey, ibid.; cf. also *Die Protokolle der Reichstagfraktion und des Fraktionsvorstands der Deutschen Zentrumspartei 1926-1933*, (Mainz: Matthias-Grünewald Verlag, 1969), Docs. 741, 742, 743, pp. 621-624.

[47] Bullock, ibid., p.229.

[48] *Memoirs*, p. 275. Papen is in error when he states that "if the Law had not been passed, it would have been much more difficult to abolish constitutional guarantees and much easier to oppose dictatorial methods." The decrees of February 28 were still in force, and Hitler had all the "legal" power necessary to consolidate his dictatorship under these decrees. Bracher, ibid., pp. 193, 196, 197, 208.

[49] *Memoirs*, p. 262. Hindenburg's mental and physical condition gradually deteriorated. Hitler replaced the *Stahlhelm* honor guard at Neudeck with a detachment of SA guards who were able to limit the President's callers. Even Papen often found access to the President difficult, if not impossible.

[50] Fritz Günther von Tschirschky, *Erinnerungen eines Hochveräters* (Stuttgart: Deutsche Verlags-Anstalt, n.d.), pp. 235-236. Tschirschky mentions Papen's opposition to the "Law for the Re-establishment of the Professional Civil Servants," which called for the exclusion of Jews from the professions such as medicine, law and the civil service. Papen successfully argued to protect Jews who had been civil servants before the war and Jewish doctors, while banned from public clinics, were permitted to practice medicine in private; *Memoirs*, pp. 285-287.

[51] *Memoirs*, p. 290. Papen mentions that Blomberg never spoke except in connection with military affairs. Neurath took very little part in general debates, and spoke only on foreign affairs. The same thing was true of the other ministers. Consequently, whenever a topic for general debate arose, Papen said he was the only one to speak out.

[52] Eltz-Rübenach, a devout Catholic, became an admirer of Hitler, while General Blomberg made no secret of his sympathies for National Socialism. The *Stahlhelm* leader, Franz Seldte, and Foreign Minister, Neurath were also ready supporters of Hitler in cabinet meetings.

[53] *Memoirs*, p. 290-291. "Blomberg was a weak, easily influenced personality who had little to oppose to Hitler's personality." In his memoirs he wrote in 1933 he found that which he had ceased to expect since 1919: "faith, respect for a man, and total support for an idea." Joachim Fest, *The Face of the Third Reich* (New York, Ace Books, 1970), p. 349.

[54] *Memoirs*, p. 260. If this is true, the perplexing question, why Papen continued to serve as the Sorcerer's apprentice, remains unanswered. At Nuremberg, he offered the rather weak excuse that he was, "working for the other Germany."

[55] *Memoirs*, p. 290.

[56] Goebbels wrote that "propaganda is good which leads to success, and it is bad which fails to achieve the desired result...it is not propaganda's task to be intelligent." In another passage he wrote, "Propaganda has absolutely nothing to do with truth!" Quoted in Fest, ibid., p. 137-138.

[57] Meeting between Papen, Hindenburg, and Schäffer, February 17, 1933, Minuth, ibid., Doc. # 23, pp. 87-90. Schäffer reminded Papen that while this might be the Vice Chancellor's opinion, it was neither Hitler's nor the Nazi party's view.

[58] Bullock, ibid., p. 230.

[59] It is ironic that Papen should complain about Göring's ruthless disregard for his objections when, as Chancellor, he had completely ignored the Prussian Minister President's objections to his arbitrary dismissal of Social Democrats from office.

[60] The Reorganization Act of Reich (March 31, 1933), and the Law for the Co-ordination of the States (April 7, 1933). Bullock, ibid., p. 230.

[61] *Memoirs*, pp. 276-77. Also serving in various departments were ten clerks. In June, Dr. Hermann Sabath, former member of the finance ministry in the Reich chancellery, joined the staff as director to supervise and coordinate the work of the bureau.

[62] Edgar J. Jung belonged to a group of young intellectuals who took a more or less tolerant attitude towards the Republic. As a member of the *Herrenklub*, Jung came into contact with Papen. "He was an ambitious man of action. A man of the world with excellent connections among politicians and businessmen, among the unions and in the German intelligentsia." He wrote about the "conservative revolution" as a Christian revival which would effect "the restoration of all those elementary laws and values without which man loses his ties with nature and God and without which he is incapable of building up a true order." Klemens von Klemperer, *Germany's New Conservatism* (New Jersey: Princeton University Press, 1968), pp. 120-123.

[63] Matthias, "The Social Democratic Party of Germany," Matthias & Morsey, *Das Ende der Parteien*, pp. 175-180. Goebbels correctly prophesied that "Once the Trade Unions are in our hands the other parties and organizations will not be able to hold out long...In a year's time Germany will be entirely in our hands." Goebbels, ibid., p. 280.

[64] Bullock, ibid., p. 232. Some of the SPD leaders left Germany, while others, like Severing, retired into the obscurity of private life. The party tried to establish a new committee after Göring's action, but the decree by Reich Interior Minister Frick put an end to this. "Law of July 7, 1933," in *Reichgesetztblatt*.

[65] Matthias & Morsey, *Das Ende der Parteien*, passim.

CHAPTER 11:
REVOLUTION AFTER POWER

A. The Third Reich & the Vatican

Although Papen showed little concern about the dissolution of the political parties, he did express considerable concern about the position of the Christian churches in the new regime. In his view, it was the "radical wing" of the Nazi party who sought to apply the process of *Gleichschaltung* to the churches, Protestant and Catholic alike.[1] This had led to the harassment of the clergy, Catholic youth organizations, the Catholic press, and other Catholic associations. Known for his unwavering allegiance to the Catholic church, Papen's bureau soon became a collecting point for complaints against the Nazis raised by the Catholic clergy and laity.[2] The growing number of complaints about Nazi terror tactics against the Church caused Papen to see the need for obtaining from Hitler some sort of legal guarantees protecting the church's organizations, press, places of worship, etc. For this reason he decided to visit Rome in order to "study the possibility of reaching some firm agreement."[3]

Although the circumstances under which Papen secured the appointment to undertake this mission have never come to light, it is certain that Hitler was interested in establishing friendly relations with the Vatican.[4] For one thing, when the negotiations began in early April, Hitler was still engaged in consolidating his power, and he was particularly apprehensive about the Church's strength, especially in predominantly Catholic Bavaria. An agreement with the Catholic church would help refute the charges that National Socialism was anti-Christian, and would therefore help reduce the tensions between his regime and the southern states. Moreover, an agreement with the Vatican would lend international prestige to his government, which at this time was engaged in delicate negotiations at the Geneva Disarmament Convention. Finally, as it turned out, any agreement with the Church that would bring about the permanent withdrawal of the clergy from politics, and thus spell the end of political Catholicism in Germany, was welcomed by the Führer.[5]

Although Papen was accused of going to Rome in order to set a trap for the Vatican, there is no real evidence to support this charge. Moreover, there is no question that he was sincerely motivated to undertake this commission in order to protect the Church's rights. He viewed a pact between two sovereign states as recognized by international law. Accordingly, any violation could be brought to the attention of the international community, and outside pressure brought to bear on the government. Since Hitler was anxious not to provoke the international community at this time, Papen saw this pact as a restraint on Nazi attacks against the Church. Finally, Papen was determined to prove to himself, as well as to the nation, that he still exercised some influence over Hitler's government, and that a Facist regime could live in harmony with the Church.[6] What Papen failed to realize was that Hitler had no intention of fulfilling the terms of the agreement, and that the Nazi leader's definition of "legal" did not correspond to that of the Vice Chancellor's.

Papen was not the only one who was concerned about the future of the Catholic Church in Germany. The Vatican was also interested in establishing a *modus vivendi* for the Church in Germany. Pope Pius XI had concluded a concordat with Mussolini, which reduced the tensions between the Church and the Fascist regime. He hoped that the same thing would happen in Germany, and he was encouraged in this by his Secretary of State, Msgr. Eugenio Pacelli, and the German hierarchy.[7]

Like Papen and the Vatican, the German hierarchy was quite anxious obtain guarantees, and reduce the growing acts of violence against the Catholic population and Church organizations. Until Hitler's *Reichstag* speech preceding the passage of the Enabling Act, the German bishops had forbidden the faithful to join the party

von Papen and Commerce Secretary, Eltz von Rubenzch at the head of the Corpus Christi procession, 1933

Reichstag session, January 30, 1934.
From right to left: Hitler, von Papen, von Neurath, Rudolf Hess

organizations, wear any of its insignia, or fly its flag in the churches. When Hitler, in his *Reichstag* speech, promised to respect the rights and privileges of the Church under the existing concordats, the bishops reversed their stand, and issued a pastoral letter removing these prohibitions. However, this reversal of policy did not check the anti-clerical rhetoric spread by Goebbels' yellow press, nor the harassment against members of the clergy, Church organizations, and the Catholic press. It was, therefore, the hope of the hierarchy that some sort of a treaty with the Vatican might provide a protection against these attacks.

As a member of the Catholic clergy, the Center party leader, Msgr. Ludwig Kaas, was also disturbed over the growing anti-clericalism in the Nazi ranks, and the accompanying harassment against the Church, which seemed to escalate with each passing day. As the leader of his party, Kaas was also concerned about the future of the Center party in German politics. Ever since Papen's chancellorship, the Center had attempted to draw Hitler into a coalition partnership without success. Now that the Nazi leader was in power, Kaas and the Center Executive Committee were anxious to see if Hitler would conduct himself with more moderation. They did not have long to wait. The process of *Gleichschaltung* moved relentlessly against the trade unions, the Federal states, and the political parties. By the end of March, it was very clear to Kaas that the Center was also in danger of falling victim to Hitler's cruel and uninhibited use of force under the pretense of "legality." Desperate to escape the fate of the other victims of the *Gleichschaltung*, Kaas saw an opportunity when Hitler proposed the Enabling Act. The Center votes were essential for passage of the Act, and so Hitler met with the Center Executive Committee on March 22, the day before the crucial vote was to be taken. Hitler promised not to use the new grant of power to change the Constitution, and to retain the civil servants belonging to the Center party. He also pledged to protect the confessional schools, and to respect the concordats between the Vatican and the states of Bavaria, Prussia, and Baden. He promised to mention these commitments the next day in his speech before the *Reichstag*.[8]

Kaas did not stay around to vote, but left for Rome the day before the passage of the Enabling Act, in his words, "to review the situation created by Hitler's *Reichstag* speech and examine the possibility of a broader understanding between the Church and the State."[9] Kass denied that he intended to discuss the possibility of a concordat between the Vatican and the Third Reich. However, as a personal friend and advisor to Pacelli when the latter was the *Nuncio* in the 1920s, it is not unlikely that Kaas reported his meeting with Hitler and the Führer's promises. He probably also reported the Nazi attacks against the Church, its leaders, and organizations, and expressed concern that the radical faction of the Nazi party was dictating to Hitler these terror tactics against the Church.[10]

While Kaas was in Rome, Göring and Frick were relentlessly pursuing the *Gleichschaltung* policies. An increasing number of Center party civil servants were being dismissed from the government in spite of Hitler's promises not to do so. This alarmed the party leadership to such an extent that when Kaas returned to Berlin on March 31, he spent the next seven days in conferences with Party leaders. In a private meeting with Hitler, he tried to persuade the Nazi leader to discontinue the removal of Center civil servants. Hitler assured Kaas once again that membership in the Center was not a disadvantage. There was no discussion about the possibility of a treaty with the Vatican on that occasion.[11]

While in Berlin, Kaas also learned of Papen's proposed visit to Rome but, other than rumors that the Vice Chancellor was going to attend the Four Powers Conference being held in Rome, he knew nothing else. If Kaas suspected any other reason for this trip, he does not mention it in his personal diary.[12]

On April 8, Kaas departed for Rome, in order to "get away from domestic politics."[13] While sitting in the dining car having coffee, Kaas saw Papen and his wife, Martha. Was this just a coincidence, or did he deliberately take this train because he knew that Papen was going to Rome? If this was the case, why would Kaas want to meet Papen? On the other hand, was Papen as surprised to meet Kaas as the Center leader claimed? While the answer to these questions will probably never be known, this is another example of the aura of intrigue that seemed to pervade Papen's life.[14] According to Kaas, the two men discussed a number of the issues that appeared in the final draft of the Concordat between the Vatican and Germany. By the time they arrived in Rome they had reached an understanding. Kaas offered to serve as Papen's liaison with the Vatican in the concordat negotiations, while Papen, who saw the advantage in this arrangement, agreed.[15] Papen calculated that the Center leader would be invaluable in dealing with the more sensitive issues because of his personal friendship with Pacelli.

Between April 8 and June 7, 1933, negotiations for an agreement between the Vatican and the Third Reich continued. Papen left Rome on April 18, after a number of meetings with Pacelli and Kaas, who was now invited by the Cardinal Secretary to serve as his advisor during the course of the negotiations. For the next two months the Vice Chancellor conducted negotiations through his proxy in the Vatican, Ludwig Kaas. Toward the end of April, Kaas sent Papen a draft of a concordat, which the Vice Chancellor presented to Hitler. While the Führer suggested a number of changes, the article dealing with the de-politicization of the clergy quickly became one of the major obstacles in the negotiations. Papen supported Hitler's objections to Kaas' proposal that the German bishops, and not the Vatican, should decide whether the clergy could or could not engage in political activities or be members of political parties. Their intention was quite clear, and Kaas tried unsuccessfully to oppose them. Removal of the clergy from positions of influence in political parties, especially the Center, would weaken the leadership and facilitate Hitler's plans to do away with all political opposition. But leaving the enforcement of this article up to the bishops instead of the Vatican was viewed by Hitler and Papen as less effective since they knew that some of the more influential members of the hierarchy, like Cardinal Schulte and Bishop von Preysing, whose sympathies were with the Center, would hesitate to enforce the article. For example, when the bishops were presented with a draft of the concordat on May 30, 1933, Schulte called the Hitler government "revolutionary in which there was no law or justice." With such a government it was not possible to negotiate a concordat.[16] Bishop Preysing of Eichstätt (later of Berlin), called for the bishops to disavow any connection with the "new order." He warned that Hitler intended to unite the state and the party as one entity, and he admonished the bishops that it was their duty to warn the faithful of the "danger to their faith and morals stemming from the Nazi program."[17]

A second draft was received by Papen in May and, except for Article 31, most of Kaas' recommendations were acceptable. But Papen still insisted that a *conditio sine qua non* in the negotiations was that the Holy See and not the bishops should enforce Article 31. After consultation with Hitler, Papen left for Rome where he arrived on June 29, 1933. With Ambassador Bergen, the Vice Chancellor went to see

Pacelli. Papen found the Cardinal Secretary visibly upset by reports of Nazi terror tactics against the Center and the Bavarian People's Party. Reports of the arrest of clergymen and the dismissal of Center civil servants had reached the Vatican through the foreign press. Papen tried to explain that these reports were attempts by the foreign press to discredit the National Socialists, and urged Pacelli to conclude the agreement as quickly as possible in order to bring peace and order to the Reich.[18] But Papen was also afraid that continued attacks against the Church might endanger the negotiations. Consequently, he notified Hitler of Pacelli's complaints and urged him to put a stop to the persecutions.[19]

Apparently this warning had little effect on the Führer, since the attacks actually increased during the final days of the negotiations. Why he continued to permit these attacks against the Church is not known for certain. It is possible that he might have wanted to put pressure on the Holy See to sign the agreement without further deliberation over the disputed articles. Another possible reason could have been that he wanted to destroy as many Catholic organizations as possible before an agreement protecting them was signed. One other possible reason was that Hitler no longer desired to have any arrangement with the Vatican, and hoped that the renewed attacks against the church would sabotage the negotiations.[20]

In the meantime, in accordance with "rubrics" of international law, the wording of the text was mutually agreed upon. The next day Hitler issued a press release rescinding the order that had dissolved many Catholic organizations, and called for a nullification of the coercive measures against "priests and other leaders of Catholic organizations."[21] On July 20, 1933, the Concordat was formally signed by Pacelli and Papen in the presence of Msgr. Kaas, and Rudolf Bultman, the representative of the Reich Foreign Office.

With Hitler, the Vatican, the German hierarchy, and the Center party all interested in reaching some accommodation between the Holy See and Hitler's regime, it is somewhat perplexing to accept Papen's account of his role in the negotiations. It is true that he did serve as the representative of the Hitler regime in the negotiations, and that he did influence both sides to accept compromises in the negotiations. But, when discussing his role in his *Memoirs*, he leaves the impression that the successful outcome was principally the result of his efforts. However, without the work of Msgr. Kaas, Cardinal Pacelli, and the

German bishops represented by Gröber of the Freiburg/Breisgau archdiocese, and Berning of Osnabrück, along with the advice of the Chairman of the German Bishop's Conference, Cardinal Bertram, an accord would never have been reached. Moreover, it was not Papen, but Pacelli who convinced Pope Pius XI to agree to the terms of the treaty.

When the text of the agreement was published on July 22, it was received with mixed emotions. Pacelli pessimistically commented to Ivone Kirkpatrick, the British Consul in Rome, that the Germans were bound to violate the Concordat. He added, with a touch of irony, that they "would probably not violate all of the articles at the same time."[22] There were others, however, who saw this as a victory for the Church. Among them, Archbishop Gröber and Bishop Berning. Both men were enthusiastic supporters of Hitler during the first months of his Chancellorship. If there were criticisms of the manner with which the Nazis were treating the Catholic church, these two believed that the persecution was being carried out without Hitler's consent![23] They also believed that the signing of the concordat would permit the more moderate element in the Nazi party to have greater influence over Hitler and his policies towards the Church.[24] Since this was Papen's position too, it is not too far-fetched to suspect that the Vice Chancellor had a great deal to do with influencing these bishops to support the idea of a concordat and to urge their fellow bishops to put pressure on the Vatican to sign the agreement.[25]

Papen naively believed that the Concordat would serve as a guarantee that the Catholic church could continue to coexist alongside the Nazi regime. He boasted that as long as he remained in the cabinet, until June 30, 1934, he "...retained enough influence on Hitler to see that the terms of the Concordat were honored as far as possible." In those instances in which there were violations of the agreement, Papen accepted Hitler's declaration that they were caused by the "irresponsible elements in the provinces."[26] This meant that Papen could always take the credit but not the blame.

By the summer of 1933, Hitler was in complete control of the government in which Papen remained only as a shadowy figure - a man with a title but very little else. Papen's January prediction that Hitler would be easily tamed prove to be worthless. For all of his cleverness, what had eluded the Vice Chancellor was that Hitler knew where the key to power lay. It was not, as Papen supposed, to be found in the

Presidential suite, where intrigue brought Hitler to power, and with which Papen still hoped to bind him. Nor was it to be found in the *Reichstag* chambers, where partisan politics had become so disarranged as to leave the parliamentary system with no weapons to fight totalitarianism. Hitler knew, what Papen and his aristocratic colleagues despised, that the key to power was to be found in the streets where the disillusioned German masses, willing to surrender freedom for security, yearned for a messiah to "deliver them from evil." Deceived by Hitler's tactics of legality, Papen never understood that the revolutionary character of Hitler's movement could only be revealed after Hitler came to power. Astonished and intimidated by the forces which he unwittingly helped to release, Papen now sought to justify his cooperation with Hitler, while at the same time he tried without success to channel the revolutionary wave into conservative waters. Unfortunately for Papen and the causes he espoused, Hitler had no intention of pursuing anything that deviated from his intentions to possess total control over the destiny of Germany.

B. The "Apprentice" in the "New Order"

One of Papen's greatest mistakes was to think that once Hitler came to power he would call a halt to the violence and intimidation exercised by the SA. But, under the leadership of Ernst Röhm, the SA regarded Hitler's victory in the March 5 elections as a signal that the time had arrived to settle accounts. Röhm and his followers recalled the promises made by Hitler in the days before the seizure of power. They were reinforced in this belief by a speech Hitler delivered to Nazi leaders in Berlin as late as the middle of June. "The law of the National Socialist revolution has not yet run its course. Its dynamic force still dominates development in Germany today, a development which presses forward irresistibly to a complete transformation of German life...The German Revolution will not be complete until the whole German people has been fashioned anew, until it has been organized anew and has been reconstructed."[27]

This call for violence was unlike any other form of violence which had been common enough in Germany before 1933. This time the Government itself deliberately engaged in acts of violence and intimidation as a way to govern. Government police agencies like the Gestapo were used for this reason, and the State established concentration camps where criminals and others designated by the Nazi-appointed judges as "traitors" were incarcerated.[28] This open contempt for justice by the one institution that should have upheld the rights of citizens was a further encouragement for those elements in society that had little regard for law and order. The SA set up "bunkers" in abandoned warehouses in Berlin that served as places where victims were beaten, and even killed for no other reason than to satisfy a personal grudge, to seize an apartment, or fulfill a sadistic wish. Meanwhile, the government paid scant attention to these acts of violence, and only called for amnesty in those instances where the "penal acts were committed in the name of the national revolution."[29] The way in which the wave of violence continued to spread made it appear that there would be no end until every institution in Germany had been transformed and brought under Nazi control.

While Hitler had encouraged, and even relied on this barbaric means to achieve victory, he was quick to see that this headlong rush into chaos could eventually threaten the very existence of the State that permitted it. Two dangers, to which as leader of his party and head of the government he could not remain indifferent, were the disruption of the economic organization of the country, and any attempt to interfere with the inviolability of the Army.

Nazis like the Gottfried Feder believed the time had arrived to put into practice the original economic program of the Nazi party, which called for sweeping nationalization of industry, profit-sharing, the abolition of unearned incomes and "the abolition of the rule of interest."[30] Although he was indifferent to economic issues, Hitler was perceptive enough to know that Feder's radical economic experiments at this time could throw the economy into a state of total confusion. This in turn could destroy the chances of cooperation with big business and industry to end the depression and alleviate the unemployment crisis. Such an argument, which directly touched his own power, took precedence over the nostrums disseminated by Feder.[31] The Chancellor made this perfectly clear to the Reich governors who met with him on July 6: "The revolution is not a permanent state of affairs, and it must not be allowed to develop into such a state...We must not, therefore, dismiss a business man if he is a good businessman, even if he is not yet a National Socialist...In the long run our political power will be the more secure, the more we succeed in underpinning it economically." In order to insure the support of big business, Hitler appointed two influential businessmen to the cabinet.[32] Dr. Schmitt, the director of the largest insurance company in Germany, replaced Hugenburg as Minister of Economy and Trade, and Hjalmar Schacht, President of the Reichsbank, was appointed to the same ministry without portfolio.[33]

Although Hitler wanted to call a halt to the revolution, he was far from convincing others of the necessity of his new policy. One of the most dissatisfied was Ernst Röhm, Chief of Staff of the Storm Troopers. Röhm represented hundreds of thousands of embittered Nazis who felt that they had been cheated of the vague promise that after the victory, Germany would belong to them.[34] The SA leader's open attacks against the capitalists, the Junkers, conservative politicians and stiff-necked generals created an increasingly difficult problem for Hitler. But, what proved to be the most serious issue between the Führer and Röhm, and the one that eventually cost the SA Chief his life, was his plans to amalgamate the *Reichswehr* and the SA into a National Socialist militia.

Hitler had always opposed the idea of merging the SA with the Army.[35] For one thing, he remembered how the Army's repudiation of him in 1923 had been decisive for the failed *putsch*. He was also grateful for the Army's neutrality during the struggle for power, and especially during the first months of his Chancellorship when he was engaged in crushing all resistance and arrogating more power to himself. Looking ahead to the day when Hindenburg would die, Hitler knew he would need the support of the Army if he was to succeed the Field Marshal as President. However, in order to get the Army to remain friendly towards his regime, Hitler had to grant certain concessions. Among these was a promise that the Army would never be forced into an intervention in a civil war. This would allow the Army to preserve intact its traditions and its independent position in the State.[36]

An additional fact was that the Army had nothing but contempt for Ernst Röhm, and the generals were adamant in their refusal to accept the SA on an equal footing. This was one institution, they insisted, that would not be Nazified, and Röhm's pretensions were rejected out of hand. Hitler's anxiety over the growing tensions between the SA Chief and the generals prompted him to make a series of speeches in which he assured the Army that he remained loyal to their pact. On July 1, 1933 he addressed the SA leaders at Bad Reichenhall: "This army of the political soldiers of the German Revolution has no wish to take the place of our Army or to enter into competition with it." In another speech delivered to the *Stahlhelm* on September 23, Hitler expressed his gratitude to the Army for its "benevolent neutrality" at the time he became Chancellor. He then concluded his remarks with the promise: "We can assure the Army that we shall never forget this...and that with all our heart and all our power we will support the Army."[37]

These public assurances to the Army were accompanied by a temporary check on the revolutionary activities throughout the Reich.[38] In line with this change in policy, Göring announced the dismissal of the SA and SS auxiliary police, stating that they were no longer needed. This action, however, resulted in an immediate and ominous warning from the SA chieftain. Speaking in the name of his embittered followers who felt that they had been left out in the cold, Röhm delivered an impassioned speech to fifteen thousand SA officials in the Berlin Sportspalast: "One often hears voices from the bourgeois camp to the effect that the SA have lost all reason for existence." But he declared that this old bureaucratic notion would have to be changed either "in a gentle, or if need be, in an ungentle manner."[39]

Between Hitler's promises to the Army and Röhm's hostile remarks, the confrontation that loomed between the SA and the Army proved to be a test case of a much larger issue. Labeled as the "Second Revolution," this conflict raised the question at what point should the revolution be stopped? It also faced Hitler with the problem that every revolutionary leader confronted after coming to power, how to wipe out the disreputable past and those elements that were associated with it? From the fall of 1933 to the summer of 1934, this dispute over the Second Revolution formed the dominant issue in German politics.[40]

In the meantime, Papen was not idle. In spite of the admitted ineffectiveness of his office, he continued to attend cabinet meetings, and was not afraid to speak out on those occasions when he disagreed with Hitler's decisions. Although his efforts were usually ineffective, due in part to the little or no support he received from his conservative colleagues, Papen refused to concede defeat. By temperament and background, the aristocratic, ex-cavalry officer found it intolerable "not to be in the game, even if he did not like his fellow-players."[41] His role as Hitler's representative in the Concordat negotiations with the Vatican, which he considered a great success, was one example of this eagerness to be one of the important players in the game. Never bashful about his own abilities, but often unaware of the possible consequences of his precipitous actions, Papen set for himself the goal of reconciling Hitler's movement with his own anachronistic ideas about Germany's future. It was around this course of action that he had organized the vice chancellery.

Although Papen complained that the office of vice chancellor was an anomaly, it did have certain advantages. Unlike the other cabinet ministers, the vice chancellor had no specific responsibilities. This left him free to pursue those issues or activities that he regarded as most important. Aside from responding to the flood of complaints, and protests from all parts of the community against the measures and excesses of the Nazis, Papen spent a great deal of time delivering speeches, attending various official functions, and meeting with important conservative businessmen. On many of these occasions his intention was to persuade his listeners that the Third Reich and the Catholic Church were not incompatible institutions.[42] He also tried to explain that it was a radical faction in the Nazi party that was forcing Hitler to make more and more concessions to them. According to Papen, men like Goebbels, Himmler, Heydrich and Röhm were the real culprits, while he and many others mistakenly continued to believe that Hitler's protestations of good faith were genuine.[43]

This failure to understand and publicly challenge Hitler's fraudulent behavior was not limited to Papen and his conservative friends. Other intelligent, well-informed, and responsible German citizens were also mislead by Hitler's duplicity. Nevertheless, even after it became clear to him that the Nazis - under the inspiration, and with the approval of the Führer - were bent on destroying the very Christian foundations he courageously wished to defend, Papen continued to serve the Nazi revolution.[44]

The Führer, on the other hand, had his reasons for permitting the Vice Chancellor to remain in the Government. For one thing, Papen was still Hindenburg's favorite. As long as the President was alive, Hitler could take no chances that he would be ousted from office like his predecessor, General Schleicher. Papen's role in that "palace conspiracy" was still too fresh in Hitler's memory to be ignored. Besides, as Commander-in Chief of the Army, Hindenburg, on the advice of the Vice Chancellor, was still capable of calling on the military to force Hitler and his movement from positions of power. Along with these reasons, there were still occasions in which the Chancellor needed the presence of men like Papen and Neurath -

aristocrats who gave an aura of "legitimacy" to his Government. Papen had been most useful in the negotiations with the Vatican, which Hitler had regarded as important for his image among the European nation-states. Hitler would call upon him again when the issue concerning the resolution of the Saarland was raised.[45]

Papen was pleased to receive the appointment as Reich Commissioner for the Saar on November 14, 1933. As a long-time resident of the Saar, he felt that he was the most informed person in the Government to deal with this delicate question. As a passionate advocate of German nationalism, who felt that the Versailles had been a miscarriage of justice, Papen called for the return of the Saarland to the Third Reich.

In his capacity as Reich Commissioner, Papen energetically set about the task of coordinating efforts to bring about the return of the Saar to Germany. In addition to his attendance at numerous meetings with representatives Prussia, Bavaria, the League of Nations and the French government, Papen delivered several extremely nationalistic speeches to conservative Catholic organizations, calling for their support of the Government's determination to see the Saar restored to the Fatherland.

In early November 1933, when the Government stepped up its campaign for the return of the Saar to the Reich, Papen joined in. On November 9, he delivered a speech to the Cologne branch of the AKD (German Catholic Workers Association), in which he pointed to the similarities between Catholic ideals and those of the Nazi party. While he was careful to indicate that not all differences between the Nazi ideas and those of the Catholic church had been resolved by the Concordat, he insisted that the "structural elements of the NSDAP and the Catholic *Weltanschaung* were not antithetical." Then he listed those he believed most comparable: the protection of the German nationality and language, religion and custom; the restoration of the natural order and the establishment of the principle of hierarchical authority which included the restoration of the proper relationship between the ruler and subject; the recognition of the centrality of the family and the importance of the community over the individual; and the unity of church and state as achieved in the Concordat.[46] As far as the present conflict between the Catholic church and the National Socialists was concerned, Papen argued that this had ended with the establishment of the Concordat.

Papen's assurances that the Concordat had resolved the conflict between the Catholic church and Hitler's regime were simply not true. For one thing, Papen's bureau had received hundreds of complaints from the clergy and leaders of the Catholic youth organizations charging the Nazis with harassment and violations of the Concordat agreement.[47] Papen's bureau also received numerous complaints from Catholic bishops as well as parish priests complaining of Nazi harassment. In most of these instances, Papen had his staff respond sympathetically with a promise to personally intercede with Hitler on their behalf.[48] Why then did he publicly declare that the Concordat had brought about a reconciliation between the Church and Hitler's government? The only plausible explanation for these statements must have been his hope that by pointing out what he thought were the better elements in the Nazi movement, and comparing them to Catholicism, he was appealing to Hitler's conscience to withdraw his support from the radical faction in the Party, and follow a more moderate course in the future. However, this well-intentioned, but lamentable, effort only served to strengthen Hitler's position in Germany and provided him with further support in his determination to develop a full-blown dictatorship.

One of the most pathetic examples of Papen's efforts to get German Catholics to support Hitler's government took place in Gleiwitz, Upper Silesia. Ever since the end of World War I, this city had been a hot-bed of German nationalism and a center of anti-Polish sentiment, which became even more intense with the rise of National Socialism.[49] Invited by the conservative AKD, Papen traveled in Gleiwitz where he delivered a highly nationalistic speech to an enormous crowd, including most of the top administrators of the province and many highly placed members of the local Nazi Party organization (*Gau-Gleiwitz*). Like the festivities in Westphalia, Cologne, and other places where Papen had spoken, Nazi formations in full uniform with swastika flags flying, SA and Stahlhelm units goosestepped to the martial strains of Imperial Germany's favorite themes. On a bunting-decorated podium, in a tailored, pin-stripe suit, Papen, along with other local officials, waved cheerfully to the huge, enthusiastic crowd. After two brief speeches of welcome, Papen delivered his speech entitled "Christian Principles in the Third Reich." In an unusually long speech, the Vice Chancellor told his largely Catholic audience that National Socialism under the courageous leadership of Adolf Hitler was implementing many of the economic and social programs of the Roman pontiffs, Leo XIII and Pius XI.[50]

Carefully selecting certain passages from the writings of these two popes, Papen suggested that the social structure of the Third Reich was in complete accord with papal teachings. He even declared that until Adolf Hitler, no political leader had ever attempted to incorporate the papal teachings into any political system. Touching on such issues as the relationship between capital and labor, the corporate nature of the State and the concept of property, the dangers of Marxism, Communism, and the Bolshevization of Europe, Papen declared that National Socialism was in complete harmony with the encyclicals. While he admitted, on the other hand, that there were areas of controversy in the Church-State relationship he down-played them, confidently claiming that the on-going efforts to eliminate these differences would eventually prove to be successful. Although Papen might have been sincere in his efforts to reconcile Nazism with Catholic ideology, his narrow view of society, fueled by a desire to return to some sort of a pre-French Revolutionary socio-political system, resulted in a inaccurate interpretation of these two encyclicals.[51]

Papen's campaign to bring about a reconciliation between National Socialism and Catholicism was further complicated by three interrelated problems: the President's health, the restoration of the monarchy, and the growing tension between the SA and the *Reichswehr*.

Since the first of the year, Hindenburg's declining health raised the question of his successor. Within a matter of months, or perhaps even weeks, the question of succession would have to be settled. Since neither Papen and the conservatives nor Hitler wanted a return to parliamentary democracy, the question came down to either the restoration of the monarchy or a Nazi dictatorship.   Since the early days of the Republic it had been the conservatives' dream that after Hindenburg's death the monarchy would be restored. Papen made no secret of his determination to do everything in his power to see that this dream was finally realized. Hitler, on the other hand, never seriously considered this possibility. As long as the position of President as Commander-in-Chief of the armed forces existed alongside his own, and as long as the oath of allegiance was taken to the President and not to himself, Hitler knew that his power was something less than absolute. Yet, in spite of his determination to be in sole possession of both the Presidency and the Chancellorship, he found it politic to talk in vague terms of restoring the monarchy some time in the future.[52]

Hitler had every reason to exercise patience. Effective resistance was still possible. Towards the end of December 1933, Kurt von Hammerstein, on bad terms with both Hindenburg and von Blomberg, submitted his resignation. Hitler and Blomberg wanted Major General von Reicheneau, Blomberg's chief aid and a staunch National Socialist to replace Hammerstein. Hindenburg refused to appoint Reicheneau, while at the same time he was furious with Hitler for intruding in an area that he regarded exclusively his own. Anxious not to aggravate the President further, thereby offering his enemies an opportunity to persuade Hindenburg to call for his resignation, the Führer agreed to the appointment of Papen's earlier candidate, von Fritsch.[53]

But, while Hitler exercised caution, Papen exhibited a characteristic eagerness to negotiate the next hurdle. His first step was to meet with the Chancellor in March 1934. Papen pointed out that the monarchy would leave Hitler free to be the NSDAP leader instead of being forced as President to be completely nonpartisan. This was not a very strong argument as far as Hitler was concerned. However, not willing to reveal his true feelings, he professed to be interested in the return of a Hohenzollern to the throne. After stressing that Germany had to recover her full sovereignty before the monarchy could be restored, Hitler agreed to discuss candidates. He also promised to appoint a man of Papen's choice to a post in the Chancellery in order to gain some administrative experience.[54]

Although pleased with his meeting with Hitler, apparently Papen did not completely trust the Nazi leader. He decided to travel to Neudeck in order to obtain from Hindenburg a political testament recommending the return of the monarchy. Although very sick, and growing senile in his final months, the old Field Marshal was still the one person to whom Papen and the conservatives looked to guide Germany back to what they considered Germany's true destiny. And even as he awaited the summons to wage his final battle, the Hero of Tannenberg was called upon once more to defend the Fatherland; this time to fulfill his greatest dream - the restoration of the monarchy.[55]

In his meeting with the President, Papen discussed the problem of Hindenburg's successor "quite openly." The Constitution stipulated that on the death of the President, his duties evolved to the Chancellor until a new President was elected. Papen probably had little confidence that Hitler would abide by the constitution; but in any case new elections would certainly return a majority for the Nazis, and Hitler could go ahead and do what he wanted. Therefore he suggested to the President that he should leave a political testament to the nation "recommending the return of the monarchy."[56] At Hindenburg's request Papen drew up a draft, which he presented to the President in April. Hindenburg told Papen he would look over the document and he would give this his full attention later on. According to Papen, he visited the President a few days later, and was informed that the document as prepared was unacceptable. He told Papen that the time was not yet ripe for such a proposal, and he did not want to become the subject of controversy either in life or death. Therefore, Hindenburg said he intended to divide Papen's draft into two parts: one, a "political testament" addressed to the nation, was an account of his Presidency; the other, a personal letter to the Chancellor recommending the return of the monarchy. The result was that the "political testament" was published a few days after Hindenburg's death, while the private letter to Hitler recommending the return of the monarchy was never published.

According to Papen, Hindenburg's decision to separate the two documents meant that the whole point of his strategy, that is an appeal to the nation for a return of the monarchy, was lost. Hitler was free to do as he wished, and consequently he never published the personal letter. Later on Papen admitted that even if both documents had been published it would not have mattered. "On August 1, 1934, a few hours before Hindenburg died, the cabinet met and agreed upon a law combining the offices of President and Chancellor."[57] This would have provided Hitler with all the "legal" authority he needed. Aside from this observation, Hitler's popularity with the German public, big business, and even a growing number in the military - not to mention his control over the media - made any attempt by the monarchists to appeal for public support almost certain to fail.

Although the problem of Hindenburg's successor was a sensitive issue for both Hitler and Papen, an even more serious problem was the growing tensions between the SA and the *Reichswehr*. SA Chief Ernst Röhm, kept pressing Hitler to declare a "second revolution," which meant that he wanted the SA and the *Reichswehr* to be merged with himself appointed as *Reichswehr* Minister in the cabinet. This was completely unacceptable to the Army, and the High Command presented a unanimous opposition to the Government and appealed to Hindenburg to put a stop to Röhm's attempted interference.

As a member of the Government with good connections in the *Bendlerstgrasse*, Papen tried to persuade Hitler that any concessions along the lines proposed by the SA leader would result in dire consequences, not only for Hitler but also for the nation. On those occasions, Hitler made light of Röhm's demands labeling them "the aberrations of individual party leaders."[58] Not long afterwards however, when he was informed of the declining health of the President, Hitler realized that the question of the succession would have to be settled. But in order to combine the offices of President and Chancellor, and thereby consolidate his dictatorship, he had to take steps to resolve the problem between the Army and the SA. Complicating this problem were the fierce internal rivalries in the Party, which eventually worked to Hitler's advantage. Röhm had powerful enemies in the Party as well as in the Army. Göring, who was on terrible terms with the SA chief, found an ally in SS leader, Heinrich Himmler, who was engaged in building up a police empire in the Nazi state, and who sought to remove from his path the first obstacle, Ernst Röhm. Meanwhile Hess, Borman, and Major Buch (chairman of the USCHLA), were busy collecting scandalous information about Röhm and other SA leaders, which they hoped to use as a means to either force Röhm to resign or encourage Hitler to dismiss him.[59] Röhm's only "friend" in the party leadership was Joseph Goebbels, and oddly enough the man who had him killed, Hitler. Goebbels was more of a talker about a second revolution than a doer. And at the last moment he abandoned Röhm the same way he had betrayed Strasser in 1926, when he joined forces with Hitler. Röhm's strength lay in the two and one half million Brownshirts and their leaders, who were completely dedicated to him.

Papen was undoubtedly delighted to hear about the divisions within the Nazi ranks; but this did not alleviate his fears about the future. Towards the end of May, he went to see Hindenburg for the last time. The sick old man remarked that things were going badly, and he requested Papen to see what he could do to straighten things out.

The President was correct. Things were going badly. The revolutionary tempo had not subsided, but rather seemed to be gaining momentum. Fueling this movement were rumors that Röhm was preparing a plot to overthrow Hitler and the Army, while shipments of arms from Belgium were supposedly being funneled into Brownshirt headquarters.[60] Moreover, tensions between the *Reichswehr* and the SA had reached crisis proportions by late spring 1934. Attacks directed against the churches, the aristocracy, and the conservatives by Goebbels, Rosenberg, Frick, Ley, Hess, Göring and even Hitler himself increased.

By the beginning of June, Papen was persuaded by his Staff that the only way to pressure Hitler into pursuing a more moderate course was to deliver a public warning.[61] Hindenburg's death was imminent, and the issue of his successor was still unresolved. The dying President had refused to publicly call for a restoration of the monarchy. This meant that until a decision was made to restore the monarchy, or elections were scheduled to choose a new president, Hitler would be in charge. However, nobody, including Papen, knew what Hitler intended to do. Although he probably would have continued to cooperate with Hitler's foreign policies and economic reforms, Papen could no longer remain silent in the face of the growing threat of a second revolution.

Aware of the divisions within the Nazi Party, Papen decided that this was an opportune moment to reassert his influence, and for the last time make use of his credit with the President to stage a public protest against the recent course, and, more importantly, against the future course, of events in the Third Reich. He reasoned that if Hitler refused to listen to his protest, or if it lead to trouble, he would have the support of Hindenburg, who was equally unhappy about the state of affairs in Germany. In any case, Papen counted on the President to call out the Army if the need should arise.

On Sunday, June 17, Papen ascended the podium in the Auditorium Maximum of the University of Marburg before a full assembly of students and faculty. The title of his address was "The Aims of the German Revolution." It was the last time that he would raise his voice in protest against the abuses being perpetrated by the radical faction in the Nazi movement.

The speech was drafted by Edgar Julius Jung, the young right-wing intellectual, and Papen's speech writer.[62] Filled with references to Catholic and conservative principles, the speech was "a last minute attempt to force the revolutionary wave into conservative waters."[63] Calling for an end to the revolution and a termination of the Nazi terror, Papen declared that "at some time the movement must come to a stop and a solid social structure arise..." He also called for the return of some measure of freedom, and attacked the mishandling of propaganda: "Great men are not created by propaganda, but grow until their deeds are acknowledged by history." And, in probably what was one of the major themes of this speech, Papen pleaded for a Christian Europe: "If we deny the great inheritance of our culture...we again shall miss the chance that Europe has given central Europe...If Europe wants to keep alive its claim to world leadership not an hour can be lost to use its powers for a spiritual rebirth and to bury its petty quarrels."[64]

While Papen's speech was received enthusiastically throughout Germany when it became known, Goebbels moved swiftly to suppress its publication. But even the absolute powers of the Propaganda Minister were not sufficient to keep the German people from learning about the speeches' contents. Papen's staff had provided foreign correspondents and diplomats in Berlin with copies of his speech, which, as a consequence, found their way into the foreign press.[65] The speech, which was also published verbatim in *Germania*, produced a notable sensation throughout the Reich. For example, when Papen appeared with Goebbels at the annual German Derby in Hamburg on June 24, the Vice Chancellor was greeted with cries of "Heil Marburg," while much to his chagrin, the Propaganda Minister received a rather cool reception.[66]

Papen was furious at the suppression of his speech, and in a rather heated meeting with Hitler on June 20, threatened his own and the resignation of other conservative ministers in the Cabinet. Papen told the Führer that he had spoken as "a Trustee for the President," and threatened to go to Hindenburg and inform him of his resignation unless Goebbels' ban was lifted and the Chancellor agreed to follow the recommendations Papen had listed in his speech.[67] Hitler agreed that Goebbels had made a mistake, and told him that the Propaganda Minister had reacted out of concern over the increased tensions as a result of the insubordination of the SA He said he would tell Goebbels to remove the ban, and asked Papen to withhold his resignation until they both went to Neudeck for a joint interview with the President. Papen agreed, but they never went because "Hitler kept putting off this visit quite deliberately."[68]

The Marburg speech was only one of several reminders to Hitler that he was face to face with a major crisis and that action could not be put off much longer. Under increasing pressure from Göring, Himmler, and Heydrich to get rid of the reactionaries in the Vice Chancery, Hitler decided that something had to be done. He ordered the arrest of Jung on June 25, while Göring and Himmler continued to finalize plans to launch a "second revolution" against Röhm and other SA leaders.

After his meeting with Papen, Hitler went to Neudeck to see the President. He was greeted by General von Blomberg with the unwelcome news that if he did not effect a relaxation of the current crisis, the President would declare martial law and hand over power to the Army. This news made Hitler realize that there was more at stake than the succession to the Presidency; his whole future hung in the balance.

C. Night of the Long Knives

On June 25, Papen left Berlin to attend his niece's wedding in Westphalia. While there he received a telephone call from Tschirschky, who informed him that Edgar Jung had been arrested by the Gestapo.[69] Returning to Berlin the next day, he went directly to Himmler's office and protested the arrest of Jung. He was told that Jung had been engaging in illegal contacts with foreign countries, and that an investigation was underway to determine if the allegations were true or not. Himmler also assured Papen that Jung would probably be released in a few days.[70] Four days later the storm broke.

On June 30, 1934, Hitler moved to liquidate Röhm and his lieutenants in what was given the code name "Operation Hummingbird," also called the "night of the long knives." Under the direction of Himmler and Göring, a plan to eliminate the SA chieftain and his officers had been carefully worked out.[71]

On the morning of June 30, Papen received an urgent telephone call from Tschirschky to come to the office as soon as possible. Papen arrived at his office at 9 o'clock where he was informed that Göring's adjutant, Bodenschatz, had telephoned several times requesting Papen to go immediately to the Nazi official's office. Accompanied by his adjutant, Papen went to the office of the Air Ministry where he found "the whole area full of SS guards armed with machine-guns." Göring, who was in his study with Himmler, informed Papen that the SA had started a second revolution, Hitler had flown to Munich to put down the revolt led by Röhm and his forces, and the Göring had been given complete power to crush the revolt in Berlin. Papen protested that as the Chancellor's deputy he alone had the power to deal with the revolt in the capital. There followed a heated debate which was cut short by Göring who advised Papen to return home for his own safety, and not to leave it again without the Nazi official's knowledge. Rejoined by Tschirschky, Papen drove to the Vice Chancellery where he found the SS police, Göring's secret police and the Gestapo occupying the offices. Not allowed to enter his office, Papen was ordered by the SS to return to his car and, accompanied by the police, returned to his residence. When he arrived home he found the place surrounded by SS guards, his telephone cut off, a police captain in his house who had orders not to permit the Vice Chancellor any contact with the outside world.[72]

Over the next three days Papen, along with his daughter, who was visiting him, and his son, and Franz, who was studying for his law exams, were effectively under house arrest. His wife and other two daughters were away on a boat trip with friends from Bremen. Held completely incommunicado, Papen had no idea what was going on in Berlin or anyplace else in the country.[73] Like his adjutant, Tschirschky, he also expected to be arrested. In all this uncertainty and confusion Papen tried to contact the President in order to inform him of his predicament and urge him to declare a state of emergency. This action, he thought, would have put the Army in charge of the situation, and enable the President to investigate into what was going on. Not only was he unable to reach Hindenburg while under house arrest, but when he tried to contact the President after his release, he was unable to arrange a visit on the grounds that the marshal's health would not permit it.[74]

On the evening of July 2, Papen was informed by the police that the "protective custody" had been suspended and that he and his family were free.[75] It was only then that Papen was able to piece together what had happened. He discovered from one of his staff, Dr. Sabath, that Kageneck, Savigny, Hummelsheim, and Miss Stotzingen had been arrested, that von Bose had been shot, and his body removed, and the office files seized. Armed with this information, Papen went to see Hitler on the morning of July 4. The Führer was holding a cabinet meeting at which he was offering his explanation of what happened and why. Papen recorded that he declined to take his place, and "demanded to see him alone." Angry about the mistreatment of himself and his staff, and the implications that he and his staff had been involved in the Röhm conspiracy, Papen demanded the release of his staff. Calling for an investigation and clarification of the allegations against him and his staff, Papen then insisted that Hitler accept his resignation, which he had submitted on June 18, and added that he "refused to take any further part in the work of the Government." After he refused to accept Papen's demand that his resignation be announced immediately, Hitler requested Papen to wait until things had quieted down, and he had a chance to give a public account of his actions.[76]

Leaving Hitler's office, Papen drove straight to General Fritsch where he learned that Schleicher and his wife had been shot, and that the danger of a *putsch* seemed to be over. When Papen asked Fritsch why the Army had not intervened, the General stated that is what he and other officers wanted to do, but he could not move without explicit orders from Blomberg or Hindenburg. Blomberg was opposed to any intervention, while Hindenburg could not be reached, or had been misinformed. What Papen did not know at the time was that the military had not intervened because Röhm's removal benefited the Army.[77]

After June 16, Papen claimed that he never again took part in a cabinet meeting. He also wrote three letters to Hitler, "all insisting...on the complete innocence of anyone in my office of any complicity in Röhm's plans." He then offered to withhold the announcement of his resignation "until Bose's death had been properly investigated." Papen's concern for his staff is commendable, and he did eventually manage to get them released. However, in recording these events, he leaves out passages in those letters where he praises Hitler for having taken full responsibility for everything that had occurred in putting down the revolt. "I think this...courageous and firm intervention have met with nothing but recognition throughout the entire world." He assured Hitler of his unchanged admiration and devotion, and asked him to tell the *Reichstag* that Papen's honor and authority were unimpeached.[78] While he expressed shock and disgust at the vicious murder of Jung and Bose, and referred to the entire purge as "a negation of the due processes of law," he fails to mention his gratitude to Hitler in the letter he sent to Hitler after the Führer's *Reichstag* speech in which he justified the purge. Papen wrote how he would like to clasp the Führer's hand, in order to thank him for his rescue of the country and to congratulate him "for all you have given anew to the German nation by crushing the intended second revolution." This praise was accompanied by a plea for Hitler to make a public statement on behalf of Papen's loyalty because of the preposterous charges being made against him, including the calumny that he had planned to murder men like Göring and Goebbels.[79]

What prompted Papen to congratulate Hitler in spite of the fact that he had two of Papen's aides murdered along with a number of other innocent victims? Papen justified his actions on several grounds. For one thing, he said that Göring's police had confiscated von Bose's files, which contained "an immense amount of material on the activities of the Nazi Party and the excesses of Himmler and Heydrich."[80] This material, Papen argued, could very well have been used by Hitler to trump up charges against the Vice Chancellor and his staff, charging them with complicity in the Röhm affair. If this concern was not enough to cause Papen to assume a cautious attitude towards the entire affair, the shocking news of how Schleicher and his wife were murdered would certainly have prompted him to remain silent. After all, what was to stop Himmler from murdering Papen and his entire family under the same pretext that he had used to justify the Schleicher murders? Finally, Papen claimed that he was trying to free his staff from prison, and thought a conciliatory approach would accomplish this objective.[81]

At Nuremberg, the prosecutor charged that Papen should have made a public protest against the events of June 30, and announced his resignation. Papen's answer was that, with the complete control of the press and radio under Goebbels, such an idea was "illusory." Then shifting tactics, he proceeded to lecture the prosecution. Lumping the June 30 affair together with Hitler's disregard for international treaties, Papen accused the Allies of appeasing Hitler with pacts and treaties in spite of the knowledge of these murders. With this bit of sophistry he expected the Court to believe that he was no more guilty of his continued collaboration with Hitler than the continued cooperation of the foreign powers, even after the occupation of the Rhineland, etc.

Yet, in spite of this bold defense, Papen must have felt some guilt. "For seventeen years," he confessed, "I had believed, mistakenly, that it would possible to regulate Hitler's conduct of affairs." While admitting that he might have lacked political judgment, Papen vigorously rejected the allegation at Nuremberg that he "had deliberately delivered up [his] country and its people to a rule of violence that would lead to chaos."[82]

While Papen certainly had nothing to do with the Röhm affair, and he was not on trial at Nuremberg for that issue, his continued participation in Hitler's government after this brutal purge, necessarily comes in for criticism. Justice Robert H. Jackson, at Nuremberg, summed up the contradiction in the behavior of conservative collaborators like Papen: "When we asked him why he did not halt the criminal course of the government in which he was a participant, he said he had absolutely no influence. But when we asked him why he remained a member of a criminal government, he told us that he hoped to moderate the program by remaining there."[83]

There is no satisfactory explanation of this contradiction, to which in various ways, all later attempts at self-justification by conservative collaborators eventually led. However, this does point to the homogeneous nature of the motives which, aside from all purely personal interests, caused the majority of conservatives, including Papen, to cling to an alliance with Hitler: the longing to gain back at any price the leadership of the nation, or at any rate certain leading positions. Behind this was the feeling that they were naturally called upon to govern. This feeling never left them, and when they lost their special privileges in 1918, their urge to participate again was as disgusting as it was persistent.[84]

With the pressure from the Left and the Right no longer a threat, Hitler was free to resolve the problem of the succession at his leisure. He had fulfilled his agreement with the Army, while in von Blomberg he had found an obsequious conspirator. Within an hour of Hindenburg's death on August 2, the announcement came from the Chancellors' headquarters that the office of the Presidency would henceforward be merged with that of the Chancellor, and that Hitler would become Head of State, as well as Commander-in-Chief of the armed forces. Among the signatures at the bottom of the law announcing these changes were those of Papen, Neurath, Schwerin von Krosigk, von Blomberg and Schacht: "the representatives of Conservatism acquiesced in their own defeat."[85]

On August 19, the German people were invited to express their approval of Hitler's assumption of Hindenburg's office as the Führer and Reich Chancellor, the official title by which Hitler was now to be known. The results of the plebiscite showed that more than thirty-eight million voted "yes," while four and a quarter million had the courage to vote "no;" another 870,000 destroyed their ballots.[86] His dream was fulfilled, and Hitler was now the dictator of Germany.

Although the deaths of von Bose and Jung had caused Papen great distress, Hindenburg's death affected him even more. He had always been a great admirer of the Field Marshal, and over the years had developed a close friendship with the President. As he traveled to Neudeck to pay his last respects to the old man, Papen recalled the many private and official conversations he had engaged in with him. They had shared the same traditions, the same memories of Germany's past, and the same hopes for Germany's future. Hindenburg had often referred to Papen as his favorite, and placed a great deal of trust in him throughout the last years of his Presidency.

Upon his arrival at Neudeck, Papen offered his condolences to the family, and then bade his final farewell to the President. As he looked on the rugged, but now very pale, face of the Field Marshal, Papen was reminded of a whole era of German history - from the battle of Sadowa in 1871, to the coronation of the Kaiser at Versailles. He recalled Hindenburg's willingness to take over the leadership of his country during his declining years, and his unwavering fidelity to his constitutional oath. Reflecting on the countless occasions when he called upon the President's authority to protect, as well as guide, him through stormy and often threatening circumstances, Papen felt, not only a sense of loss, but also a deep concern for his future, especially in the light of the recent events. With no recourse to the President's authority and prestige, Papen was now exposed to the unpredictable actions of the Nazi dictator. It was not long before he would discover what price he had to pay in order to survive in the Sorcerer's kingdom.

NOTES

[1] Papen was not alone in believing that the acts of violence and terror of the SA and SS were carried out under the leadership of the more radical Nazis Goebbels, Göring, Himmler, and Röhm, and not at Hitler's command. Report of Ernst Föhr: Conference of Church Province Representatives Meeting in Berlin, April 25, 1933, Bernhard Stasiewski, *Akten Deutscher Bischöfe über die Lage der Kirche 1933-1945* (Mainz: Mattthias-Grünewald Verlag, 1968), Doc. 32/II, pp. 104-115.

[2] Cf. *Bestand Kanzlei des Stellvertreters des Reichskanzlers*, "*Akten betreffend Bittschriften und Beschwerden von Einzelpersonen und in kirchlichen Angelegenheiten, 1933-34*," R 53, pp. 413-499 1/I, Bundesarchiv, Koblenz (Hereafter cited as *Bestand des Stellvertreters*.)

[3] *Memoirs*, p. 278.

[4] Counselor Fritz Menshausen in the German Foreign Office, stated it was "now possible to conclude a *Reichskonkordat*, the realization of which until now has always failed because of the objection of the *Reichstag*." Menshausen's Memorandum April 7, 1933, Alfons Kupper, *Staatliche Alten die Reichskonkordats-verhandlungen 1933* (Mainz: Matthias-Grünewald Verlag, 1969), Doc. 3, pp. 9-11.

[5] In order to get Hitler to go along with the idea of a pact with the Vatican, Papen proposed that one of the chief points in the negotiations should be an agreement that the clergy would surrender all rights to vote or participate in political activities. "Menhausen's Memo to the Foreign Office, April 7, 1933. Kupper, ibid., Doc. 3, pp. 9-11. In his *Memoirs*, Papen mentions all of the advantages gained by the Church, but he completely omits this condition, which brought to an end the influence of the Catholic church in the political arena.

[6] *Memoirs*, pp. 278-279. Cf. also Richard W. Rolfs, S.J., "The Role of Adolf Cardinal Bertram in the Third Reich: 1933-1938" (Ph.D. dissertation, University of California, Santa Barbara, 1976), pp. 67-70.

[7] Pacelli had served as *Nuncio* to Bavaria from 1917 to 1920, during which time he concluded a concordat with the German State. He then served as *Nuncio* to the Weimar Republic, and managed to negotiate agreements with Prussia in 1924 and Baden in 1932. However, he was unable to reach any agreement with the Republic due to strong opposition from the radical factions on the Right and the Left. Cf. Ludwig Volk, *Das Reichskonkordat vom 20 Juli 1933* (Mainz: Matthias-Grünewald Verlag, 1972), p. 50.

[8] Morsey, "*Zentrumspartei*," pp. 358-363; Morsey, *Protokolle*, Docs. 741, 742, 743, pp. 621-624.

[9] Letter of Kaas to Bergen, November 19, 1935. Printed in Kupper, ibid., Appendix #19, p. 496. Kaas never returned to Germany, but remained in Rome. There has never been a satisfactory explanation for this behavior, but it is possible that he might have feared reprisals by Hitler against him personally.

[10] Rudolf Morsey, "*Tagebuch 7-20. April 1933, Ludwig Kaas. Aus dem Nachlass von Prälat Ludwig Kaas*," *Stimmen der Zeit* 166 (1950/60), 422-430.

[11] Ludwig Volk, *Das Reichskonkordat vom 20. Juli 1933* (Mainz: Matthias-Grünewald Verlag, 1972), *Konkordat*, p. 97.

[12] "Kaas Memorandum to Bergen, October 12, 1933,": in Ludwig Volk, *Kirchliche Akten über die Reichskonkordatsverhandlungen 1933* (Mainz: Matthias-Grünewald Verlag, 1969), Doc. 8, pp. 300-304; Volk, ibid., pp. 8-84.

[13] "Kaas Memorandum to Bergen, October 12, 1933," in Ludwig Volk, *Kirchliche Akten*, Doc. 8, pp. 300-304; Kupper, *Staatliche Akten*, Doc. 4, pp. 12-16. The fact that he never set foot in Germany again suggests that he might have feared reprisals by Hitler against him personally. Gunther Lewy, *The Catholic Church in Nazi Germany*, maintains that Kaas was about to be arrested for violation of fiscal laws (p. 62).

[14] In his *Memoirs*, Papen conveniently omits this meeting and the subsequent conversation with Kaas. Did Papen wish to diminish Kaas' role in the negotiations in order to take more credit for himself? Or did he wish to keep secret that he and Kaas had planned to meet on this train in order to chart a strategy with which to approach the Holy See? The latter scenario would certainly fit in with Papen's typical pattern of intrigue. From Kaas' account it is highly plausible that this interpretation is closer to the truth.

[15] Kupper, ibid., Doc. 4, pp. 12-16; Volk, ibid., pp. 98-99.

[16] Papen to Kaas, April 27, 1933. Kupper, ibid., Doc. 14, p. 31; Rolfs, ibid., pp. 72-76. Ludwig Volk, *Der Bayerische Episkopat und der Nationalsozialismus 1930-1934* (Mainz: Matthias-Grünewald Verlag, 1966), pp. 110-113.

[17] Preysing to the Fulda Bishops' Conference, May 31, 1933, in Stasiewski, ibid., Doc. 44, p. 238.

[18] Bergen to the Foreign Office, June 30, 1933. Kupper, ibid., Doc. 56, p. 124. Cardinal Faulhaber of Munich had also complained to Pacelli as well as to Hitler. Cf. Stasiewski, ibid., Doc. 47, pp. 250-253.

[19] Papen to Hitler, July 2, 1933. Kupper, ibid., Doc. 60, pp. 128-131.

[20] Kupper, ibid., Doc. 58, p. 126. It was no secret among diplomatic circles that Goebbels, Himmler, and Göring wanted to prevent any agreement between the Vatican and Germany. It is therefore possible that they pressured Hitler to discontinue the negotiations. After all, the political parties had disappeared by

July, and the Nazis were in control of the state governments, as well as the media.

[21] Volk, *Episkopat*, pp. 114-115. Among the more complex issues left undecided was the question of the future of the Catholic organizations. Archbishop Gröber of Freiburg and Bishop Berning of Osnabrück were assigned to draw up a list of organizations that would be allowed to continue to exist. All that Hitler promised was that the government would not force members of Catholic organizations to join Nazi formations. The Vatican accepted this promise *without* a list of protected organizations.

[22] Rolfs, ibid., p. 85.

[23] There was a general belief among the German bishops that in the Nazi movement there were two ideologies. One, favored by Himmler, Heydrich and Goebbels, called for the complete suppression of the Church. The other, headed by moderates like Kerrl, the Minister for Ecclesiastical Affairs, Ambassador von Bergen, and Foreign Minister Neurath, favored a program that encouraged some form of a compromise with the Holy See, but at the same time desired to see the end of "political Catholicism."

[24] Cardinal Bertram expressed this view to Pacelli in a letter of August 18, 1934. Archdiocese Archives, Breslau, I A 25/v 4.

[25] Papen mentions his close association with Gröber during the course of the negotiations. Both Gröber and Berning represented a wing of the hierarchy that had favored the approval of the Nazi party in 1930, and had urged the bishops to rescind the order prohibiting Catholics for joining or voting for Nazis. Gröber was also a sponsoring member of Himmler's SS because of his donations to that organization. Later on, he was completely disillusioned with the Nazi movement, and even became the object of Nazi persecution. Cf. Hans Buchheim, "*Fördernde Mitgliedschaft bei der SS,*" *Gutachten des Institute für Zeitgeschichte* (München: Im Selbstverlag, 1958), pp. 350-351.

[26] *Memoirs*, p. 282.

[27] Speech to the *Führertagung*, June 14, 1933 in Norman Baynes (ed), *The Speeches of Adolf Hitler, 1922-1939*, Vol. 1 (London: Oxford University Press, 1942), p. 223 & pp. 481-483.

[28] The Gestapo was established by Göring to serve as an intelligence gathering agency for the Prussian State Police. The first concentration camps (KZ) were set up at Oranienburg and Dachau, but were soon established in other parts of Germany.

[29] Bullock, ibid., p. 236.

[30] Gottfried Feder was one of the original members of the German Worker's Party. His economic theories occupied a prominent place in the NSDAP program in the 1920s. For a more complete analysis of Feder's policies see

Henry Ashby Turner's excellent study, *German Big Business & the Rise of Hitler*, pp. 62ff.

[31] All programs were a means to an end, to be taken or dropped as needed. "Any idea," he wrote in *Mein Kapmf*, "may be a source of danger if looked upon as an end in itself." (quoted in Bullock, ibid., p. 184.)

[32] Hitler's speech to the *Reichstatthälter* July 6, 1933, Baynes, Vol. 1, pp. 865-866. Quoted in Bullock, ibid., pp. 239-240. Henry Ashby Turner Jr. correctly states that big business did not put Hitler in power. However, big business did cooperate with the Nazis after they came to power in 1933.

[33] Like Papen, Schacht thought Hitler would be tamed after becoming Chancellor, and that he could be taught the principles of a sound economy. He became the Minister of Economics in 1934 and remained in that position until 1937. Arrested in July 1944, he spent the next four years in twenty-three prisons. He was tried and acquitted at Nuremberg.

[34] By the end of 1933 the SA numbered between two and three million men, more than twenty times the size of the *Reichswehr*.

[35] Hitler had never envisioned the Brown Shirts as an auxiliary, let alone a rival, of the Army. After the failed *putsch* in 1923, Röhm wanted to hand over the entire SA as an organization to the Army. This was totally unacceptable to Hitler. It was on these grounds that Hitler broke with Röhm in May 1925 - a breach that lasted five years.

[36] The General Staff was opposed to the Army's mixing in politics, as it had under Schleicher. They wanted a return to von Seeckt's policy of non-intervention in domestic affairs. Therefore, Hitler's promise was a tempting offer that they could not refuse.

[37] Hitler's speech to the *Stahlhelm*, September 23, 1933 in Baynes, ibid., p. 556. "In the long run Hitler would treat the Army just as Röhm would have done. But in 1933-34 he needed the support of the Army, and was not about to permit Röhm and the SA spoil his plans." Bullock, ibid., p. 244.

[38] It was not because Hitler had lost his appetite for violence that he issued his "cease fire" command. As long as Hindenburg was alive Hitler wanted to take no chances that the President might call on the Army to defend the State, and remove him as Chancellor.

[39] Quoted in Bullock, ibid., pp. 244-245. The SA chief delivered other speeches designed to arouse his para-military forces.

[40] Bullock, ibid., pp. 241-242.

[41] Quoted in Joachim Fest, *The Face of the Third Reich*, p. 236.

[42] Although many of his files were destroyed in the "Night of the Long Knives," on June 30, 1934, those that did survive include letters from Catholic bishops reporting violations of the Concordat, Nazi intimidation of the clergy

and Catholic youth organizations, SA invasion and destruction of Church property, etc. Cf. *Bestand des Stellvertreters*, R 53 413-4991/I, BA, Koblenz.
[43] *Memoirs*, p. 304.

[44] *Memoirs*, p. 327. After the brutal murders committed by the SA and SS in June 1934, Papen admitted that he had mistakenly believed it would be possible to "regulate Hitler's conduct of affairs." He also confessed that he had lacked "political judgment" in his assessment of Hitler.

[45] The Saar basin, the rich coal-mining area lying north of Lorraine and forming part of Prussia, was detached from Germany under the Versailles Treaty, and the rights of exploitation were granted to France for a period of fifteen years as part of the reparations imposed upon Germany. During this period, the Saar was administrated by a special commission appointed by the League of Nations. At the end of the period the people of the Saar were to decide whether they wished to return to Germany or remain autonomous.

[46] The entire speech was published in *Germania*, Saturday, November 11, 1933. Cf. "*Akten betreffend Reisen und Reden von Papens, 1933-34.*" *Bestand Kanzlei des Stellvertreters*, R 53,397-410/I BA, Koblenz.

[47] Although many files of the Vice Chancellery were destroyed, there still exists ample evidence that supports Papen's claim that his office received "thousands of complaints, protests and warnings." *Bestand des Stellvertreters des Reichskanzlers*, "*Akten betreffend Bittschriften und Beschwerden von Einzelpersonen und in kirchlichen Angelegenheiten, 1933-34. R 53 413-4991/*," BA, Koblenz. Adolf Cardinal Bertram's files also contain copies of letters of complaint to various government bureaus with copies to Papen e.g., *Erzbischöfliches Archiv Breslau*, "Complaints vs. violations of Concordat," IA/25b #110; "Gestapo action vs. Catholic Youth organizations," IA/25g #32.

[48] *Bestand des Stellvertreters*, BA, Koblenz; Stasiewski, *Akten Deutscher Bischöfe passim*; Ludwig Volk, *Kirchliche Akten, passim*; Volk, *Episkopat passim*; Papen, *Memoirs*, p. 305. *EA Breslau*, IA/25 b-z.

[49] Gleiwitz was the place selected by Heydrich in August 1939, where an "attack" by the Nazi Security forces was staged in order to provide an excuse for Hitler to attack Poland.

[50] Leo XIII's Encyclical "*Rerum Novarum*" was a classic appeal for a more just society in which a respect for the worker was combined with a plea for a proper use of property. Pius XI's encyclical entitled "*Quadragesimo Anno*," dedicated to Leo's letter forty years later, reflected many of Leo's proposals for a more just society. Both popes condemned the abuses committed by unchallenged capitalism, as well as the false solutions to those abuses as proposed by Marxism.

[51] This speech can be found in *Bestand Kanzlei des Stellkvertreters*, "*Reisen u. Reden von Papens*," R 53 397-410/I.

[52] Even before he came to power, Hitler had suggested to Hindenburg the possibility of restoring the monarchy, and as Chancellor he kept assuring the President that he hoped eventually to restore the monarchy.

[53] Cf. Dorpalen, ibid., pp. 474-475.

[54] Dorpalen, ibid., p. 477.

[55] *Memoirs*, pp. 330-331.

[56] *Memoirs*, p. 329-330.

[57] *Memoirs*, p. 333.

[58] *Memoirs*, p. 306.

[59] The USCHLA had been formed by Hitler in 1926 for the purpose of disciplining party members who got out of line.

[60] The whole story of an imminent *coup* was a lie, invented later either by Hitler in order to justify the murders, or a scheme devised by Himmler and Göring in order to trick Hitler into moving against Röhm. cf. Bullock, ibid., pp. 250-253.

[61] *Memoirs*, p. 314.

[62] In his *Memoirs*, Papen makes no mention of Jung in the preparation of this speech. Despite those who defend Papen as the author, Larry Jones has provided sufficient proof that the speech was the intellectual property of Jung. Larry E. Jones, "Edgar Julius Jung," ibid., pp. 171-72.

[63] Jones, ibid., pp. 171-172; von Klemperer, ibid., p. 210. Jones speculates that Papen probably never looked at the speech until he had boarded the train for Marburg (p. 171).

[64] "Speech by Vice Chancellor von Papen before the University Society Marburg, 17 June 1934," *IMT*, Vol,. XL, pp. 543-558.

[65] Bose managed to have certain parts of the speech broadcast live in certain parts of Germany. He also saw to it that copies of the speech were distributed at home and abroad in advance. Tschirschky, ibid., p. 171.

[66] *Memoirs*, p. 311. William E. Dodd, *Ambassador Dodd's Diary*, ed. by W.E. Dodd, Jr., and Martha Dodd (Harcourt Brace, 19412), entries for June 20 and 21, 1934, p. 114.

[67] *Memoirs*, p. 310. Unfortunately, Papen did not follow through on this threat, and the Marburg speech proved to be his first and last act of high civil courage. One of his closest aides later expressed his disappointment: "I am convinced that all he [Papen] did until 18 June 1934, he did out of genuine conviction...it was only after the Marburg speech...that he failed. This points clearly to the fact that he was weak and not of strong character." Fritz von Tschirschsky, *Errinerungen*, p. 231.

[68] *Memoirs*, p. 311. Another version has it that Papen tried to see the President but that he was prevented from doing so under orders from the Führer himself. Dorpalen, ibid., p. 479.

[69] Tschirschky, ibid., p. 181-89, for a more reliable account of Jung's arrest and the events in the Vice Chancery.

[70] *Memoirs*, p. 312.

[71] The story of the purge has been told and retold from every point of view. And while Hitler's role in the murders was secondary, Göring and Himmler would never have gone ahead with the plot without the approval of the Führer. Cf. Bullock, ibid., pp. 258-267.

[72] Tshirschky, ibid., pp. 181-89; *Memoirs*, pp. 315-317.

[73] Papen recalled that the one "tenuous link with the outside world" was the US Ambassador who, having learned of Papen's arrest, drove slowly past the house looking for signs of life. *Memoirs*, p. 317.

[74] *Memoirs*, pp. 318-323.

[75] It was only later that Papen came to know why he had been spared. Apparently Göring protected him because of his relationship with Hindenburg, and probably because he thought Papen's liquidation would only add to the problems Hitler faced as a result of this purge. Hitler was also inclined to protect Papen in order to use his influence with Hindenburg in the matter of the succession issue. As it turned out, Papen did become a pawn in Hitler's scheme to prevent the public from learning about Hindenburg's "political testament."

[76] *Memoirs*, p. 317-318.

[77] Others murdered in this purge included Erich Klausner, General von Bredow, Gregor Strasser, and Edgar Jung, Papen's assistant. The exact number of those killed in the purge will probably never be known. In his speech to the *Reichstag*, Hitler estimated that fifty eight were executed while another nineteen lost their lives. A *White Book* published in Paris gave a total of four hundred and one, and listed one hundred and sixteen by name. Cf. Bullock, ibid., p. 262.

[78] "Papen to Hitler, July 12, 1934," United States, Department of State, Office, Chief Counsel for Prosecution of Axis Criminality, *Nazi Conspiracy and Aggression*, Supplement A, Doc. D-716.

[79] Papen to Hitler, July 14, 1934, Ibid., Doc. D-718.

[80] *Memoirs*, p. 322. Bose was a former intelligence officer in the Army, and very skillful in collecting information. Bose also knew a great deal about the organization of the Gestapo and the conflict that had been going on between the SS and the SA. Papen speculates that he was probably shot because he knew too much.

[81] *Memoirs*, p. 321.

[82] *Memoirs*, p. 327.

[83] Fest, *The Face of the Third Reich*, p. 237.

[84] Fest, ibid., p. 237.

[85] Bullock, ibid., p. 266. At Nuremberg Papen asserted that he had neither "signed the laws or had any part in their composition." He speculated that it was either a forgery or "the stationary office had committed an error." He also testified that he had not attended a Cabinet meeting since June 16, 1934. Cf. Papen, *Memoirs*, p. 335.

[86] Bullock, ibid., p., 267.

CHAPTER 12:
THE AUSTRIAN QUESTION

A. The July Crisis -1934

The revolutionary impulse of Nazism did not cease with "Operation Hummingbird." Hitler's conquest of Germany was the first step in his dream of a German-dominated Europe. Ever since his boyhood days, he had been an intense German nationalist. The defeat in 1918 was a personal disaster. From the beginning of his political career therefore, he identified his own ambition with the re-establishment and extension of German power. If ever he came to power there was little doubt that his first objective would be to tear up the Treaty of Versailles. He said it quite plainly in *Mein Kampf*: "German-Austria must return to the great German mother country...Never will the German nation possess the moral right to engage in colonial politics until, at least, it embraces its own sons within a single state."[1]

Between 1930 and 1933, while Hitler was on his way to becoming the dictator of Germany, there was a revival of National Socialism in Austria.[2] The leader of this revival was Alfred Eduard Frauenfeld, a thirty-year-old bank clerk in Vienna, who joined the long list of the unemployed after his bank collapsed in 1930. For the next three years he devoted all his time to increasing the Austrian Nazi Party membership. By 1933, the Austrian Party had grown from three hundred to forty thousand members. The Austrian Nazis who formed part of the German Party under Hitler's leadership, lived and worked for the day when the two countries would be united. With the help of Theo Habicht, a member of the German *Reichstag* and the man Hitler appointed as Inspector of the Austrian Party, Frauenfeld and other local party leaders carried on a program of violence, terror and intimidation.[3] From Munich, the Nazis sent radio messages attacking the Dollfuss government. Money and arms were smuggled across the frontier and into Austrian Nazi hands. German planes dropped Nazi propaganda leaflets over Austrian towns and villages calling for union with the Fatherland. When Dollfuss countered by imposing a ban on the party and its activities, Hitler retaliated with a tourist boycott whereby all German visitors to Austria were assessed a special tax of 1,000 Marks.

Although Hitler always claimed that the Austrian affair was between Germany and Austria, such was not the case. The Italian dictator, Benito Mussolini, was a firm supporter of Chancellor Engelbert Dollfuss' government.[4] Moreover, France, as an ally of Czechoslovakia, was also concerned about Germany's policy in Central Europe. Consequently, the Austrian Nazis call for union with Germany, coupled with information of Nazi plans for a *putsch*, combined to produce a sense of apprehension among the Western powers.

With Mussolini's encouragement, France and Great Britain joined Italy in publishing a declaration proclaiming the necessity of maintaining Austria's independence.[5] Exactly one month later, on March 17, 1934, Mussolini signed the Roman Protocols with Austria and Hungary. This agreement strengthened the political ties between Italy and her two client states on the Danube.

However, this agreement did not stop the Austrian Nazis from attempting to overturn the Dollfuss regime. On July 25, less than one month after the Röhm affair, a squad of Nazi thugs swarmed into the Austrian chancellery and fatally wounded Dollfuss as he tried to escape. Other Nazis occupied the radio station and announced the appointment of Anton Rintelin as Chancellor. However, since neither the Government troops nor the population came to the Nazi's support, the *putsch* was quickly suppressed. The leaders, along with several thousand Nazis, escaped to Germany with the assistance of the German Foreign Minister, Kurt Rieth. More important for Hitler was the news

*Ambassador von Papen and his wife with their guests at a memorial
service for Prince Eugene of Savoy - Vienna, Austria.*

that Mussolini had dispatched Italian troops to the Austrian border. *Il Duce* also sent a telegram to the Austrian government promising Italian support in the defense of their independence.

Hitler was attending the Wagner Festival in Bayreuth when he received word of the attempted *putsch*. According to Friedelind Wagner, who was sitting in Hitler's box, the Führer "...could scarcely wipe the delight from his face." But in order to avoid any indication that he approved of this *coup*, he told his guests that he had to attend the prepared dinner, "...or people will think I had something to do with this."[6]

Meanwhile, Papen along with his son, Franz Jr., had just returned to Berlin from a hunting expedition, when he received word that the Führer urgently requested him to telephone him immediately at Bayreuth.[7] and suspicious, but also very curious, Papen decided to contact Hitler in order to find out what this "urgent matter" was all about.[8]

Placing the call to Bayreuth, Papen was put into immediate contact with Hitler. In an extremely agitated voice the Führer almost shouted, "Herr von Papen, you must go immediately as Minister to Vienna, the situation is extremely serious. You must accept the post." Hitler then described the murder of Dollfuss, and added that Mussolini had ordered Italian divisions to the Austrian frontier. In a voice that bordered on hysteria, Hitler then exclaimed: "We are faced with a second Sarajevo!"[9]

In the light of the murder of two of his assistants, it would not have come as a surprise if Papen had flatly refused to help Hitler out of this predicament. But instead, he agreed to fly to Bayreuth in Hitler's private plane to "talk the matter over with him personally."

As he prepared to fly to Bayreuth, Papen reflected on the reasons why the Führer had approached him. Germany was not prepared for a war against Mussolini who would be supported by France and Britain. Hitler also knew that he was on friendly terms with the Italian dictator, and his contacts with the French went back to his participation in German-French dialogues after World War I. Furthermore, none of the Nazi leaders like Goebbels, Göring, or Hess would be acceptable since the Austrians believed that the German Nazi party had been involved in the assassination. As a non-Nazi and a Catholic, Hitler saw Papen as the ideal person to represent his government in a nation whose population was predominantly Catholic. Moreover, the Führer also knew that Papen had been a good friend of the slain Chancellor. His opposition to the 1,000 mark tax, and his protests against terrorist methods by the Nazi underground in Austria were well known. Finally, his Marburg speech, which had been published in the foreign press, served to leave the impression that he was his own man, and could be relied on to follow his own conscience.[10]

When he arrived at Bayreuth, Papen went immediately to meet Hitler. The Führer gave him the full details of the attempted *putsch* including the role of the German minister, Dr. Kurt Rieth, which implicated the German legation in Vienna, and therefore the German government. Pointing to the possible serious international consequences of this crisis, Hitler appealed to Papen's diplomatic talents, his interest in German-Austrian relations, and his patriotism. Papen responded that he was not prepared at that moment to accept the invitation to go to Vienna. He reminded Hitler of the murder of two of his assistants by members of Hitler's own Party, and of the ransacking of his office by the Gestapo and the SS, and of his own house arrest. How could he now trust Hitler? The Führer replied that he had complete confidence in him, and appealed once more to his patriotism to accept this important assignment.

Moved by Hitler's appeals, and confident that he could save the situation, Papen agreed to go to Vienna, but only under certain conditions, which he presented to Hitler after consulting with his associates.[11]

> (1) Habicht was to be dismissed, and steps taken to ensure that his contacts with Austria and Austrian Nazis were completely broken.
> (2) The German Nazi Party was to be forbidden to interfere in the internal Austrian affairs.
> (3) The problem of Austrian union with Germany must never be resolved by force, but only by evolutionary methods.
> (4) His mission was to end as soon as normal, friendly relations had been restored between Austria and Germany. For this purpose he was to receive the appointment as "Minister on special mission."
> (5) He was not to come under the jurisdiction of the German Foreign Office, but was to be responsible to Hitler alone.[12]

Although there is no record that Hitler signed an agreement, he did, in fact, fulfill the conditions. Habicht was dismissed in the presence of Papen. Hitler ordered the immediate dissolution of the Austrian Nazi Party bureau in Munich on August 3, 1934. The *Kampfring* (Austrian Nazi organization in Germany) was to be reorganized in such a way as to exclude any interference in Austria's internal affairs, and it was ordered to become completely separated from the German Party organization.[13] Finally as promised, Hitler announced Papen's resignation from the cabinet, and allowed Papen to publish his reasons for this step.[14] Although in his *Memoirs* Papen claimed that he told Hitler he intended to resign because of the murder of his two assistants, his press release completely omitted that reason.[15] Instead, he said he was resigning because Goebbels, a junior minister, had issued a ban on an official speech of a senior member in the Cabinet, who was speaking as a trustee for the President.

Why, then, in spite of the murder of Jung and Bose, did Papen agree to accept Hitler's entreaty? He maintained that he wanted to "...prevent radical elements in the Nazi party both in Germany and Austria from pursuing any policy which would likely lead to international complications." He said he was also convinced that there was a need to rebuild the dike against the Bolshevik tidal wave that was sweeping throughout Western Europe in underground movements.[16]

These might well have been some of the reasons why he accepted the Vienna assignment. But there were other equally important grounds for this decision, which Papen conveniently omitted. For one thing, the events of June 30 were still very fresh in his mind, and he was quite concerned for the safety of his family. By relocating them in Vienna, at least until he was certain that the revolution was really over, they would be safe.[17] However, perhaps the most compelling reason that he decided to accept the assignment was his burning ambition to be an important player in the game. Here was an opportunity to bring about the fulfillment of one of his fondest dreams - the unification of Austria and Germany. He readily admitted that he was "fascinated by the magnitude of the task." However, as long as Austria felt threatened by Germany, she would seek aid from other nations, and any hope of unification would vanish. In order to bring about the *Anschluss* (annexation), he believed that his first goal would be to remove Austria's fear of German intervention in her internal affairs. This program of pacification would be accompanied by mutual cooperation in the cultural and economic fields. Once Austria realized the benefits from these exchanges, Papen expected that she would take the initiative towards full union of her own free will.[18]

Papen's insatiable appetite to be involved in affairs of state might have stemmed from a sincere desire to do what he thought was in the best interests of Germany. However, he also possessed the unwavering conviction that he always knew what was best for the nation, and therefore he was better qualified than anyone else to handle situations like the Austrian crisis. Criticized later for encouraging the *Anschluss*, and therefore exposing Austria to the methods of a brutal dictatorship, he argued that "...the desire of the two countries for union could not be set aside merely because a certain man and a certain party ruled Germany." He was also convinced that in 1934, it was still possible to regard the Nazi rule as a short-term manifestation in the life of the German people; there was no reason to abandon the idea of unification.[19] For Papen, historical necessity was more important than the notion of the Austrians living under Nazi tyranny.

B. Schuschnigg's Dilemma

Meanwhile, Kurt von Schuschnigg, the conservative Catholic leader of the Christian Social party, was appointed to succeed the murdered Dollfuss as Chancellor. As an ardent nationalist, he dreamed of a united German empire along the lines of the former Holy Roman Empire. However, as a believer in Pan-Germanism, he was torn between union with Germany and opposition to Hitler's Germany. This ambivalence led him to pursue a policy of appeasement, which would provide Hitler with a pretext to pursue his goal of uniting the two nations under the Swastika.

Aside from the strained relations between Austria and Germany in 1934, Schuschnigg faced a number of serious domestic challenges. Although the Austrian Nazi Party had been banned by Dollfuss, and the radical leaders had either been arrested or fled to Germany after the abortive *putsch* in June of 1934, there were still many in Austria who remained faithful to the movement. These exiled Nazis established a base in Munich and formed what was called the "Austrian Legion." With the backing of the German Nazis, this organization maintained an intricate system of communications with their colleagues across the border. They also continued to agitate for union between the two nations. Consequently, Schuschnigg viewed this threat of another Nazi revolt as always a possibility.[20]

Aside from this problem, Schuschnigg had inherited another one. In the middle of March 1933, Dollfuss had done away with the constitutional government and replaced it with the so-called "Fatherland Front." This was a coalition government around which, Dollfuss hoped, Austrians of all creeds and beliefs could rally.[21] In order to protect his government against his enemies, Dollfuss had come to rely heavily on the support of a private military organization, the *Heimwehr*. In May 1933, the leader of the *Heimwehr*, Prince Ernest Rudiger Starhemberg, an aristocrat of the old school who was opposed to the unification of Germany and Austria, placed his organization at the disposal of Dollfuss.[22] With this promised support, Dollfuss ordered the dissolution of the Socialist-controlled Vienna City Council. He also disarmed the Socialist paramilitary organization, the *Schutzbund*. This led to open revolt in Vienna, which spread to the provinces. For four days, from February 12 to 15, 1934, civil war raged in the streets of Vienna between government troops supported by the *Heimwehr*, vs. the *Schutzbund*. It ended in the defeat of the Socialists, but strengthened the influence of the *Heimwehr*.

When Schuschnigg agreed to become the Chancellor, he not only accepted Starhemberg as the Vice Chancellor, but also the head of the "Fatherland Front," while Schuschnigg agreed to serve as second in command. However, this arrangement merely postponed the eventual conflict between two political forces attempting to govern Austria.[23]

From the very beginning, Schuschnigg wanted to create an independent position for himself. But with financial support from Mussolini, Starhemberg's organization was able to retain its independence, and prevent Schuschnigg from accomplishing his goal. The only way the Chancellor could break out of this arrangement was to come to terms with the Nazis and loosen Austria's ties with Italy. Such a course, however, was fraught with danger. Mussolini's patronage of Austria was one of the major reasons why Hitler had rejected the idea of using force to accomplish the *Anschluss*. The loss of Italian support would expose Austria to a more aggressive German policy. Therefore, in order to avoid this possibility, Schuschnigg embarked on a dual policy. On the one hand he continued to seek the support of Mussolini, while on the other he undertook to obtain the backing of England and France in case the Italian dictator abandoned Austria to the Third Reich. Unfortunately, he failed to accomplish either of these objectives.

Meanwhile, Schuschnigg's efforts to break with the *Heimwehr* found immediate response in local Nazi circles. After the abortive *putsch*, a more conciliatory faction under the leadership of Anton Reinthaller was left in charge of the Party.[24] Unlike the radical wing, Reinthaller envisioned a national movement which would be independent of Germany. He wanted to adopt the Nazi program as its basis, but he also sought to rally the Pan-Germans and the *Landbund* around the Nazi party.[25] Schuschnigg was willing to work with this moderate faction of the Party because he saw their cooperation as an additional aid in his efforts to oust Starhemberg and the *Heimwehr* from power.[26] Reinthaller, who hoped to obtain the government's approval of this proposed coalition, forbade any contacts between Austrian Nazis and their leaders in Germany.[27]

It was this very complicated political situation that faced Papen as Hitler's Special Envoy to Vienna. However, it was a situation that not only whetted his appetite for power, but was tailored to his talents for intrigue. And, while he viewed this appointment as an opportunity to serve Germany, he failed to recognize that in serving Germany he was promoting Hitler and the Nazi movement.

C. Hitler's Special Envoy

Papen's assumption of the diplomatic post in Vienna was not accomplished without some difficulty. Hitler was so anxious to resolve the tensions which had resulted from the Dollfuss assassination, that he announced Papen's appointment before obtaining the approval of the Austrian Government.[28] Austria regarded this violation of normal diplomatic procedure as an attempt by Germany to ignore her sovereign rights. Consequently, the Schuschnigg government delayed the approval of Papen's appointment until assured that this was not the case.

However, this diplomatic *faux pas* was not the only reason for the delay. On July 29, the Austrian President, Anton Miklas, received a letter of protest from Cardinal Innitzer. Writing on behalf of the Austrian bishops, Innitzer called the President's attention to Papen's Gleiwitz speech of January 14, 1934, in which he accused the Vice

Chancellor of unjustly criticizing the Christmas pastoral letter of the Austrian bishops.[29] As a consequence, the Cardinal pointed out, the speech had resulted in painful embarrassment for the Austrian hierarchy. He went on to declare that, "In light of the murder of Dr. Dollfuss, the [negative] opinion of the Austrian bishops about the Nazi movement [as expressed in the Pastoral Letter]...was confirmed."[30] Turning to the appointment of Papen to Vienna, Innitzer warned that, "The appointment...will give rise to strong objections, if an appropriate and satisfactory explanation is not forthcoming." Furthermore, the trust Papen would require, "in order to accomplish his mission," would not be present if the President accepted the appointment without fulfilling this request. Innitzer concluded with the pointed remark that he intended to consult the Holy See for its opinion about this matter.[31]

The Austrian prelate's letter was not the only protest registered with the Schuschnigg government. The Legation Counselor in Rome, Herr Roter, sent a strictly confidential telegram to Theodore von Hornbostel, the Head of the Political Department in the Foreign Ministry, in which he quoted the Italian Under Secretary, who referred to Papen as, "a dangerous intriguer, and one of the most thoughtless persons next to the [German] Foreign Minister that I know."[32] In another report, Roter quoted Mussolini as advising the Government not to be in a hurry to accept Papen. *Il Duce* also strongly recommended that regardless of what policy he chose to follow, Schuschnigg's government should insist on sticking to the course laid down by Dollfuss.[33]

Another warning came from the Austrian Counsel General in Paris, who reported on July 27, that the French thought Papen's appointment indicated an "...insidious change of direction," which for the moment, gave the appearance that propaganda directed against Austria had ceased. But, "as far as the French government was concerned, this did not indicate any change in the National Socialist policy concerning Austria." Papen was characterized as a "bold but overly-hasty" person who justifiably wanted to get out of Germany and away from Goebbels' revenge. The communiqué also quoted the French government's opinion about Papen, whom, they believed, had been silent too long before he gave his Marburg speech to be reformed. In conclusion, the French urged the Austrian government to flatly turn down the appointment because the "German Nancy-boys are capable of anything."[34]

In spite of these objections, Schuschnigg's government, under pressure from the German Foreign Office, finally approved the appointment of Papen in mid-August.[35] Accompanied by von Tschirschky, Papen arrived by plane in Vienna on August 15, 1934. It was a grey and drizzly day, and the empty streets along the route which he traveled to the German embassy, were cordoned off as if the government had anticipated a demonstration.[36] Arriving at the old German Embassy in the *Metternichgasse*, Papen was greeted by the Legation Staff, which included Prince Victor Erbach who was the Legation's chief Counselor, two secretaries, von Heinz and von Haeften, and the military attaché, Lt. Colonel Muff. Joining Papen from his Berlin staff, besides von Tschirschsky and von Kettler, were his secretaries, Baroness Stotzingen and Miss Rose. Graf Kageneck remained in Berlin where he took charge of the residence on *Lennestrasse* and served as a liaison officer providing Papen with much useful information about conditions in Berlin.[37]

While Papen was aware of the difficult assignment he had accepted, it became even more painfully obvious to him when he made his first official visit to the *Ballhaus Platz*. As he entered the grounds, he noticed that the entire area was "ringed around with machine-gun posts like a fortress, and the famous old palace, in which the Congress of Vienna had met in 1815, provided an icy reception." On entering reception room he noticed the death mask of the slain Dollfuss on a window ledge, which seemed a portent of his first meeting with President Miklas, Schuschnigg, and the Foreign Minister Berger-Waldenegg. When his goodwill speech evoked no response, Papen was convinced that the reason for this cold reception was that the Austrian officials were ignorant of what his role as Chancellor and later as the Vice Chancellor had been. He thought these officials regarded him as the one "...who had broken the back of Germany's Zentrum, who had plotted the downfall of Brüning, and raised Hitler to power." He also thought they accused him of having trapped the Vatican into signing the Concordat, "...and of being a Catholic in wolf's clothing, against whom everyone must be on their guard." This perception of what the Austrian officials believed about his activities in German politics, is an indication of how little information Papen had about the Austrian leaders, and the Austrian Foreign Office.[38]

The following day, Papen met with Chancellor Schuschnigg and Foreign Minister Berger-Waldenegg. Like the previous day, this reception was also rather cool. Hoping to break the ice, Papen opened the discussion with the remark that he saw as his principle task the restoration of peace between Germany and Austria. He could only accomplish this if certain conditions were fulfilled: an end to the yellow press and radio campaign, the dismissal of the *Landesleiter* (Habicht), and the dissolution of the Austrian Legion.[39] Papen then brought up the possibility of amnesty for the Austrian Nazis in exile, and urged the Government to permit the national groups (not the National Socialists!) to continue to meet unharmed. In his reply, Schuschnigg declared that Austria would never allow any interference in her internal affairs. Furthermore, until it was very clear that the German Government was sincere in its efforts to have peaceful relations with Austria, the amnesty issue was out of the question.[40]

Papen left this interview more than ever convinced that his first task was to assure the Austrian government that Germany had no intentions of interfering in its internal affairs. However, this did not mean that he intended to give up on the idea of a peaceful *Anschluss*.[41] While he acknowledged that there were certain "obstacles" standing in his way, he was confident that he possessed the skills to accomplish this mission. Confidence was one quality that he possessed in abundance, even if he did not always temper it with prudence.

One of the least effective barriers to Papen's evolutionary scheme was the so-called Austrian Legion.[42] Although this association of exiled Austrian Nazis was supposed to be dissolved, according to the July Agreement, it continued to exist.[43] The Austrian government complained to Papen and the Foreign Office on numerous occasions, but nothing came of these protests.[44] Papen claimed that he did not have sufficient evidence to warrant any action on his part. However, the reason he probably did not register any objections was because he realized that they would go unheard in Berlin. It is also possible that he hoped the Legion's activities would bring pressure to bear on Schuschnigg to come to some sort of an agreement with him.

A more serious adversary to Papen's schemes for a peaceful *Anschluss* came from the Austrian Nazis under the leadership of Captain Josef Leopold.[45] At first, Papen thought that Leopold would be an ally. In his report to Hitler in April, 1935, he expressed his satisfaction with the choice to reassign Leopold as the leader of the Austrian Nazi Party.[46] By 1936, however, the apparent differences between the Papen and Leopold surfaced. Papen expected that the role of the Austrian Nazis was to win large sections of the population to a pro-German policy. He stressed that the ultimate decision with regard to Austria lay outside of Austria, and therefore Leopold's party played only a passive role.[47] However, Leopold opposed this approach. He insisted that it was up to the Austrian Nazis to decide what form cooperation with the Schuschnigg government should take.[48]

In order to register his stubborn opposition to Papen's policy Leopold issued a public statement in the *Völkischer Beobachter*, the official organ of the Austrian Nazi party: "...the party has, in the immediate jurisdiction of Vienna, temporarily broken off social relations with the *Metternichgasse*. This measure applies to the person of the Ambassador, whose mission, in the opinion of the Austrian National Socialists, ended on July 11, 1936."[49] Papen tried without success to bring about a retraction. And, when Leopold refused to see him, Papen retaliated by ordering the members of his legation to break off relations with the Nazi leader and his agents.[50]

However, in spite of this action, Leopold continued to wage a campaign of criticism against Papen. Eventually Hitler turned against Leopold for two reasons: first, Leopold and his followers openly defied the Führer's policy of pacification; secondly, and more importantly, after the meeting with Schuschnigg in Berchtesgaden in 1938, Hitler no longer needed the pressure which Leopold had exerted upon the Austrian Chancellor.[51]

While Leopold's opposition might have been an obstacle to Papen's evolutionary approach, the friction that existed between Schuschnigg, and Starhemberg aided his cause. By May of 1935, it was clear to Papen that a serious rift existed between the two officials. Therefore, in a report to Hitler, he proposed a scheme for pitting the two against each other. The Austrian Nazis should ally themselves with "the Pan-German wing of the Christian-Socialist Party." Then, if the Reich would refrain from interfering with the activities of this alliance, a coalition government could emerge. This would gradually help to break down the barriers between the two countries, and facilitate unification.

Hitler agreed with Papen's scheme, and decided to go along with the recommendation. In a speech to the *Reichstag* on May 21, he stated that "Germany had neither the intention nor the wish to interfere in Austrian internal affairs or to force the annexation or incorporation of Austria into Germany.[52] Hitler was not only trying to placate Austria, but he also wanted to reassure Mussolini who had consistently opposed any interference in Austrian affairs by Germany.

This conciliatory speech found its echo in Vienna. On May 29, before the Austrian parliament, Schuschnigg dismissed the allegation that Austrian was pursuing an anti-German policy: "We have never ceased to regard ourselves as a German state, and we consider the sympathy and respect of our friends abroad always as pro-Austrian, never as anti-German."[53] However, this declaration was not intended to be interpreted as a sign that Austria was prepared to discuss the question of unification. At no time did Schuschnigg want to unite with Hitler's Germany.

Papen interpreted Schuschnigg's conciliatory remarks regarding Austro-German relations as an opportunity to enter into negotiations for an agreement between the two countries. Therefore, on July 11, 1935, he submitted a draft of an agreement to the Austrian Foreign Minister. In order to alleviate any anxieties, on the part of the Austrians, that he might have received orders from Hitler or the German Nazi Party, Papen emphasized that this draft was entirely his own idea. He also reminded Berger that he had the authority from Hitler personally to negotiate with the Austrian government on all questions. The draft reiterated the positions taken by Hitler and Schuschnigg. It also called for the regulation of press and radio, the permission to use German emblems in Austria, the lifting of tourist restrictions by both sides, and the setting up of a committee to deal with questions arising from the agreement.[54]

Although Papen's suggestions found no immediate response, he did manage to negotiate a press truce with the Austrians.[55] Then, after waiting almost two months, Papen decided to press the Austrians for a reply. In a meeting with Berger, Papen stated that Hitler had authorized him to negotiate in the name of the German government. Eventually this move had the desired effect. On October 1, Berger handed Papen the Austrian counter-proposal which accepted almost all of Papen's original draft, with one essential reservation, that "the government had not yet taken a position."[56] This reservation was intended to serve as a signal to Mussolini, who was still Austria's benefactor, that Austria would make no move without consulting *Il Duce*.

Papen's hopes for an early success faded away when Mussolini's troops invaded Abyssinia on October 3. This naked act of aggression strengthened rather than weakened the pro-Italian *Heimwehr* wing in

Schuschnigg's cabinet. Austria and Hungary stood by Italy in accordance with their obligations stemming from the Rome protocols. When the League of Nations imposed economic sanctions against Italy, only Austria, Hungary and Albania voted against the fifty-two member nations. Although this anti-League policy found a great deal of criticism in Austrian government circles, Schuschnigg felt that he had no other course of action.[57]

One result of the disagreements over this pro-Italian policy was the reconstruction of the cabinet on October 17.[58] This led to strengthening the authority of the government and increasing the power of Starhemberg and the *Heimwehr*. Those cabinet members who opposed Austria's pro-Italian policy of non-support for the League's sanctions against Italy were dropped.[59]

Papen knew that as long as Starhemberg's position was firmly established, there was no chance of success for his proposal. Nevertheless, he continued to be optimistic. In his report to Hitler he wrote that from Germany's point of view "...the change in affairs is only too welcome. Every new weakening of the system is of advantage, even if at first it seems, in fact, to be directed against us." He hoped to set Schuschnigg free from his dependence on Starhemberg, and recommended that influence in this direction be brought to bear by the German press, and Goebbels' Propaganda Ministry: "...it will be a good thing to torment by clever and tactful handling via the Press the growing popular feeling against Italian policy, but without giving the government any valid occasion...of stirring up a new campaign against us."[60]

Ultimately, however, Papen knew that only a reversal of Mussolini's Austrian policy would provide Schuschnigg with full freedom of action to reach an agreement with Germany. This, however, depended in great measure on a change in the international scene. With this in mind, Papen concluded: "I am convinced that the shift of power on the European chess-board will quite soon permit us actively to tackle the question of our obtaining influence in the South East of Europe."[61]

* * *

Mussolini's decision to embark on an aggressive foreign policy, spear-headed by his attack on Abyssinia, shifted the whole question of

Austria's independence. The Italian dictator now made his Abyssinian policy the test-case for his future attitude towards other European countries.[62] The Austrian question was the only obstacle that stood in the way of a rapprochement between Italy and Germany. However, he had no intention of allowing his foreign policy to be determined by the Austrian question. Therefore, he reminded France and England that he could easily come to terms with Germany by settling the Austrian problem with her.[63]

Hitler was quick to see the advantages to be gained from the Abyssinian war. With Italy preoccupied in Africa, the Führer knew that Mussolini's attention would be diverted from Austria. Therefore, insisting on complete neutrality, Hitler issued orders prohibiting the German press from unsympathetic comments about the conflict. When the Emperor Haile Selassie, requested military equipment, the German Minister in Addis Ababa was instructed to give an evasive reply. Mussolini noted this restraint with approval, and he mentioned to Baron von Plessen in the German Legation that Germany's refusal to deliver arms to Abyssinia was evidence that "Germany was not supporting Italy's enemies."[64]

Papen was also aware of the advantages to be gained from *Il Duce's* pro-German policy. He was confident that if Mussolini turned away from Austria, Starhemberg's position would be seriously weakened. Schuschnigg could then marshall the nationalist forces against the *Heimwehr* leader, and gain sole control of the government. With Starhemberg gone, Papen believed that he would have a better chance of persuading Schuschnigg that union with Germany would be beneficial for Austria.

However, it was not from Papen, but from the German Ambassador in Rome, Ulrich von Hassell, that Hitler received the news he had anxiously awaited. Hassell reported to Hitler that on January 6, 1936, he met with Mussolini, who told him that "Austria had lost confidence in Italy's ability to protect her." Afraid that Austria would be driven into the arms of Czechoslovakia, and therefore ultimately France, Mussolini said he preferred an alignment of Austria with Germany, "because of Germany's benevolent neutrality" in the Abyssinian affair. Upon hearing this, Hitler summoned Hassell to Berlin to on January 17, 1936. Hassell reported that Bernardo Attolico, Italian Ambassador to Berlin, had reaffirmed to him Mussolini's desire for an agreement between Vienna and Berlin. Hitler welcomed this bit of news, but he cautioned Hassell and Neurath that "on the German side we must continue to keep our eyes open in Vienna and see whether the Austrian side, and particularly Starhemberg, displayed willingness to restore links with Berlin on an acceptable basis."[65]

Informed by Neurath of this meeting, Papen received instructions to "...watch closely and see whether the Austrian side exhibited any inclination to pick up the threads with Berlin on a basis acceptable to us." As a check on Mussolini's intentions, he was instructed to observe whether *Il Duce* was encouraging Austria to reach an agreement with Berlin. He was also encouraged to maintain his contacts with Prince Starhemberg, just in case Schuschnigg should lose his influence and be forced to resign.[66]

In the meantime, Schuschnigg had gone to Rome on March 23, 1936, to attend the annual conference of the three signatories to the Rome protocols. At that meeting, Schuschnigg discovered that a complete change of position had taken place from that of a year earlier. Whereas in 1935, Mussolini had tried to develop a closer relationship between the Danubian countries to the exclusion of Germany, Schuschnigg was now told that the Austrian question, which had stood in the way of a close alliance between Italy and Germany, had to be settled.[67]

The Austrian Chancellor drew two conclusions from this advice. First, Starhemberg was no longer an obstacle to an Austro-German settlement. Mussolini's decision to withdraw his support from Starhemberg signified the end of dualism in Austria. Secondly, Schuschnigg realized that Austria was politically isolated. The priority of Italian interests had changed; support from Hungary was luke-warm; British interests were non-existent and therefore France was paralyzed; the League of Nations no longer counted. Finally, the domestic and economic situation was desperate. For all of these reasons, therefore, the Chancellor decided that it was time to reach an agreement with the Third Reich.[68]

Returning from his conference with Mussolini, Schuschnigg decided to deal the first blow against the *Heimwehr*. On April 1, 1936, the Austrian Assembly passed Schuschnigg's bill introducing compulsory military service. Since the army was an integral part of the Fatherland Front, this expansion of the army strengthened Schuschnigg, and considerably weakened the Heimwehr.[69] At the end of May, after Schuschnigg had already begun negotiations with Papen,

Starhemberg was dismissed from the cabinet and stripped of his leadership in the Fatherland Front.[70]

With Starhemberg out of office, and the *Heimwehr* reduced to impotence, Schuschnigg was free to make a settlement with Germany. Therefore, the Austrian Chancellor approached Papen and declared that the moment had arrived for reaching an agreement. However, for the present, he requested that the plans should remain secret because he feared unwanted resistance.[71] The "resistance" he referred to would probably have come from Italy. Schuschnigg wanted to discuss his proposal with Mussolini so that *Il Duce* would have the opportunity to make concessions to Germany without abandoning the principle of Austria's independence.

On June 5 and 6, Schuschnigg met Mussolini in the latter's country villa at Rocca delle Caminate. The Austrian Chancellor revealed the principles of his future policy towards Germany, and the agreement on which it should be based: (1) participation of one or two nationalists in the Austrian government; (2) amnesty for the Austrian Nazis; (3) suppression of all propaganda on both sides, and (4) German recognition of Austria's independence.[72] Mussolini agreed with the proposal. He then added that since Italy was tied up elsewhere, Austria would have to stand on its own two feet. He could help the Austrians more easily if Italy and Austria had good relations with Germany.[73]

Returning from Rome with Mussolini's blessings, Schuschnigg met with Papen. Once the final negotiations began they moved ahead rapidly. Although Papen alone drew up the draft of what he called the "Gentleman's Agreement," he received plenty of advice from Hitler and the Foreign Office.[74] A series of meetings between the two men continued throughout the rest of May and into the month of June. On the basis of Papen's proposals of the previous year, Schuschnigg produced a counter-proposal on June 19, which fundamentally agreed with Papen's draft. Papen reported almost daily to Hitler and the Foreign Office as the negotiations drew to a close. On July 7 or 8, Papen went to Obersalzburg with Glaise-Horstenau as Schuschnigg's representative, and secured Hitler's approval of the text.[75] Then in Vienna, on July 11, in the Federal Chancellor's office at the *Ballhaus Platz*, Papen and Schuschnigg signed and exchanged copies of the documents, which contained the following points: Germany's recognition of Austria's independence; a promise of non-intervention in her internal affairs; and an acknowledgment that Austria would conduct her foreign policy parallel to Germany's. However, this last point would not affect Austria's special relationship with Italy and Hungary established in the Rome protocols of 1934. On internal affairs, Schuschnigg's most important concession was that the "national opposition" was to be represented in the government.[76]

In addition to these agreements, secret clauses called for a relaxation of the Press war between the two countries; amnesty for political prisoners in Austria, and measures for dealing with the Austrian Nazi refugees in Germany. The agreement also called for the resumption of normal economic relations, and German removal of all restrictions on tourist traffic between the two countries.[77]

After a final meeting with Schuschnigg, Papen composed a report in which he gave a summary of his mission to Vienna. The July Agreement, Papen wrote, was a decisive step toward a peaceful union between the two countries. He also expressed his personal appreciation to the Führer for entrusting this historical mission to him. He concluded his report with the offer to resign since his temporary assignment had been fulfilled.[78]

The next day Papen flew from Berlin to Bayreuth where he joined Hitler, Goebbels, Neurath and others, to celebrate their victory. When Papen arrived at Bayreuth, Hitler greeted him with expressions of appreciation for his successful negotiations with the Austrian government. Then, as a reward for his loyal service, the Führer offered him the position of Ambassador to Austria. Although Papen referred to this appointment as a "doubtful honor," he continued to use the title until his dismissal from the post in 1938.[79]

During his stay in Bayreuth, Papen mixed business with pleasure. At Hitler's invitation he attended several Wagner performances, followed by lavish receptions at which the Führer commended Papen for his achievements in Vienna. These social events were interspersed with business meetings at which Hitler and Neurath discussed with Papen the implementation of the July Agreement. Finally, after several days of relaxation at Bayreuth, Papen returned to Vienna to assume his new post as German Ambassador to Austria.[80]

NOTES

[1] *Mein Kampf*, p. 529.

[2] Bullock, ibid., p. 110 ff. In 1910, the *Deutschsoziale Arbeiterpartei* was founded by Dr. Walter Riehl, an Austrian lawyer, and a railway engineer, Rudolf Jung. In May 1918, this Austrian party named itself "German National Socialist Worker's Party," and began to use the swastika (*Hakenkreuz*), as its symbol. In 1926 this Austrian party submitted to the leadership of Hitler.

[3] Theodor Habicht was appointed by Hitler as Inspector of the Austrian NSDAP in the summer of 1931. He set up a terrorist network designed to bring the Austrian government to its knees and thus force the *Anschluss*. Although Habicht was removed from this position in July 1934, he continued to promote terrorist activities from Germany.

[4] The Austrian Chancellor, Dollfuss, had done away with parliamentary democracy in Austria in March 1933, and with the assistance of Starhemberg organized the "Fatherland Front," a fascist organization which stood above parties making them superfluous. From this point on, the Government under the semi-dictatorial rule of Dollfuss, relied largely on the support of a the *Heimwehr* (Home Guard), a para-military organization under the leadership of Prince Ernest Rudiger Starhemberg.

[5] On February 17, 1934, the three nations signed this agreement. "Drummond to Simon, February 17, 1934, Great Britain Foreign Office," *DBFP*, 2nd Ser., Vol. VI, No. 290.

[6] Quote of Friedelind Wagner in *The Royal Family of Bayreuth* in Bullock, ibid., p. 283. At Nuremberg, Göring testified that Hitler gave his approval based on false information that the Austrian armed forces supported the *coup*, and were prepared to take action to support the *Anschluss*. Göring Testimony, March 11, 1946, *IMT*, IX, 102.

[7] According to the Austrian Foreign Minister, Egon Berger-Waldenegg, Papen received word of the attempted *coup* while on a hunting trip in Silesia. Egon Berger-Waldenegg to the Austrian Chancellor, "Conversation about Papen's Vienna Mission, Berlin, 21 August 1934," *Bundeskanzleramt*, Z1. 191/Pol, Austrian Staatsarchiv, Vienna.

[8] *Memoirs*, p. 337.

[9] Ibid.

[10] *Memoirs*, pp. 338-339.

[11] His son Franz Jr., Wilhelm von Kettler, and Graf Kageneck had accompanied Papen to Bayreuth. They pointed out that acceptance of this mission would appear to many as an incomprehensible act in light of the

disgraceful events of June 30. Papen acknowledged this possibility, but replied that, "...a statesman with a true sense of responsibility must sometimes be ready to face the unjust censure of his friends." *Memoirs*, p. 340.

[12] Ibid., pp. 340-342.

[13] Memo from Hitler to Hess, August 19, 1934, *DGFP*, Ser. C., Vol. III, No. 165. Hitler directed Hess to reorganize the *Kampfring* and convert it into a relief society concerned solely with the cultural, social, and economic welfare of its members. However, this did not stop the organization from pressing for *Anschluss*.

[14] Hüffer Memorandum, August 7, 1934, *DGFP*, ibid., No. 149; Hitler to Hess, August 19, 1934, ibid., No. 165; "Guiding Principles," ibid., encl. 2 in No. 167; ibid., (p. 310).

[15] *Memoirs*, pp. 341-342

[16] Ibid., p. 346-47.

[17] Papen's assistant, Edgar Jung, is reported to have said that it was Papen's idea to go to Vienna because he no longer felt secure in Germany, and sought a foreign assignment at any price. Apparently, Papen had every reason to fear for his life. Goebbels was so incensed over Papen's Marburg speech he wanted the Führer "to dispose of him." Report of Austrian Foreign Correspondent, Andreas Hemberger, to the *Bundeschancellor*, Vienna, 8.8. 1934, *Bundeskanzleramt, Oesterreichisches Staatsarchiv*.

[18] Papen's desire for union of the two nations reflected the romantic aspiration expressed in the *Grossdeutsch* movement of the mid-19th century: "...no German statesman was prepared to renounce the *Anschluss* idea." *Memoirs*, p. 348; Pre-trial testimony, Nuremberg, *NCA*, Suppl. B., pp. 1472-1474.

[19] *Memoirs*, p. 347.

[20] Innsbruck, Styria, and Carinthia were all hot-beds of Nazi party activity, even though the Nazis were legally banned. Papen knew this, but he made several trips to these areas, gave speeches in which he encouraged unification, and was received with great outbursts of applause.

[21] "To create political unity, to overcome the spirit of the party, was the one idea of the Fatherland Front." Kurt von Schuschnigg, *My Austria*, trans. John Sugrue (New York: A.A. Knopf, 1938) p. 205.

[22] Charles A. Gulich, *Austria: From Habsburg to Hitler*, Vol. II (Berkeley: University of California Press, 1948), 1018-1027.

[23] Guido Zernatto, *Die Wahrheit über Österreich* (New York: Longman, Green and Co., 1938), p. 151.

[24] Reinthaller was a member of the *Landbund*. He joined the Nazis in 1930, and became *Gauleiter* for Upper Austria. Habicht removed him from this post.

But he retained his influence, and encouraged reconciliation with the government. Gehl, ibid., p. 106.

[25] Reinthaller's efforts culminated in an agreement reached with Herman Foppa of the Pan-German Party, and Franz Hueber's *Heimschutz*, on March 5, 1935. This led to the formulation of the "National Front," who offered to cooperate with the Fatherland Front. Franz Langroth, *Kampf um Österreich* (Wels: Welsermuhl, 1951), pp. 178-181.

[26] Reinthaller had served with Schuschnigg in the same regiment in World War I. After the *putsch* of July 25, 1935, this former association took on new significance. Cf. Gehl, ibid.

[27] Reinthaller sent a memo to Rudolf Hess, the Nazi secretary, requesting that no more orders or instructions be sent to party comrades in Austria in order to convince the Austrian Chancellor that all ties with the German Nazi party had been severed. Reinthaller to Hess, September 15, 1934, "Unpublished Documents of German Foreign Policy," Public Record Office, London, No. 8658/E606194-197; *DGFP*, Ser C, Vol. III, No. 17.

[28] *Memoirs*, p. 342-343.

[29] The pastoral letter condemned National Socialism, and set forth four fundamental errors in the Nazi ideology: race hatred, radical anti-semitism, ultra nationalism, and efforts to establish a national church to replace the Catholic Church. Papen, defending Nazi ideology, accused the bishops of false judgments and charged them with performing a great disservice to the German people of both nations. He said they should have attacked the injustices of the Versailles Treaty, which had plunged Germany and Austria into humiliating misery.

[30] Cardinal Innitzer to the *Bundespresident*, July 29, 1934, *Bkamt*, Präes. Kzl. Zl. 9283, Oestereichisches Staatsarchiv, Vienna.

[31] Innitzer to Miklas, ibid. The Vatican *Nuncio* to Austria was Cardinal Sibilia, who submitted some guidelines to "leading Austrian Catholic Statesmen," (i.e., to Miklas and Schuschnigg among others) in November 1935. Sibilia noted that the Holy See would continue to support Austrian independence. Correspondence between the German consulate in Vienna and the Foreign Office, Berlin, "*Abschrift, 14.11.1935*," *Geheim Akten*, E 272717-22, Political Archives of the German Foreign Office, Bonn. As long as Sibilia remained in Vienna, Innitzer refused to receive Papen or accept any of his invitations to meet him. Furthermore, it was because of Innitzer's influence that Schuschnigg had misgivings about Papen.

[32] Telegram from Herr Roter to General Secretary, Hornbostel, Rome, August 3, 1934, *Bkamt*, Z. 46/56522. Oesterreichisches Staatsarchiv, Vienna.

[33] Telegram from Herr Roter to *Bundeskanzleramt*, Rome, July 28, 1934, *Bkamt*, Abt., 13/pol., Z 41, ibid.

[34] Telegram from Herr Bischoff to Bundeskanzleramt, Paris, July 30, 1934, *Bkamt*, Z.90/56373, ibid.

[35] The German Foreign Office informed the Austrian government that a refusal to accept Papen would be regarded "as a declaration of diplomatic war." Bülow's memorandum, August 3, 1934, *DGFP*, Ser. C, Vol. III, No. 146.

[36] *Memoirs*, p. 350.

[37] Ibid.

[38] Ibid., p. 351. The records in the Austrian State Archives indicate that Vienna was very well briefed on what was going on in Berlin. The Government also knew about the role that Papen played in concluding the Concordat with the Vatican. Moreover, it was through the German bishops as well as the Vatican, that the Austrian Government was informed about the Nazi persecution of German Catholics.

[39] Papen's testimony at Nuremberg, *IMT*, XVI, p. 301.

[40] When Berger also demanded Hitler to dissolve the *Kampfring*, Papen responded, with remarkable naiveté, that he had never heard of the organization. Conference with Ambassador von Papen, Wien, am August 17, 1934, present: *Bundeskanzler* Dr. Schuschnigg, *Bundesminister*, Berger-Waldenegg, Ambassador von Papen. *Bkamt*, 57110, Österr. 5/ii, ibid.

[41] Papen to Hitler, Vienna, August 17, 1934, *DGFP*, Ser. C., Vol. III, No. 167.

[42] Jürgen Gehl speculated that the Austrian Legion, as a force, was not significant enough to exert any pressure on the Schuschnigg government or carry any weight in political decisions. Gehl, ibid., p. 103.

[43] This agreement was signed by Schuschnigg on July 11. Cf. pp. 323-324 for the terms of this agreement.

[44] The Foreign Minister to the Chief of Staff of the SA, January 11, 1935, draws attention to the complaints from Vienna concerning the activities of the Austrian Legion (*DGFP*, Ser. C. Vol. III, No. 424).

[45] *Memoirs*, p. 384. Leopold, a former Austrian non-commissioned officer, was given the honorary rank of Captain for his long service and good conduct in World War I. In 1925 he joined the Nazi party, and eventually reached the top of the party. As one of the leaders in the July *putsch*, he was imprisoned and spent the next two years in concentration camps. In the amnesty of 1936, he returned to Austria and, after a struggle with the moderate faction, resumed the leadership of the party. In 1938, he was removed from his position by Hitler because he refused to cooperate with the pacification program.

[46] Papen to Hitler, April 4, 1935, *NCA*, Suppl. A, Doc. D-687. Three years later Papen would write to Hitler demanding that he remove Leopold from Austria.

Papen revealed his low esteem for Leopold: "His education was limited, and he was dogmatic and stubborn in character - a typical unintelligent non-commissioned officer." *Memoirs*, ibid.

[47] Papen to the German Foreign Minister, March 13, 1937, *DGFP*, Ser. D, Vol. I, No. 216.

[48] Gehl, ibid., p. 149. Despite Hitler's orders not to interfere, Leopold issued orders to the Austrian Nazis that "...such interference is a vital necessity for us and...that we absolutely do not need to go to the Reich for counsel & aid."

[49] Papen's memorandum, June 3, 1937, *DGFP*, ibid., enclosure in No. 229. July 11, 1936.

[50] Gehl, ibid., p. 154. Papen's version of this encounter differs. He wrote that Leopold came to his office where there was a "stormy meeting," during which Papen told the Nazi leader that "it was not his business to decide when an agreement between two countries was to be abrogated." Papen told Leopold that he wanted nothing further to do with him and ordered him never to set foot again on the legation premises. Papen said he wanted to "show Schuschnigg how I stood in the matter." Papen's Memorandum to Hitler, *DGFP*, Vol. I, encl. to No. 229; *Memoirs*, pp. 403-404.

[51] Keppler's memorandum, February 22, 1938, *DGFP*, ibid., 318; Gehl, ibid., pp. 153-161; 180-181. In a stormy meeting with Hitler in February 1938, Leopold was told that Hubert Klausner was replacing him, and he was to remain in Germany.

[52] Baynes, *Hitler's Speeches*, Vol. II, p. 1239.

[53] Royal Institute of International Affairs, *Documents on International Affairs* (London: Oxford University Press, 1935), Vol. II, No. 185.

[54] Enclosure of Minutes of Papen-Berger conversation, July 11, 1935, *DGFP*, ibid. No. 203; Papen, *Memoirs*, pp. 362-364.

[55] A joint communiqué was issued on August 27, 1935. The text of the agreement can be found in a memorandum of a telephone conversation between Papen and the Austrian State Secretary, von Bülow, in *DGFP*, ibid., pp. 589-590.

[56] Berger-Waldenegg to Papen, October 1, 1935, *DGFP*, ibid., No. 319; Papen, *Memoirs*, ibid.

[57] Schuschnigg, *Austrian Requiem*, pp. 120-121. A chief proponent of the pro-Italian policy was the Foreign Minister, Berger.

[58] Schuschnigg maintains that the changes were made for two inter-connected reasons. First, tensions between Starhemberg and Fey had visibly increased. Secondly, important differences arose between the Minister for Social Welfare, Neustädtler-Stürmer and the Chancellor, *The Brutal Takeover*, pp. 116-117.

[59] Papen's Report to Hitler, October 18, 1935, Wien, Nr. A 2391. *PAAA*, GW., *Amt*, No. E272134. Schuschnigg mentioned that the Minister of Public Security, Major Emil Fey, who was also the head of the Vienna *Heimwehr*, and Starhemberg's rival for control of the *Heimwehr* was removed at Starhemberg's suggestion. However, his quarrel with Starhemberg continued, and he remained the leader of the Vienna *Heimwehr*. Two of Fey's closest associates, State Secretary Baron Karl von Karwinsky and Odo Neustädter-Stürmer, State Secretary for "work creation," were also dismissed from the cabinet. *The Brutal Takeover*, p. 117.

[60] Papen to Hitler, October 18, 1935, *DGFP*, ibid., No. 363; *NCA*, VII, pp. 929-929.

[61] Ibid.

[62] Gehl, ibid., p. 117.

[63] *Documents of International Affairs, 1931-1938* (London: Oxford University Press, for R.I.I.A., 1932-1941), Vol. 1, p. 178. Up until the Abyssinian invasion, France and England had encouraged Italy to retain its close relationships with Austria in order to keep Germany out of Austria. However, when the League condemned Italy for the invasion, Mussolini issued this statement, probably as a threat, hoping that the French and British would back off of their sanctions against him.

[64] Plessen's report, May 26, 1936, *German Documents of the Auswärtiges Amt*, London, 8069/E57906 (Hereafter cited: *GDAA*).

[65] Hassell memorandum on meeting with Hitler, January 20, 1936, *DGFP*, ibid., No. 506.

[66] Neurath to Papen, January 23, 1936, ibid., No. 515. Hitler was aware through Papen of the conflict between Schuschnigg and Starhemberg, and was waiting to see which one of them would win out. Papen did meet with the *Heimwehr* leader, and reported that he had suggested a united front between Italy, Austria, Germany, and Hungary be formed to "combat the Jewish-Freemason-Bolshevist common enemy." Papen to Hitler, February 12, 1936, ibid., No. 556.

[67] There were several reasons why Mussolini advised Schuschnigg to seek a settlement with Germany. The Abyssinian adventure did not develop as smoothly as he had anticipated, either militarily or politically. The failure of the Hoare-Laval Plan, and the imposition of League sanctions forced Mussolini to contemplate the possibility that Italy might become isolated. Finally, the attempts by Czechoslovakia, supported by France, to attract Austria had to be checked.

[68] Schuschnigg, *The Brutal Takeover*, p. 138.

[69] Guido Zernatto, ibid., p. 168, thought that Schuschnigg made a grave mistake in forcing the dissolution of the *Heimwehr*. By eliminating his rival, Schuschnigg had deprived himself of the one military instrument that could effectively support his regime. The strength of his government was no longer based on *opposition* to the Nazis, but on a compromise with them.

[70] Starhemberg made several final efforts to remain in power. On May 10, he sent a flattering telegram to Mussolini congratulating him on his capture of Addis Ababa. Mussolini remained unmoved. On May 15, he traveled to Rome to plead for support, but *Il Duce* advised him to restrain himself. Starhemberg even tried to meet with Göring to make an agreement, thus hoping to cut off Schuschnigg's negotiations with Germany. That meeting never took place. Gehl, ibid., pp. 126-129.

[71] Papen to Hitler, May 14, 1936, *GD*, 1744/402742; *Memoirs*, p. 369.

[72] Hassell's report, June 6, 1936, *GDAA*, 1744/402761.

[73] Ibid. In order to make sure his new policy was carried out, Mussolini replaced State Secretary, Fulvio Suvich, an opponent of the *Anschluss*, with his son-in-law, Count Ciano, who held the opposite view.

[74] Papen was in constant contact with Hitler concerning the progress in the negotiations, e.g., Papen to the Foreign Ministry, Vienna, May 4, 1936, *DGFP*, ibid., No. 304; Memorandum of the Foreign Minister, Berlin, May 13, 1936, ibid., No. 321; Memorandum by Papen on Conversation with Schuschnigg, June 19, 1936, Ibid., No. 389; Papen to Neurath, Vienna, June 24, 1936, Ibid., No. 401; Memorandum of Political Div. VI (Altenburg), Berlin, June 29, 1936, No. 408; Telegrams of Neurath to Papen, June 27, 1936, & Papen to Neurath, June 30, 1936, Ibid., No. 410; Telegrams of Neurath to Papen, July 3, and Papen to Neurath, July 3, 1936, Ibid., No. 423, 424.

[75] *Memoirs*, p. 369. Papen suggested to Schuschnigg that someone from the Austrian government should accompany him to see Hitler. But the Austrian Chancellor "did not respond." Papen is mistaken about where the meeting took place, which took place in Obersalzburg, not in Berlin.

[76] Ibid., pp. 362-364; Text of the German-Austrian Communiqué, July 11, 1936, *DGFP*, ibid., No. 153.

[77] Ibid., p. 369; *DGFP*, ibid., No. 152.

[78] Papen to Hitler, Berlin, July 16, 1936, *DGFP*, ibid., No. 455. In his *Memoirs*, Papen claims that he submitted his resignation because Hitler had accused him of making too many concessions. But then he said that he finally decided to join Hitler at Bayreuth after the Führer had apologized for his accusations. (*Memoirs*, pp. 370-71). If this is what happened, how does Papen explain the fact that the Führer already approved both drafts in his meeting at Obersalzburg with Papen and Glaise-Horstenau on July 7? Even more

puzzling, why would Papen decide nine years later that the version in his *Memoirs* is the correct one?

[79] *Memoirs*, p. 372.

[80] The Austrian government ignored the appointment when Hitler refused to raise the status of the Vienna legation to that of an embassy.

CHAPTER 13: THE *ANSCHLUSS*

A. "Gentleman's" Agreement

Although Papen's diplomatic dexterity during the course of the negotiations had been sorely tested, the fulfillment of the terms of the accord proved to be even more difficult. From the very outset there were many complaints on both sides. The Reich charged the Austrians with foot-dragging when it came to the appointment of persons from the national opposition to positions of political responsibility. The Austrians, on the other hand, complained that Germany never took the non-interference obligation seriously. An example of this was the fact that the Reich continued to encourage, direct, and finance the illegal Nazi party under Leopold's leadership. Moreover, the Austrian Legion was still in existence in Germany, and the German press had taken little notice of the agreement to "refrain from exerting and political influence on conditions in the other country..."[1] While all of these complaints raises the question about the sincerity with which both sides entered in to the accord, the fundamental problem was that both sides had completely different ideas about the purpose of the agreement. Germany - or at least Papen - saw it as a first stage in the process of eliminating Austria as an independent state. He was convinced that this could be accomplished by means of tactful diplomacy. Like many in Germany he justified this conviction on the premise that the Reich had some prescriptive right to Austria based on history, economic common sense, nature's law of nationalism and political expediency.[2]

Austria, on the other hand, viewed the agreement as a temporary means of preserving her independence. Neither Schuschnigg nor any of his advisors thought the accord would cause Hitler to desist from pursuing the idea of unification. The Austrians thought that the agreement would buy them a little time, during which they hoped the Great Powers "would not give way to further illusions about the dangerous nature of Berlin's policy, and would combine to form another 'Stresa Front.'"[3] This did not mean that Schuschnigg's government was opposed to unification. What he opposed was union with Hitler's Germany. But this distinction was acknowledged neither by the Germans, nor by many Austrian nationalists who, influenced by Nazi propaganda enthusiastically called for union between the two countries.

During the next two years, therefore, Papen concentrated his efforts on winning Schuschnigg's confidence in order to convince him that unification with the Reich was in Austria's best interests. Perhaps, if he had been allowed the opportunity to pursue this evolutionary policy Papen might have succeeded in bringing about a peaceful *Anschluss*. However, more radical factions continually interfered with his plans. Eventually, Hitler yielding to those elements simply marched into Austria and claimed it for the Reich.

When Papen returned to Vienna at the end of August 1936, he sent a report to Hitler in which he outlined the strategy he intended to pursue in implementing the terms of the agreement. While counseling patience, he also called for "intensified pressure directed at changing the regime." For this task, he expected to enlist the help of Leopold and the illegal Austrian Nazi Party. He also reported that he hoped to see, "...personalities having the support and confidence of the [National Socialist] movement," occupy positions in the Fatherland Front. Aiding him in this endeavor was Glaise-Horstenau, whom he described as a "willing collaborator."[4]

In line with this policy, Papen met with Schuschnigg and supported the Chancellor's decision to replace the last *Heimwehr* representatives in the government with spokesmen from the "national opposition."[5] Horstenau became Interior Minister, while Odo Neustädter-Stürmer, was appointed Minister of Public Safety.[6] Both of these positions were crucial because between them they controlled the entire police and intelligence apparatus of the State. Unfortunately, Schuschnigg failed to realize that in spite of their avowed nationalism, they were not prepared to divorce themselves from the National Socialist Party.[7] On the other hand, these appointments furnished Papen with a pipe-line into the Schuschnigg cabinet, and consequently a distinct advantage in his negotiations with the Austrian government.

Papen also proposed that the Reich Foreign Office take advantage of Austria's economic crisis. He knew that one of Schuschnigg's primary reasons for signing the July agreement was to obtain a favorable trade treaty with Germany. Papen regarded this as an opportunity to force Schuschnigg to fulfill the terms of the July accord more quickly. The German Foreign Office regarded this as a chance to put additional pressure on the Austrian government to grant even further political concessions.[8]

Papen agreed with this policy, and after receiving a set of instructions from the Foreign Office, presented State Secretary Guido Schmidt with a list of complaints together with a draft of a proposal designed to resolve these differences. The Reich charged that the Austrian government continued to persecute the Nationals; failed to include the Austrian refugees residing in Germany in the amnesty; refused to withdraw the ban on German newspapers and books; forbade Reich-Germans from wearing party insignia or giving the Hitler salute. The proposed draft contained recommendations designed to resolve these complaints along with certain economic incentives. Papen also "advised" Schmidt that the Reich would delay any further settlement in the commercial field if Austria failed to cooperate.[9]

Faced with this alternative, Schmidt agreed to go to Berlin with Papen to discuss the draft proposal with Hitler and representatives from the Foreign Office. On November 19 they met with Hitler, Neurath, the Austrian Minister in Berlin, Tauschitz, and State Secretary Meissner. Hitler explained his analysis of the situation emphasizing the need for cooperation between Austria and Germany in the face of the Bolshevik threat to European security.[10] Cleverly sandwiched in between the negotiations were tours of the War Academy, the Air Ministry, and the elite *Richthofen* Squadron by Göring. Naturally, these tours were intended to impress the Austrian minister with the Reich's military prowess. They also served as a subtle hint of what might happen if Austria refused to cooperate. This tactic had the desired result. At the end of his visit, Schmidt and Neurath signed a secret protocol which supplemented the July Agreement regulating Austro-German relations in minute detail. Among the specific rights guaranteed to German citizens residing in Austria were the permission to wear the Nazi insignia, hoist the Reich flag, and give the Hitler salute under certain conditions. In return, the Reich government agreed to open its borders to Austrian trade.[11]

The application of economic pressures by Germany, along with the infiltration of pro-Nazi sympathizers in the government, threatened to undermine Schuschnigg's resolve to remain independent of the Reich. Caught in this situation, Schuschnigg received advice from two different sources that he should come to terms with the Nazis under Leopold's leadership. Within his government Neustädter-Stürmer supported this course in order to get some backing against the ecclesiastical block in the Fatherland Front.[12] Schuschnigg received similar advice from the recently appointed Counsellor to the German legation in Vienna, Otto von Stein.[13] In late November 1936, Stein had an interview with Schuschnigg in which he told the Chancellor that the only really large national opposition movement in Austria was the Nazi Party under Leopold's leadership. Stein recommended that the Chancellor come to terms with Leopold.[14]

Schuschnigg decided to follow the advice of Stein and Neustädter-Stürmer. The result was the formation of the *Deutsch-sozialer Volksbund* (DSV), an association that was to unify all national forces with the Nazis as its core. In order to gather all the "nationals" in Austria to form a representative body, a "Committee of Seven" was established. It consisted of three Nazis, all associates of Leopold; two representatives from Minister Neustädter-Stürmer, one representative from Minister Glaise-Horsetnau, and one independent member. However, pressure from within the Fatherland Front prevented Schuschnigg from going along completely with the plan. Consequently, he offered to grant the Committee *de facto* recognition, remain in contact with it, and see that its activities were not impeded. In return, the formation of the DSV would be dropped. Leopold agreed to go along with this compromise in return for assurances that the Nazis would be protected from the police in Vienna and the provinces. Schuschnigg also agreed to release 145 imprisoned National Socialists.[15]

With this compromise it appeared that relations between Schuschnigg and the Nazi opposition were settled. It also looked like Papen's strategy had been defeated by Leopold. However, such was not the case. A combination of Leopold's intransigence, Papen's tenacity, and some unexpected assistance from the Fatherland Front temporarily worked in favour of Papen's pacification policies.

Leopold and the illegal Nazi Party immediately took advantage of their new found freedom of action. The Committee of Seven set up its office in the *Teinfaltstrasse* in Vienna. Gradually, Leopold turned the office into a Nazi headquarters under the direction of Dr. Leopold Tavs, the *Gauleiter* in Vienna. Disagreements between the non-Nazi members of the Committee and Leopold soon resulted in the resignation of the former.

The resignation of the non-Nazi members of the Committee of Seven was followed by occasional Nazi acts of terrorism inspired by Leopold and the *Tienfaltstrasse* radicals.[16] Schuschnigg now realized that the basis on which the Committee of Seven was formed had not been met, and therefore saw that any further attempts to collaborate with it was useless.[17] Influencing the Chancellor to come to this conclusion was Guido Zernatto, the General Secretary of the Fatherland Front. With the backing of the "ecclesiastical block" in the Fatherland Front, Zernatto called for the resignation of the "crypto-Nazi" Neustädter-Stürmer, who had supported the policy of cooperation with Leopold. As a result of this pressure, Schuschnigg abandoned Neustädter-Stürmer, and in March 1937, took over the Ministry of Public Security himself. He also accepted Zernatto's suggestion to appoint Arthur Seyss-Inquart to the Federal State Council.[18] Later, in explaining his reasons for appointing Seyss, Schuschnigg said that he "was an avowed Nazi, but favored - at that time, at least - the moderate wing of the movement."

The appointment of Seyss-Inquart met with Papen's approval. He described the Viennese lawyer as "conscientious, prudent, tolerant, and unlikely to indulge in any wild adventures." Although Seyss was convinced that the reunion of the German peoples was a desirable ideal, Papen noted that he recognized the necessity for maintaining Austria's independence.[19] However, "independence" as defined by Papen did not mean the abandonment of the *Anschluss*. He simply meant that Austria's decision to unite with the Reich should be a free and independent one, albeit under the "influence" of Papen and all the other forces favoring his evolutionary plan. In other words, in Seyss-Inquart, Papen found another ally in his plans for a peaceful *Anschluss*.

The resignation of Neustädter-Stürmer signified the end of attempts by the Nazi party and the Austrian government to settle the dispute independently of Germany. It also spelled the beginning of the end of Leopold's position in the Austrian Nazi Party. Although he continued to oppose Papen's presence and activities in Vienna, a combination of forces working against him led to his undoing. First of all, Papen had no place in his policy for a strong illegal party. This led to a confrontation between him and Leopold in May 1937, which resulted in a complete break in relations between the legation and Leopold and his agents. Moreover, Leopold's personal feud with Seyss-Inquart further weakened his position, and ultimately resulted in his recall to Berlin by Hitler himself in October 1937.[20]

Leopold's defeat signaled a victory for Papen. Since the beginning of his assignment to Vienna in 1934, Papen had insisted to Hitler that the settlement of the "German question" could only be resolved by Germany. The Austrian Nazis, he argued, must recognize "that bringing about a new political relationship between Austria and the Reich is not their responsibility."[21] With Leopold's influence diminished, Papen hoped to complete his evolutionary policy for the union of the two countries.

However, Papen was frustrated in these designs by the constant delaying tactics of the Austrian Chancellor. Desperately trying to avoid the *Anschluss*, Schuschnigg engaged in every type of ploy to escape the inevitable. Fearing that Hitler would lose patience with his evolutionary policy, and yield to a more radical solution, Papen warned the Chancellor that his refusal to implement the terms of the July Agreement were fueling the opposition. In a meeting with Schuschnigg in May 1937, Papen tried to "rouse him from his passive attitude." He warned that the growing number of incidents combined with continued delays in the implementation of the July Agreement might cause Hitler to change his mind about Papen's special mission to Austria.[22]

While Papen was sincere in his efforts to persuade Schuschnigg to comply more fully with the terms of the agreement, he was also thinking of his own position and his determination to be successful in this mission. Should his evolutionary plans go awry, and a more radical solution lead to the *Anschluss*, his reputation as a diplomat would be questioned. This type of a set-back would not only injure his pride, but might jeopardize his own future in the Reich. He knew that he was not popular with radical Nazis like Himmler, Heydrich, Goebbels, and Borman. The murders of his colleagues in the Röhm *putsch* were proof of this. He became even more convinced of this when two of his assistants became targets of the Gestapo in Vienna.[23]

In the meantime tensions continued to mount. Seyss-Inquart's efforts to bring more representatives from the national opposition into the government met with stubborn delays on the part of Schuschnigg.[24] When Papen questioned the Chancellor over these delays, Schuschnigg replied that the fault lay with the radical Austrian Nazis who had provoked the Fatherland Front. He said that the persecution of Catholics in Germany served to increase opposition to reconciliation in the Fatherland Front. Schuschnigg also reminded Papen that in the July Agreement, the Reich had acknowledged that the Austrian Nazi Party was an internal Austrian affair, yet Reich interference had never ceased. He then called Papen's attention to Leopold's recent meeting with Hitler, and the fact that he had received instructions from Göring regarding a more aggressive course of action. Papen's response to these allegations was to point out that he was instructed by Hitler to declare that any violation of the agreement was contrary to the Führer's wishes, and if the Austrian government would produce evidence of any violation, Hitler would take immediate action. No doubt Papen's defense of Hitler contained some truth, but it did not eliminate the fact that other Nazis like Göring, Himmler, Heydrich, and Borman continued to supply the "Illegals" with directives, and even financial support.[25]

Papen's efforts to accomplish a peaceful unification were not only hampered by Schuschnigg's hesitancy, Leopold's antics, and the Fatherland Front's opposition. Of all the Nazi leaders including Hitler, Herman Göring was the strongest advocate of a quick solution to the Austrian question. As early as October 1936, he met with Schuschnigg in Budapest during the funeral for General Gömbos. Applying a mixture of threats and persuasions, Göring told Schuschnigg that if Germany had so desired, the *Anschluss* could have been accomplished long ago.[26] Again in November 1936, Göring literally banged his fists on the table in anger when discussing with foreign diplomats the Austrian problem and Italy's patronage of Vienna: "It is simply inadmissable," he shouted, "that Italy should push herself between the two German states...Italy's interest in maintaining Austrian independence is laughable...The *Anschluss* will come one day, in one way or another."[27]

Impatient with Papen's pacification program, Göring decided to pursue his own policy with regard to the Austrian question. Convinced of the inevitability of the *Anschluss*, he was determined to give destiny an early helping hand in the form of a firm push in the back. As Hitler's *Reichsjaegermeister* - one of his many titles and offices in the Third Reich - Göring played host to the International Sporting Exhibition held in Berlin from November 2 - 21, 1937. Sportsmen and politicians from all over Europe were present, including Guido Schmidt and Papen. In the context of this sporting event, Göring seized the opportunity on occasion to talk politics. On November 17, for example, after an exchange of pleasantries about hunting, he complained of Austria's defensive preparations and asked: "Do you really think that if the Führer wanted to force the *Anschluss*, Austria would be able to defend herself?" Then he added, "I may as well tell you that this union will be carried out no matter what happens."[28] In the meantime, on the domestic front in Austria as the fateful year 1938 approached, Schuschnigg recalled:

> Towards the end of 1937 the Nazi underground terror was again in full swing. Telephone booths exploded, tear gas bombs were thrown, and mass demonstrations were arranged in order to induce the Austrian police to intervene. Once the police dispersed the crowds, Berlin protested that we did not keep our share of the bargain and allowed the persecution of National Socialism.[29]

In a report to Hitler on December 21, 1937, Papen informed him that he had advised Schuschnigg and Schmidt that German-Austrian relations "were not developing favorably." He also reminded them that Germany was embarked on a movement of the greatest historical significance, and that Austria had better get aboard the Reich victory train. Then he added with a note of warning: "The sole aim of my policy pursuant to my instructions from the Führer, was to promote a solution of the German problem by way of evolution, in order to forestall any solution by force."[30] Schuschnigg and Schmidt did not misunderstand the message. If they did not play the game by his "gentleman's rules," Papen would be unable to call off the Nazi radicals who would throw the rule book away. The evidence of the possibility of force to achieve the *Anschluss* was only too plain for them to ignore. Witness the threats of Göring to Schmidt in Berlin, and the recent terrorist activities of the local Austrian Nazis.

All along, Schuschnigg had banked on support from the other European powers to prevent Germany from forcefully annexing Austria. That was one of the reasons he had refused to leave the League of Nations along with Germany in 1933. However, by December, 1937, he discovered that Austria was isolated. His neighbors to the West and South had left him alone to face the colossus from the North.[31] It is little wonder, then, that Papen could confidently conclude his report by stating that all that remained to promote the German mission in Austria, was to subject the Austrian Chancellor to the strongest possible pressure.[32] But while Papen saw victory within sight, a storm was about to break that would sweep his efforts away.

By the fall of 1937, if not earlier, the extremist propaganda and the resumption of terrorism by the Austrian Nazis aggravated the already strained relations between Austria and the Reich. Further efforts to normalize relations between the two countries met with meager results. In July, for example, Schuschnigg had initiated a meeting of the commission provided for in the Gentleman's Agreement.[33] The Commission met in Vienna on July 5, 1937 under the chairmanship of Ernst von Weisäcker. Included in the German delegation were Ambassador Papen and Wilhelm Keppler.[34] The Austrians were represented by Guido Schmidt and Theodore Hornbostel. Unfortunately, the negotiations focussed on minor details, such as whether or not to allow the sale of Hitler's *Mein Kampf* in Austria. When Weizsäcker left Vienna on July 12, no major problem had been solved.[35]

By September 1937, Papen saw little evidence that Schuschnigg's government was making any effort to fulfill the terms of the Agreement. Schuschnigg on the other hand, was upset with the growing radical activities of the Austrian Nazis and the encouragement they were receiving from their German colleagues across the border.[36] In an attempt to put pressure on the Reich to call for an end to these activities, Schuschnigg ordered that no more Nazis were to be admitted to the Fatherland Front. Papen interpreted the Chancellor's action as unwillingness to fulfill the terms of the July Agreement, and was afraid that such tactics would soon place Germany in an untenable position. What he really meant was that his own evolutionary policy might be scrapped because of Schuschnigg's procrastination. In order to prevent this from happening, Papen proposed to bring about a change of Chancellors. Since President Miklas had been sharply critical of Schuschnigg's policy for along time, Papen suggested that Miklas be used as "the opening wedge."[37] After all, this scheme had worked in his favour when he plotted the demise of Schleicher in 1933. And Hitler, who had been the favorable recipient of that success, would certainly agree that a repetition of such tactics could be equally successful. However, nothing came of this scheme to oust Schuschnigg. Apparently Hitler or the Foreign Office, or both, decided that this was too risky.

In the meantime, Papen pursued another tactic designed to safeguard his evolutionary policy. The growing deadlock between the two governments was a signal to Papen that the relations between them could be restored only outside of the usual diplomatic channels. Moreover, the radical Nazis under Leopold's leadership were threatening to undermine his entire plan. Therefore, at the end of December 1937, he suggested to Schuschnigg that the time was ripe for a meeting between the Austrian Chancellor and Hitler. However, Schuschnigg declined because he felt that any complaint that he might raise about German interference in Austria's internal affairs would be ignored.[38] In spite of this rejection, Papen did not lose hope. He made the same suggestion to Hitler who, attracted by the idea, declared himself ready to have a meeting with Schuschnigg, which was then scheduled to take place at the end of January, 1938.[39]

With the Führer's consent, Papen resubmitted his proposal to Schuschnigg on January 7, 1938. Since the invitation now came from Hitler, Schuschnigg regarded the time had come to have a frank discussion and "take the bull by the horns." Over the objections of Schmidt and Hornbostel, therefore, he agreed to meet under certain conditions. He demanded a formal invitation, safeguards against a subsequent cancellation of the meeting, and the arrangement of a formal agenda.[40]

When Schuschnigg decided to meet with Hitler he also resolved to take action against Leopold's radical faction. Although the reasons why he decided to so on this occasion are not clear, it is possible that by checking the activities of the illegal party he thought he would strengthen his hand at the meeting with Hitler. But even if this were not the case, he hoped to isolate Leopold's movement and therefore reduce the risk of counter-measures.

The immediate occasion for taking action was furnished by the results of a police raid on the Nazi headquarters in the *Tienfaltstrasse* on January 25, 1938. Falling into the hands of a shocked Schuschnigg were plans calling for a *putsch* against the government. Known as the "Tavs Plan," the conspiracy outlined a program of provocation and sabotage to be carried out by the Austrian Nazis. These revolutionary activities would compel Schuschnigg to call on his Army to put down the disorder. This in turn, would cause the Reich to serve an ultimatum demanding that the Austrian Nazis share equal power with the Fatherland Front in the formation of a new government. One detail of the plot even called for the assassination of either Papen or the German military attache in order to provoke the German government into action.[41]

Schushnigg's reaction to the discovery of this plot was to call for the arrest of Leopold, and to shut down the Nazi headquarters. The day after the raid, Schmidt proposed to Papen that the three most compromised Austrian Nazis, Tavs, Leopold and In der Maur, should be sent to Germany. Papen, who had already fallen out with Leopold and his crowd, was pleased to cooperate with this recommendation. However, it took the efforts of Seyss-Inquart along with Wilhelm Keppler to convince Hitler to recall the radical leader and order him to remain in Germany.[42]

In the meantime, Papen feared that the Tavs conspiracy would torpedo his efforts to bring Hitler and Schuschnigg to the bargaining table. But his fears subsided when he received a telegram from Neurath informing him that Hitler was prepared to meet with Schuschnigg on February 15, at his mountain retreat in Obersalzburg. More importantly, Papen was delighted to learn that Schuschnigg decided to cooperate with Seyss-Inquart, and agreed to accept Seyss-Inquart's "Little Program." The terms of which called for: 1) the release of all persons in jail as a result of the July 1934 *putsch;* 2) the development of military, economic, and political relations with the Reich through the inclusion of representatives from the National Opposition; 3) control over various government committees to be granted to Seyss-Inquart; 4) that the form of the press communique be agreed upon ahead of time; and 5) that strict secrecy be guarranteed. [43] But, when Schuschnigg offered Seyss a full ministerial post in the cabinet, Papen advised him to decline the invitation for the time being. He told Seyss-Inquart that this could be one of the barganing chips in the negotiations at Obersalzburg. [44]

In the meantime, unknown to Papen, Hitler had decided to eliminate the non-Nazi personnel in the Foreign Office. On the evening of February 9, 1938, Papen received a telephone call from Hans Heinrich Lammers, State Secretary of the Chancellery in Berlin: "The Führer wishes me to inform you that your mission in Vienna has ended." Then Lammers added, "I wanted to tell you this before you read it in the newspapers." When a shocked Papen asked for a reason for this sudden decision, and why Hitler did not tell him this when he was in Berlin the previous week, Lammers replied: "The decision has just been taken." He also informed Papen that Foreign Minister von Neurath, ambassadors Hassel in Rome, and Dirckson in Tokyo, had also been relieved. [45]

This news left Papen depressed. For four years he had struggled to deal with a problem that he considered of vital importance for Germany's foreign policy. In spite of opposition from the local Nazi party, as well as interference from people in his own legation, Papen felt that he had finally localized the "Austrian question." Even Mussolini had abandoned his original objections to the idea of union.

After discussing this with his family, he concluded that his evolutionary policy was being jettisoned, and he would be replaced by some radical member of the Nazi party. However, if Hitler now decided to use force to accomplish the *Anschluss*, Papen wanted to make sure that the world knew that he had nothing to with "the whole train of events." He therefore instructed his assistant Wilhelm von Kettler, to find a safe place for all of his correspondence with Hitler so that they would not be destroyed by the Gestapo. He figured that these reports would exonerate him of any blame, and prove that he was actually working to achieve a peaceful resolution of the tensions between the two countries. [46]

Aside from his determination not to be accused cooperating with a policy of force against Austria, Papen must also have been concerned for his own and the safety of his family. Had not the Nazis murdered two of his assistants in the Blood Purge of June 30, 1934? More recently the Gestapo sought to arrest, and probably murder, von Tschirschky. [47] He also knew that his telephones were bugged and he was under constant surveillance by the Gestapo. And finally, the discovery of the "Tavs Plan," in which he was targeted for assassination, was further evidence that his life was in danger.

Although Blomberg, Fritsch, Neurath and others left their posts without a murmur, Papen, who had been in tight spots before and always managed to escape, was not so submissive. [48] The thought that all of his groundwork for a peaceful resolution of the *Anschluss* question was threatened, prompted him to go immediately to Berchtesgaden and confront the Führer. He might have lacked prudence, but he certainly did not lack courage.

The only version of this meeting with Hitler on February 5, comes from Papen. He found the Führer "exhausted and distrait (sic!)," unable to focus on anything. Papen expressed his regret that Hitler had decided to abandon a moderate and responsible policy towards Austria. He also remarked that his successor would have a difficult time trying to gain the confidence of the Austrian Chancellor, and a number of influential Austrians. Then reminding Hitler of the planned meeting with Schuschnigg, he recommended as his "last official act," that the Führer should go ahead with the meeting. This was undoubtedly a subtle suggestion that the Führer ought to reinstate him. This appeal had its desired effect. Hitler requested Papen to go back to Vienna and arrange for the meeting. When he raised the rather weak objection that he could hardly return to Vienna since the Austrian government, and in fact the whole world, knew of his dismissal, Hitler replied that it made no difference to him.[49]

Although this decision to return to Vienna has been severely criticized, Papen justified it on the grounds that his presence might help to prevent the Reich from adopting "a policy of naked threats." He also agreed to return to Vienna with what was probably a sincere, if ironic sounding intention, "...to render one last service to the solution of the Austro-German problem..."[50]

Meanwhile, the announcement of Papen's withdrawal as ambassador to Austria came as an unpleasant bit of news to Schuschnigg. He was almost certain that Hitler intended to replace Papen with someone, probably a Nazi, who favored rougher methods in achieving the *Anschluss*. However, before the Chancellor had an opportunity to learn the background for Papen's dismissal, the Ambassador was back in Vienna.

Papen immediately set to work on Schuschnigg, realizing that his personal future depended on a resounding success from Hitler's point of view. In a meeting with the Austrian Chancellor, Papen explained that Hitler had assured him personally that any discussion would be confined to the difficulties both sides had in fulfilling the 1936 agreement. Papen also told Schuschnigg that he had been explicitly instructed to say that Hitler's interest lay in the renewal, reinforcement and perpetuation of the July agreement, and that no new demands would be made. Finally, Papen added that he had been commissioned by the Führer to say that "...whatever the course of the negotiations, in no case would they alter Austro-German relations to the disadvantage of Austria nor lead to any aggravation of the Austrian situation." The worst thing that could happen, Papen assured Schuschnigg, would be that everything would remain the same. Then offering a personal opinion, he told Schuschnigg that the moment was favorable for a settlement of the differences between the two countries: Hitler was in a difficult position at home as a result of the dismissal of the army officers and the shake-up in the foreign office; he needed a period of calm abroad, and therefore the concessions he was prepared to make now would probably never be repeated in the future.[51] On that same evening therefore, Schuschnigg notified Schmidt and Zernatto that he had accepted Hitler's invitation to attend the meeting, which was now rescheduled for February 12, at Berchtesgaden.

Although Papen's persuasive methods exercised a great deal of influence on Schuschnigg's decision to go to Berchtesgaden, the Chancellor had another important motive for accepting the invitation. According to reports he received from his foreign office, negotiations for a settlement between England and Italy were underway at that very moment.[52] If a settlement of the Italo-British difficulties, stemming from Mussolini's Abyssinian adventure, could be resolved, Austria might count on a determined diplomatic *démarche* by the Great Powers that would cause Germany to back off of a forceful invasion of Austria.[53] The meeting with Hitler would give Schuschnigg more time for this situation to develop. This was wishful thinking on Schuschnigg's part, since Mussolini had no intention of resuming his patronage of Austria at the expense of a pact with Hitler. Moreover, neither the British nor the French were prepared to invest in the future of Austria. England's Chamberlain had already determined to pursue a policy of appeasement and not use force to prevent changes that Hitler wanted in Austria and Czechoslovakia.[54]

B. The Eagle's Nest

When Papen returned to Vienna on February 7, only five days remained in which Schuschnigg could prepare for the meeting with Hitler. Other than the general assurances he had received from Papen, Schuschnigg had not received a specific agenda from the German Foreign Office.[55] In spite of Papen's assurances, Schuschnigg expected Hitler to make further demands at Berchtesgaden. He therefore instructed Zernatto, in cooperation with Seyss-Inquart, to work out the basis for cooperation between the national groups (including the Nazi Party) and the Fatherland Front. If he could make an agreement with the national opposition, which included the Nazis, prior to the meeting, he would be able to forestall any attempt by Hitler to use this group as a bargaining chip for more concessions.[56]

Seyss-Inquart and Zernatto entered into negotiations on February 10, two days before Schuschnigg's arrival at Berchtesgaden. The fruits of their labors resulted in the so-called *punktationen* (draft treaty). The core of Zernatto's draft was the concession that "national socialism not tied to a party undoubtedly contained basic conceptions which could become part of the state ideology of the new Austria." The *punktationen* envisaged the installation of Seyss-Inquart as arbitrator in all matters concerning the opposition, a gradual amnesty of all Nazis still under arrest, military cooperation between Germany and Austria, and the appointment of representatives from the national opposition to different government and local offices.[57] Schuschnigg viewed this proposal as the extreme limit of concession to which the Austrian government was prepared to go in order to meet the German complaint that Austria was not fulfilling its obligations under the July 1936 Agreement. It was also obvious from the tone of the *punktation*, that Schuschnigg had worked on the basic assumption that Seyss and the "moderate" Nazis were on his side. The idea of splitting the Nazi camp into two, absorbing the moderate element into the Fatherland Front, and isolating the radicals, made sense - though in terms of practical politics, this plan was visionary. In all fairness to Schuschnigg, however, neither he nor any other European statesman comprehended the passionate loyalty that the Führer's followers, including the "moderates," were prepared to give him.

Although Schuschnigg's failure to realize the dedication of the Nazis to their Führer was, perhaps, excusable, in light of subsequent developments, his decision to trust Seyss-Inquart proved to be most unfortunate. But here too, the Chancellor was betrayed. In their initial meeting, Seyss told Schuschnigg that he had accepted the principle of Austrian independence, and the current Austrian constitution which ruled out any reactivation of the National Socialist Party.[58] However, like Papen, Seyss favored a gradual policy leading to the *Anschluss*. Also unknown to the Chancellor was the fact that Seyss was in close contact with Wilhelm Keppler, who was sent by Hitler to "engineer the *Anschluss* and pave the way for a 'peaceful' seizure of power by national socialism in Austria..."[59]

Perhaps Schuschnigg should have been more cautious given the fact that Seyss-Inquart, Keppler, the Austrian Nazis, and even Papen were committed to the *Anschluss* policy. Certainly the Austrian Chancellor's tactics during the final hours before his departure for Berchtesgaden are subject to criticism. On the afternoon of February 11, less than twenty-four hours before his scheduled meeting with Hitler, Schuschnigg met with Seyss-Inquart and showed him the terms of the *punktationen*. As it turned out, by negotiating with Seyss prior to the meeting with Hitler, Schuschnigg had given his trump cards away before he even got to the conference table.[60]

Throughout the afternoon of February 11, and into the evening, Schuschnigg met with Seyss-Inquart and Zernatto. During a break in the negotiations, Seyss summoned Kajetan Mühlmann, one of the Austrian Nazi leaders, and gave him an outline of the ten points in the *punktationen*. He was also directed to leave at once for Berchtesgaden with this information.[61] Later that same evening, Seyss met with Rainer and other Nazis in his office and gave them the details of his meeting with Schuschnigg.[62]

This information was relayed to Berchtesgaden through two channels. Rainer teletyped his report to Munich where a Nazi official handed the information to Keppler who was on his way to Berchtesgaden.[63] Mühlmann arrived at the *Berghof* at 7 a.m. on February 12, and told his story to Papen and Keppler over breakfast. Papen had arrived at Berchtesgaden on February 11, in order to prepare for the Austrian delegation. Papen claimed that he was completely unaware of the *punktationen* until Mühlmann's breakfast report.[64] Realizing how important this information could be in the course of the negotiations, Papen and Keppler decided to inform the newly-appointed foreign minister, von Ribbentrop, who in turn, immediately went to Hitler with this information.[65]

Later that same morning, Papen hurried off to the Salzburg frontier where he met Schuschnigg and welcomed him to Germany in the name of the Führer. As they continued by car, some fifteen miles to the *Berghof*, Papen casually mentioned that "a few German generals had arrived quite accidentally at Hitler's villa." Schuschnigg replied that he didn't mind, and added: "especially since I had not much choice in the matter."[66] On their arrival at the *Berghof*, Hitler greeted the Austrian party in polite and even friendly terms.

Looking back at the entire day, Schuschnigg wrote that "the general impression in the *Berghof* was unmistakable; every decision was Hitler's alone; neither diplomats nor the generals were allowed to argue; they did as they were told. We heard practically nothing from Hitler's entourage that day except 'that is for the Führer to decide,' and 'yes, my Führer.'"[67]

The first part of the discussion was carried on by Schuschnigg and Hitler alone.[68] They had scarcely sat down when Hitler launched into an angry tirade against the whole course of Austrian policy. Schuschnigg's efforts to interrupt and defend himself were shouted down. Working himself into a towering rage, Hitler crowed that he had achieved everything he had set out to accomplish, and for this reason has become perhaps the greatest German in history. Strutting back and forth, he then turned and pointed to a shocked Schuschnigg, and declared that Austria was alone; neither France, Britain, nor Italy would lift a finger to save her. Then in a threatening tone he warned Schuschnigg that if he was not prepared to agree at once to all that he demanded, he would settle the matter by force. Schuschnigg was finally able to interrupt the monologue with the request: "Herr *Reichskanzler*, what exactly are your wishes?" The Führer impatiently replied that they could discuss the details in the afternoon. In other words the Führer had no idea at that moment just what demands he intended to make. Nevertheless, Schuschnigg was now convinced that what Hitler really meant was satellite status for Austria and a camouflaged *Anschluss*.[69]

After lunch, Schuschnigg and Schmidt were left to themselves talking to the generals. No doubt Hitler had ordered them to appear in order to demonstrate that the recent military shakeup had left his position unaffected. Perhaps even more importantly, Hitler intended to leave the impression with Schuschnigg that he was able to back up his threats with force.

While Schuschnigg was engaged in desultory conversation with the other guests, Hitler met with Ribbentrop, Papen, and Keppler, drafting the German demands.[70] Ever since early morning Hitler had been in possession of the *punktationen*, which the traitor Seyss-Inquart had sent him. This fact, plus the highly satisfactory "softening-up" session with Schuschnigg, left no doubt in the Führer's mind that Austria was ready for the "kill."

At 4 p.m., the blow was delivered. Schuschnigg and Schmidt were ushered into a room where they found Ribbentrop and Papen facing them across the table. The Reich Foreign Minister presented the Chancellor with two typewritten pages containing the German demands, along with the remark that they contained the limit of the concessions the Führer was willing to make.[71] Known as the "Keppler Protocol," the demands looked strangely familiar to Schuschnigg. The major section consisted of the same measures which had been conceded in principle during the previous negotiations between Seyss-Inquart and Zernatto. In addition to these demands, the draft requested the appointment of Glaise-Horstenau as Minister of the Armed Forces, and Seyss-Inquart as Minister of Public Security, with full control over the Austrian police forces. The remaining provisions were simply extensions of the Austrian concessions worked out by Zernatto in his ten-point draft. Ribbentrop declared that all of these demands were to be carried out the week of February 18.[72]

However, the Chancellor was not ready to surrender without a fight. He protested that Hitler's terms flouted the pledge given to him only four days before by Papen on the Führer's behalf. Quoting Papen, Schuschnigg said that "no additional political demands" would be made at Berchtesgaden. Papen interrupted Schuschnigg in tones of "outraged innocence" that he too had been taken "completely by surprise." Then, in spite of this broken pledge, Schuschnigg asked whether Germany could be counted on to keep its side of the bargain. Naturally, both Papen and Ribbentrop answered affirmatively, and assured the Austrian Chancellor that Hitler's only aim was to solve the Austrian problem quietly and peacefully. Of course what Papen and the Führer meant by "solving the Austrian problem" was a far cry from what Schuschnigg defined as the "problem." Nevertheless, apparently Schuschnigg was satisfied with this answer. Given the tactical mistakes

Schuschnigg committed prior to the meeting, plus his rather naive attitude during the negotiations, is it any wonder that the Austrians had unwittingly helped to dig their own grave at Berchtesgaden?

Schuschnigg's conversation with Papen and Ribbentrop was interrupted by a summons from Hitler, who told him that he had to accept the terms immediately. When the Austrian Chancellor replied that he was willing to sign, but that he could not, by the Austrian Constitution, guarantee ratification, or the time limit for the amnesty, Hitler flung open the door, and dismissing Schuschnigg shouted for General von Keitel.

Von Keitle's testimony at Nuremberg leaves no doubt that this summons had been the purest bluff. When the chief of the OKW entered the room Hitler simply motioned him to take a seat, and remarked that he had "nothing in particular to discuss."[73] The mere presence of the chief of the army with Hitler for a few minutes was the only active part the generals played during the conference. Of course the Austrians did not know this. Waiting outside of Hitler's study, Schmidt whispered that he would not be surprised if both of them were arrested within the next five minutes.[74]

In the meantime, according to Papen, Schuschnigg and Schmidt requested him to intervene, which he agreed to do. He pointed out to Hitler that some of the demands were obviously unacceptable. He also suggested that it would be more feasible to obtain Schuschnigg's agreement to as many measures as possible. Apparently Hitler agreed to allow Papen to try and break the deadlock. The Austrians met with Papen who, according to Schuschnigg, "acted as a helpful mediator."[75] While there were some adjustments as a result of Papen's intercession, from the Austrian standpoint there was no marked nor decisive improvement in the document as a whole.[76]

With the signature of the final protocol the difficult day in the *Berghof* came to an end. However, the Austrians got one final rebuff before leaving. Schuschnigg had agreed to the meeting on Papen's promise that the talks would publicly reaffirm as their basis the compromise agreement of July, 1936. He now sought to have this point written into the joint press release. However, Hitler would have none of it. He knew that he had won a diplomatic victory of the first magnitude, and he was determined that he alone would exploit its propaganda value at the time of his own choosing. The result was a short paragraph in which the day's stormy events were described as "an informal meeting prompted by the mutual desire to talk over all questions pertaining to the relations between Germany and Austria."[77]

After putting their signatures to the agreement, Schuschnigg and Schmidt bade their farewells. Anxious to get away, Schuschnigg declined Hitler's invitation to stay to a late supper. The Austrians were silent as they drove towards Salzburg. Accompanying them was the ubiquitous Papen who could not refrain from trying to cheer them up. "Well now," he remarked to Schuschnigg, "you have seen what the Führer can be like at times. But the next time I am sure it will be different. You know, the Führer can be absolutely charming."[78] The "next time" that Hitler contacted Schuschnigg was through the Gestapo!

When Schuschnigg returned to Vienna he had only three days in which to implement the terms in the Berchtesgaden agreement. The approval of President Miklas was vital. Schuschnigg had secured the additional three days of grace solely on the grounds that cabinet appointments were the sole prerogative of the President. When he met with Miklas on February 13, Schuschnigg presented him with the terms of the Agreement, and then listed three possible courses of action: (1) either he resign and a new government be formed, which would not be bound by the Agreement; (2) appoint a new Chancellor to carry out the directives of the protocol; or (3) he could remain in office and fulfill his own agreement with Hitler.[79] Since there was no other candidate willing to assume political responsibility at this late hour, Miklas was left no other choice than to accept Schuschnigg's third alternative.

The next day, February 14, Schuschnigg proceeded with the reorganization of his government. Seyss-Inquart became Minister of the Interior and Security. As a counter-balance to Seyss, Schuschnigg retained State Secretary Skubl, whom he could trust, and made him, in addition to his post as Director of Security, Inspector General for the Police. He also brought into the government a number of his closest political followers including General Zehner as State Secretary of National Defense. There was even an attempt to join hands with the long dormant Social Democrats like Watzek, who became Secretary of Labor.[80]

The first measure which the new government acted upon was a proclamation of general amnesty. While this included the Austrian Socialists, the main beneficiaries were the Nazis. Not only the participants of the July, 1934, *putsch* released, but so were Tavs and his cronies.

Having implemented these major concessions, Schuschnigg now had to decide how much of the details of the Berchtesgaden agreement should be revealed to the Austrian public. He decided to spread a harmless version of the meeting.[81] A directive was issued to the various Austrian embassies insisting that the Chancellor had succeeded in overcoming a difficult stage of Austro-German relations without any internal and external repercussions of a serious nature.[82] Schuschnigg also sought Papen's advice about publishing a joint statement of the meeting. Papen was happy to oblige with a face-saving statement that deceived the world as to what had really taken place at Berchtesgaden.

The joint communique, which Hitler approved, described the talks at Berchtesgaden as "an attempt between two Chancellors to clear up the difficulties which had arisen in implementing the July pact." This was followed by a declaration that "both Germany and Austria are determined to adhere to the basic principles of this pact, and to treat it as the starting point for the development of satisfactory relations between the two states." The communique ended with two sentences composed by Papen the night before:

> ...with this object, both sides agreed after the discussion of February 12, 1938, to put into immediate operation measures which will ensure that close and friendly ties between the two states are established, as befits their history and general interests of the German people. Both statesmen are convinced that the steps that they have agreed upon also constitute an effective contribution towards the peaceful development of the European situation.[83]

These sentences probably represented Papen's concept of what he thought the Berchtesgaden meeting *ought* to have been, however wildly they misrepresented what had actually gone on there. Schuschnigg's contribution was more naive than deceptive since he ignored both the devastating impact that Seyss-Inquart's appointment would inevitably produce, and the impossibility of preventing the details of the meeting with Hitler from leaking out.[84] The British, French and American newspapers available in Vienna filled in the gaps that Schuschnigg left blank. Consequently, the Austrians were able to read for the first time another version of the Berchtesgaden meeting.

Naturally, the communique made Berlin's task much easier. When protests at Schuschnigg's treatment came in, the German government could point out that according to Schuschnigg himself the agreement had settled the Austro-German differences. On the other hand, when the foreign press revealed the sordid details of the meeting, a mood of panic and disillusionment resulted. Telegraphing Berlin in the early hours of February 18, Papen described Vienna as "an ant-hill," with the banks under heavy pressure, the stock exchange uneasy, and thousands of Jews packing their bags to emigrate.[85]

Hitler, in the meantime, began to fulfill some of his obligations, as he understood them, under the terms of the agreement. With his typical duplicity, he ordered his deputy, Rudolf Hess to issue instructions to all Nazi party officials. They were not to meddle in the internal affairs of Austria, or carry on Nazi propaganda across the border, or issue directives to Austrian Nazis.[86]

In spite of this apparently conciliatory action, Hitler was gathering force for a counter-swing towards violence. In his *Reichstag* speech on February 20, the Führer expressed his "sincere thanks to the Austrian Chancellor for his great understanding and the warmhearted willingness with which he accepted my invitation and worked with me..." But in that same three hour speech he referred to the "ten million Germans" living on the borders of the Reich who were "subjected to continuous suffering because of their sympathy and solidarity with the whole German race and its ideology."[87] When he announced in that same speech that he would not allow them to be deprived of the "right of racial self-determination," the warning did not fall on deaf ears in Vienna. Except of course Papen, who records in his *Memoirs* eight years later: "I still contend that in speaking thus Hitler meant what he said...By speaking in such friendly terms he certainly wished to make things easier for the Austrian chancellor."[88]

While Hitler's *Reichstag* speech caused Schuschnigg to become disillusioned, the appointment of the radical Nazi, Franz Klausner, as chief of the illegal party in Austria came as a severe blow. Schuschnigg thought he had a clear understanding in February that all Nazi affairs would be handled by the "moderate" minister of the interior, Seyss-Inquart. For Hitler, however, this understanding only meant that Leopold would be recalled, and he would be replaced by another of his stamp. Once again, in commenting on Klausner's appointment, Papen choose to ignore any sinister motives behind Hitler's actions, and speaks only of the Führer's peaceful intentions.[89]

In the meantime, the Austrian Nazis made full use of their newly gained liberties. After Hitler's *Reichstag* speech on February 20, the Austrian Nazis demonstrated in the streets of Vienna. In Graz they virtually took possession of the city. The situation threatened to get out of hand and on February 21, the Austrian government banned all demonstrations. As Minister of the Interior, Seyss-Inquart supported this measure in a broadcast on February 22. In his appeal, he requested the Austrian Nazis not to display the swastika or sing the German national anthem. Although he managed to persuade the local Nazi leaders in Graz to cancel a demonstration scheduled for February 27, this did not mean that the ultimate aim had been abandoned, as Keppler observed: "at present we are inclined to put the brakes to the movement, in order to wring more and more concessions from Schuschnigg. It seems the prime necessity, for the time being, to secure for the future further possibilities of organizing legally and for that reason to forego a parade or two."[90]

C. Operation Otto

While Papen choose either to ignore or cover up Hitler's determination to use force if necessary to achieve the *Anschluss*, Schuschnigg began to see the true state of affairs. Hitler's reference to "ten million Germans along our borders," and Klausner's appointment did nothing to reassure the Chancellor. Fearing the need to restore his own shaken authority inside the Fatherland Front, Schuschnigg decided to switch from silence into eloquence and from passivity into defiance.

On February 24, 1938, he delivered a speech to the Austrian parliament in which he declared that Austria had gone to the very limit of concessions to Germany. Austria, he declared, would never voluntarily give up its independence, and he concluded with a stirring call: "red-white-red [the Austrian national colors] until we're dead!"[91]

Papen's reaction to Schuschnigg's speech was one of hurt bewilderment, "he [Schuschnigg] made little attempt to respond to Hitler's overtures."[92] Nevertheless, in his last report to Hitler from Vienna, Papen tried to excuse Schuschnigg's tone. The Chancellor, he telegraphed, had expressed his strong nationalist feelings in order to retrieve his domestic position; there were plots in Vienna to overthrow him because of his concessions at Berchtesgaden. "In the meantime," Papen reported, "the work of Seyss-Inquart in conjunction with the leading Austrian National Socialists is proceeding according to plan...The discipline of the Party members in yesterday's February 24 meeting was excellent."[93] It was obvious that Papen was afraid that Hitler might resort to force in retaliation against Schuschnigg's speech, and this would defeat his evolutionary approach to the *Anschluss*.

Papen's reference to "party discipline" is particularly interesting. If "discipline" is measured by the expert manner in which the Nazis in Graz muzzled Schuschnigg's speech by putting the loudspeaker out of action, and then with the help of the police hoisting the swastika alongside the Austrian colors on the roof of the town hall, Papen's definition is accurate. However, Schuschnigg hardly regarded Seyss-Inquart's activities in the same light. In fact, the Chancellor began to feel the burden of carrying Seyss as his Interior Minister. He could no longer rely on the Austrian police to enforce the rules laid down by the Fatherland Front.[94]

Two days after Schuschnigg's speech at Graz, Papen paid a farewell call on the Chancellor. In his *Memoirs* he describes the meeting. After several pleasantries, Papen launched into a severe reproach over Schuschnigg's behavior. He complained that the speech had raised the Austrian problem once again as the center of discussion in Europe. He warned Schuschnigg than "an Austrian independence supported by French or Czech crutches was unbearable for Germany." Immediately retreating, Schuschnigg agreed that the effects of the French debate had been most disturbing to him. He even agreed to publish a special article in the official *Wiener Zeitung* "which would draw a clear line between the problem of Austrian independence and French interests."[95] When Schuschnigg remarked that he had acted under brutal pressure at Berchtesgaden, Papen, at his hypocritical best, recorded: "after all, I had been present myself and had been able to ascertain that he [Schuschnigg] had always at every point possessed complete freedom of decision."[96] Papen concluded his account of his last official function in Vienna:

> ...when taking my leave of the Chancellor, I asked him not
> to delude himself into believing that Austria could ever
> maintain her position with the aid of non-German

European alliances. The Austrian question would be decided only by the interests of the German people. He assured me that he was convinced of this too, and that he would let this conviction guide his actions.[97]

Following his final conversation with Schuschnigg, Papen left for Kitzbühl to enjoy a few days skiing and rest before returning to Germany, where he met Graf Kageneck, and von Kettler. Papen had requested Kettler to bring all of his important correspondence with the Austrian government with him. He wanted to store them in Switzerland "in case they should ever be required as proof of my policy."[98] No doubt Papen was beginning to suspect that Hitler might be ready to use force to annex Austria. Therefore, he was determined to protect his own position in the eyes of the international community as well as in Austria and in Germany.

In the meantime, Schuschnigg, now fully aware that the Reich had only compromised in order to consolidate its position, decided to force a decision. Although it was a gamble, he saw a direct appeal to the Austrian people as the last stand against an *Anschluss*. If they declared in favour of independence it would forestall the revolutionary method and probably prevent German armed intervention. Schuschnigg was gambling that Hitler would not dare to act counter to the declared will of the population if it decided against an *Anschluss*.[99]

On March 4, Schuschnigg held a conference with several of the political leaders in his cabinet and the mayor of Vienna. He informed them of his intention to hold a plebescite on the *Anschluss* question.[100] After obtaining the consent of the President, he informed Seyss-Inquart, but requested him to keep the information secret until he had announced the plebescite the following day, March 7.[101]

Meanwhile, hopeing to obtain foreign support, Schuschnigg informed one of the signatories of the Rome Protocols, Hungary, of his intention to hold a plebescite. Kalman Kanya, the Hungarian Foreign Minister told Schuschnigg he was confident that Hitler was only bluffing.[102] When informed of this idea, Mussolini was less optimistic, and described it as "a bomb which would burst in Schuschnigg's hands."[103] However, Schuschnigg felt it was too late to turn back, and on that same evening he announced the holding of a plebescite on the coming Sunday, March 13. The formula was broadcast immediately after his speech, and called for a "yes" - "no" vote on the question of whether Austria should remain independent.

The news of the plebescite reached Hitler on the morning of March 9, through a telephone call from Rainer to Keppler in Berlin.[104] According to Keppler, Hitler received the news with "utter incredulity." Within an hour he sent Keppler to Vienna to bring Schuschnigg to his senses. When he returned to Berlin on the morning of March 10, empty handed, Hitler immediately sent for General Keitel and other generals and stated that he would not tolerate a plebescite. Then Keitel reminded the Führer of the existence of "Plan Otto," which had been prepared the previous summer as a precaution against the return of Otto of Habsburg to Austria. Hitler now ordered Keitel to draw up operational plans to cross the Austrian border in force.

In the meantime, Papen had left Vienna on February 26. His work there was finished, and he returned to his estate in Wallerfangen. When news of the plebescite reached him, Papen's first thoughts were to obtain a postponement in order "to allow proper time for its preparation, and to have the question phrased more objectively." Although he was no longer in an official position, he was eager to get back into action. He was confident that he could persuade Schuschnigg either to cancel the plebescite, or at least modify the wording in such a way as to avoid a violent solution. He was also convinced that he could calm Hitler's anger and determination to apply force against Austria. With his typical boldness, Papen sent Schuschnigg a telegram offering his suggestions, which were turned down by the Austrian Chancellor.[105] Meanwhile, he received a telephone call from the Reich Chancellery ordering him to go immediately to Berlin.[106] Once again, the "sorcerer" commanded and the "apprentice" obeyed. He arrived at the Chancellery on March 11, at about nine o'clock. He recorded his impressions of the meeting:

> ...there was that tension in the air that I had so often noticed as an accompaniment to Hitler's actions... Everyone, who by reason of duty, curiosity, employment or intrigue, that had any connection with the subject discussed, seemed to be present.[107]

When Papen was ushered into Hitler's presence he found the Führer in a state "bordering on hysteria." Hitler shouted, "the situation has become unbearable...Schuschnigg has betrayed the greater German ideal...He cannot be allowed to succeed and he will not succeed." After urging moderation, Papen warned Hitler of possible reaction by the other western powers if Germany should take military measures against Austria: "the only solution that would have historical justification," Papen argued, "would be one arrived at by peaceful means, not by the use of the sword." Having said his piece, Papen took a seat in the ante-room of the chancellery "without playing any part in the dramatic events of the day."[108]

While Papen sat in the ante-room of the Reich Chancellery, the final tragic hours of Austrian independence slipped away. Waiting at the airport on the morning of March 11, Seyss-Inquart received Hitler's ultimatum, which he then delivered to Schuschnigg. The Chancellor was given from noon until 2 p.m. to accept the Führer's ultimatum. After discussion with his cabinet, Schuschnigg decided to bow to the German demands, and call off the plebescite.

At this point Göring, who had been pressing for an invasion all along, decided to take action. He called for Scuschnigg's resignation and the appointment of Seyss-Inquart who was to form a new cabinet within two hours! When this news reached him, Schuschnigg knew that all was finished, and he submitted his resignation at 3:30 p.m.[109]

President Miklas was not as willing to surrender. Despite Göring's threats of immediate invasion by the Wehrmacht, Miklas remained adamant. Hitler lost all patience, and flashed the invasion order at 8:45 p.m.[110] Göring then sent a telegram to Seyss-Inquart with the order that he "invite" the German army to come in and establish peace and order, and help prevent bloodshed. Such an invitation would provide Göring with the "legal" excuse to invade Austria. When Seyss-Inquart refused to go along with this scheme, Keppler, without having obtained Seyss-Inquart's consent, called back to Berlin: "tell the Field Marshal that Seyss-Inquart agrees."

On the morning of March 12, German troops rolled over the border into Austria. Hitler crossed the border near Braunau am Inn, his birthplace, at 3:50 p.m. The enthusiastic reception he received at Linz, he later claimed, was what convinced him to immediately carry out the *Anschluss*. On Sunday, March 13 - ironically the day on which Schuschnigg's plebescite was to have been held - President Miklas stepped down from office, and Seyss-Inquart signed the *Anschluss* law. The Austrian Republic ceased to exist.

Back in Berlin, Papen described his mood: "like everyone else, I was caught up in the general enthusiasm and overwhelmed by the historical magnitude of the occasion - the union of the two German peoples."[111] Later that day he received a telegram from Hitler requesting him to go to Vienna. The same day the German radio announced that "in honor of his valuable services," the ex-ambassador had been made a member of the Nazi Party and given one of its highest awards, the Golden Badge of Honor.[112]

Papen arrived in Vienna on March 14, and joined Hitler in the reviewing stand opposite the Hofburg, the ancient palace of the Habsburgs. A large, enthusiastic crowd lined the sidewalks while Papen and Hitler received the "Sieg Heils" of the German and Austrian military units as they marched past. During a pause in the parade, Papen, in an attempt to square his service to Hitler's foreign policy towards Austria and his Catholic conscience, he turned to Hitler and suggested a meeting between the Führer and the Primate of Austria, Cardinal Theodor Innitzer.[113] Hitler agreed, and told Papen to go ahead with the necessary arrangements.

On March 15, Papen brought the Cardinal to Hitler's hotel suite where the two of them discussed the place of Austrian Catholicism in the new order. Innitzer, who had been so opposed to the idea of the *Anschluss* now revealed another side of his character. Obsequiously declaring that "German thoughts and German feelings had never lacked in Austria," the Primate promised that Austria's Catholics would become "the truest sons of the great Reich into whose arms they had been brought back on this momentous day." In Papen's words: "Hitler was delighted with the Cardinal's patriotic words, shook his hand warmly, and promised him everything."[114] If Innitzer had known what Hitler's promises really meant he would have walked out without a further word.[115] As it was, the Cardinal was so compromised that the Vatican, unhappy over the his servile conduct, summoned him to Rome to explain his behavior.[116] Unfortunately, by then the clergy and faithful had their orders, and the damage was done. Thus Papen, who told Hitler he was grateful for the opportunity to perform this last service to Austria, had truly fulfilled his pledge before departing from Vienna.

When the national plebescite took place, the results revealed an overwhelming victory for the Führer.[117] Meanwhile, having given his final performance in Vienna, Papen returned to temporary retirement at his estate at Wallerfangen. He would remain there until summoned once again by the Sorcerer. Looking back at Papen's service in the cause of the Führer, it is difficult to understand how, without protest, he accepted the manner with which the *Anschluss* was achieved. Was not Hitler's forceful annexation of Austria a complete repudiation of his evolutionary policy? Did he not spend four years trying to pacify the Austrian government to the point that it would see the advantages of union with the Reich? Even if he was sincere, what can be said about his methods? Perhaps Schuschnigg's cryptic comments on the reich ambassador made in 1967 are still an indictment of Papen's role in the *Anschluss*:

> In my judgement he accepted the maxim: "the end justifies the means" - in politics and in diplomacy. This explains... the ambiguous duplicity characteristic of his professional behavior. As to his background, he belonged to the German-national Catholics whose nationalism, perhaps even opportunism, overshadowed his basic conservatism.[118]

NOTES

[1] Article III of the Gentleman's Agreement, July 11, 1936, *DGFP*, ibid., No. 152.

[2] *Memoirs*, pp. 343-346. Papen recites a litany of historical reasons why Germany and Austria should be united. He justified the *Anschluss* on the romantic notion about the restoration of something like the Holy Roman Empire. Together, Germany and Austria would resume their historic role "as the main dike holding back the Slavic flood," (ibid., p. 346).

[3] Schuschnigg, ibid., p. 141. The Stresa Conference between Britain, France & Italy in April 1935, condemned Hitler's announcement that he no longer intended to abide by the military clauses of the Versailles Treaty. The three nations intimated that they would stand firm against further treaty violations.

[4] Papen's report to Hitler, September 1, 1936, *NCA*, Vol. IV, No. 2246-PS. Glaise-Horstenau was a leading representative of the National Opposition in Austria. He was in complete sympathy with the idea of the *Anschluss*. Appointed by Schuschnigg as Minister without Portfolio after the July Agreement, he remained in the cabinet as Vice Chancellor under Seyss-Inquart. In 1946 he committed suicide at Nuremberg when threatened with extradition to Yugoslavia. Cf. Schuschnigg, ibid., p. 334.

[5] It is not clear that Papen had a direct influence on the appointment of these "crypto-Nazis." However, if his report to Hitler on November 4, is accurate, Schuschnigg probably listened to his advice. In that report Papen maintained that Schuschnigg had postponed a meeting with him shortly after the cabinet shake-up: "...in order not to have the reorganization appear as under pressure of my representation." Report of the German Ambassador in Austria (Papen) to the Führer and Chancellor, November 4, 1936, *DGFP*, Ser C, Vol. I, No. 171, p. 314.

[6] Neustädter-Stürmer was a *Heimwehr* member of the parliament during Dollfuss' government. He became a minister in the Dollfuss cabinet. He also helped to mediate the free conduct agreement with the July conspirators. A victim of the purge of the cabinet in October 1935, he was then reappointed by Schuschigg in the November cabinet shake-up. This "crypto-Nazi" also advised Schuschnigg to come to terms with the Austrian Nazi party. But in 1937, when Schuschnigg was pressured by the clerical circles in the Fatherland Front to discontinue cooperation with the Nazis, Neustädt-Stürmer was dismissed.

[7] To what extent Glaise-Horstenau took orders from Germany can be seen in a conversation he had with the German Military Attaché in Vienna, Lieutenant-

General Muff. The Austrian minister remarked that he would not give up his position until he was expressly authorized or directed to do so by the Reich. Office Minute by Günther Altenberg, October, 1936, *DGFP*, Ser D, Vol. I, No. 166.

[8] Papen's report to Hitler September 1, 1936, *NCA*,Vol. IV, No. 2246-PS: "The proposed conference on economic relations...will be a very useful tool for the realization of some of our projects."   The response to this proposal came November 5, 1936: "We are primarily concerned with conducting the economic and political discussions in such a manner as to contribute indirectly towards furthering the...conversations regarding the political execution of the July 11 agreement." The German Foreign Ministry to the German Legation in Austria, *DGFP*, ibid.,No.172.

[9] Memorandum of Altenburg, Berlin, November 13, 1936, *DGFP*, ibid., No. 178.

[10] Meissner's memo, November 19, 1936, *DGFP*, ibid., encl. No. 181.

[11] Text of the Protocol, November 21, 1936, *DGFP*, ibid., No. 182. Austria also agreed not to participate in more extensive economic conditions in the Danube area without consulting Germany.

[12] Gehl, *Austria, Germany & the Anschluss*, p. 150

[13] Otto von Stein was a Nazi "plant" in the Vienna Legation. He was in constant contact with Leopold, providing him with directives and financial assistance from Berlin. Papen had no respect for Stein, claiming that he was unaware at the time of Stein's improper activities. No doubt Stein also served as an informer for the Foreign Office in Berlin. Ribbentrop and Papen were not on the best of terms, especially because of Papen's independent and direct contact with Hitler.

[14] Papen thought that Stein "followed a policy diametrically opposed to [his] own." *Memoirs*, p. 382. However, every indication points to the fact that both men were following similar courses of action to achieve an *Anschluss*. Their differences were limited to the personalities involved. Papen advised Schuschnigg to negotiate with the moderate element, which included Glaise-Horstenau, Reinthaller, and Seyss-Inquart, whereas Stein favored the radical group led by Leopold.

[15] Gehl, ibid., p. 152.

[16] On January 25, 1938, the *Teinfaltstrasse* office was the scene of a police raid in which a plan to overthrow the Schuschnigg government was discovered. Known as the Tavs Plan, because the plot was found among his papers, Tavs was arrested and charged with treason. However, he was never convicted, because the *Anschluss* took place less than two months later. Schuschnigg, ibid., pp. 165-167. Papen observed that among the papers was a plan to

assassinate either himself or the military attaché "...in order to provide an excuse for German intervention," *Memoirs*, p. 404.

[17] Schuschnigg to Seyss-Inquart, June 16, 1937, *GDA*, 1788/498158-159.

[18] Gehl, ibid., pp. 152-155. Seyss-Inquart was a successful Vienna lawyer. Like Schuschnigg, he was a Catholic intellectual, and shared the Chancellor's ideas about the historic need for an Austro-German partnership. In February 1938, he became Minister of the Interior. From March 12 to 14, 1938, he was Federal Chancellor, and then Reich Regent. From 1939 to 1940 he was Deputy Governor-General in Poland and then, until 1945, Reich Commissioner in the Netherlands. For his activities in the Netherlands he was condemned to death at Nuremberg on October 1, 1946.

[19] *Memoirs*, p. 395. Papen speculated that if Schuschnigg had taken Seyss-Inquart into his confidence "all might have been well." This would have worked to Papen's advantage. However, Schuschnigg thought that "this idea was incompatible with Austrian independence." Cf. Gehl, ibid., p. 163.

[20] This entire episode is another example of how Hitler would allow rivalries to develop between the various departments and personalities. The application of "divide and rule" might have reduced efficiency, but it strengthened his position by allowing him to play off one department or personality against the other.

[21] Papen to Hitler, January 12, 1937, *DGFP*. ibid., No. 196.

[22] In July 1937, a demonstration took place in Wels during a parade of ex-servicemen from both countries. Papen was in attendance, but left when he saw the growing confrontation. As the parade marched past the reviewing stand the Austrian band played the Austrian national anthem. The huge crowd sang the words to *Deutschland, Deutschland über Alles* - the melodies are the same. The Austrian police had to dispel the crowd by force. The Austrian Nazis reported the incident to Hitler who was furious about the suppression of the Nazi demonstration. Papen, *Memoirs*, pp. 397-98.

[23] Tschirschky and Kettler became targets of the Gestapo's dislike for Papen. Tschirschky refused to appear in Berlin on trumped-up charges of homosexuality, and fled to Switzerland. Von Kettler was not as lucky. Shortly before the *Anschluss* he disappeared, and his body was later found floating in the Danube, presumably murdered by the Gestapo.

[24] After assuming office, Seyss established contact with the moderate element in the Austrian Nazi party, and set about to arrange the gradual integration of the Nazis and the Fatherland Front.

[25] Papen's Report to Hitler, May 26, 1937, *GDA*, E/272610-1.

[26] Unsigned Memorandum on Göring-Schuschnigg meeting, October 3, 1936, *DGFP*, ibid., No. 169.

[27] Göring quoted in Brook-Shepherd, *The Anschluss*, p. 2, from an unpublished telegram, November 24, 1936, in the Austrian Foreign Office Archives.

[28] Revertera affidavit, *Schmidt Trial*, pp. 292-297.

[29] Schuschnigg, *Austrian Requiem*, p. 9.

[30] Papen's Report to Hitler, December 21, 1937, *DGFP*, Ser. D, Vol. I, No. 273.

[31] On the international front signs were not encouraging. Neville Chamberlain replaced Stanley Baldwin in May 1937, and gave a new impulse to the policy of appeasement. Mussolini's state visit to Germany in September strengthened the Rome-Berlin axis, and told Ribbentrop that if a crisis should arise in Austria, Italy would do nothing. With the solidarity of England and Italy lacking, Schuschnigg could expect no action from France.

[32] Papen to Hitler, ibid.

[33] Gentleman's Agreement July 11, 1936, Article X, "Procedure for Objections and Complaints," *DGFP*, Ser. D.,Vol. I, No. 152.

[34] Weizsäcker was a representative from the Foreign Office. Keppler was the Chief of the Central Party Office for economic questions. He was also authorized by Hitler to serve as a mediator between the Austrian Nazis and Schuschnigg's regime.

[35] Gehl, ibid., p. 157.

[36] As early as August 1936, the Austrian Foreign Ministry learned that Theo Habicht was once again busying himself with the Austrian question. On numerous occasions Papen complained about the interference of the Austrian Nazis, especially Leopold, who was constantly interfering in his [i.e. Papen's] efforts to bring about a peaceful *Anschluss*.

[37] Papen's report to Foreign Minister Neurath, September 1, 1937, *DGFP*, ibid., No. 251.

[38] Schuschnigg, *The Brutal Takeover*, p. 172. Schuschnigg demanded the dissolution of the illegal Nazi Party, and the fulfillment of all those obligations which, in the Austrian view, were still outstanding from the July Agreement.

[39] *Memoirs*, p. 409.

[40] Gehl, ibid., pp. 166-167.

[41] Papen's Report to the German Foreign Ministry, January 27, 1938, *DGFP*, ibid., No. 279; Papen, ibid., p. 404; Gehl, ibid., pp. 167-168. It is unlikely that anyone in the *Tienfaltstrasse* would have drawn up such a bold plot without someone in the German hierarchy knowing and approving of it. According to Zernatto, some of the captured documents contained the initials "R. H.," which he believed stood for Rudolf Hess, Hitler's Deputy. If Hitler knew of the plan there is no documentary evidence to prove this. Zernatto, ibid., pp. 182-185;

Schuschnigg's affidavit, November 19, 1945, *NCA*,Vol.V, Doc. 2995-PS, for details of the "Tavs Plan."

[42] On June 16, 1937, Schuschnigg had appointed Seyss-Inquart to the Federal State Council for the purpose of integrating the Nazi party and the Fatherland Front. Keppler had been sent by Hitler to resolve the differences between Leopold and Seyss-Inquart. Hitler recalled Leopold to Berlin in October 1937, and after criticizing Leopold for his intransigence, ordered him not to interfere with Seyss-Inquart's activities in any way. Cf. Keppler Memorandum, October 8, 1937, *DGFP*, ibid., No. 260.

[43] A full report of these demands can be found in Keppler's report to Neurath, February 2, 1938, *DGFP*, ibid., No. 282.

[44] Papen's Report to Hitler, February 4, 1938, *DGFP*, ibid., No. 284.

[45] *Memoirs*, p. 406.

[46] Ibid., p. 407. While the world did not require proof of his desire to see a peaceful *Anschluss* at that time, his reports stood him in good stead at Nuremberg, and probably contributed a great deal to his acquittal of the charges that he had cooperated in waging an offensive (aggressive) war.

[47] Ibid., pp. 433-437.

[48] Bullock, ibid., pp. 363-367. Blomberg was removed because of his "scandalous" marriage to a former prostitute. Commander-in-Chief of the Army, General Fritsch, was sacked on the trumped-up charge of homosexuality, and sixteen other generals were also dismissed. The plot to eliminate the two generals was arranged between Hitler, Himmler, and Göring. Hitler was irritated with Fritsch's opposition to his *KVVK], d, KD* policy expressed at a meeting in November 1937. Himmler despised Fritsch because he blocked his attempts to extend the power of the S.S. into the army. Göring was ambitious to replace Blomberg.

[49] *Memoirs*, pp. 407-408.

[50] Ibid. Once again, in assuming the role of the Apprentice, Papen pulled himself from the brink of disaster, and agreed to do the Sorcerer's bidding.

[51] Schuschnigg, *The Brutal Takeover*, pp. 178-179; Papen, ibid., p. 411.

[52] Mussolini told Schuschnigg that the Italian Foreign Minister in London was on the verge of an agreement with the British, and expected a successful outcome in about two weeks. Schuschnigg, ibid., p. 179.

[53] Ibid. According to Schuschnigg, there was little hope that the British or Italians would provide military support against a possible invasion by Hitler's *Wehrmacht*.

[54] In November 1937, the French Foreign Minister Yvon Delbos, conceded that France "had no essential objection to further assimilation of certain of

Austria's domestic institutions with Germany's..." Cf. Welczek's report, November 27, 1937, *DGFP*, ibid., No. 46.

[55] Later Schuschnigg accused Papen of failing to keep his word to provide an agenda for the meeting. Papen claimed that from the very beginning of the negotiations he had declined this request because He "felt there should be no limit to the matters discussed." Papen, ibid., p. 411. It doesn't seem probable that the Austrian Chancellor would have entered into negotiations without an agenda.

[56] Zernatto, ibid., p. 200.

[57] *Schmidt Trial*, p. 559 for the full text of the *Punktationen*.

[58] Schuschnigg, ibid., p. 181.

[59] Keppler visualized a gradual escalation of political demands culminating in an avalanche that would quickly sweep away all the clutter of treaty commitments in order to create a new situation and force Austria into the status of a satellite.

[60] Schuschnigg was unaware that in late January, the Nazis Rainer and Globocnik (subsequently *Gauleiter* of Vienna), both close associates of Seyss-Inquart, had gone to Berlin to present the demands of the Austrian Nazi Party.

[61] Mühlmann testimony, *Schmidt Trial*, p. 249.

[62] Seyss-Inquart testimony, *IMT*, Vol. XVI, p. 161. In his testimony at the Schmidt trial, Seyss-Inquart maintained that he had not been briefed about the Keppler plan. He said he told some friends (Dr. Rainer?) about the substance of the agreements contained in the *Punktationen*, and he assumed that Rainer would inform the Reich. (Seyss-Inquart testimony, *Schmidt Trial*, p. 338. This testimony is in conflict with the proven fact that Seyss was in continuous contact with Keppler, and therefore was certainly familiar with the outline of the Plan. Schuschnigg explains this apparent conflict by suggesting that Seyss might have left the detail work on the list to Rainer and Globocink. It is very likely that Seyss wanted to avoid tying his hands too soon in order to safeguard his role as mediator. Schuschnigg, ibid., p. 183.

[63] After receiving the information from Seyss, Rainer telephoned Berlin to inform Keppler. However, Keppler had already embarked for Berchtesgaden by train, and was scheduled to pass through Munich on February 11.

[64] *Memoirs*, p. 411. At Nuremberg, Guido Schmidt confirmed Papen's claim that he had no knowledge of the *Punktationen* worked out by Schuschnigg and Zernatto, and that Papen was very surprised when the terms were revealed at Berchtesgaden.

[65] Ribbentrop's testimony, *IMT*, Vol. X, pp. 218-219. According to Michael Bloch, *Ribbentrop A Biography*, the recently appointed Foreign Minister had very little to do with the Austrian affair. Bloch maintained that it was

Schuschnigg's minister, Guido Schmidt, and Papen who played the most important roles in this entire affair, pp. 163-165.

[66] Schuschnigg, *Austrian Requiem*, p. 11. The generals turned out to be von Keitel who had just been appointed to head the High Command of the *Wehrmacht*, von Reichenau, in command of the motorized forces stationed in Dresden, and General of the Air Force in Bavaria, Hugo Sperrle.

[67] Schuschnigg, *The Brutal Takeover*, p. 192.

[68] Both Schuschnigg and Papen have written an account of the Berchtesgaden meeting. On most of the essential points the two are in agreement. However, according to Schuschnigg, Papen's version tends to leave his involvement at the meeting in a more neutral position than he actually held.

[69] Schuschnigg, ibid. p. 193.

[70] Ribbentrop testimony, *IMT*, Vol. X, pp. 218-219. Papen omits any mention of his participation in this meeting.

[71] Schuschnigg, *Austrian Requiem*, p. 21.

[72] For the text of Hitler's draft proposals (Keppler protocol) see *DGFP*, ibid., No. 294. In his efforts to cover up his error in showing Seyss-Inquart the draft, Schuschnigg claims that the Keppler "protocol" bore no resemblance to the *Punktationen*. His claims are correct only insofar as the Keppler document spelled out in detail what the *Punktationen* laid down in principle.

[73] Keitel testimony, *IMT*, Vol. X, pp. 567-568; Schuschnigg, *Austrian Requiem*, p. 29.

[74] Schuschnigg found himself under considerable pressure, but his claim that Hitler's demands were a complete surprise is without any foundation; he was presented with his own concessions.

[75] Schsuschnigg, *The Brutal Takeover*, p. 198.

[76] Schuschnigg, *Austrian Requiem*, p. 25; Text of the final protocol, February 12, 1938, *DGFP*, ibid., No. 295.

[77] Ibid.

[78] Schuschnigg, *Austrian Requiem*, p. 27.

[79] Schuschnigg, ibid., p. 29; Schuschnigg to Papen, February 15, 1938, *DGFP*, ibid., No. 299.

[80] Stein's Report, February 17, 1938, *DGFP*, ibid., No. 306.

[81] Schuschnigg, ibid., p. 30.

[82] Telegram to the various Austrian missions, February 15, 1938, *DGFP*, ibid., enclosure in No. 322.

[83] Press release, February 15, 1938, *DGFP*, ibid., No. 298.

[84] Why did Schuschnigg agree to publish such a false picture of the meeting? One author suggests that he "was inhibited by his own dread of histrionics, by a quixotic desire to keep faith with the leader of the other Germany, by

uneasiness over his own role, and by the fear that the facts might arouse even more panic than patriotism among his countrymen." Gordon Brook-Shepherd, *The Anschluss*, p. 73.

[85] Papen to the German Foreign Ministry, *DGFP*, ibid., No. 309.

[86] Personal Adjutant of the Führer's Deputy to the Foreign Minister, February 16, 1938, *DGFP*, ibid., No. 304.

[87] For the text of Hitler's *Reichstag* speech see Baynes, *Hitler's Speeches*, Vol. 2, pp. 1407-1407.

[88] *Memoirs*, p. 422. In quoting Hitler's reference to Austria, Papen completely ignores the ominous warnings of the Führer which were made later in the same speech

[89] Ibid., p. 423. "The radical elements had got to be kept in check and it must be realized that from time to time Seyss-Inquart might even have to order the arrest of certain Nazis. *These measures hardly confirm the arguments of those who suggest that Hitler was already plotting the Anschluss by force*" (emphasis added).

[90] Memorandum of Keppler's trip to Vienna on March 3 to 6, 1938, *DGFP*, ibid., No. 335. Hitler had not ruled out force in the *Anschluss* issue. In reply to Keppler's question about the future of the *Hilfswerk Nordwest*, a para-military invasion force composed of Austrian Nazis and based in Germany, Hitler said he did not want to dissolve the unit yet since intervention by force was still a possibility.

[91] Schuschnigg's speech is printed in *Documents on International Affairs, 1931-1938* (Oxford University Press, for R.I.I.A., 1932-1941), Vol. II, 1938, pp. 53-62.

[92] *Memoirs*, p. 422.

[93] Papen to the German Foreign Ministry, February 25, 1938, *DGFP*, ibid., No. 325.

[94] Schuschnigg, *Austrian Requiem*, pp. 30-32; 34.

[95] Papen memorandum, February 26, 1938, *DGFP*, ibid., No. 327. In Paris the entire foreign affairs debate in the Chamber of Deputies was colored by Schuschnigg's firmness. Yvon Delbos, the Foreign Minister, described Austria's independence as "an indispensable element in the European balance," and one deputy was even moved to declare that "France's fate would be decided on the banks of the Danube." Cf. Brook-Shepherd, ibid., p. 103. *Memoirs*, pp. 424-425.

[96] It was true that Schuschnigg did have complete freedom of action. However, in light of his fears for Austria, one could hardly say that Hitler's screams for Keitel, the presence of Army officers, the Führer's threats that the Luftwaffe was not far from Vienna, etc., did not *in fact* inhibit his freedom.

[97] Papen memorandum, February 26, 1938, *DGFP*, ibid., No. 327.

[98] *Memoirs*, ibid.

[99] Schuschnigg, *Austrian Requiem*, pp. 36-37.

[100] *Memoirs*, p. 425. Papen maintained that the French Minister in Vienna, M. Puaux, proposed the idea of a plebescite to Schuschigg, who firmly denied this *The Brutal Takeover*, p. 225.

[101] Schuschigg, ibid., He decided the plebescite as a way of demonstrating the unequivocal determination of the Austrians to cling to independence.

[102] Schuschnigg, *Austrian Requiem*, pp. 37-38.

[103] Colonel Liebitzky, Austrian Military Attache in Rome, submitted this in his testimony at the *Schmidt Trial*, p. 223.

[104] Rainer Report, July 6, 1938, *DGFP*, ibid., No. 339.

[105] *Memoirs*, p. 426.

[106] Ibid., p. 427.

[107] Ibid. Papen recorded the meeting erroneously. Among those present were Neurath, Frick, Goebbels, Himmler, Generals Brautchitsch and Keitel.

[108] Ibid., p. 428.

[109] Transcript of telephone conversation prepared by Göring's *Forschungsamt*, *NCA*, Vol. V, Doc. 2949-PS; also cf. Schuschnigg, *Austrian Requiem*, pp. 41-55.

[110] Instruction No. 2 for Operation Otto, *NCA*, Vol. VI, Doc. C-182.

[111] *Memoirs*, p. 431.

[112] Ibid. Papen does not mention that he was also made a member of the Nazi Party. Although he never acknowledged the award and never wore the badge, he never gave it back either.

[113] During his first two years in Vienna neither Innitzer nor his bishops had received Papen, and had refused all invitations in protest against the Nazi persecution of German Catholics. After the July Agreement, however, a thaw in their relations set in, and Papen was on more or less good terms with the Austrian hierarchy.

[114] Papen testimony, *Schmidt Trial*, p. 133. Two days after Innitzer's meeting with Hitler, the Catholic bishops of Austria issued a statement praising the accomplishments of German National Socialism in the arenas of internal and foreign policy. They requested the faithful to approve the union between the two countries in the forthcoming plebescite. Schultess, ibid., No.79 (1938), pp. 80-81.

[115] Some of the most violent persecution - even more so than in Germany - against the Austrian Catholics was undertaken by the Nazi controlled government.

[116] Innitzer was made to sign a statement, published by *L'Osservatore Romano* on April 7. It stated that the earlier declaration of the Austrian bishops was not to be understood as an approval of what was incompatible with the laws of God; nor was it to be regarded as binding on the faithful.
[117] On April 10, when the ballot boxes were emptied, a majority of 99.73% in favor of Hitler was claimed. According to the official figures, 4,453,000 out of 4,484,000 had voted "yes" and a bare 11,929 had voted "no."
[118] Letter from Kurt von Schuschnigg to William Joseph Leavey, August 12, 1967. Quoted in Leavy, *Hitler's Envoy "Extraordinary*," p. 141.

CHAPTER 14:
MISSION TO ANKARA

A. Prelude to World War II

When Papen left Vienna in March 1938, he joined his family at Wallerfangen. He spent the next twelve months relaxing with his family, going on several hunting expeditions, and attending numerous social events. While he enjoyed being with his family freed from the pressures of responsibility, Papen moved restlessly between his estate in Wallerfangen and Berlin. Through daily newspaper and radio reports he carefully followed the course of events going on in the international world as well as in Germany itself.

In the meantime, Hitler's war plans were beginning to take shape. Now that Austria was united to the Reich, the next step in Hitler's *Lebensraum* policy was Czechoslovakia. The lever with which he planned to undermine the Czech republic was the existence inside the Czech borders of a German minority. As former subjects of the Hapsburg Empire, they had been separated from Austria under the terms of the Versailles Treaty after the First World War. The grievances of these Sudeten Germans and their traditional hostility against the Czechs was intensified by the rise of Nazi power across the border. Just as they had done in Austria, the German Nazis spread their ideas and organization among the Sudeten Germans, and secretly subsidized the Sudeten German Party under the leadership of Konrad Henlein.

Like most everyone else in Germany, Papen closely followed the events in the Sudetenland. On September 12, 1938, he listened to Hitler's explosive speech against Czechoslovakia demanding self-determination for the Sudeten Germans. Three days later he read in the newspaper that the British Prime Minister, Neville Chamberlain, was meeting with Hitler at Berchtesgaden. The diplomatic situation took a turn for the worse after Chamberlain's second meeting with Hitler in Godesberg. Europe appeared to be heading for war. As a reserve officer, Papen was notified by the military authorities that in case of war he would be called on to take command of a reserve regiment. Then, when Hitler met with Chamberlain, Mussolini, and the French Foreign Minster, Daladier, in Munich, on September 29 and 30, an agreement was reached that resulted in peace - at least for a time. Although Papen, who was still in the service of the Reich as an ambassador-at-large, had nothing to do with these negotiations, he did send the Führer a telegram begging him to reach an agreement with Great Britain. He also sent Chamberlain a long letter of congratulations, and described the great relief felt by the German people at the news of the compromise.[1]

However, Chamberlain's policy of appeasement did nothing but encourage Hitler to proceed with his expansionist aims. On the afternoon of March 13, 1939, one year and a day after the *Anschluss*, Papen heard over the radio that the German troops had marched into Prague. Two days later, on March 15, Hitler affirmed the claim of the Germans to the territories of Bohemia and Moravia. His revenge was complete - Czechoslovakia became the second victim of his *Lebensraum* policy.

With the disappearance of Czechoslovakia from the map of Europe, the winds of war swept northward towards Poland.[2] Adding to the tension was the invasion of Albania by Italian troops on April 7, 1939. Papen, who was in Dresden taking a cure at the time, received an urgent telephone call from Ribbentrop informing him of the Italian invasion. The inference of course, was that Papen should go to Turkey much the same as he had gone to Vienna five years earlier in order to mollify the Turks regarding their apprehensions over Mussolini's ambitions in the Mediterranean. Impatient to get back into action, he readily agreed to come to Berlin to get a clearer picture of the situation.[3]

When he arrived in Berlin, Papen met with Ribbentrop to discuss the effect of the Italian invasion on Turkish policy, and on the Anglo-Turkish treaty negotiations which were going on at the same time. After considerable "soul-searching," Papen agreed to accept the embassy post in Ankara. His recollections with regard to this decision are remarkably similar to the thoughts he recorded prior to his appointment to Vienna in 1934:

> Once more I was haunted by the reflections that had plagued me at Bayreuth in 1934, when after the murder of Dollfuss, I had been called to undertake the difficult mission to Vienna...After taking much advice I now came to the same conclusion - that a final effort, in which I would do my utmost to save Germany and the outside world from threatening catastrophe, would be better than to put on my old uniform and fight a hopeless war on the Siegfried Line.[4]

When questioned at Nuremberg, why he agreed to go to Turkey after all of the terrible things that had happened to him and his office assistants, Papen replied: "After March 15, the entry into Prague, we knew we were sitting on a powder keg. In this European problem, there were two possibilities of conflict, one was the Polish problem, where I could do nothing, the other was the Southeast problem, which had become acute...I felt that I could do something here and could contribute to the maintenance of peace in Europe."[5] Ribbentrop suggests a more practical reason for Papen's assignment: "The Führer sent Papen to Ankara on my advice. His instructions were to keep Turkey out of the war..."[6]

While Papen's decision to continue serving Hitler has been rightly criticized, one should remember his background. He was born and educated during the pre-war era of the Kaiser, when the highest form of patriotism was to applaud Germany's right to her "place in the sun." Unfortunately, this impaired his ability to distinguish between that expression of nationalism and Hitler's notion of *Lebensraum*. Added to these motives was his conviction that his earlier experiences in Turkey would be of invaluable service in the interests of the Fatherland.[7]

However, underneath this mantle of patriotism, and sincere, albeit misdirected, protestations that he "served the Fatherland but not the Nazis," existed an ambitious and incredibly self-confident personality who seized every opportunity he could to be an important player in the game.

B. Turkey, 1938-1939

Turkey's geographical location situated her at an extremely important crossroads between the West and the East. A country of twenty million, Turkey was situated at the meeting place of three great power blocs: the Axis powers overshadowing the Balkans to the west, the Soviet Union to the north, and the British and her allies who were predominant in the Arab world. Moreover, Turkey controlled vital lines of communication between these power blocs: the sea route between the Aegean and the Black Sea, whose control had been the source of serious controversy ever since the rise of Russia to a Great Power status in the eighteenth century; and the Bagdad Railway connecting the Balkans with the Middle East, whose construction had been an important factor in the events leading to World War I.

The Turkish government, which was established after the Kemalist revolution in 1921, was a one party, authoritarian system. Conscious of the pains with which she had been building up since the revolution, Turkey wanted to preserve the framework undamaged at all costs. Moreover, their experience during World War I made them profoundly distrusting of Great Power politics. And while they were ready to enter into alliances to protect their sovereignty and territorial integrity, they took great pains to provide for escape clauses in case the obligations incurred by the treaty should afterwards be found to conflict with the national interests. Masters at prolonged bargaining, Turkey was able to successfully walk a very thin diplomatic line between Allied pressures and German threats until the very last days of World War II.

In view of the events of 1938, Turkey's relations with Germany were extremely delicate. Under pressure from Germany to enter into closer political relations in exchange for more favorable commercial agreements, the Turks engaged in protracted negotiations leading to a trade agreement without political commitments.[8] However, in order to insure that her economic security, as well as her political independence, did not depend on Germany alone, Turkey concluded a trade agreement with the British.[9] Over the next five years, until the last two months of the war in 1944, the Turkish Government successfully negotiated commercial agreements in exchange for war materials with both Germany and the Western Powers. At the same time, through artful but effective bargaining, she was able to avoid any firm political commitment to either side.

For example, when Germany tried to draw Turkey into a closer political commitment through generous trade arrangements, the Turkish position pointed out to Ribbentrop in April, 1938, was "one of conciliation and neutrality towards all sides;" Turkey wanted to keep out of a coalition. This became quite clear to the German Foreign Minister in his discussions with the Turkish Ambassador, Numan Menemencioglu, in July 1938. The outcome of those meetings was summed up in a circular from the German Foreign Ministry to diplomatic missions on August 10, 1938: "The German-Turkish relations...were unchanged...Turkey still hesitates to give German-Turkish relations a new and more intimate form, at least at the present time."[10] During the next seven months Germany made no further effort to establish closer political relations with Turkey, but pursued a policy of building up economic relations as a basis for a continued Turkish guarantee of neutrality. It was Mussolini's occupation of Albania on April 7, 1939, that threatened Germany's relations with Turkey, and improved British efforts to draw Turkey into a closer political as well as economic commitment.[11]

When the news of the Italian invasion of Albania reached London, the British, fearing that Italy would move against Greece next, made it a matter of priority to ascertain whether Turkey would support the Greeks against an Italian attack. The Turkish Government responded to British inquiries that they wanted stronger assurances than England had initially offered.[12] After protracted negotiations, the British agreed to help Turkey against Italy in return for Turkish support if Britain were to get involved in a war with Italy.

Despite these assurances, Turkey was reluctant to abandon the status of neutrality prematurely or without reservations. As it turned out, the Turkish government agreed to publicly declare that they were following a policy in close sympathy with the British. Privately the Turkish Foreign Secretary, Saracoglu, assured Great Britain that Turkey would cooperate with the British in a general war, and not merely one limited to the Mediterranean and the Balkans.[13] The British regarded this reply as a basis for an arrangement which would be a valuable reinforcement of what was called the "peace front." Therefore, in the circumstances, Britain decided to encourage the Turkish government to concentrate on consolidation and enlargement of the Balkan Entente.[14]

German reaction to Britain's proposal to Turkey for a "peace" front came swiftly. The German Government interpreted this move as an attempt by the British to conclude an alliance with Turkey, and thus "encircle" the Reich. Therefore, the Foreign Office issued a circular to several European Embassy's soliciting reactions. Dr. Kroll, the Chargé in Ankara, replied that, "the Turkish Government's policy had not budged an inch" from the position which he had repeatedly explained to the Reich Foreign Minister, that is Turkey intended to remain neutral.[15] However, the Turkish Government was not exactly honest with Kroll. On March 31, the Turkish ambassador in London was engaged in serious negotiations with the British Foreign Ministry, while in Berlin, the Turkish ambassador continued to assume diplomatic innocence. He assured Ribbentrop that any rumors about Turkey adopting a favorable attitude towards British proposals were "without foundation."[16]

This "cat-and-mouse" game continued throughout the spring of 1939. While Germany tried to draw a reluctant Turkey into a closer relationship, the Turks balanced this off with efforts to get the British to provide them with a firmer commitment in case of a war with Italy. Meanwhile, Kroll warned the Foreign Office that further action by Italy in the Balkans "would inevitably drive Turkey into the ranks of our opponents." He urged Ribbentrop to get Rome to make a clear statement that Italy's policy in the Balkans, "...had no territorial ambitions." Such a declaration would strengthen Turkey's "neutral attitude."[17]

While Turkey played the "reluctant bride" role with Germany and the British, her relations with the Soviet Union in the prewar years, if not cordial, were not marked by any special crisis. Whatever "friendship" existed between the two countries was based upon a Treaty of Neutrality and Non-Aggression signed in 1923 and renewed in 1935 for a period of ten years. Just prior to the outbreak of World War II, the Turks had accepted a Russian proposal to begin negotiations for a mutual assistance pact.[18] However, after Hitler concluded a his agreement with Stalin, the Turks backed down from the Russian offer, and turned to Britain for support.

It was this very complex political situation that Papen faced on his arrival in Ankara. But, just like his assignment to Vienna, he relished the challenges, and was completely confident that he could fulfill the commission to keep Turkey neutral.

C. Duel for Turkey

Accompanying Papen on his arrival in Ankara on April 27, 1939, were his daughter Isabella, his secretary Fräulein Rose and his valet. After meeting with the German Chargé, and other members of the Embassy staff, Papen went that evening to meet with the Turkish Foreign Minister, Sükrü Saracoglu. He told the Turkish minister that the Axis powers wanted to settle all problems peacefully, and that Germany was opposed to the idea of a Turkish-British agreement. Only a policy of Turkish neutrality was acceptable, for which in return, the Reich was ready to provide armaments for Turkish defense.[19]

The next day Papen met with President Ismet Inönü. Both men agreed that friendly relations between the two countries was most desirable. Inönü expressed concern over Mussolini's invasion of Albania, and was particularly anxious to know why there were so many Italian "occupation forces" in such a small country. Obviously, the Turkish President interpreted this as a preparation for future invasions of other areas in the Balkans, particularly Greece. When Papen questioned Inönü about the agreement with Britain and France, the President replied that it still had to be ratified. The German Ambassador then requested Inönü to hold off the ratification until he had time to persuade Hitler to use his influence on Mussolini with a view to easing the situation. The President agreed to await the results of Papen's intervention.[20]

In these initial meetings, Papen enunciated the fundamental policy which he had been commissioned to pursue. However, during his five and one-half year assignment, he would encounter severe opposition to the manner with which he conducted his diplomatic activities. For one thing, his mission to Ankara operated under somewhat different rules than in Vienna. Papen did not have the "open wire" to Hitler that he enjoyed during his four years in Austria. All of his correspondence, telegrams and courier messages went directly to *Wilhelmnstrasse* in

Berlin and into the hands of Foreign Minister Ribbentrop. It was common knowledge that the relationship between Papen and Ribbentrop was anything but friendly, and time and again Papen incurred the wrath of his chief. However, Ribbentrop was not the only obstacle Papen faced in his post as Ambassador to Turkey. He was also under constant surveillance by the Gestapo, just as he had been in Vienna. Moreover, in his efforts to keep Turkey neutral, Papen faced persistent opposition from the British government, who was trying to persuade Turkey to join the Allies. Although he was no Bismarck, to his credit Papen did manage to juggle a number of glass balls, which resulted in Turkish neutrality until the very last months of the war.

When he left that first meeting with the President, Papen felt that he had not come too late to restore the situation. What he failed to realize was that the Anglo-Turkish negotiations were almost concluded. In fact, only two days after his arrival, Berlin learned from a "reliable source" that the British had offered, and the Turks had agreed, to enter a mutual assistance pact.[21]

The Anglo-Turkish Declaration of May 12 was a bitter blow for Germany. However, Papen refused to accept this announcement as a *fait accompli*. He meant to change Turkey's attitude before they committed themselves to a definite agreement with the Allies. The key to the problem, as Papen saw it, was Italy's Balkan ambitions. The day following the Declaration, Papen continued to express optimism in a telegram to the Foreign Ministry, "yesterday's Declaration formed the basis for a policy which could be changed at any time," Representing Italy as the villain, he concluded that Turkey put all the blame on Italy, "Germany is not mentioned at all."[22] Not satisfied that the Foreign Office fully understood, Papen decided to go to Berlin on May 15 to give a personal assessment of the situation.

When he arrived in the capital, Papen found himself caught up in the festivities that marked the signing of the "Pact of Steel" between Italy and Germany.[23] When Papen saw Ribbentrop, he handed him a memorandum entitled "The Military-Political Situation of Turkey and the Axis Powers." He hoped that the Foreign Minister would use this information in his conversations with Count Ciano when the Italian Foreign Minister came to Berlin to sign the Pact. The memorandum pointed out that "the Axis Powers must attempt to lead Turkey back to her previous attitude of strict neutrality," otherwise Germany could be faced in the event of war with a very unfavorable military-political predicament.[24] The report also contained Papen's military assessment if Turkey fought on the British side, and urged that if unwilling to alter her policies, at least Italy should "disguise the development of her position in Albania." In conclusion he observed that twenty years of hard work in building Germany's "powerful influence" in Turkey would be lost if "the Italian-Turkish tension cannot be relieved."[25] While Ribbentrop seemed to agree with Papen's ideas, he was unable to convince Ciano. The Italian Foreign Minister was able to convince Ribbentrop that Turkish hostility was also directed against Germany, and that Papen's view was erroneous.

Italy's refusal to go along with Papen's proposal made him aware that a new approach was necessary in order to retain good relations with Turkey. Before he left Berlin, he attended a high level inter-departmental conference, at which it was decided that if economic pressures on Turkey were applied, they would make her realize the folly of negotiating with the Allies.[26] After all, this tactic had been very successful in "persuading" Schuschnigg to reach an accommodation with the Reich in 1938.

Papen returned to Ankara in early June. Throughout the summer he was involved in frequent discussions with Saracoglu and Menemcioglu in order to persuade Turkey not to enter into a definitive agreement with the Western Powers. Moreover, while he assured them of Germany's peaceful intentions, he warned that any Anglo-Turkish Pact would "in the sphere of trade policy...take only our own (i.e., Germany's) interests into account."[27]

Papen's "softer" approach was countered by a much harder line coming from Ribbentrop in Berlin. The German Foreign Minister told the Turkish Ambassador, Arpag, that if Turkey was determined to pursuing an aggressive policy towards Germany, "...we would have to take note of this and act accordingly."[28] While the diplomats were bargaining for better positions, Hitler was gearing up for war. Throughout the summer of 1939, the remilitarization of Danzig, the training of the local SS and SA. with arms smuggled across the frontier, and a series of incidents designed to provoke the Poles, continued with little respite. In June Goebbels appeared in the city and made two violent speeches, reaffirming Germany's claims to its return.

Accompanying these activities, Ribbentrop and Hitler were planning to lure Stalin into a non-aggression pact. The basis for a deal was obvious. The last thing Hitler wanted was a two-front war - Russia in the East and France and Britain in the West. Stalin, on the other hand, saw the policy of appeasement exercised by the West a failure. He also distrusted the Western Powers, and suspected them of trying to embroil Russia in a war with Germany. He saw a deal with Germany as an opportunity to buy time, and possibly secure more important territorial and strategic advantages in Eastern Europe. These could be used to strengthen Russia against the day when Hitler would decide to attack Russia.[29]

On August 15, Papen received word of the death of his mother. The next day, accompanied by his daughter Stefanie, he left by plane for Germany. Following the funeral he went to see Hitler at Berchtesgaden to discuss the problem of economic relations with Turkey. Arriving at the *Berghof* on August 20, Papen was astounded to learn that Ribbentrop was flying to Moscow to sign a non-aggression Pact with the Soviet Union.[30] Startled by this news, Papen's first reaction was that peace was now secure. With Russia allied to Germany, Poland would have to come to some reasonable agreement over the Corridor problem.[31] This thought prompted Papen to congratulate Hitler on what he called "a brilliant diplomatic victory." Little did Papen know at that time, that the Führer had already determined to overrun Poland and divide the booty with Russia.

Papen returned to Istanbul convinced that the worst was over, and that he could now assure the Turks that the Pact with the USSR would contribute to a peaceful settlement of the German-Polish question.

* * *

On September 1, 1939, at 4:45 a.m., Hitler's forces invaded Poland. A depressed Papen heard the news on the radio at the Embassy in Ankara. Turning to his Secretary, Fräulein Rose, he said: "Mark my words, this war is the worst crime and the greatest madness that Hitler and his clique have ever committed. Germany can never win this war. Nothing will be left but ruins."[32]

It would seem that if he was so opposed to the war, Papen would have resigned his post and gone to a neutral country like Switzerland. Instead, he thought he was faced with several choices. He could protest to the world in general. But, he rejected this with the puzzling explanation that this "would indicate a moral weakening in Germany." He would also have to take at least temporary asylum in Turkey. He called this a "useless" move; probably because he would still be in danger of arrest from the Gestapo. He also argued that even the most burning patriots could do nothing to shorten the war or bring peace. His second choice would be to resign his post, put on his uniform, and lead his regiment. But he had already rejected this idea when he decided to go to Ankara. Therefore he opted for the third choice, which was to remain at his post in Ankara, using the same type of rationalization that allowed him to serve Hitler in Vienna: "Ankara...seemed to offer the best chance of deflecting the coming catastrophe." While he could do nothing to prevent the war, he thought he could try and limit the conflict by preventing Turkey from entering the war on either side.[33] And to his credit, from Germany's standpoint, he actually did mange to keep Turkey out of the war until the very end. On the other hand, his activities in Turkey hardly promoted peace.

When he returned to Turkey, Papen was relieved to learn that the Turkish Government was not greatly disturbed by the announcement of the German-Soviet Non-Aggression Pact. The reason was that Turkey had already contemplated entering into a bilateral agreement with Russia for mutual assistance before the outbreak of the war. The attack on Poland served to encourage the dialogue between Russia and Turkey to continue. For one thing, Stalin wanted to prevent Turkey from concluding an alliance with the West. As the "gate-keeper" of the Straits leading into the Black Sea, Turkey was able to permit or prohibit warships from passing through the Straits as long as she was a non-belligerent, "...or considered herself threatened by imminent danger of war."[34] The control of the Straits had been a serious security issue for Russia ever since the days of the Tsars. A friendship treaty with the "gate-keeper" would serve to block any threat from the British navy against the Soviet Union's southern ports on the Black Sea. With this consideration in mind, Moscow readily agreed to cooperate with Germany in working for the permanent neutrality of Turkey.[35] Through its Ambassador in Moscow, Germany also warned Molotov that the British were attempting to draw Rumania into an alliance. Therefore it would be wise if Russia pressured Turkey to close the Straits to British and French ships.[36]

Meanwhile, in a report to Ribbentrop, Papen suggested that Germany should take advantage of her early diplomatic and military successes, and influence Turkish foreign policy. The reason Turkey had entered into the agreement with Britain and France in May 1939,

Papen contended, was based on the assumption that the encirclement of Germany would lead to active participation by Russia. However, the conclusion of the German-Soviet Pact and the declaration of Italy's neutrality completely upset these assumptions.[37] Although Papen did not believe Turkey would renounce her commitments to the Western Powers, he still felt that with sufficient inducements, Turkey, in the long run, could be detached from her present commitment. As he saw it, Turkey could be brought within the framework of "natural relations" with the powers whose interests she is also "geographically" connected.[38]

The struggle by Germany and the Soviet Union to prevent Turkey from entering into an agreement with England and France continued throughout the months of September and October 1939. In Berlin, Ribbentrop continued to put pressure on Moscow to obtain from Turkey a treaty in which she would not permit any passage through the Straits of Anglo-French war material or troops.[39] In Moscow, Molotov demanded from the Turkish Foreign Minister, Saracoglu, that Turkey close the Straits, and that the Soviet Union would not become involved in hostilities under any circumstances.[40] In Ankara, Papen met with President Inönü and argued for Turkey's return to absolute neutrality. Papen also "advised" the President that under the present war conditions such a pact would be "viewed differently by Germany than before the outbreak of the war."[41]

Nevertheless, in spite of all these pressures, the Turkish Government concluded a mutual assistance pact with Britain and France on October 19, 1939. Perhaps the most important reason for Turkey's decision was that after months of negotiation, she was able to obtain generous commercial arrangements.[42] Later on, Papen would engage in a similar tactic in an effort to woo Turkey away from her alliance with the Allies.

When the war broke out in September, the Western Powers and Turkey were still trying to reach an agreement.[43] However, in the psychological atmosphere of the first weeks of war, the financial arrangements which had carried so much weight in London previously, were now replaced by political considerations. The Treaty of Mutual Assistance now seemed worth buying at a price not very much lower than what the Turks were demanding. Finally, seven weeks into the war, Britain, France and Turkey signed a Special Agreement on Financial and Economic Question, along with the Treaty of Mutual

Assistance.[44] Included in the Treaty was an escape clause, which provided that the Treaty was not to come into force until Turkey had been supplied with the war material that she needed to defend her borders.[45]

When Hitler was informed of the Treaty, he immediately summoned Papen to Berlin for a conference. When Papen arrived in Berlin, he found that he was in trouble on two accounts. He had failed to keep Turkey out of the allied bloc, and, against Ribbentrop's instructions, he had discussed peace plans with Hitler.

Papen's interest in a peace plan had its origins at the end of the Polish campaign; at the beginning of the period known as the *Sitzkrieg*, or "phony war." In several conversations with Dr. Philip C. Visser, the Netherlands Minister to Turkey, Papen discussed the possibility of finding a peaceful settlement to the war. He considered the lull in the fighting as an opportunity to try and find a way to prevent the extension of the war into the West. He told Visser of his plan, which included the restoration of an independent Poland, with the return of the western provinces to Germany; the re-establishment of Czech sovereignty; the recognition of the annexation of the Sudetenland to the Reich; German guarantees against any threat to the Balkan states and the Eastern Mediterranean. Visser replied that his government would be willing to act as intermediaries in presenting this plan to the British Government.[46] When Papen was informed by Visser that his Government was prepared to act as an intermediary, he informed Ribbentrop, who turned down the entire project.[47]

The Dutch Minister's conversation with Papen in early October was part of a whole series of peace maneuvers going on in the neutral capitals of Europe after the collapse of Poland.[48] Hitler himself actually gave the impetus to a "peace offensive." On September 26, in an interview with a Swedish businessman, Berger Dahlerus, he listed the conditions whereby Germany would be willing to bring an end to the war. "The British can have peace if they want it," the Führer told Dahlerus, "but they will have to hurry."[49] Again in a *Reichstag* speech on October 6, Hitler proposed peace to both France and Britain. Every paper in Germany at once broke into headlines: "Hitler's Peace Offer. No war aims against France and Britain. Reduction of armaments. Proposal of a conference." As propaganda, it was a well-conceived deception since there was not one single concrete proposal other than - by implication - general recognition of Germany's conquests. His main purpose in making the speech seems to have been to convince the German public that if the war continued, it was not his fault. When Chamberlain and Daladier rejected the peace offer, Hitler had his alibi.[50]

In the meantime, encouraged by all of these peace signs, Papen decided to broach the subject of peace with Hitler when he returned to Berlin. However, when he arrived in Berlin on October 18, he received a message from Ribbentrop that he was not to discuss any peace plans with Hitler under any circumstances. In spite of this order, Papen had a long discussion with Hitler about the possibility of initiating peace moves through the mediation of the Dutch Government. Hitler's only reaction was to request Papen to meet with him again after the Ambassador returned from a visit to his family in the Saar.[51]

Ribbentrop, however, was furious when he heard of Papen's flagrant disregard for his orders. In a rage, he circulated an order forbidding any official in his ministry to receive Papen or engage him in any political discussions.[52] When Papen returned to Berlin he had another meeting with Hitler, in which he bitterly complained about Ribbentrop's "ridiculous order." The Führer told Papen not to take the matter too seriously. Somewhat calmed, Papen plunged into the details of a plan that he had received from the Dutch Ambassador Visser, and which the Dutch had proposed to Great Britain as well. Hitler's response quickly crushed all of Papen's hopes: "No my dear Herr von Papen, such an opportunity to revise the Peace of Westphalia will never present itself again. We must not be deterred now."[53] Then after listening to a rambling monologue about Germany's rightful position in Central Europe, Papen left the chancellery completely disillusioned. He realized that Hitler was not interested in peace.

When Papen saw Ribbentrop he was even more depressed. The Foreign Minister told him that the letter sent by the Queen of the Netherlands, offering to serve as a mediator in peace talks, "would not even be answered." Upset by this bit of news, he went to see Göring. The Reich Marshal told him that Ribbentrop and Hitler had made up their minds to have it out with Britain, and then added that he (Göring) favored ending the war. With this response, Papen left for Ankara realizing that the "peace offensive" had collapsed.[54] There would be other times and other occasions in which he claimed that he tried to bring about an end to the hostilities, but without success.

Before he left Berlin, however, Papen was given written instructions from Ribbentrop calling for a "new line of action" vis-à-vis Turkey. The Ambassador was to inform Saracoglu that "despite previous warnings" Turkey had concluded a pact with England and France for the purpose of encircling Germany. Germany considered this a grave violation of a neutral and an intentional affront to Germany.[55] Papen was to warn the Turkish Government that "the German Government must reserve the right to take the measures it sees fit should the treaty just concluded lead to practical consequences against Germany."[56]

After Papen delivered this veiled threat to Saracoglu, he had a conversation with the Soviet Ambassador, in which they discussed the possibility of a forced entry into the Bosporus by the British. In his report to Berlin, Papen urged joint German-Soviet large scale operations against England in the spring "for the purpose of reducing British influence in the Balkans and restoring German prestige in Turkey."[57] Thus, in a rather amazingly short period of time, Papen apparently got over his disappointment that his peace proposal was not well-received in Berlin. Like the Führer, he was equally adept at speaking of peace to the neutrals and expressing quite militant sentiments to the Foreign Office.

On April 9, 1940, Hitler's *Blitzkrieg* rolled through Denmark, seized the capital, and launched paratroopers against Norway. Within forty-eight hours Norway was under effective German control. Then on May 10, the *Wehrmacht* struck the Low Countries with full force. By the end of May the German Panzer units had rolled victoriously over Luxembourg, Holland, and Belgium, and fought dogged British and French rear guard units to the beaches of Dunkirk, where 340,000 managed to escape, thanks to the intrepidity of the British small craft that took them off the beach to the British Isles. Although this was a disappointment for the Germans they had no time to dwell on it. Without a perceptible pause the Panzer divisions pierced the crumbling French front on the Somme, bypassed the Maginot Line, and broke the spirit of a brave French army. On June 22, 1940, a reconstituted government signed the armistice, and France was out of the war.[58]

Meanwhile in Ankara, after delivering his *démarche* to Saracoglu, Papen decided to pursue his own line of action in an effort to improve the Reich's relations with Turkey. While he could do nothing about halting Ribbentrop's "power politics," Papen continued to pursue his "evolutionary" tactics with some success. Taking a cue from the British, he was convinced that the duel for Turkey could best be won on the economic front. Therefore, he spent the next seven months waging an incessant campaign with the Foreign Office to conclude an economic agreement with Turkey.[59] During those months of tireless negotiations, Papen was opposed by Ribbentrop, and frustrated by the procrastination of the Turkish government which was counseled by the British not to do business with Hitler.[60] Nevertheless, Papen doggedly pursued his goal and finally, aided by the spectacular military successes of the German war machine, Papen concluded a new commercial treaty with Turkey on July 25, 1940, after the collapse of France.[61]

Although Papen's ability to reach an agreement with the Turks was a victory, the British and French continued to be Turkey's principal customers and suppliers. By June 1941, Germany's share in Turkish trade had dropped from about fifty percent before the war to about ten percent.[62]

Meanwhile two other events in 1940 challenged Papen's diplomatic efforts to keep Turkey neutral. On June 10, 1940, Italy entered the war, thus facing Turkey with the problem of her obligation under the terms of her alliance with the Western Powers. But, an even more serious threat to Papen's mission was Italy's attack on Greece on October 28, 1940.

In May 1940, Papen had drawn up a comprehensive political report for the Foreign Office on the subject of "Italy's entry into the war and Turkey."[63] Papen stated that "...the desire of leading [Turkish] political circles to keep out of the conflict grows with the increase of German victories." Turkey would remain neutral, Papen continued, "...if Italy can be kept out of the Balkans, particularly Greece and Yugoslavia." Papen also suggested strong Russian pressure in order to force Turkey to withdraw from her obligations to the Western Powers. He concluded his report with a promise that his office would continue to "intimidate" the Turks.[64]

True to his word, Papen warned the Turks that a war between Turkey and Italy would bring Germany in on the side of her ally.[65] Papen's tactics worked. The Turks decided to hide under Protocol No. 2 of the Anglo-French Treaty, which allowed her to remain neutral in any threat of war in which the Soviet Union was involved. On June 13, 1940, Papen reported that "the game has been won. . . . The Council of

Ministers sees no reason for entering the conflict because of Italy's declaration of war."[66]

Papen had scarcely managed to obtain Turkey's assurances to remain neutral when another crisis occurred. This time the issue centered around Bulgaria and the Italo-Greek war. Once again, the question of Turkish neutrality was tested. Papen seemed confident that as long as Bulgaria stayed out of the conflict, Turkey would remain neutral. One hopeful sign of this, was the conclusion of a non-Aggression Pact between Bulgaria and Turkey on February 17, 1941.[67] When Papen discussed this treaty with Saracoglu, the Foreign Minster replied that he was very satisfied with it, and thought of it as a "...convenient weapon against English pressure."[68]

Meanwhile, Mussolini's adventure in Greece had become a dangerous liability. The Italian attack had led to the British sending troops from Egypt to aid the stubborn defenders. Although at first Hitler had resisted the idea of entering a Balkan war, the presence of British troops plus Mussolini's inability to defeat the Greeks, prompted the Führer to change his mind.[69]

However, between Germany and Greece lay four countries - Hungary, Yugoslavia, Rumania and Bulgaria - whose compliance had to be secured before Hitler could reach the Greek frontier. Hungary and Rumania had already accepted the status of German satellites, and German troops had been moving across Hungary and into Rumania throughout the winter. In Bulgaria a sharp struggle for influence took place between Germany and Russia. The Germans won, and on the night of February 28, 1941, German and Rumanian forces crossed the Danube into Bulgaria. The next day Bulgaria signed the Tripartite Pact.[70]

Before the German troops marched into Bulgaria, Ribbentrop instructed Papen to explain to Saracoglu that a personal letter of explanation from Hitler to the Turkish President was on its way.[71] On March 4, 1941, İnönü received a letter from the Führer, in which he explained that the German troop movements into Bulgaria were not directed against Turkey. Hitler promised that his troops would not go near the Turkish border. He also assured İnönü that Germany had no territorial ambitions in the Balkans.[72] In his reply to Hitler, the Turkish President confirmed Hitler's resolve to invade Greece and Yugoslavia without heeding any advice from Turkey.[73] Papen attempted to dispel İnönü's doubts about Hitler's promises by stating that he would not retain his post for another hour if he were not convinced that "on this occasion he intended to keep his word."[74] For one of the few times in his life Hitler did keep his word. On April 6, 1941, German divisions operating from Bulgaria began the invasion of Greece. On April 22, the British troops began their evacuation. On April 23, the Greeks, after six months of heroic resistance, were forced to capitulate. By the beginning of May, the Balkan wars, started by Mussolini, had ended in a German victory.

The suddenness with which the German armed forces swept through Yugoslavia and Greece furnished Papen with the perfect psychological moment to pressure the Turks into a new and more advantageous agreement.[75] However, before Papen was able to propose a new agreement with Turkey to the Foreign Office, Hitler requested him to join him in his special train located near Vienna. Ostensibly the reason was to take part in the negotiations between Hitler and King Boris of Bulgaria concerning certain territorial demands the Bulgarian monarch made as a reward for aiding Germany against Yugoslavia. After this brief meeting in which Papen defended Turkish interests over and against Bulgarian demands, he went on to Berlin.[76]

Although he intended to return to Ankara after meeting with Hitler and King Boris, Papen was called to Berlin by Ribbentrop to discuss how to ensure a continuing supply of chromium from Turkey. However, during his one month stay in Berlin, Papen had a series of meetings with various Turkish and German officials concerning the current situation and discussions about the future relationships between the Reich and Turkey. One of the more important topics discussed was a proposal to enter into a friendship agreement with Turkey. Naturally, both Hitler and Ribbentrop were interested in such a treaty, especially since the Führer was in the final stages of planning the attack against Russia. A non-aggression pact with Turkey would protect Germany's southern flank when the attack against the Soviet Union came in June.[77] Papen claims that he knew nothing of "Operation Barbarossa" (the code name for the invasion of Russia), until the attack actually began on June 22.[78] However, there is some evidence that indicates he was fully cognizant of the impending operation against the Russians, probably as early as December 1940, almost certainly during his long stay in Berlin in April 1941.[79]

Armed with this knowledge, Papen was anxious to reach a new agreement with Turkey, before "Operation Barbarossa" got underway.[80] With little time remaining, Ribbentrop was also anxious to conclude a treaty with Turkey. Therefore, in spite of his annoyance with Papen for what he called "interference in my job," he authorized the Ambassador to enter immediately into negotiations with the Turkish government for the purpose of concluding a non-aggression pact.[81] Among the instructions Papen received was a secret protocol that would allow German arms and materials to pass through Turkey escorted by German troops.[82] As the zero hour for Operation Barbarossa drew closer, Ribbentrop and Papen continued to argue over the terms of proposal. The Foreign Minister insisted that no agreement could be signed, which mentioned in any way Turkey's obligations to Great Britain. Realizing that Saracoglu would never sign a pact which conflicted with other Turkish commitments, Papen insisted that there be a specific mention in the treaty of "current obligations."[83] Finally, in a flurry of telegrams to the Foreign Minister on June 12, 13, and 14 to withdraw his objections, Ribbentrop gave approval to Papen to sign the treaty of friendship. The Treaty pledged mutual respect for the integrity and inviolability of their territories; they also agreed to consult one another on all questions affecting their common interests; the treaty was to remain in force for ten years.[84]

Papen believed that the main argument he used to convince Ribbentrop to sign the treaty was summed up in one sentence: "I remain firmly convinced that once the first step is made, we will be confronted with an entirely different situation in the autumn."[85] This seems to be a reference to the expected success in the forthcoming Russian campaign, which was only ten days away. This is also another reason to question Papen's statement that he knew nothing of the Russian campaign until it actually took place on June 22, 1941. Nevertheless, Papen had brought about a diplomatic coup. The Treaty was interpreted by the West, especially after the June 22 attack on the Soviet Union, as Hitler's insurance policy against an attack on his southern flank.[86]

The German invasion of the USSR opened an entirely new avenue of approach for Papen in his diplomatic approaches to Turkey. Instead of just trying to improve Germany's economic relations with Turkey, Papen now sought to persuade the Turkish Government to join the Axis. Over the course of the next sixteen months, therefore, he did his utmost to fan the traditional fears of the Soviet Union. As far as his own personal opinion was concerned, Papen was delighted to see the

Soviet Union on the "other side." As an ardent Catholic, Papen vigorously opposed atheistic communism; he could now look at the war as a crusade. Unfortunately, every diplomatic success he was able to achieve in Turkey meant a success for Hitler's *Lebensraum* policy. But, he was blind to this reality, and continued to do the bidding of the Sorcerer.

One of the first issues to face Papen in the new atmosphere of Turkish-German relations was the question of the passage of Soviet ships through the Straits. Ribbentrop instructed Papen to persuade Saracoglu to refuse permission for Soviet warships and merchant vessels to pass through the Straits.[87] After a series of meetings with the Turkish Foreign Minister, and numerous communications with the Foreign Office in Berlin, Papen was able to persuade the Turks to prohibit the passage of Russian warships through the Straits, but they refused to impose the same prohibition on merchant ships.[88]

In other areas during the early stages of the Soviet offensive, Papen did all in his power to nourish Turkey's pro-German attitude. One way was to point out that Turkey's own interest in the elimination of the Bolshevik system naturally brought her over to the German side. He also suggested that the Reich should permit Turkey to take the initiative in a peace proposal to England in the event of a German victory over Russia. The advantage in allowing this, Papen argued, would be that if England refused any peace offer through Turkey, the Turks could more easily give up their alliance with England, and develop a closer friendship with Germany.[89]

Ribbentrop would have nothing to do with this proposal. He informed Papen that Germany would not make a peace offer either through the Turks or otherwise. Moreover, the idea of using Turkey as a mediator with respect to England in order to entice her into the German camp was "illusionary." The only effective way to accomplish this was through the use of "power politics."[90] In his rebuttal, Papen argued that the war against Russia had created an entirely new situation in Europe, "the problem of the destruction of Bolshevism had created for the first time a United European Front." Power politics was not the answer, but rather a "wise exploitation of our position of power combined with diplomatic accommodation" to secure for Germany the most important position in the Near East "without striking a blow."[91] In addition, Papen argued, there were definite military advantages to this tactic, viz., the neutralization of fifty Turkish divisions, which would be essential if, after the Russian campaign, a final attack on Egypt were to be launched from there. The only way this objective could be reached was through diplomacy. Papen finished his report with a threat to resign if Ribbentrop thought he was not doing his job as Ambassador to Turkey.[92]

Ribbentrop backed down a little from his previous position, and stated that he did not mean to challenge Papen's diplomatic skill. However, he stubbornly insisted that Papen's proposal was too idealistic. With a more realistic view towards Turkish ambitions, Ribbentrop argued that the Reich's position of power in southeastern Europe, along with offers to the Turks of new territories after the defeat of the Russians, would win them over more easily than Papen's "soft" policies. He also repeated his warning that no peace feelers with respect to England were to be undertaken.[93]

In the meantime, the duel for Turkish loyalty had not abated as a result of the German invasion of Russia. On the contrary, Ankara was a hot-bed of intrigue, spying, and double-dealing. For example, the Soviet and British ambassadors presented their reassurances to the Turkish Government that they had "no aggressive intentions or claims whatever with regard to the Straits." Moreover, they were prepared to "scrupulously observe the territorial integrity of the Turkish Republic." Finally, they were prepared to "render every help and assistance in the event of their being attacked by a European Power."[94]

These assurances combined naturally caused the Turks to be more cautious about a commitment to Germany. However, this was not the only impediment in Papen's efforts to win Turkey over to the Axis cause. Two other events that occurred in the final days of 1941 made his task even more difficult. On December 3, 1941, President Roosevelt announced that the defense of Turkey was vital to the defense of the United States. Therefore, he had directed the Lend-Lease Administrator, Earl R. Stettinius, to see to it that the Turkish defense needs were filled as fast as possible.[95] Papen, who had been made aware of the Lend-Lease program by Saracoglu, reported to the Foreign Ministry that even though Turkey had become a full member of the American Lend-Lease arrangement, she would not move "one inch away from the policy which is dictated by Turkey's own well-understood interests."[96] The other event that would have a shattering effect on Papen's mission to Ankara was the United States entrance into the War on December 7, 1941.

D. Tangled Webs and Crooked Trails

Papen's first two and one-half years in Ankara, if not crowned with complete success, were noteworthy in many areas. Not only was he able to keep Turkey out of the war, but he managed to conclude the German-Turkish Treaty of Friendship. Coming as it did just five days prior to the Nazi attack on Russia, it guaranteed Germany's southern flank from attack. However, when the Hitler attacked the Soviet Union, Berlin's policy of keeping Turkey neutral shifted to a policy of bringing Turkey into the Axis camp.

While Papen was optimistic about his chances of winning the Turks over to the Axis, he was also aware of the obstacles that stood in his way. The entrance of the United States into the war, the extension of the Lend-Lease Law to Turkey, the beginning of military defeats in eastern Europe and Africa, and the continual pressures on Turkey to adhere to the agreements with Great Britain were among the more difficult challenges testing Papen's diplomatic skills. Added to this were his disagreements with Ribbentrop over the tactics used to win the Turks to the Axis cause. The Foreign Minister favored "power politics" as a means of forcing Turkey into an alliance with Germany, as opposed to Papen's "evolutionary" approach. This feud resulted in sending conflicting signals to the Turkish Government, who naturally took advantage of this in its negotiations with the Reich. One other annoying obstacle for the Ambassador was the interference of the Gestapo in his diplomatic activities. Papen had run into the same problem in Austria. Most, if not all, of the embassy staff were members of the Nazi Party; how many of them also acted as spies for Himmler is unknown. The same cannot be said of Bohle's *Auslandsorganisation*. Bohle was the author of many reports sent to the Foreign Office which Papen charged were unreliable and often created unnecessary and even harmful duplication.[97] One other, but more serious interference came from Dr. Victor Friede, the Nazi Party head in Turkey.[98] In the summer of 1942, at a Nazi party meeting, Friede allegedly attacked Papen and even suggested that he be shot or at least sent to a concentration camp![99] When Papen appealed to Berlin to have Friede recalled he was told the matter was pending.[100]

Papen knew most of his opponents within the German colony, and was able to keep an eye on them. His experience with tactics of intimidation, threats, and even murder had taught him to be extremely careful. However, he was not prepared for what happened to him on February 24, 1942. On that morning about 10 a.m. Papen, accompanied by his wife, was walking as usual from his home to the Embassy. As the couple walked along the Attaturk Avenue their casual conversation was violently interrupted by a loud explosion a short distance behind them hurling both of them to the ground. Papen described the scene:

> ...I picked myself up immediately, then helped my wife, who was somewhat shaken, to her feet, noting with some satisfaction that no bones seemed to be broken.. 'Don't go a step further,' I shouted. I could only assume that we had set off a mine. . . . at this moment a taxi stopped near us. I shouted to the driver to go to the Embassy and ring the police. . . . Members of the excellent Turkish security service were soon on the spot and began a detailed investigation.[101]

The only injury the Ambassador incurred was a cut knee and a torn trouser leg. However, the noise and force of the explosion injured his eardrum which continued to give him some discomfort for several weeks. His wife, Martha, was unhurt, but the back of her dress was stained with blood from what Papen presumed was that of the vanished assailant.[102]

When news of the attempted assassination became known, rumors and accusations spread like wild-fire. Ribbentrop charged that it was the work of the British Secret Service with the cooperation of the Bolsheviks.[103] The British and Russians accused the Gestapo. Meanwhile, the very efficient Turkish police undertook a thorough investigation, and announced on March 5, 1942, that the person who happened to be behind the Papens and was torn to bits by the explosion was not a woman as first believed, but a man who was carrying the bomb wrapped in a cloth. The man was identified as Omer Tokat, a Macedonian Communist. His accomplices were communist natives of Yugoslavia. They were arrested, and from their interrogation it appeared that "certain foreigners in Ankara and Istanbul had been plotting against two personalities of a foreign power," one of whom was the German Ambassador von Papen.[104]

On the night of March 5, the Turkish police raided the Soviet non-diplomatic offices in Ankara and demanded of the Soviet Consul-General the surrender of a suspect who was hiding out in the Consulate. On his refusal, the police threw up a cordon around the Consulate with the threat that they would force an entry if the suspect was not handed over within forty-eight hours. Within three hours of the deadline the suspect was turned over to the police for trial.[105]

After completing their investigation, the Turkish authorities had rounded up four suspects, two Russians and two Turks of Macedonian origin.[106] Even before the trial opened on April 1, the Soviet Embassy exerted strong pressure on the Turkish Government to have the two Russians released, claiming that the entire affair was a "frame-up" by the Germans. *Pravda* published an article on April 5, declaring that there had been no attempt on Papen, but instead a "manifest and insolent" Nazi attempt to pervert Turkish justice.[107] During the next two and one-half months and twelve hearings, the Soviet press continued to publish a stream of offensive propaganda, while the Soviets, attempting to intimidate the Turkish Government, called the trial an "unfriendly act." In spite of this pressure, however, the trial continued. On June 17, the court found the accused guilty, and sentenced the two Russians to twenty years in prison and the two Turks to ten years.[108]

While the attempted assassination left Papen with an injured eardrum for several weeks, it did not dampen his efforts to win Turkey over to the Axis camp. In spite of incidents like the explosion, Ribbentrop's recalcitrant attitude, and the annoying interference of Nazis like Bohle and Friede, Papen stuck to his guns. While other factors certainly aided Papen in his efforts to reach an agreement with Turkey, his role between 1942 and 1944 cannot be over-emphasized. Through patient, skillful diplomacy and flexibility, Papen was able to influence the Turks to conclude three successive trade agreements. By early 1944, Germany was receiving four times more exports, including chromium, from Turkey than Great Britain.

Aiding Papen in these diplomatic successes was his understanding of the Turkish mind and the political circumstances in which Turkey found herself. To the allies, Turkey rationalized that she was receiving supplies from Germany that would provide her with the ability to resist a German attack. The armaments received would also deprive Germany of valuable equipment and therefore help the allied military cause. In fact by 1943, the fear of German attack against Turkey had all but disappeared. However, as the Allied forces continued to be victorious, Turkish fears of the Russian colossus increased. Thus the military supplies Turkey received from Germany in return for chromium were looked upon as defenses against a Russian attack. Thus partly from fear of a Russian attack, partly from economic policy, and no doubt, partly from greed, Turkey continued to trade in both camps. Papen had a strong appreciation and understanding of this Turkish attitude, and felt confident that he could win them over by exploiting all of these desires. Until the battle of el-Alamein in October 1942, and very soon afterwards at Stalingrad, Papen's expectations appeared to be coming to fruition. However, as the tide of battle began to favor the Allies the tone of Turkish opinion seemed to quickly adjust itself to the new circumstances.

In November 1942, Churchill had entertained hopes of bringing Turkey into the war by the following spring. In the course of the Casablanca Conference, held in January, 1943, Churchill said that if the Turks remained recalcitrant he would be prepared to tell them that if they did not come into the war he would not try to control the Russians in the Dardanelles.[109] Also at Casablanca, President Roosevelt gave Churchill primary responsibility in "playing cards" with Turkey. This in effect gave the British a relatively free hand in dealing with the Turkish attitude toward the war.[110]

Following Casablanca, Churchill met with the Turkish prime minister, Saracoglu, at Adana on January 30-31, 1943. The British Prime Minister proposed that Turkey assume the same position the United States had before Pearl Harbor, viz., "a departure from strict neutrality." Under such an arrangement Turkey could permit the use of her airfields from which the allies could bomb the oil fields in Rumania as well as the enemy-occupied Dodecanese Islands and Crete. While Turkey appeared to be interested in this proposal, she also expressed fears of future Soviet policy. Churchill assured the Turkish minister that if Turkey became a full partner of the allies in the war, the strength of an international organization (Roosevelt's pet program) would keep Russia in line, and she would receive the fullest aid and have the right to all guarantees for her territory after the war. At the conclusion of the meeting, these results were embodied in a military agreement.[111]

However, just when the Allies thought they had won Turkey over to their side, the Turks suddenly did an about face. When the British

Air, Army, and Naval Commanders-in-Chief visited Ankara in February 1943, to discuss the details of the military agreement concluded at Adana, the Turks showed an "inability and unwillingness" to produce any reliable estimate of their civil or military needs.[112] One of the main reasons for this change of heart stemmed from Papen's assurances to the Turks that Germany had no aggressive intentions against Turkey. Again, after March 5, 1943, when Papen returned from one of his visits to Berlin with further messages of assurances from Hitler, the British negotiators experienced even more difficulties.[113] The British suspected that Papen had threatened the Turks with an aerial bombardment against Istanbul, which would have been catastrophic because of its largely wooden structures and huge population.[114] Whatever the reason, by spring the Turks had drawn back into their shell, and the word "neutrality" again appeared.

Another set-back for the Allies was the surrender to the Germans of the garrisons on the Dodecanese Islands, and the evacuation of Samos and the minor islands. This military defeat at Turkey's doorstep even further diminished her desire to enter the war. In reply to the British threats of a blockade if they did not join the Allies, the Turks insisted on adequate defense against large scale German attack. Anthony Eden summed up the Turkish position: "In principle the Turks accepted their country's entry into the war, but in practice they refused to move until the military implications had been cleared up."[115]

About this time, mid-November 1943, Papen came into a new source of information that became one of the most sensational spy stories to come out of the war. Given the code name "Operation Cicero" by Papen, an Albanian citizen, Elysea Bazna, the valet to the British Ambassador, regularly opened Knatchbull-Hugessen's safe, photographed top-secret papers, and sold them to the German Embassy.[116] A representative of the Gestapo in the Ankara mission, L. C. Moyzisch, served as the German contact for Cicero. Although the stolen material should have been passed through Gestapo channels to Berlin, Papen was successful in having most of the material pass through his hands before it was sent on to Berlin.[117] From November 1943 through February 1944, the information passed on to Papen from Cicero could have been invaluable had it been used judiciously by the German High Command. However, Ribbentrop regarded the flood of information as an attempt by the British to mislead the German government, and therefore ignored it.

Despite Berlin's skepticism, Papen was able to utilize the information to further his own objective of keeping Turkey out of the war. For example, he was aware of the decision reached at the Foreign Minister's meeting in Moscow, October 18 - November 2, 1942, at which they decided to compel Turkey to declare war by the end of the year. Papen also learned that this information was communicated to the British Ambassador in Ankara on November 19, and the Ambassador's reply, which said in part that Turkey's entry in the war might take place within two weeks of the Allied landings in Western Europe.[118]

Cicero information was also helpful to Papen after the Teheran Conference of November 28 - December 1, 1943. At that Conference it was decided to conduct the Second Front in the west, and not through the Balkans as Churchill had recommended.[119] It was also agreed that Turkey should come into the war by the end of the year - "...if necessary by the scruff of the neck," Stalin added.

As a result of this decision, President İnönü was invited to a conference with FDR and Churchill in Cairo lasting from December 4-6, 1943. Presented with the decision made at Teheran, İnönü said Turkey would join the allies under two conditions. One, he wanted a joint military plan of action, and second, he desired a "peep" into the more distant political future. The President insisted on these two points, especially the latter one, because of the information Papen received from Cicero about the Teheran Conference, and passed on to İnönü the eve of his meeting with the Allied leaders. It seems that at Teheran, the Allies wanted Turkey in the war as a pawn, i.e., Churchill insisted that if the Second Front was to be launched in the West, Turkey would have to come into the war. None of the Big Three apparently though very much about the final consequences for that country after the war. The Teheran decision divided Europe north and south, which meant that Turkey would find herself in the Soviet sphere of influence. This was precisely what İnönü wanted to avoid, and about which Papen had warned him, thanks to Cicero. Whatever the Turks had in mind, certainly the above considerations contributed to the breakdown of an agreement. However, Churchill was as stubborn as the Turks. He insisted on another meeting, and finally an arrangement was reached whereby the Turkish Government would state their position on the use of the Turkish air bases by February 15, 1944.[120]

Also thanks to Cicero, Papen knew what had happened between İnönü and Churchill at Cairo. He therefore warned the Turkish Foreign

Minister that compliance with the British requests would "inevitably lead to German reprisals" whose "least consequences would be the complete destruction" of Istanbul and Izmir.[121] Cicero also furnished Papen with the information that in a note to the British on December 12, 1943, the Turkish Government had refused to commit themselves.[122] When the British countered with a proposal to establish eighteen RAF squadrons and ten aircraft regiments to forestall German air attacks, the Turks played for time. Eventually the British air delegation left Turkey on February 3, 1944.[123] In a telegram to Ribbentrop Papen triumphantly stated, "this round in the campaign for Turkey has been won by us...a Balkan offensive could not now take place."[124] The Cicero operation came to an end in February 1944 when Cicero simply failed to supply anymore material to Papen. An American "mole," planted in the Reich Foreign Ministry, became aware of the Cicero activities in Ankara and tipped off his superior, Allen Dulles, OAS Chief in Switzerland. Dulles notified his British counterpart, and as a result the British Embassy in Ankara tightened its security.[125]

While the Cicero operation helped Papen to defeat British policies in the Middle East, this was countered by the defection of one of the Abwehr's principal agents in Ankara, Dr. Vermehren, to the British. Papen was shocked by this news, but was not surprised since Vermheren had a profound distaste for the Nazi regime. Since Vermeheren's wife was a distant relative of Papen's, he naturally feared that this defection would cause his enemies in Berlin to charge him with complicity in the affair, and clamor for his arrest. However, nothing came of this, and once more, Papen escaped certain punishment, and possibly execution.[126]

When the United States entered the war after Pearl Harbor, Papen said he "was faced with a whole set of problems." He asked himself if there was any way "...to free the German people from a regime which was leading their country and Europe to disaster?" Then he added that "this fateful problem was to occupy me for the next three years."[127]

By the end of 1942, Papen believed that it was now impossible for Germany to achieve a military victory. Whatever local successes the Nazi war machine enjoyed, including the Blitzkrieg victories over the West and reaching the gates of Moscow - they would not lead to final victory. It was with this realization that he once again decided to send out a peace feeler to the West. This time he enlisted the aid of an old friend, Baron von Lersner.[128] In April 1942, Lersner met with Monsignor Roncalli, the Papal Nuntius to Turkey, to discuss the possibility of a compromise peace via the Vatican.[129] Lersner went to Rome where he met with the Secretary of State Msgr. Maglioni and his deputy, Msgr. Montini. Delivering Papen's message, Lersner told the two prelates that "steps would have to be taken to ensure that they were conducted with a different German regime, if a real possibility of negotiations existed."[130] Lersner must have also presented Papen's peace plan, which was most probably the same one he had proposed to the Dutch Ambassador and to Hitler. However, Maglioni told him that he did not think the Western Powers would have any interest in Papen's proposal. There were fears that Stalin, who was demanding a second front, might reach a compromise with Hitler. "For this reason alone...no thought of peace talks could be entertained."[131] Lersner returned to Ankara empty-handed, and consequently this peace initiative went no further.

In mid-April, Papen went to Berlin where he discovered that the morale was "at zero" level. Two Nazis, Helldorf, Berlin's chief of police, and Gottfried Bismarck, a local government head, told Papen that Hitler was introducing methods that could only result in the complete collapse of Germany. Helldorf described for Papen the terrible prison conditions, in which hundreds of people were being held under sentence of death for minor offenses. Moreover, "Special Courts" had been established, and were passing wholesale sentences with no right of appeal. Papen realized that Germany's external situation was not the only threat, but that the country had reached a stage that required desperate counter-measures.[132]

Following this meeting, Papen had dinner at the Union Club, where he met with a small group headed by Colonel Beck, former Chief of Staff. At that meeting, Papen learned for the first time of a plot to remove Hitler. Before they were prepared to carry out this plan, however, they wanted to discover what attitude the Western Powers would adopt towards a Germany liberated from Hitler. Papen was requested to undertake the task of finding out if the Allies would abandon the formula of unconditional surrender, and whether they would "grant to the German Government, which met democratic requirements, the rights to which Germany's history and position entitled her."[133]

After he returned to Ankara, Papen asked his friend Lersner to get in touch with George H. Earle, the United States Naval Attaché in Istanbul.[134] Both Papen and Earle believed that the real threat to Europe was the Soviet Union. If German capitulation to the Allies was unavoidable, both thought that a compromise peace could be reached in which Germany would join Britain and the United States in protecting the eastern frontiers of Europe against the Bolsheviks.[135] When Lersner got in touch with Earle, he submitted Papen's peace proposal which consisted of the following points: Hitler would be removed from power and he would be tried by an international court; the "unconditional surrender" would be modified; hostilities in the west would cease, and German forces would be transported to the eastern front in order to prevent the Soviet forces from occupying territory in the Balkans and Germany; and there were assurances on the part of the German conspirators that the bargain would be carried out following Roosevelt's agreement. When Earle presented this proposal in Washington, he was told that only General Eisenhower was authorized to discuss surrender with the German Government. The proposal, therefore, was rejected.

Not long after Earle's efforts failed, Papen received another request to serve as a peace-broker between the Allies and Germany. This time it was not through Earle, but through a certain Theodore Morde.[136] In two interviews with Papen, on October 5 and 6, 1943, Morde discussed a plan which, among other things, called for a federation of European states. During the course of the second interview, Papen discussed his own peace plan, which was the same one he had proposed to Earle. He also added that he would take no further steps until he had written proof from Roosevelt that the American President was prepared to negotiate.[137] As in the Earl case, nothing came of this incident, and Papen never did know just who sponsored this man, or how he intended to approach FDR with the plan.[138]

By the spring of 1944, Papen was desperate. He knew that the end was near. Therefore, he decided to try once again through Lersner to contact George Earle with a final proposal. This time Lersner was instructed to tell Earle that Papen was prepared to fly the American secretly to some neutral place for a meeting with Helldorf and Bismarck "to decide what steps were necessary for the neutralization of Hitler and his eventual surrender to a properly constituted international court." The offer also contained Papen's other proposals previously presented to Earle. Like the previous offer, Roosevelt turned this one down, according to Earle, ruling that any negotiations with Germany had to be made through General Eisenhower.[139]

E. The End of a Career

On June 6, 1944, the invasion of Western Europe by the Allied forces against Germany and her allies began with landings on the Normandy Beach. Two days later the British Ambassador in Ankara was informed by his agents that a heavily armed German war transport, the *Kassel*, and three small Ems-type ships were about to pass through the Straits from the Black Sea. Immediately Knatchbull-Hugesen demanded that the Turkish Government stop and search the vessels, in accordance with the terms of the Montreaux Convention. The Foreign Minister, Menemencioglu, requested from Papen, and received assurances that these were not warships. However, the Turkish Government inspected the *Kassel*, and discovered that it was heavily armed. The result was that the pro-German Menemencioglu was forced to resign, and Saracoglu replaced him on a temporary basis. Papen, who was the villain in this entire affair, remarks in his *Memoirs*, "No one regretted his resignation more than I did." He then added that his only consolation was "that our personal relationship was not affected by this incident."[140]

On July 21, 1944, Papen was informed of the attempted assassination of Hitler in the Wolf's Lair in East Prussia. The Berlin broadcast implied that the Gestapo was tracking down the conspirators and others who might have known of the plot. Miraculously, Papen's name was never mentioned in the reports. However, Papen had every reason to fear that he might come under investigation because of his peace proposals, as well as his connection with several of the conspirators. The Gestapo methods of obtaining information were well-known to him by now, and there was certainly an abundance of evidence that could be introduced against him.

Shortly after the assassination attempt against Hitler, after four years of skillfully treading the thin diplomatic wire between a friendship treaty with the Allies and a non-aggression pact with Germany, the Turkish government made the decision to break her diplomatic relations with the Third Reich.

When Papen received the news of the Turkish parliament's decision, he prepared to depart his post in Ankara. He confessed that his own fate was by no means certain. When he received a report of Churchill's remarks during a speech in the House of Commons on August 2, Papen became even more anxious about his future. After describing the successes of the Allies, Churchill remarked that "Herr von Papen may be sent back to Germany to meet the blood bath he so narrowly escaped at Hitler's hands in 1934."[141] Anxious to find out if Churchill might have some inside information about his fate, Papen was reported as having questioned several people about what the English Prime Minister might know.[142] As he was about to depart from Ankara, according to Papen, the head of one of the neutral nations told Papen that the Allies warned him not to leave Turkey, and that they were prepared to offer him protection. However, Papen turned this offer down: "There were still some Germans," he proudly proclaimed, "who considered it unworthy to save their own skins and abandon their country in her hour of need."[143]

After packing his personal belongings, and bidding good-bye to President Inönü, Papen paid a farewell visit to Monsignor Roncalli. It was through Papen's efforts that Roncalli was able to get a transport ship with 1500 Jewish children through the Straits and on to Israel before the Gestapo was able to seize the vessel and pack the children off to a concentration camp where they would certainly have been killed.

On August 5, 1944, Papen departed from Ankara. After passing through Bulgaria, his train went on to Budapest, which was completely untouched by the war. As the train approached the German border, Papen had mixed emotions. For one thing, he thought he was going to be arrested by the Gestapo because of his connection with the men who had attempted to assassinate Hitler. He therefore gave his granddaughter, who was traveling with him, a final message to his wife. Arriving at the border everything was normal. Leaving his granddaughter at Dresden, Papen went on to Berlin. Instead of the Gestapo, however, he was greeted by a delegation from the Foreign Office headed by the chief of protocol. He was informed, to his great relief, that he had no reason to fear arrest, although some of the people who had been with Papen in Vienna had been taken into custody, including Schulenburg the former Ambassador to Moscow.[144]

After receiving instructions that the Führer wanted to see him, Papen took a night train to Hitler's headquarters. On August 6, 1944, he met with the Führer for the last time. After waiting a few minutes Hitler came into the room "ashen pale, one arm in a sling, trembling in every limb." Papen recalled that Hitler was nervous wreck. His first remarks were about the plot, but he suddenly switched and asked for news about Turkey. Papen gave his report and described his final audience with the Turkish president. Then, he tried one last attempt to persuade Hitler to reach an agreement with the West. Hitler reacted violently, and said there could be no compromise. As he was about was about to leave, Hitler suddenly handed Papen a little case containing the Knight's Cross of the Military Merit Order: "You have rendered many services to your country, and it is certainly no fault of yours that your mission to Turkey has come to an end...And he held out his hand. Our last meeting was at an end."[145]

Papen spent a few days in Berlin, during which time he tried unsuccessfully to intercede with Himmler on behalf of some arrested in the July plot. He left for Wallerfangen in September where he was to face another and much more difficult ordeal.

NOTES

[1] Papen, *Memoirs*, pp. 441-442.

[2] On April 3, 1939, Hitler issued a new directive to his commanders which was given the code name of "Operation White" (war with Poland). He also outlined a plan for the seizure of Danzig, and set September 1, 1939 as the actual date of the German invasion of Poland. Bullock, ibid., p. 445.

[3] Ibid., p. 444. Ribbentrop tried on two previous occasions to get Papen to accept the ambassadorial assignment in Turkey, but Papen had refused.

[4] Ibid.

[5] Papen's testimony at Nuremberg, *IMT*, Vol. XVI, pp. 325-326.

[6] Joachim von Ribbentrop, *The Ribbentrop Memoirs*, trans. Oliver Watson (London: Weidenfeld and Nicolson, 1954), p. 164, note.

[7] Papen, ibid., p. 445. It will be recalled that Papen served in Turkey during World War I, where he was highly esteemed by the Turks.

[8] For the credit negotiations see *DGFP*, Ser. D, Vol. V, Nos. 552, 553, 554, 555, 557. The German trade agreement with Turkey was due to expire on August 3, 1938. Germany wanted to include Austria within the scope of a new German-Turkish economic agreement. The Turkish Government agreed to a ten-year credit of 150 million Reich Marks, provided that nearly half of the total should be allocated for the purchase of war material. The agreement was signed on July 25, 1938, and was to remain in force until August, 1939.

[9] The agreement called for a British credit of 16 million pounds in return for a commitment from the Turks to deliver raw materials equivalent to the amount of the credit. For an account of these economic negotiations. *DGFP*, ibid., Nos. 545, 546, 547, & 549.

[10] Foreign Ministry Circular, August 16, 1938, ibid., No. 550.

[11] The British Government's first approach for a formal agreement with Turkey came in March 1934. As a result of the good will that developed between the two countries, Britain had a distinct advantage over Germany in 1939.

[12] On April 10, 1939, the British Ambassador, Sir Hugh Knatchbull-Hugessen informed the Turkish Foreign Minister that he had received assurances from the Italian Government that they had no intention of occupying Corfu or attacking Greece. The Turkish Minister was not favorably impressed by this rather vague guarantee, and demanded something more definite and encouraging. C. Knatchbull-Hugessen to Halifax, April 10, 1939, *Documents of British Foreign Policy, 1919-1939*, Third Series, Vol. V, Doc. No. 121 (hereafter cited *DBFP*).

[13] Knatchbull-Hugessen to Halifax, April 16, 1939, ibid., No. 190.

[14] Knatchbull-Hugessen to Halifax, April 18, 1939, ibid., No. 203. The British also kept the French Government informed of their progress with Turkey. However, because of differences over the French Mandate, Alexandretta, negotiations between Turkey and France were at a standstill. Britain tried to encourage the French to acquiesce to Ankara's demands, and permit the union of Alexandretta to Turkey.

[15] Kroll to the Foreign Ministry, March 31, 1939, *DGFP*, ibid., No. 134.

[16] Ribbentrop memorandum of conversation with Turkish Ambassador, April 4, 1939, *DGFP*, ibid., No. 151.

[17] Kroll to the Foreign Ministry, April 18, 1939, ibid., No. 226.

[18] Knatchbull-Hugessen to Halifax, August 7, 1939, *DBFP*, VI, No. 579. The Turkish Foreign Minister, Saracoglu, made it clear to the Russians that any pact would apply only to the regions contiguous to both Russia and Turkey; Knatchbull-Hugessen to Halifax, August 26, 1939, ibid., Nos. 341, 712.

[19] Report of Sir Knatchbull-Hugessen to Viscount Halifax, April 29, 1939, *DBFP*, V, Doc. # 302.

[20] Papen to the Foreign Ministry, Ankara, April 29, 1939, *DGFP*, VI, No. 288.

[21] *Weizsäcker* circular, May 2, 1939, *DGFP*, ibid., No. 305. This pact called for mutual assistance between Britain and Turkey in the event of (a) a war between Turkey and Italy; (b) a war between Britain and Italy; (c) any Axis aggression in the Balkans. However, this pact depended on the approval of the Soviet Union as agreed upon in the Treaty of Neutrality between the USSR and Turkey, which was signed in 1929. When the Russian Deputy Commissar for Foreign Affairs arrived in Ankara on April 28, the British Ambassador was told that Russia "applauded" Turkey's understanding with Great Britain. Knatchbull-Hugessen to Halifax, May 5, 1939, *DBFP*, ibid., No. 379.

[22] Papen to the Foreign Ministry, May 13, 1939, *DGFP*, VI, No. 374.

[23] The details of the Pact had been arranged between Ribbentrop and the Italian Foreign Minister, Count Ciano in the first week of May. Hitler was convinced that the announcement of an alliance with Italy would further weaken the British and French resolution to stand by Poland. C. Bullock, ibid., pp. 453-454.

[24] Papen memorandum, May 20, 1939, *DGFP*, VI, No. 413.

[25] Ibid.

[26] Minutes for the Inter-Departmental Conference, May 24, 1939, *DGFP*, ibid., No. 435; Clodius memorandum, May 30, 1939, ibid., No. 454. It was decided that no heavy guns would be delivered to Turkey in spite of the fact that they had been contracted and paid for in advance. They also agreed to delay the extension of the Turkish-German Trade Agreement of 1938 (due to expire on

August 31, 1939), and that no negotiations on the subject would be conducted for the present.

[27] Papen to the Foreign Ministry, June 5, 7 and 8, 1939, ibid. Nos. 475, 489, 495. It is also interesting to note that these meetings between Papen and the Turkish officials were reported by the British Ambassador, Knatchbull-Hugessen, to the Foreign Office in London; Reports to Halifax on April 28, May 6, and June 7, 1939, *DBFP*, V, Nos. 302, 387, 738.

[28] Unsigned memorandum of Ribbentrop conversation with the Turkish Ambassador, June 8, 1939, *DGFP*, VI, No. 496.

[29] Bullock, ibid., p. 459, note # 1. In the long run Hitler's *Lebensraum* policy called for an attack against the Soviet Union. But in the short run, a pact with Stalin would avoid encirclement, and allow Hitler to complete the first stage of that policy.

[30] *Memoirs*, pp. 451-452. Papen's presence at the airport in Salzburg to see Ribbentrop off to Moscow gave rise to the rumor that he had been involved in the negotiations. C. Oswald Dutch, *The Errant Diplomat* (London: Edward Arnold & Co., 1940), pp. 268-276). However, there is no evidence to support that charge, and there is every reason to believe that Hitler insisted on complete secrecy in order to prevent the British from interfering.

[31] The negotiations between Germany and Poland over the question of Danzig widened in June of 1939. Not only Danzig was claimed by Germany, but the whole of the Corridor, and even Posen and Upper Silesia.

[32] Papen, ibid., p. 453.

[33] Ibid., p. 453.

[34] One of the articles of the Montreaux Convention, which had been signed in 1936, stated that if Turkey was a belligerent, "...or considered herself threatened by imminent danger of war, she had complete discretion about allowing warships through the Straits," Royal Institute of International Affairs, (London: Oxford University Press, 1936-1937) *Documents on International Affairs*, 1936, pp. 656-658. For the history of the Montreaux Convention see D. A. Routh, "The Montreaux Convention Regarding the Regime of the Black Sea Straits," Royal Institute of International Affairs, *Survey of International Affairs, 1936* (London: Oxford University Press, 1937), pp. 631-636, 641.

[35] On September 2, 1939, Molotov told the German Ambassador to Moscow, Friedrich Schulenburg, that the USSR was prepared to work for the permanent neutrality of Turkey, as desired by Germany. C. Schulenburg to the Foreign Ministry, September 2, 1939, *DGFP*, VII, No. 551.

[36] Schulenburg to the Foreign Ministry, September 5, 1939, ibid., No. 6. Molotov replied that the USSR was exerting her influence on Turkey as requested by Germany.

[37] When Mussolini was informed of Germany's decision to attack Poland he sent Hitler a letter in which he declined to join the Reich in the war. C. Bullock, ibid., pp. 477-478.

[38] Ambassador Papen to Foreign Minister Ribbentrop, September 14, 1939, *DGFP*, VII, No. 69. Papen also recommended that Russia, Italy and Germany guarantee Turkey's possessions and status quo in the Balkans.

[39] Ribbentrop to the Embassy in the Soviet Union, September 29, 1939, Ibid., VII, No. 167.

[40] Schulenburg to the Foreign Ministry, October 17, 1939, ibid., VII, No. 268. A detailed account of Saracoglu's negotiations in Moscow was prepared by Ernst Wörmann, Director of the Political Department of the German Foreign Office. C. Wörmann memorandum, November 2, 1939, *Unpublished German Documents/FO, Turkey*, B.I, "Ribbentrop," Nr. 531.

[41] Papen to the Foreign Ministry, October 4, 1939, ibid., VII, No. 189.

[42] In July the Turks proposed a credit of thirty-five million pounds for armaments, a gold loan of fifteen million pounds, and an immediate credit of ten million pounds to be used for urgent armament purchases, and to free the frozen balances due by Turkey to countries with free currency. The British thought this too high and countered with an offer of ten million pounds credit. Owing to a heavy loss of gold and foreign exchanges, the British said it was impossible to give Turkey credit for purchases in other countries. The haggling went on for several more weeks, with each side conceding, then revising, then reconsidering, etc. British Ambassador, Knatchbull-Hugessen to Halifax in the Home Office, *DBFP*, Vol. VI.

[43] While Turkey and England haggled over the economic issues in the treaty, Hitler and Stalin were engaged in diplomatic negotiations that resulted in the German-Soviet non-aggression pact. With the fear of having to wage a two-front war no longer present, Hitler was ready to march against Poland.

[44] The economic articles of the Treaty awarded Turkey twenty-five million pounds for war materials, a gold loan of fifteen million pounds, and a loan of three and one-half million pounds for transfer of commercial credits recorded in clearing accounts. Great Britain, Foreign Office, *Treaty of Mutual Assistance between the United Kingdom, the French Republic and the Turkish Republic*, Cmd. 6165.

[45] W.N. Medlicott, *The Economic Blockade* (London: H. M. S. O., 1952), Vol. I., p. 272. It was this clause that allowed Turkey to remain neutral, even after Italy's attack against Greece gave Britain and France the right to demand Turkish support in accordance with the Joint Declaration and Treaty of Mutual Assistance.

[46] Papen to the Foreign Ministry, October 1, 1939, *UPGD/Turkey*, I, "Papen," No. 175.

[47] Papen, ibid., pp. 456-457. Ribbentrop was eager for war, and was convinced that Britain and France would never offer more than nominal support to Poland.

[48] The Netherlands, Belgium, Finland, Norway, and Sweden, offered to serve as mediators in the interest of peace. C. German Foreign Ministry memorandum, October 11, 1939, *DGFP*, VII, No. 242.

[49] Schmidt memorandum of the conversation, September 26, 1939, ibid., No. 138.

[50] Hitler had no intention of stopping the war. On September 27, he had met with the commanders-in-chief of the *Wehrmacht* and informed them of his decision to "attack in the West as soon as possible, since the Franco-British Army is not yet prepared." C. Brauchitsch's testimony, *IMT*, 1946, Vol. XX, p. 573.

[51] Papen, *Memoirs*, p. 457.

[52] Weizäcker memorandum, October 21, 1939, *DGFP*, VIII, No. 288.

[53] The Peace of Westphalia in 1648, along with the Treaty of Münster resulted in the loss of political power for the German states (there was no united Germany at that time), and the Holy Roman Empire under the Hapsburgs. For the next 150 years, these treaties had a significant political impact on Germany.

[54] Papen, ibid., p. 458. Göring, unlike Hitler, was not at all eager for war, even a local war. He preferred a dictated settlement in which Britain and France should take the responsibilities for forcing the Poles to accept the German demands. The rivalry between Göring and Ribbentrop further complicated the history of this last stage of the crisis. C. Bullock, ibid., pp. 479-480

[55] Ribbentrop to Papen, November 3, 1939, *DGFP*, VIII, No. 324.

[56] Papen to the Foreign Ministry, November 9, 1939, ibid., No. 338.

[57] Ibid.

[58] Papen did his utmost to impress the Turkish officials with reports of German military victories in order to convince them of the desirability of a Turco-German agreement. C. Papen to the Foreign Ministry, June 3, 1940, ibid., No. 375.

[59] See Ribbentrop memorandum, November 11, 1939; unsigned memorandum of the Economic Policy Department, November 1939; Ribbentrop to Papen December 1, 1939; Wiehl to Papen, January 9, 1940; Clodius memorandum, March 17, 1940, ibid., VIII, Nos. 347, 391, 408, 516, 681; see also Clodius memorandum, May 17, 1940, ibid., IX, Nos. 30 and 264.

[60] For Papen's difficulties which he met during the winter of 1939-1940 c. Papen to Foreign Ministry, November 17, 1939, January 6, 1940, February 21, 1940, and March 14, 1940, *DGFP*, VII, Nos. 339, 366, 390, 512, 625, and 674.

[61] The treaty was valid for one year and included the following points: Turkish and German exports were fixed at $20,000,000. Certain complicated provisions to insure the exports were also included. However, one of the most important raw materials for the making of munitions, chromium, was not included in the agreement. In January 1940, the Allies had been given the right to purchase all of Turkey's chrome exports for two years, with an option of renewal for another year.

[62] Report of U. S. Ambassador MacMurray to Secretary of State Cordell Hull, December 1940, *Foreign Relations of the United States 1940*, Vol II, pp. 987-990. One of the main reasons for this decline was the German refusal to deliver heavy guns unless Turkey increased chromium sales to the Reich. The Turks refused to do this because they had agreed to sell most of their chrome to Britain.

[63] Papen to the Foreign Ministry, May 17, 1940, *DGFP*, IX, No. 265.

[64] Ibid. As a result of Papen's suggestion, Ribbentrop requested Molotov to apply pressure on Turkey to remain neutral, Ribbentrop to Schulenberg, June 5, 1940, ibid., No. 388.

[65] Papen to the Foreign Ministry, June 4, 1940, ibid., IX, No. 383.

[66] Papen to the Foreign Ministry, June 13, 1940, ibid., No. 424. On June 26, the Turkish Prime Minister formally announced Turkey's policy of neutrality.

[67] Richthofen to the Foreign Ministry, January 20, and 27, 1941, ibid., Nos. 671, 702; February 14, 1941, No. 715.

[68] Papen to the Foreign Ministry, February 20, 1941, ibid., XII, No. 67.

[69] Hitler had another reason for attacking Greece. In December 1940, he issued Directive No. 21 which called for the preparation of the German Armed Forces to crush Soviet Russia. Since the spring of 1941, perhaps earlier, he had decided to sweep the British out of the Balkans as a preliminary action to the greatest of all his schemes, the attack on Russia. Therefore, a decisive victory against the Greeks who were being supported by British troops, would see the accomplishment of this first stage against Russia. C. Bullock, ibid., p. 573.

[70] Ibid., pp. 570-571.

[71] Ribbentrop to Papen, February 27, 1941, *DGFP*, XII, No., 102.

[72] Hitler to Inönü, March 1, 1941, ibid., No. 113.

[73] The President of the Turkish Republic to Adolf Hitler, March 12, 1941, ibid., No. 161.

[74] Papen, *Memoirs*, p. 473. Of course, this was a promise he could easily keep since he knew that Hitler's plans were to attack the Soviet Union. Aside from

clearing the area of British troops, the Greek invasion was simply another excuse to station more troops on the Russian border without arousing Stalin's suspicions.

[75] Papen to State Secretary Weizsäcker, April 8, 1941, ibid., XI, No. 295. Papen proposed a German-Turkish non-Aggression Pact to preclude Soviet-Turkish rapprochement. The Soviets were trying to persuade the Turks to make a pact with them because the real reason Germany attacked Greece was to get control of the Straits.

[76] Papen, ibid., pp. 473-474. Naturally Papen's defense of Turkish interests improved his relationships with the Turkish Government, and made it easier for him to gain their trust.

[77] Papen memorandum, April 25, 1941, ibid., No. 404.

[78] Papen, ibid., p. 479.

[79] In a letter to Ribbentrop, sent immediately after he returned to Ankara, Papen refers to a question from Saracoglu regarding German-Russian relations, he uses the phrase "in accordance with instructions," to describe his answer, c. Papen to Ribbentrop, May 13, 1941, *DGFP*, ibid., Vol. XII, No. 514. Papen mentioned agreements that could be made between Turkey and Germany over the issue of Russia, but added, "only when we can speak about them openly." Papen to Ribbentrop, May 17, 1941, ibid., No. 531. Both the US and Britain believed that Papen was fully aware of the planned German attack on the Soviet Union which was set for June 1941, C. MacMurray to Hull, June 22, 1941, *FRUS, 1941*, pp. 870-873.

[80] In his initial discussion with Saracoglu, Papen reported that "we can very definitely and also very quickly find a treaty instrument with Turkey preparing the transition of Turkey to our camp." Papen to Ribbentrop, May 14, 1941, *DGFP*, XII, No. 514. Why the sudden need for a quick resolution if not because Papen knew about the deadline for the attack against Russia?

[81] In his *Memoirs*, Papen says his talks with Ribbentrop in April focused on the need for more chromium from Turkey. Yet in Ribbentrop's urgent instructions to Papen to speed up the process of a non-aggression pact, there is no mention of chromium. Is this another proof that Papen knew exactly what was going to happen in June?

[82] Ribbentrop to Papen, May 17, 1941, ibid., No. 529. The alleged reason for this secret protocol was to lend support to the Arabian freedom movement, especially Iraq. Rashad Ali Garlani had ousted the pro-English Iraqi Government, and the Germans saw an opportunity to assist the revolutionary movement in Baghdad and at the same time gain control of the oil fields in the Persian Gulf. The revolt in Iraq ended on May 30, so the "excuse" to support the revolutionaries was no longer justified. This would seem to indicate that

German interest in a non-aggression pact with Turkey was predicated on the forthcoming military attack against the Soviet Union.

[83] Ribbentrop to Papen, June 3, 1941, June 9, 1941, June 13, 1941, ibid., XII, Nos. 588, 607, and 623.

[84] German-Turkish Treaty, June 18, 1941, ibid., No. 648.

[85] Papen to Ribbentrop, June 12, 1941, ibid., No. 620.

[86] *New York Times*, June 21, 1941, Sect. IV, p. 1.

[87] Under the terms of the Montreaux Convention, Turkey could refuse to let warships pass through the Straits, but under the Convention freedom of passage was permitted to merchant vessels.

[88] Papen to Ribbentrop, August 23, 1941, ibid., No. 230.

[89] Papen to Ribbentrop, July 14, 1941, ibid., No. 125.

[90] Ribbentrop to Papen, July 24, 1941, ibid., No. 145.

[91] Papen to Ribbentrop, July 28, 1941, ibid., No. 161.

[92] Ibid. Ribbentrop would love to have had Papen resign, but the Ambassador was only testing the Foreign Minister's power. In fact, Ribbentrop would have been afraid to fire Papen because Hitler still wanted to keep him in Ankara. This is another example of the Führer's tactics to divide and conquer. As long as Papen and Ribbentrop were competing with one another, Hitler could serve as mediator and judge, thereby retaining complete control.

[93] Ribbentrop to Papen, August 11, 1941, *DGFP*, XIII, No. 194.

[94] Annex to the Edminster memorandum to Hull, August 13, 1941, *FRUS, 1941*, III, pp. 891-892.

[95] *New York Times*, December 4, 1941, p. 1. Turkey had been receiving war material out of American deliveries to England. (In return for this "favor," the United States had been receiving the bulk of Turkish chromium which had been contracted to Britain under the terms of the trade agreement of 1939.) The new law would make Turkey a direct recipient of Lend-Lease goods.

[96] Papen to Ribbentrop, November 18, 1941, *DGFP*, XIII, No. 471.

[97] Papen, *Memoirs*, p. 489. It will be recalled that Papen ran into the same problem with Bohle in Austria, where Papen was unable to stop Bohle's activities. However he was able to have Bohle's activities curtailed in Turkey.

[98] After his arrival in Ankara, Papen tried to get Friede recalled to Germany because of his interference with Embassy personnel and Papen's activities. In 1942, it was reported by *Reuters* that in a speech to a group of Nazis in Ankara, Friede allegedly attacked Papen, accusing him of self-seeking intrigues, and indirectly calling for his dismissal as ambassador to Turkey. Papen was never able to have Friede recalled to Germany because Himmler, Bormann and Ribbentrop refused to do anything about it.

[99] Ibid., p. 490.

[100] Papen suspected that because Friede had the support of Himmler, Bormann, and Ribbentrop, Hitler would never hear of the case. It is not clear why Freide was eventually removed. But in all probability, it was because he was useful to the Party someplace else.

[101] Papen, ibid., p. 486. Papen gives the wrong date.

[102] Ibid.

[103] Ribbentrop to Papen, Berlin, February 24, 1942, *German Documents of the Auswärtiges Amt, Political Archives & Historical Section*, Bonn, No. 342.

[104] Steinhardt to Hull, March 6, 1942, *FRUS, 1942*, IV, p. 824. Steinhardt was appointed U. S. Ambassador to Turkey on March 1 when MacMurray resigned. He had previously been the US Ambassador to the USSR

[105] Steinhardt to Hull, March 11, 1942, ibid., p. 825; c. also Papen to Ribbentrop, March 6, 1942, *UPGD/Turkey*, V, "Papen," No. 351.

[106] The two Russians were officials of the Soviet trade commission at Istanbul, Georgi Pavlov, and Leonard Kornilov. The two Turkish subjects were medical student Abd ur-Rahman Saymanul, and a barber, Sulaeman Sav. The Turks had come to Turkey three years previously, and had acted as Communist couriers between Turkey and Yugoslavia. The two Russians had taught them to use firearms and explosives for the purpose of assassinating an important German official, and so provoking a war between Germany and Turkey.

[107] *New York Times*, April 6, 1942, p. 7, for extracts of the *Pravda* article entitled "German Provocateurs before the Turkish Courts."

[108] *New York Times*, April 2, 1942. For published details of the opening sessions of the trial, c., ibid., June 18, 1942, p. 3.

[109] Robert E. Sherwood, *Roosevelt and Hopkins* (New York: Harper and Brothers, 1948), p. 683.

[110] Leahy to Hull, July 16, 1943, *FRUS, 1943*, VI, pp. 1069-1070.

[111] Winston S. Churchill, *The Second World War* (Boston: Houghton Mifflin, Co., 1953), Vol. IV, pp. 710-711. Turkey was offered twenty-five British and American air squadrons immediately on her entrance into the war.

[112] H. Maitland Wilson, *Eight Years Overseas* (London: Oxford University Press, 1949), pp. 155-158.

[113] Papen to Ribbentrop, May 5, 1943, *UPGD/FO*, VIII, "Papen," No. 432.

[114] Knatchbull-Hugessen, *Diplomat in Peace and War* (London: John Murray, 1949), p. 191. There is no such evidence in Papen's reports that he ever directed such a threat towards Turkey. Given his entire service in Turkey, it seems highly unlikely that Papen would have used such a blatant form of intimidation. This smacks more of Ribbentrop's "power politics," than of Papen's "evolutionary" campaign.

[115] Anthony Eden, *The Memoirs of Anthony Eden: The Reckoning* (Boston: Houghton Mifflin Co., 1965), p. 490.

[116] L. C. Moyzisch, Operation Cicero (London: Wingate, 1950). Twentieth Century Fox made a movie in 1950 with James Mason in the feature role of Cicero.

[117] Papen, ibid., p. 511; Moyzisch, ibid., p. 117.

[118] Papen to Ribbentrop, November 20, 1943, *UPGD/Turkey*, IX, "Papen," No. 1683.

[119] This information alone would have been invaluable from a military standpoint. Instead of concentrating so many forces in the East, or even in the South, Germany could have focused more on the West.

[120] Minutes of the Churchill-Inönü meeting, December 7, 1943, *FRUS*, VI, pp. 751-756.

[121] Papen to Ribbentrop, December 18, 1943, *UPGD/Turkey*, IX, "Papen," No. 1842.

[122] Papen to Ribbentrop, December 18, 1943, ibid., No. 1845.

[123] Papen to Ribbentrop, February 2, 1944, *DGFP*, XIII, No. 206. Papen's information from Cicero was so accurate that he was able to report the departure of the British delegation the day before they actually left!

[124] Papen to Ribbentrop, February 11, 1944, ibid., No. 222.

[125] Papen did not know exactly what happened to Cicero, alias Elias. Moyzisch claims to have seen him once in Istanbul in August 1944, and at various times Egyptian newspapers reported that he was being sought by the police. As late as 1951 Papen says that Ribbentrop's brother-in-law, Jenke, who had introduced Cicero to Papen in October 1943, reported that he saw Cicero in Pera a couple of time in 1951. *Memoirs*, p. 519.

[126] Ibid., pp. 520-521. Papen claims he tried unsuccessfully to prevent the Abwehr organization from being transferred from Canaris to Himmler. He also said he learned later that the Gestapo was planning to send a plane-load of reliable SS plain clothes men to Ankara in order to kidnap him and return him to Berlin. He thought that Hitler stepped in to prevent this. However, there is no evidence to support either his claims or Hitler's alleged intervention.

[127] Ibid., p. 484. However, it seems that this twinge of conscience was more the product of his imagination as an author, than as a diplomat who, for four years, worked tirelessly in Turkey to promote a German victory. Not only did he help to prolong the war and the misery that accompanied it, but his actions did precious little to "free the German people" from the tyranny of Hitler's brutal dictatorship. That would come, no thanks to Papen, from the allied forces.

[128] Lersner, it will be remembered, had been a close friend of Papen since their days together before World War I. They had served together in the United

States and Mexico, had been in touch on the Western Front after Papen was requested to leave the U. S. in 1916. He represented Germany at Versailles in 1918. During Hitler's regime Lersner became a member of the Abwehr, and joined Papen in Ankara as President of the Orient Association, a cover for Canaris' Abwehr organization. He testified on Papen's behalf at Nuremberg.

[129] In 1934, Roncalli became the Vatican representative to Turkey and Greece in 1934. He met Papen in 1939. When Pope Pius XII died in 1958, Roncalli was elected his successor on the eleventh ballot, and took the name John XXIII.

[130] Papen, ibid., p. 489.

[131] Papen's peace proposal included a provision that would make the Ukraine an independent state. Stalin would never have accepted such a provision, which would have been enough to drive him to make a compromise peace with Hitler.

[132] Ibid., p. 498. Both Helldorf and Bismarck had joined the Nazi party in its early days from what Papen described as "idealistic motives."

[133] Ibid, p. 499.

[134] Earle was friend of Roosevelt, and had been the first Democratic Governor of Pennsylvania for over fifty years. He was a minister to Vienna, and had served as Roosevelt's representative in Sofia in 1941-1942.

[135] A report in the service newspaper *Stars and Stripes* for Wednesday, March 27, 1946, stated that in 1943 a peace feeler by Papen through Earle to President Roosevelt had been made, in which Papen proposed a joint German-Allied army be maintained on the Eastern Front "to hold off the forces of the Soviet Union."

[136] Theodor Morde was a member of Robert Sherwood's staff in Cairo under the Coordinator of Information, and then with the Office of War Information. He resigned his post in Cairo and took a job with the *Reader's Digest*. Sherwood was very suspicious of Morde's claims that General Pat Hurly was sponsoring him to go to Istanbul and make a peace offer to Papen. He sent a memo to William "Wild Bill" Donovan, Director of the OSS, stating that General Hurley denied any association with Morde and suggested that Morde be refused a passport to travel outside of the United States. "Memorandum for the President," October 26, 1943, *PSF, # 167*, FDR Library, Hyde Park, N. Y.

[137] Meeting No. 2 between Morde and Papen, October 6, 1943, *PSF, No. 167, 1941-1943*, FDR Library, Hyde Park, N. Y. Papen's account of this meeting is fairly accurate, but adds that he thought Morder might have been sent by Earle, which was a possibility; Papen, *Memoirs*, pp. 503-505.

[138] Morde claimed that he was sponsored by General Pat Hurley. Hurley denied that he had anything to do with this. Robert Sherwood of the OWI, sent a

memo to Roosevelt informing him of Morde's background, and warning the President about the man. Apparently there were people in the US Government who, like Earle, believed that the United States and Germany should combine their efforts against what they perceived to be a threat from the Soviet Union. William Donovan, Director of the OSS, was in favor of Morde's trip to Istanbul. See a Memo of William Donovan to President Roosevelt, October 29, 1943, *PSF, No. 167, 1941-1943*, FDR Library, Hyde Park, N. Y.

[139] Papen, ibid., p. 522. In an article published in the *Philadelphia Enquirer*, January 30, 1949, Earle gave his version of the proposal and Roosevelt's rejection. Earle also added that he told the President he was going to denounce his foreign policy and declare that it was Russia, not Germany, that presented the real threat to the United States. After this direct violation of FDR's specific order that he was not to make disparaging remarks about an ally (i.e., Russia), Earle was forced to resign his commission.

[140] Ibid., p. 527. Under the circumstances, this comment is a bit incredulous.

[141] Churchill's Speech to the House of Commons, August 2, 1944, *House of Commons Debates*, 5th. ser., Vol. CCCL, Cols. 1726-1733; Papen, ibid., p. 528.

[142] Knatchbull-Hugessen, *Diplomat in Peace and War* (London: John Murray, 1949), pp. 202-203.

[143] Papen, ibid. The alleged offer to help Papen is not substantiated in official U. S. diplomatic correspondence.

[144] 145. Ibid., p. 530.

[145] 146. Ibid., pp. 531-532.

CHAPTER 15: THE FINAL YEARS

A: <u>From Ankara to Nuremberg</u>

When Franz von Papen returned to his estate in Wallerfangen in September 1944, the reality of war came home to him. Until now, he had followed the war through newspaper accounts, radio reports, and correspondence with the Foreign Office in Berlin. Now he witnessed first hand the relentless bombardment of the once-peaceful villages and towns in the Saarland by the Allied air force. The quiet country roads were now crowded with frightened, fleeing villagers in carts, trucks, and even on foot, loaded with the few possessions that they were able to take with them. As the von Papen's watched this stream of fleeing humanity, they knew that it was only a question of time before they too would have to leave.

On November 29, the guns of the Third U. S. Army could be heard firing at the German defenses a few kilometers from Wallerfangen in the valley below. That same morning, Papen received a telephone call that the time had come to evacuate his estate. Accompanied by his wife, Papen crossed the Saar and went to Gemünden near Coblenz, where he sought refuge in a friend's home. A few hours later his son Franz and two daughters Isabella and Margarete joined them.[1]

From this point on, Papen became not just a refugee, but a fugitive. As the American forces advanced, Papen was forced to flee again, this time alone, leaving his wife and daughter Margarete in Gemünden.[2] Papen now attempted to avoid capture by seeking refuge at his married daughter's home at Stockhausen in Westphalia. Within a matter of days, however, the American forces had surrounded the entire Ruhr, so Papen hid out in a small lodge in the woods. Finally, on April 9, 1945, the main house was surrounded and searched from top to bottom. The next day an American platoon reached the lodge where Papen was hiding. When questioned as to his identity, Papen admitted who he was, and the sergeant placed him under arrest.[3] Although he did not know it at the time, Papen was to spend the next four years under guard either in prison or in a labor camp.

Together with his son and son-in-law, under heavy guard, Papen passed through the towns and villages he had known and loved in more peaceful times: his birthplace, Werl, which had been untouched by the ravages of war; Dülmen, where he had been honorary mayor, had been reduced to rubble. They were taken by plane from Haltern to Wiesbaden, headquarters of the American Army. It was at Wiesbaden that Papen learned of the shocking conditions in the concentration camps, and the horrible slaughter of millions of innocent men, women, and children. Papen knew of the camps, but not what went on in them. Like many Germans, he was unaware of the brutal and inhuman experiments being practiced, especially on the Jews. At the Nuremberg Trials, when forced to view the horror of the camps, Papen became sick to his stomach.

While Papen cannot be associated with radical anti-Semites like Streicher, Hitler, Goebbels, Himmler or Bormann, he believed that too many Jews were in public office and in the professions. In a speech in Gleiwitz in January 1934, he said every country had a right to protect its blood. He wanted the Jews to be treated like foreigners in Germany. They were not to be citizens, but their rights would be defined and safeguarded by law, and when excesses occurred one could protest against them. However, he also said that for a Christian there was no place for racism.[4] When the Nuremberg Laws were promulgated, Papen raised no voice in protest, but he was pleased that Hitler exempted from certain sections of the Law, Jewish veterans of World War I, and civil servants employed prior to the war.[5] It seems that if Papen entertained any antipathy towards the Jews it was not based on the perverted notions of social Darwinism as preached by the Nazis, but rather on political and economic issues.

However, Papen's attitude towards the Jews should not come as a surprise. As a devout, Catholic conservative, he reflected the attitudes of many Catholic bishops both in Germany and Austria. The Austrian Bishop, Aloys Hudal, a good friend of Papen, wrote that the Nuremberg Laws were a necessary measure of self-defense against the influx of foreign elements.[6] The Vicar General of Mainz, Dr. Mayer, thought that Hitler's *Mein Kampf* had appropriately described the bad influence of the Jews in press, theater and literature. Still, Mayer contended, it was un-Christian to hate other races and to subject the Jews and foreigners to disabilities through discriminatory legislation that would bring reprisals from other countries.[7] On the other hand, the assistance Papen gave to Msgr. Roncalli in Turkey that resulted in free passage of 1500 Jews from Rumania to Israel, is an indication that he had compassion for the plight of the Jewish people.[8] Papen's sympathy for the Jews, and his willingness to undertake risks to help them is certainly to his credit. However, his continued service in the interests of a government whose ideology called for the extermination of an entire race, poses a dilemma that he was never able to resolve.

From Wiesbaden he was transported to the Chateau de Lesbioles near Spa.[9] In May, he was moved again, this time to a small hotel near Luxembourg where he remained until August.

As a prisoner, Papen was not only moved from place to place, but he underwent numerous interrogations. In the course of one of these inquiries, Papen inappropriately proposed that he would be happy to lend his name in any appeal to Germany that might lead to the end of hostilities. He even proposed that he be taken to the front where he could get in touch with the German Army command, and find out which one of the Generals was "prepared to consider proposals for an armistice."[10]

Finally, at the beginning of August, Papen joined Göring, Ribbentrop, Rosenberg and Streicher in the Mondorf prison located near Luxembourg. Taken to the Luxembourg airport, the prisoners were loaded aboard two C-47s. and, contrary to Papen's account, were accompanied by two armed guards on each plane.[11] When the planes landed, they were loaded on trucks and driven through a city in complete ruins - it was Nuremberg, the city where Hitler had held all the great Nazi Party celebrations. Once again, Nuremberg would be the focus of international acclaim; this time not for the celebration of National Socialism, but for its final condemnation.

It was a typically gray and drizzly fall day in Nuremberg. The prisoners were rushed off the transports into enclosed ambulances and taken to the Palace of Justice, where one wing of the prison had been prepared for them. The prisoners cells were located in the wing nearest the courthouse where the trials were to take place. Papen describes his cell, No. 47, in which he was to remain from August 12, 1945 until October 15, 1946:

> Instead of the cell window, high in the wall, there were thick iron bars, and the lighting installation in the ceiling had been removed. In one corner there was a collapsible wooden bed with a grey blanket. The only other furniture was a small table and stool. The hatch in the door, through which the meals were passed, was kept open, so that the guards outside could keep us continually under observation.[12]

The stone walls and floors, cool in the summer but freezing in the winter made conditions even more depressing. At night the only light in the cells was provided by a bare bulb with a metal reflector directed into the ceiling through a rectangular hatch in the thick solid door, which was always open. A guard was stationed outside of each door, and the prisoners were kept under constant observation as a precaution against suicide.[13]

The accused were not permitted to speak to each other or to the guards, received no news of the outside world, and were forbidden to receive parcels from the outside. Each day they were allowed to exercise, which consisted of walking single-file, without speaking or stopping, around a square in the yard.

Although the conditions were depressing enough, even worse was the fact that Papen still did not know what the charges against him were. Added to this was his anxiety over the fate of his daughters who had been serving as nurses on the Russian front. It was not until September that he learned that his wife and daughters had arrived in Nuremberg where they had obtained lodgings.[14]

While Papen had been interrogated almost from the moment of his capture until he arrived at Nuremberg, the official pre-trial interrogations began on September 3. Thomas J. Dodd was Papen's American interrogator, who, according to Papen was "polite, correct, even kind." Because of the nature of the charges brought against him,

Dodd attempted to find out how culpable Papen was in bringing Hitler to power, and what role Papen played in the *Anschluss*.[15]

One question that continued to surface, not only in these sessions, but also in his trial, was why Papen continued to serve Hitler in spite of the violence, terror, and persecution that were the hallmarks of Nazi Germany. As examples of this, Dodd mentioned the murder of two of his associates and Papen's house arrest during the Röhm affair; the forced *Anschluss*, which Papen said he had consistently opposed; the murder of his close associate, von Kettler by the Gestapo; the constant surveillance and even harassment Papen endured in Vienna and Turkey; the brutal treatment of Jews on *Krystallnacht*, and other acts of Nazi terror and violence.[16] Papen's only reply to these questions was that he was a good German patriot, and he had acted according to his conscience, which was to his way of thinking, for the good of Germany, and not for the good of the Nazi Party or Hitler.[17]

It was not until October 19, that Papen learned for the first time the charges against him. There were four categories of crimes with which the accused were charged. Papen, to his relief, was not charged with war crimes or crimes against humanity, but only with conspiring to prepare for a war of aggression. He expected his trial to be quite short, since he was confident that it would be fairly easy to prove his complete innocence of this charge. He even wrote to his wife that he expected the proceedings to last two or three days, and he would be with her by the end of November. What he did not expect was that they would all be tried together, and not separately.[18]

Along with the indictment, Papen was given a list of German lawyers from which he was to choose a defense counsel. Unfamiliar with all but one of the listed attorneys, Papen sought and received the advice of his friend, Count Schaffgotsch, who recommended the Breslau lawyer, Dr. Egon Kubuschok, who agreed to take over Papen's case. Since Franz Junior was also a lawyer, Papen was able to have him released from his status as a prisoner-of-war, to help him prepare his father's defense.[19]

In general, the German defense attorneys worked almost wholly dependent on the Allies, in a dimly lighted room confronted with thousands of documents of which they had no advanced knowledge. They were treated with a mixture of tolerance and goodwill, as pariah Germans. In the early days of the trial, the accused met for conferences with their lawyers in a single room under the surveillance of American

MPs. The stain of collective guilt was on the lawyers too. The court spoke in different tones to them than the prosecution. They were told to move along with their cases, to pay attention, and to stop talking about irrelevant matters like the Versailles Treaty or Allied misbehavior.[20]

The trial date was set for November 20, 1945. At 9 a.m. the prisoners, dressed in proper suits, shirts and ties, were escorted from their cells to an elevator one by one under guard. They were brought into the courtroom which was located on the second floor of the Palace of Justice, where they took their seats on two long wooden benches divided by an aisle. Papen, wearing a pin-stripe suit with a white handkerchief in his breast pocket, sat between General Alfred Jodl, who had planned all of Hitler's major campaigns, and Papen's old friend from Austria, the tall, introverted Seyss-Inquart, who had led Austria into the *Anschluss* with Germany. Ten guards, outfitted in white helmets, white belts, and white billy clubs were positioned behind and to the side of the dock. The four judges and their alternates appeared dressed in judicial robes, with the exception of the Russians, who wore military uniforms.[21]

The opening session which lasted from 9:30 a.m. until 5 p.m., was limited to reading the indictment followed by the court's request for pleas from the accused, which they did in several languages, all pleading not guilty. For the next four months the prosecution presented its case and witnesses. This was followed by the presentation of the defense cases and witnesses.

After some eight weeks, on January 23, 1946, the case against Papen was introduced by Major I. Harcourt-Barrignton, a British assistant prosecutor. Papen was charged with crimes against peace, which included not only conspiracy to wage war, but also his role in the acquisition and consolidation of power by the Nazi Party. The prosecution concentrated its attack on Papen's activities between June 1, 1932, and the *Anschluss* in March 1938.[22]

The British prosecutor charged Papen with using his personal influence to facilitate Hitler's assumption of power. To this end he intended to introduce as evidence a long affidavit by the Cologne banker, Baron von Schröder, at whose house Papen met with Hitler on January 4, 1933. According to the prosecution, it was on that occasion that Papen and Hitler made a pact which resulted in Hitler's appointment as chancellor. Papen stated that in his conversation with Hitler, he discussed the Führer's participation in the Schleicher

von Papen horseback riding in the zoological gardens, Berlin.

government, but not anything about Hitler becoming chancellor. However, Papen's lawyer was able to prevent the evidence from being admitted.[23]

Other efforts were made by the prosecution to prove that Papen helped to consolidate the dictatorship of the Nazi Party in his role in the cabinet, e.g., by approving the establishment of special courts, the amnesty decrees, and the passage of other decrees that resulted in the complete control of the state governments by the Nazi Party. He was also charged with sabotaging the *Reichskonkordat* with the Vatican. Finally the prosecution charged Papen with failing to stop Hitler at the time of his Marburg speech. The British lawyer argued that if Papen had defied the Nazis and told the whole world the truth, the world would have been spared much suffering.[24]

When it came to present Papen's involvement in the *Anschluss* issue, the prosecution lawyers attacked him sharply for his behavior. Using Papen's reports to Hitler as evidence, the prosecution charged that the Austro-German Friendship Treaty of 1936 was a scheme between Hitler and Papen to deceive the Austrians, since it resulted in putting Austrian Nazis in key positions in the Government. This in turn, it was argued, weakened Schuschnigg's position, and eventually resulted in his being forced into meeting with Hitler at Berchtesgaden. Papen, who was present at that meeting, was accused of cooperating with Hitler in the game of intimidation which resulted in further concessions by Schuschnigg.[25]

In an effort to prove that Papen had conspired with Hitler, the prosecution unsuccessfully attempted to introduce the affidavits of the former American Minister to Vienna, George Messersmith. His affidavit stated in part the following:

> ...in the baldest and most cynical manner [Papen]
> proceeded to tell me that all of Southeastern Europe, to the
> borders of Turkey, was Germany's natural hinterland, and
> that he had been charged with the mission of facilitating
> German economic and political control over all of this
> region for Germany. He blandly and directly said that
> getting control of Austria was to be the first step.[26]

Messersmith also charged Papen with using his reputation as a loyal Catholic to mislead and influence Cardinal Innitzer who subsequently went along with the idea of the *Anschluss*.[27]

When Papen's case had been completed, the prosecution took another six weeks to complete the rest of the cases. Then, on the afternoon of March 13, 1946, the defense took the stage. Starting with Herman Göring, all the accused with the exception of Hess and Frick, took the stand in their defenses. It was not until June 14, 1946, that Papen's turn came to take the witness stand, and for his lawyer, Kubuschok, to present the defense.

Papen's defense consisted of two important points. First, he had to prove that his activities between 1932 and 1934 did not serve to bring Hitler to power or strengthen his position. Secondly, he had to prove that he did not intend to undermine Schuschnigg's Government by subversive methods, but that he had, on the contrary, done all he could to oppose the Nazis' plans for a forced *Anschluss*. The only way he could do this, since he had no documents, files, or archives at his disposal, was to call on former friends, and associates to submit responses to a questionnaire, which was permitted by the Court in lieu of witnesses. Papen received affidavits from Monsignor Roncalli, former Papal Delegate to Turkey; the Dutch Minister to Turkey, Mr. Visser; Admiral Horthy, Regent of Hungary; his life-long friend, Baron Lersner; his former adjutant in Vienna, von Tschirschky; Prince Erbach, Papen's legation counselor in Vienna; his private secretary Fräulein Rose; Count Kageneck and Conrad Josten, two of Papen's assistants during his chancellorship, and others.[28]

When Papen was called before the court to testify on his own behalf, he began with a long discourse on the historical background leading to the formation of the Third Reich, and the events leading up to World War II. The President of the Court, Lord Lawrence, had to constantly interrupt Papen's digressions, and admonish him to stick to the events in which he was involved between June 1, 1932, and March 15, 1938. The only time Papen was not interrupted was when he gave his reasons for the Marburg speech.

Most helpful to Papen's defense with regard to his Austrian activities, had been Göring's testimony in which, under cross-examination, he accepted the complete responsibility for the *Anschluss*.[29] Also coming to Papen's defense were the statements made by the Austrian State Secretary, Guido Schmidt, who was involved in the arrangements for the Berchtesgaden meeting as well as his presence at that meeting.[30]

When it came time for the cross-examination, the most effective questioning came from the Deputy Chief Prosecutor for the United Kingdom, Sir David Maxwell Fyfe. Papen considered him the most able jurist in the entire trial. In his cross-examination, Fyfe accused Papen of helping to bring Hitler to power even though he knew the true nature of National Socialism. This can be proven, Fyfe argued, from the fact that Papen continued to serve Hitler even after the Röhm *putsch*. Fyfe also brought up Papen's correspondence with Hitler while serving as ambassador in Vienna. He charged that the reports indicated an attempt to deceive the Austrian government. Finally, in summing up his cross-examination, Fyfe did not concentrate on whether or not Papen was guilty of crimes against peace and security. Instead, Fyfe said Papen's crime was his continued service in Hitler's government even though he knew of all the crimes committed by the Nazis; he had seen the murder of his own associates, the persecution of many innocent Germans, and the reign of terror conducted by the Gestapo and Himmler's SS. Nevertheless, Fyfe continued, the only reason Papen took one job after another was because he sympathized and wanted to carry on with the Nazi work.

When it came turn for Papen to respond to these charges, he replied that he had followed his conscience, and that he had not served the Nazis but he had served the German people - "the other Germany." It was out of love of country and people, Papen declared, that he continued to serve the Nazi regime. He accepted prominent positions because he considered it his duty, and because be believed that he could steer National Socialism into responsible channels. He went to Austria because he wanted to prevent what actually came to pass in spite of his efforts. The same was true with regard to Turkey, as he said his reports indicated.[31]

The final weeks of the trial had now passed, and it was time for the verdicts. On Saturday, September 28, the visits of families, which had been permitted, came to an end. Sunday there was a deep despondency in the cells. Monday the prosecution summed up the arguments, most of which were accepted by the Tribunal.

On Tuesday, October 1, the prisoners were brought back into the courtroom, and took their usual places in the dock. The atmosphere in the court was extraordinarily tense. The Lord Justice began with a presentation of the Court's findings. Then each of the justices read a section of the prepared statement which included findings on the law of the case, the verdict on the organizations, the review of the evidence, and justification in support of their decision to accept most of it.

The weather seemed to match the gloom of the courtroom. Nuremberg was shrouded in a light fog through which the broken towers and piles of rubble appeared and disappeared in shifting surrealistic images. None of the defendants had slept much that night, and they all looked haggard. The faces of judges burdened with this task, were as taunt as the defendants.

The defendants were all subdued. Göring, his eyes - like those of Frank, Doenitz, and Schirach - hidden behind dark glasses, was slumped over his head bowed, the earphones held to his right ear. Hess stared off into space indifferent to all around him, as he had been throughout the trial. Keitel remained rigid and expressionless, while Funk twisted and fidgeted, as usual. Streicher, arms crossed, leaned back belligerently. Papen sat slightly slumped to one side, but his face showed neither fear nor anxiety. He wore the same neat pin-stripe suit with a white handkerchief neatly folded in his breast pocket. His eyes were downcast, and there were deep shadows underneath - a sign that he had very little sleep the previous night.

At 9:30 a.m., the first verdict against organizations in the Third Reich was delivered. Then the prisoners turn came next. They collectively heard the general judgment of the Tribunal as well as the verdicts. These procedures lasted the entire day, and part of the next, before the Tribunal dealt individually with the fate of each of the defendants. When it came his turn to summarize the trials, the Chief Counsel for the United States, Robert H. Jackson was particularly hostile towards Papen: "Franz von Papen, pious agent of an infidel regime, held the stirrup while Hitler vaulted into the saddle, lubricating the Austrian annexation, and devoting his diplomatic cunning to the service of the Nazi objectives abroad."[32]

Finally, after what must have seemed an eternity to him, Papen was called before the bench to hear his fate. The Lord Justice, Lawrence, looking down at Papen noted that while Papen "engaged in both intrigue and bullying...the Charter does not make criminal such offenses against political morality, however bad these may be."[33] Along with Schacht and Fritzsche, Papen was acquitted, and ordered to be released at the end of the session.

When the court recessed at midday, the press was permitted access to the three acquitted men. Schacht became the center of a flock of reporters and photographers. He swapped his comments and autographs for cigarettes and chocolates. Dodd, who had been Papen's interrogator, congratulated him and presented him with a box of Havana cigars. Fritzsche was so overcome that he was hardly able to speak. He had doubted that the Tribunal, as a matter of policy, would acquit anyone. If Papen spoke to the press, there is no record of what he might have said, and he gives no indication of this in his *Memoirs*. After the press conference the three men had lunch together. The other eighteen defendants stole envious glances at the places of Schacht, Fritzsche and Papen where Colonel Andrus had placed three oranges. As a gesture of sympathy, Papen sent his orange to Neurath; Fritzsche gave his to Schirach. With no one to relate to among the defendants, Schacht simply peeled and ate his.

In the meantime, Andrus was prepared to release the three acquitted men as soon as their attorneys arranged for transportation. However, as the afternoon wore on, an angry crowd of Germans, protesting the acquittals, gathered in front of the Palace of Justice. Among the most outraged was the Bavarian Prime Minister, Wilhelm Högner, who had no intention of being as indulgent as the Americans. He ordered the arrest of Schacht, Papen and Fritzsche who were to be tried by a denazification court, as soon as the Americans relinquished custody of them. On the advice of Schacht's attorney, the three decided to remain in the prison, where they were given unlocked rooms on the third floor.[34]

Papen decided to write to the French and British military governments requesting permission to live either in Gemünden or Westphalia. He also asked the American Military Government to grant him safe conduct to his destination. In the meantime, impatient to leave, Fritzsche and Schacht were taken into custody by the Bavarian police the minute they stepped out of the Palace of Justice. Several weeks later, after receiving no answer to his letters Papen left the prison and was placed under police surveillance and ordered not to leave Nuremberg. Once again, he found himself facing another ordeal - this time at the hands of the very Germans for whom he claimed he had continued to serve the Nazi regime.

B. Denazification

After he was released by the Bavarian authorities, Papen managed to locate his wife and daughter, Margarete, who were living with a Mr. Adam, one of his former army colleagues. Papen was invited to remain with the former police official until the authorities decided how to proceed.

The ordeal of the prison had taken its toll on Papen's health, and at sixty-five, he was not physically or mentally as strong as he had been. He therefore expressed a wish to go to a sanatorium just outside of the city, but his request was refused. Eventually he was able to get a bed in St. Theresa hospital, run by Catholic sisters, where he remained for some months. However, he continued to be under surveillance by a policeman - a reminder that his ordeal was far from over.

About the middle of January 1947, Papen was notified by the Bavarian Denazification Minister, Loritz, that his case was to begin immediately. The Court (*Spruchkammer*), located in Nuremberg, consisted of the President, Dr. Camille Sachs, and six other judges.[35] Since the Court could not change the judgment of the International Tribunal, it could only attempt to prove that Papen had aided and abetted Hitler's rise to power. One of the key pieces of evidence supporting this allegation was the testimony of the Cologne banker, Kurt von Schröder, and the letters of the Nazi Wilhelm Keppler.[36] According to these witnesses, it was Papen who arranged for the meeting with Hitler at the Cologne banker's home. According to Keppler, Papen told Schröder that Hitler's becoming chancellor was essential, and that he would back the Führer's candidacy. Papen denied this was the way things developed, stating that he had only offered Hitler the vice chancellorship. However, the Court accepted the argument that neither Keppler nor Hitler would have agreed to a meeting in which Papen would have offered the Führer the same position he had turned down in August 1932.[37]

The Court also charged Papen with conspiring with Oskar von Hindenburg and Meissner to overcome President Hindenburg's objections to the appointment of Hitler as chancellor. Moreover, the Court accused Papen of deliberately preventing the other political parties from participating in the formation of a new cabinet in which Hitler became the chancellor.[38]

The Court found Papen guilty of the charges, and sentenced him to eight years in a labor camp, confiscated his wealth except for 5,000 German Marks, and permanently deprived him of his civil rights.[39] However, because of his poor health Papen was sent to a Nuremberg labor camp hospital at Fürth, where his lawyers began the long process of appeals in an effort to change the verdict of the denazification court.

From April 1947 until February 1949, Papen was moved from one labor camp to another. From Fürth he was sent to Garmisch, and then to a tougher camp at Regensburg. Because of heart trouble he was sent to another hospital in May 1948. At that hospital he was attacked and brutally beaten by one of the inmates. He was carried into the operating room unconscious where a skilled surgeon operated successfully on multiple fractures.[40]

In the meantime, his lawyers had presented an appeal from the verdict of the denazification court of the First Instance. The court of appeal (*Spruch der Berufungskammer*) in Nuremberg-Fürth was presided over by Johann Sauerländer, a retired ministry councilor, and three other judges. Papen was presented by Dr. Kubuschok and his son, Franz Junior.[41]

The mass of documentation that had accumulated since his first trial were now presented by both sides. Similar arguments, testimonies of witnesses, etc. were also introduced. The Court's decision classified Papen as "incriminated in Category II." He was assessed thirty-thousand German Marks as a contribution to the *Wiedergutmachung* (i.e., reparations for crimes committed by Hitler and the National Socialists). He was also deprived of his right to vote, receive a pension from the state, hold any political office, drive a car, or work at anything but ordinary labor.[42]

Both the court of first instance and the appeals court contended that Papen had thrown his full support to the Nazis at critical times. Without his help, Hitler might never have succeeded in becoming chancellor by legal means. This matter of legality had always been of great importance to Hitler, and it always played a decisive role in the Führer's way of thinking.

C. The Last Days

Once his trials were over, and he was able to rejoin his family and settle down in their new home in Obersasbach, on the edge of the Black

Forest, Papen spent most of his time defending his position and activities during Hitler's twelve-year reign of terror and violence. From 1952 until his death on May 2, 1969, Papen tried to refute the bitter recriminations and charges made against him. In spite of two books (his memoirs), numerous articles, speeches, newspaper articles, and other written and personal arguments with professional historians, political scientists, reporters, journalists, and political party officials, he failed to completely exculpate himself from the charges made against him in the International Tribunal as well as the denazification courts.[43]

Eventually he did manage to have some of the punishments inflicted on him by the denazification courts reduced or diminished. In May 1964, his pension as a former member of the German army in World War I was renewed.[44] Then in May 1965, the highest court in Bavaria reviewed his case, and removed him from Group II to Group III, the classification of the least incriminated, which restored his civil rights. Yet, in spite of these favorable decisions, Papen continued to try and justify his reasons for serving Hitler and National Socialism. Unfortunately, he was no match for the professional writers and scholars, and his amateurish, and often erroneous rebuttals to their criticisms failed to alter his image.

Papen's last years are a tragic record of a man who professed to follow his own conscience, but refused to acknowledge his contribution to Hitler's totalitarian system. Although he completely rejected the Nazi ideology, his willingness to continue to serve Hitler weakened all of his protestations and criticisms of National Socialism. Perhaps his greatest sin was not one of commission, but rather of omission. His one opportunity to have been a true defender of what he always professed - Christian values - was his Marburg speech. Unfortunately after that display of courage, his role as Apprentice to the Sorcerer was firmly established.

NOTES

[1] Papen, *Memoirs*, pp. 533-535. Franz Junior, who was attached to a headquarters company located north of Wallerfangen, was forced to retreat as the allies approached. He finally sought refuge at his sister's home in Stockhausen, where he was taken as a prisoner of war by the Americans on April 9, 1945.

[2] Although he could have become an American prisoner, Papen decided to flee because he said he did not want his family to be taken hostage by the Gestapo. He does not offer any reason why this would occur.

[3] Ibid., p. 536. The *New York Times*, April 14, 1945, Vol. LXIV, reported Papen's capture made by Lt. Thomas McKinley. According to the *Times*, when he was captured he exclaimed, "I wish this war were over." "So do 11,000,000 other guys," was the reply of Sergeant Hugh Frederick.

[4] Papen's Gleiwitz Speech, January 14, 1934. Quoted in *IMT*, vol. XVI, pp. 274-275.

[5] The Nuremberg Laws of 1935 contained a provision that Jews could not serve in any civil service position. Papen claimed a victory when he persuaded Hitler to exempt non-Aryan officers who had served in World War I, and those Jews who were civil servants or government officials before the start of the war. However, this exemption was due more to Hitler's need to move slowly in the face of Hindenburg's allegiance to German front-line soldiers, than to any suggestions from Papen.

[6] Aloys Hudal, *The Foundations of National Socialism* (Leipzig-Vienna: Johannes Günther Verlag, 1937), pp. 75 & 88. Papen even gave a copy of this book to Hitler who was extremely interested in it. However, Goebbels and Bormann told Hitler the book "...would have a most unfortunate effect on the party," (*Memoirs*, p. 383).

[7] Dr. Mayar, "*Kann ein Katholik Nationalsozialist sein?*" Printed in Hans Müller, *Kirche und Nationalsozialismus: Dokumente 1930-1935* (München: Deutscher Taschenbuch Verlag, 1965), p. 15. In his speech in Gleiwitz, Papen used almost the same words as Mayar in his reference to the Jews and the need for Christian toleration.

[8] In the written transcript of the Bavarian Supreme Court, Papen is commended for his successful efforts in preventing 10,000 Jews from being shipped to concentration camps in Eastern Europe, "*Schriftlichen Verfahren, Hauptkammer, München, 16 Mai 1956,*" *Amtsgericht* KV-P, Q 14, München.

[9] It was at Chateau de Lesbioles that Papen wrote out an eighty-page report giving the background and history of the *Anschluss*, and his role it. *IMT*,

Supplement A, 3300-PS. At Nuremberg, Papen tried to have the court listen to a recounting of this history, but he was cut off by the President of the Court, and told to just stick to the salient points.

[10] Ibid., p. 540. Nothing came of this wild scheme.

[11] Ibid. p. 544: "I went under heavily armed guard with Streicher, Rosenberg, Frank and others." When the American commander emphasized the importance and safety of the prisoners, the lieutenant in charge remarked: "You mean no leaving the plane without a chute, sir?" Robert, E. Conot, *Justice at Nuremberg* (New York: Harper & Row, Publishers, 1983), p. 34.

[12] Ibid., p. 545.

[13] The observation of the prisoners was tightened up after Dr. Conti, leader of the Nazi medical association, and Dr. Ley, chief of the Labor Front, had succeeding in killing themselves in their cells.

[14] Papen, *Memoirs*, pp. 545-546.

[15] Papen was formally accused on only one count of the indictment: of having taken part in the preparation for the waging of aggressive warfare in violation of international treaties.

[16] Dodd interrogation of Papen, September 3, 19, October 8, 12, 1945, *Nazi Conspiracy and Aggressions*, Supplement B, pp. 1449-1486 (Hereafter cited, *NCA*, etc.).

[17] Papen, *Memoirs*, pp. 547-548.

[18] Ibid., p. 547.

[19] Papen, ibid., p. 548.

[20] Eugene Davidson, *The Trial of the Germans* (New York: The MacMillan Company, 1966), pp. 34-35. In spite of the manner with which these defense attorney's were treated, nothing could conceal from them, the spectators, or even the defendants that this trail was being conducted with decorum and fairness, in comparison with the "kangaroo courts" under the Nazi system of justice.

[21] The four judges representing the Four Powers were: Lord Justice Geoffrey Lawrence for England, who was President of the Court; Attorney General Francis Biddle represented the United States; Professor Donnedieu de Vabres for the French Republic; Major General Niktchenko for the USSR. The alternates were: Sir William Birkett for England; John Parker for the US; M. Falco for France; Lt. Col. Volchkov for the USSR. In addition, each nation had a chief prosecutor, several assistants, and junior counselors. Cf. Davidson, ibid., p. 21, note.

[22] Papen tried to introduce material from pre-world war one Germany, and his activities as Ambassador to Turkey from 1939 to 1945. However, the Court kept reminding him that his case had nothing to do with these periods.

[23] *Memoirs*, p. 560. Kuboschok was able to have the affidavit rejected by the court on the grounds that Schröder intended to use it in his own defense, therefore it was prejudiced. If the court should decide to admit it, Papen's attorney insisted on the right to cross-examine Schröder. Why the prosecution declined to present Schröder is not clear.

[24] Papen's lawyer stated that Papen's conduct after the Marburg speech and the Röhm purge were proof enough that he was opposed to the way things were developing in Germany. For example, his opposition to Hitler and the Nazis was shown by what happened to his staff and himself in the events of June 30, 1934; his resignation and refusal to participate in the cabinet sessions and the *Reichstag* after June 30; his rejection of the ambassadorship to the Vatican; his attempts to bring about the intervention of the *Wehrmacht* through General Fritsch and then Hindenburg, which was blocked by the SS and the "palace guard."

[25] In his defense, Papen used the testimony of Guido Schmidt, the Austrian Foreign Secretary. Schmidt testified that the negotiations leading up to the July Agreement had been entered into as much on Austrian initiative as Papen's. When asked whether he thought the July Agreement had been signed as an attempt to deceive, Schmidt replied "no." This did not help Papen's cause. However, Schuschnigg admitted much later that he thought Papen was acting in good faith when he invited him to meet with Hitler in Berchtesgaden.

[26] Messersmith affidavit, *IMT*, vol. 28, 1760-PS, p.24.

[27] Messersmith affidavit, *IMT*, vol. 28, 2385-PS, pp. 5-7. The Court was prepared to admit Messersmith's testimony when Papen's lawyer requested the right to cross examine him. The prosecution argued that he was too old, and not in good health. When Papen's lawyer expressed doubt about the reliability of an old man's memory, the prosecution changed its "excuse," stating that Messersmith was unavailable because he was serving as ambassador to Mexico. Consequently, the affidavits were not admitted as evidence.

[28] More than a hundred documents including affidavits, letters, questionnaires, excerpts from newspapers, calendars of events, and copies of Papen's speeches were presented by Papen's lawyer. Count Kageneck and Dr. Kroll testified in person, and other witnesses who had been called in for Seyss-Inquart's defense served to support Papen in their cross-examination. Copies of these affidavits along with translations into English are found in the archives of the *Institut für Zeitgeschichte*, NG/1948, IMT; also cf. "Papen Documents," *IMT*, vol. XL, pp. 159-160; 521-523;543-592; cf. Dr. Kubuschok's defense of Papen, June 17-19, 1946, *IMT*, XVI, pp. 236-333; 338-429. It is interesting to note that many of the respondents were extremely cautious in their responses, no doubt because many of them feared reprisals against themselves.

[29] Göring testimony, *IMT*, Vol. IX, pp. 103-104: "...From this time forwards [March 11, 1938], I must take the responsibility for what happened 100 per cent on my shoulders, for it was...myself who set the pace here and forced things to a decision against his [Hitler's] doubts."

[30] Papen's testimony vs. Messersmith, *IMT*, Vol. XVI, pp. 301 ff. In his own case, Seyss-Inquart told the Tribunal that he did not think Papen ever considered that his job was to bring about the *Anschluss*, but rather that he was only there to relax the terrible tensions that existed between the two countries after the Dollfuss murder. Seyss-Inquart testimony, *IMT*, Vol. V, pp. 961-992.

[31] Final plea by Franz von Papen, *NCA*, Supplement B, pp. 842-843.

[32] Statement of Robert H. Jackson, US Chief Counsel, *NCA*, Suppl. A, p. 27.

[33] The American judges Biddle and Parker split with the French and Russian judges. The Americans argued that Papen had not been a conspirator, that he had not promoted the *Anschluss*, and had been as surprised as everyone else. The French contended that Papen's complicity had been greater than Schacht's. Papen was immoral and corrupt, and the practical effect of his actions had been to make him an accomplice in events leading to war. Another judge commented that "we come down to the dislike of the kind of man Papen is." Lord Justice Lawrence said he was disturbed because he disliked Papen more than Schacht, but felt compelled to vote for acquittal. The result as a 2-2 tie, and according to the prearranged rule, Papen got off scot free. Conot, ibid., p. 491.

[34] Conot, ibid., p. 499; Papen, *Memoirs*, p. 575.

[35] Sachs and his deputy were Jews who had, under the Nuremberg laws, been dismissed from the legal profession. Besides Sachs and his deputy, the Court consisted of one Communist, two Social Democrats, one Liberal and one Christian Democrat. Given Papen's past relationships with these political groups, it is little wonder that he received such a harsh conviction.

[36] *Entnazifizierungsverfahren* Franz von Papen, *Urteil 1 Instanz, Spruchkammer* Nuremberg, February 24, 1947, Bd III: *Sitzungs Protokoll 1, Spruch 1 Instanz, Amstgericht, Registrar S, Abt. 4, München* (hereafter cited: *Spruchkammer*, etc.). It will be remembered that Papen's lawyer was able to prevent this testimony from being admitted as evidence in the war crime's trial in 1946. Keppler was the man who made the arrangements for Papen to meet Hitler at Schröder's home in Cologne on January 4, 1933.

[37] Ibid.

[38] Ibid. According to the Court, Brüning offered to serve in a new cabinet, but Papen ignored this offer, and formed a cabinet without any political party representation.

[39] Ibid.

[40] *Memoirs*, p. 578. Papen recalled that the attacker was a former SS man who was mentally unstable and had a record of attacking others.

[41] *Spruch der Berufungskammer I, Nüremberg-Fürth im Verfahren gegen ehemaligen Reichskansler Franz von Papen, 26 Januar 1949, Berufungsverhandlung F. von Papen, January 1949, Dok. Buch II, KV-Prozesse, IMT, Q 15, Staatsarchiv, Nüremberg.* (Herafter cited: *Berufungskammer*, etc.)

[42] *Berufungskammer*, ibid.

[43] His *Memoirs*, which have been referred to in this study, are replete with factual errors, unwarranted justifications, and unjust charges against others without adequate evidence. Papen was urged not to publish his remembrances by friends and associates. However, he needed to try and recuperate some of his tarnished image. Unfortunately, his *Memoirs* only served to further condemn him as a pariah in his own land.

[44] The administration court in Mannheim rendered a decision in May 1964, that ordered the state of Baden-Württemberg to pay Papen as a retired carrier officer a subsistence of 680 Marks monthly, retroactive to September 1957. Article in *Der Spiegel*, June 10, 1964, p. 41.

BIBLIOGRAPHY

I. Archives

Amtsgericht, Munich
Archdiocesan Archives, Wroclaw, Poland
Bayerisches Hauptstaatsarchiv, Munich
Bundesarchiv - Koblenz
Bundesarchiv - *Militärarchiv*, Freiburg/B
Deutsches Adelsarchiv, Marburg
Deutsches Zentralarchiv, Potsdam
Franklin Delano Roosevelt Library, Hyde Park, N.Y.
Geheimes Staatsarchiv Preussischer Kulturbesitz, Berlin
Hauptstaatsarchiv, Stuttgart
Institut für Zeitgeschichte, Munich
Institut für Zeitungsforschung der Stadt Dortmund
National Archives, Washington, D. C.
Oesterreichisches Staatsarchiv, Vienna
Politisches Archiv des Auswärtigen Amts, Bonn
Public Record Office, London
Staatsarchiv Nuremberg

II. Government Publications, Printed Documentary Collections

Albrecht, Dieter. *Der Notenwechsel zwischen dem Heiligen Stuhl und der deutschen Reichsregierung, 1937-1945.* Kommission für Zeitgeschichte, Katholische Akademie in Bayern, Reihe A: Quellen Vol. II. Mainz: Matthias-Grünewald Verlag, 1967.

Austrian Courts. *Der Hochverrätsprozess gegen Guido Schmidt.* Wien: Staatsdrükerei, 1947.

German Courts. *Preussen contra Reich vor dem Staatsgerichtshof in Leipzig von 10. bis 12. Oktober 1932.* Berlin: J.H.W.Dietz, 1933.

Great Britain, Command Papers: Cd. 8012. Miscellaneous No. 16 (1915) *Austrian and German Papers found in Possession of Mr. James Archibald, Falmouth, August 30, 1915.* London: H.M Stationary Office, 1915.

_____ Foreign Office. *Documents of British Foreig Policy, 1919-1939.* Third Series, Vols. IV - VI. London: H. M. S. O., 1951.

_____ Foreign Office. *Selection from Papers found in Possession of Captain Franz von Papen, late German Military Attaché, Washington. Falmouth, January 2 & 3, 1916.* London: Harrison & Sons, 1916.

Hubatsch, Walther. *Hindenburg und der Staat: Aus den Papieren des Generalfeldmarschalls und Reichspräsidenten von 1878 bis 1934.* Göttingen: Musterschmidt Verlag, 1966.

International Military Tribunal, Nuremberg, *Trial of the Major War Criminals Before the International MIlitary Tribunal, Nuremberg, 14 November 1945 to 1 October 1946.* 42 vols. Nuremberg: 1947-1949.

Kent, George, ed., *Catalogue of Files and Microfilms of the German Foreign Ministry.* 4 vols. Stanford: University of Stanford Press, 1962-1973.

Kupper, Alfons, ed., *Staatliche Akten die Reichskonkordats-verhandlungen 1933.* Kommission für Zeitgeschichte, Katholische Akademie in Bayern, Reihe A. Band 2. Mainz: Matthias-Grünewald Verlag, 1969.

Mayar, Dr. *Kann ein Katholik Nationalsozialist Sein?"* in Hans Müller, ed. *Kirche und Nationalsozialismus: Dokumente 1930- 1935.* München: Deutscher Taschenbuch Verlag, 1965.

Michaelis Herbert; Schraepler, Ernst; Scheel, Guenter, ed., *Ursachen und Folgen vom Deutschen Zusammenbruch 1918 und 1945 bis zur Staatlichen Neuordnung Deutschlands in der Gegenwart: Eine Urkunden und Dokumentsammlung zur Zeitgeschichte.* 9 vols. Berlin: Dokumenten Verlag Herbert Wendler & Co., n.d.

Minuth, Karl-Heinz, ed. *Akten der Reichskanzlei Regierung Hitler 1933-1938.* Band I: *30 Januar bis 31 August* 1933. Band II: *12 September 1933 bis 27 August 1934.* Boppard am Rhein: Harald Boldt Verlag, 1983.

Morsey, Rudolf, eds., *Die Protokolle der Reichstagfraktion und des Fraktionsvorstands der Deutschen Zentrumspartei.* Kommission für Zeitgeschichte, Katholische Akademie in Bayern, Reihe A: Band 9. Mainz: Matthias-Grünewald Verlag, 1969.

"Papen Stammtafel," Gothaischen Genealogischen Taschenbuch. Marburg: Deutsches Adelsarchiv, 1933.

Preussische Landtag, *Sitzungberichte des Preussischen Landtäges, 1932-1933.* Berlin: 1932-1933.

Royal Institute of International Affairs. Documents *of International Affairs, 1931-1938.* vol. 1. London: Oxford University Press for R. I. I. A., 1932-1941.

Stasiewski, Bernhard. *Akten Deutscher Bischöfe über die Lage der Kirche 1933-1945.* Vol. 1. Mainz: Matthias-Grünewald Verlag, 1968.

Thurauf, Ulrich, ed., *Schulthess' Europäischer Geschichtskalendar 1932.* V 3. München: C. H. Beck'sche Verlagsbuchhandlung, 1933.

US Chief Counsel for the Prosecution of Axis Criminality. *Nazi Conspiracy and Aggression.* 8 vols. & Supplements A & B. Washington: G. P. Office, 1946-1948.

US Department of State. *Documents on German Foreign Policy 1918-1945.* Series C: II, III, IV. Series D: I, V, VII, VIII, IX, XII, XIII. Washington: G. P. O., 1957.

_____ *Foreign Relations of the United States: Diplomatic Papers, 1931-1933.* Washington: G. P. Office, 1946-1950.

Volk, Ludwig, ed., *Kirchliche Akten über die Reichskonkordat-verhandlung 1933.* Kommission fuer Zeitgeschichte, Katholische Akademie in Bayern, Reihe A: Bd. 11, Mainz: Matthias-Grünewald Verlag, 1969.

Woodward, E.L. & Butler, Rohan, eds., *Documents on British Foreign Policy 1919-1939*. 2nd. Series, Vols. II - IV: 1932- 1933; 3rd. Series, Vols. IV - VI: 1933-1939, London: H.M.S.O., 1947-1956.

III. Memoirs, Autobiographies, Speeches

Aretin, Erwein Frh. von. *Krone und Ketten: Erinnerungeneines Bayerischen Edelmannes*. Eds. Karl Bucheim & Otmar Aretin München: Südeutscher Verlag, 1955.

Baynes, Norman H., ed., *Hitler's Speeches, 1922-1939*. 2 vols. London: Oxford University, 1942.

Braun, Otto. *Vom Weimar zu Hitler*. 2nd ed. New York: Europe Verlag, 1940.

Brüning, Heinrich, *Memorien 1918-1934*. Stuttgart: Deutsche Verlags-Anstalt, 1970.

Carnegie Endowment for International Peace. *Official German Documents Relating to the World War*. 2 vols. New York: Oxford University Press, 1923.

Diels, Rudolf. *Lucifer ante Portas: es spricht der erste Chef der Gestapo* Stuttgart: Deutsche Verlags-Anstalt, 1950.

Dodd, William. *Ambassadore Dodd's Diary, 1933-1938*. Ed. by William Dodd, Jr. & Martha Dodd. New York: Harcourt-Brace,1941.

Francois-Poncet, Andre. *Souvenirs d'une Ambassade a Berlin, Septembre 1931 - Octobre 1938*. Paris: Flammarion, 1946.

Goebbels, Joseph. *Vom Kaiserhof zur Reichskanzlei: Eine Historische Darstellung in Tagebuchblättern vom 1 Januar bis zum 1 Mai 1933*. München: Zentralverlag der NSDAP, Franz Eber, Nachf., 1934.

_____ *The Goebbels Diaries 1942-1943*. New York: Lochner, Louis. ed., trans. Doubleday & Company, Inc., 1948.

Grzesinski, Albert. *Inside Germany*. Translated by Alexander Lipschitz. New York: E. P. Dutton & Co., Inc., 1939.

Herriot, Edouard. *Jadis: D'une guerre a l'autre 1914-1936.* Paris: Flammarion, 1952.

Hindenburg, Paul. *Aus meinen Leben.* Leipzig: Volksausg., 1934.

Hitler, Adolf. *Mein Kampf.* München: Zentralverlag der N.S.D.A.P. Frz. Eher Nachff., 1943.

House of Commons Debates. Vol. CCCL. *Churchill's Speech* to *the House of Commons, August 2, 1944*, London: H. M. S. O., 1944.

Joos, Joseph. *So Sah ich Sie: Menschen und Geschnisse.* Augsburg: Verlag Winfried-Werk, 1958.

Kessler, Harry. *Tagebücher 1918-1937.* Frankfurt/M.: Wolfgang Pfeiffer-Belli Verlag, 1961.

Knatchbull-Hugessen, Hughe Sir, KCMG. *Diplomat in Peace and War.* London: John Murray, 1949.

Lobe, Paul. *Errinnerungen eines Reichstags Präsidenten.* Berlin: Arani Verlag, 1949.

Meissner, Otto. *Staatssekretär uunter Ebert, Hindenburg, Hitler; der Schickalsweg des deutschen Volkes von 1918-1945, wie ich ihn erlebte.* 3rd. ed. Hamburg: Hoffman und Campe, 1950.

Papen, Franz von. *Memoirs.* Translated by Brian Connell. New York: E.P.Dutton & Company, Inc., 1953.

_____ *Die Wahrheit Eine Gasse.* München: Paul List Verlag, 1952.

_____ *Vom Scheitern einer Demokratie 1930-1933.* Mainz: V. Hase & Köhler Verlag, 1968.

Pünder, Herman. *Politik in der Reichkanzlei: Aufzeichnungen aus den Jahren 1929-1932,* ed. Thilo Vogelsang. Stuttgart: Deutsche Verlags-Anstalt, 1961.

Ribbentrop, Joachim von. *The Ribbentrop Memoirs,* translated by Oliver Watson. London: Weidenfeld & Nicolson, 1954.

Schmidt, Paul. *Statist auf diplomatischer Bühne, 1923-1945. Erlebnisse des Chefdolmentschers im Auswärtigen Amt mit den Staatsmännern Europas.* Bonn: Athenaeum Verlag, 1950.

Severing, Carl. *Mein Lebensweg II.* Köln: Greven Verlag, 1950.

Schuschnigg, Kurt von. *Austrian Requiem.* New York: G.P. Putnam's Sons, 1946.

_____ *My Austria.* Translated by John Sugrue. New York: A. A. Knopf, 1938.

_____ *The Brutal Takeover.* Translated by Richard Barry. London: Weidenfeld & Nicolson, 1969.

Schwerin-Krosigk, Lutz Graf. *Es geschah in Deutschland, Menschen Bilder Unserer Jahrhunderts.* Tübingen und Stuttgart: Rainer Wunderlich Verlag, Hermann Leins, 1951.

Simon, John. *Retrospect: The Memoirs of the Rt. Hon. Viscount Simon.* London: Hutchinson, Ltd., 1952.

Tschirschky, Fritz Günter von. *Errinerungen eines Hochverräters.* Stuttgart: Deutsche Verlags-Anstalt, n.d.

Wilson, Maitland H. *Eight Years Overseas.* London: Oxford University Press, 1949.

IV. Secondary Literature

Adams, Henry M. & Robin K. *Rebel Patriot: A Biography of Franz von Papen.* Santa Barbara: McNally & Loftin, 1987.

Bach, Jürgen. *Franz von Papen in der Weimarer Republik* Düsseldorf: Droste Verlag, 1977.

Bay, Juergen. *Der Preussenkonflikt, 1932/33. Ein Kapital der Verfassungsgeschichte der Weimarer Republik.* Ph.D. dissertation, Friedrich-Alexander Universität, 1965.

Beck, Earl R. *The Death of the Prussian Republic.* Florida State University Press, 1959.

Bloch, Michael. *Ribbentrop, A Biography.* New York: Crown Publishers, Inc., 1992.

Blood-Ryan, H. W. *Franz von Papen: His Life and Times.* London: Rich & Cowan Ltd., 1940.

Braatz, Werner E. *Neo-Conservatism in Crisis at the End of the Weimar Republic: Franz von Papen and the Rise and Fall of the 'New State,' June to December, 1932.* Ph.D. dissertation, University of Wisconsin, 1969.

Bracher, Karl Dietrich; Sauer, Wolfgang; Schulz, Gerhard. *Die Nationalsozialistische Machtergreifung: Studien zur Errichtung der totalitären Herrschaftssystems in Deutschland, 1933-1934.* Köln: Westdeutscher-Verlag, 1960.

_____ *Die Auflösung der Weimarer Republik: Eine Studie zum Problem des Machtverfalls in der Demokratie.* 3rd. rev. ed. Villingen/Schwarzwald: Ring Verlag, 1960.

Brecht, Arnold. *Federalism and Regionalism: The Division Of Prussia.* London: Oxford University Press, 1945.

_____ *Prelude to Silence - The End of the German Republic.* New York: Oxford University Press, 1944.

Brooke-Shepherd, Gordon. *The Anschluss: The Rape of Austria.* London: MacMillan & Co., 1963.

Bullock, Alan. *Hitler A Study in Tyranny.* rev. ed. New Bantam Books, 1961.

Conot, Robert E. *Justice at Nuremberg.* New York: Harper & Row, Publishers, 1983.

Conway, John B. *The Nazi Persecution of the Churches 1933-1935.* New York: Basic Books, 1968.

Childers, Thomas. *The Nazi Voter.* Chapel Hill: University of North Carolina Press, 1983.

Churchill, Winston. *The Second World War.* vol. IV. Boston: Houghton Mifflin, Co., 1953.

Craig, Gordon A. *Germany 1866-1945.* New York: Oxford University Press, 1978.

Davidson, Eugene. *The Trial of the Germans*. New York: The MacMillan Company, 1966.

Dodd, Martha. *Through Embassy Eyes*. New York: Harcourt-Brace, 1939.

Dorpalen, Andreas. *Hindenburg and the Weimar Republic*. New Jersey: Princeton University Press, 1964.

Dutch, Oswald. *The Errant Diplomat*. London: Edward Arnold & Co., 1940.

Evans, Ellen Lovell. *The German Center Party 1870-1933*. Carbondale: Southern Ilinois University Press, 1981.

Eyck, Erich. *A History of the Weimar Republic*, 2 vols. Translated by Harlan P. Hanson & Robert G. L. Waite. New York: Atheneum Press, 1970.

Fest, Joachim. *The Face of the Third Reich*. Translated by Michael Bullock. New York: Ace Books, 1970.

Feuchtwanger, E.J. *From Weimar to Hitler Germany, 1918-1933*. New York: St. Martin's Press, 1993.

Gehl, Juergen. *Austria, Germany and the Anschluss*. London: Oxford University Press, 1963.

Halperin, S. William. *Germany Tried Democracy*. New York: W.W. Norton & Company, Inc., 1946.

Hamilton, Richard F. *Who Voted for Hitler?* Princeton, N. J.: Princeton University Press, 1982.

Hoemig, Herbert. *Das Preussische Zentrum in der Weimarer Republik*. Kommission für Zeitgeschichte, Katholische Akademie in Bayern, Reihe B. Band 28. Mainz: Matthias-Grünewald Verlag, 1979.

Horkenbach, Cuno, ed., *Das Deutsche Reich vom 1918 bis Heute* Bnd. III. Berlin: Verlag für Presse Wirtschaft, 1933.

Kirk, George, ed., *The Middle East in the War*. Part IV: "Russia and the Middle East: (1) Turkey." *Survey of International Affairs 1939-1946*. London: Oxford University Press, 1952.

Klemperer, Klemens von. *Germany's New Conservatism*. Princeton, New Jersey: Princeton University Press, 1968.

Langroth, Franz. *Kampf um Oesterreich*. Wels: Welsermuhl, 1951.

Leavey, William Joseph. *Hitler's Envoy Extraordinary--Franz von Papen: Ambassador to Austria, 1934-1938 and Turkey,1939-1944* Ph.D. dissertation, St. John's University, 1968.

Matthias, Erich, Morsey, Rudolf. eds., *Das Ende der Parteien 1933*. Düsseldorf: Athenaeum/Droste Verlag, 1979.

Medlicott, W. N. *The Economic Blockade*. Vol 1. London: H.M.S.O., 1952.

Meissner, Hans Otto & Wilde, Harry. *Die Machtergreifung: Ein Bericht über die Technik des nationalsozialistischen Staatsstreich*. Stuttgart: J. G. Cotta, 1958.

Miller, Max. *Eugen Bolz: Staatsmann und Bekenner*. Vol. II. Stuttgart: Schwabenverlag, 1951.

Moeller, Robert. *German Peasants & Agrarian Politics 1914-1924*. Chapel Hill: University of North Carolina Press, 1986.

Morsey, Rudolf. *Die Deutsche Zentrumspartei 1917-1923*. Düsseldorf: Droste Verlag, 1966.

Moyzisch, L. C. *Operation Cicero*. London: Wingate Press, 1950.

Papen, F.F. *29.10.79 Zum Geburtstag meines Vaters Franz von Papen*. Privatdrück, n.d.

Picker, Harry. *Hitler's Tischgespräche im Führer-Hauptquartier, 1941-1944*. Gerhard Ritter, ed. Munich: Athenaum Verlag, 1951.

Rauschnigg, Hermann. *The Revolution of Nihilism: Warning to the West*. New York: Alliance Book Corporation/Longman's Green & Co., 1939.

Rein, Hans. *Franz von Papen im Zwielicht der Geschichte*. Baden-Baden: Nomos Verlagsgesellschaft, 1979.

Rintelen, Franz von. *The Dark Invader*. London: Penguin Books, 1936.

Rolfs, Richard W. "The Role of Adolf Cardinal Bertram in the Third Reich: 1933-1938," Ph.D. dissertation, Santa Barbara: University of California, 1976.

Routh, D. A. *The Montreaux Convention Regarding the Regime of the Black Sea Straits* Royal Institute of International Affairs, *Survey of International Affairs, 1936.* London: Oxford University Press, 1937.

Schotte, Walter. *Das Kabinett Papen, Schleicher, Gayl.* Leipzig: R. Kittler Verlag, 1932.

_____ *Der Neue Staat.* Berlin: Neufeld & Henius Verlag, 1932.

Smith, Bradley F. *Reaching Judgement at Nuremberg.* New York: Basic Books, Inc., 1977.

Sterling, Michael C. *The Herrenreiter in Politics: The Government of Franz von Papen, May 31, 1932 - December 2, 1932.* Ph.D. dissertation, Indiana University, 1979.

Trumpp, Thomas. *Franz von Papen, der preussich-deutsche Dualismus u. 20 Juli 1932; ein Beitrag zur Vorgeschichte, 20 Juli 1932,* Ph.D. dissertation, Tübingen Universität, 1963.

Turner, Henry Ashby Jr. *German Big Business and the Rise of Hitler.* New York & Oxford: Oxford University Press, 1985.

Volk, Ludwig. *Der Bayerische Episkopat und der Nationalsozialismus 1930-1934.* Mainz: Matthias-Grünewald Verlag, 1966.

_____ *Das Reichskonkordat vom 20. Juli 1933.* Mainz: Matthias-Grünewald Verlag, 1972.

Vogelsang, Thilo. *Reichswehr, Staat und NSDAP: Beitrage zurdeutschen Geschichte 1930-1932.* Stuttgart: Deutsche-Verlag Anstalt, 1962.

Waite, Robert G. L. *Vanguard of Nazism: The Free Corps Movement in Postwar Germany, 1910-1923.* Cambridge: Harvard University Press, 1952.

Wheeler-Bennett, John W. *The Nemisis of Power: The Germany Army in Politics, 1918-1945.* New York: St. Martin's Press, Inc., 1954.

_____ *The Pipedream of Peace: The Story of the Collapse of Disarmament.* New York: William Morrow & Company, 1935.

Zernatto, Guido. *Die Wahrheit über Oesterreich.* New York: Longman, Green and Co., 1938.

V. Journal Articles

Aretin, Karl Otmar von. "*Prälat Kaas, Franz von Papen und das Reichskonkordat von 1933.*" *Vierteljahrshefte für Zeitgeschichte* 14 (1966): 252-269.

Braatz, Werner E. "Franz von Papen and the Preussenschlag, 20 July 1932: a Move by the 'New State' toward Reichsreform," *European Studies Review* 2 (April 1973): 157-180.

Bracher, Karl Dietrich. "*Der 20 Juli 1932.*" *Zeitschrift für Politik* 3 (1956): 243-251.

Colm, Gerhard. "Why the Papen Plan for Economic Recovery Failed." *Social Research* 1 (February 1934): 83-96.

Deist, Wilhelm. "*Schleicher und die deutsche Abrüstungspolitik im Juni/Juli 1932,*" *Vierteljahrshefte für Zeitgeschichte* VIII (1959): 164-169.

Eschenberg, Theodor. "Franz von Papen." *Vierteljahrshefte für Zeitgeschichte* I (April 1953): 153-169.

Houghton, W.F. "The Albert Portfolio." *Saturday Evening Post* (August 17, 1929).

Jones, Larry. "Edgar Julius Jung: The Conservative Revolution in Theory and Practice." *Central European History* 21, #2 (June 1988): 142-174.

Kleist-Schmenzin, Ewald von. "Die Letzte Möglichkeit: Zur Erennung Hitler's zum Reichskanzler am 30. Januar 1933." *Politische Studien* 1066 (February 1959): 89-92.

Klepper, Otto. "Das Ende der Republik," *Die Gegenwart,* 42/43 (September 30, 1947): 20-22.

Kluke, Paul. "Der Fall Potempa." *Vierteljahrshefte für Zeitgeschichte* 3 (July 1957): 279-297.

Kohler, Eric D. "The Successful Center-Left: Joseph Hess the Prussian Center Party," *Central Europoean History* 23 #4 (December 1990): 313-348.

Kuhn, Axel, *"Die Unterredung zwischen Hitler u. Papen in Hause des Barons von Schröder,"* *Geschichte in Wissenschaft u. Unterricht,* 12 (January, 1973): 709-72.

Kupper, Alfons. *"Zur Geschichte des Reichskonkordats."* *Stimmen der Zeit* 163 (1959): 278-302.

_____ *"Zur Geschichte des Reichskonkordats."* *Stimmen der Zeit* 171 (1963): 25-500.

Lindheim, Hermann von. *"Zu Papens Staatsstreich vom 20 Juli 1932." Geschichte in Wissenschaft und Unterricht* 3 (March 1960): 154-164.

Morsey, Rudolf. *"Tagebuch 7. - 20. April 1933, Ludwig Kaas. Aus dem Nachlass von Prälat Ludwig Kaas." Stimmen der Zeit* 166 (1959-60): 422-430.

_____ *"Zur Geschichte des Preussenschlags am 20 Juli 1932." Vierteljahrshefte für Zeitgeschichte* 4 (October 1961): 430-439.

_____ *"Der Beginn der Gleichschaltung in Preussen." Vierteljarhshefte für Zeitgeschichte* (Jan 1963): 85-97.

Muth, Heinrich. *"Das Kölner Gespräch am 4. Januar." Geschichte in Wissenschaft und Unterricht* 37 #8 (1986): 463-480; 529-541.

Neebe, Reinhard. *"Unternehmerverbände und Gewerkschaften in den Jahren der Grossen Krise 1929-33." Geschichte und Gesellschaft* 9 (1983): 302-330.

Petzold, Joachim. *"Der Staatsstreich vom 20 Juli 1932 in Berlin." Zeitschrift für Geschtsswissenschaft* 6 (1956): 1146-1186.

Schäffer, Fritz. "*Die Bayrische Volkspartei (BVP)*." *Politische Studien* 147 (Jan-Feb 1963), 58-61.

Sontheimer, Kurt. "*Antidemokratisches Denken in der Weimarer Republik*." *Vierteljarhshefte für Zeitgeschichte* 1 (January 1957): 42-62.

Turner, Henry Ashby, Jr. "The *Ruhrlade*, Secret Cabinet of Heavy Industry in the Weimar Republic." *Central European History* 3 (S'70): 195-228.

_____ "*Grossuunternehmertum und Nationalsozialismus 1931-1933. Kritisches u. Ergänzendes zu zwei neuen Forschungsbeiträgen*." *Historische Zeitschrift* Band 221, Heft I (August 1975): 18-68.

Vogelsang, Thilo. "*Neue Dokumente zur Geschichte der Reichswehr 1930-1933*." *Vierteljahrshefte für Zeitgeschichte* 4 (October 1954): 397-435.

_____ "*Zur Politik Schleichers gegenüber der NSDAP 1932*." *Vierteljahrshefte für Zeitgeschichte* 1 (January 1958): 85-118.

Zeender, John K. "The Presidential Election of 1925." *Journal of Modern History* 35 (1963): 366-381.

VI. Newspapers

Der Angriff
Augsburger Postzeitung
Berliner Tageblatt
Der Ring
Frankfurter Allgemeine
Germania
Junge Nation
Kölnische Zeitung
Die Lokalanzeiger
L'Osservatore Romano

The New York World
The Observer
San Francisco Chronicle
Stars and Stripes
Tägliche Rundschau
Der Volkische Beobachter
Vorwärts
Vossische Zeitung
Wolff's Telegraphisches Büro
The New York Times

INDEX